SSH, the Secure Shell

The Definitive Guide

Other computer security resources from O'Reilly

SECOND EDITION

SSH, the Secure Shell

The Definitive Guide

Daniel J. Barrett, Richard E. Silverman,
and Robert G. Byrnes

O'REILLY®

Beijing · Cambridge · Farnham · Köln · Paris · Sebastopol · Taipei · Tokyo

SSH, the Secure Shell: The Definitive Guide™

by Daniel J. Barrett, Richard E. Silverman, and Robert G. Byrnes

Copyright © 2005, 2001 O'Reilly Media, Inc. All rights reserved.
Printed in the United States of America.

Published by O'Reilly Media, Inc., 1005 Gravenstein Highway North, Sebastopol, CA 95472.

O'Reilly books may be purchased for educational, business, or sales promotional use. Online editions are also available for most titles (*safari.oreilly.com*). For more information, contact our corporate/institutional sales department: (800) 998-9938 or *corporate@oreilly.com*.

Editor:	Mike Loukides
Production Editor:	Mary Brady
Cover Designer:	Ellie Volckhausen
Interior Designer:	David Futato

Printing History:

February 2001:	First Edition.
May 2005:	Second Edition.

 This book uses RepKover™, a durable and flexible lay-flat binding.

ISBN: 0-596-00895-3

[M]

Table of Contents

Preface . . . . **xi**

1. Introduction to SSH **1**
    1.1 What Is SSH?   1
    1.2 What SSH Is Not   3
    1.3 The SSH Protocol   3
    1.4 Overview of SSH Features   5
    1.5 History of SSH   9
    1.6 Related Technologies   10
    1.7 Summary   15

2. Basic Client Use **16**
    2.1 A Running Example   16
    2.2 Remote Terminal Sessions with ssh   16
    2.3 Adding Complexity to the Example   18
    2.4 Authentication by Cryptographic Key   21
    2.5 The SSH Agent   28
    2.6 Connecting Without a Password or Passphrase   32
    2.7 Miscellaneous Clients   33
    2.8 Summary   34

3. Inside SSH **36**
    3.1 Overview of Features   36
    3.2 A Cryptography Primer   39
    3.3 The Architecture of an SSH System   43
    3.4 Inside SSH-2   45
    3.5 Inside SSH-1   68

3.6 Implementation Issues   69
3.7 SSH and File Transfers (scp and sftp)   81
3.8 Algorithms Used by SSH   84
3.9 Threats SSH Can Counter   91
3.10 Threats SSH Doesn't Prevent   93
3.11 Threats Caused by SSH   97
3.12 Summary   98

4. Installation and Compile-Time Configuration **99**
4.1. Overview   99
4.2 Installing OpenSSH   106
4.3 Installing Tectia   111
4.4 Software Inventory   124
4.5 Replacing r-Commands with SSH   125
4.6 Summary   127

5. Serverwide Configuration **128**
5.1 Running the Server   129
5.2 Server Configuration: An Overview   132
5.3 Getting Ready: Initial Setup   141
5.4 Authentication: Verifying Identities   171
5.5 Access Control: Letting People In   184
5.6 User Logins and Accounts   198
5.7 Forwarding   201
5.8 Subsystems   206
5.9 Logging and Debugging   209
5.10 Compatibility Between SSH-1 and SSH-2 Servers   223
5.11 Summary   226

6. Key Management and Agents **227**
6.1 What Is an Identity?   227
6.2 Creating an Identity   233
6.3 SSH Agents   242
6.4 Multiple Identities   260
6.5 PGP Authentication in Tectia   262
6.6 Tectia External Keys   264
6.7 Summary   265

7. Advanced Client Use **266**

    7.1 How to Configure Clients 266

    7.2 Precedence 276

    7.3 Introduction to Verbose Mode 277

    7.4 Client Configuration in Depth 278

    7.5 Secure Copy with scp 313

    7.6 Secure, Interactive Copy with sftp 323

    7.7 Summary 325

8. Per-Account Server Configuration **326**

    8.1 Limits of This Technique 326

    8.2 Public-Key-Based Configuration 328

    8.3 Hostbased Access Control 346

    8.4 The User rc File 348

    8.5 Summary 348

9. Port Forwarding and X Forwarding **349**

    9.1 What Is Forwarding? 350

    9.2 Port Forwarding 351

    9.3 Dynamic Port Forwarding 373

    9.4 X Forwarding 377

    9.5 Forwarding Security: TCP-wrappers and libwrap 389

    9.6 Summary 395

10. A Recommended Setup **396**

    10.1 The Basics 396

    10.2 Compile-Time Configuration 397

    10.3 Serverwide Configuration 397

    10.4 Per-Account Configuration 403

    10.5 Key Management 404

    10.6 Client Configuration 404

    10.7 Remote Home Directories (NFS, AFS) 404

    10.8 Summary 407

11. Case Studies **408**

    11.1 Unattended SSH: Batch or cron Jobs 408

    11.2 FTP and SSH 415

    11.3 Pine, IMAP, and SSH 436

    11.4 Connecting Through a Gateway Host 444

11.5   Scalable Authentication for SSH   452

11.6   Tectia Extensions to Server Configuration Files   468

11.7   Tectia Plugins   479

12. Troubleshooting and FAQ **495**

12.1   Debug Messages: Your First Line of Defense   495

12.2   Problems and Solutions   497

12.3   Other SSH Resources   513

13. Overview of Other Implementations **515**

13.1   Common Features   515

13.2   Covered Products   516

13.3   Other SSH Products   516

14. OpenSSH for Windows **521**

14.1   Installation   521

14.2   Using the SSH Clients   522

14.3   Setting Up the SSH Server   522

14.4   Public-Key Authentication   524

14.5   Troubleshooting   525

14.6   Summary   525

15. OpenSSH for Macintosh **526**

15.1   Using the SSH Clients   526

15.2   Using the OpenSSH Server   526

16. Tectia for Windows **531**

16.1   Obtaining and Installing   532

16.2   Basic Client Use   533

16.3   Key Management   534

16.4   Accession Lite   536

16.5   Advanced Client Use   539

16.6   Port Forwarding   542

16.7   Connector   543

16.8   File Transfers   551

16.9   Command-Line Programs   552

16.10 Troubleshooting   554

16.11 Server   555

17. SecureCRT and SecureFX for Windows 563

    17.1 Obtaining and Installing   563

    17.2 Basic Client Use   564

    17.3 Key Management   564

    17.4 Advanced Client Use   568

    17.5 Forwarding   570

    17.6 Command-Line Client Programs   572

    17.7 File Transfer   572

    17.8 Troubleshooting   574

    17.9 VShell   574

    17.10 Summary   575

18. PuTTY for Windows 576

    18.1 Obtaining and Installing   576

    18.2 Basic Client Use   576

    18.3 File Transfer   578

    18.4 Key Management   580

    18.5 Advanced Client Use   583

    18.6 Forwarding   587

    18.7 Summary   589

A. OpenSSH 4.0 New Features 591

B. Tectia Manpage for sshregex 595

C. Tectia Module Names for Debugging 604

D. SSH-1 Features of OpenSSH and Tectia 609

E. SSH Quick Reference 612

Index 629

Preface

Welcome to the second edition of our book on SSH, one of the world's most popular approaches to computer network security. Here's a sampling of what's new in this edition:

- Over 100 new features, options, and configuration keywords from the latest versions of OpenSSH and SSH Tectia (formerly known as SSH Secure Shell or SSH2 from *ssh.com*)
- Expanded material on the SSH-2 protocol and its internals, including a step-by-step tour through the transport, authentication, and connection phases
- Running OpenSSH on Microsoft Windows and Macintosh OS X
- All-new chapters on Windows software such as Tectia, SecureCRT, and PuTTY
- Scalable authentication techniques for large installations, including X.509 certificates
- Single sign-on between Linux and Windows via Kerberos/GSSAPI
- Logging and debugging in greater depth
- Tectia's metaconfiguration, subconfiguration, and plugins, with examples

...and much more! You might be surprised at how much is changed, but in the past four years, SSH has significantly evolved:

SSH-2 protocol triumphant
Back in 2001, only a handful of SSH products supported the relatively new SSH-2 protocol, and the primary implementation was commercial. Today, the old SSH-1 protocol is dying out and all modern SSH products, free and commercial, use the more secure and flexible SSH-2 protocol. We now recommend that everyone avoid SSH-1.

The rise of OpenSSH
This little upstart from the OpenBSD world has become the dominant implementation of SSH on the Internet, snatching the crown from the original, SSH Secure Shell (now called SSH Tectia, which we abbreviate as Tectia). Tectia is

still more powerful than OpenSSH in important ways; but as OpenSSH is now included as standard with Linux, Solaris, Mac OS X, and beyond, it dominates in pure numbers.

The death of telnet and the r-tools

The insecure programs *telnet*, *rsh*, *rcp*, and *rlogin*—long the standards for communication between computers—are effectively extinct.* FTP is also on the way out, except when operated behind firewalls or over private lines.

An explosion of Windows products

In 2001, there were a handful of SSH implementations for Windows; now there are dozens of GUI clients and several robust servers, not to mention a full port of the free OpenSSH.

Increased attacks

The Internet has experienced a sharp rise in computer intrusions. Now more than ever, your servers and firewalls should be configured to block all remote accesses except via SSH (or other secure protocols).

Protect Your Network with SSH

Let's start with the basics. SSH, the Secure Shell, is a reliable, reasonably easy to use, inexpensive security product for computer networks and the people who use them. It's available for most of today's operating systems.

Privacy is a basic human right, but on today's computer networks, privacy isn't guaranteed. Much of the data that travels on the Internet or local networks is transmitted as plain text, and may be captured and viewed by anybody with a little technical know-how. The email you send, the files you transmit between computers, even the passwords you type may be readable by others. Imagine the damage that can be done if an untrusted third party—a competitor, the CIA, your in-laws— intercepted your most sensitive communications in transit.

SSH is a small, unassuming, yet powerful and robust solution to many of these issues. It keeps prying eyes away from the data on your network. It doesn't solve every privacy and security problem, but it eliminates several of them effectively. Its major features are:

- A secure, client/server protocol for encrypting and transmitting data over a network

- Authentication (recognition) of users by password, host, or public key, plus optional integration with other popular authentication systems, such as PAM, Kerberos, SecurID, and PGP

---

* Not counting secure versions of these tools, e.g., when enhanced with Kerberos support. [1.6.3]

- The ability to add security to insecure network applications such as Telnet, NNTP, VNC, and many other TCP/IP-based programs and protocols
- Almost complete transparency to the end user
- Implementations for most operating systems

Intended Audience

We've written this book for system administrators and technically minded users. Some chapters are suitable for a wide audience, while others are thoroughly technical and intended for computer and networking professionals.

End-User Audience

Do you have two or more computer accounts on different machines? SSH lets you connect one to another with a high degree of security. You can remotely log into one account from the other, execute remote commands, and copy files between accounts, all with the confidence that nobody can intercept your username, password, or data in transit.

Do you connect from a personal computer to an Internet service provider (ISP)? In particular, do you connect to a Unix shell account at your ISP? If so, SSH can make this connection significantly more secure. An increasing number of ISPs are running SSH servers for their users. In case your ISP doesn't, we'll show you how to run a server yourself.

Do you develop software? Are you creating distributed applications that must communicate over a network securely? Then don't reinvent the wheel: use SSH to encrypt the connections. It's a solid technology that may reduce your development time.

Even if you have only a single computer account, as long as it's connected to a network, SSH can still be useful. For example, if you've ever wanted to let other people use your account, such as family members or employees, but didn't want to give them unlimited use, SSH can provide a carefully controlled, limited-access channel into your account.

Prerequisites

We assume you are familiar with computers and networking as found in any modern business office or home system with an Internet connection. Ideally, you are familiar with network applications like Telnet and FTP. If you are a Unix user, you should be familiar with standard network applications (e.g., *ftp*) and the basics of writing shell scripts and Perl scripts.

System-Administrator Audience

If you're a Unix or Macintosh OS X system administrator, you probably know about SSH already. It's less well known in the Windows world, where secure logins are usually accomplished with *radmin* (Remote Administrator) and other remote desktop applications, and network file transfers are done using network shares. In contrast, SSH is more focused on the command line and is therefore more scriptable than the usual Windows techniques. SSH also can increase the security of other TCP/IP-based applications on your network by transparently "tunneling" them through SSH-encrypted connections. You will love SSH.

Prerequisites

In addition to the end-user prerequisites in the previous section, you should be familiar with user accounts and groups, networking concepts such as TCP/IP and packets, and basic encryption techniques.

Reading This Book

This book is divided roughly into three parts. The first three chapters are a general introduction to SSH, first at a high level for all readers (Chapters 1 and 2), and then in detail for technical readers (Chapter 3).

The next nine chapters cover SSH for Unix and similar operating systems (OpenBSD, Linux, Solaris, etc.). The first two (Chapters 4 and 5) cover SSH installation and serverwide configuration for system administrators. The next four (Chapters 6–9) cover advanced topics for end users, including key management, client configuration, per-account server configuration, and forwarding. We complete the Unix sequence with our recommended setup (Chapter 10), some detailed case studies (Chapter 11), and troubleshooting tips (Chapter 12). The remaining chapters cover SSH products for Windows and the Macintosh, plus brief overviews of implementations for other platforms.

Each section in the book is numbered, and we provide cross-references throughout the text. If further details are found in Section 7.1.2.2, we use the notation [7.1.2.2] to indicate it.

Our Approach

This book is organized by concept rather than syntax. We begin with an overview and progressively lead you deeper into the functionality of SSH. So, we might introduce a topic in Chapter 1, show its basic use in Chapter 2, and reveal advanced uses in Chapter 7. If you prefer the whole story at once, Appendix E presents all commands and configuration options in one location.

We focus strongly on three levels of server configuration, which we call compile-time, serverwide, and per-account configuration. Compile-time configuration (Chapter 4) means selecting appropriate options when you build the SSH clients and servers. Serverwide configuration (Chapter 5) applies when the SSH server is run and is generally done by system administrators, while per-account configuration (Chapter 8) can be done anytime by end users. It's vitally important for system administrators to understand the relationships and differences among these three levels. Otherwise, SSH may seem like a morass of random behaviors.

Although the bulk of material focuses on Unix implementations of SSH, you don't have to be a Unix user to understand it. Fans of Windows and the Macintosh may stick to the later chapters devoted to their platforms, but a lot of the meaty details are in the Unix chapters, so we recommend reading them, at least for reference.

Which Chapters Are for You?

We propose several "tracks" for readers with different interests and skills:

System administrators
> Chapters 3–5 and 10 are the most important for understanding SSH and how to build and configure servers. However, as the administrator of a security product, you should read the whole book.

Unix users (not system administrators)
> Chapters 1 and 2 provide an overview, and Chapters 6–9 discuss SSH clients in depth.

Windows end users
> Read Chapters 1, 2, 13, 14, and 16–18 for starters, and then others as your interests guide you.

Macintosh end users
> Read Chapters 1, 2, 13, and 15 for starters, and then others as your interests guide you.

Users of other computer platforms
> Read Chapters 1, 2, and 13 for starters, and then others as your interests guide you.

Even if you are experienced with SSH, you'll likely find value in Chapters 3–12. We cover significant details the Unix manpages leave unclear or unmentioned, including major concepts, compile-time flags, server configuration, and forwarding.

Supported Platforms

This book covers Unix, Windows, and Macintosh implementations of SSH.

 When we say "Unix" in this book, we mean the whole family of Unix-like operating systems such as Linux, OpenBSD, and Solaris.

SSH products are also available for the Amiga, BeOs, Java, OS/2, Palm Pilot, VMS, and Windows CE, and although we don't cover them, their principles are the same.

This book is current for the following Unix SSH versions:

OpenSSH	3.9a
SSH Tectia	4.2

a See Appendix A for a preview of new features in OpenSSH 4.0.

Version information for non-Unix products is found in their respective chapters.

Disclaimers

We identify some program features as "undocumented." This means the feature isn't mentioned in the official documentation but works in the current release and/or is clear from the program source code. Undocumented features might not be officially supported by the software authors and can disappear in later releases.

Conventions Used in This Book

The following typographical conventions are used in this book:

Constant width
> For configuration files, things that can be found in configuration files (such as keywords and configuration file options), source code, and interactive terminal sessions.

Constant width italic
> For replaceable parameters on command lines or within configuration files.

Italic
> For filenames, URLs, hostnames, command names, command-line options, and new terms where they are defined.

A_K
> In figures, the object labeled A has been secured using a cryptographic key labeled K. "Secured" means encrypted, signed, or some more complex relationship, depending on the context. If A is secured using multiple keys (say, K and L), they are listed in the subscript, separated by commas: $A_{K, L}$.

This icon indicates a tip, suggestion, or general note.

 This icon indicates a warning or caution.

Comments and Questions

Please address comments and questions concerning this book to the publisher:

O'Reilly Media, Inc.
1005 Gravenstein Highway North
Sebastopol, CA 95472
(800) 998-9938 (in the United States or Canada)
(707) 829-0515 (international/local)
(707) 829-0104 (fax)

There is a web page for this book, which lists errata, examples, or any additional information. You can access this page at:

http://www.oreilly.com/catalog/sshtdg2/

To comment or ask technical questions about this book, send email to:

bookquestions@oreilly.com

For more information about books, conferences, Resource Centers, and the O'Reilly Network, see the O'Reilly web site at:

http://www.oreilly.com

Safari Enabled

 When you see a Safari® Enabled icon on the cover of your favorite technology book, it means the book is available online through the O'Reilly Network Safari Bookshelf.

Safari offers a solution that's better than e-books. It's a virtual library that lets you easily search thousands of top technology books, cut and paste code samples, download chapters, and find quick answers when you need the most accurate, current information. Try it for free at *http://safari.oreilly.com*.

Acknowledgments

Our biggest thanks go to the two parties who made this second edition a reality: the many readers who purchased the first edition, and our editor Mike Loukides. We couldn't have done this without you!

We thank the O'Reilly "tools" team for Frame typesetting advice, and Rob Romano for turning our hasty sketches into polished illustrations. Special thanks to the O'Reilly production team, Keith Fahlgren, John Bickelhaupt, Audrey Doyle, and Mary Brady, for their hard work creating the final package.

We thank our excellent technical reviewers for their thorough reading and insightful comments: Markus Friedl and Damien Miller of the OpenSSH team, Paul Lussier, Drew Simonis, and Mike Smith. Big thanks also to several vendors of SSH products who provided us with free copies of their software, reviewed the manuscript, and answered our questions. From SSH Communications Security, maker of SSH Tectia, we thank Nicolas Gabriel-Robez, Tommi Lampila, Sami J. Lehtinen, Timo J. Rinne, Janne Saarikko, Petri Sakkinen, Vesa Vatka, and Timo Westerberg. From VanDyke Software, maker of SecureCRT, SecureFX, and VShell, we thank Jill Christian, Maureen Jett, Marc Orchant, and Tracy West. SSH Communications Security also kindly gave us permission to include the *sshregex* manpage (Appendix B) and the *sshdebug.h* error codes (Appendix C).

Dan Barrett thanks Lisa and Sophie for bearing the late-night writing and hacking sessions required for this book. He also thanks Alex Schowtka and Robert Dulaney of VistaPrint, his employer, for their kind permission to work on this project. Bob Byrnes thanks Alison and Rebecca for all of their help and understanding throughout the many nights and weekends when he was glued to his keyboard. Richard Silverman thanks his coauthors for their unfailing good humor and patience—even when a sudden decision to change jobs and move out of state threw his book schedule into chaos. He also thanks his various friends, especially Bob Stepno, for listening to his endless chatter about The Book. It's truly a wonder they still speak to him at all.

## CHAPTER 1

Introduction to SSH

Many people today have multiple computer accounts. If you're a reasonably savvy user, you might have a personal account with an Internet service provider (ISP), a work account on your employer's local network, and a few computers at home. You might also have permission to use other accounts owned by family members or friends.

If you have multiple accounts, it's natural to want to make connections between them. For instance, you might want to copy files between computers over a network, log into one account remotely from another, or transmit commands to a remote computer for execution. Various programs exist for these purposes, such as *ftp* for file transfers, *telnet* for remote logins, and *rsh* for remote execution of commands.

Unfortunately, many of these network-related programs have a fundamental problem: they lack security. If you transmit a sensitive file via the Internet, an intruder can potentially intercept and read the data. Even worse, if you log onto another computer remotely using a program such as *telnet*, your username and password can be intercepted as they travel over the network. Yikes!

How can these serious problems be prevented? You can use an *encryption program* to scramble your data into a secret code nobody else can read. You can install a *firewall*, a device that shields portions of a computer network from intruders, and keep all your communications behind it. Or you can use a wide range of other solutions, alone or combined, with varying complexity and cost.

1.1 What Is SSH?

SSH, the Secure Shell, is a popular, powerful, software-based approach to network security.* Whenever data is sent by a computer to the network, SSH automatically encrypts (scrambles) it. Then, when the data reaches its intended recipient, SSH

---

* "SSH" is pronounced by spelling it aloud: S-S-H.

automatically decrypts (unscrambles) it. The result is *transparent* encryption: users can work normally, unaware that their communications are safely encrypted on the network. In addition, SSH uses modern, secure encryption algorithms and is effective enough to be found within mission-critical applications at major corporations.

SSH has a client/server architecture, as shown in Figure 1-1. An SSH *server* program, typically installed and run by a system administrator, accepts or rejects incoming connections to its host computer. Users then run SSH *client* programs, typically on other computers, to make requests of the SSH server, such as "Please log me in," "Please send me a file," or "Please execute this command." All communications between clients and servers are securely encrypted and protected from modification.

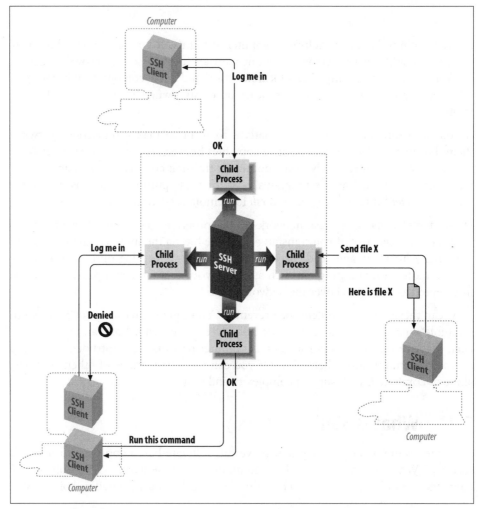

Figure 1-1. SSH architecture

Our description is simplified but should give you a general idea of what SSH does. We'll go into depth later. For now, just remember that SSH clients communicate with SSH servers over encrypted network connections.

SSH software is very common today. It comes with most Linux distributions, Macintosh OS X, Sun Solaris, OpenBSD, and virtually all other Unix-inspired operating systems. Microsoft Windows has plenty of SSH clients and servers, both free and commercial. You can even find it for PalmOS, Commodore Amiga, and most other platforms. [13.3]

Many SSH clients are inspired by old Unix programs called the "r-commands:" *rsh* (remote shell), *rlogin* (remote login), and *rcp* (remote copy). In fact, for many purposes the SSH clients are drop-in replacements for the r-commands, so if you're still using them, switch to SSH immediately! The old r-commands are notoriously insecure, and the SSH learning curve is small.

1.2   What SSH Is Not

Although SSH stands for Secure Shell, it is not a true shell in the sense of the Unix Bourne shell and C shell. It is not a command interpreter, nor does it provide wildcard expansion, command history, and so forth. Rather, SSH creates a channel for running a shell on a remote computer, with end-to-end encryption between the two systems.

SSH is also not a complete security solution—but then, nothing is. It won't protect computers from active break-in attempts or denial-of-service attacks, and it won't eliminate other hazards such as viruses, Trojan horses, and coffee spills. It does, however, provide robust and user-friendly encryption and authentication.

1.3   The SSH Protocol

SSH is a *protocol,* not a product. It is a specification of how to conduct secure communication over a network.*

The SSH protocol covers authentication, encryption, and the integrity of data transmitted over a network, as shown in Figure 1-2. Let's define these terms:

Authentication
> Reliably determines someone's identity. If you try to log into an account on a remote computer, SSH asks for digital proof of your identity. If you pass the test, you may log in; otherwise, SSH rejects the connection.

---

* Although we say "the SSH protocol," there are actually two incompatible versions of the protocols in common use: SSH-1 (a.k.a. SSH-1.5) and SSH-2. We distinguish these protocols later.

Encryption

Scrambles data so that it is unintelligible except to the intended recipients. This protects your data as it passes over the network.

Integrity

Guarantees the data traveling over the network arrives unaltered. If a third party captures and modifies your data in transit, SSH detects this fact.

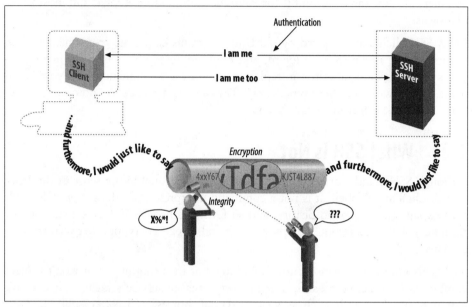

Figure 1-2. Authentication, encryption, and integrity

In short, SSH makes network connections between computers, with strong guarantees that the parties on both ends of the connection are genuine. It also ensures that any data passing over these connections arrives unmodified and unread by eavesdroppers.

1.3.1   Protocols, Products, Clients, and Confusion

The first SSH product, created by Tatu Ylönen for Unix, was simply called "SSH." This caused confusion because SSH was also the name of the protocol. In this book, we use more precise terminology to refer to protocols, products, and programs, summarized in the sidebar "Terminology: SSH Protocols and Products." In short:

- Protocols are denoted with dashes: SSH-1, SSH-2.
- Products are denoted in mixed case, without dashes: OpenSSH, Tectia, PuTTY, etc.
- Client programs are in lowercase: *ssh*, *scp*, *putty*, etc.

Terminology: SSH Protocols and Products

SSH

A generic term referring to SSH protocols and software products.

SSH-1

The SSH protocol, Version 1. This is the original protocol, and it has serious limitations, so we do not recommend its use anymore.

SSH-2

The SSH protocol, Version 2, the most common and secure SSH protocol used today. It is defined by draft standards documents of the IETF SECSH working group. [3.4]

SSH1

The granddaddy of it all: the original SSH product created by Tatu Ylönen. It implemented (and defined) the SSH-1 protocol and is now obsolete.

SSH2

The original SSH-2 product, created by Tatu Ylönen and his company, SSH Communications Security (*http://www.ssh.com*).

ssh (all lowercase letters)

A client program run on the command line and included in many SSH products, for running secure terminal sessions and remote commands. On some systems it might be named *ssh1* or *ssh2*.

OpenSSH

The product OpenSSH from the OpenBSD project, *http://www.openssh.com*.

Tectia

The successor to SSH2, this refers to the product suite "SSH Tectia" from SSH Communications Security. We abbreviate the name as simply "Tectia." Since Tectia is available for both Unix and Windows, when we write "Tectia" we generally mean the Unix version unless we say otherwise.

1.4   Overview of SSH Features

So, what can SSH do? Let's run through some examples that demonstrate the major features of SSH, such as secure remote logins, secure file copying, and secure invocation of remote commands.

1.4.1   Secure Remote Logins

Suppose you have login accounts on several computers on the Internet. Common programs like *telnet* let you log into one computer from another, say, from your home PC to your web hosting provider, or from one office computer to another. Unfortunately, *telnet* and similar programs transmit your username and password in plain text over the Internet, where a malicious third party can intercept them.* Additionally, your entire *telnet* session is readable by a network snooper.

Terminology: Networking

Local computer (local host, local machine)
> A computer on which you are logged in and, typically, running an SSH client.

Remote computer (remote host, remote machine)
> A second computer you connect to via your local computer. Typically, the remote computer is running an SSH server and is accessed via an SSH client. As a degenerate case, the local and remote computers can be the same machine.

Local user
> A user logged into a local computer.

Remote user
> A user logged into a remote computer.

Server
> An SSH server program.

Server machine
> A computer running an SSH server program. We sometimes simply write "server" for the server machine when the context makes clear (or irrelevant) the distinction between the running SSH server program and its host machine.

Client
> An SSH client program.

Client machine
> A computer running an SSH client. As with the server terminology, we simply write "client" when the context makes the meaning clear.

~ or $HOME
> A user's home directory on a Unix machine, particularly when used in a file path such as *~/filename*. Most shells recognize ~ as a user's home directory, with the notable exception of the Bourne shell. *$HOME* is recognized by all shells.

SSH completely avoids these problems. Rather than running the insecure *telnet* program, you run the SSH client program *ssh*. To log into an account with the username smith on the remote computer *host.example.com*, use this command:

```
$ ssh -l smith host.example.com
```

The client authenticates you to the remote computer's SSH server using an encrypted connection, meaning that your username and password are encrypted before they leave the local machine. The SSH server then logs you in, and your entire login

---

* This is true of standard Telnet, but some implementations add security features.

session is encrypted as it travels between client and server. Because the encryption is transparent, you won't notice any differences between *telnet* and the *telnet*-like SSH client.

1.4.2 Secure File Transfer

Suppose you have accounts on two Internet computers, *me@firstaccount.com* and *metoo@secondaccount.com*, and you want to transfer a file from the first to the second account. The file contains trade secrets about your business, however, that must be kept from prying eyes. A traditional file-transfer program, such as *ftp*, doesn't provide a secure solution. A third party can intercept and read the packets as they travel over the network. To get around this problem, you can encrypt the file on *firstaccount.com* with a program such as Pretty Good Privacy (PGP), transfer it via traditional means, and decrypt the file on *secondaccount.com*, but such a process is tedious and nontransparent to the user.

Using SSH, the file can be transferred securely between machines with a single secure copy command. If the file were named *myfile*, the command executed on *firstaccount.com* might be:

```
$ scp myfile metoo@secondaccount.com:
```

When transmitted by *scp*, the file is automatically encrypted as it leaves *firstaccount. com* and decrypted as it arrives on *secondaccount.com*.

1.4.3 Secure Remote Command Execution

Suppose you are a system administrator who needs to run the same command on many computers. You'd like to view the active processes for each user on four different computers—*grape*, *lemon*, *kiwi*, and *melon*—on a local area network using the Unix command */usr/bin/w*. Many SSH clients can run a single remote command if you provide it at the end of the command line. This short shell script does the trick:

```
#!/bin/sh
for machine in grape lemon kiwi melon
do
    ssh $machine /usr/bin/w          Execute remote command by ssh
done
```

Each *w* command and its results are encrypted as they travel across the network, and strong authentication techniques may be used when connecting to the remote machines.

1.4.4 Keys and Agents

Suppose you have accounts on many computers on a network. For security reasons, you prefer different passwords on all accounts; but remembering so many passwords is difficult. It's also a security problem in itself. The more often you type a password, the more likely you'll mistakenly type it in the wrong place. (Have you ever accidentally typed your password instead of your username, visible to the world? Ouch! And on many systems, such mistakes are recorded in a system log file, revealing your password in plain text.) Wouldn't it be great to identify yourself only once and get secure access to all the accounts without continually typing passwords?

SSH has various authentication mechanisms, and the most secure is based on *keys* rather than passwords. Keys are discussed in great detail in Chapter 6, but for now we define a key as a small blob of bits that uniquely identifies an SSH user. For security, a key is kept encrypted; it may be used only after entering a secret *passphrase* to decrypt it.

Using keys, together with a program called an *authentication agent*, SSH can authenticate you to all your computer accounts securely without requiring you to memorize many passwords or enter them repeatedly. It works like this:

1. In advance (and only once), place special, nonsecure files called *public key files* into your remote computer accounts. These enable your SSH clients (*ssh*, *scp*) to access your remote accounts.

2. On your local machine, invoke the *ssh-agent* program, which runs in the background.

3. Choose the key (or keys) you will need during your login session.

4. Load the keys into the agent with the *ssh-add* program. This requires knowledge of each key's secret passphrase.

At this point, you have an *ssh-agent* program running on your local machine, holding your secret keys in memory. You're now done. You have passwordless access to all your remote accounts that contain your public key files. Say goodbye to the tedium of retyping passwords! The setup lasts until you log out from the local machine or terminate *ssh-agent*.

1.4.5   Access Control

Suppose you want to permit another person to use your computer account, but only for certain purposes. For example, while you're out of town you'd like your secretary to read your email but not to do anything else in your account. With SSH, you can give your secretary access to your account without revealing or changing your password, and with only the ability to run the email program. No system-administrator privileges are required to set up this restricted access. (This topic is the focus of Chapter 8.)

1.4.6   Port Forwarding

SSH can increase the security of other TCP/IP-based applications such as *telnet*, *ftp*, and the X Window System. A technique called *port forwarding* or *tunneling* reroutes a TCP/IP connection to pass through an SSH connection, transparently encrypting it end to end. Port forwarding can also pass such applications through network firewalls that otherwise prevent their use.

Suppose you are logged into a machine away from work and want to access the internal news server at your office, *news.yoyodyne.com*. The Yoyodyne network is connected to the Internet, but a network firewall blocks incoming connections to most ports, particularly port 119, the news port. The firewall does allow incoming SSH connections, however, since the SSH protocol is secure enough that even Yoyodyne's rabidly paranoid system administrators trust it. SSH can establish a secure tunnel on an arbitrary local TCP port—say, port 3002—to the news port on the remote host. The command might look a bit cryptic at this early stage, but here it is:

```
$ ssh -L 3002:localhost:119 news.yoyodyne.com
```

This says "*ssh*, please establish a secure connection from TCP port 3002 on my local machine to TCP port 119, the news port, on *news.yoyodyne.com*." So, in order to read news securely, configure your news-reading program to connect to port 3002 on your local machine. The secure tunnel created by *ssh* automatically communicates with the news server on *news.yoyodyne.com*, and the news traffic passing through the tunnel is protected by encryption. [9.1]

1.5 History of SSH

SSH1 and the SSH-1 protocol were developed in 1995 by Tatu Ylönen, a researcher at the Helsinki University of Technology in Finland. After his university network was the victim of a password-sniffing attack earlier that year, Ylönen whipped up SSH1 for himself. When beta versions started gaining attention, however, he realized his security product could be put to wider use.

In July 1995, SSH1 was released to the public as free software with source code, permitting people to copy and use the program without cost. By the end of the year, an estimated 20,000 users in 50 countries had adopted SSH1, and Ylönen was fending off 150 email messages per day requesting support. In response, Ylönen founded SSH Communications Security Corp., (SCS, *http://www.ssh.com/*) in December of 1995 to maintain, commercialize, and continue development of SSH. Today he is a board member and technical advisor to the company.

Also in 1995, Ylönen documented the SSH-1 protocol as an Internet Engineering Task Force (IETF) Internet Draft, which essentially described the operation of the SSH1 software after the fact. It was a somewhat ad hoc protocol with a number of problems and limitations discovered as the software grew in popularity. These problems couldn't be fixed without losing backward compatibility, so in 1996, SCS introduced a new, major version of the protocol, SSH 2.0 or SSH-2, that incorporates new algorithms and is incompatible with SSH-1. In response, the IETF formed a working group called Secure Shell (SECSH) to standardize the protocol and guide its development in the public interest. The SECSH working group submitted the first Internet Draft for the SSH-2.0 protocol in February 1997.

In 1998, SCS released the software product SSH Secure Shell (SSH2), based on the superior SSH-2 protocol. However, SSH2 didn't replace SSH1 in the field: it was missing some features of SSH1 and had a more restrictive license, so many users felt little reason to switch, even though SSH-2 is a better and more secure protocol.

This situation changed with the appearance of OpenSSH (*http://www.openssh.com/*), a free implementation of the SSH-2 protocol from the OpenBSD project (*http://www. openbsd.org/*). It was based on the last free release of the original SSH, 1.2.12, but developed rapidly into one of the reigning SSH implementations in the world. Though many people have contributed to it, OpenSSH is largely the work of software developer Markus Friedl. It has been ported successfully to Linux, Solaris, AIX, Mac OS X, and other operating systems, in tight synchronization with the OpenBSD releases.

SCS has continued to improve its SSH products, in some cases beyond what OpenSSH supports. Its product line now carries the name Tectia. And nowadays there are dozens of SSH implementations, both free and commercial, for virtually all platforms. Millions of people use it worldwide to secure their communications.

1.6   Related Technologies

SSH is popular and convenient, but we certainly don't claim it is the ultimate security solution for all networks. Authentication, encryption, and network security originated long before SSH and have been incorporated into many other systems. Let's survey a few representative systems.

1.6.1   rsh Suite (r-Commands)

The Unix programs *rsh*, *rlogin*, and *rcp*—collectively known as the *r-commands*—are the direct ancestors of the SSH clients *ssh*, *slogin*, and *scp*. The user interfaces and visible functionality are nearly identical to their SSH counterparts, except that SSH clients are secure. The r-commands, in contrast, don't encrypt their connections and have a weak, easily subverted authentication model.

An r-command server relies on two mechanisms for security: a network naming service and the notion of "privileged" TCP ports. Upon receiving a connection from a client, the server obtains the network address of the originating host and translates it into a hostname. This hostname must be present in a configuration file on the server, typically */etc/hosts.equiv*, for the server to permit access. The server also checks that the source TCP port number is in the range 1–1023, since these port numbers can be used only by the Unix superuser (or root uid). If the connection passes both checks, the server believes it is talking to a trusted program on a trusted host and logs in the client as whatever user it requests!

These two security checks are easily subverted. The translation of a network address to a hostname is done by a naming service such as Sun's Network Information Service (NIS) or the Internet Domain Name System (DNS). Most implementations and/or deployments of NIS and DNS services have security holes, presenting opportunities to trick the server into trusting a host it shouldn't. Then, a remote user can log into someone else's account on the server simply by having the same username.

Likewise, blind trust in privileged TCP ports represents a serious security risk. A cracker who gains root privilege on a trusted machine can simply run a tailored version of the *rsh* client and log in as any user on the server host. Overall, reliance on these port numbers is no longer trustworthy in a world of desktop computers whose users have administrative access as a matter of course, or whose operating systems don't support multiple users or privileges (such as Windows 9x and Macintosh OS 9).

If user databases on trusted hosts were always synchronized with the server, installation of privileged programs (setuid root) strictly monitored, root privileges guaranteed to be held by trusted people, and the physical network protected, the r-commands would be reasonably secure. These assumptions made sense in the early days of networking, when hosts were few, expensive, and overseen by a small and trusted group of administrators, but they have far outlived their usefulness.

Given SSH's superior security features and that *ssh* is backward-compatible with *rsh* (and *scp* with *rcp*), we see no compelling reason to run the r-commands anymore. Install SSH and be happy.

1.6.2 Pretty Good Privacy (PGP) and GNU Privacy Guard (GnuPG)

PGP is a popular encryption program available for many computing platforms, created by Phil Zimmerman. It can authenticate users and encrypt data files and email messages. GnuPG is a more powerful successor to PGP with less-restrictive licensing.

SSH incorporates some of the same encryption algorithms as PGP and GnuPG, but applied in a different way. PGP is file-based, typically encrypting one file or email message at a time on a single computer. SSH, in contrast, encrypts an ongoing session between networked computers. The difference between PGP and SSH is like that between a batch job and an interactive process.

 PGP and SSH are related in another way as well: Tectia can optionally use PGP keys for authentication. [5.4.5]

More PGP and GnuPG information is available at *http://www.pgp.com/* and *http://www.gnupg.org/*, respectively.

1.6.3   Kerberos

Kerberos is a secure authentication system for environments where networks may be monitored, and computers aren't under central control. It was developed as part of Project Athena, a wide-ranging research and development effort at the Massachusetts Institute of Technology (MIT). Kerberos authenticates users by way of *tickets,* small sequences of bytes with limited lifetimes, while user passwords remain secure on a central machine.

Kerberos and SSH solve similar problems but are quite different in scope. SSH is lightweight and easily deployed, designed to work on existing systems with minimal changes. To enable secure access from one machine to another, simply install an SSH client on the first and a server on the second, and start the server. Kerberos, in contrast, requires significant infrastructure to be established before use, such as administrative user accounts, a heavily secured central host, and software for networkwide clock synchronization. In return for this added complexity, Kerberos ensures that users' passwords travel on the network as little as possible and are stored only on the central host. SSH sends passwords across the network (over encrypted connections, of course) on each login and stores keys on each host from which SSH is used. Kerberos also serves other purposes beyond the scope of SSH, including a centralized user account database, access control lists, and a hierarchical model of trust.

Another difference between SSH and Kerberos is the approach to securing client applications. SSH can easily secure most TCP/IP-based programs via a technique called port-forwarding. Kerberos, on the other hand, contains a set of programming libraries for adding authentication and encryption to other applications. Developers can integrate applications with Kerberos by modifying their source code to make calls to the Kerberos libraries. The MIT Kerberos distribution comes with a set of common services that have been "kerberized," including secure versions of *telnet, ftp,* and *rsh*.

If the features of both Kerberos and SSH sound good, you're in luck: they've been integrated. [11.4] More information on Kerberos can be found at *http://web.mit.edu/ kerberos/www/*.

1.6.4   IPSEC and Virtual Private Networks

Internet Protocol Security (IPSEC) is an Internet standard for network security. Developed by an IETF working group, IPSEC comprises authentication and encryption implemented at the IP level. This is a lower level of the network stack than SSH addresses. It is entirely transparent to end users, who don't need to use a particular program such as SSH to gain security; rather, their existing insecure network traffic is protected automatically by the underlying system. IPSEC can securely connect a single machine to a remote network through an intervening untrusted network (such as the Internet), or it can connect entire networks (this is the idea of the Virtual Private Network, or VPN).

SSH is often quicker and easier to deploy as a solution than IPSEC, since SSH is a simple application program, whereas IPSEC requires additions to the host operating systems on both sides if they don't already come with it, and possibly to network equipment such as routers, depending on the scenario. SSH also provides user authentication, whereas IPSEC deals only with individual hosts. On the other hand, IPSEC is more basic protection and can do things SSH can't. For instance, in Chapter 11 we discuss the difficulties of trying to protect the FTP protocol using SSH. If you need to secure an existing insecure protocol such as FTP, which isn't amenable to treatment with SSH, IPSEC is a way to do it.

IPSEC can provide authentication alone, through a means called the Authentication Header (AH), or both authentication and encryption, using a protocol called Encapsulated Security Payload (ESP). Detailed information on IPSEC can be found at *http://www.ietf.org/html.charters/ipsec-charter.html*.

1.6.5   Secure Remote Password (SRP)

The Secure Remote Password (SRP) protocol, created at Stanford University, is a security protocol very different in scope from SSH. It is specifically an authentication protocol, whereas SSH comprises authentication, encryption, integrity, session management, etc., as an integrated whole. SRP isn't a complete security solution in itself, but rather, a technology that can be a part of a security system.

The design goal of SRP is to improve on the security properties of password-style authentication, while retaining its considerable practical advantages. Using SSH public-key authentication is difficult if you're traveling, especially if you're not carrying your own computer, but instead are using other people's machines. You have to carry your private key on a portable storage device and hope that you can get the key into whatever machine you need to use.

Carrying your encrypted private key with you is also a weakness, because if someone steals it, they can subject it to a dictionary attack in which they try to find your passphrase and recover the key. Then you're back to the age-old problem with passwords: to be useful they must be short and memorable, whereas to be secure, they must be long and random.

SRP provides strong two-party mutual authentication, with the client needing only to remember a short password which need not be so strongly random. With traditional password schemes, the server maintains a sensitive database that must be protected, such as the passwords themselves, or hashed versions of them (as in the Unix */etc/passwd* and */etc/shadow* files). That data must be kept secret, since disclosure allows an attacker to impersonate users or discover their passwords through a dictionary attack. The design of SRP avoids such a database and allows passwords to be less random (and therefore more memorable and useful), since it prevents dictionary attacks. The server still has sensitive data that should be protected, but the consequences of its disclosure are less severe.

SRP is also intentionally designed to avoid using encryption algorithms in its operation. Thus it avoids running afoul of cryptographic export laws, which prohibits certain encryption technologies from being shared with foreign countries.

SRP is an interesting technology we hope gains wider acceptance; it is an excellent candidate for an additional authentication method in SSH. The current SRP implementation includes secure clients and servers for the Telnet and FTP protocols for Unix and Windows. More SRP information can be found at *http://srp.stanford.edu/*.

1.6.6 Secure Socket Layer (SSL) Protocol

The Secure Socket Layer (SSL) protocol is an authentication and encryption technique providing security services to TCP clients by way of a Berkeley sockets-style API. It was initially developed by Netscape Communications Corporation to secure the HTTP protocol between web clients and servers, and that is still its primary use, though nothing about it is specific to HTTP. It is on the IETF standards track as RFC-2246, under the name "TLS" for Transport Layer Security.

An SSL participant proves its identity by a *digital certificate,* a set of cryptographic data. A certificate indicates that a trusted third party has verified the binding between an identity and a given cryptographic key. Web browsers automatically check the certificate provided by a web server when they connect by SSL, ensuring that the server is the one the user intended to contact. Thereafter, transmissions between the browser and the web server are encrypted.

SSL is used most often for web applications, but it can also "tunnel" other protocols. It is secure only if a "trusted third party" exists. Organizations known as *certificate authorities* (CAs) serve this function. If a company wants a certificate from the CA, the company must prove its identity to the CA through other means, such as legal documents. Once the proof is sufficient, the CA issues the certificate.

For more information, visit the OpenSSL project at *http://www.openssl.org/*.

1.6.7 SSL-Enhanced Telnet and FTP

Numerous TCP-based communication programs have been enhanced with SSL, including *telnet* (e.g., SSLtelnet, SRA telnet, SSLTel, STel) and *ftp* (SSLftp), providing some of the functionality of SSH. Though useful, these tools are fairly single-purpose and typically are patched or hacked versions of programs not originally written for secure communication. The major SSH implementations, on the other hand, are more like integrated toolsets with diverse uses, written from the ground up for security.

1.6.8   stunnel

stunnel is an SSL tool created by Micha Trojnara of Poland. It adds SSL protection to existing TCP-based services in a Unix environment, such as POP or IMAP servers, without requiring changes to the server source code. It can be invoked from *inetd* as a wrapper for any number of service daemons or run standalone, accepting network connections itself for a particular service. *stunnel* performs authentication and authorization of incoming connections via SSL; if the connection is allowed, it runs the server and implements an SSL-protected session between the client and server programs.

This is especially useful because certain popular applications have the option of running some client/server protocols over SSL. For instance, email clients like Microsoft Outlook and Mozilla Mail can connect to POP, IMAP, and SMTP servers using SSL. For more *stunnel* information, see *http://www.stunnel.org/*.

1.6.9   Firewalls

A *firewall* is a hardware device or software program that prevents certain data from entering or exiting a network. For example, a firewall placed between a web site and the Internet might permit only HTTP and HTTPS traffic to reach the site. As another example, a firewall can reject all TCP/IP packets unless they originate from a designated set of network addresses.

Firewalls aren't a replacement for SSH or other authentication and encryption approaches, but they do address similar problems. The techniques may be used together.

1.7   Summary

SSH is a powerful, convenient approach to protecting communications on a computer network. Through secure authentication and encryption technologies, SSH supports secure remote logins, secure remote command execution, secure file transfers, access control, TCP/IP port forwarding, and other important features.

CHAPTER 2
Basic Client Use

SSH is a simple idea but it has many parts, some of them complex. This chapter is designed to get you started with SSH quickly. We cover the basics of SSH's most immediately useful features:

- Logging into a remote computer over a secure connection
- Transferring files between computers over a secure connection

We also introduce authentication with cryptographic keys, a more secure alternative to ordinary passwords. Advanced uses of client programs, such as multiple keys, client configuration files, and TCP port forwarding, are covered in later chapters. Our examples in this chapter work with OpenSSH and Tectia on Linux and other Unix-inspired operating systems.

2.1   A Running Example

Suppose you're out of town on a business trip and want to access your files, which sit on a Unix machine belonging to your ISP, *shell.isp.com*. A friend at a nearby university agrees to let you log into her Linux account on the machine *local.university. edu*, and then remotely log into yours. For the remote login you could use the *telnet* program, but as we've seen, this connection between the machines is insecure. (No doubt some subversive college student would grab your password and turn your account into a renegade web server for pirated software and death metal MP3s.) Fortunately, both your friend's machine and your ISP's have an SSH product installed.

In the example running through the chapter, we represent the shell prompt of the local machine, *local.university.edu*, as a dollar sign ($) and the prompt on *shell.isp.com* as shell.isp.com>.

2.2   Remote Terminal Sessions with ssh

Suppose your remote username on *shell.isp.com* is pat. To connect to your remote account from your friend's account on *local.university.edu*, you type:

```
$ ssh -l pat shell.isp.com
pat's password: ******
Last login: Mon Aug 16 19:32:51 2004 from quondam.nefertiti.org
You have new mail.
shell.isp.com>
```

This leads to the situation shown in Figure 2-1. The *ssh* command runs a client that contacts the SSH server on *shell.isp.com* over the Internet, asking to be logged into the remote account with username pat.[*] You can also provide *user@host* syntax instead of the *–l* option to accomplish the same thing:

```
$ ssh pat@shell.isp.com
```

Figure 2-1. Our example scenario

On first contact, SSH establishes a secure channel between the client and the server so that all transmissions between them are encrypted. The client then prompts for your password, which it supplies to the server over the secure channel. The server authenticates you by checking that the password is correct and permits the login. All subsequent client/server exchanges are protected by that secure channel, including everything you type into the SSH application and everything it displays to you from *shell.isp.com*.

It's important to remember that the secure channel exists only between the SSH client and server machines. After logging into *shell.isp.com* via *ssh*, if you then *telnet* or *ftp* to a third machine, *insecure.isp.com*, the connection between *shell.isp.com* and *insecure.isp.com* is not secure. However, you can run another *ssh* client from *shell.isp. com* to *insecure.isp.com*, creating another secure channel, which keeps the chain of connections secure.

We've covered only the simplest use of *ssh*. Chapter 7 goes into far greater depth about its many features and options.

2.2.1   File Transfer with scp

Continuing the story, suppose that while browsing your files, you encounter a PDF file you'd like to print. In order to send the file to a local printer at the university, you

---

[*] If the local and remote usernames are identical, you can omit the *–l* option (*–l pat*) and just type ssh shell. isp.com.

must first transfer the file to *local.university.edu*. Once again, you reject as insecure the traditional file-transfer programs, such as *ftp*. Instead, you use another SSH client program, *scp*, to copy the file across the network via a secure channel.

First, you write the attachment to a file in your home directory on *shell.isp.com* using your mail client, naming the file *printme.pdf*. When you've finished reading your other email messages, log out of *shell.isp.com*, ending the SSH session and returning to the shell prompt on *local.university.edu*. You're now ready to copy the file securely.

The *scp* program has syntax much like the traditional Unix *cp* program for copying files.* It is roughly:

```
scp name-of-source name-of-destination
```

In this example, *scp* copies the file *printme.pdf* on *shell.isp.com* over the network to a local file in your friend's account on *local.university.edu*, also called *printme.pdf*:

```
$ scp pat@shell.isp.com:printme.pdf printme.pdf
```

The file is transferred over an SSH-secured connection. The source and destination files may be specified not only by filename, but also by username ("pat" in our example) and hostname (*shell.isp.com*), indicating the location of the file on the network. Depending on your needs, various parts of the source or destination name can be omitted, and default values used. For example, omitting the username and the at sign (pat@) makes *scp* assume that the remote username is the same as the local one.

Like *ssh*, *scp* prompts for your remote password and passes it to the SSH server for verification. If successful, *scp* logs into the pat account on *shell.isp.com*, copies your remote file *printme.pdf* to the local file *printme.pdf*, and logs out of *shell.isp.com*. The local file *printme.pdf* may now be sent to a printer.

The destination filename need not be the same as the remote one. For example, if you're feeling French, you could call the local file *imprime-moi.pdf*:

```
$ scp pat@shell.isp.com:printme.pdf imprime-moi.pdf
```

The full syntax of *scp* can represent local and remote files in powerful ways, and the program also has numerous command-line options. [7.5]

2.3 Adding Complexity to the Example

The preceding example session provided a quick introduction to the most often-used client programs—*ssh* and *scp*—in a format to follow while sitting at your computer. Now that you have the basics, let's continue the example but include situations and complications glossed over the first time. These include the "known hosts" security feature and the SSH escape character.

---

* Actually it's modeled after the old *rcp* program for copying files insecurely between machines.

If you're following at the computer as you read, your SSH clients might behave unexpectedly or differently from ours. As you will see throughout the book, SSH implementations are highly customizable, by both yourself and the system administrator, on either side of the secure connection. Although this chapter describes common behaviors of SSH programs based on their installation defaults, your system might be set up differently.

If commands don't work as you expect, try adding the *-v* ("verbose") command-line option, for example:

```
$ ssh -v shell.isp.com
```

This causes the client to print lots of information about its progress, often revealing the source of the discrepancy.

2.3.1 Known Hosts

The first time an SSH client encounters a new remote machine, it may report that it's never seen the machine before, printing a message like the following:

```
$ ssh -l pat shell.isp.com
The authenticity of host 'shell.isp.com (192.168.0.2)' can't be established.
RSA key fingerprint is 77:a5:69:81:9b:eb:40:76:7b:13:04:a9:6c:f4:9c:5d.
Are you sure you want to continue connecting (yes/no)?
```

Assuming you respond yes (the most common response), the client continues:

```
Warning: Permanently added 'shell.isp.com,192.168.0.2' (RSA) to the list of known
hosts.
```

This message appears only the first time you contact a particular remote host. The message is a security feature related to SSH's concept of *known hosts*.*

Suppose an adversary wants to obtain your password. He knows you are using SSH, and so he can't monitor your connection by eavesdropping on the network. Instead, he subverts the naming service used by your local host so that the name of your intended remote host, *shell.isp.com*, translates falsely to the IP address of a computer run by him! He then installs an altered SSH server on the phony remote host and waits. When you log in via your trusty SSH client, the altered SSH server records your password for the adversary's later use (or misuse, more likely). The bogus server can then disconnect with a preplanned error message such as "System down for maintenance—please try again after 4:00 p.m." Even worse, it can fool you completely by using your password to log into the real *shell.isp.com* and transparently pass information back and forth between you and the server, monitoring your entire session. This hostile strategy is called a man-in-the-middle attack. [3.9.4] Unless you

---

* Depending on your client configuration, *ssh* might print a different message and automatically accept or reject the connection. [7.4.3.1]

think to check the originating IP address of your session on the server, you might never notice the deception.

The SSH *known-host mechanism* prevents such attacks. When an SSH client and server make a connection, each of them proves its identity to the other. Yes, not only does the server authenticate the client, as we saw earlier when the server checked Pat's password, but the client also authenticates the server by public-key cryptography. [3.4.3.6] In short, each SSH server has a secret, unique ID, called a *host key*, to identify itself to clients. The first time you connect to a remote host, a public counterpart of the host key gets copied and stored in your local account (assuming you responded "yes" to the client's prompt about host keys, earlier). Each time you reconnect to that remote host, the SSH client checks the remote host's identity using this public key.

Of course, it's better to have recorded the server's public host key before connecting to it the first time, since otherwise you are technically open to a man-in-the-middle attack that first time. Administrators can maintain systemwide known-hosts lists for given sets of hosts, but this doesn't do much good for connecting to random new hosts around the world. Until a reliable, widely deployed method of verifying such keys securely exists (such as secure DNS, or X.509-based public-key infrastructure), this record-on-first-use mechanism is an acceptable compromise.

If authentication of the server fails, various things may happen depending on the reason for failure and the SSH configuration. Typically a warning appears on the screen, ranging from a repeat of the known-hosts message:

```
Host key not found from the list of known hosts.
Are you sure you want to continue connecting (yes/no)?
```

to more dire words:

```
@@@@@@@@@@@@@@@@@@@@@@@@@@@@@@@@@@@@@@@@@@@@@@@@@@@@@@@@@@@
@    WARNING: REMOTE HOST IDENTIFICATION HAS CHANGED!    @
@@@@@@@@@@@@@@@@@@@@@@@@@@@@@@@@@@@@@@@@@@@@@@@@@@@@@@@@@@@
IT IS POSSIBLE THAT SOMEONE IS DOING SOMETHING NASTY!
Someone could be eavesdropping on you right now (man-in-the-middle attack)!
It is also possible that the RSA host key has just been changed.
The fingerprint for the RSA key sent by the remote host is
77:a5:69:81:9b:eb:40:76:7b:13:04:a9:6c:f4:9c:5d.
Please contact your system administrator.
Add correct host key in /home/smith/.ssh/known_hosts to get rid of this message.
Offending key in /home/smith/.ssh/known_hosts:36
```

If you answer yes, *ssh* allows the connection, but disables various features as a security precaution and doesn't update your personal known-hosts database with the new key; you must do that yourself to make this message go away.

As the text of the message says, if you see this warning, you aren't necessarily being hacked: for example, the remote host key may have legitimately changed for some reason. In some cases, even after reading this book, you won't know the cause of these messages. If you need assistance, contact your system administrator or a knowledgeable friend, rather than take a chance and possibly compromise your password. We'll cover these issues further when we discuss personal known hosts databases and how to alter the behavior of SSH clients with respect to host keys. [7.4.3]

2.3.2 The Escape Character

Let us return to the *shell.isp.com* example, just after you'd discovered the attachment in your remote email message and saved it to the remote file *printme.pdf*. In our original example, you then logged out of *shell.isp.com* and ran *scp* to transfer the file. But what if you don't want to log out? If you're using a workstation running a window system, you can open a new window and run *scp*. But if you're using a lowly text terminal, or you're not familiar with the window system running on your friend's computer, there is an alternative. You can temporarily interrupt the SSH connection, transfer the file (and run any other local commands you desire), and then resume the connection.

ssh supports an *escape character,* a designated character that gets the attention of the SSH client. Normally, *ssh* sends every character you type to the server, but the escape character is caught by the client, alerting it that special commands may follow. By default, the escape character is the tilde (~), but you can change it. To reduce the chances of sending the escape character unintentionally, that character must be the first character on the command line, i.e., following a newline (Control-J) or return (Control-M) character. If not, the client treats it literally, not as an escape character.

After the escape character gets the client's attention, the next character entered determines the effect of the escape. For example, the escape character followed by a Control-Z suspends *ssh* like any other shell job, returning control to the local shell. Such a pair of characters is called an *escape sequence*. We cover these in detail in a later chapter. [7.4.6.8]

To change the *ssh* escape character, use the *–e* command-line option. For example, type the following to make the percent sign (%) the escape character when connecting to *shell.isp.com* as user pat:

```
$ ssh -e "%" -l pat shell.isp.com
```

2.4 Authentication by Cryptographic Key

In our running example, the user pat is authenticated by the SSH server via login password. Passwords, however, have serious drawbacks:

- In order for a password to be secure, it should be long and random, but such passwords are hard to memorize.

- A password sent across the network, even protected by an SSH secure channel, can be captured when it arrives on the remote host if that host has been compromised.
- Most operating systems support only a single password per account. For shared accounts (e.g., a superuser account), this presents difficulties:
  - Password changes are inconvenient because the new password must be communicated to all people with access to the account.
  - Tracking usage of the account becomes difficult because the operating system doesn't distinguish between the different users of the account.

To address these problems, SSH supports *public-key authentication*: instead of relying on the password scheme of the host operating system, SSH may use cryptographic *keys*. [3.2.2] Keys are more secure than passwords in general and address all the weaknesses mentioned earlier.

2.4.1   A Brief Introduction to Keys

A key is a digital identity. It's a unique string of binary data that means "This is me, honestly, I swear." And with a little cryptographic magic, your SSH client can prove to a server that its key is genuine, and you are really you.

An SSH identity uses a pair of keys, one private and one public. The *private key* is a closely guarded secret only you have. Your SSH clients use it to prove your identity to servers. The *public key* is, like the name says, public. You place it freely into your accounts on SSH server machines. During authentication, the SSH client and server have a little conversation about your private and public key. If they match (according to a cryptographic test), your identity is proven, and authentication succeeds.

The following sequence demonstrates the conversation between client and server. [3.4.2.4] (It occurs behind the scenes, so you don't need to memorize it or anything; we just thought you might be interested.)

1. Your client says, "Hey server, I'd like to connect by SSH to an account on your system, specifically, the account owned by user smith."
2. The server says, "Well, maybe. First, I challenge you to prove your identity!" And the server sends some data, known as a *challenge,* to the client.
3. Your client says, "I accept your challenge. Here is proof of my identity. I made it myself by mathematically using your challenge and my private key." This response to the server is called an *authenticator*.
4. The server says, "Thanks for the authenticator. I will now examine the smith account to see if you may enter." Specifically, the server checks smith's public keys to see if the authenticator "matches" any of them. (The "match" is another cryptographic operation.) If so, the server says, "OK, come on in!" Otherwise, the authentication fails.

Before you can use public-key authentication, some setup is required:

- You need a private key and a public key, known collectively as a *key pair*. You also need a secret passphrase to protect your private key. [2.4.2]
- You need to install your public key on an SSH server machine. [2.4.3]

2.4.2 Generating Key Pairs with ssh-keygen

To use cryptographic authentication, you must first generate a key pair for yourself, consisting of a private key (your digital identity that sits on the client machine) and a public key (that sits on the server machine). To do this, use the *ssh-keygen* program to produce either a DSA or RSA key. The OpenSSH version of *ssh-keygen* requires you to specify the key type with the *–t* option (there is no default):

```
$ ssh-keygen -t dsa
Generating public/private dsa key pair.
Enter file in which to save the key (/home/dbarrett/.ssh/id_dsa): press ENTER
Enter passphrase (empty for no passphrase): ********
Enter same passphrase again: ********
Your identification has been saved in /home/pat/.ssh/id_dsa.
Your public key has been saved in /home/pat/.ssh/id_dsa.pub.
The key fingerprint is:
14:ba:06:98:a8:98:ad:27:b5:ce:55:85:ec:64:37:19 pat@shell.isp.com
```

On Tectia systems, *ssh-keygen* produces a DSA key by default, and also accepts the *–t* option:

```
$ ssh-keygen
Generating 2048-bit dsa key pair
   1 ..oOo.oOo.oO
   2 o.oOo.oOo.oO
   3 o.oOo.oOo.oO
        The program displays a "ripple" pattern to indicate progress; the characters are actually
overwritten on a single line
  28 o.oOo.oOo.oO
Key generated.
2048-bit dsa, pat@shell.isp.com, Wed Jan 12 2005 20:22:21 -0500
Passphrase : *************
Again      : *************
Private key saved to /home/pat/.ssh2/id_dsa_2048_a
Public key saved to /home/pat/.ssh2/id_dsa_2048_a.pub
```

Normally, *ssh-keygen* performs all necessary mathematics to generate a key, but on some operating systems you might be asked to assist it. Key generation requires some random numbers, and if your operating system doesn't supply a random-number generator, you may be asked to type some random text or wiggle your mouse around. *ssh-keygen* uses the timings of your keystrokes to initialize its internal random-number generator. On a 3.2 GHz Pentium 4 system running Linux, a 1024-bit RSA key generates in less than one second; if your hardware is slower or heavily loaded, generation could take minutes. It can also take longer if the process runs out of random bits and *ssh-keygen* waits to collect more.

ssh-keygen then creates your local SSH directory (*~/.ssh* for OpenSSH or *~/.ssh2* for Tectia) if it doesn't already exist, and stores the private and public components of the generated key in two files there. By default, their names are *id_dsa* and *id_dsa.pub* (OpenSSH) or *id_dsa_2048_a* and *id_dsa_2048_a.pub* (Tectia). SSH clients consider these to be your default identity for authentication purposes.

 Never reveal your private key and passphrase to anyone. They are just as sensitive as your login password. Anyone possessing them can impersonate you!

When created, the identity file is readable only by your account, and its contents are further protected by encrypting them with the passphrase you supplied during generation. We say "passphrase" instead of "password" both to differentiate it from a login password, and to stress that spaces and punctuation are allowed and encouraged. We recommend a passphrase at least 10–15 characters long and not a grammatical sentence.

ssh-keygen has numerous options for managing keys: changing the passphrase, choosing a different name for the key file, and so forth. [6.2]

2.4.3   Installing a Public Key on an SSH Server Machine

When passwords are used for authentication, the host operating system maintains the association between the username and the password. For cryptographic keys, you must set up a similar association manually. After creating the key pair on the local host, you must install your public key in your account on the remote host. A remote account may have many public keys installed for accessing it in various ways.

Returning to our running example, you must install a public key into the pat account on *shell.isp.com*. This is done by editing a file in the SSH configuration directory: *~/.ssh/ authorized_keys* for OpenSSH or *~/.ssh2/authorization* for Tectia.

2.4.3.1   Instructions for OpenSSH

Create or edit the remote file *~/.ssh/authorized_keys* and append your public key—i.e., the contents of the *id_dsa.pub* file you generated on the local machine. A typical *authorized_keys* file contains a list of public-key data, one key per line. The example contains only two public keys, each on its own line of the file, but they are too long to fit on this page. The line breaks inside the long numbers are printing artifacts; if they were actually in the file, it would be incorrectly formatted and wouldn't work:

```
ssh-dss AAAAB3NzaC1kc3MAAACBAMCiL15WEI+OdFJZ9InMSh4PAZ3eFO7YJBFZ6ybl7ld+807z/
jnXGghYVuvKbHdNlRYWidhdFWtDW3l5v8Ce7nyYhcQU7x+j4JeUf7qmLmQxluOv+O5rlg7L5U2RuW94yt1BGj
+xk7vzLwOhKHE/+YFVz52sFNazoYXqPnm1pRPRAAAAFQDGjroMj+ML= jones@client2.com
```

```
ssh-rsa
AAAAB3NzaC1yc2EAAAABIwAAAIEAvpB4lUbAaEbh9u6HLig7amsfywD4fqSZq2ikACIUBn3GyRPfeF93l/
weQh7O2ofXbDydZAKMcDvBJqRhUotQUwqV6HJxqoqPDlPGUUyo8RDIkLUIPRyqypZxmK9aCXokFiHoGCXfQ9i
mUP/w/jfqb9ByDtG97tUJF6nFMP5WzhM= smith@client.net
```

The first entry is a DSA key and the second is RSA. [8.2.1]

2.4.3.2 Instructions for Tectia

For Tectia you need to edit two files, one on the client machine and one on the server machine. On the client machine, create or edit the file ~/.ssh2/identification and insert a line to identify your private-key file:

```
IdKey id_dsa_2048_a
```

On the server machine, create or edit the file ~/.ssh2/authorization, which contains information about public keys, one per line. But unlike OpenSSH's authorized_keys file, which contains copies of the public keys, the authorization file lists only the file-name of the key:

```
Key id_dsa_2048_a.pub
```

Finally, copy id_dsa_2048_a.pub from your local machine to the remote Tectia server machine, placing it in ~/.ssh2.

Regardless of which SSH implementation you use, make sure your remote SSH directory and associated files are writable only by your account:*

```
# OpenSSH
$ chmod 755 ~/.ssh
$ chmod 644 ~/.ssh/authorized_keys

# Tectia
$ chmod 755 ~/.ssh2
$ chmod 644 ~/.ssh2/id_dsa_2048_a.pub
$ chmod 644 ~/.ssh2/authorization
```

The SSH server is picky about file and directory permissions and may refuse authentication if the remote account's SSH configuration files have insecure permissions. [5.3.2.1]

You are now ready to use your new key to access the pat account:

```
$ ssh -l pat shell.isp.com
Enter passphrase for key '/home/you/.ssh/id_dsa': ************
Last login: Mon Aug 16 19:44:21 2004 from quincunx.nefertiti.org
You have new mail.
shell.isp.com>
```

If all goes well, you are logged into the remote account. Figure 2-2 shows the entire process.

---

* We make files world-readable and directories world-searchable, to avoid NFS problems. [10.7.2] But if StrictModes is enabled in the server, you'll need to make these permissions more restrictive. [5.3.2.1]

Installing OpenSSH Keys with ssh-copy-id

OpenSSH includes a program, *ssh-copy-id*, that installs a public key automatically on a remote server with a single command, placing it into *~/.ssh/authorized_keys*:

```
ssh-copy-id -i key_file [user@]server_name
```

For example, to install the key *mykey* in the dulaney account on *server.example.com*:

```
$ ssh-copy-id -i mykey dulaney@server.example.com
```

You don't need to list the *.pub* extension of the key file; or more specifically, you can provide either the private or public-key file, and the public key is copied to the remote server.

In order for the copy to take place, you'll need an account on the remote machine, of course, and you'll need to authenticate somehow. If you've never set up public-key authentication on *server.example.com* before, you'll be prompted for your login password.

ssh-copy-id is convenient, but it has some subtle issues:

- If you have no *authorized_keys* file on the remote machine, *ssh-copy-id* creates one containing your new key; otherwise, it appends the new key.
- If you do already have a remote *authorized_keys* file, and it does not end with a newline character, *ssh-copy-id* blindly appends your new key onto the last public key in the file, with no newline between them. This effectively corrupts the last two keys in *authorized_keys*. Moral: always make sure *authorized_keys* ends with a newline. (This is easy to overlook, especially when running OpenSSH on Windows. [14.4])
- The syntax of *ssh-copy-id* is similar to that of *scp*, the secure copy program, but there's an important difference: *scp* follows the hostname of the remote machine with a colon. Don't use a colon with *ssh-copy-id* or you'll get an error message, "Name or service not known," as the hostname lookup fails.

Before you use *ssh-copy-id* to simplify or hide the details of public-key authentication, we recommend that you understand how to set it up manually. This point is often true of security-related software: you should know how and why it works.

Note the similarity to the earlier example with password authentication. [2.2] On the surface, the only difference is that you provide the passphrase to your private key, instead of providing your login password. Underneath, however, something quite different is happening. In password authentication, the password is transmitted to the remote host. With cryptographic authentication, the passphrase serves only to decrypt the private key to create an authenticator. [2.4.1]

Public-key authentication is more secure than password authentication because:

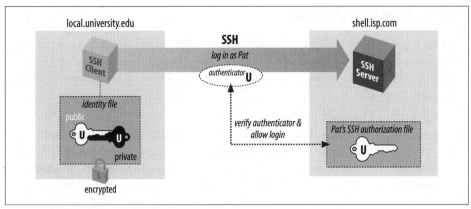

Figure 2-2. Public-key authentication

- It requires two secret components—the identity file on disk, and the passphrase in your head—so both must be captured in order for an adversary to access your account. Password authentication requires only one component, the password, which might be easier to steal.

- Neither the passphrase nor the key is sent to the remote host, just the authenticator discussed earlier. Therefore, no secret information is transmitted off the client machine.

- Machine-generated cryptographic keys are infeasible to guess. Human-generated passwords are routinely cracked by a password-guessing technique called a *dictionary attack*. A dictionary attack may be mounted on the passphrase as well, but this requires stealing the private-key file first.

A host's security can be greatly increased by disabling password authentication altogether and permitting only SSH connections by key.

2.4.4   If You Change Your Key

Suppose you have generated a key pair, *id_dsa* and *id_dsa.pub*, and copied *id_dsa.pub* to a bunch of SSH server machines. All is well. Then one day, you decide to change your identity, so you run *ssh-keygen* a second time, overwriting *id_dsa* and *id_dsa. pub*. Guess what? Your previous public-key file is now invalid, and you must copy the new public key to all those SSH server machines again. This is a maintenance headache, so think carefully before changing (destroying!) a key pair. Some caveats:

- You are not limited to one key pair. You can generate as many as you like, stored in different files, and use them for diverse purposes. [6.4]

- If you just want to change your passphrase, you don't have to generate a new key pair. *ssh-keygen* has command-line options for replacing the passphrase of an existing key: *–p* for OpenSSH [6.2.1] and *–e* for Tectia [6.2.2]. In this case your public key remains valid since the private key hasn't changed, just the passphrase for decrypting it.

2.5   The SSH Agent

Each time you run *ssh* or *scp* with public-key authentication, you have to retype your passphrase. The first few times you might not mind, but eventually this retyping gets annoying. Wouldn't it be nicer to identify yourself just once and have *ssh* and *scp* remember your identity until further notice (for example, until you log out), not prompting for your passphrase? In fact, this is just what an *SSH agent* does for you.

An agent is a program that keeps private keys in memory and provides authentication services to SSH clients. If you preload an agent with private keys at the beginning of a login session, your SSH clients won't prompt for passphrases. Instead, they communicate with the agent as needed. The effects of the agent last until you terminate the agent, usually just before logging out. The agent program for both OpenSSH and Tectia is called *ssh-agent*.

Generally, you run a single *ssh-agent* in your local login session, before running any SSH clients. You can run the agent by hand, but people usually edit their login files (for example, *~/.login* or *~/.xsession*) to run the agent automatically. SSH clients communicate with the agent via a local socket or named pipe whose filename is stored in an environment variable, so all clients (and all other processes) within your login session have access to the agent. [6.3.4] To try the agent, type:

```
$ ssh-agent $SHELL
```

where SHELL is the environment variable containing the name of your login shell. Alternatively, you could supply the name of any other shell, such as *sh*, *bash*, *csh*, *tcsh*, or *ksh*. The agent runs and then invokes the given shell as a child process. The visual effect is simply that another shell prompt appears, but this shell has access to the agent.

Once the agent is running, it's time to load private keys into it using the *ssh-add* program. By default, *ssh-add* loads the key from your default identity file:

```
$ ssh-add
Enter passphrase for /home/you/.ssh/id_dsa: ********
Identity added: /home/you/.ssh/id_dsa (/home/you/.ssh/id_dsa)
```

Now *ssh* and *scp* can connect to remote hosts without prompting for your passphrase. Figure 2-3 shows the process.

ssh-add reads the passphrase from your terminal by default or, optionally, from standard input noninteractively. Otherwise, if you are running the X Window System with the DISPLAY environment variable set, and standard input isn't a terminal, *ssh-add* reads your passphrase using a graphical X program, *ssh-askpass*. This behavior is useful when calling *ssh-add* from X session setup scripts.

 To force *ssh-add* to use X to read the passphrase, type *ssh-add < /dev/ null* at a command line.

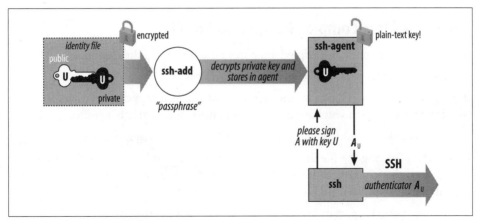

Figure 2-3. How the SSH agent works

ssh-add has further capabilities and can operate with multiple identity files. [6.3.3] For now, here are a few useful commands. To load a key other than your default identity into the agent, provide the filename as an argument to *ssh-add*:

```
$ ssh-add my-other-key-file
```

You can also list the keys the agent currently holds:

```
$ ssh-add -l
```

delete a key from the agent in memory:

```
$ ssh-add -d name-of-key-file
```

or delete all keys from the agent in memory:

```
$ ssh-add -D
```

When running an SSH agent, don't leave your terminal unattended while logged in. While your private keys are loaded in an agent, anyone may use your terminal to connect to any remote accounts accessible via those keys, without needing your passphrase! Even worse, a sophisticated intruder can extract your keys from the running agent and steal them.

If you use an agent, make sure to lock your terminal if you leave it while logged in. You can also use *ssh-add -D* to clear your loaded keys and reload them when you return. In addition, *ssh-agent* can be "locked" by *ssh-add*, to protect the agent from unauthorized users. [6.3.3]

2.5.1 Agents and Automation

Suppose you have a batch script that runs *ssh* to launch remote processes. If the script runs *ssh* many times, it prompts for your passphrase repeatedly, which is inconvenient for automation (not to mention annoying and error-prone). If you run an agent, however, your script can run without a single passphrase prompt. [11.1]

2.5.2   A More Complex Passphrase Problem

In our running example, we copied a file from the remote to the local host:

```
$ scp pat@shell.isp.com:printme.pdf imprime-moi.pdf
```

In fact, *scp* can copy a file from the remote host *shell.isp.com* directly to a third host running SSH on which you have an account named, say, "psmith":

```
$ scp pat@shell.isp.com:printme.pdf psmith@other.host.net:imprime-moi.pdf
```

Rather than copying the file first to the local host and then back out again to the final destination, this command has *shell.isp.com* send it directly to *other.host.net*. However, if you try this, you run into the following problem:

```
$ scp pat@shell.isp.com:printme.pdf psmith@other.host.net:imprime-moi.pdf
Enter passphrase for RSA key 'Your Name <you@local.org>': ************
You have no controlling tty and no DISPLAY.  Cannot read passphrase.
lost connection
```

What happened? When you run *scp* on your local machine, it contacts *shell.isp.com* and internally invokes a second *scp* command to do the copy. Unfortunately, the second *scp* command also needs the passphrase for your private key. Since there is no terminal session to prompt for the passphrase, the second *scp* fails, causing the original *scp* to fail. The SSH agent solves this problem: the second *scp* command simply queries your local SSH agent, so no passphrase prompting is needed.

The SSH agent also solves another, more subtle, problem in this example. Without the agent, the second *scp* (on *shell.isp.com*) needs access to your private-key file, but the file is on your local machine. So, you have to copy your private key file to *shell. isp.com*. This isn't ideal; what if *shell.isp.com* isn't a secure machine? Also, the solution doesn't scale: if you have a dozen different accounts, it is a maintenance headache to keep your private key file on all of them. Fortunately, the SSH agent comes to the rescue once again. The remote *scp* process simply contacts your local SSH agent and authenticates, and the secure copy proceeds successfully, through a process called agent forwarding.

2.5.3   Agent Forwarding

In the preceding example, the remote instance of *scp* has no direct access to your private key, since the agent is running on the local host, not the remote host. SSH provides *agent forwarding* [6.3.5] to address this problem.

When agent forwarding is turned on,* the remote SSH server masquerades as a second *ssh-agent*, as shown in Figure 2-4. It takes authentication requests from your SSH client processes there, passes them back over the SSH connection to the local

---

* It is on by default in Tectia, but off in OpenSSH.

agent for handling, and relays the results back to the remote clients. In short, remote clients transparently get access to the local *ssh-agent*. Since any programs executed via *ssh* on the remote side are children of the server, they all have access to the local agent just as if they were running on the local host.

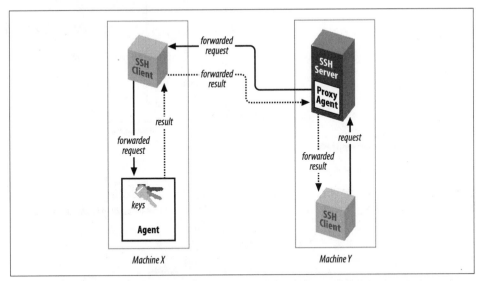

Figure 2-4. How agent forwarding works

In our double-remote *scp* example, here is what happens when agent forwarding comes into play (see Figure 2-5):

1. You run the command on your local machine:

   ```
   $ scp pat@shell.isp.com:printme.pdf psmith@other.host.net:imprime-moi.pdf
   ```

2. This *scp* process contacts your local agent and authenticates you to *shell.isp.com*.

3. A second *scp* command is automatically launched on *shell.isp.com* to carry out the copy to *other.host.net*.

4. Since agent forwarding is turned on, the SSH server on *shell.isp.com* poses as an agent.

5. The second *scp* process tries to authenticate you to *other.host.net* by contacting the "agent" that is really the SSH server on *shell.isp.com*.

6. Behind the scenes, the SSH server on *shell.isp.com* communicates with your local agent, which constructs an authenticator proving your identity and passes it back to the server.

7. The server verifies your identity to the second *scp* process, and authentication succeeds on *other.host.net*.

8. The file copying occurs.

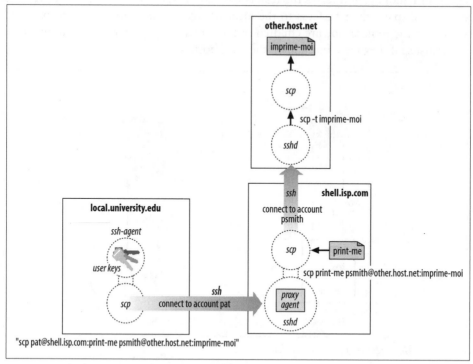

Figure 2-5. Third-party scp with agent forwarding

Agent forwarding works over multiple connections in a series, allowing you to *ssh* from one machine to another, and then to another, with the agent connection following along the whole way. These machines may be progressively less secure, but agent forwarding doesn't send your private key to the remote host: it just relays authentication requests back to the first host for processing. Therefore, you don't have to copy your private key to other machines.

2.6 Connecting Without a Password or Passphrase

One of the most frequently asked questions about SSH is: "How can I connect to a remote machine without having to type a password or passphrase?" As you've seen, an SSH agent can make this possible, but there are other methods as well, each with different trade-offs. Here we list the available methods with pointers to the sections discussing each one.

To use SSH clients for *interactive sessions* without a password or passphrase, you have several options:

- Public-key authentication with an agent [2.5] [6.3]
- Hostbased authentication [3.4.3.6]
- Kerberos authentication [11.4]

 Another way to achieve passwordless logins is to use an unencrypted private key with no passphrase. Although this technique can be appropriate for automation purposes, never do this for interactive use. Instead, use the SSH agent, which provides the same benefits with much greater security. Don't use unencrypted keys for interactive SSH!

On the other hand, noninteractive, unattended programs such as *cron* jobs or batch scripts may also benefit from not having a password or passphrase. In this case, the different techniques raise some complex issues, and we discuss their relative merits and security issues later. [11.1]

2.7 Miscellaneous Clients

Several other clients are included in addition to *ssh* and *scp*:

- *sftp*, an *ftp*-like client
- *slogin*, a link to *ssh*, analogous to the *rlogin* program

2.7.1 sftp

The *scp* command is convenient and useful, but many users are already familiar with FTP (File Transfer Protocol), a more widely used technique for transferring files on the Internet.* *sftp* is a separate file-transfer tool layered on top of SSH. The OpenSSH *sftp* can run over either SSH-1 or SSH-2, whereas the Tectia version runs over SSH-2 only due to implementation details.

sftp has several advantages:

- It is secure, using an SSH-protected channel for data transfer.
- Multiple commands for file copying and manipulation can be invoked within a single *sftp* session, whereas *scp* opens a new session each time it is invoked.
- It can be scripted using the familiar *ftp* command language.
- In other software applications that run an FTP client in the background, you can try substituting *sftp*, thus securing the file transfers of that application. You might need to run an agent, however, since programs that normally invoke *ftp* might not recognize the *sftp* passphrase prompt, or they might expect you to have suppressed FTP's password prompt (using a *.netrc* file, for example).

---

* Due to the nature of the FTP protocol, FTP clients are difficult to secure using SSH port forwarding. It is possible, however. [11.2]

Anyone familiar with FTP will feel right at home with *sftp*, but *sftp* has some additional features of note:

- Command-line editing using GNU Emacs-like keystrokes (Control-B for backward character, Control-E for end of line, and so forth).*
- Wildcards for matching filenames. OpenSSH uses the same "globbing" syntax that is supported by most common shells, while Tectia uses an extended regular expression syntax described in Appendix B.
- Several useful command-line options:

  –b filename (OpenSSH)
  –B filename (Tectia)
  > Read commands from the given file instead of the terminal.

  –S path
  > Locate the *ssh* program using the given path.

  –v
  > Print verbose messages as the program runs.

  –V (OpenSSH)
  > Print the program version number and exit.

In addition, many of the command-line options for ssh can also be used for *sftp*.

The OpenSSH version of *sftp* supports only the binary transfer mode of standard FTP, in which files are transferred without modification. Tectia's *sftp* also supports ASCII transfer mode, which translates end-of-line characters between systems that might use different conventions, e.g., carriage return plus newline for Windows, newline (only) for Unix, or carriage return (only) for Macintosh.

2.7.2 slogin

slogin is an alternative name for *ssh*, just as *rlogin* is a synonym for *rsh*. On Linux systems, *slogin* is simply a symbolic link to *ssh*. Note that the *slogin* link is found in OpenSSH but not Tectia. We recommend using just *ssh* for consistency: it's found in all these implementations and is shorter to type.

2.8   Summary

From the user's point of view, SSH consists of several client programs and some configuration files. The most commonly used clients are *ssh* for remote login, and *scp* and *sftp* for file transfer. Authentication to the remote host can be accomplished

---

* OpenSSH 4.0 and higher.

using existing login passwords or with public-key cryptographic techniques. Passwords are more immediately and easily used, but public-key authentication is more flexible and secure. The *ssh-keygen*, *ssh-agent*, and *ssh-add* programs generate and manage SSH keys.

CHAPTER 3

Inside SSH

SSH secures your data while it passes over a network, but how exactly does it *work?* In this chapter, we move firmly onto technical ground and explain the inner workings of SSH. Let's roll up our sleeves and dive into the bits and bytes.

This chapter is written for system administrators, network administrators, and security professionals. Our goal is to teach you enough about SSH to make an intelligent, technically sound decision about using it. Mostly, we deal with SSH-2 as the current and recommended SSH protocol; our treatment of the old and deprecated SSH-1 is limited to a summary of its differences and limitations. When we refer to "the SSH protocol," we mean SSH-2.

Of course, the ultimate references on SSH are the protocol standards and the source code of an implementation. We don't completely analyze the protocols or recapitulate every step taken by the software. Rather, we summarize them to provide a solid, technical overview of their operation. If you need more specifics, you should refer to the standards documents. The SSH Version 2 protocol is in draft status on the IETF standards track; it is available at:

> *http://www.ietf.org/*

The older SSH-1 protocol is called Version 1.5 and is documented in a file named *RFC* included in the source package of the now-obsolete SSH1.

3.1   Overview of Features

The major features and guarantees of the SSH protocol are:

- *Privacy* of your data, via strong encryption
- *Integrity* of communications, guaranteeing they haven't been altered
- *Authentication,* i.e., proof of identity of senders and receivers
- *Authorization,* i.e., access control to accounts
- *Forwarding* or *tunneling* to encrypt other TCP/IP-based sessions

3.1.1 Privacy (Encryption)

Privacy means protecting data from disclosure. Typical computer networks don't guarantee privacy; anyone with access to the network hardware, or to hosts connected to the network, may be able to read (or *sniff*) all data passing over the network. Although modern switched networks have reduced this problem in local area networks, it is still a serious issue; passwords are easily stolen by such sniffing attacks.

SSH provides privacy by encrypting data that passes over the network. This end-to-end encryption is based on random keys that are securely negotiated for that session and then destroyed when the session is over. SSH supports a variety of encryption algorithms for session data, including such standard ciphers as AES, ARCFOUR, Blowfish, Twofish, IDEA, DES, and triple-DES (3DES).

3.1.2 Integrity

Integrity means assuring that data transmitted from one end of a network connection arrives unaltered on the other end. The underlying transport of SSH, TCP/IP, does have integrity checking to detect alteration due to network problems (electrical noise, lost packets due to excessive traffic, etc.). Nevertheless, these methods are ineffective against deliberate tampering and can be fooled by a clever attacker. Even though SSH encrypts the data stream so that an attacker can't easily change selected parts to achieve a specific result, TCP/IP's integrity checking alone can't prevent, say, an attacker's deliberate injection of garbage into your session.

A more complex example is a *replay attack*. Imagine that Attila the Attacker is monitoring your SSH session and also simultaneously watching over your shoulder (either physically, or by monitoring your keystrokes at your terminal). In the course of your work, Attila sees you type the command *rm -rf* * within a small directory. He can't read the encrypted SSH session data, of course, but he could correlate a burst of activity on that connection with your typing the command, and capture the packets containing the encrypted version of your command. Later, when you're working in your home directory, Attila inserts the captured bits into your SSH session, and your terminal mysteriously erases all your files!

Attila's replay attack succeeds because the packets he inserted are valid; he could not have produced them himself (due to the encryption), but he can copy and replay them later. TCP/IP's integrity check is performed only on a per-packet basis, so it can't detect Attila's attack. Clearly, the integrity check must apply to the data stream as a whole, ensuring that the bits arrive as they were sent: in order and with no duplication.

The SSH protocol uses cryptographic integrity checking, which verifies both that transmitted data hasn't been altered and that it truly comes from the other end of the connection. It uses keyed hash algorithms based on MD5 and SHA-1 for this purpose: well-known, widely trusted algorithms.

3.1.3 Authentication

Authentication means verifying someone's identity. Suppose I claim to be Richard Silverman, and you want to authenticate that claim. If not much is at stake, you might just take my word for it. If you're a little concerned, you might ask for my driver's license or other photo ID. If you're a bank officer deciding whether to open a safe-deposit box for me, you might also require that I possess a physical key, and so on. It all depends on how sure you want to be. The arsenal of high-tech authentication techniques is growing constantly and includes DNA-testing microchips, retina and hand scanners, and voice-print analyzers.

Every SSH connection involves two authentications: the client verifies the identity of the SSH server (*server authentication*), and the server verifies the identity of the user requesting access (*user authentication*). Server authentication ensures that the SSH server is genuine, not an impostor, guarding against an attacker's redirecting your network connection to a different machine. Server authentication also protects against man-in-the-middle attacks, wherein the attacker sits invisibly between you and the server, pretending to be the client on one side and the server on the other, fooling both sides and reading all your traffic in the process!

User authentication is traditionally done with passwords, which unfortunately are a weak authentication scheme. To prove your identity you have to reveal the password, exposing it to possible theft. Additionally, in order to remember a password, people are likely to keep it short and meaningful, which makes the password easier for third parties to guess. For longer passwords, some people choose words or sentences in their native languages, and these passwords are likely to be crackable. From the standpoint of information theory, grammatical sentences contain little real information (technically known as *entropy*): generally less than two bits per character in English text, far less than the 8–16 bits per character found in computer encodings.

SSH supports authentication by password, encrypting the password as it travels over the network. This is a vast improvement over other common remote-access protocols (Telnet, FTP) which generally send your password in the clear (i.e., unencrypted) over the network, where anyone with sufficient network access can steal it! Nevertheless, it's still only simple password authentication, so SSH provides other stronger and more manageable mechanisms: per-user public-key signatures, and an improved *rlogin*-style authentication with host identity verified by public key. In addition, various SSH implementations support some other systems, including Kerberos, RSA Security's SecurID tokens, S/Key one-time passwords, and the Pluggable Authentication Modules (PAM) system. An SSH client and server negotiate to determine which authentication mechanism to use, based on their configurations, and a server can even require multiple forms of authentication.

3.1.4 Authorization

Authorization means deciding what someone may or may not do. It occurs after authentication, since you can't grant someone privileges until you know who she is. SSH servers have various ways of restricting clients' actions. Access to interactive login sessions, TCP port and X Window forwarding, key agent forwarding, etc., can all be controlled, though not all these features are available in all SSH implementations, and they aren't always as general or flexible as you might want. Authorization may be controlled at a serverwide level (e.g., the */etc/ssh/sshd_config* file for OpenSSH), or per account, depending on the authentication method used (e.g., each user's files ~/.ssh/authorized_keys, ~/.ssh2/authorization, ~/.shosts, ~/.k5login, etc.).

3.1.5 Forwarding (Tunneling)

Forwarding or tunneling means encapsulating another TCP-based service, such as Telnet or IMAP, within an SSH session. This brings the security benefits of SSH (privacy, integrity, authentication, authorization) to other TCP-based services. For example, an ordinary Telnet connection transmits your username, password, and the rest of your login session in the clear. By forwarding *telnet* through SSH, all of this data is automatically encrypted and integrity-checked, and you may authenticate using SSH credentials.

SSH supports three types of forwarding:

TCP port forwarding
    Secures any TCP-based service [9.2]

X forwarding
    Secures the X11 protocol (i.e., X Windows) [9.4]

Agent forwarding
    Permits SSH clients to use SSH private keys held on remote machines [6.3.5]

From these basic facilities, some SSH products build more complex services, such as SOCKS proxies and special-purpose forwarders that can handle difficult protocols like FTP.

3.2 A Cryptography Primer

We've covered the basic properties of SSH. Now we focus on cryptography, introducing important terms and ideas regarding the technology in general. There are many good references on cryptographic theory and practice, and we make no attempt here to be comprehensive. (For more detailed information, check out Bruce Schneier's excellent book, *Applied Cryptography*, published by John Wiley & Sons.) We introduce encryption and decryption, plaintext and ciphertext, keys, secret-key and public-key cryptography, and hash functions, both in general and as they apply to SSH.

Encryption is the process of scrambling data so that it can't be read by unauthorized parties. An *encryption algorithm* (or *cipher*) is a particular method of performing the scrambling; examples of currently popular encryption algorithms are RSA, AES, DSA, and Blowfish. The original, readable data is called the *plaintext,* or data "in the clear," while the encrypted version is called the corresponding ciphertext.

The goal of an encryption algorithm is to convert plaintext to ciphertext. To do this, you pass two inputs to the encryption algorithm: the plaintext itself, and a *key,* a string that is typically a secret known only to you. From these inputs, the algorithm produces the ciphertext. An encryption algorithm is considered secure if it is infeasible for anyone to read (or *decrypt*) the encrypted ciphertext without the key. An attempt to decrypt data without its key is called *cryptanalysis.*

3.2.1 How Secure Is Secure?

It's important to understand the word "infeasible" in the previous paragraph. Today's most popular and secure ciphers are vulnerable to *brute-force* attacks: if you try every possible key, you eventually succeed in decryption. However, when the number of possible keys is large, a brute-force search requires a great deal of time and computing power. Based on the state of the art in computer hardware and algorithms, it is possible to pick sufficiently large key sizes to render brute-force key-search unreasonable for your adversary. What counts as infeasible, though, depending on how valuable the data is, how long it must stay secure, and how motivated and well-funded your adversary is. Keeping something secret from your rival startup for a few days is one thing; keeping it secret from a major world government for 10 years is quite another.

Of course, for all this to make sense, you must be convinced that brute force is the only way to attack your cipher. Encryption algorithms have structure and are susceptible to mathematical analysis. Over the years, many ciphers previously thought secure have fallen to advances in cryptanalysis. It isn't currently possible to *prove* a practical cipher secure. Rather, a cipher acquires respectability through intensive study by mathematicians and cryptographers. If a new cipher exhibits good design principles, and well-known researchers study it for some time and fail to find a practical, faster method of breaking it than brute force, then people will consider it secure.*

---

* In his pioneering works on information theory and encryption, the mathematician Claude Shannon defined a model for cipher security and showed there is a cipher that is perfectly secure under that model: the so-called *one-time pad.* It is perfectly secure: the encrypted data gives an attacker no information whatsoever about the possible plaintext. The ciphertext literally can decrypt to any plaintext at all with equal likelihood. The problem with the one-time pad is that it is cumbersome and fragile. It requires that keys be as large as the messages they protect, be generated perfectly randomly, and never be reused. If any of these requirements are violated, the one-time pad becomes extremely insecure. The ciphers in common use today aren't perfectly secure in Shannon's sense, but for the best of them, brute-force attacks are infeasible.

3.2.2 Public- and Secret-Key Cryptography

Encryption algorithms as described so far are called *symmetric* or *secret-key* ciphers; the same key is used for encrypting and decrypting. Examples are Blowfish, AES, 3DES, and RC4. Such a cipher immediately introduces the key-distribution problem: how do you get the key to your intended recipient? If you can meet in person every once in a while and exchange a list of keys, that's all well and good, but for dynamic communication over computer networks, this doesn't work.

Public-key, or *asymmetric,* cryptography replaces the single key with a pair of related keys: public and private. They are related in a mathematically clever way: data encrypted with one key may be decrypted only with the other member of the pair, and it is infeasible to derive the private key from the public one. You keep your private key, well, private, and give the public key to anyone who wants it, without worrying about disclosure. Ideally, you publish it in a directory next to your name, like a telephone book. When someone wants to send you a secret message, they encrypt it with your public key. Other people may have your public key, but that won't allow them to decrypt the message; only you can do that with the corresponding private key. Public-key cryptography goes a long way toward solving the key-distribution problem.*

Public-key methods are also the basis for *digital signatures:* extra information attached to a digital document to provide evidence that a particular person has seen and agreed to it, much as a pen-and-ink signature does with a paper document. Any asymmetric cipher (RSA, ElGamal, Elliptic Curve, etc.) may be used for digital signatures, though the reverse isn't true. For instance, the DSA algorithm is a signature-only public-key scheme and is not intended to be used for encryption. (That's the idea, anyway, although it's easy to use a general DSA implementation for both RSA and ElGamal encryption. That was not the intent, however.)

Secret- and public-key encryption algorithms differ in another way: performance. All common public-key algorithms are enormously slower than secret-key ciphers—by orders of magnitude. It is simply infeasible to encrypt large quantities of data using a public-key cipher. For this reason, modern data encryption uses both methods together. Suppose you want to send some data securely to your friend Bob Bitflipper. Here's what a modern encryption program does:

1. Generate a random key, called the *bulk key*, for a fast, secret-key algorithm like 3DES (a.k.a. the *bulk cipher*).

2. Encrypt the plaintext with the bulk key.

---

* There is still the issue of reliably determining whose public key is whose; but that gets into public-key infrastructure, or PKI systems, and is a broader topic.

3. Secure the bulk key by encrypting it with Bob Bitflipper's public key, so only Bob can decrypt it. Since secret keys are small (a few hundred bits long at most), the speed of the public-key algorithm isn't an issue.

To reverse the operation, Bob's decryption program first decrypts the bulk key, and then uses it to decrypt the ciphertext. This method yields the advantages of both kinds of encryption technology, and in fact, SSH uses this technique. User data crossing an SSH connection is encrypted using a fast secret-key cipher, the key for which is shared between the client and server using public-key methods.

3.2.3   Hash Functions

In cryptography (and elsewhere in computing and network technology), it is often useful to know if some collection of data has changed. Of course, one can just send along (or keep around) the original data for comparison, but that can be prohibitively expensive both in time and storage. The common tool addressing this need is called a *hash function*. Hash functions are used by SSH-1 for integrity checking (and have various other uses in cryptography we won't discuss here).

A hash function is simply a mapping from a larger set of data values to a smaller set. For instance, a hash function H might take an input bit string of any length up to 50,000 bits, and uniformly produce a 128-bit output. The idea is that when sending a message m to Alice, I also send along the hash value $H(m)$. Alice computes $H(m)$ independently and compares it to the $H(m)$ value I sent; if they differ, she concludes that the message was modified in transit.

This simple technique can't be completely effective. Since the range of the hash function is strictly smaller than its domain, many different messages have the same hash value. To be useful, H must have the property that the kinds of alterations expected to happen to the messages in transit, must be overwhelmingly likely to cause a change in the message hash. Put another way: given a message m and a typical changed message m', it must be extremely unlikely that $H(m) = H(m')$.

Thus, a hash function must be tailored to its intended use. One common use is in networking: datagrams transmitted over a network frequently include a message hash that detects transmission errors due to hardware failure or software bugs. Another use is in cryptography, to implement digital signatures. Signing a large amount of data is prohibitively expensive, since it involves slow public-key operations as well as shipping along a complete encrypted copy of the data. What is actually done is to first hash the document, producing a small hash value, and then sign that, sending the signed hash along instead. A verifier independently computes the hash, then decrypts the signature using the appropriate public key, and compares them. If they are the same, he concludes (with high probability) that the signature is valid, and that the data hasn't changed since the private-key holder signed it.

These two uses, however, have different requirements, and a hash function suitable for detecting transmission errors due to line noise might be ineffective at detecting deliberate alterations introduced by a human attacker! A cryptographic hash function must make it computationally infeasible to find two different messages having the same hash or to find a message having a particular fixed hash. Such a function is said to be *collision-resistant* (or *collision-proof,* though that's a bit misleading), and *pre-image-resistant*. The Cyclic Redundancy Check (CRC) hash commonly used to detect accidental data changes (e.g., in Ethernet frame transmissions) is an example of a noncollision-resistant hash. It is easy to find CRC-32 hash collisions, and a well-known attack on SSH-1 is based on this fact. [3.5] Examples of cryptographically strong hash functions are MD5 and SHA-1.

3.3   The Architecture of an SSH System

SSH has about a dozen distinct, interacting components that produce the features we've covered. [3.1] Figure 3-1 illustrates the major components and their relationships to one another.

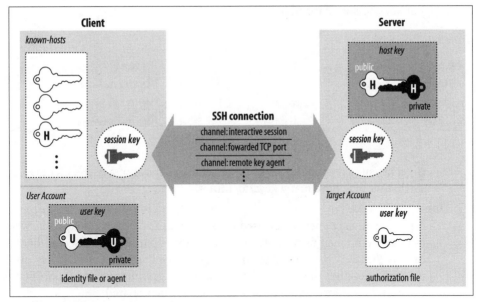

Figure 3-1. SSH architecture

By "component" we don't necessarily mean "program": SSH also has keys, sessions, and other fun things. In this section we provide a brief overview of all the components, so you can begin to get the big picture of SSH:

Server

A program that allows incoming SSH connections to a machine, handling authentication, authorization, and so forth. In most Unix SSH implementations, the server is *sshd.*

Client

A program that connects to SSH servers and makes requests, such as "log me in" or "copy this file." In OpenSSH and Tectia, the major clients are *ssh*, *scp*, and *sftp*.

Session

An ongoing connection between a client and a server. It begins after the client successfully authenticates to a server and ends when the connection terminates. Sessions may be interactive or batch.

Key

A relatively small amount of data, generally from tens of to 1,000 or 2,000 bits, used as a parameter to cryptographic algorithms such as encryption or message authentication. The key binds the algorithm operation in some way to the key holder: in encryption, it ensures that only someone else holding that key (or a related one) can decrypt the message; in authentication, it allows you to verify later that the key holder actually signed the message. There are two kinds of keys: symmetric or secret key, and asymmetric or public key. [3.2.2] An asymmetric key has two parts: the public and private components. SSH has several types of keys, as summarized in Table 3-1.

Table 3-1. Keys, keys, keys

Name	Lifetime	Created by	Type	Purpose
User key	Persistent	User	Public	Identify a user to the server
Host key	Persistent	Administrator	Public	Identify a server/machine
Session key	One session	Client (and server)	Secret	Protect communications

User key

A persistent, asymmetric key used by clients as proof of a user's identity. (A single user may have many keys/identities.)

Host key

A persistent, asymmetric key used by a server as proof of its identity, as well as by a client when proving its host's identity as part of hostbased authentication. [3.4.3.6] If a machine runs a single SSH server, the host key also uniquely identifies the machine. (If a machine is running multiple SSH servers, each may have a different host key, or they may share.)

Session key

A randomly generated, symmetric key for encrypting the communication between an SSH client and server. It is shared by the two parties in a secure manner during the SSH connection setup so that an eavesdropper can't discover it. Both sides then have the session key, which they use to encrypt their communications. When the SSH session ends, the key is destroyed.

An SSH connection has several session keys: each direction (server to client, and client to server) has keys for encryption and others for integrity checking. In our discussions we treat all the session keys as a unit and speak of "the session key" for convenience; they are all derived from a single master secret, anyway. If the context requires it, we identify the individual key we mean.

Key generator
A program that creates persistent keys (user keys and host keys) for SSH. OpenSSH and Tectia have the program *ssh-keygen*.

Known-hosts database
A collection of host keys. Clients and servers refer to this database to authenticate one another.

Agent
A program that caches user keys in memory, so users needn't keep retyping their passphrases. The agent responds to requests for key-related operations, such as signing an authenticator, but it doesn't disclose the keys themselves. It is a convenience feature. OpenSSH and Tectia have the agent *ssh-agent*, and the program *ssh-add* loads and unloads the key cache.

Signer
A program that signs hostbased authentication packets. We explain this in our discussion of hostbased authentication. [3.4.3.6]

Random seed
A pool of random data used by SSH components to initialize software pseudo-random number generators.

Configuration file
A collection of settings to tailor the behavior of an SSH client or server.

Not all these components are required in an implementation of SSH. Certainly servers, clients, and keys are mandatory, but many implementations don't have an agent, and some don't even include a key generator.

3.4 Inside SSH-2

The SSH protocol has two major, incompatible versions, called Version 1* and Version 2. [1.5] We refer to these as SSH-1 and SSH-2. The SSH-1 protocol is now a relic; it is less flexible than SSH-2, has unfixable security weaknesses, and has been deprecated for years. Its implementations see no real development aside from bug fixes, and the default protocol for most SSH software has been SSH-2 for some time now. In this chapter, as we describe "the SSH protocol," we are talking about SSH-2. We limit our

---

* SSH Version 1 went through several revisions, the most popular known as Versions 1.3 and 1.5.

treatment of SSH-1 to a summary of its design, its differences with SSH-2, and its weaknesses.

The SSH protocol is actually divided into four major pieces, formally described as four separate protocols in different IETF documents, and in principle independent of one another. In practice, they are layered together to provide the set of services most users associate with SSH as a whole. These are:

- SSH Transport Layer Protocol (SSH-TRANS)
- SSH Authentication Protocol (SSH-AUTH)
- SSH Connection Protocol (SSH-CONN)
- SSH File Transfer Protocol (SSH-SFTP)

There are other documents that describe other aspects of, or extensions to, the protocols, but the preceding ones represent the core of SSH. As of this writing, these documents are still "Internet-Drafts," but after much effort by the IETF SECSH working group, they have been submitted to the IESG for consideration as proposed standards and may soon be published as Internet RFCs.

Figure 3-2 outlines the division of labor between these protocols, and how they relate to each other, application programs, and the network. Elements in italics are protocol extensions defined in separate Internet-Draft documents, which have attained fairly widespread use.

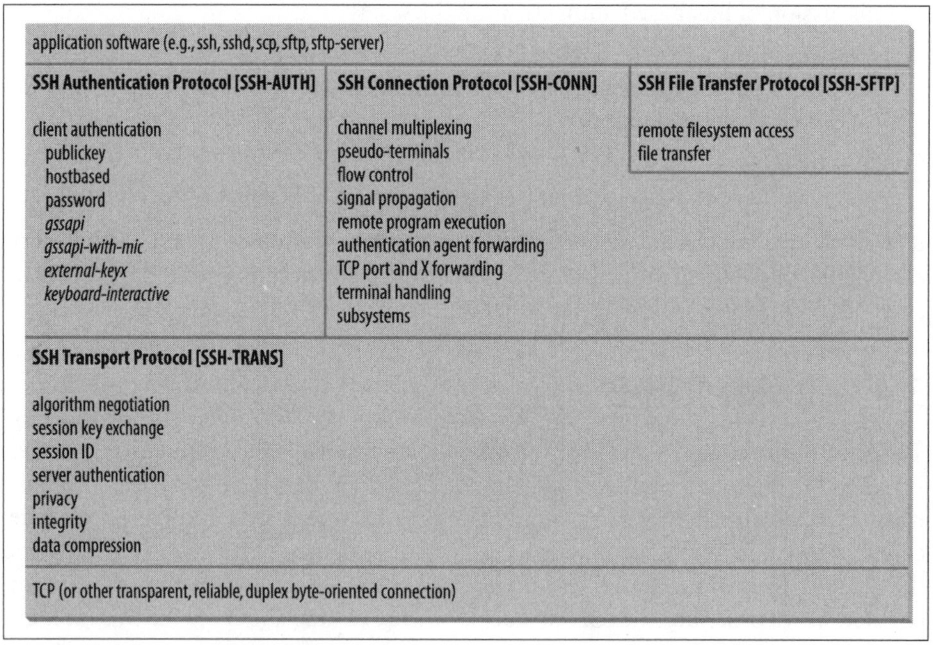

application software (e.g., ssh, sshd, scp, sftp, sftp-server)		
SSH Authentication Protocol [SSH-AUTH]	**SSH Connection Protocol [SSH-CONN]**	**SSH File Transfer Protocol [SSH-SFTP]**

client authentication
  publickey
  hostbased
  password
  gssapi
  gssapi-with-mic
  external-keyx
  keyboard-interactive
	channel multiplexing
	pseudo-terminals
	flow control
	signal propagation
	remote program execution
	authentication agent forwarding
	TCP port and X forwarding
	terminal handling
	subsystems
		remote filesystem access
		file transfer

SSH Transport Protocol [SSH-TRANS]		
algorithm negotiation session key exchange session ID server authentication privacy integrity data compression		
TCP (or other transparent, reliable, duplex byte-oriented connection)		

Figure 3-2. SSH-2 protocol family

SSH is designed to be modular and extensible. All of the core protocols define abstract services they provide and requirements they must meet, but allow multiple mechanisms for doing so, as well as a way of easily adding new mechanisms. All the critical parameters of an SSH connection are negotiable, including the methods and algorithms used in:

- Session key exchange
- Server authentication
- Data privacy and integrity
- User authentication
- Data compression

Client and server negotiate the use of a common set of methods, allowing broad interoperability among different implementations. In most categories, the protocol defines at least one *required* method, to further promote interoperability. Note that this only means a conforming implementation is required to support the method in its code; any particular method may in fact be turned off by the administrator in a particular environment. So, the fact that public-key authentication is required by SSH-AUTH doesn't mean it's always available to clients from any particular running SSH server; it merely means it must be available and *could* be turned on, if need be.

3.4.1   Protocol Summary

SSH-TRANS is the fundamental building block, providing the initial connection, record protocol, server authentication, and basic encryption and integrity services. After establishing an SSH-TRANS connection, the client has a single, secure, full-duplex byte stream to an authenticated peer.

Next, the client can use SSH-AUTH over the SSH-TRANS connection to authenticate itself to the server. SSH-AUTH defines a framework within which multiple authentication mechanisms may be used, fixing such things as the format and order of authentication requests, conditions for success or failure, and how a client learns the available methods. There may be any number of actual methods implemented, and the protocol allows arbitrary exchanges as part of any particular mechanism so that protocol extensions are easily defined to incorporate any desired authentication method in the future. SSH-AUTH *requires* only one method: public key with the DSS algorithm. It further defines two more methods: password and hostbased. A number of other methods have been defined in various Internet-Drafts, and some of them have gained wide acceptance.

After authentication, SSH clients invoke the SSH-CONN protocol, which provides a variety of richer services over the single pipe provided by SSH-TRANS. This includes everything needed to support multiple interactive and noninteractive sessions: multiplexing several streams (or *channels*) over the underlying connection; managing X,

TCP, and agent forwarding; propagating signals across the connection (such as SIG-INT, when a user types ^C to interrupt a process); terminal handling; data compression; and remote program execution.

Finally, an application may use SSH-SFTP over an SSH-CONN channel to provide file-transfer and remote filesystem manipulation functions.

It's important to understand that the arrangement, layering, and sequencing of these protocols is a matter of convention or need, not design; although they are typically used in a particular order, other arrangements are possible. For instance, note that SSH-CONN is not layered on top of SSH-AUTH; they are both at the same level above SSH-TRANS. Typically, an SSH server requires authentication via SSH-AUTH before allowing the client to invoke SSH-CONN—and also typically, clients want to use SSH-CONN in order to obtain the usual SSH services (remote terminal, agent forwarding, etc.). However, this need not be the case. A specialized SSH server for a particular, limited purpose might not require authentication, and hence could allow a client to invoke an application service (SSH-CONN, or perhaps some other locally defined service) immediately after establishing an SSH-TRANS connection. An anonymous SFTP server might be implemented this way, for example. However, such nonstandard protocol arrangements are probably seen only in a closed environment with custom client/server software. Since most SFTP clients in the world expect to do SSH-AUTH, they probably won't interoperate with such a server. An anonymous SFTP server for general use would use SSH-AUTH in the usual fashion and simply report immediate success for any attempted client authentication.

That said, these protocols were conceived as a group and rely on each other in practice. For instance, SSH-SFTP on its own provides no security whatsoever; it is merely a language for conducting remote-filing operations. It's assumed to be run over a secure transport if security is needed, such as an SSH session. However, using the *sftp -S* option of OpenSSH and Tectia, for example, you could connect the *sftp* client to an *sftp-server* running on another host using some other method: over a serial line, or some other secure network protocol...or *rsh* if you want to be perverse. Similarly, SSH-AUTH mechanisms rely on a secure underlying transport to varying degrees. The most obvious is the "password" mechanism, which simply sends the password in plaintext over the transport as part of an authentication request. Obviously, that mechanism would be disastrous over an insecure transport.

Another important point is that the SSH protocol deals *only* with communication "on-the-wire"—that is, its formats and conventions apply only to data being exchanged dynamically between the SSH client and server. It says nothing at all, for instance, about:

- Formats for storing keys on disk
- User authorization (e.g., ~/.ssh/authorized_keys)
- Key agents or agent forwarding

...and many other things that people typically think of as part of SSH. These facets are *implementation-dependent*: they are not specified by the standard, and hence may be done differently depending on what software you're using. And in fact they do differ: OpenSSH and Tectia use different file formats for keys. Even if you convert one to the other, you'll find that OpenSSH keys belong in ~/.ssh/authorized_keys, whereas each Tectia key goes in its own file, listed by reference in yet another file, ~/.ssh2/authorization. And although both products sport a private-key agent—with the same name even, *ssh-agent*—they are incompatible.

Now that we have an overview of the major components of SSH, let's dive in and examine each of these protocols in detail. To give structure and concreteness to an otherwise abstract description of the protocols, we frame our discussion by following a particular SSH connection from beginning to end. We follow the thread of debugging messages produced by *ssh -vv*, explaining the significance of the various messages and turning aside now and then to describe the protocol phases occurring at that point.

Since this *–vv* level of verbosity produces quite a few messages not relevant to our protocol discussion, we omit some for the sake of clarity.

3.4.2   SSH Transport Layer Protocol (SSH-TRANS)

3.4.2.1   Connection

We begin by running an SSH client in verbose mode, requesting a connection to *host.foo.net*:

```
$ ssh -vv host.foo.net
OpenSSH_3.6.1p1+CAN-2003-0693, SSH protocols 1.5/2.0, OpenSSL 0x0090702f
debug1: Reading configuration data /Users/res/.ssh/config
debug1: Applying options for com
debug1: Applying options for *
debug1: Reading configuration data /etc/ssh/ssh_config
debug1: Connecting to host.foo.net [10.1.1.1] port 22.
debug1: Connection established.
```

The client is a version of OpenSSH running on a Macintosh. It reads its configuration files, then makes a TCP connection to the remote side, which succeeds.

3.4.2.2   Protocol version selection

As soon as the server accepts the connection, the SSH protocol begins. The server announces its protocol version using a text string:

```
debug1: Remote protocol version 2.0, remote software version 4.1.0.34 SSH Secure
Shell
```

You can see this string yourself by simply connecting to the server socket, e.g., with *telnet*:

```
$ telnet host.foo.net 22
Trying 10.1.1.1...
Connected to host.foo.net
Escape character is '^]'.
SSH-2.0-4.1.0.34 SSH Secure Shell
^]
telnet> quit
Connection closed.
```

The format of the announcement is:

```
SSH-<protocol version>-<comment>
```

In this case, the server implements the SSH-2 protocol, and the software version is 4.1.0.34 of SSH Secure Shell from SSH Communications Security. Although the comment field can contain anything at all, SSH servers commonly put their product name and version there. This is useful, as clients often recognize specific servers in order to work around known bugs or incompatibilities. Some people don't like this practice on security grounds, and try to remove or change the comment. Be aware that if you do, you may cause more trouble than it's worth, since previously working SSH sessions may suddenly start failing if they had relied on such workarounds.

The protocol version number "1.99" has special significance: it means the server supports both SSH-1 and SSH-2, and the client may choose either one.

Next, OpenSSH parses the comment:

```
debug1: no match: 4.1.0.34 SSH Secure Shell
debug1: Enabling compatibility mode for protocol 2.0
debug1: Local version string SSH-2.0-OpenSSH_3.6.1p1+CAN-2003-0693
```

but does not find a match in its list of known problems to work around. It elects to proceed with SSH-2 (the only choice in this case), and sends its own version string to the server, in the same format. If the client and server agree that their versions are compatible, the connection process continues; otherwise, either party may decide to terminate the connection.

At this point, if the connection proceeds, both sides switch to a nontextual, record-oriented protocol for further communication, which is the basis of SSH transport. This is often referred to as the SSH *binary packet protocol*, and is defined in SSH-TRANS.

3.4.2.3 Parameter negotiation

Having established a connection and agreed on a protocol version, the first real function of SSH-TRANS is to arrange for the basic security properties of SSH:

- Privacy (encryption)
- Integrity (nonmodifiability and origin assurance)
- Server authentication (man-in-the-middle and spoofing resistance)
- Compression (not a security property per se, but included in this negotiation)

But first, the two sides must agree on session parameters, including the methods to achieve these properties. The whole process happens in the protocol phase called the *key exchange*, even though the first part also negotiates some parameters unrelated to the key exchange per se.

```
debug1: SSH2_MSG_KEXINIT sent
debug1: SSH2_MSG_KEXINIT received
```

The client sends its KEXINIT ("key exchange initialization") message, and receives one from the server. Here are the choices it gives to the server:

```
debug2: kex_parse_kexinit: gss-group1-sha1-toWM5Slw5Ew8Mqkay+al2g==,
                gss-group1-sha1-A/vxljAEU54gt9a48EiANQ==,
                diffie-hellman-group-exchange-sha1,
                diffie-hellman-group1-sha1
```

These are the key exchange algorithms the client supports, which are:

diffie-hellman-group1-sha1
> This algorithm is defined and required by SSH-TRANS; this specifies the well-known Diffie-Hellman procedure for key agreement, together with specific parameters (Oakley Group 2 [RFC-2409] and the SHA-1 hash algorithm).

diffie-hellman-group-exchange-sha1
> Similar, but allows the client to choose from a list of group parameters, addressing concerns about possible attacks based on a fixed group; defined in the IETF draft document "secsh-dh-group-exchange."*

gss-group1-sha1-toWM5Slw5Ew8Mqkay+al2g==
gss-group1-sha1-A/vxljAEU54gt9a48EiANQ==
> These odd-looking names are partially encoded in Base64—they represent two variants of a Kerberos-authenticated Diffie-Hellman exchange as defined in IETF draft "secsh-gsskeyex." These are useful where a Kerberos infrastructure is available, providing automatic and flexible server authentication without maintaining separate SSH host keys and known-hosts files. The Kerberos authentication

---

* A *group* is a mathematical abstraction relevant to the Diffie-Hellman procedure; see a reference on group theory, number theory, or abstract algebra if you're curious.

proceeds by way of GSSAPI, and the name suffixes are the Base64 encoding of the MD5 hash of the ASN.1 DER encoding of the underlying GSSAPI mechanism's OID. Say that five times fast.

In terms of abstract requirements, an SSH key exchange algorithm has two outputs:

- A shared secret, *K*
- An "exchange hash," *H*

K is the master secret for the session: SSH-TRANS defines a method for deriving from secret *K* the various keys and other cryptographic parameters needed for specific encryption and integrity algorithms used in the SSH connection. The exchange hash *H* does not have to be secret, although it should not be divulged unnecessarily. It should be unique to each session, and computed in such a way that neither side can force a particular value of hash *H*. We'll see the significance of that later.

The key exchange should also perform server authentication, in order to guard against spoofing and *man-in-the-middle* (MITM) attacks. There is an inherent asymmetry in the SSH client/server relationship: the server accepts connections from as-yet unknown parties, whereas a client always has a particular server as the target of its connection. The server may demand secret information as part of user authentication (e.g., password). The client is the first party to rely on the identity of the other side, and hence server authentication comes first. Without server authentication, an attacker might redirect the client's TCP connection to a host of his choice (perhaps by subverting the DNS or network routing) and trick the user into logging into the wrong host; this is called *spoofing*. Or, he might interpose himself between the client and the (legitimate) server, executing the SSH protocol as server on one side and client on the other, passing messages back and forth and reading all the traffic! This is a *man-in-the-middle attack*.

The key exchange phase of SSH-TRANS may be repeated later in a connection, in order to replace an aging master secret or re-authenticate the server. In fact, the draft recommends that a connection be re-keyed after each gigabyte of transmitted data or after each hour of connection time, whichever comes sooner. However, the hash output *H* of the very first key exchange is used as the "session identifier" for this SSH connection; we'll see its use later.

Next, the client offers a choice of SSH host key types it can accept:

```
debug2: kex_parse_kexinit: ssh-rsa,ssh-dss,null
```

In this case, it offers RSA, DSA, and "null," for no key at all. It includes "null" because of its support of Kerberos for host authentication; if a Kerberos key exchange is used, no SSH-specific host key is needed for server authentication.

After that, the client lists the bulk data encryption ciphers it supports:

```
debug2: kex_parse_kexinit: aes128-cbc,3des-cbc,blowfish-cbc,cast128-cbc,arcfour,
        aes192-cbc,aes256-cbc,rijndael-cbc@lysator.liu.se
```

The selected cipher is used for privacy of data flowing over the connection. Bulk data is never enciphered directly with public-key methods such as RSA or DSA because they are far too slow. Instead, we use a symmetric cipher such as those listed, protecting the session key for that cipher with public-key methods if appropriate. The names here indicate particular algorithms and associated cryptographic parameters; for instance, aes128-cbc refers to the Advanced Encryption Standard algorithm, with a 128-bit key in cipher-block-chaining mode.

Note the use of a private algorithm name as well: rijndael-cbc@lysator.liu.se. This email-address-like syntax is defined in the SSH Architecture draft ("secsh-architecture"), and allows any individuals or organizations to define and use their own algorithms or other SSH protocol identifiers without going through the IETF to have them approved. Identifiers that don't contain an @ sign are global and must be centrally registered.

The draft also defines the "none" cipher, meaning no encryption is to be applied. While there are legitimate reasons for wanting such a connection (including debugging!), some SSH implementations do not support it, at least in their default configuration. Often, recompiling the software from source with different flags, or hacking the code itself, is needed to turn on support for "none" encryption.* The reason is that it's deemed just too dangerous. If a user can easily turn off encryption, so can an attacker who gains access to a user's account, even briefly. Imagine surreptitiously adding this to an OpenSSH user's client configuration file, ~/.ssh/config:

```
# OpenSSH
Host *
 Ciphers none
```

or simply replacing the *ssh* program on a compromised machine with one that uses the "none" cipher, and issues no warnings about it. Bingo! All the user's SSH sessions become transparent, until he notices the change (if ever). If the client doesn't support "none," then this simple config file hack won't work; if the server doesn't, then the client-side Trojan horse won't work, either.

Next, the client presents its list of available integrity algorithms:

```
debug2: kex_parse_kexinit: hmac-md5,hmac-sha1,hmac-ripemd160,
            hmac-ripemd160@openssh.com,hmac-sha1-96,hmac-md5-96
```

The integrity algorithm is applied to each message sent by the SSH record protocol, together with a sequence number and session key, to produce a *message authentication code* (MAC) appended to each message. The receiver can use the MAC and its own copy of the session key to verify that the message has not been altered in transit,

---

* OpenSSH has no support for the "none" cipher; it can't even be enabled at compile time. In contrast, Tectia fully supports the "none" cipher, but it is not enabled by default; it needs to be explicitly included using the Ciphers keyword. [5.3.5]

is not a replay, and came from the other holder of the session key; these are the message integrity properties.

SSH-TRANS defines several MAC algorithms, and requires support for one: "hmac-sha1," a 160-bit hash using the standard keyed HMAC construction with SHA-1 (see RFC-2104, "HMAC: Keyed-Hashing for Message Authentication").

Finally, the client indicates which data-compression techniques it supports:

```
debug2: kex_parse_kexinit: none,zlib
```

The draft does not require any compression to be available (i.e., "none" is the required type). It does define "zlib": LZ77 compression as described in RFC-1950 and in RFC-1951. Although it does not appear here, SSH speakers also at this point also can negotiate a *language tag* for the session (as described in RFC-3066), e.g., to allow a server to provide error messages in a language appropriate to the user.

Having sent its negotiation message, the client also receives one from the server, listing the various parameters it supports in the same categories:

```
debug2: kex_parse_kexinit: diffie-hellman-group1-sha1
debug2: kex_parse_kexinit: ssh-dss,x509v3-sign-rsa
debug2: kex_parse_kexinit: aes128-cbc,3des-cbc,twofish128-cbc,cast128-cbc,
                           twofish-cbc, blowfish-cbc,aes192-cbc,aes256-cbc,
                           twofish192-cbc,twofish256-cbc,arcfour
debug2: kex_parse_kexinit: hmac-sha1,hmac-sha1-96,hmac-md5,hmac-md5-96
debug2: kex_parse_kexinit: none,zlib
```

Note that this server supports a much smaller set of key exchange algorithms: only the required one, in fact. It has two host key types to offer: plain DSS, and RSA with X.509 public-key certificate attached. It does not support a null host key since its single key exchange algorithm requires one.

Next, each side chooses a cipher/integrity/compression combination from the other side's set of supported algorithms:

```
debug1: kex: server->client aes128-cbc hmac-md5 none
debug1: kex: client->server aes128-cbc hmac-md5 none
```

In this case, the choices in both directions are the same; however, they need not be. The choice of these mechanisms is entirely independent, and they are independently keyed, as well. Data flowing in one direction might be encrypted with AES and compressed, while the return stream could be encrypted with 3DES without compression.

3.4.2.4 Key exchange and server authentication

At this point, we are ready to engage in the actual key exchange:

```
debug2: dh_gen_key: priv key bits set: 131/256
debug2: bits set: 510/1024
debug1: sending SSH2_MSG_KEXDH_INIT
```

The client chooses an exchange algorithm from the server's advertised set; in this case, the server offers only one, and we go with it. We generate an ephemeral key as part of the Diffie-Hellman algorithm, and send the initial message of the `diffie-hellman-group1-sha1` exchange, simultaneously letting the server know which method we're using, and actually starting it.

Next the client expects, and the server sends, its reply to our KEXDH_INIT message:

```
debug1: expecting SSH2_MSG_KEXDH_REPLY
debug1: Host 'host.foo.net' is known and matches the DSA host key.
debug1: Found key in /Users/res/.ssh/known_hosts:169
debug2: bits set: 526/1024
debug1: ssh_dss_verify: signature correct
```

Contained in the reply is the server's SSH public host key, of a type we said we'd accept in the earlier parameter negotiation (DSA), along with a signature proving it holds the corresponding private key. The signature is verified, of course, but that by itself is meaningless; for all we know, the server just generated this key. The crucial step here is to check that the public key identifies the server we wanted to contact. In this case, the client finds a record associating the name *foo.host.net* with the key supplied by the server, at line 169 in the user's OpenSSH *known_hosts* file.

Note that the approach used to verify the host key is entirely unspecified by the SSH protocol; it's completely implementation-dependent. Most SSH products provide some version of the known-hosts file method used here: simple, but limiting and cumbersome for large numbers of hosts, users, or different SSH implementations. A client could do anything that makes sense to verify the host key, perhaps taking advantage of some existing secure infrastructure, for example; look it up in a trusted LDAP directory.

Of course, the problem of verifying the owner of a public key is hardly a new one; that's what Public Key Infrastructure (PKI) systems are for, such as the X.509 standard for public-key certificates. SSH-2 supports PKI, defining a number of key types which include attached certificates:

`ssh-rsa`	Plain RSA key
`ssh-dss`	Plain DSS key
`x509v3-sign-rsa`	X.509 certificates (RSA key)
`x509v3-sign-dss`	X.509 certificates (DSS key)
`spki-sign-rsa`	SPKI certificates (RSA key)
`spki-sign-dss`	SPKI certificates (DSS key)
`pgp-sign-rsa`	OpenPGP certificates (RSA key)
`pgp-sign-dss`	OpenPGP certificates (DSS key)

Many SSH products handle only plain DSS/RSA keys, but some (such as Tectia) offer PKI support as well. Recall that earlier, the server offered a key type of `x509v3-sign-rsa` along with plain DSS. Our OpenSSH client does not support certificates, and so selected the DSS key. However, with PKI support, the client could verify the host key by its accompanying certificate. New hosts could be added and existing keys changed, without having to push out new known-hosts files to all clients every time—often a practical impossibility anyway, when you consider laptops, many different SSH clients with different ways of storing host keys, etc. Instead, clients only need a single key; that of the authority issuing your host key certificates. We'll cover PKI in more detail in a case study. [11.5]

3.4.2.5 Server authentication and antispoofing: some gory details

As noted earlier, we're avoiding diving too deeply into protocol details, instead attempting a technical overview that covers the issues SSH administrators most need to understand to deploy effective systems. However, it's worth going a little deeper here regarding the actual mechanism of server authentication, since our description begs the question. Simply saying that the server "provides a signature" to prove its identity doesn't cut it. Here's a naive protocol:

1. Client sends a challenge.
2. Server returns challenge signed with its host key.
3. Client verifies the signature and the server/key binding and takes this as proof of the server's identity.

We're being at least moderately clever here; by using a random challenge, we assure that the response can't be replayed by an attacker, i.e., is not a reply from an earlier session. Not bad, but no cigar: this simple procedure does not prevent MITM attacks! An MITM attacker can simply pass along the challenge to the server, get the signature, and pass it back to the client. All this protocol really proves to the client is that the entity at the other end of its connection can *talk* to the real server, when what the client wants to verify is that entity actually *is* the real server. So, here's how it's done: instead of a random challenge, the server signs the SSH session identifier, which we described earlier. Recall that the identifier is unique to each session, and that neither side can force a particular value for it. In order to do MITM, our attacker has to execute the SSH protocol independently on two sides: once with the client, and again with the server. The identifiers for those two connections are guaranteed to be different, no matter what the attacker does. He needs to produce the client-side identifier signed by the server in order to fool the client, but all he can get is the server-side identifier; he can't force the server to sign the wrong identifier.

Cryptographers are devious people. We like them.

3.4.2.6 Wonder security powers, activate!

Back to our debug trace example: we've sent and received a single key-exchange message on each side now, and this key-exchange method in fact only requires the two messages. Other exchange mechanisms could take any number and form of messages, but ours is now complete. Based on the contents of these messages, both sides compute the needed shared master secret K and exchange hash H, in such a way that an observer can't feasibly discover them (we leave the mathematical details to your perusal of the actual draft document, if you're that curious). Having authenticated the exchange using the server's host key, we are convinced that we have shared keys with the server we really wanted to talk to, and now everything is in place to turn on security in the form of encryption and integrity checking.

Using a procedure defined in the draft, the client derives appropriate encryption and integrity keys from the master secret; the server does the same to produce matching keys:

```
debug2: kex_derive_keys
debug2: set_newkeys: mode 1
debug1: SSH2_MSG_NEWKEYS sent
debug1: expecting SSH2_MSG_NEWKEYS
debug2: set_newkeys: mode 0
debug1: SSH2_MSG_NEWKEYS received
```

Both sides then send the NEWKEYS message, each which marks taking the new keys into effect in its own direction; all messages after NEWKEYS are protected using the new set of keys just negotiated. With a functioning SSH-TRANS session at hand, the client now requests the first service it wants access over the connection: user authentication.

```
debug1: SSH2_MSG_SERVICE_REQUEST sent
debug2: service_accept: ssh-userauth
debug1: SSH2_MSG_SERVICE_ACCEPT received
```

3.4.3   SSH Authentication Protocol (SSH-AUTH)

Compared to SSH-TRANS, SSH-AUTH is a relatively simple affair, defined in a mere 12 pages as opposed to the 28 of the SSH-TRANS document (and that's not counting various extensions!). As with SSH-TRANS and key-exchange methods, the authentication protocol defines a framework within which arbitrary authentication exchanges may take place. It then defines a small number of actual authentication mechanisms, and allows for easy extension to define others. The three defined methods are password, public-key, and host-based authentication, of which only public-key is required.

3.4.3.1   The authentication request

The authentication process is driven by the client, framed by client requests and server responses. A request contains the following parts:

Username U
> The authorization identity the client is claiming. For most SSH systems, this means a user account in the usual sense: for instance, in Unix, granting the right to create processes with a particular uid. However, it might have some other meaning in other contexts; its interpretation is not defined by the protocol.

Service name S

> The facility to which the client is requesting access, and hence implicitly the protocol to be started over the SSH-TRANS connection after authentication succeeds. There might be several authenticated services available, but typically there is only one: "ssh-connection," requesting access to the various services provided via the SSH-CONN protocol: interactive login, remote command execution, file transfer, port forwarding, and all the other things users actually want to do with SSH.

Method name M, and method-specific data D

> The particular authentication method being used in this request—say, "password" or "publickey"—and the method-specific data convey whatever is needed to start this particular authentication exchange, e.g., an actual password to be verified by the server. As with key-exchange names in SSH-TRANS, names with "@domain" syntax may be used by anyone to implement local methods, while names without @-signs must be globally registered SSH authentication methods.

Once a particular authentication method starts, it may include any number of other message types specific to its needs. Or in the simplest case, the data carried by the initial request is enough, and the server can respond right away. In any case, after the request and some number of subsequent method-specific messages back and forth, the server issues an authentication response.

Note that, strictly speaking, calling this an "authentication request" is not quite accurate; this request actually mixes authentication and authorization. It requests verifying an authentication identity via some method, and simultaneously asks the server to check that identity's right to access a particular account: an authorization decision. If the attempt fails, the client doesn't know whether this was because authentication failed (e.g., it supplied the wrong password), or authentication succeeded but authorization failed (e.g., the password was right but the account was disabled). A human-readable error message might make that clear, but the situations are indistinguishable as far as the protocol is concerned (in general, but individual methods may provide more information, as we will see later with the public-key method).

3.4.3.2 The authentication response

An SSH-AUTH authentication response comes in two flavors: SUCCESS and FAILURE (an early version of the protocol had chocolate, too, which was unfortunately abandoned). A SUCCESS message carries no other data; it simply means that authentication was successful, and the requested service has been started; further SSH-TRANS messages sent by the client should be defined within that service's protocol, and the SSH-AUTH run is over.

A FAILURE message has more structure:

- A list of authentication methods that can continue
- A "Partial success" flag

The name "failure" is actually a bit misleading here. If the partial success flag is false, then this message does mean the preceding authentication method has failed for some reason (e.g., a supplied password was incorrect, a mismatched public key produced an incorrect signature, the requested account is locked out, etc.). If the flag is true, however, the message means that the method *succeeded*; however, the server requires that additional methods also succeed before granting access. Thus, the protocol allows an SSH server to require multiple authentication methods—although not all implementations provide the feature; Tectia does, for instance, while OpenSSH currently does not.*

In either case, the message also supplies the list of authentication methods the server is willing to accept next. This allows for much flexibility; if it wants, the server can completely control the authentication process by only allowing one method at any time. But it can also specify multiple methods, allowing the client to choose them in an order which makes sense for the user. For instance, given a choice, a SSH client usually first tries methods that allow automatic authentication, such as Kerberos or public key with an agent, before those that require user intervention, such as entering a password or key passphrase.

3.4.3.3   Getting started: the "none" request

One thing is missing from all this: if the client drives the authentication process by making requests, but the list of available authentication methods is contained in server responses, then how does the client pick a first method to try? Of course, it could always just try any method and see what happens; the worst that could happen is that it fails or isn't available, and the client gets a correct list to pick from. But that's messy, and there's a standard way to do it: the "none" method. The protocol reserves the method name "none," and gives it a special meaning: if authentication is required at all, then this method must always fail. A client typically starts SSH-AUTH by sending a "none" request, expecting failure and getting back the list of available non-"none" methods to try. Of course, if the account in question does *not* require authentication, the server may respond with SUCCESS, immediately granting access.

Here, the client, having already sent the "none" request to start with, now receives its initial list of methods to try:

```
debug1: Authentications that can continue: publickey,password
```

---

* The OpenSSH team is working on multiple authentication support.

If you're debugging on the server side, you see something like this (with the OpenSSH server):

```
debug1: userauth-request for user res service ssh-connection method none
debug1: attempt 0 failures 0
Failed none for res from 10.1.1.1 port 50459 ssh2
```

This message is confusing if you're debugging some other problem, as it appears to show some mysterious failure.

The client continues, choosing public-key authentication to try first, with a DSS key stored in the SSH agent:

```
debug1: Next authentication method: publickey
debug1: Offering agent key: res-dsa
debug2: we sent a publickey packet, wait for reply
```

3.4.3.4 Public-key authentication

A public-key authentication request carries the method name "publickey" and may have different forms depending on a flag setting. One form has this method-specific payload:

- Flag = FALSE
- Algorithm name
- Key data

The usable public-key algorithms are the same set defined in SSH-TRANS, and the format key data depends on the type; e.g., for "ssh-dss" it contains just the key, whereas for x509v3-sign-rsa it contains an X.509 public-key certificate.

With the flag set to FALSE, this message is merely an authorization test: it asks the server to check whether this key is authorized to access the desired account, without actually performing authentication. If it is, a special response message comes back; this is an example of the possible method-specific SSH-AUTH messages we mentioned earlier. If the key is not authorized, the response is simply FAILURE.

The second form is:

- Flag = TRUE
- Algorithm name
- Key data - signature

This actually requests authentication; the signature is computed over a set of request-specific data which includes the session ID, which binds the request to this SSH session and gives the public-key method its own measure of MITM resistance, similar to that described earlier for key exchange.

The reason for providing both forms of request is that computing and verifying public-key signatures are compute-intensive tasks, which might also require interaction with the user (e.g., typing in a key passphrase). Hence, it makes sense to test a key first, to see whether it's worth going to the trouble of using it.

The way a server actually authorizes a key for access to an account is outside the scope of the protocol, and can be anything at all. The usual way is to list or refer to the key in some file in the account, as with the OpenSSH ~/.ssh/authorized_keys file. However, the server might access any type of service to do this; again, checking an entry in an LDAP directory comes to mind. Or again, certificates might be used: just as with host authentication, the key here might include a certificate, and any of the certificate's data might be used to make the authorization decision.

Coming back to our debug trace, we see that the server accepts the offered key:

```
debug1: Server accepts key: pkalg ssh-dss blen 435 lastkey 0x309a40 hint -1
debug2: input_userauth_pk_ok: fp 63:24:90:03:cb:78:85:e6:59:71:49:26:55:81:f5:70
debug1: Authentication succeeded (publickey).
```

Then it logs the key's fingerprint and returns the final SUCCESS message, indicating that access is granted and the SSH-AUTH session is finished.

Before moving on to the final protocol phase, let's examine two other methods defined in SSH-AUTH: password and hostbased authentication.

3.4.3.5 Password authentication

The password method is very simple: its name is "password," and the data is, surprise, the password. The server simply returns success or failure messages as appropriate. The method it uses to verify the password is implementation-dependent, and varies a great deal: PAM, Unix password files, LDAP, Kerberos, NTLM; all these are available in various products.

The password is passed in plaintext, at least as far as SSH-AUTH is concerned; hence, it is critical that this method be used over an encrypted connection (as is usually the case with SSH). Furthermore, since this method reveals the password to the server, it is crucial that the server not be an impostor. Even if an SSH product may warn of, but allow, a connection to an unauthenticated server in SSH-TRANS, it usually disallows password authentication in SSH-AUTH for this reason. Compare this with the public-key method, which doesn't reveal the user's key in the authentication process.

It should be mentioned that "password authentication" is a pretty broad term, and might be construed as encompassing other, better methods. If you think of it as describing any mechanisms that rely on secrets that can be easily memorized and typed by a human, then there are "password" methods with much better security properties than the trivial one described here; the Secure Remote Password protocol

(SRP, *http://srp.stanford.edu/*) is one. [1.6.5] In this book, however, when we talk about "password" authentication, we mean as defined in SSH-AUTH.

SSH-AUTH also has a set of messages for password changing—for example, allowing a user whose password has expired to set a new one before logging in.

3.4.3.6 Hostbased authentication

Hostbased authentication is fundamentally different from its public-key and password cousins, in that the server actually delegates responsibility for user authentication to the client host. In short, hostbased authentication establishes trust relationships between machines. Rather than directly verifying the user's identity, the SSH server verifies the identity of the client *host*—and then believes the host when it says the user has already authenticated on the client side. Therefore, you needn't prove your identity to every host that you visit. If you are logged in as user andrew on machine A, and you connect by SSH to account bob on machine B using hostbased authentication, the SSH server on machine B doesn't check your identity directly. Instead, it checks the identity of host A, making sure that A is a trusted host. It further checks that the connection is coming from a trusted program on A, one installed by the system administrator that won't lie about andrew's identity. If the connection passes these two tests, the server takes A's word that you have been authenticated as andrew and proceeds to make an authorization check that *andrew@A* is allowed to access the account *bob@B*.

This sort of authentication makes sense only in a tightly administrated environment with less stringent security requirements, or when deployed for very specific and limited purposes, such as batch jobs. It demands that all participating hosts be centrally administered, making sure that usernames are globally selected and coordinated. If not, you could get access to someone else's account just by adding an account with the same name to your own machine! Also, there's the problem of transitive compromise: once one host is broken, the attacker automatically gets access to all accounts accessible via hostbased authentication from there, without any further work.

Nevertheless, hostbased authentication has advantages. For one, it is simple: you don't have to type passwords or passphrases, or generate, distribute, and maintain keys. It also provides ease of automation. Unattended processes such as *cron* jobs may have difficulty using SSH if they need a key, passphrase, or password coded into a script, placed in a protected file, or stored in memory. This isn't only a potential security risk but also a maintenance nightmare. If the authenticator ever changes, you must hunt down and change these hardcoded copies, a situation just begging for things to break mysteriously later on. Hostbased authentication gets around this problem neatly.

The "hostbased" request looks like:

- Host key algorithm
- Client host key

- Client hostname
- Client-side username, C
- Signature

Note that this request has two usernames: the requested server-side account name U present in every SSH-AUTH request, and the client-side username C specific to the hostbased request. The interpretation is that user C on the client is requesting access to account U on the server, and the client's authentication as C is vouched for by the signature of the client host key. The mapping of which client usernames may access which accounts on the server is up to the implementation. Unix products tend to use semantics similar to the historical *rhosts* syntax, in the files */etc/shosts.equiv* and *~/.shosts*. These can implement global identity mappings, allowing matching usernames automatic access, as well as more complicated or limited access patterns.

In order to perform this authentication, the server must verify the client host identity—that is, it must check that the supplied key matches the claimed client hostname (e.g., with a known-hosts file). Having checked that and verified the signature, it then uses that same hostname in the authorization check (e.g., in */etc/shosts.equiv*), to see if the requested client/server name pair is allowed access from this client host. Some implementations also check that the client's network address actually maps to the given hostname via the local naming service (DNS, NIS, etc.), but this is not really necessary; the meat of the authorization is in the association of the verified hostname supplied in the request, and the authorization rules. In fact, the address check may cause more trouble than it's worth, in the presence of poorly maintained DNS, network complications such as NAT, firewalls, proxying, etc.

Of course, for this whole scenario to make any sense at all, there are yet more administrative burdens to be met. The signature, after all, is supplied by the client; and yet it is interpreted here as a trusted third party—the client *host* as a separate entity—vouching for the user's identity. But the user is behind the SSH client; how does this work? The answer is that the client host and SSH software must be arranged so that the user is *not* fully in control of what's going on. The private client host key must not be accessible to the user; rather, there must be a trusted service whereby the user can obtain the needed signature for the hostbased authentication request, and such signatures are only issued as appropriate. In a Unix context, usually the private host key file is readable only by the root account, and some part of SSH is installed with special privileges by the sysadmin ("setuid root"; typically this is a separate program called *ssh-signer*, which serves only this purpose). This trusted program checks the uid of the user running it, and issues signatures only for the corresponding username. This effectively translates the local authentication that allowed the person to log in to begin with, into an SSH certificate which can be transmitted and trusted as part of hostbased authentication. This description makes it even more clear how the whole arrangement is predicated on a very centrally controlled and consistently administrated system. One should evaluate very carefully whether hostbased authentication is the right choice.

3.4.4   SSH Connection Protocol (SSH-CONN)

In its final, successful authentication request, the client specified a service name of "ssh-connection"; this is not visible in the OpenSSH client debug trace but shows up on the server as:

```
debug1: userauth-request for user res service ssh-connection method publickey
```

Since it authenticated the client, the server now starts that service, and we move on to the SSH Connection Protocol. This layer actually provides the capabilities that users want to employ directly and that define SSH for most people: remote login and command execution, agent forwarding, file transfer, TCP port forwarding, X forwarding, etc.

There is a lot of detail in the connection protocol, but much of it is too low-level for our present discussion; we give a fairly high-level description here, sufficient to interpret most debugging messages and to understand how an SSH product provides its services using SSH-CONN. Unlike the earlier protocols, a really detailed understanding of SSH-CONN is not usually needed for debugging everyday SSH problems.

3.4.4.1   Channels

The basic service SSH-CONN provides is *multiplexing*. SSH-CONN takes the single, secure, duplex byte-stream provided by SSH-TRANS, and allows its clients to create dynamically any number of logical SSH-CONN *channels* over it. Channels are identified by *channel numbers*, and may be created or destroyed by either side. Channels are individually flow-controlled, and each channel has a *channel type* which defines its use. Types and other items in SSH-CONN are named in the same extensible manner as other SSH namespaces (key exchanges, key algorithm and authenticated method names, etc.). The defined types are:

session
> The remote execution of a program.
>
> Merely opening a session channel does not start a program; that is done using subsequent requests on the channel. An SSH-CONN session may have multiple session channels open at once, simultaneously supporting several terminal, file-transfer, or program executions at once. Various Windows-based SSH products have used this ability for some time now; it has only recently appeared in OpenSSH with the ControlMaster/ControlPath feature. [7.4.4.2]

x11
> An X11 client connection.
>
> One of these is opened from server to client, for each X11 program using X forwarding as established by an *x11-req* on a session channel (discussed later).

forwarded-tcpip
> An inbound connection to a remotely forwarded port.
>
> When a connection arrives on a remotely forwarded TCP port, the server opens this channel back to the client to carry the connection.

---

direct-tcpip
>   An outbound TCP connection.
>
>   This directs the peer to open a TCP connection to a given socket, and attach the channel to that connection. The socket may be specified using a domain name or IP address, allowing a name to be resolved on the remote side in a possibly different namespace than the client. These channels are used to implement local TCP forwarding (*ssh -L*). Preparing for local forwarding is purely a client-side affair: the client simply starts listening on the requested port.* The server first hears of it when a connection actually arrives on the port, whereupon the client opens a *direct-tcpip* channel with the appropriate target socket. This means that if certain local forwardings are disallowed by the server, this isn't noticed on connection setup, but only when a connection is actually attempted

Channel semantics are richer than a traditional Unix file handle; the data they carry can be typed, and this facility is used to distinguish between stdout and stderr output from a program on a single channel.

3.4.4.2 Requests

In addition to an array of channel operations—open, close, send data, send urgent data, etc.—SSH-CONN defines a set of *requests*, with global or channel scope. A global request affects the state of the connection as a whole, whereas a channel request is tied to a particular open channel. The global requests are:

tcpip-forward
>   Request a remote TCP port forwarding.
>
>   If the user requests a TCP port be forwarded on the remote side back to the local side (as with "ssh -R"), the SSH client issues this global request. In response, the server starts listening on the indicated port and starts a "forwarded-tcpip" channel back to the client for each connection.
>
>   This request actually contains the full socket to be bound on the remote: an (*address,port*) pair and not just a port number. This allows the client to be selective in remote-forwarding remote ports on a multihomed server, or to implement local-only remote forwardings by binding only the loopback address (127. 0.0.1), on a per-request basis. Not all implementations take advantage of this feature, however; Tectia does, but OpenSSH currently does not.†

cancel-tcpip-forward
>   Cancel an existing remote forwarding.

---

* Unlike remote forwarding, no initial setup is required on the remote side.

† The OpenSSH team is working on adding this feature.

Now let's summarize the channel requests; except as indicated, most operations refer to the remote side of a session channel:

pty-req
> Allocate a *pty*, including window size and terminal modes.
>
> This creates a pseudo-terminal for the channel, generally required for interactive applications; the pseudo-terminal is a virtual device which makes it appear that the remote program is directly connected to a terminal.

x11-req
> Set up X11 forwarding.
>
> Do the preparation necessary for X11 forwarding on the remote; usually involves listening on a socket (TCP or otherwise) for X11 connections, setting the DISPLAY variable to point to that socket, and setting up proxy X11 authentication.

env
> Set an environment variable.
>
> Although useful, this feature is also a potential security problem. It has not been widely supported by SSH implementations until recently and is generally carefully controlled.

shell, exec, subsystem
> Run the default account shell, an arbitrary program, or an abstract service, respectively.
>
> These requests start a program running on the remote side, and connect the channel to the program's standard input/output/error streams. The "subsystem" request allows a remote program to be named abstractly, rather than being depended on by a particular remote filename. For instance, an SFTP file transfer is usually started by sending a subsystem request with the name "sftp." The SSH server is configured to execute the correct server program in response to the request; this way, the location of the SFTP server program can change without affecting clients. Or indeed, SFTP could be implemented internal to the SSH server itself, rather than being a separate program, and this, too, would be transparent to clients; this is an option with Tectia.

window-change
> Change terminal window size.

xon-xoff
> Use client-side ^S/^Q flow control.

signal
> Send a specified signal to a remote process (as in the Unix *kill* command).

exit-status
> Return the program's exit status to the initiator.

exit-signal
> Return the signal that terminated the program (e.g., if a remote program dies by signal, as from a segmentation fault or manual *kill -9* command).

Theoretically, all these requests are symmetric; that is, the protocol allows the server to open a session channel to the client and request a program to be started on it, for example. However, in most SSH implementations as a remote-login tool, this simply doesn't make sense, and is an obvious security risk to boot! So, such requests are usually not honored by clients (and the SSH-CONN draft recommends as much).

3.4.4.3 The finish line

With all this behind us, we can easily make sense of the remainder of the connection setup. The client opens a session channel with id 0:

```
debug1: channel 0: new [client-session]
debug2: channel 0: send open
debug1: Entering interactive session.
```

This session is a terminal login, so next we request a pseudo-terminal on the session channel:

```
debug1: channel 0: request pty-req
```

X forwarding is turned on, so the client first gets the local X11 display key by running the *xauth* program on this side, then requests X forwarding on the remote by sending an *x11-req* global request:

```
debug2: x11_get_proto: /usr/X11R6/bin/xauth list :0 2>/dev/null
debug1: Requesting X11 forwarding with authentication spoofing.
debug1: channel 0: request x11-req
```

Agent forwarding is also turned on, so we open a channel for that as well:

```
debug1: Requesting authentication agent forwarding.
debug1: channel 0: request auth-agent-req@openssh.com
```

But wait... we didn't mention agent forwarding anywhere in SSH-CONN, nor the channel type that appears here, auth-agent-req@openssh.com. Indeed, that's because it's not there; key agents are an implementation detail outside the purview of the protocol. This channel type is an example of the naming extension syntax; it is particular to the OpenSSH implementation. An OpenSSH server accepts such a channel request and sets up an agent-forwarding socket on the remote end (whose details are specific to the OpenSSH program suite). A non-OpenSSH server would refuse the unrecognized request, and agent forwarding would not be available.

Finally, the client issues a "shell" request on the session channel:

```
debug1: channel 0: request shell
```

directing the remote account's default command be started. And at long last...

```
debug1: channel 0: open confirm rwindow 100000 rmax 1638
Last login: Mon Aug 30 2004 18:04:10 -0400 from foo.host.net
$
```

...we're logged in!

3.5   Inside SSH-1

With a solid understanding of the current SSH protocol behind us, we now quickly summarize SSH-1 in terms of its differences, weaknesses, and shortcomings in comparison with SSH-2:

Non-modular
> SSH-1 is defined as a single monolithic protocol, rather than the modular approach taken with the SSH-2 suite.

Less negotiation
> SSH-1 has more fixed parameters; in fact, only the bulk cipher is negotiated. The integrity algorithm, host key type, key-exchange methods, etc., are all fixed.

Ad hoc naming
> SSH-1 lacks the well-defined naming syntax for SSH-2 entities which allows for smooth, implementation-specific extensions.

Single authentication
> SSH-1's user authentication process allows only one method to succeed; the server can't require multiple methods.

RhostsRSA authentication
> SSH-1's RhostsRSA authentication, analogous to hostbased, is in principle limited to using a network address as the client host identifier. This limits its usefulness in the face of network issues such as NAT, proxying, mobile clients, etc.

Less flexible remote forwarding
> SSH-1 remote forwarding specifies only a port, not a full socket, so can't be bound to different addresses on multihomed servers, and the *gatewayhosts* option must be set globally for all remote forwardings rather than per port.

Weaker integrity checking
> SSH-1 uses a weak integrity check, the CRC-32 algorithm. CRC-32 is not cryptographically strong, and its weakness is the basis of the Futoransky/Kargieman "insertion attack"; see *http://seclists.org/lists/firewall-wizards/1998/Jun/0095.html*.

Server keys
> The fixed key exchange of SSH-1 employs an extra asymmetric key called the *server key*, not to be confused with a host key. [3.6.1] The server key is an ephemeral public/private key pair, regenerated once per hour and used to provide forward secrecy for the session key. Forward secrecy means that even if long-term secrets such as user or host private keys are compromised later, these can't be used to decrypt SSH sessions recorded earlier; the use of an extra key which is never written to disk assures this. The Diffie-Hellman algorithm which is the basis of all the SSH-2 key exchanges provides forward secrecy by itself, and so an extra "server key" is not needed.

Weak key exchange

    The SSH-1 key exchange is weak in that the client alone determines the session key, and simply sends it to the server. A Trojaned client can easily use weak keys to compromise all its sessions undetectably.

3.6 Implementation Issues

There are many differences among the current crop of SSH implementations: features that aren't dictated by the protocols, but are simply inclusions or omissions by the software authors. Here we discuss a few implementation-dependent features of various products:

- Host keys
- Authorization in hostbased authentication
- SSH-1 backward compatibility
- Randomness
- Privilege separation

3.6.1 Host Keys

SSH host keys are long-term asymmetric keys that distinguish and identify hosts running SSH, or instances of the SSH server, depending on the SSH implementation. This happens in two places in the SSH protocol:

- Server authentication verifying the server host's identity to connecting clients. This process occurs for every SSH connection.*
- Authentication of a client host to the server; used only during RhostsRSA or hostbased user authentication.

Unfortunately, the term "host key" is confusing. It implies that only one such key may belong to a given host. This is true for client authentication but not for server authentication, because multiple SSH servers may run on a single machine, each with a different identifying key.† This so-called "host key" actually identifies a running instance of the SSH server program, not a machine.

OpenSSH maintains a single database serving both server authentication and client authentication. It is the union of the system's *known_hosts* file (*/etc/ssh/ssh_known_hosts*), together with the user's *~/.ssh/known_hosts* file on either the source machine (for server authentication) or the target machine (for client authentication). The

---

* In SSH-1, the host key also encrypts the session key for transmission to the server. However, this use is actually for server authentication, rather than for data protection per se; the server later proves its identity by showing that it correctly decrypted the session key. Protection of the session key is obtained by encrypting it a second time with the ephemeral server key.

† Or sharing the same key, if you wish, assuming the servers are compatible with one another.

database maps a hostname or address to a set of keys acceptable for authenticating a host with that name or address. One name may be associated with multiple keys (more on this shortly).

Tectia, on the other hand, maintains two separate maps for these purposes:

- The *hostkeys* map for authentication of the server host by the client
- The *knownhosts* map for authentication of the client host by the server

Hooray, more confusing terminology. Here, the term "known hosts" is reused with slightly different formatting ("knownhosts" versus "known_hosts") for an overlapping but not identical purpose.

While OpenSSH keeps host keys in a file with multiple entries, Tectia stores them in a filesystem directory, one key per file, indexed by filename. For instance, a *knownhosts* directory looks like this:

```
$ ls -l /etc/ssh2/knownhosts/
total 2
-r--r--r--  1 root    root         697 Jun  5 22:22 wynken.sleepy.net.ssh-dss.pub
-r--r--r--  1 root    root         697 Jul 21  1999 blynken.sleepy.net.ssh-dss.pub
```

Note that the filename is of the form *<hostname>.<key type>.pub*.

The other map, *hostkeys*, is keyed not just on name/address, but also on the server's TCP listening port; that is to say, it is keyed on TCP sockets. This allows for multiple keys per host in a more specific manner than before. Here, the filenames are of the form *key_<port number>_<hostname>.pub*. The following example shows the public keys for one SSH server running on *blynken*, port 22, and two running on *wynken*, ports 22 and 220. Furthermore, we've created a symbolic link to make "nod" another name for the server at *wynken*:22. End users may add to these maps by placing keys (either manually or automatically by client) into the directories *~/.ssh2/knownhosts* and *~/.ssh2/hostkeys*.

```
$ ls -l /etc/ssh2/hostkeys/
total 5
-rw-r--r--  1 root    root         757 May 31 14:52 key_22_blynken.sleepy.net.pub
-rw-r--r--  1 root    root         743 May 31 14:52 key_22_wynken.sleepy.net.pub
-rw-r--r--  1 root    root         755 May 31 14:52 key_220_wynken.sleepy.net.pub
lrwxrwxrwx  1 root    root          28 May 31 14:57 key_22_nod.pub -> key_22_wynken.
sleepy.net.pub
```

Even though it allows for multiple keys per host, Tectia is missing one useful feature of OpenSSH: multiple keys *per name*. This sounds like the same thing, but there's a subtle difference: names can refer to more than one host. A common example is a set of load-sharing login servers hidden behind a single hostname. A university might have a set of three machines intended for general login access, each with its own name and address:

login1.foo.edu → 10.0.0.1
login2.foo.edu → 10.0.0.2
login3.foo.edu → 10.0.0.3

In addition, there is a single generic name that carries all three addresses:

login.foo.edu → {10.0.0.1, 10.0.0.2, 10.0.0.3}

The university computing center tells people to connect only to *login.foo.edu*, and the university's naming service hands out the three addresses in round-robin order (e.g., using round-robin DNS) to share the load among the three machines. SSH has problems with this setup by default. Each time you connect to *login.foo.edu*, you have a two-thirds chance of reaching a different machine than you reached last time, with a different host key. SSH repeatedly complains that the host key of *login.foo.com* has changed and issues a warning about a possible attack against your client. This soon gets annoying. With OpenSSH, you can edit the *known_hosts* file to associate the generic name with each of the individual host keys, changing this:

```
login1.foo.edu 1024 35 1519086808544755383...
login2.foo.edu 1024 35 1508058310547044394...
login3.foo.edu 1024 35 1087309429906462914...
```

to this:

```
login1.foo.edu,login.foo.edu 1024 35 1519086808544755383...
login2.foo.edu,login.foo.edu 1024 35 1508058310547044394...
login3.foo.edu,login.foo.edu 1024 35 1087309429906462914...
```

With Tectia, however, there's no general way to do this; since the database is indexed by entries in a directory, with one key per file, it can't have more than one key per name.

It might seem that you're losing some security by doing this, but we don't think so. All that's really happening is the recognition that a particular name may refer to different hosts at different times, and thus you tell SSH to trust a connection to that name if it's authenticated by any of a given set of keys. Most of the time, that set happens to have size 1, and you're telling SSH, "When I connect to this name, I want to make sure I'm connecting to this particular host." With multiple keys per name, you can also say, "When I connect to this name, I want to make sure that I get one of the following set of hosts." That's a perfectly valid and useful thing to do.

Another way to solve this problem is for the system administrators of *login.foo.com* to install the same host key on all three machines. But this defeats the ability of SSH to distinguish between these hosts, even if you want it to. We prefer the former approach.

3.6.2   Authorization in Hostbased Authentication

The most complicated aspect of hostbased authentication is not the method itself, but the implementation details of configuring it, particularly authorization. We'll discuss:

- Hostbased access files
- Control file details
- Netgroups as wildcards

3.6.2.1 Hostbased access files

Two pairs of files on the SSH server machine provide access control for hostbased authentication, in both its weak and strong forms:

- /etc/hosts.equiv and ~/.rhosts (weak)
- /etc/shosts.equiv and ~/.shosts (strong)

The files in /etc have machine-global scope, while those in the target account's home directory are specific to that account. The hosts.equiv and shosts.equiv files have the same syntax, as do the .rhosts and .shosts files, and by default they are all checked.

 If any of the four access files allows access for a particular connection, it's allowed, even if another of the files forbids it.

The /etc/hosts.equiv and ~/.rhosts files originated with the insecure r-commands. For backward compatibility, SSH can also use these files for making its hostbased authentication decisions. If you're using both the r-commands and SSH, however, you might not want the two systems to have the same configuration. Also, because of their poor security, it's common to disable the r-commands, by turning off the servers in your inetd.conf files and/or removing the software. In that case, you may not want to have any traditional control files lying around, as a defensive measure in case an attacker managed to get one of these services turned on again.

To separate itself from the r-commands, SSH reads two additional files, /etc/shosts. equiv and ~/.shosts, which have the same syntax and meaning as /etc/hosts.equiv and ~/.rhosts, but are specific to SSH. If you use only the SSH-specific files, you can have SSH hostbased authentication without leaving any files the r-commands would look at.*

All four files have the same syntax, and SSH interprets them very similarly—but not identically—to the way the r-commands do. Read the following sections carefully to make sure you understand this behavior.

3.6.2.2 Control file details

Here is the common format of all four hostbased control files. Each entry is a single line, containing either one or two tokens separated by tabs and/or spaces. Comments begin with #, continue to the end of the line, and may be placed anywhere; empty and comment-only lines are allowed.

```
# example control file entry
[+-][@]hostspec  [+-][@]userspec  # comment
```

---

* Unfortunately, you can't configure the server to look at one set but not the other. If it looks at ~/.shosts, then it also considers ~/.rhosts, and both global files are always considered.

The two tokens indicate host(s) and user(s), respectively; the *userspec* may be omitted. If the at sign (@) is present, then the token is interpreted as a netgroup (see the sidebar "Netgroups") and is looked up using the innetgr( ) library call, and the resulting list of user or hostnames is substituted. Otherwise, the token is interpreted as a single host or username. Hostnames must be canonical as reported by gethostbyaddr( ) on the server host; other names won't work.

If either or both tokens are preceded by a minus sign (–), the whole entry is considered negated. It doesn't matter which token has the minus sign; the effect is the same. Let's see some examples before explaining the rules.

The following *hostspec* allows anyone from *fred.flintstone.gov* to log in if the remote and local usernames are the same:

```
# /etc/shosts.equiv
fred.flintstone.gov
```

The following *hostspec*s allow anyone from any host in the netgroup "hostbasedusers" to log in, if the remote and local usernames are the same, but not from *evil. empire.org*, even if it is in the hostbasedusers netgroup:

```
# /etc/shosts.equiv
-evil.empire.org
@hostbasedusers
```

This next entry (*hostspec* and *userspec*) allows *mark@way.too.trusted* to log into any local account! Even if a user has *-way.too.trusted mark* in *~/.shosts*, it won't prevent access since the global file is consulted first. You probably never want to do this.

```
# /etc/shosts.equiv
way.too.trusted mark                    Don't do this!!
```

On the other hand, the following entries allow anyone from *sister.host.org* to connect under the same account name, except mark, who can't access any local account:

```
# /etc/shosts.equiv
sister.host.org -mark
sister.host.org
```

Remember, however, that a target account can override this restriction by placing sister.host.org mark in *~/.shosts*. Note also, as shown earlier, that the negated line must come first; in the other order, it's ineffective.

This next *hostspec* allows user wilma on *fred.flintstone.gov* to log into the local wilma account:

```
# ~wilma/.shosts
fred.flintstone.gov
```

This entry allows user fred on *fred.flintstone.gov* to log into the local wilma account, but no one else—not even *wilma@fred.flintstone.gov*:

```
# ~wilma/.shosts
fred.flintstone.gov fred
```

Netgroups

A netgroup defines a list of (*host*, *user*, *domain*) triples. Netgroups are used to define lists of users, machines, or accounts, usually for access-control purposes; for instance, one can usually use a netgroup to specify what hosts are allowed to mount an NFS file-system (e.g., in the Solaris *share* command or BSD *exportfs*).

Different flavors of Unix vary in how they implement netgroups, though you must always be the system administrator to define a netgroup. Possible sources for netgroup definitions include:

- A plain file, e.g., */etc/netgroup*
- A database file in various formats, e.g., */etc/netgroup.db*
- An information service, such as Sun's YP/NIS

On many modern Unix flavors, the source of netgroup information is configurable with the Network Service Switch facility; see the file */etc/nsswitch.conf*. Be aware that in some versions of SunOS and Solaris, netgroups may be defined only in NIS; it doesn't complain if you specify "files" as the source in *nsswitch.conf*, but it doesn't work either. Recent Linux systems support */etc/netgroup*, though C libraries before *glibc* 2.1 support netgroups only over NIS.

Some typical netgroup definitions might look like this:

```
# defines a group consisting of two hosts: hostnames "print1" and
# "print2", in the (probably NIS) domains one.foo.com and two.foo.com.
print-servers      (print1,,one.foo.com) (print2,,two.foo.com)
# a list of three login servers
login-servers      (login1,,foo.com) (login2,,foo.com) (login1,,foo.com)
# Use two existing netgroups to define a list of all hosts, throwing in
# another.foo.com as well.
all-hosts          print-servers login-servers (another,,foo.com)
# A list of users for some access-control purpose.  Mary is allowed from
# anywhere in the foo.com domain, but Peter only from one host.  Alice
# is allowed from anywhere at all.
allowed-users      (,mary,foo.com) (login1,peter,foo.com) (,alice,)
```

When deciding membership in a netgroup, the thing being matched is always construed as an appropriate triple. A triple (x, y, z) matches a netgroup N if there exists a triple (a, b, c) in N which matches (x, y, z). In turn, you define that these two triples match if and only if the following conditions are met:

—continued—

> $x = a$ **or** x is null **or** a is null
>
> **and**:
>
> $y = b$ **or** y is null **or** b is null
>
> **and**:
>
> $z = c$ **or** z is null **or** c is null
>
> This means that a null field in a triple acts as a wildcard. By "null," we mean missing; that is, in the triple $(, user, domain)$, the host part is null. This isn't the same as the empty string: $("", user, domain)$. In this triple, the host part isn't null. It is the empty string, and the triple can match only another whose host part is also the empty string.
>
> When SSH matches a username U against a netgroup, it matches the triple $(, U ,)$; similarly, when matching a hostname H, it matches $(H , ,)$. You might expect it to use $(, U, D)$ and $(H, , D)$ where D is the host's domain, but it doesn't.

These entries allow both fred and wilma on *fred.flintstone.gov* to log into the local wilma account:

```
# ~wilma/.shosts
fred.flintstone.gov fred
fred.flintstone.gov
```

Now that we've covered some examples, let's discuss the precise rules. Suppose the client username is C, and the target account of the SSH command is T. Then:

1. A *hostspec* entry with no *userspec* permits access from all *hostspec* hosts when $T = C$.

2. In a per-account file (*~/.rhosts* or *~/.shosts*), a *hostspec userspec* entry permits access to the containing account from *hostspec* hosts when C is any one of the *userspec* usernames.

3. In a global file (*/etc/hosts.equiv* or */etc/shosts.equiv*), a *hostspec userspec* entry permits access to any local target account from any *hostspec* host, when C is any one of the *userspec* usernames.

4. For negated entries, replace "permits" with "denies" in the preceding rules.

Note Rule #3 carefully. You never, ever want to open your machine to such a security hole. The only reasonable use for such a rule is if it is negated, thus disallowing access to any local account for a particular remote account. We present some examples shortly.

The files are checked in the following order (a missing file is simply skipped, with no effect on the authorization decision):

1. */etc/hosts.equiv*

2. */etc/shosts.equiv*

3. *~/.shosts*

4. *~/.rhosts*

SSH makes a special exception when the target user is root: it doesn't check the global files. Access to the root account can be granted only via the root account's */.rhosts* and */.shosts* files. If you block the use of those files with the IgnoreRootRhosts server directive, this effectively prevents access to the root account via hostbased authentication.

When checking these files, there are two rules to keep in mind. The first rule is: the first accepting line wins. That is, if you have two netgroups:

```
set     (one,,) (two,,) (three,,)
subset  (one,,) (two,,)
```

the following */etc/shosts.equiv* file permits access only from host three:

```
-@subset
@set
```

But this next one allows access from all three:

```
@set
-@subset
```

The second line has no effect, because all its hosts have already been accepted by a previous line.

The second rule is: if any file accepts the connection, it's allowed. That is, if */etc/shosts.equiv* forbids a connection but the target user's *~/.shosts* file accepts it, then it is accepted. Therefore, the sysadmin *cannot rely on the global file to block connections*. Similarly, if your per-account file forbids a connection, it can be overridden by a global file that accepts it. Keep these facts carefully in mind when using hostbased authentication.*

3.6.2.3 Netgroups as wildcards

You may have noticed the rule syntax has no wildcards; this omission is deliberate. The r-commands recognize bare + and − characters as positive and negative wildcards, respectively, and a number of attacks are based on surreptitiously adding a "+" to someone's *.rhosts* file, immediately allowing anyone to *rlogin* as that user. So, SSH deliberately ignores these wildcards. You'll see messages to that effect in the server's debugging output if it encounters such a wildcard:

```
Remote: Ignoring wild host/user names in /etc/shosts.equiv
```

However, there's still a way to get the effect of a wildcard: using the wildcards available in netgroups. An empty netgroup:

```
empty  # nothing here
```

---

* By setting the server's IgnoreRhosts keyword to yes, you can cause the server to ignore the per-account files completely and consult the global files exclusively instead. [5.4.4]

matches nothing at all. However, this netgroup:

```
wild  (,,)
```

matches everything. In fact, a netgroup containing (,,) anywhere matches every-thing, regardless of what else is in the netgroup. So, this entry:

```
# ~/.shosts
@wild
```

allows access from any host at all,* as long as the remote and local usernames match. This one:

```
# ~/.shosts
way.too.trusted @wild
```

allows any user on *way.too.trusted* to log into this account, while this entry:

```
# ~/.shosts
@wild @wild
```

allows any user access from anywhere.

Given this wildcard behavior, it's important to pay careful attention to netgroup defi-nitions. It's easier to create a wildcard netgroup than you might think. Including the null triple (,,) is the obvious approach. However, remember that the order of ele-ments in a netgroup triple is (*host,user,domain*). Suppose you define a group "oops" like this:

```
oops         (fred,,) (wilma,,) (barney,,)
```

You intend for this to be a group of usernames, but you've placed the usernames in the host slots, and the username fields are left null. If you use this group as the user-spec of a rule, it acts as a wildcard. Thus, this entry:

```
# ~/.shosts
home.flintstones.gov @oops
```

allows anyone on *home.flintstones.gov*, not just your three friends, to log into your account. Beware!

3.6.2.4 Summary

Hostbased authentication is convenient for users and administrators, because it can set up automatic authentication between hosts based on username correspondence and interhost trust relationships. This removes the burden of typing passwords or dealing with key management. However, it is heavily dependent on the correct administration and security of the hosts involved; compromising one trusted host can give an attacker automatic access to all accounts on other hosts. Also, the rules for the access control files are complicated, fragile, and easy to get wrong in ways

---

* If strong hostbased authentication is in use, this means any host verified by public key against the server's known hosts database.

that compromise security. In an environment more concerned with eavesdropping and disclosure than active attacks, it may be acceptable to deploy hostbased authentication for general user authentication. In a more security-conscious scenario, however, it is probably inappropriate, though it may be acceptable for limited use in special-purpose accounts, such as for unattended batch jobs. [11.1.3]

3.6.3 SSH-1 Backward Compatibility

The Tectia server can provide backward compatibility for the SSH-1 protocol, as long as another package supporting SSH-1 (such as OpenSSH) is also installed on the same machine. When the Tectia server encounters a client requesting an SSH-1 connection, it simply runs the SSH-1 server.* This is rather cumbersome. It's also wasteful and slow, since each new *sshd1* needs to generate its own server key, which otherwise the single master server regenerates only once an hour. This wastes random bits, sometimes a precious commodity, and can cause noticeable delays in the startup of SSH-1 connections to a Tectia server. Further, it is an administrative headache and a security problem, since one must maintain two separate SSH server configurations and try to make sure all desired restrictions are adequately covered in both.

OpenSSH, on the other hand, supports both SSH-1 and SSH-2 in a single set of programs, an approach we prefer.

3.6.4 Randomness

Cryptographic algorithms and protocols require a good source of random bits. Randomness is used in various ways:

- To generate data-encryption keys
- As plaintext padding and initialization vectors in encryption algorithms, to help foil cryptanalysis
- For check-bytes or *cookies* in protocol exchanges, as a measure against packet-spoofing attacks

Randomness is harder to achieve than you might think; in fact, even defining randomness is difficult (or picking the right definition for a given situation). For example, "random" numbers that are perfectly good for statistical modeling might be terrible for cryptography. Each of these applications requires certain properties of its random input, such as an even distribution. Cryptography, in particular, demands *unpredictability*, so an attacker reading our data can't guess our keys.

---

* Or it can use an internal SSH-1 compatibility mode.

True randomness—in the sense of complete unpredictability—can't be produced by a computer program. Any sequence of bits produced as the output of a program eventually repeats itself. For true randomness, you have to turn to physical processes, such as fluid turbulence or the quantum dice of radioactive decay. Even there, you must take great care that measurement artifacts don't introduce unwanted structure.

There are algorithms, however, that produce long sequences of practically unpredictable output, with good statistical randomness properties. These are good enough for many cryptographic applications, and such algorithms are called *pseudo-random number generators*, or *PRNGs*. A PRNG requires a small random input, called the *seed*, so it doesn't always produce the same output. From the seed, the PRNG produces a much larger string of acceptably random output; essentially, it is a randomness "stretcher." So, a program using a PRNG still needs to find some good random bits, just fewer of them, but they had better be quite unpredictable.

Since various programs require random bits, some operating systems have built-in facilities for providing them. Some Unix variants (including Linux and OpenBSD) have a device driver, accessed through */dev/random* and */dev/urandom*, that provides random bits when opened and read as a file. These bits are derived by all sorts of methods, some quite clever. Correctly filtered timing measurements of disk accesses, for example, can represent the fluctuations due to air turbulence around the drive heads. Another technique is to look at the least significant bits of noise coming from an unused microphone port. And of course, they can track fluctuating events such as network packet arrival times, keyboard events, interrupts, etc.

SSH implementations make use of randomness, but the process is largely invisible to the end user. Here's what happens under the hood. OpenSSH and Tectia, for example, use a kernel-based randomness source if it is available, along with their own sampling of (one hopes) fluctuating system parameters, gleaned by running such programs as *ps* or *netstat*. It uses these sources to seed its PRNG, as well as to "stir in" more randomness every once in a while. Since it can be expensive to gather randomness, SSH stores its pool of random bits in a file between invocations of the program, as shown in the following table:

	OpenSSH	Tectia
Server	/etc/ssh/ssh_random_seed	/etc/ssh2/random_seed
Client	~/.ssh/random_seed	~/.ssh2/random_seed

These files should be kept protected, since they contain sensitive information that can weaken SSH's security if disclosed to an attacker, although SSH takes steps to reduce that possibility. The seed information is always mixed with some new random bits before being used, and only half the pool is ever saved to disk, to reduce its predictive value if stolen.

In OpenSSH and Tectia, all this happens automatically and invisibly. OpenSSH links against the OpenSSL library and uses its randomness source, a kernel source if available. When building OpenSSH on a platform without */dev/random*, you have a choice. If you have installed an add-on randomness source, such as the Entropy Gathering Daemon (EGD, *http://www.lothar.com/tech/crypto/*), you can compile OpenSSH to use it with the --with-egd-pool compile-time configuration option. Or you can use the OpenSSH entropy-gathering mechanism. You can tailor which programs are run to gather entropy and "how random" they're considered to be, by editing the file */etc/ssh/ssh_prng_cmds*. Also, note that the OpenSSH random seed is kept in the *~/.ssh/prng_seed* file, even the daemon's, which is just the root user's seed file. Earlier versions of OpenSSH use this method internally and automatically if there is no */dev/random* and no pool specified. OpenSSH 3.8 and later have the random generator factored into a separate program, *ssh-rand-helper*, selected with the --with-rand-helper compile-time configuration option.

3.6.5   Privilege Separation in OpenSSH

A persistent problem in the world of Unix security is the lack of fine-grained permissions when it comes to process capabilities. Basically, either you're God (that is, "root") or you're not. The "Church" of Unix is missing the hosts of angels, archangels, cherubim, etc., that fill other pantheons and smooth the relationship between mere mortals and the divine, embodied for us in the mystical uid 0. This means that in order to accomplish some common tasks, such as listening on port 22 or creating processes under other uid's, the SSH server must also take on all the other powers of the root account. This flies in the face of a basic rule of security engineering: the Principle of Least Privilege, which says that a process should have only the privileges it needs, only when it needs them, and no more. If a serious vulnerability is found in the code of a server running as root, you can kiss your system goodbye, because when an attacker gets in, he has complete control.

In order to address this general problem, OpenSSH has a feature called *privilege separation*. The developers have factored out those server functions which require root privilege, and placed them in a separate process. The main server does not run as root; it gives up that privilege as soon as possible after startup, leaving a separate privileged "monitor" process with which it can communicate. The monitor opens the server listening socket which the main server inherits, but then closes its copy so that it does not communicate directly with clients (i.e., potential attackers). It communicates only by a private pipe to the main server and obeys a strict protocol, performing only those privileged operations necessary from time to time for the operation of the main server, and nothing else. This design mitigates the problem by restoring the Principle of Least Privilege, at least as much as is possible given the limitations of Unix.

Privilege separation is a complicated feature to implement, however, due to many small differences among Unix platforms with regard to the exact behavior of relevant system calls such as setuid, seteuid, setgid, etc., as well as difficulties with related software such as PAM. The early implementations of privilege separation in OpenSSH were notorious for causing mysterious errors in the operation of the server. Things have improved a great deal, but if you run into odd problems you can't explain—especially having to do with a privilege or access violation on the part of the server—you could do worse than to disable privilege separation and see what happens.

For more information on privilege separation, see:

- *http://www.citi.umich.edu/u/provos/ssh/privsep.html*
- "Preventing Privilege Escalation," Niels Provos, Markus Friedl, and Peter Honeyman, 12th USENIX Security Symposium, Washington, D.C., August 2003, *http://www.citi.umich.edu/u/provos/papers/privsep.pdf*.

3.7   SSH and File Transfers (scp and sftp)

The first thing to understand about SSH and file transfers is this: SSH doesn't really *do* file transfers. That is, the core SSH protocol as implemented by a program such as *ssh* (SSH-TRANS, SSH-AUTH, and SSH-CONN) has no file-transfer capability at all. Following good modular design, file transfer is simply one of many services that might be run over an SSH connection channel. In fact, the file-transfer programs bundled with most Unix-based SSH products, *scp* and *sftp*, typically don't even implement SSH in themselves; they simply run *ssh* in a subprocess to connect to the remote host, start the remote file-transfer agent, and talk to it.

Historically, the first file-transfer mechanism implemented with SSH was the program *scp*, included with the original SSH1 product. *scp* is simply an "ssh-ification" of the venerable Unix *rcp* program; just as *rcp* runs the *rsh* program to contact the remote host, *scp* runs *ssh* instead. If existing *rsh* software had supported a switch to select a different program than the default *rsh* (like *scp -S*), *scp* might never have been written; there would have been no need.

The *rcp* protocol used by *scp* is very limited. In a single session it can only transfer a set of whole files in one direction; there's no directory browsing, partial transfer, resumption of interrupted transfers, multiple transfer directions—in other words, it's nothing like FTP. When SSH Communications Security (SCS) defined the first version of the SSH-2 protocol and delivered its implementation, it wanted to include a much better file-transfer utility. To that end, it defined a completely new remote-filing protocol, designed to work easily over a single, reliable, secure, duplex byte-stream connection—that is, over SSH. The utility was called *sftp*. As with SSH-2, this initially undocumented and proprietary protocol was eventually moved onto the standards track of the IETF SECSH working group, as the "SSH File Transfer Protocol" (SSH-SFTP). Once that happened it began to appear in other implementations as well—for example, the *sftp* program in OpenSSH—first as a client only for compatibility with SCS servers, with *sftp-server* following later.

The name "SFTP" is unfortunate in two respects. First, it suggests that SFTP has something to do with the FTP protocol as defined in RFC-959 et al. It doesn't: they are completely different. Indeed, that's largely the point; as with *rcp*: were FTP amenable to use over SSH, SFTP might never have been written. But SSH and FTP are not a good match [11.2], so SFTP was born. It is a common mistake to think you can somehow use an *sftp* program to connect securely to an FTP server—a reasonable enough supposition, given the name—but you can't; they're entirely incompatible.

The name "SFTP" is also misleading in that it suggests security; many assume it stands for "Secure FTP." This isn't so. The SFTP protocol has no security features at all; implementations derive their security by speaking the protocol over an SSH connection.

3.7.1 What's in a Name?

So far, this isn't too bad. There are two file-transfer protocols commonly used over SSH—RCP and SFTP, usually implemented on the client side by the programs *scp* and *sftp*. The situation is a bit more complicated, though, because of the way the Tectia software operates. Although Tectia includes a program named *scp2*, it does *not* use the RCP protocol; instead, it uses SFTP. The Tectia programs *scp2* and *sftp2* are simply two different frontends for the SFTP protocol. They merely provide different user interfaces: *scp2* acts like *rcp/scp*, and *sftp2* is deliberately similar to an FTP client.

None of this confusing terminology is made any easier by the fact that when installed, Tectia makes symbolic links allowing you to use the plain names *scp*, *ssh*, etc., instead of *scp2* or *ssh2*. Even more bizarrely, *scp2* has a *-1* option that causes it to run a program named *scp1* for backward compatibility (of a sort). The upshot is that typing "scp" may get you either of two entirely different protocols, depending on what software is installed, and how it was installed. In our discussion, we ignore this complication; when we refer to *scp*, we mean an OpenSSH-style *scp* which uses the RCP protocol.

3.7.2 scp Details

When you run *scp* to copy a file from client to server, it invokes *ssh* with various options, like so:

```
/usr/bin/ssh -x -o ForwardAgent=no -o ClearAllForwardings=yes server-host scp ...
```

Earlier versions of *scp* actually searched your PATH for the *ssh* program rather than specifying it completely. This was a problem if multiple SSH software packages were installed, since it could run mismatched pieces of software together.

This runs another copy of *scp* on the remote host. That copy is invoked with the undocumented switches *–t* and *–f* (for "to" and "from"), putting it into SCP server mode. This next table shows some examples; Figure 3-3 shows the details.

This client scp command:	Runs this remote command:
scp foo server:bar	scp -t bar
scp server:bar foo	scp -f bar
scp *.txt server:dir	scp -d -t dir

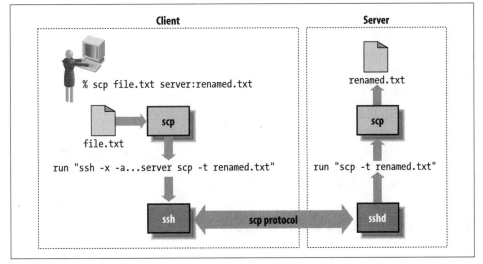

Figure 3-3. scp operation

If you run *scp* to copy a file between two remote hosts, it simply executes another *scp* client on the source host to copy the file to the target. For example, this command:

```
scp source:music.au target:playme
```

runs this in the background:

```
ssh -x -o ClearAllForwardings=yes -n source scp music.au target:playme
```

Note that the options are changed appropriately: agent forwarding is not turned off, as that may be needed by the remote *scp* client in order to contact the target host.

3.7.3   scp2/sftp Details

When you run *scp2* or *sftp* under Unix, it also runs an *ssh* program behind the scenes, as with *scp*.* The exact details vary depend on which software is in use; remember that *sftp* comes with both OpenSSH and Tectia. However, they both look like:

```
ssh [options] server-host -s sftp
```

Instead of a remote command, this uses an SSH-2 subsystem request to start the *sftp* server on the remote host. This insulates the client from the details of how SFTP is implemented on the server, rather than embed the *sftp-server* pathname in the command (which might change), or relaying on the remote PATH setting to find it (which might not work). Unlike *scp*, here the command line doesn't specify the files to be transferred; that information is carried inside the SFTP protocol.

Using a subsystem means that the SSH server must be specifically configured to handle SFTP. For OpenSSH:

```
# sshd_config
subsystem sftp /usr/libexec/sftp-server
```

Tectia can either execute an external SFTP server in the same way:

```
# sshd2_config
subsystem-sftp /usr/libexec/sftp-server2
```

or run the SFTP protocol within the SSH server process itself:

```
# sshd2_config
subsystem-sftp internal://sftp-server
```

Figure 3-4 shows more details of how *sftp* operates.

3.8   Algorithms Used by SSH

We now summarize each of the algorithms we have mentioned. Don't treat these summaries as complete analyses, however. You can't necessarily extrapolate from characteristics of individual algorithms (positive or negative) to whole systems without considering the other parts. Security is complicated that way.

3.8.1   Public-Key Algorithms

3.8.1.1   Rivest-Shamir-Adleman (RSA)

The Rivest-Shamir-Adleman (RSA) public-key algorithm is the most widely used asymmetric cipher. It derives its security from the difficulty of factoring large integers

---

* Tectia for Windows simply integrates SSH into these programs.

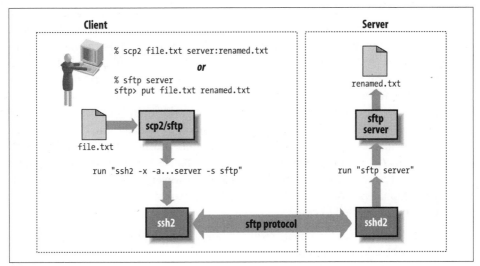

Figure 3-4. scp2/sftp operation

that are the product of two large primes of roughly equal size. Factoring is widely believed to be intractable (i.e., infeasible, admitting no efficient, polynomial-time solution), although this isn't proven. RSA can be used for both encryption and signatures.

Until September 2000, RSA was claimed to be patented in the U.S. states by Public Key Partners, Inc., a company in which RSA Security, Inc. is a partner. (The algorithm is now in the public domain.) While the patent was in force, PKP claimed that it controlled the use of the RSA algorithm in the U.S., and that the use of unauthorized implementations was illegal. Until the mid-1990s, RSA Security provided a freely available reference implementation, RSAref, with a license allowing educational and broad commercial use (as long as the software itself was not sold for profit). Since RSA is now in the public domain, RSAref has disappeared.

The SSH-1 protocol specified use of RSA explicitly. SSH-2 can use multiple public-key algorithms, but originally defined only DSA. [3.8.1.2] The SECSH working group added the RSA algorithm to SSH-2 shortly after the patent expired.

3.8.1.2 Digital Signature Algorithm (DSA)

The Digital Signature Algorithm (DSA) was developed by the U.S. National Security Agency (NSA), and promulgated by the U.S. National Institute of Standards and Technology (NIST) as part of the Digital Signature Standard (DSS). The DSS was issued as a Federal Information Processing Standard, FIPS-186, in May 1994. It is a public-key algorithm, based on the Schnorr and ElGamal methods, and relies on the difficulty of computing discrete logarithms in a finite field. It is designed as a signature-only scheme that can't be used for encryption, although a fully general implementation may easily perform both RSA and ElGamal encryption.

DSA has also been surrounded by a swirl of controversy since its inception. The NIST first claimed that it had designed DSA, then eventually revealed that the NSA had done so. Many question the motives and ethics of the NSA, with ample historical reason to do so.[*] Researcher Gus Simmons discovered a subliminal channel in DSA that allows an implementor to leak information—for instance, secret key bits—with every signature.[†] Since the algorithm was to be made available as a closed hardware implementation in smart cards as part of the government's Capstone program, many people considered this property highly suspicious. Finally, the NIST intended DSA to be available royalty-free to all users. To that end it was patented by David Kravitz (patent #5,231,668), then an employee of the NSA, who assigned the patent to the U.S. government. There have been claims, however, that DSA infringes existing cryptographic patents, including the Schnorr patent. To our knowledge, this issue has yet to be settled in court.

The SSH-2 protocol uses DSA as its required (and currently, only defined) public-key algorithm for host identification.

3.8.1.3   Diffie-Hellman key agreement

The Diffie-Hellman key agreement algorithm was the first public-key system published in the open literature, invented by Whitfield Diffie, Martin Hellman, and Ralph Merkle in 1976. It was patented by them in 1977 (issued in 1980, patent #4,200,770); that patent has now expired, and the algorithm is in the public domain. Like DSA, it is based on the discrete logarithm problem, and it allows two parties to derive a shared secret key securely over an open channel. That is, the parties engage in an exchange of messages, at the end of which they share a secret key. It isn't feasible for an eavesdropper to determine the shared secret merely from observing the exchanged messages.

SSH-2 uses the Diffie-Hellman algorithm as its required (and currently, its only defined) key-exchange method.

3.8.2   Secret-Key Algorithms

3.8.2.1   International Data Encryption Algorithm (IDEA)

The International Data Encryption Algorithm (IDEA) was designed in 1990 by Xuejia Lai and James Massey,[‡] and went through several revisions, improvements, and renamings before reaching its current form. Although relatively new, it is considered

---

[*] See James Bamford's book, *The Puzzle Palace* (Penguin), for an investigative history of the NSA.

[†] G. J. Simmons, "The Subliminal Channels in the U.S. Digital Signature Algorithm (DSA)." *Proceedings of the Third Symposium on: State and Progress of Research in Cryptography*, Rome: Fondazione Ugo Bordoni, 1993, pp. 35–54.

[‡] X. Lai and J. Massey, "A Proposal for a New Block Encryption Standard," *Advances in Cryptology—EUROCRYPT '92 Proceedings*, Springer-Verlag, 1992, pp. 389–404.

secure; the well-known cryptographer Bruce Schneier in 1996 pronounced it "the best and most secure block algorithm available to the public at this time."

IDEA is patented in Europe and the U.S. by the Swiss company Ascom-Tech AG.* The name "IDEA" is a trademark of Ascom-Tech. The attitude of Ascom-Tech toward this patent and the use of IDEA in the U.S. has changed over time, especially with regard to its inclusion in PGP. It is free for noncommercial use. Government or commercial use may require a royalty, where "commercial use" includes use of the algorithm internal to a commercial organization, not just directly selling an implementation or offering its use for profit. Here are two sites for more information:

- *http://vmsbox.cjb.net/idea.html*
- *http://home.ecn.ab.ca/~jsavard/crypto/co040302.htm*

3.8.2.2   Advanced Encryption Standard (AES)

In 1997, the NIST began a program to develop a replacement for the existing government-standard symmetric encryption algorithm, DES, which was beginning to show its age. The process involved soliciting designs from the worldwide cryptographic community, and pitting them against one another in a design contest of sorts. After a five-year process, the winner was finally selected. The algorithm designed by Joan Daemen and Vincent Rijmen and originally known as Rijndael became the Advanced Encryption Standard, codified in FIPS-197. AES is a symmetric block cipher with key sizes of either 128, 192, or 256 bits. You can find more information at the following site:

http://csrc.nist.gov/publications/fips/fips197/fips-197.pdf

3.8.2.3   Data Encryption Standard (DES)

The Data Encryption Standard (DES) is the old workhorse of symmetric encryption algorithms, now finally put out to pasture, replaced by AES. Designed by researchers at IBM in the early 1970s under the name Lucifer, the U.S. government adopted DES as a standard on November 23, 1976 (FIPS-46). It was patented by IBM, but IBM granted free worldwide rights to its use. It has been used extensively in the public and private sectors ever since. DES has stood up well to cryptanalysis over the years and is increasingly viewed as outdated only because its 56-bit key size is too small relative to modern computing power. A number of well-publicized designs for special-purpose "DES-cracking" machines have been put forward, and their putative prices are falling more and more into the realm of plausibility for governments and large companies. It seems sure that at least the NSA has such devices.

---

* U.S. patent #5,214,703, 25 May 1993; international patent PCT/CH91/00117, 28 November 1991; European patent EP 0 482 154 B1.

3.8.2.4 Triple-DES

Triple-DES, or 3DES, is a variant of DES intended to increase its security by increasing the key length. It has been proven that the DES function can increase its security by encrypting multiple times with independent keys.[*] 3DES encrypts the plaintext with three iterations of the DES algorithm, using three separate keys. The effective key length of 3DES is 112 bits, a vast improvement over the 56-bit key of plain DES.

3.8.2.5 ARCFOUR (RC4)

Ron Rivest designed the RC4 cipher in 1987 for RSA Data Security, Inc. (RSADSI); the name is variously claimed to stand for "Rivest Cipher" or "Ron's Code." It was an unpatented trade secret of RSADSI, used in quite a number of commercial products by RSADSI licensees. In 1994, though, source code claiming to implement RC4 appeared anonymously on the Internet. Experimentation quickly confirmed that the posted code was indeed compatible with RC4, and the cat was out of the bag. Since it had never been patented, RC4 effectively entered the public domain. This doesn't mean that RSADSI won't sue someone who tries to use it in a commercial product, so it is less expensive to settle and license than to fight. We aren't aware of any test cases of this issue. Since the name "RC4" is trademarked by RSADSI, the name "ARCFOUR" has been coined to refer to the publicly revealed version of the algorithm.

ARCFOUR is very fast but less studied than many other algorithms. It uses a variable-size key; SSH-1 employs independent 128-bit keys for each direction of the SSH session. The use of independent keys for each direction is an exception in SSH-1, and crucial: ARCFOUR is essentially a pad using the output of a pseudo-random number generator. As such, it is important never to reuse a key because to do so makes cryptanalysis trivially easy. If this caveat is observed, ARCFOUR is considered secure by many, despite the dearth of public cryptanalytic results.

3.8.2.6 Blowfish

Blowfish was designed by Bruce Schneier in 1993, as a step toward replacing the aging DES. It is much faster than DES and IDEA, though not as fast as ARCFOUR, and is unpatented and free for all uses. It is intended specifically for implementation on large, modern, general-purpose microprocessors and for situations with relatively few key changes. It isn't particularly suited to low-end environments such as smart cards. It employs a variable-size key of 32 to 448 bits; SSH-2 uses 128-bit keys. Blowfish has received a fair amount of cryptanalytic scrutiny and has proved impervious to attack so far. Information is available from Counterpane, Schneier's security consulting company, at:

http://www.schneier.com/blowfish.html

---

[*] Because it doesn't form a group over its keys. See W. Campbell and M. J. Wiener, "DES Is Not a Group," *Advances in Cryptology—CRYPTO '92 Proceedings*, Springer-Verlag, pp. 512–520.

3.8.2.7 Twofish

Twofish is another design by Bruce Schneier, together with J. Kelsey, D. Whiting, D. Wagner, C. Hall, and N. Ferguson. It was submitted in 1998 to the NIST as a candidate for the Advanced Encryption Standard, to replace DES as the U.S. government's symmetric data encryption standard. It was one of the five finalists in the AES selection process, out of 15 initial submissions, but eventually lost to Rijndael. Like Blowfish, it is unpatented and free for all uses, and Counterpane has provided uncopyrighted reference implementations, also freely usable.

Twofish admits keys of lengths 128, 192, or 256 bits; SSH-2 specifies 256-bit keys. Twofish is designed to be more flexible than Blowfish, allowing good implementation in a larger variety of computing environments (e.g., slower processors, small memory, in-hardware). It is very fast, its design is conservative, and it is likely to be quite strong. You can read more about Twofish at:

http://www.schneier.com/twofish.html

You can read more about the NIST AES program at:

http://www.nist.gov/aes/

3.8.2.8 CAST

CAST was designed in the early 1990s by Carlisle Adams and Stafford Tavares. Tavares is on the faculty of Queen's University at Kingston in Canada, while Adams is an employee of Entrust Technologies of Texas. CAST is patented, and the rights are held by Entrust, which has made two versions of the algorithm available on a worldwide royalty-free basis for all uses. These versions are CAST-128 and CAST-256, described in RFC-2144 and RFC-2612, respectively. SSH-2 uses CAST-128, which is named for its 128-bit key length.

3.8.3 Hash Functions

3.8.3.1 CRC-32

The 32-bit Cyclic Redundancy Check (CRC-32), defined in ISO 3309,[*] is a noncryptographic hash function for detecting accidental changes to data. The SSH-1 protocol uses CRC-32 (with the polynomial 0xEDB88320) for integrity checking, and this weakness admits the "insertion attack" discussed elsewhere. [3.5] The SSH-2 protocol employs cryptographically strong hash functions for integrity checking, obviating this attack.

---

[*] International Organization for Standardization, *ISO Information Processing Systems—Data Communication High-Level Data Link Control Procedure—Frame Structure*, ISO 3309, October 1984, 3rd Edition.

3.8.3.2 MD5

MD5 ("Message Digest algorithm number 5") is a cryptographically strong, 128-bit hash algorithm designed by Ron Rivest in 1991, one of a series he designed for RSADSI (MD2 through MD5). MD5 is unpatented, placed in the public domain by RSADSI, and documented in RFC-1321. It has been a standard hash algorithm for several years, used in many cryptographic products and standards. A successful collision attack against the MD5 compression function by den Boer and Bosselaers in 1993 caused some concern, and though the attack hasn't resulted in any practical weaknesses, there is an expectation that it will, and people are beginning to avoid MD5 in favor of newer algorithms. RSADSI recommends moving away from MD5 in favor of SHA-1 or RIP-EMD-160 for future applications demanding collision-resistance.[*]

3.8.3.3 SHA-1

SHA-1 (Secure Hash Algorithm) was designed by the NSA and the NIST for use with the U.S. government Digital Signature Standard. Like MD5, it was designed as an improvement on MD4, but takes a different approach. It produces 160-bit hashes. There are no known attacks against SHA-1, and, if secure, it is stronger than MD5 simply for its longer hash value. It has replaced MD5 in some applications; for example, SSH-2 uses SHA-1 as its required MAC hash function, as opposed to MD5 in SSH-1.[†]

3.8.3.4 RIPEMD-160

Yet another 160-bit MD4 variant, RIPEMD-160, was developed by Hans Dobbertin, Antoon Bosselaers, and Bart Preneel as part of the European Community RIPE project. RIPE stands for RACE Integrity Primitives Evaluation;[‡] RACE, in turn, was the program for Research and Development in Advanced Communications Technologies in Europe, an EC-sponsored program which ran from June 1987 to December 1995. RIPE was part of the RACE effort, devoted to studying and developing data integrity techniques. Hence, RIPEMD-160 should be read as "the RIPE Message Digest (160 bits)." In particular, it has nothing to do with RIPEM, an old Privacy-Enhanced Mail (PEM) implementation by Mark Riordan.

RIPEMD-160 isn't defined in the SSH protocol, but it is used for an implementation-specific MAC algorithm in OpenSSH, under the name `hmac-ripemd160@openssh.com`. RIPEMD-160 is unpatented and free for all uses. You can read more about it at:

> *http://www.esat.kuleuven.ac.be/~bosselae/ripemd160.html*

---

[*] RSA Laboratories Bulletin #4, 12 November 1996, *ftp://ftp.rsasecurity.com/pub/pdfs/bulletn4.pdf*.

[†] As this book went to press, the NIST announced plans to phase out SHA-1 by the year 2010, in favor of stronger algorithms like SHA-256 and SHA-512.

[‡] Not to be confused with another "RIPE," Réseaux IP Européens ("European IP Networks"), a technical and coordinating association of entities operating wide area IP networks in Europe and elsewhere (*http://www.ripe.net*).

3.8.4   Compression Algorithms: zlib

zlib is currently the only compression algorithm defined for SSH. In the SSH protocol documents, the term "zlib" refers to the "deflate" lossless compression algorithm as first implemented in the popular *gzip* compression utility, and later documented in RFC-1951. It is available as a software library called ZLIB at:

> *http://www.zlib.net/*

3.9   Threats SSH Can Counter

Like any security tool, SSH has particular threats against which it is effective and others that it doesn't address. We'll discuss the former first.

3.9.1   Eavesdropping

An *eavesdropper* is a network snooper who reads network traffic without affecting it in any way. SSH's encryption prevents eavesdropping. The contents of an SSH session, even if intercepted, can't be decrypted by a snooper.

3.9.2   Name Service and IP Spoofing

If an attacker subverts your naming service (DNS, NIS, etc.), network-related programs may be coerced to connect to the wrong machine. Similarly, an attacker can impersonate a host by stealing use of its IP address(es). In either case, you're in trouble: your client program can connect to a false server that steals your password when you supply it. SSH guards against this attack by cryptographically verifying the server host identity. When setting up a session, the SSH client validates the server's host key against a local list associating server names and addresses with their keys. If the supplied host key doesn't match the one on the list, SSH complains. This feature may be disabled in less security-conscious settings if the warning messages get annoying. [7.4.3.1]

The SSH-2 protocol allows for including PKI certificates along with keys. In the future, we hope that implementation of this feature in SSH products along with more common deployment of PKI will ease the burden of key management and reduce the need for this particular security trade-off.

3.9.3   Connection Hijacking

An "active attacker"—one who not only can listen to network traffic, but also can inject his own—can hijack a TCP connection, literally stealing it away from one of its legitimate endpoints. This is obviously disastrous: no matter how good your authentication method is, the attacker can simply wait until you've logged in, then steal your connection and insert his own nefarious commands into your session. SSH can't prevent hijacking, since this is a weakness in TCP, which operates below SSH. However, SSH renders it ineffective (except as a denial-of-service attack). SSH's integrity checking detects if a session is modified in transit, and shuts down the connection immediately without using any of the corrupted data.

3.9.4 Man-in-the-Middle Attacks

A *man-in-the-middle attack* is a particularly subtle type of active attack and is illustrated in Figure 3-5. An adversary sits between you and your real peer (i.e., between the SSH client and server), intercepting all traffic and altering or deleting messages at will. Imagine that you try to connect to an SSH server, but Malicious Mary intercepts your connection. She behaves just like an SSH server, though, so you don't notice, and she ends up sharing a session key with you. Simultaneously, she also initiates her own connection to your intended server, obtaining a separate session key with the server. She can log in as you because you used password authentication and thus conveniently handed her your password. You and the server both think you have a connection to each other, when in fact you both have connections to Mary instead. Then she just sits in the middle, passing data back and forth between you and the server (decrypting on one side with one key and re-encrypting with the other for retransmission). Of course, she can read everything that goes by and undetectably modify it if she chooses.

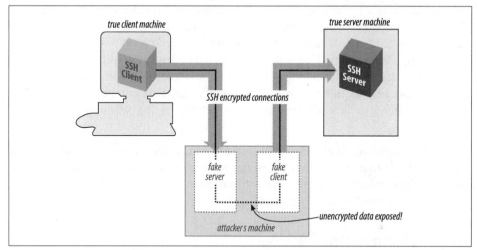

Figure 3-5. Man-in-the-middle attack

SSH counters this attack in two ways. The first is server host authentication. Unless Mary has broken into the server host, she is unable to effect her impersonation, because she doesn't have the server's private host key. Note that for this protection to work, it is crucial that the client actually check the server-supplied public host key against its known hosts list; otherwise, there is no guarantee that the server is genuine. If you connect for the first time to a new server and let *ssh* accept the host key, you are actually open to a man-in-the-middle attack. However, assuming you aren't spoofed that one time, future connections to this server are safe as long as the server host key isn't stolen.

The second protection SSH affords is via certain user authentication methods. The password method is obviously vulnerable, but publickey and hostbased authentication resist MITM attacks. Mary can't discover the session key simply by observing the key exchange; she must perform an active attack in which she carries out separate exchanges with each side, obtaining separate keys of her own with the client and server. In both SSH-1 and SSH-2, the key exchange is designed so that if she does this, the session identifiers for each side are different. When a client provides a digital signature for either public-key or hostbased authentication, it includes the session identifier in the data signed. Thus, Mary can't just pass on the client-supplied authenticator to the server, nor does she have any way of coercing the client into signing the other session ID.*

If you don't verify the server name/key correspondence, Mary can still perform the man-in-the-middle attack, even though she can't log in as you on the server side. Perhaps she can log into her own account or another she has cracked. With some cleverness, she might still deceive you long enough to do damage.

3.10 Threats SSH Doesn't Prevent

SSH isn't a total security solution. We'll now present some examples of attacks that SSH wasn't designed to prevent.

3.10.1 Password Cracking

SSH dramatically improves password security by encrypting your password as it passes over the network. Nevertheless, a password is still a weak form of authentication, and you must take care with it. You must choose a good password, memorable to you but not obvious to anyone else, and not easily guessable. You must also avoid having your password stolen, since possession alone is sufficient to grant access to your account. So, watch out: the guy at the next terminal might be surreptitiously "shoulder surfing" (watching as you type). That computer kiosk you're about to use may have been tricked up to log all keystrokes to Cracker Central Command. And the nice-sounding fellow who calls from Corporate IT and asks for your password to "fix your account" might not be who he claims.

---

* This is not true of the older SSH-1 protocol, however.

Consider public-key authentication instead, since it is *two-factor*: a stolen passphrase is useless without the private-key file, so an attacker needs to steal both. Of course, the SSH client on the computer you're borrowing can be rigged to squirrel away your key after you blithely supply your passphrase to decrypt it. If you're that worried, you shouldn't use strange computers. In the future, one hopes, cryptographic smartcards and readers will be ubiquitous and supported by SSH so that you can carry your keys conveniently and use them in other computers without fear of disclosure.

If you must use password authentication because of its convenience, consider using a one-time password scheme such as S/Key to reduce risk. [5.4.5]

3.10.2 IP and TCP Attacks

SSH operates on top of TCP, so it is vulnerable to some attacks against weaknesses in TCP and IP. The privacy, integrity, and authentication guarantees of SSH limit this vulnerability to denial-of-service attacks.

TCP/IP is resistant to network problems such as congestion and link failure. If the enemy blows up a router, IP can route around it. It wasn't designed to resist an adversary injecting bogus packets into the network, however. The origin of TCP or IP control messages isn't authenticated. As a result, TCP/IP has a number of inherent exploitable weaknesses, such as:

SYN flood
> SYN stands for "synchronize," and is a TCP packet attribute. In this case, it refers to the initial packet sent to start the setup of a TCP connection. This packet often causes the receiver to expend resources preparing for the coming connection. If an attacker sends large numbers of these packets, the receiving TCP stack may run out of space and be unable to accept legitimate connections.

TCP RST, bogus ICMP
> Another TCP packet type is RST, for "reset." Either side of a TCP connection can send an RST packet at any time, which causes immediate teardown of the connection. RST packets may be injected easily into a network, immediately disconnecting any target TCP connection.
>
> Similarly, there is ICMP, the Internet Control Message Protocol. ICMP allows IP hosts and routers to communicate information about network conditions and host reachability. But again, there is no authentication, so injecting bogus ICMP packets can have drastic effects. For instance, there are ICMP messages that say a particular host or TCP port is unreachable; forging such packets can cause connections to be torn down. There are also ICMP messages that communicate routing information (redirects and router discovery); forging such messages can cause sensitive data to be routed through unintended and possibly compromised systems.

TCP desynchronization and hijacking

By clever manipulation of the TCP protocol, an attacker can desynchronize two sides of a TCP connection with respect to data byte sequence numbers. In this state, it is possible to inject packets that are accepted as a legitimate part of the connection, allowing the attacker to insert arbitrary information into the TCP data stream.

SSH provides no protection against attacks that break or prevent setup of TCP connections. On the other hand, SSH's encryption and host authentication are effective against attacks that involve inappropriate routing that would otherwise permit reading of sensitive traffic or redirect a connection to a compromised server. Likewise, attacks that hijack or alter TCP data will fail, because SSH detects them, but they also break the SSH connection, because SSH responds to such problems by termination.

Because these threats focus on problems with TCP/IP, they can be effectively countered only by lower, network-level techniques, such as hardware link encryption or IPSEC. [1.6.4] IPSEC is the IP Security protocol that is part of the next-generation IP protocol, IPv6, and available as an add-on to the current IP standard, IPv4. It provides encryption, integrity, and data origin-authentication services at the IP packet level.

3.10.3 Traffic Analysis

Even if an attacker can't read your network traffic, he can glean a great deal of useful information by simply watching it—noting the amount of data, the source and destination addresses, and timing. A sudden increase in traffic with another company might tip him off that an impending business deal is in the works. Traffic patterns can also indicate backup schedules or times of day most vulnerable to denial-of-service attacks. Prolonged silence on an SSH connection from a sysadmin's desktop might indicate that she's stepped out, and that now is a good time to break in, electronically or physically.

SSH doesn't address traffic-analysis attacks. SSH connections are easily identifiable as they generally go to a well-known port, and the SSH protocol makes no attempt to obfuscate traffic analysis. An SSH implementation could conceivably send random, no-op traffic over a connection when it's otherwise idle, to frustrate activity correlation. OpenSSH, in fact, sends no-op packets in response to keystrokes when a program turns off tty echo (e.g., the *su* program prompting for a password). This makes it harder for an attacker to identify the keystrokes of value in a session.

 Although the SSH protocol doesn't specifically deal with traffic analysis, some implementations take steps against it. OpenSSH, for example, hides the fact that terminal echoing has been turned off by sending fake echo packets, making it harder to recognize signatures of non-echoing commands, such as typing the root password after an *su* prompt.

A more serious concern regarding traffic analysis arises from recent work by U.C. Berkeley researchers Dawn Song, David Wagner, and Xuqing Tian. At the 10th Usenix Security Symposium (Washington D.C., August 2001), they presented a paper titled "Timing Analysis of Keystrokes and Timing Attacks on SSH":

http://www.usenix.org/publications/library/proceedings/sec01/song.html

The paper applies traffic-analysis techniques to interactive SSH connections to infer information about the encrypted contents. The authors conclude that the keystroke timing data observable from existing SSH implementations reveals a dangerously significant amount of information about user terminal sessions—enough to locate typed passwords in the session data stream and reduce the computational work involved in guessing those passwords by a factor of 50. While this work describes a very sophisticated attack which has yet to yield any practical exploits (that we know of!), this area bears watching.

3.10.4   Covert Channels

A *covert channel* is a means of signaling information in an unanticipated and unnoticed fashion. Suppose that one day, Sysadmin Sally decides her users are having too much fun, and she turns off email and instant messaging so that they can't chat. To get around this, you and your friend agree to put messages to each other into world-readable files in your home directories, which you'll check every once in a while for new messages. This unanticipated communication mechanism is a covert channel.

Covert channels are hard to eliminate. If Sysadmin Sally discovers your file-based technique, she can make all home directories unreadable and unsearchable by anyone but their owners, and prevent the owners from changing this restriction. While she's at it, she can also make sure you can't create files anywhere else, like */tmp*. (Most of your programs don't work now, but that doesn't matter to Sally.) Even so, you and your friend can still list each other's home directory nodes themselves, which reveals the directory modification date and number of files, so you devise a secret code based on these visible parameters and communicate by modifying them. This is a more complex covert channel, and you can imagine even more outlandish ones in the face of further restrictions from Sally.

SSH doesn't attempt to eliminate covert channels. Their analysis and control are generally part of highly secure computer systems, such as those designed to handle information safely at various security classification levels within the same system. Incidentally, the SSH data stream itself can be used perfectly well as a covert channel: the encrypted contents of your SSH session might be a recipe for chocolate chip cookies, while a secret message about an impending corporate merger is represented in Morse code using even/odd packet lengths for dashes and dots.

3.10.5 Carelessness

> *Mit der Dummheit kämpfen Götter selbst vergebens.*
> *(Against stupidity, even the Gods struggle in vain.)*
> —Friedrich von Schiller

Security tools don't secure anything; they only help people to do so. It's almost a cliché, but so important that it bears any amount of repeating. The best cryptography or most secure protocols in the world won't help if users pick bad passwords, or write their passphrases on Post-it notes stuck to the undersides of their keyboards. They also won't help sysadmins who neglect other aspects of host security, allowing host-key theft or wiretapping of terminal sessions.

As Bruce Schneier is fond of saying, "Security is a process, not a product." SSH is a good tool, but it must be part of an overall and ongoing process of security awareness. Other aspects of host integrity must still be attended to; security advisories for relevant software and operating systems monitored, appropriate patches or workarounds applied promptly, and people educated and kept aware of their security responsibilities. Don't just install SSH and think that you're now secure; you're not.

3.11 Threats Caused by SSH

We can hear the chorus now..."What? I'm using SSH to improve security; what do you mean it *causes* threats!?" Calm down, we're just being complete here. There are no new threats that SSH causes per se, but there are existing issues that it perhaps exacerbates.

To employ SSH, your users must be able to make outbound TCP connections: and really, that gives them the power to do just about anything. Think you can restrict which Internet hosts they can contact? Think again: all they need is a proxy on a host they *can* reach to redirect their traffic. Think they can only use TCP because that's all the firewall lets through? Not at all: there are freely available tools that can operate a full-blown VPN over a TCP (e.g., OpenVPN). Think you're safe from inbound attacks because you allow only outbound connections? Don't be naive: that "outbound" connection is a two-way street once established and can be connected to anything at all.

The only things that keep people from violating your security policy with this access, aside from respecting the policy itself, are ignorance and inconvenience. Your users might not know how to play any of the preceding tricks, or it might be too much trouble if they do. SSH, however, makes some of these things very easy: tunneling outbound connections to "forbidden" TCP ports, reverse forwarding to tunnel *back* through your firewall and circumvent it, etc...and everything nicely encrypted so that you can't see what's happening!

The important lesson here is not that SSH is dangerous, but that truly limiting network access is a very difficult proposition: usually impossible, in fact, with any kind of reasonable effort (and if you want to get any other work done). When there are convenient tools like SSH lying around tempting people to get around annoying limitations, you can no longer rely on ignorance and inconvenience to enforce your security policy. Ultimately, you must gain the trust and cooperation of your users to have an effective security policy.

3.12 Summary

The SSH protocol uses openly published, strong cryptographic tools to provide network connections with privacy, integrity, and mutual authentication. The original SSH-1 protocol (a.k.a. SSH 1.5) was wildly popular, despite being somewhat ad hoc: essentially a documentation of SSH1's program behavior. It had a number of shortcomings and flaws, of which the weak integrity check and resulting Futoransky/Kargieman insertion attack is perhaps the most egregious example. The current protocol version, SSH-2, is far superior, but was slow to take off due to the dearth of implementations, licensing restrictions, and the continued availability of the free SSH1 software for many commercial purposes. Thankfully, the tide has now turned, due primarily to the gargantuan and mostly unpaid efforts of the OpenSSH team in bringing forth a free implementation of the SSH-2 protocol.

SSH counters many network-related security threats, but not all. In particular, it is vulnerable to denial-of-service attacks based on weaknesses in TCP/IP, its underlying transport...though now that IPSec is widespread, these weaknesses can be addressed if need be. SSH also doesn't address attacks such as traffic analysis and covert channels, which may be of concern depending on the environment.

## CHAPTER 4

Installation and Compile-Time Configuration

Now that you know what SSH is and how it works, where do you get it and how do you install it? This chapter surveys several popular and robust implementations of SSH and explains how to obtain, compile, and install them:

OpenSSH
> A free implementation, originally part of OpenBSD, and available for many other operating systems including Linux, Solaris, Mac OS X, and Windows.

Tectia
> A suite of commercial products from SSH Communications Security Corp., that run on a variety of platforms including Linux, Solaris, HP-UX, AIX, and Windows. Formerly known as SSH2 and SSH Secure Shell.

Non-Unix implementations of SSH are covered in Chapters 13–18.

4.1. Overview

The first question to consider when installing any implementation of SSH is whether to use a binary or source distribution.

Binary distributions are already configured and compiled, and are therefore easy to use. They are available for popular SSH implementations like OpenSSH and Tectia on a variety of common platforms. The packaging technology and installation instructions vary according to the target system—consult the documentation provided by your vendor for details. For example, on Linux systems, binary distributions are usually shipped as RPM packages, and can be installed using a single command like:

```
$ rpm -Uhv openssh-3.9p1-1.i386.rpm
```

Installation on Unix systems typically requires root access, to install files in system directories, and to update the databases that keep track of installed packages.

Binary distributions are often cryptographically signed, to ensure that no one has tampered with the files. Signatures can be provided as separate files, or (depending on the package format) embedded within the binary distribution files, and the technique to verify the signature depends on how the files were signed. For example, on RPM-based Linux systems, first import the vendor's public key, which is distributed by keyservers or the vendor's web site:

```
$ rpm --import http://www.redhat.com/security/db42a60e.txt
```

Then use the public key to check the signature:

```
$ rpm --checksig -v openssh-3.9p1-1.i386.rpm
```

 Always check the signatures of binary distributions before installing. Imagine the havoc that could be caused if a maliciously hacked version of SSH was unwittingly used on your system.

Source distributions require more work to install, but allow many more configuration options. They can also be used on platforms for which no binary distributions are available.

To install from sources, perform the following general steps; we'll cover specific details for OpenSSH and Tectia in subsequent sections.

4.1.1   Install the Prerequisites

Some SSH implementations rely on other software packages; these must be obtained and installed first. The precise requirements sometimes depend on the configuration options chosen: e.g., support for hardware authentication devices (smartcards) might require special libraries.

4.1.2   Obtain the Sources

Source code for open source SSH implementations can be downloaded from each project's web site, and often a large number of mirror sites. Sources for commercial products are sometimes provided on the distribution media, or are available on vendors' password-protected web sites.

4.1.3   Verify the Signature

Sources should be distributed with a signature file that guarantees the distribution is genuine and has not been modified. [1.6.2] The precise steps used to verify the signature depend on how the source file was signed.

Always check the signature before installing sources. Otherwise, you can be fooled by a hacked version created by an untrusted third party. If you blindly install a source without checking the signature, you can seriously compromise your system's security.

4.1.4   Extract the Source Files

Source distributions are almost invariably packaged in compressed tar format.* File-names ending in *.tar.gz* (or sometimes *.tgz*) are compressed using gzip, and can be extracted using a command like:

```
$ tar xzvf openssh-3.9p1.tar.gz
```

If your version of tar does not support the *z* option for running gunzip automatically, try:

```
$ gunzip < openssh-3.9p1.tar.gz | tar xvf -
```

gzip (and gunzip) can be obtained, if you don't already have them, from *http://www.gzip.org/*.

Similarly, filenames ending in *.tar.bz2* are compressed using bzip2, and can be extracted using a command like:

```
$ tar xjvf openssh-3.9p1.tar.bz2
```

If your version of tar does not support the *j* option for running bunzip2 automatically, try:

```
$ bunzip2 < openssh-3.9p1.tar.bz2 | tar xvf -
```

bzip2 (and bunzip2) can be obtained from *http://sources.redhat.com/bzip2*.

In all cases, the result is a new subdirectory containing all files in the distribution. The name of the source directory is usually the same as the tar file, e.g., *openssh-3.9p1*.

To list the contents of the tar file, without extracting, use the *t* option instead of *x*; for example:

```
$ tar tzvf openssh-3.9p1.tar.gz
```

4.1.5   Perform Compile-Time Configuration

Most SSH implementations have dozens of configuration options you can set at compile time. It's a good idea to carefully consider each one, instead of blindly accepting the defaults. In fact, the flexibility provided by this compile-time configuration process is a primary motivation for installing from source distributions.

---

* Often called a "tarball."

Compile-time configuration is performed by running a script named `configure` that is usually found in the top-level source directory.* Roughly speaking, the `configure` script accomplishes two tasks:

- It examines the local system, setting various platform-specific and operating-system-specific options. For example, `configure` notices which header files and libraries are available and whether your C compiler is ANSI or not. It does this by compiling and running a series of carefully constructed, small test programs, examining system files, etc. This happens automatically in most cases, so you can just sit back and watch the script announce what it discovers as it runs.

- It includes or excludes certain features found in the SSH source code. For example, `configure` can keep or remove support for Kerberos authentication.

We'll discuss only the second task, since it's SSH-specific, and cover only the configuration options that are directly related to SSH or security. For example, we won't cover options that relate to the compiler (e.g., whether warnings should be printed or suppressed) or operating system (e.g., whether particular Unix library functions should be used). To see the full set of configure options, use the command:

```
$ configure --help
```

Also, read the installation documentation, which is often found in files named *README* and *INSTALL* in the source directory.

The behavior of SSH servers can be controlled at three levels. The first is compile-time configuration as discussed in this chapter. In addition, *serverwide configuration* (Chapter 5) controls global settings for a running SSH server, and *per-account configuration* (Chapter 8) controls settings for each user account accepting SSH connections. Figure 4-1 illustrates where compile-time configuration fits into the whole spectrum. We'll remind you of this picture each time we introduce a new type of configuration.

Compile-time configuration affects both the SSH server and client programs. Changing the configuration requires recompiling and reinstalling, which is neither easy nor convenient, so for most aspects of server and client operation, it's more appropriate to edit configuration files after installation. Nevertheless, there are some good reasons to use compile-time configuration:

- Some configuration options can only be set at compile time.

- Features that are disabled at compile time can't be accidentally enabled by erroneous configuration files. Inflexibility can be an asset.

---

* The `configure` script is generated by a Free Software Foundation package called autoconf. You don't need to know this to compile SSH, but if you're interested in learning more about autoconf, visit the GNU web site at *http://www.gnu.org/software/autoconf/*.

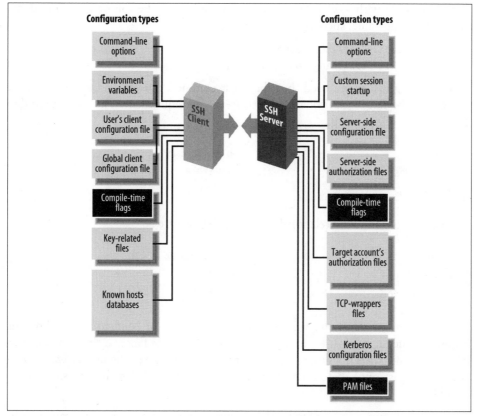

Figure 4-1. SSH compile-time configuration (highlighted parts)

- Removing code for unused features improves security—you can't be burned by security holes in code that you don't compile!

- Similarly, code removal sometimes yields a performance advantage, since less memory and disk space is used.

The `configure` script accepts command-line flags, each beginning with a double dash (--), to control its actions. Flags are of two types:

With/without flags

Include a package during compilation. These flags begin with `--with` or `--without`. For example, support for the X Window System can be included using the flag `--with-x` and omitted using `--without-x`.

Enable/disable flags

Set the default behavior of SSH. These flags begin with `--enable` or `--disable`. For example, the X forwarding feature in Tectia is enabled by the flag `--enable-X11-forwarding` or disabled with `--disable-X11-forwarding`. Some of these defaults can be overridden later by serverwide or per-account configuration.

Flags beginning with --with or --enable may optionally be followed by an equals sign and a string value, such as:

```
--with-etcdir=/usr/local/etc
--enable-X11-forwarding=no
```

Various string values are used, but the most common are yes and no. For a given package *P*, the flags --with-*P* and --with-*P*=yes are equivalent. The following table illustrates the relationship:

If you write:	It's equivalent to:
--with-*P*=yes	--with-*P*
--with-*P*=no	--without-*P*

This next table shows the relationships for a given feature *F*:

If you write:	It's equivalent to:
--enable-*F*=yes	--enable-*F*
--enable-*F*=no	--disable-*F*

In the sections that follow, we show many examples of *configure* with different command-line flags. Most examples demonstrate only one flag at a time, but keep in mind that other flags might be present on the command line. The proper way to run *configure* is just once, before compilation, with all desired flags on the same command line.

The *configure* script uses directory information from its own location to embed pathnames into the *Makefiles*, header files, etc., that it creates. Relying on the PATH environment variable to find the *configure* script is therefore a bad practice. If you choose to compile within the source directory, specify the current directory explicitly when you run *configure*:

```
$ ./configure ...options...
```

Alternately, you can compile in a different directory, which is convenient if the source directory is used for multiple platforms. To do this, create a separate, empty build directory, and run *configure* there, specifying the source directory for the *configure* pathname:

```
$ mkdir -p /elsewhere/build/ssh
$ cd /elsewhere/build/ssh
$ /somewhere/src/ssh/configure ...
```

In our examples, we'll omit the directory components from the *configure* pathname, but remember that they should be included when you run the script.

Specifying Options for the configure Script

Be careful when specifying *configure* options, or you might waste a lot of time. The *configure* script is not very smart, performing little or no sanity checking on its input. For example, if you provide an invalid value, *configure* can naively run for several minutes, handling 100 other configuration options, before finally reaching the bad value and dying. Now you have to run the script all over again.

Unrecognized command-line options are silently ignored, which makes typos especially dangerous. Be sure to check the messages produced by *configure* as it runs, and especially the configuration summary printed at the end to verify that your options were understood as you intended.

Don't depend on default values, since they might differ among SSH implementations. For maximum security and control, explicitly specify all the options you care about when running *configure*.

The `--no-create` option causes the *configure* script to perform all of its checks, but not to create any output files in the build directory. This can be useful if you need to debug an unexpected interpretation of the other options.

4.1.6   Compile Everything

This is simple—just type:

```
$ make
```

Compiling can take a while, depending on the speed of your system.

The *make* command should be run in the same directory where the *configure* script ran.

 If *make* fails when you attempt to use a separate build directory (i.e., different from the source directory), then you might need to upgrade your version of the *make* program. A good choice is GNU *make*, available from *http://www.gnu.org/software/make/*.

4.1.7   Install the Programs and Configuration Files

You need root privileges to install files in system directories, which is the usual location:

```
$ su
Password: ********
# make install
```

4.2   Installing OpenSSH

OpenSSH is a free implementation of the SSH-1 and SSH-2 protocols, obtained from the OpenSSH web site:

> *http://www.openssh.com/*

OpenSSH is a very complete implementation and includes:

- Client programs for remote logins, remote command execution, and secure file copying across a network, all with many runtime options
- A highly configurable SSH server
- Command-line interfaces for all programs, facilitating scripting with standard Unix tools (shells, Perl, etc.)
- Numerous, selectable encryption algorithms and authentication mechanisms
- An SSH agent, which caches keys for ease of use
- Support for SOCKS proxies
- Support for TCP port forwarding and X11 forwarding
- History and logging features to aid in debugging
- Example configuration files */etc/ssh/ssh_config* and */etc/ssh/sshd_config*

Since it is developed by the OpenBSD Project, the main version of OpenSSH is specifically for the OpenBSD Unix operating system, and is in fact included in the base OpenBSD installation. As a separate but related effort, another team maintains a "portable" version that compiles on a variety of Unix flavors and tracks the main development effort. The supported platforms include Linux, Solaris AIX, IRIX, HP/UX, FreeBSD, NetBSD, and Windows via the Cygwin compatibility library. The portable version carries a "p" suffix. For example, 3.9p1 is the first release of the portable version of OpenSSH 3.9.

4.2.1   Prerequisites

OpenSSH depends on two other software packages: OpenSSL and zlib. OpenSSL is a cryptographic library available at *http://www.openssl.org/*; all the cryptography used in OpenSSH is pulled from OpenSSL. zlib is a library of data-compression routines, available at *http://www.gzip.org/zlib/*. These packages must be on your system before you build OpenSSH.

4.2.2   Downloading and Extracting the Files

Distributions are packaged in gzipped *tar* format and are extracted with the *tar* command in the usual way. [4.1.4] The results are stored in a directory with a name like *openssh-3.9p1*.

4.2.2.1 Verifying with GnuPG

Along with each OpenSSH distribution is a GnuPG (Gnu Privacy Guard) signature. The file *openssh-3.9p1.tar.gz*, for example, is accompanied by *openssh-3.9p1.tar.gz. sig* containing the GnuPG signature. To verify the file is genuine, you need GnuPG installed (*http://www.gnupg.org/*). Then:

1. If you have not done so previously, obtain the GnuPG public key for the distribution, available from various keyservers on the Internet, such as:

   http://www.keyserver.net
   http://pgp.mit.edu

   Add the key to your GnuPG key ring by running:

   ```
   $ gpg --keyserver keyserver --search-keys openssh
   ```

   and following the instructions.

2. Download both the distribution file (e.g., *openssh-3.9p1.tar.gz*) and the signature file (e.g., *openssh-3.9p1.tar.gz.sig*).

3. Verify the signature with the command:

   ```
   $ gpg --verify openssh-3.9p1.tar.gz.sig openssh-3.9p1.tar.gz
   ```

   If no warning messages are produced, the distribution file is genuine.

Always check the GnuPG signatures.

4.2.3   Building and Installing

Building and installing OpenSSH follows the familiar pattern for Unix open source software: *configure*, *make*, and *make install*. [4.1.6] Read the file *INSTALL* in the top-level source directory for full instructions.

4.2.4   Configuration Options

OpenSSH's *configure* script understands a wide range of options to customize its operation. We cover the most significant ones.

4.2.4.1   File locations

`--prefix`   *Determine where to install the software*

The *make install* command installs OpenSSH in the */usr/local* hierarchy by default, placing *ssh* into */usr/local/bin*, *sshd* into */usr/local/sbin*, configuration files into */usr/local/etc*, and so forth. You can specify a different installation hierarchy, such as */usr*, with:

```
$ configure --prefix=/usr
```

Other options offer more fine-grained control over installation directories, such as
--bindir for the executables normally placed in a *bin* directory, --sbindir for the
sbin files, --sysconfdir for the *etc* files, --mandir for manpages, and so on: run *configure* --help for the full list.

--with-default-path=*PATH*	*Default server PATH*
--with-superuser-path=*PATH*	*Superuser's server PATH*

You can set the default command search path for OpenSSH when attempting to run
a subprogram, and an alternative path for the superuser.

--with-ssl-dir=*PATH*	*Set path to OpenSSL installation*

If OpenSSL isn't installed in the usual place, */usr/local/ssl*, use this option to indicate
its location.

--with-xauth=**PATH**	*Set path to xauth program*

In OpenSSH, the default location of the *xauth* program for X authentication is a
compile-time parameter.

--with-pid-dir=*PATH*	*Specify location of ssh.pid file*

The location of the OpenSSH pid file, where it stores the pid of the currently running daemon, can be changed via the --with-pid-dir option. The default is */var/run/sshd.pid*.

4.2.4.2   Random number generation

--with-random=*FILE*	*Read random bits from given file, normally /dev/urandom*
--with-rand-helper	*Use external program to generate randomness*

OpenSSH normally relies on the OpenSSL library to provide a stream of random bits
for its cryptographic needs. The OpenSSL pseudo-random number generator
(PRNG) needs to be "seeded" to start with, and then periodically, with an initial segment of unpredictable bits (as truly random as is available). If the operating system
supplies random bits, OpenSSL uses this to seed itself; for example, many Unix variants provide random bits via a device driver accessible through */dev/random* or */dev/urandom*.

If your platform doesn't provide any randomness source, you need to build
OpenSSH with:

```
configure --with-rand-helper
```

OpenSSH then runs the external program *ssh-rand-helper* to seed the PRNG.

--with-prngd-port=*PORT*	*Read entropy from PRNGD/EGD TCP localhost:PORT*
--with-prngd-socket=*FILE*	*Read entropy from PRNGD/EGD socket FILE (default= /var/run/egd-pool)*

If your system is running the Entropy Gathering Daemon (EGD) package (*http://www.lothar.com/tech/crypto/*), you can use it with the `--with-prngd-port` and `--with-prngd-socket` options.

The *ssh-rand-helper* program uses a configurable set of commands that monitor changing aspects of system operation, mixing their output together to produce its random bits. You can control which commands are used and how, with the file */etc/ssh/ssh_prng_cmds*.

> **--with-egd-pool=**FILE   *Read randomness from EGD pool FILE (default none)*

If you install EGD as described earlier, use the `--with-egd-pool` option to have OpenSSH use EGD as its randomness source.

4.2.4.3 Networking

> **--with-ipaddr-display**   *Use IP address instead of hostname in $DISPLAY*

In X forwarding, use DISPLAY values of the form 192.168.10.1:10.0 instead of *hostname*:10.0. This option works around certain buggy X libraries that do weird things with the hostname version, using some sort of IPC mechanism for talking to the X server rather than TCP.

> **--with-ipv4-default**   *Use IPv4 unless "-6" is given*
> **--with-4in6**   *Check for and convert IPv4 in IPv6 mapped addresses*

OpenSSH supports IPv6, the next-generation TCP/IP protocol suite that is still in the development and very early deployment stages on the Internet (the current version of IP is IPv4). The default configuration of OpenSSH attempts to use IPv6 where possible, and sometimes this results in problems. If you encounter errors mentioning "af=10" or "address family 10," that's IPv6, and you should try the –4 runtime option, or compiling `--with-ipv4-default`.

4.2.4.4 Authentication

> **--with-pam**   *Enable PAM support*
> **--without-pam**   *Disable PAM support*

PAM, the Pluggable Authentication Modules system, is a generic framework for authentication, authorization, and accounting (AAA). The idea is that programs call PAM to perform AAA functions, rather than implementing these functions themselves. This allows the sysadmin to configure individual programs to use various kinds of authentication, apply account restrictions, do logging, etc., via dynamically loaded libraries. PAM-aware services can be configured to do almost anything in the way of AAA, in a consistent manner and without having to change the services themselves. See the manpage for *pam* or visit *http://www.kernel.org/pub/linux/libs/pam/* for more information on PAM.

In order for OpenSSH to use PAM, the support must be compiled in. PAM is very common these days, so most OpenSSH binary packages include support; if your's doesn't, use the --with-pam option. Actually, *configure* detects PAM if you have it, so the option is often not necessary.

In addition, you must set the UsePAM configuration keyword in the SSH server:

```
# sshd_config
UsePAM yes
```

(This is off by default.) Setting UsePAM causes *sshd* to do three separate things:

- Enable the PAM "device" for keyboard-interactive authentication [5.4.6]
- Verify password authentication using PAM
- Execute all system PAM modules configured for *ssh* (usually found in */etc/pam.d/ssh*)

Note that the execution action is a very powerful feature; you can customize *sshd*'s behavior in many ways with PAM modules. Look on your system for the PAM modules available and their documentation, e.g., */lib/security* and */usr/share/doc/libpam-doc*.

Generally, if a program uses PAM, some host configuration is necessary to describe how PAM should behave for that program. The PAM configuration files are usually in the directory */etc/pam.d*, or in the single file */etc/pam.conf*. Most OpenSSH packages automatically add the requisite PAM configuration for *sshd*; otherwise, you'll need to do it, usually by copying the appropriate *sshd.pam* file from the *contrib* directory to */etc/pam.d/sshd*. Samples for various operating systems are included in the *contrib* directory of the OpenSSH source. Note that you don't need to restart *sshd* if you change its PAM configuration; the configuration files are checked on every use of PAM.

--with-md5-passwords	*Enable use of MD5 passwords*
--without-shadow	*Disable shadow password support*

These options control OpenSSH's treatment of the Unix account database (a.k.a. passwd map). They are relevant only if OpenSSH isn't using PAM, since otherwise PAM deals with reading the account information, not the OpenSSH code proper.

Enable --with-md5-passwords if your system uses MD5 instead of the traditional *crypt* function to hash passwords, and you are not using PAM.

"Shadow passwords" refers to the practice of keeping the hashed password in a restricted file, */etc/shadow* (*/etc/passwd* must be world-readable). Use --without-shadow to suppress reading of the */etc/shadow* file, should it be necessary.

--with-kerberos5=*PATH*	*Enable Kerberos-5 support*
--with-skey	*Enable S/Key support*

The `--with-kerberos5` option installs Kerberos support [11.4], and the `--with-skey` option enables support for the S/Key one-time password system for password authentication. [5.4.5]

4.2.4.5   Access control

--with-tcp-wrappers	*Include TCP-wrappers support*
--without-tcp-wrappers	*Remove TCP-wrappers support*

These options include support for TCP-wrappers, providing the path to the wrapper library, *libwrap.a*. If the library and header file for TCP-wrappers are not installed in the standard locations, you can provide a pathname as an argument. The pathname can either be a build directory that contains both the library and header file:

```
$ configure --with-tcp-wrappers=/var/tmp/build/tcp-wrappers
```

or it can be an installation directory with *lib* and *include* subdirectories:

```
$ configure --with-tcp-wrappers=/usr/local/tcp-wrappers
```

If your Unix installation doesn't include the TCP-wrappers library, you can retrieve and compile it yourself from *ftp://ftp.porcupine.org/pub/security/index.html*. For more information on TCP-wrappers, read the manpages for *tcpd* and *hosts_access*.

4.3   Installing Tectia

Tectia is a commercial implementation of the SSH-2 protocol, with some limited support for compatibility with the older (and deprecated) SSH-1 protocol. Binary distributions can be downloaded for evaluation (with a limited license that is valid for 30 days) from the SSH Communications Security web site:

http://www.ssh.com/

Fully licensed Tectia products, with distribution media and documentation, can be purchased from the same web site.

Tectia is designed for deployment across large corporate networks, and offers tremendous flexibility, power, and reliability. The products include:

- Client programs for remote logins, remote command execution, and secure file copying across a network, all with many runtime options
- A highly configurable SSH server
- Command-line interfaces for all programs, facilitating scripting with standard Unix tools (shells, Perl, etc.)
- Numerous, selectable encryption algorithms and authentication mechanisms
- An SSH agent, which caches keys for ease of use

- Support for SOCKS proxies
- Support for TCP port forwarding and X11 forwarding
- History and logging features to aid in debugging
- FIPS 140-2 certification for U.S. government applications

4.3.1 Prerequisites

Tectia is fully self contained, and requires no other packages if installed on one of the supported platforms. Some configuration options require you to install other software packages, however; these are discussed below.

4.3.2 Obtaining and Extracting the Files

Binary distributions are packaged according to the target platform, and can be installed according to the documentation provided for each system.

Source distributions are packaged in gzipped *tar* format. For Version 4.1 and earlier, the sources are included with the distribution media for the Tectia Server for Unix product. Starting with Version 4.2, the sources are available only for commercial licenses and only upon request, via a protected area of the SSH Communications Security web site. No sources are provided for the Windows products.

To extract the files, use the *tar* command in the usual way. [4.1.4] The results are stored in a directory with a name like *ssh-4.2.1.1-commercial*.

4.3.3 Verifying with md5sum

Binary and source distribution files are protected from tampering by MD5 message digests. Each file is accompanied by a separate file with an extra *.md5* suffix containing the digest.

To verify the integrity of the files, use the *md5sum* command to compute the digest, and compare the result to the contents of the corresponding *.md5* file:

```
$ md5sum ssh-4.1.0.34-commercial.tar.gz
0c7be85eb79e80e893d4c258df8443f0  ssh-4.1.0.34-commercial.tar.gz
$ cat ssh-4.1.0.34-commercial.tar.gz.md5
0c7be85eb79e80e893d4c258df8443f0
```

Here's a brash one-liner for verification in a single step:

```
$ md5sum ssh-4.1.0.34-1.i386.rpm | cut -c 1-32 | cmp - ssh-4.1.0.34-1.i386.rpm.md5
```

If the command succeeds silently, the message digests are equal.

Unfortunately, Tectia doesn't sign installers for binary package formats (like RPM) that support embedded signatures. MD5 message digests are provided for these installers, however.

4.3.4   Building and Installing

To build and install Tectia, use the standard steps that we have described previously: *configure*, *make*, and *make install*. [4.1.6] The following files are installed:

- The server program *sshd2*, and a link to it called *sshd*.
- The secure FTP server program *sftp-server2*, and a link to it called *sftp-server*.
- The clients *ssh2*, *scp2*, and *sftp2*, and links to them called *ssh*, *scp*, and *sftp*, respectively.
- Support programs *ssh-add2*, *ssh-agent2*, *ssh-askpass2*, *ssh-keygen2*, *ssh-probe2*, and *ssh-signer2*, and links to them called *ssh-add*, *ssh-agent*, *ssh-askpass*, *ssh-keygen*, *ssh-probe*, and *ssh-signer*, respectively.
- The additional support programs *sshd-check-conf* and *ssh-dummy-shell*.
- The standard crypto library *libsshcrypto-std* and the FIPS-compliant library *libsshcrypto-fips* if supported for the target system. The library filenames will have a platform-dependent suffix, e.g., *libsshcrypto.a* or *libsshcrypto.so*.
- The *ssh-crypto-library-chooser* script used to switch between standard and FIPS mode. [5.3.5]
- The password change plugin *ssh-passwd-plugin* [5.4.2.3] and (if configured) the SecurID plugins *ssh-securidv4-plugin* and *ssh-securidv5-plugin*. [5.4.5.2]
- A newly generated host key pair, created by *ssh-keygen2* and placed by default into */etc/ssh2/hostkey* (private key) and */etc/ssh2/hostkey.pub* (public key).
- The server configuration file, */etc/ssh2/sshd2_config* by default [5.2.1], plus sample subconfiguration files in */etc/ssh2/subconfig*.
- The client configuration file, */etc/ssh2/ssh2_config* by default. [7.1.2]
- The password plugin configuration file, */etc/ssh2/plugin/passwd_config*. [5.4.2.3]
- Manpages for the various programs.

4.3.5   Configuration Options

Tectia's *configure* script understands a wide variety of options to customize its operation. We cover the most significant ones.

4.3.5.1   File locations and permission

    `--prefix`   *Determine where to install the software*

The *make install* command installs Tectia in the */usr/local* directory by default. Programs that are normally run by users (e.g., *ssh*) are installed in the *bin* subdirectory, programs run by sysadmins (e.g., *sshd*) in the *sbin* subdirectory, manpages in the *man* subdirectory, etc. Use the `--prefix` option to specify a different parent directory, such as */usr/local/tectia*:

```
$ configure --prefix=/usr/local/tectia
```

If your system uses an unusual layout for specific subdirectories, options such as `--bindir`, `--sbindir`, and `--mandir` allow more precise control over the location of individual components. The *configure --help* command lists all of the options for the subdirectories.

`--with-foreign-etcdir`	*Specify directory for system configuration files*
`--with-etcdir`	*Specify directory for Tectia configuration files*

By default, Tectia assumes that the standard location for system configuration files is the */etc* directory, and installs its own configuration files in a subdirectory, */etc/ssh2*. To change the system configuration directory (continuing to use an *ssh2* subdirectory for Tectia's files by default), use the `--with-foreign-etcdir` option:

```
$ configure --with-foreign-etcdir=/usr/local/etc
```

To independently change Tectia's configuration directory, use the `--with-etcdir` option:

```
$ configure --with-etcdir=/usr/local/etc/ssh2
```

`--with-piddir`	*Specify directory for pid files*

The Tectia server stores its process ID (pid) in a file to facilitate sending signals. [5.3.1.3] By default, the pid file is created in the */var/run* directory. Use the `--with-piddir` option to change this directory:

```
$ configure --with-piddir=/var/local/pid
```

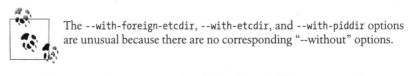 The `--with-foreign-etcdir`, `--with-etcdir`, and `--with-piddir` options are unusual because there are no corresponding "`--without`" options.

`--enable-suid-ssh-signer`	*Install ssh-signer setuid root*
`--disable-suid-ssh-signer`	*Install ssh-signer unprivileged*

Tectia uses a separate *ssh-signer* program to sign authentication packets for trusted-host authentication. Normally this program is installed with setuid root permissions so it can read the local host key file, which is readable only by the superuser.

You can install the program without setuid root permissions to eliminate possible security holes, but then hostbased authentication fails. [3.4.3.6]

4.3.5.2 Random number generation

`--with-ansi-rng`	*Use ANSI X9.62 random number generator*
`--without-ansi-rng`	*Use SSH random number generator*

Tectia uses its own random number generator by default. The `--with-ansi-rng` option configures Tectia to use the ANSI X9.62 random number generator (a.k.a. the Elliptic Curve Digital Signature Algorithm, or ECDSA) instead. This might be required for FIPS-standard compliance in some deployments.

4.3.5.3 Networking

`--with-ipv6`	*Include IPv6 support*
`--without-ipv6`	*Remove IPv6 support*

Tectia supports IPv6, the next generation of IP protocols, in addition to IPv4, the current standard. You can remove IPv6 support if you don't need it or if you experience problems with it on your operating system.

`--enable-tcp-nodelay`	*Enable Nagle Algorithm*
`--disable-tcp-nodelay`	*Disable Nagle Algorithm*

If you plan to operate Tectia over a wide-area network as opposed to a speedy Ethernet connection, you might consider disabling TCP/IP's NODELAY feature, a.k.a. the Nagle Algorithm, for SSH connections. The Nagle Algorithm reduces the number of TCP segments sent with very small amounts of data, such as the small byte sequences of a terminal session. You can disable it at compile time with the `--disable-tcp-nodelay` flag. Alternatively, you can enable or disable it during serverwide configuration using the `NoDelay` configuration keyword. [5.3.3.9]

`--with-libwrap`	*Include TCP-wrappers support*
`--without-libwrap`	*Remove TCP-wrappers support*

TCP-wrappers is a security feature for applying access control to incoming TCP connections based on their source address. [9.5] For example, TCP-wrappers can verify the identity of a connecting host by performing DNS lookups, or it can reject connections from given addresses, address ranges, or DNS domains. Although Tectia already includes some of this kind of control with features such as `AllowHosts`, `DenyHosts`, etc., TCP-wrappers is more complete. It allows some controls not currently implemented in any SSH version, such as restricting the source of forwarded X connections.

Tectia includes support for TCP-wrappers if the flag `--with-libwrap` is given at compile time. If the TCP-wrappers library and header file were not installed in the standard locations, provide a pathname as an argument. The pathname can refer to the library in a build directory:

```
$ configure --with-libwrap=/var/tmp/build/tcp-wrappers/libwrap.a
```

in which case the *tcpd.h* header file is assumed to be located in the same directory. Alternately, the pathname can refer to the directory where the library was installed:

```
$ configure --with-libwrap=/usr/local/lib
```

in which case the *tcpd.h* header file is assumed to be in a directory with its last component replaced by "include" (for the previous command, */usr/local/include*).

If your Unix installation doesn't include the TCP-wrappers library, you can retrieve and compile it yourself from:

ftp://ftp.porcupine.org/pub/security/index.html

For more information on TCP-wrappers, read the manpages for *tcpd* and *hosts_ access*.

`--with-ssh-connection-limit`	*Specify maximum number of simultaneous connections*

You can instruct Tectia to limit the maximum number of simultaneous connections it supports. By default, it accepts an unlimited number of connections, but if you want to conserve resources on the server machine, you can set a limit. The appropriate flag is --with-ssh-connection-limit with a nonnegative integer argument; for example:

```
$ configure --with-ssh-connection-limit=50
```

You can override this value at runtime with the serverwide configuration keyword MaxConnections. [5.3.3.7]

4.3.5.4   X Window System

`--with-x`	*Include X Window System support*
`--without-x`	*Remove X Window System support*

If you plan to use SSH to communicate between hosts running the X Window System, make sure to include support for X at compile time. (By default, it is included.) Conversely, if you never have anything to do with X, you can leave out the support, thereby saving some memory and disk space. Few people have a strong need to eliminate X support.

`--enable-X11-forwarding`	*Enable X forwarding*
`--disable-X11-forwarding`	*Disable X forwarding*

These options enable or disable support for X forwarding, which allows X applications opened on the SSH server machine to appear on the SSH client machine's display. [9.4] These flags set Tectia's default behavior only. X forwarding can be further enabled or disabled through serverwide configuration using the ForwardX11 configuration keyword. [9.4.3]

`--with-x11-security`	*Use the X SECURITY extension*
`--without-x11-security`	*Don't use the X SECURITY extension*

By default, Tectia uses the X SECURITY extension (if supported by your X installation) to control the level of display access granted to X clients through forwarded connections. The `--without-x11-security` option causes Tectia to treat all X clients as trusted, which grants full access to the display. Trusted X clients can use their display access to capture information from other clients, so you should carefully consider the ramifications of disabling the X SECURITY extension.

4.3.5.5   TCP port forwarding

`--enable-tcp-port-forwarding`	*Enable port-forwarding support*
`--disable-tcp-port-forwarding`	*Disable port-forwarding support*

Port forwarding enables Tectia to encrypt the data passing through any TCP/IP-based program. [9.2] This feature can be disabled at compile time if desired. X Window forwarding isn't affected by these general port-forwarding flags.

4.3.5.6   Encryption

`--with-rsa`	*Include support for RSA encryption*
`--without-rsa`	*Remove support for RSA encryption*

By default, Tectia includes an implementation of the RSA encryption algorithm for public-key authentication. [3.8.1.1] You can remove support for RSA if you'll never need it. The option was formerly used to avoid infringing a patent that expired in 2000. Now that the algorithm is in the public domain, it is rarely desirable to remove RSA support.

4.3.5.7   Authentication

`--with-passwd-plugin`	*Include support for password-change plugins*
`--without-passwd-plugin`	*Remove support for password-change plugins*

Tectia can run a separate password-change plug-in program to manage the process of changing expired passwords during authentication. [5.4.2.3] The configuration option `--with-passwd-plugin` includes support for this mechanism in the server, and also builds a generic plugin named `ssh-passwd-plugin`. The option `--without-passwd-plugin` can be used to remove these features if they are not needed.

`--enable-server-kbd-interactive`	*Include support for keyboard-interactive authentication in the server*
`--disable-server-kbd-interactive`	*Remove support for keyboard-interactive authentication from the server*
`--enable-client-kbd-interactive`	*Include support for keyboard-interactive authentication in the client*
`--disable-client-kbd-interactive`	*Remove support for keyboard-interactive authentication from the client*

Keyboard-interactive authentication is an extensible, general-purpose mechanism for implementing a variety of authentication techniques that require interaction with the remote user. Support for keyboard-interactive authentication is included by default, but it can be removed from the Tectia server and client using separate configure options.

Note that other authentication techniques such as SecurID and PAM are based on keyboard-interactive authentication, so if you remove support for it, these techniques will not work.

`--with-serversecurid`   *Include support for SecurID authentication*

SecurID is an authentication mechanism in which users carry electronic cards, approximately the size of a credit card, that display randomly changing integers. During authentication, the user is prompted to type whatever number appears on the card at the time, in addition to a username and password.

To compile Tectia with SecurID support, use the flag --with-serversecurid, providing the path to the directory containing SecurID's header files and libraries:

```
$ configure --with-serversecurid=/usr/local/ace
```

SecurIDv5 is the most recent version at press time.

`--enable-serversecurid-submethod`   *Include SecurID support in the server*
`--disable-serversecurid-submethod`   *Use an external plugin for SecurID support*

By default, SecurID support is built into the Tectia server, and is used as a keyboard-interactive submethod. Alternately, SecurID can be supported by an external program, *ssh-securidv5-plugin*. [5.4.5.2]

`--with-serversecuridv4`   *Include support for SecurIDv4 plugin authentication*

Support for the older SecurIDv4 can be included by specifying the --with-serversecuridv4 option. The SecurIDv4 installation directory must be provided as an argument:

```
$ configure --with-serversecuridv4=/usr/local/ace4
```

`--enable-legacy-securid`   *Include support for old SecurID clients*

Very old SecurID clients can be supported by a legacy securid-1@ssh.com keyboard-interactive submethod.

`--with-daemonpam`   *Include support for PAM authentication in the server*
`--without-daemonpam`   *Remove support for PAM authentication from the server*
`--with-clientpam`   *Include support for PAM authentication in the client*
`--without-clientpam`   *Remove support for PAM authentication from the client*

Normally PAM support is included for both the SSH server and client if it is provided by the target system. This support can be removed using separate options for the server or client, but it is rarely desirable to do so.

> `--with-daemon-pam-service-name`   *Specify PAM service name*

By default, Tectia uses "sshd2" as the PAM service name: this refers to Tectia in the PAM configuration files. You can change the name by providing it as an argument for the `--with-daemon-pam-service-name` option:

```
$ configure --with-daemon-pam-service-name=tectia
```

> `--with-pgp`   *Include support for PGP authentication*
> `--without-pgp`   *Remove support for PGP authentication*

Pretty Good Privacy, or PGP, is a popular encryption and authentication program available for many computing platforms. [1.6.2] Tectia optionally authenticates users based on their PGP keys, so long as those keys comply with the OpenPGP standard (RFC-2440, "OpenPGP Message Format"; some PGP versions, especially older ones, might not be OpenPGP-compliant). PGP support is included by default. [6.5]

> `--with-kerberos5`   *Include support for Kerberos-5 authentication*
> `--without-kerberos5`   *Remove support for Kerberos-5 authentication*

Kerberos is an authentication mechanism that passes around tickets, small sequences of bytes with limited lifetimes, in place of user passwords. [11.5.2.2] The configuration flags `--with-kerberos5` and `--without-kerberos5` control whether Kerberos support is included or excluded during the build. Tectia's Kerberos-5 support is experimental, and is not included by default.

If Kerberos was installed in a nonstandard location, the installation directory can be provided as an argument:

```
$ configure --with-kerberos5=/usr/local/kerberos5
```

> `--with-gssapi`   *Include support for GSSAPI authentication*
> `--without-gssapi`   *Remove support for GSSAPI authentication*

GSS (Generic Security Services) is an emerging standard that facilitates negotiation of security parameters among a wide variety of platforms. [11.5.2.2] Tectia can be compiled to use GSSAPI libraries and header files to support this standard. If the GSSAPI installation is in a nonstandard location, specify the directory (with *lib* and *include* subdirectories) as an argument for the `--with-gssapi` option:

```
$ configure --with-gssapi=/usr/local/gssapi
```

> `--enable-gssapi-dynamic`   *Enable dynamic loading of GSSAPI libraries*
> `--disable-gssapi-dynamic`   *Force static linking of GSSAPI libraries*

By default, GSSAPI libraries are linked statically into the SSH server and client. The libraries can optionally be loaded dynamically at runtime: this allows new security mechanisms to be added by replacing the libraries, without recompiling Tectia.

4.3.5.8 SOCKS proxies

`--with-socks-server` *Specify default SOCKS server*

SOCKS is a network protocol for proxies. A *proxy* is a software component that masquerades as another component to hide or protect it. For example, suppose a company permits its employees to surf the Web but doesn't want the hostnames of its internal machines to be exposed outside the company. A proxy server can be inserted between the internal network and the Internet so that all web requests appear to be coming from the proxy. In addition, a proxy can prevent unwanted transmissions from entering the internal network, acting as a firewall.

Tectia supports both Versions 4 and 5 of the SOCKS protocol,* and no external library or special configuration options are needed. The SOCKS feature is controlled by the SocksServer client configuration keyword. [7.4.7] In addition to the usual methods of setting this in a configuration file or on the command line with -o, you can also set it using the SSH_SOCKS_SERVER environment variable.

SocksServer has an empty default value, causing Tectia to assume there's no SOCKS server. The configuration flag `--with-socks-server` gives nonempty default value to this parameter, allowing you to set up a Tectia installation that assumes the presence of a SOCKS server. Note that this isn't the same as using the SocksServer keyword in the global client configuration file, because the keyword overrides the environment variable. If you use the compilation option, users can specify an alternate SOCKS server with SSH_SOCKS_SERVER; if you use the global file, they can't (although they can still override using their own SocksServer directive).

See *http://www.socks.permeo.com/* for more information on SOCKS. [7.4.7]

4.3.5.9 Debugging

`--enable-debug` *Enable light debugging*
`--disable-debug` *Disable light debugging*
`--enable-debug-heavy` *Enable heavy debugging*
`--disable-debug-heavy` *Disable heavy debugging*

Tectia programs (both the server and client) produce detailed debugging output on demand. [5.9] If desired, Tectia can be compiled with or without two levels of debugging output. Without the debugging code, the programs might experience a

---

* Except for SOCKS5 authentication methods.

slight increase in performance, but with it, the programs are easier to maintain. We recommend including at least some debugging code, because you never know when you'll need to diagnose a problem.

"Light" and "heavy" debugging are two levels of debugging that you can specify in the source code. Light debugging output is controlled by the *configure* flags --enable-debug and --disable-debug (the default). Heavy debugging output is controlled by the *configure* flags --enable-debug-heavy and --disable-debug-heavy (the default). Heavy debugging automatically enables light debugging. We recommend turning on heavy debugging or else the messages will contain too little information to be useful.

--enable-efence	*Use the Electric Fence memory allocation debugger*

Tectia's memory allocations can be tracked by Electric Fence, a freely distributable memory allocation debugger created by Bruce Perens. You must have Electric Fence installed on the server machine in order for this to work.

The --enable-efenceflag causes Tectia's programs to be linked with the Electric Fence library, *libefence.a*, which provides instrumented versions of malloc(), free( ), and other memory-related functions. Electric Fence is available from *http://www.perens.com/FreeSoftware/*.

--with-purify	*Use Rational Purify to track memory accesses*

Rational Purify is a commercial product that supports tracking of memory accesses at runtime. It is able to detect memory leaks and corruption due to buffer overruns, etc.

The --with-purify flag includes support for Rational Purify. When the Tectia programs run, they produce a report about memory activity that can be analyzed after each program exits.

Rational Purify is available from *http://www.ibm.com/software/awdtools/purify/*.

4.3.5.10 SSH-1 protocol compatibility

--with-internal-ssh1-compat	*Include SSH-1 protocol support in the client*
--without-internal-ssh1-compat	*Remove SSH-1 protocol support from the client*

The Tectia SSH client can support the older (and deprecated) SSH-1 protocol by running a separate client program named *ssh1*, which must be installed separately. [5.10] By default, the Tectia SSH client also supports SSH-1 directly using its own implementation. If you don't use the SSH-1 protocol, use the --without-internal-ssh1-compat option to remove the internal SSH-1 support and save some space in the client.

--with-ssh-agent1-compat	*Include SSH-1 protocol support in the agent*
--without-ssh-agent1-compat	*Remove SSH-1 protocol support from the agent*

SSH agents [2.5] that use the protocols SSH-1 and SSH-2 are normally not compatible. That is, each version of the agent can't store keys or forward connections from the other. However, the Tectia agent has an optional feature to serve SSH-1 protocol applications, if it is run with the option -1 (that's a one, not a lowercase L).

SSH-1 protocol support is included in the Tectia agent by default, but you can use the --without-ssh-agent1-compat option to remove it if you never plan to use SSH-1 clients.

RSA support must be included (either by default, or using the --with-rsa configure option) for the agent to support the SSH-1 protocol.

4.3.6   SSH-1 Compatibility Support for Tectia

The Tectia server only supports the SSH-2 protocol, but it can be configured to run a separate SSH-1 server to support clients that are still using the older protocol. [5.10] The Tectia client can similarly run a separate SSH-1 client program, or it can use its own internal SSH-1 implementation.

If separate SSH-1 programs are used, they must be obtained and installed. OpenSSH is a good choice for SSH-1 client support, but for SSH-1 server support, only versions earlier than 3.7 can be used.

An alternative is the latest SSH1 implementation, which is quite old and (even worse) is no longer being actively maintained, but at least is designed to be integrated seamlessly with Tectia.

To install SSH1, download the tar file and associated signature file from *ftp://ftp.ssh. com/pub/ssh/*. At press time, these were *ssh-1.2.33.tar.gz* and *ssh-1.2.33.tar.gz.sig*, respectively.

To verify the signature, you also need to download the key, in the file *SSH1-DISTRIBUTION-KEY-RSA.asc*. Import the key into your key ring:

```
$ gpg --import SSH1-DISTRIBUTION-KEY-RSA.asc
```

Then check the integrity of the tar file:

```
$ gpg --verify ssh-1.2.33.tar.gz.sig
```

Extract the files from the tar file in the usual way to create a source directory named *ssh-1.2.33*. [4.1.4]

Run the *configure* script. We won't go over its options because they are obsolete for the most part, and because fancy features are presumably not needed (or even desirable) if SSH1 is only going to be employed as part of a transition strategy until older SSH-1 clients can be upgraded to use SSH-2. You can, however, remove unneeded features to prevent them from being exploited if any security holes are lurking in the code (which becomes increasingly likely as the software continues to age). As usual, see the output from *configure --help* for details.

You can install SSH1 in the same directory as Tectia using the same *configure* `--prefix` option for each. [4.1.5] Finally, compile everything with *make*, and install (typically as root) with *make install*. [4.1.6] The following files are installed:

- The server program, *sshd1*, and a link to it called *sshd*
- The clients *ssh1* and *scp1*, and respective links called *ssh* and *scp*
- The symbolic link *slogin1*, pointing to *ssh1*, and likewise a link called *slogin* pointing to *slogin1*
- Support programs *ssh-add1*, *ssh-agent1*, *ssh-askpass1*, and *ssh-keygen1*, and links to them called *ssh-add*, *ssh-agent*, *ssh-askpass*, and *ssh-keygen*, respectively
- The support program *make-ssh-known-hosts*
- A newly generated host key pair, created by *ssh-keygen1* and placed by default into */etc/ssh/ssh_host_key* (private key) and */etc/ssh/ssh_host_key.pub* (public key)
- The server configuration file, */etc/ssh/sshd_config* by default [5.2.1]
- The client configuration file, */etc/ssh/ssh_config* by default [7.1.2]
- Manpages for the various programs

Notice that SSH1 and Tectia create some files with the same names, such as the link *sshd*. What happens if you install both SSH1 and Tectia on the same machine? Happily, everything works out, even if you install the two products into the same *bin* and *etc* directories, provided you install the most recent versions. Each of their *Makefiles* is constructed to check for the existence of the other version and respond appropriately.*

Specifically, both SSH1 and Tectia create symbolic links called *sshd*, *ssh*, *scp*, *ssh-add*, *ssh-agent*, *ssh-askpass*, and *ssh-keygen*. If you install SSH1 and then Tectia, the Tectia *Makefile* renames these files by appending the suffix *.old* and then creates new symbolic links pointing to its own Tectia programs. For instance, *ssh* originally points to *ssh1*; after installing Tectia, *ssh* points to *ssh2*, and *ssh.old* points to *ssh1*. This is appropriate since Tectia is considered a later version than SSH1.

On the other hand, if you install Tectia and then SSH1, the SSH1 *Makefile* leaves Tectia's links untouched. As a result, *ssh* remains pointing to *ssh2*, and no link points to *ssh1*. This is consistent with the practice of installing SSH1 to allow Tectia to provide fallback SSH1 support.

You need to set up the SSH1 configuration files in addition to the Tectia configuration files, and then keep them synchronized. [5.10.1]

---

* Installers for Tectia binary distributions behave the same way when integrating with SSH1 installations.

4.4   Software Inventory

Table 4-1 provides a reference to the many files and programs installed with SSH.

Table 4-1. Software inventory

Component	OpenSSH	Tectia
Server config	/etc/ssh/sshd_config	/etc/ssh2/sshd2_config
Global client config	/etc/ssh/ssh_config	/etc/ssh2/ssh2_config
Host private key	/etc/ssh/ssh_host_dsa_key	/etc/ssh2/hostkey
Host public key	/etc/ssh/ssh_host_dsa_key.pub	/etc/ssh2/hostkey.pub
Client host keys	/etc/ssh/ssh_known_hosts ~/.ssh/known_hosts	/etc/ssh2/hostkeys ~/.ssh2/hostkeys/*
Remote host keys	~/.ssh/known_hosts	~/.ssh2/knownhosts/*
libwrap control files	/etc/hosts.allow /etc/hosts.deny	/etc/hosts.allow /etc/hosts.deny
Authorization for login via public key	~/.ssh/authorized_keys	~/.ssh2/authorization
Authorization for login via trusted host	/etc/hosts.equiv /etc/shosts.equiv ~/.shosts ~/.rhosts	/etc/hosts.equiv /etc/shosts.equiv ~/.shosts ~/.rhosts
Default key pair for public-key authentication	SSH-2/RSA: ~/.ssh/id_rsa{.pub} SSH-2/DSA: ~/.ssh/id_dsa{.pub}	(No default)
Random seed	~/.ssh/prng_seed[a]	~/.ssh2/random_seed /etc/ssh2/random_seed
Commands for generating randomness	/etc/ssh/ssh_prng_cmds	–
Terminal client	ssh slogin link to ssh	ssh2[b]
Secure file copy client	scp	scp2[b]
Signer program	ssh-keysign	ssh-signer2[b]
sftp2/scp2 server	sftp-server	sftp-server2[b]
Authentication agent	ssh-agent	ssh-agent2[b]
Key generator	ssh-keygen	ssh-keygen2[b]
Key add/remove	ssh-add	ssh-add2[b]

Table 4-1. Software inventory (continued)

Component	OpenSSH	Tectia
Find SSH servers	*ssh-keyscan*	*ssh-probe2*[b]
Get passphrase via terminal or X	*ssh-askpass*	*ssh-askpass2*[b]
	x11-ssh-askpass	
Server program	*sshd*	*sshd2*[b]

[a] Present only if using OpenSSH's internal entropy-gathering mechanism (i.e., no */dev/random* or equivalent on system).
[b] A symbolic link without the "2" suffix is also installed.

4.5 Replacing r-Commands with SSH

SSH and the r-commands (*rsh*, *rcp*, *rlogin*) can coexist peacefully on the same machine. Since the r-commands are insecure, however, system administrators should replace them by their SSH counterparts (*ssh*, *scp*, *slogin*). This replacement has two parts:

- Installing SSH and removing *rsh*, *rcp*, and *rlogin*; requires some user retraining
- Modifying other programs or scripts that invoke the r-commands

The r-commands are so similar to their analogous SSH commands, you might be tempted to rename the SSH commands as the r-commands (e.g., rename *ssh* as *rsh*, etc.). After all, common commands like these are practically identical in syntax:

```
$ rsh -l jones remote.example.com
$ ssh -l jones remote.example.com

$ rcp myfile remote.example.com:
$ scp myfile remote.example.com:
```

Why not just rename? Well, the two sets of programs are incompatible in some ways. For example, some old versions of *rcp* use a different syntax for specifying remote filenames.

In the following sections, we discuss some common Unix programs that invoke the r-commands and how to adapt them to use SSH instead.

4.5.1 Concurrent Versions System (CVS)

CVS is a *version-control system*. It maintains a history of changes to sets of files, and helps coordinate the work of multiple people on the same files. It can use *rsh* to connect to repositories on remote hosts. For example, when you check in a new version of a file:

```
$ cvs commit myfile
```

if the repository is located on a remote machine, CVS can invoke *rsh* to access the remote repository. For a more secure solution, CVS can run *ssh* instead of *rsh*. Of course, the remote machine must be running an SSH server, and if you use public-key authentication, your remote account must contain your key in the appropriate place.[*]

To make CVS use *ssh*, simply set the environment variable `CVS_RSH` to contain the path to your *ssh* client:

```
# Bourne shell family
# Put in ~/.profile to make permanent.
CVS_RSH=/usr/bin/ssh
export CVS_RSH

# C shell family
# Put in ~/.login to make permanent.
setenv CVS_RSH /usr/bin/ssh
```

This approach has one problem: each time you check in a file, the logger's name is the remote account owner, which might not be your own. The problem is solved by manually setting the remote `LOGNAME` variable using the `environment` option in your remote *authorized_keys* file. [8.2.5.1]

4.5.2 GNU Emacs

The Emacs variable `remote-shell-program` contains the path to any desired program for invoking a remote shell. Simply redefine it to be the full path to your *ssh* executable. Also, the *rlogin* package, *rlogin.el*, defines a variable `rlogin-program` you can redefine to use *slogin*.

4.5.3 Pine

The Pine mail reader uses *rsh* to invoke mail-server software on remote machines. For example, it might invoke the IMAP daemon, *imapd*, on a remote mail server. Another program can be substituted for *rsh* by changing the value of a Pine configuration variable, `rsh-path`. This variable holds the name of the program for opening remote shell connections, normally */usr/bin/rsh*. A new value can be assigned in an individual user's Pine configuration file, *~/.pinerc*, or in the systemwide Pine configuration file, typically */usr/local/lib/pine.conf*. For example:

```
# Set in a Pine configuration file
rsh-path=/usr/local/bin/ssh
```

A second variable, `rsh-command`, constructs the actual command string to be executed for the remote mail server. The value is a pattern in the style of the C function `printf( )`. Most likely, you won't need to change the value because both *rsh* and *ssh* fit the default pattern, which is:

```
"%s %s -l %s exec /etc/r%sd"
```

---

[*] CVS also has a remote-access method involving its own server, called *pserver*. This mechanism can be secured using SSH port forwarding instead; read Chapter 9 for the general technique.

The first three "%s" pattern substitutions refer to the rsh-path value, the remote hostname, and the remote username. (The fourth forms the remote mail daemon name, which doesn't concern us.) So, by default, if your username is *alice* and the remote mail server is *mail.example.com*, rsh-command evaluates to:

```
/usr/bin/rsh mail.example.com -l alice ...
```

By changing the rsh-path, it becomes instead:

```
/usr/local/bin/ssh mail.example.com -l alice ...
```

As we said, you probably don't need to do anything with rsh-command, but just in case, we've included it for reference. We present a detailed case study of integrating Pine and SSH later. [11.3]

4.5.4   rsync, rdist

rsync and *rdist* are software tools for synchronizing sets of files between different directories on the same machine or on two different hosts. Both can call *rsh* to connect to a remote host, and both can easily use SSH instead: simply set the RSYNC_RSH environment variable or use the *–e* command-line option for *rsync*, and use the *–P* option with *rdist*. *rsync* with SSH is a particularly simple and effective method to securely maintain remote mirrors of whole directory trees.

4.6   Summary

OpenSSH and Tectia can be tailored in various ways by compile-time configuration with the *configure* script. We've covered the SSH-specific flags, but remember that other operating-system-specific flags might also apply to your installation, so be sure to read the installation notes supplied with the software.

Once installed, SSH software can replace the insecure r-commands on your Unix system, not only when run directly, but also within other programs that invoke *rsh*, such as Emacs and Pine.

CHAPTER 5
Serverwide Configuration

After installing an SSH server (*sshd*),[*] it's time to make informed decisions about your server's operation. Which authentication techniques should be permitted? How many bits should the server key contain? Should idle connections be dropped after a time limit or left connected indefinitely? These and other questions must be considered carefully. *sshd* has reasonable defaults, but don't accept them blindly. Your server should conform to a carefully planned security policy. Fortunately, *sshd* is highly configurable, so you can make it do all kinds of interesting tricks.

This chapter covers *serverwide configuration*, in which a system administrator controls the global runtime behavior of the SSH server. This includes a large, rich set of features, such as TCP/IP settings, encryption, authentication, access control, and error logging. Some features are controlled by modifying a serverwide configuration file, and others by command-line options passed to the server at invocation.

Serverwide configuration is just one of three levels for controlling the behavior of SSH servers. The other two levels are compile-time configuration (Chapter 4), in which the server is compiled with or without certain functionality; and per-account configuration (Chapter 8), in which the server's behavior is modified by end users for their accounts only. We'll discuss the distinction between the three levels in more detail later. [5.2]

This chapter covers only the OpenSSH and Tectia servers, focusing on the Unix implementations (including Unix variants such as Linux and OpenBSD). We've tried to indicate which features are present or absent in each flavor of *sshd*, but these will certainly change as new versions appear, so read each product's documentation for the latest information.

---

[*] Tectia's server might also be named *sshd2*, with *sshd* being a symbolic link to *sshd2*. See the upcoming sidebar "Tectia's File-Naming Conventions."

5.1 Running the Server

Ordinarily, an SSH server is invoked when the host computer is booted, and it is left running as a daemon. This works fine for most purposes. Alternatively, you can invoke the server manually. This is helpful when you're debugging a server, experimenting with server options, or running a server as a nonsuperuser. Manual invocation requires a bit more work and forethought but might be the only alternative for some situations.

Most commonly, a computer has just one SSH server running on it. It handles multiple connections by spawning child processes, one per connection.* You can run multiple servers if you like: for example, two copies of *sshd* listening on different TCP ports, or even several versions of *sshd* at once.

5.1.1 Running sshd as the Superuser

The SSH server is invoked by simply typing its name:

```
$ sshd
```

The server automatically runs in the background, so no ampersand is required at the end of the line.

To invoke the server when the host computer boots, add appropriate lines to an appropriate startup file on your system, such as */etc/rc.local* on Linux. For example:

```
# Specify the path to sshd.
SSHD=/usr/local/sbin/sshd
# If sshd exists and is executable, run it and echo success to the system console.
if [ -x "$SSHD" ]
then
    $SSHD && echo 'Starting sshd'
fi
```

Both OpenSSH and Tectia come with a startup or boot script (i.e., a System-V-style *init* control script) found in the appropriate directory for each Unix variant. For Linux, for example, the scripts are */etc/init.d/sshd* for OpenSSH and */etc/init.d/sshd2* for Tectia.†

5.1.2 Running sshd as an Ordinary User

Any user can run *sshd* if several steps are completed beforehand:

1. Get permission from your system administrator.
2. Generate a host key.

---

* Or *sshd* can be invoked by *inetd*, creating one *sshd* process per connection. [5.3.3.2]

† OpenSSH also includes */usr/sbin/rcsshd*, a symbolic link to the startup script in */etc/init.d*.

Tectia's File-Naming Conventions

At first glance, Tectia's filenames might seem rather inconsistent, but actually they follow conventions designed for flexibility and ease of use:

- Most filenames contain a "2" suffix, e.g., *sshd2*. These filenames distinguish the SSH-2 protocol implementation provided by Tectia from other implementations (e.g., OpenSSH). As a result, you could install SSH-1 protocol programs (not provided by Tectia) with filenames containing a "1" suffix, even in the same directories used by Tectia, without conflicts.

- Tectia installs symbolic links so that you can omit the "2" suffix when referring to programs, manpages, etc. For example, there's a symbolic link *sshd* pointing to *sshd2*. You can set up search paths so that Tectia is the preferred implementation, hiding other implementations that might be installed in other directories.

- On platforms like Microsoft Windows that don't support symbolic links, the program names all have the "2" suffix.

There are a few exceptions:

- Configuration files that live (at least by default) in fixed locations use *only* filenames with the "2" suffix, e.g., */etc/ssh2* or *~/.ssh2*, with no corresponding symbolic links. This avoids confusing other SSH implementations that refer to similar locations without the "2" suffix (e.g., */etc/ssh* or *~/.ssh*).

- Files unique to Tectia have *only* filenames that omit the "2" suffix. Strictly speaking, the "2" suffix is unnecessary in this case, but the convention is unfortunate, because it sometimes leads to unexpected filename comparisons. For example, the Tectia program for verifying *sshd2* configuration files is called *sshd-check-conf*, even though the default files it checks are named */etc/ssh2/sshd2_config* and *~/.ssh2/sshd2_config*. [5.2.2]

3. Select a port number.

4. Create a server configuration file (optional but strongly recommended).

Before starting, ask your system administrator if you may run an SSH server. While this isn't necessary from a technical standpoint, it is a wise idea. An administrator might not appreciate your creating a new avenue for logins behind his back. Likewise, if the administrator has disabled SSH or certain SSH features, there's probably a good security reason and you shouldn't just work around it!

Next, generate your own host key. Any other existing host key is probably readable only by the superuser. Host keys are generated with the program *ssh-keygen*. [6.2] For now, to create a 1024-bit DSA host key and store it in the file *~/myserver/hostkey*, type the following for OpenSSH:

```
# OpenSSH: Note the -N value is two single quotes, not a double-quote
$ ssh-keygen -N '' -b 1024 -t dsa -f ~/myserver/hostkey
```

This command generates the files *hostkey* and *hostkey.pub* in the directory *~/myserver* (so make sure the directory exists). Here's the analogous command for Tectia:

```
# Tectia
$ ssh-keygen -P -b 1024 -t dsa ~/myserver/hostkey
```

The *–N* (OpenSSH) and *–P* (Tectia) options cause the generated key to be left unencrypted because *sshd* expects to read it without a passphrase.

Third, select a port number on which the SSH server listens for connections. The port number is set with the *–p* command-line option of *sshd* or the Port keyword in the configuration file, as we discuss later. Your server can't listen on port 22, the default, because only the superuser may run processes to listen on that port. Your port number must be greater than or equal to 1024, as lower port numbers are reserved by the operating system for use by privileged programs. [3.4.3.6] The port number also must not conflict with those in use by other programs on the server computer; if it does, you get an error message when you try to start the server:

```
error: bind: Address already in use
```

If you receive this error, try another integer in the free range (above 1024). Avoid numbers mentioned in the computer's services map (usually */etc/services* or the Network Information Service [NIS] "services" map, which you can view with the Unix command *ypcat –k services*). These numbers have been designated by the system administrator for use with particular programs or protocols, so you might cause trouble if you steal one. The command *netstat -a* lists all ports in use; add the *–n* option to see numeric values for the ports instead of service names.

Finally, create your own SSH server configuration file. Otherwise, your server will use built-in defaults or a systemwide configuration file (if one exists) and might not operate as you intend.

Assuming you have generated a host key in *~/myserver/hostkey*, selected the port number 2345, and created a configuration file in *~/myserver/config*, the server is invoked with the command:

```
$ sshd -h ~/myserver/hostkey -p 2345 -f ~/myserver/config
```

A server run by an ordinary user has some disadvantages:

- It runs under the uid of the ordinary user, not root, so it can connect only to that user's account.

- It is invoked manually, rather than automatically when the computer boots. As a result, to run the server, you must connect once without SSH to the computer. And each time the computer is rebooted, the server dies, and you need to redo this step. Conceivably you can set up a *cron* job to keep it running automatically.

- While setting up a server, consider running it in debug mode and reading the diagnostic messages it prints, in case something isn't working right. By default, your server's log messages are written to the system log files, which you don't own and possibly can't access. This is because *sshd* does its logging via the syslog service; ordinary users can't control where the log messages are sent, usually */var/adm/messages*, */var/log/messages*, or someplace else depending on how *syslogd* is set up, and you need appropriate permissions to read these files. Running the server in debug mode gets around this annoyance. Messages will appear on your terminal (as well as in the system logs). [5.9] This way, you can more easily see error messages until you get the server working.

Nevertheless, for many users, the advantages of SSH outweigh these inconveniences. Assuming your system administrator approves, you can secure your logins with *sshd* even if you aren't a superuser.

5.2   Server Configuration: An Overview

As mentioned at the beginning of the chapter, the behavior of the server, *sshd*, may be controlled at three levels:

- *Compile-time configuration* (Chapter 4) is accomplished when *sshd* is built. For example, a server may be compiled with or without support for *rhosts* authentication.

- *Serverwide configuration*, the subject of this chapter, is performed by a system administrator and applies to a running instance of the server. For instance, an administrator may deny SSH access by all hosts in a given domain or make the server listen on a particular port.

   Serverwide configuration may depend on compile-time configuration. For example, a server's hostbased authentication options work only if the server is compiled with hostbased authentication support included. Otherwise, the options have no effect. We identify such dependencies throughout the book. Figure 5-1 highlights the serverwide configuration tasks.

- *Per-account configuration* (Chapter 8) is performed by the end user, specifically, the owner of the account to which an SSH connection has been requested. For example, users may permit or deny access to their own accounts from particular hosts, overriding the serverwide configuration.

Suppose user deborah on the machine *client.unc.edu* invokes an SSH client. The client's behavior is determined by several factors:

- The compile-time options selected when the software was built
- The machinewide client configuration file on *client.unc.edu*
- User deborah's own client configuration file
- The command-line options used by deborah when invoking the client

An SSH server running on *server.unc.edu* accepts deborah's connection to the account charlie. The server's behavior is determined by the compile-time options used when

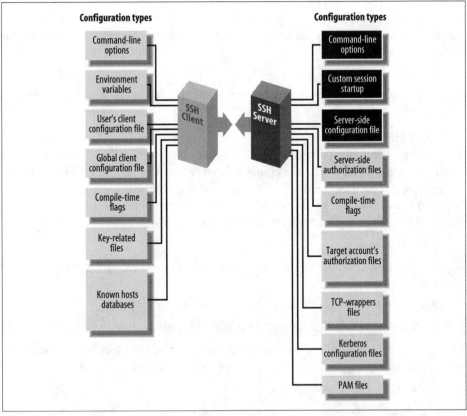

Figure 5-1. Serverwide configuration (highlighted parts)

sshd was built, the machinewide server configuration file on *server.unc.edu*, the command-line options used when the SSH server was run, and charlie's personal server configuration file (e.g., an *authorized_keys* file), plus several files that set environment variables for the successful login session.

With three levels of server configuration, and multiple entry points for modifying the behavior at each level, things can get complicated. In particular, different options may work together or cancel each other. For example, user charlie can configure his account on *server.unc.edu* to accept connections from *client.unc.edu*, while the system administrator of *server.unc.edu* can configure the SSH server to reject them. (In this case, Charlie loses.) Administrators must understand not only how to configure the server themselves, but also how their choices interact with compile-time and per-account settings.

5.2.1   Server Configuration Files

Serverwide configuration is accomplished in two ways: through a server configuration file, or through command-line options. In a *server configuration file*, numerous configuration variables, called *keywords*, may have their values set. For example, to set the TCP port on which the server will listen, a configuration file can contain the line:

```
Port 1022
```

You may also separate the keyword and value by an equals sign (with optional whitespace):

```
Port = 1022
```

The configuration file is typically */etc/ssh/sshd_config* for OpenSSH or */etc/ssh2/ sshd2_config* for Tectia.* The file contains keywords and their values, as in the Port example, with one pair (keyword and value) per line. Keywords are case-insensitive: Port, port, and PoRt are all treated identically. Comments may appear in the file as well: any line beginning with a hash sign (#) is a comment:

```
# This is a comment
```

Comments cannot be appended to keyword lines. For example, the following does not work:

```
Port 1022   #  This comment is not allowed here, so don't do this
```

Empty lines (or lines containing only whitespace) are also ignored as comments.

To use a configuration file other than the default, invoke *sshd* with the –*f* command-line option, providing the alternative filename as an argument:

```
$ sshd -f /usr/local/ssh/my_config
```

Tectia supports some extensions to configuration files that we cover in a detailed case study: [11.6]

Metaconfiguration information

Structured comments at the top of the server configuration file that define syntax rules for the rest of the file. For example, the REGEX-SYNTAX metaconfiguration statement selects one of several different regular expression standards: grep style (egrep), filename globbing (zsh_fileglob), and others.

Subconfiguration files

Alternative configuration files specific to particular local accounts or remote hosts. The keywords UserSpecificConfig and HostSpecificConfig define the associations between subconfiguration files and the affected accounts and hosts, respectively. For example, the line:

```
# Tectia
UserSpecificConfig smith /usr/local/ssh/smith.config
```

states that all connection attempts to the smith account must adhere to the configuration in file */usr/local/ssh/smith.config*.

---

* On Windows, Tectia's configuration files are located in the SSH Tectia Server installation folder.

Quoted values

Tectia has unusual rules for quoted strings, namely, that quotes are largely ignored. The following *sshd2_config* lines are equivalent:

```
# Tectia
Port 1022
Port "1022"
Port "10"22
```

5.2.2   Checking Configuration Files

After you've changed a server configuration file (or constructed an initial version of the file), how do you know it's going to work and have the effects you intend? Later, when you upgrade the server to a more recent version, how can you detect incompatible changes in the meaning of keywords that you've been using?

The most thorough way to verify the server configuration, of course, is to run the server exactly as you plan to deploy it, and test all of the functionality that you expect to use. This kind of testing can be time-consuming, however, and you might not be able to afford interrupting service on a busy production machine.

Alternately, you could use some other test machine, or run the server on a different port [5.3.3.1] while the old configuration is still being used on the original machine. These approaches are almost as good, but they can be complicated if the server configuration refers to network characteristics of the machine where it will be deployed, or by firewalls that block access to nonstandard ports.

Both OpenSSH and Tectia have test features to help with these situations, or to just provide a quick check of the server configuration before more rigorous testing.

5.2.2.1   Checking OpenSSH configuration files

If the OpenSSH server is started with the –*t* (test) option, it starts up, checks the validity of its host keys and the server configuration file, and then immediately exits without performing any other actions. When no problems are found, the server silently returns a zero exit status to indicate successful operation. Otherwise, error messages are printed to the standard error and the server exits with a nonzero status:

```
# OpenSSH
$ sshd -t
/etc/ssh/sshd_config: line 33: Bad configuration option: BlurflPox
/etc/ssh/sshd_config: Bad yes/no argument: maybe
```

The server must be run by a user (typically root) who has read access to the host key files and the server configuration file. Any other server options can be used in conjunction with –*t*, such as –*h* options [5.3.1.1] to specify new host key files, the –*f* option [5.2.1] to specify a new configuration file, or –*d* options [5.9] for more detailed debugging output (even if no errors are detected).

5.2.2.2   Checking Tectia configuration files

Tectia provides a separate program, *sshd-check-conf*, to check server configuration files.* Supply a hypothetical user and remote host, and *sshd-check-conf* will describe its access control decisions for them:

```
# Tectia
$ sshd-check-conf rebecca@client.friendly.org
Verifying rebecca@client.friendly.org[10.1.2.3]...
   Logins from client.friendly.org[10.1.2.3] allowed.
   Hostbased can be used from client.friendly.org[10.1.2.3].
   Login by user rebecca allowed.
   User rebecca will not be chrooted.
   TCP forwarding by user rebecca allowed.
```

sshd-check-conf is especially helpful for verifying policies described by complicated patterns and subconfiguration files. [11.6.2] It uses the same code as *sshd* to parse the server configuration files and understands metaconfiguration information. [11.6.1]

If any errors are detected, *sshd-check-conf* prints messages to the standard error, as *sshd* would:

```
# Tectia
$ sshd-check-conf rebecca@client.friendly.org
Warning: Unrecognized configuration parameter 'BlurflPox'.
Warning: Illegal IdleTimeout value 'never'.
Warning: Failed to parse some variables from config file '/etc/ssh2/sshd2_config'.
FATAL: Failed to read config file "/etc/ssh2/sshd2_config"
```

It is not necessary to run *sshd-check-config* as root, as long as the server configuration files can be read. By default, */etc/ssh2/sshd2_config* is used if the program is run by the superuser, or *$HOME/.ssh2/sshd2_config* otherwise. As for *sshd*, the *–f* option specifies a different configuration file:

```
# Tectia
$ sshd-check-conf -f /tmp/sshd2_config_new rebecca@client.friendly.org
```

The hypothetical SSH sessions are described by one or more [*user@*]*host* arguments on the command line. A numerical user ID can be used in place of a username, or the username can be omitted entirely to check only the remote host. In this case, *sshd-check-conf* substitutes UNKNOWN for the username when it analyzes the access controls:

```
# Tectia
$ sshd-check-conf client.friendly.org
Verifying UNKNOWN@client.friendly.org[10.1.2.3]...
   Logins from client.friendly.org[10.1.2.3] allowed.
   Hostbased can be used from client.friendly.org[10.1.2.3].
   Login by user UNKNOWN denied.
```

An IP address can be used instead of a hostname: both the hostname and IP address are checked.

---

* *sshd-check-conf* doesn't read or verify host keys.

If a hostname resolves to multiple IP addresses, then only the first IP address is used, and a warning is printed by *sshd-check-conf*.

Here's a brash one-liner to check the access controls for all local users:

```
# Tectia
$ sed -e "s/:.*/@`hostname`/" /etc/passwd | xargs sshd-check-conf
```

You can also run *sshd-check-conf* interactively: just don't supply any *[user@]host* arguments on the command line. The program prompts for *[user@]host* strings, permits Emacs-style editing of the strings as you enter them (using the GNU readline library), and maintains a history of previously entered values.

In addition, *sshd-check-conf* recognizes a *dump* command to print keywords and values for the server configuration:

```
# Tectia
$ sshd-check-conf
...
ssh-check-conf> dump
# General
Port = 22
ProtocolVersionString = 4.1.3.2 SSH Secure Shell
MaxConnections = 0
...
# Authentication and authorization
AllowedAuthentications = publickey,password
IgnoreRhosts = no
...
# Forwardings
ForwardX11 = yes
ForwardAgent = yes
...
# Miscellaneous user setup
UserConfigDirectory = %D/.ssh2
PrintMOTD = yes
...
sshd-check-conf> quit
$
```

Tectia's *sshd-check-conf dump* command prints most configuration keywords and values, but not all of them.

To exit from interactive mode, use the quit command, or type the end-of-file character (usually ^D), or just kill the program (typically with ^C). The quit and dump commands are case-insensitive.

Because *sshd-check-conf* matches patterns for subconfiguration files [11.6.2], it reads the main configuration file only when a *[user@]host* string has been given. Therefore, the dump command can't be used before then:

```
# Tectia
$ sshd-check-conf
sshd-check-conf> dump
No config data to dump; input <user@host> first.
```

The *sshd-check-conf* program accepts the debug options *–d* and *–v* [5.9] to print more detailed debugging information as it reads the configuration files and analyzes access control decisions.

5.2.3 Command-Line Options

Additionally, when invoking the server, you may supply command-line options. For example, the port value may be specified on the command line with the *–p* option:

```
$ sshd -p 1022
```

Command-line options override settings in the configuration file. Thus, if the configuration file says port 1022 but the server is invoked with -p 2468, the port used will be 2468.

Most command-line options duplicate the features found in the configuration file, for convenience, while a few provide unique functionality. For instance, the *–f* option instructs *sshd* to use a different configuration file, a feature that's useless to put in a configuration file.

On the other hand, most keywords don't have command-line equivalents. However, the *–o* option lets you specify any keyword and its value on the command line; for example, to set the TCP port number by this method:

```
$ sshd -o "Port 1022"
```

The argument for the *–o* option should be a keyword and value, exactly as specified in the configuration file.* An equals sign (with optional whitespace) can also be used:

```
$ sshd -o "Port = 1022"
```

You can omit the quotes if you avoid characters special to the shell (including the whitespace around the equals sign):

```
$ sshd -o Port=1022
```

You can repeat the *-o* option to set values for multiple keywords on the same command line.

---

* Except for comments, which will not work, e.g., *sshd -o "# Your message here"*. But this would be silly.

Tectia servers always use the default *egrep* syntax for regular expressions on the command line. Unlike configuration files, command-line options have no way to change this via metaconfiguration, e.g., for *-o* options.

Command-line options can be repeated, but the effects of such repetition vary and even differ depending on the server implementation. In almost all cases, only the last repeated option is used, and all earlier instances of the same option are (silently) ignored. For example, an attempt to read two configuration files:

```
$ sshd -f /usr/local/ssh/main.conf -f /usr/local/ssh/alt.conf
Beware! Does not read both files!
```

will actually read only *alt.conf* and ignore *main.conf*.

The "last option wins" rule can be handy for scripting. Suppose you launch the server from a shell script called *launch-sshd*:

```
# launch-sshd:
sshd -f /usr/local/ssh/main.conf "$@"
```

Since the $@ is replaced by options from the command line, you can substitute a different configuration file when using the script:

```
$ launch-sshd -f /usr/local/ssh/alt.conf
```

We have seen that the *–o* option is an exception: it can be repeated to set values for as many keywords as needed. There are only a few other exceptions, all for OpenSSH. The *–p* option can be repeated to listen on multiple ports: [5.3.3.1]

```
# OpenSSH
$ sshd -p 2222 -p 3333
```

The *–h* option can be used multiple times to specify different types of host keys in separate files: [5.3.1.1]

```
# OpenSSH
$ sshd -h /usr/local/ssh/my_dsa_key -h /usr/local/ssh/my_rsa_key -h /usr/local/ssh/
my_old_ssh1_key
```

Repeating the *–d* option increases the level of verbosity for debugging: [5.9]

```
# OpenSSH
$ sshd -d -d -d
```

Tectia is more consistent than OpenSSH: it *always* uses the last instance of each option on the command line.

5.2.4   Changing the Configuration

sshd reads its configuration file at startup. Therefore, if you modify the file while the server is running, the changes don't affect the server. You must force the server to reread the file in order to accept the changes. This is done by sending a SIGHUP signal to the server process. The pid of the server is found in a file, usually */var/run/sshd.pid* for OpenSSH or */var/run/sshd2_22.pid* for Tectia. [5.3.1.3]

Suppose the pid file is */var/run/sshd.pid*, the default for OpenSSH. To send the SIGHUP signal, run the Unix *kill* command:

```
$ cat /etc/sshd.pid
19384
$ kill -HUP 19384
```

or more succinctly, with backquotes:

```
$ kill -HUP `cat /etc/sshd.pid`
```

or on systems with the *pidof* command, which prints pids of given, named processes:

```
$ kill -HUP `pidof sshd`
```

Linux systems (and others) have boot scripts that can signal the SSH server. For example, instead of explicitly sending SIGHUP to *sshd*, you can run:

```
$ /etc/init.d/sshd reload
```

Regardless of how it's sent, the SIGHUP signal restarts *sshd* (with a different pid) but doesn't terminate existing SSH connections, so you can send it safely while clients are connected. The new *sshd* process reads and conforms to the new configuration.

The SIGHUP technique affects settings defined in the configuration file, not command-line options. To change those, you must kill and restart the server with the new options. For example:

```
$ kill 19384
$ sshd new_options
```

Command-line options are often specified in boot scripts that are used to start *sshd*. For example, some Linux systems read an OPTIONS variable assignment from the file */etc/sysconfig/sshd* (if it exists). You may need to edit such options files if you want to permanently change the command-line options used to start the SSH server at boot time. After doing this, you can use the boot script to restart the server with the new command-line options:

```
$ /etc/init.d/sshd restart
```

Boot scripts can perform other useful functions. To determine whether the SSH server is running, use:

```
$ /etc/init.d/sshd status
```

To start or stop the server, use:

```
$ /etc/init.d/sshd start
$ /etc/init.d/sshd stop
```

Some configuration keywords refer to external files. If the contents of those files change, you might wonder if it is necessary to signal the SSH server. In almost all cases, the answer is no: only the filenames are recorded when the configuration file is read, and the external file's contents are reread each time they are needed. The host key file is an important exception, because it is normally read only when the server starts. [5.3.1.1]

5.2.5 A Tricky Reconfiguration Example

Because command-line options override their configuration file equivalents, some interesting situations can arise. Suppose the configuration file sets the TCP port number to be 2222:

```
Port 2222
```

but the server is invoked with the *-p* command-line option, overriding this value with 3333:

```
$ sshd -p 3333
```

The server uses TCP port 3333. Now, suppose you restart *sshd* with SIGHUP:

```
$ kill -HUP `pidof sshd`
```

forcing *sshd* to reread the configuration file. What do you think happens to the port number? Does the server use port 2222 after rereading the configuration file, or does the command-line option remain in effect for port 3333? In fact, the command-line option takes precedence again, so port 3333 is reused. *sshd* saves its argument vector[*] and reapplies it on restart.

5.3 Getting Ready: Initial Setup

We now embark on a detailed discussion of SSH server configuration, using both keywords and command-line options. Please keep in mind that modern SSH products are actively developed and their features may change. Be sure to read their documentation for the latest information.

We begin with initial setup decisions, such as: where should important files be kept? What should their permissions be? What TCP/IP settings should be used? Which encryption algorithms should be supported?

---

[*] argv, to C programmers.

5.3.1   File Locations

sshd expects certain files to exist, containing the server's host key, the random seed, and other data. The server looks for these files in default locations, or you may override them with keywords and command-line options as described later.

Although you may place these files anywhere you like, we strongly recommend keeping them on a local disk on your server machine, not on a remotely mounted disk (e.g., via NFS). This is for security reasons, as NFS will gleefully transmit your sensitive files unencrypted across the network. This would be especially disastrous for the unencrypted private host key!

As a running example, we use an invented directory, */usr/local/ssh*, as our preferred (nondefault) location for the SSH server's files.

5.3.1.1   Host key files

The host key of *sshd* uniquely identifies a server to SSH clients. The host key is stored in a pair of files, one containing the private key and the other the public key. OpenSSH has distinct host keys in DSA (*/etc/ssh/ssh_host_dsa_key*) and RSA (*/etc/ssh/ssh_host_rsa_key*) formats, as well as a legacy SSH-1 protocol key, */etc/ssh/ssh_host_key*. These private keys are readable only by privileged programs such as the SSH server and clients. Their locations may be changed with the HostKey keyword:[*]

```
# OpenSSH
HostKey /usr/local/ssh/my_dsa_key
HostKey /usr/local/ssh/my_rsa_key
HostKey /usr/local/ssh/my_old_ssh1_key
```

Each private key has a corresponding public key, stored in a second file with the same name but with *.pub* appended. So, in the above example, the public keys would be */usr/local/ssh/my_dsa_key.pub*, */usr/local/ssh/my_rsa_key.pub*, and */usr/local/ssh/my_old_ssh1_key.pub*.

For Tectia, the default private key file is */etc/ssh2/hostkey* if the server is run by the superuser or *~/.ssh2/hostkey* if run by any other user. To specify a different private key file, use the HostKeyFile keyword:

```
# Tectia
HostKeyFile /usr/local/ssh/key
```

The server's public key file, normally */etc/ssh2/hostkey.pub* for superusers or *~/.ssh2/hostkey.pub* for others, may be changed independently with the PublicHostKeyFile keyword:

```
# Tectia
PublicHostKeyFile /usr/local/ssh/pubkey
```

---

[*] HostKey has the aliases HostRsaKey and HostDsaKey, but they are deprecated and might be removed in a future version of OpenSSH.

If you prefer command-line options, *sshd* supports the *–h* command-line option to specify the private key file:

```
$ sshd -h /usr/local/ssh/key
```

Once again, the public key filename is derived by appending *.pub* to the private key filename, in this case, */usr/local/ssh/key.pub*.

OpenSSH allows each type of host key to be specified with a separate *–h* option (and detects the type of each key automatically):

```
# OpenSSH
$ sshd -h /usr/local/ssh/my_dsa_key -h /usr/local/ssh/my_rsa_key -h /usr/local/ssh/
my_old_ssh1_key
```

For Tectia, if the –h option is repeated, only the last file is used and all earlier –h options are ignored. This is consistent with its usual behavior with command-line options. [5.2.3]

5.3.1.2 Random seed file

The SSH server generates pseudo-random numbers for cryptographic operations. [3.6.4] It maintains a pool of random data for this purpose, derived either from the operating system if provided (e.g., */dev/random* on Linux) or from various bits of changing machine state (e.g., clock time, statistics on resource use by processes, etc.). This pool is called the *random seed*.

If running on a system with a random-bit source, such as */dev/urandom*, OpenSSH doesn't create a random seed file. Tectia stores a random seed in */etc/ssh2/random_ seed*, and the location may be overridden with the RandomSeedFile keyword:

```
# Tectia
RandomSeedFile /usr/local/ssh/seed2
```

5.3.1.3 Process ID file

The OpenSSH server's pid is stored in */var/run/sshd.pid*, and you can override this location with the PidFile keyword:

```
# OpenSSH
PidFile /usr/local/ssh/pid
```

OpenSSH doesn't record the process ID when it runs in debug mode. [5.9]

There is no corresponding keyword for Tectia. Its pid file is always named */var/run/ sshd2_N.pid*, or if there is no */var/run* directory, */etc/ssh2/sshd2_N.pid*, where *N* is the TCP port number of the server.* Since the default port is 22, the default pid file is *sshd2_22.pid*. If multiple *sshd2* processes are run simultaneously on different ports of

---

* More precisely, *N* is the value for the Port keyword, even if ListenAddress keywords cause the server to use different ports. [5.3.3.1]

the same machine, their pid files can be distinguished by this naming convention. The directory used to store pid files can be changed by the *configure* option --with-piddir. [4.3.5.1]

5.3.1.4 Server configuration file

The server configuration file is normally */etc/ssh/sshd_config* for OpenSSH and */etc/ssh2/sshd2_config* for Tectia. An alternative configuration file can be specified with the *–f* command-line option:

```
$ sshd -f /usr/local/ssh/config
```

This is useful when testing a new server configuration: create a new file and instruct *sshd* to read it. It is also necessary if you are running multiple *sshd*s on the same machine and want them to operate with different configurations.

Only a single configuration file is read. If you provide multiple *–f* options, the last one is used and all others are ignored.

5.3.1.5 User SSH directory

Tectia's *sshd* expects a user's SSH-related files to be in the directory *~/.ssh2* by default, but this can be changed with the UserConfigDirectory keyword. (OpenSSH has no such capability.) The directory name may be literal, as in:

```
# Tectia
UserConfigDirectory /usr/local/ssh/my_dir
```

or it may be specified with printf-like patterns, as in:

```
# Tectia
UserConfigDirectory %D/.my-ssh
```

The %D pattern expands to the user's home directory. So, the preceding example expands to *~/.my-ssh*. The following table shows the available patterns:

Pattern	Meaning
%D	User's home directory
%U	User's login name
%IU	User's uid (Unix user ID)
%IG	User's gid (Unix group ID)

If the % character is followed by any other characters, it is left unchanged.[*]

For the system administrator, the UserConfigDirectory keyword provides a quick way to override all users' Tectia preferences. Specifically, you can cause *sshd* to

---

[*] You need not double the percent sign (%%) to get a literal percent character, i.e., as required for the C function printf.

ignore everybody's ~/.ssh2 directories, substituting your own instead. For instance, the line:

```
# Tectia
UserConfigDirectory /usr/sneaky/ssh/%U
```

tells *sshd* to seek the preferences for each user in */usr/sneaky/ssh/<username>* instead of ~/.ssh2. This powerful feature can also be misused if your machine is compromised. If an intruder inserted the following line into *sshd2_config*:

```
# Tectia
UserConfigDirectory /tmp/hack
```

and uploaded his own public key file into */tmp/hack*, he would gain SSH access to every user's account.

5.3.1.6   Per-account authorization files

The OpenSSH server expects to find a user's public-key authorization file in ~/.ssh/ *authorized_keys*. This location can be changed with the `AuthorizedKeysFile` keyword, followed by the new location:

```
# OpenSSH
AuthorizedKeysFile .ssh/permitted_keys
```

Filenames can be absolute or are relative to the user's home directory. Additionally, the location can contain a few special symbols: `%h` to mean the user's home directory, `%u` for the username, or `%%` for a percent sign. So, when user smith authenticated on a server machine with this line in */etc/ssh/sshd_config*:

```
# OpenSSH
AuthorizedKeysFile /usr/local/access/%u
```

the authorization filename would expand to */usr/local/access/smith*.

The Tectia server uses a different key file layout than OpenSSH. [6.1.2] Its authorization file, normally ~/.ssh2/*authorization*, contains names of separate public key files, rather than the keys themselves. *sshd* can be instructed to find the authorization file elsewhere via the keyword `AuthorizationFile`:

```
# Tectia
AuthorizationFile my_public_keys
```

Filenames can be absolute or are relative to each user's Tectia configuration (.*ssh2*) directory. The preceding example specifies the file ~/.ssh2/*my_public_keys*.

5.3.1.7   utmp file structure

The *utmp* file (e.g., */var/run/utmp*) contains information about users currently logged in, such as their username, tty, and most notably for us, the hostname from which they've logged in (for remote logins). OpenSSH's *sshd* can limit the length of hostname information written to the *utmp* file. (It's inspired by a similar feature in the telnet daemon *telnetd*.)

```
# OpenSSH
$ sshd -u 25          Limit hostnames to 25 characters or less
```

If a remote hostname is longer than this limit, the host's IP address will be written instead. Why is this useful? For two reasons:

- Hostnames longer than the default length—which may vary on different systems—will normally be truncated in the *utmp* file. While you cannot increase the *utmp* length with the *–u* option, you can notify *sshd* of the length limitation so that IP addresses get used in place of long hostnames. This way, you'll accurately record the host's identity. See */usr/include/utmp.h* to learn the length limit for your system.

- If you specify -u0, IP addresses will always be used in place of hostnames. This has the side effect of forcing *sshd* not to make DNS requests for these hostname lookups. (It will not entirely suppress DNS, however, since it might be needed for authentication.)

5.3.2   File Permissions

As security products, OpenSSH and Tectia require certain files and directories on the server machine to be protected from unwanted access. Imagine if your *authorized_keys* or *.rhosts* file were world-writable; anyone on that host could modify them and gain convenient access to your account. *sshd* has several configuration keywords for reducing this risk.

5.3.2.1   Acceptable permissions for user files

Users aren't always careful to protect important files and directories in their accounts, such as their *.rhosts* file or personal SSH directory. Such lapses can lead to security holes and compromised accounts. To combat this, you can configure *sshd* to reject connections to any user account that has unacceptable permissions.

The StrictModes keyword, with a value of yes (the default), causes *sshd* to check the permissions of important files and directories. They must be owned by the account owner or by root, and group and world write permission must be disabled. For OpenSSH, StrictModes checks:

- The user's home directory
- The user's *~/.rhosts* and *~/.shosts* file
- The user's SSH configuration directory, *~/.ssh*
- The user's SSH *~/.ssh/authorized_keys* file
- The user and system "known hosts" files

For Tectia, the list is smaller and is checked only for hostbased authentication: [3.4.3.6]

- The user's home directory
- The user's *~/.rhosts* and *~/.shosts* file

If any check fails, the server rejects SSH connection attempts to the account. If StrictModes is given the value no, these checks aren't performed:

```
StrictModes no
```

However, we strongly suggest you leave these checks enabled.

Tectia recognizes an undocumented keyword, StrictModes.UserDirMaskBits, to control the checks more precisely. The value is an octal number representing the file permission bits that must be disabled. For example, to require that files grant no group or world access (read, write, or execute):

```
# Tectia
StrictModes.UserDirMaskBits 077
```

The default value is 022, indicating that group and world write permission must be disabled.

Even if StrictModes is enabled, it can be defeated by using POSIX access control lists (ACLs), which are supported in Solaris and some other flavors of Unix, to set file permissions with greater precision. *sshd* doesn't check ACLs, so one could argue that StrictModes is an incomplete test.

Boolean Values in Configuration Files

Many keywords, such as StrictModes, require Boolean values. OpenSSH and Tectia have different standards for these values.

OpenSSH recognizes either yes or true to enable the behavior described by a keyword, as well as the opposite values no or false to disable. These values cannot be abbreviated, and must be lowercase.

Tectia is much more lenient: it recognizes any word starting with the letters y (yes), t (true), or k (*kyllä*: Finnish for "yes") in lowercase or uppercase to enable, and anything else to disable.

We use yes and no in our examples because they are accepted by both products, and we recommend you do the same.

5.3.3   TCP/IP Settings

Since the SSH protocol operates over TCP/IP, *sshd* permits control over various parameters related to TCP/IP.

5.3.3.1 Port number and network interface

By default, *sshd* listens on TCP port 22. The port number may be changed with the Port keyword:

```
Port 9876
```

or the *–p* command-line option:

```
$ sshd -p 9876
```

If you repeat the Port keyword or *–p* option, OpenSSH listens on all of the specified ports:

```
# OpenSSH
$ sshd -p 22 -p 9876
```

Tectia, on the other hand, allows only a single port setting: if multiple Port keywords or *–p* options are specified, the server uses only the last one and ignores all earlier instances.*

You may also configure *sshd* to bind its listening port on a particular network interface. By default, the port is bound on all active network interfaces on the host. The ListenAddress keyword limits *sshd* to listen only on specific interfaces; the default value is 0.0.0.0.

For example, suppose a computer has two Ethernet cards and is attached to two different networks. One interface has the address 192.168.10.23, and the other, 192.168.11.17. By default, *sshd* listens on both interfaces; therefore, you can reach the server by connecting to port 22 at either address. However, this may not always be what you want; perhaps you want to provide SSH service only to hosts on one network and not the other:

```
ListenAddress 192.168.10.23
```

Of course, this represents a real restriction only if the two networks aren't otherwise connected together (say, by a router) so that port 22 on 192.168.10.23 is not reachable from the network 192.168.11.24.

To listen on multiple, specific interfaces, repeat the ListenAddress keyword:

```
ListenAddress 192.168.10.23
ListenAddress 192.168.11.17
```

For even more precise control, you can also specify the port for listening on a given interface. The syntax differs for OpenSSH and Tectia:

```
# OpenSSH
ListenAddress 192.168.11.17:12345   Port 12345. Notice the colon between the address and the port.
```

```
# Tectia
ListenAddress 192.168.11.17 12345   Port 12345. Notice the space between the address and the port.
```

---

* The port setting (either explicit or the default value, 22) is used in the name of the process ID file. [5.3.1.3] Tectia servers can listen on multiple ports, but this requires use of the ListenAddress keyword.

The address 0.0.0.0 means to listen on all interfaces:

```
ListenAddress 0.0.0.0
```

optionally qualified by a port number:

```
# OpenSSH
ListenAddress 0.0.0.0:9876

# Tectia
ListenAddress 0.0.0.0 9876
```

OpenSSH servers allow the address to be omitted (meaning all interfaces) if the port is specified:

```
# OpenSSH
ListenAddress :9876
```

 For OpenSSH, a ListenAddress of 0.0.0.0:2222 will listen on port 2222 only on IPv4 interfaces, whereas :2222 means to listen on both IPv4 and IPv6 addresses. Additionally, you can specify IPv6 addresses with colons, but to avoid ambiguity between the address and the port specification, enclose the IPv6 part in square brackets, e.g., ListenAddress [::1]:2222.

Tectia servers recognize the address any for all interfaces, with or without a port:

```
# Tectia
ListenAddress any
ListenAddress any 9876
```

Since Tectia uses only a single Port value, the only way to configure the server to listen on multiple ports is to use multiple ListenAddress keywords.

OpenSSH also permits hostnames in place of numeric addresses:

```
ListenAddress server.example.com
```

If the hostname lookup yields multiple addresses, then they are all used.

If a `ListenAddress` value has no port specified, then the value (or possibly multiple values, for OpenSSH) of the `Port` keyword is used for that address. In such a case, the `Port` keyword(s) must precede that `ListenAddress` keyword.

Additionally, the *–p* command-line option overrides all `Port` and `ListenAddress` keywords in the configuration file. The server listens on all interfaces if any *–p* options are used. Use one or several *–o* options with the `ListenAddress` keyword to indicate specific interfaces on the command line.

5.3.3.2   Invocation by inetd or xinetd

sshd normally runs as a daemon, listening for incoming connection requests, and forking whenever it accepts a connection from a client. This spawns a separate child process (a copy of the parent *sshd* process) to handle each session. The child process exits when the session ends.

Alternatively, the server may be invoked by *inetd* or *xinetd*, like many other network daemons. In this case, the general-purpose network daemon listens for and accepts the SSH connections. It then starts a new instance of *sshd* for each session with the already-connected socket attached to the standard input, output, and error streams of *sshd*. Each *sshd* invocation is responsible for a single session.

If you prefer this behavior, place an appropriate line in the *inetd* or *xinetd* configuration file to describe the SSH service, invoking *sshd* with the *–i* command-line option. For *inetd*, add a single line to */etc/inetd.conf*:

```
ssh stream tcp    nowait root    /usr/local/sbin/sshd    sshd -i
```

Or if you're using *xinetd*, create a new file */etc/xinetd.d/ssh* containing:

```
service ssh
{
        socket_type = stream
        protocol    = tcp
        wait        = no
        user        = root
        server      = /usr/local/sbin/sshd
        server_args = -i
        disable     = no
}
```

You will also need an entry for SSH in the server machine's TCP/IP services database, usually */etc/services* (or sometimes */etc/inet/services*), such as:

```
ssh    22/tcp    # SSH Remote Login Protocol
```

The *–i* option causes *sshd* to:

- Ignore all `Port` and `ListenAddress` keywords and the *–p* command-line option, because *inetd* or *xinetd* itself is responsible for listening
- (OpenSSH only) Ignore all `MaxStartups` keywords

- (OpenSSH only) Direct debug output to syslog [5.9] instead of the standard error stream, since stderr is attached to the SSH socket by *inetd* or *xinetd*, and debug output would confuse the SSH client at the other end of the connection

The *inetd/xinetd* approach has advantages and disadvantages. On the up side, it allows a wrapper program to invoke *sshd*, should that be needed, and *xinetd* particularly supports many options that can complement the SSH server configuration. Also, *inetd* and *xinetd* provide a single, centralized point of control for all types of network connections, which simplifies maintenance. If you want to forbid all types of TCP/IP connections, for example, you can simply disable *inetd/xinetd* instead of running around killing other daemons. On systems where SSH connections are rare, using *inetd/xinetd* for the SSH service saves resources (memory and a process slot) otherwise consumed by the SSH server as it listens for incoming connections. Finally, starting a new *sshd* instance for each connection can make attacks more difficult by introducing additional randomness. On the down side, *inetd/xinetd*-based SSH connections may be slower to start up.*

5.3.3.3 Restarting the SSH server for each connection

SSH servers use randomness extensively for cryptographic algorithms and protocols, typically relying on the operating system (or other external state) to provide a source of random bits. [3.6.4] Some operating systems also support Address Space Layout Randomization (ASLR), which protects against certain kinds of attacks that require knowledge of predictable memory locations. ASLR causes random offsets to be used when program segments or shared libraries are loaded, memory regions are dynamically allocated, etc.

Most of the randomness introduced by ASLR occurs when a program is initially loaded and starts running. Even on systems without ASLR, dynamic memory allocations that primarily occur in the early stages of program execution can be affected by the global state of the system's virtual memory, which is hard to predict. In contrast, when a long-running program merely forks to create many child processes, all of the children inherit the memory layout (and even contents) from the parent process. Restarting the child processes after each fork mitigates the risks associated with attacks that are based on guessing memory locations.

By default, the OpenSSH server restarts itself after it accepts each connection from a client, and forks to create a separate child process to handle the session.† Relative pathnames can't be used for server restarts, since *sshd* changes its working directory shortly after it begins running:

```
# OpenSSH
$ ./sshd
sshd re-exec requires execution with an absolute path
```

---

* Only if you use the SSH-1 protocol, where *sshd* generates a new server key each time it's invoked. But you're not using SSH-1, are you?

† This feature is new in OpenSSH 3.9.

We'll continue to use the relative pathname "sshd" for our examples as an abbreviation, since the full, absolute pathname usually isn't relevant to our discussions about the *sshd* command line. Nevertheless, an absolute pathname is recommended in practice, and newer versions of OpenSSH now enforce this, as shown in the preceding example.

If the server restart fails for some other reason (e.g., the executable file used originally to start *sshd* was renamed or removed), then the child process continues to run after forking, but produces a warning (which is usually sent to syslog):

```
error: rexec of /usr/sbin/sshd failed: No such file or directory
```

Before it restarts, the child process adds the undocumented –*R* option at the end of its command line: this is used by the new process to detect that it has been restarted, and should therefore use the already connected socket that it inherits from its parent for communication with the client.* The parent process (i.e., the one that listens for incoming connections) sends a copy of its configuration and the SSH-1 server key (if one is used) via another socket to the restarted child process, which knows to read the data because of the same –*R* option. The child process then proceeds to handle the session normally.

If OpenSSH is started by *inetd* or *xinetd*, then there is no need to restart the SSH server, because a new instance of *sshd* is started by *inetd/xinetd* for each connection. [5.3.3.2] In fact, the function of the restarted child process is so similar to the operation of the server with *inetd/xinetd* that the –*R* option enables the same side effects as the –*i* option: notably, debug output is forced to syslog instead of the standard error.

The restart mechanism can be disabled by the undocumented, lowercase –*r* option:

```
# OpenSSH
$ sshd -r
```

This is useful in conjunction with server debugging features, since restarts are an inconvenient complication, and the side effect of sending debug output to syslog after the child process restarts is undesirable. [5.9] The –*r* option can also be used to avoid the slight performance cost for server restarts, especially on systems without ASLR, where such restarts provide little or no additional randomness. There is no configuration option to disable the server restart feature at build time.

5.3.3.4 Keepalive messages

The keepalive feature (TCPKeepAlive in OpenSSH, KeepAlive in Tectia) is concerned with recognizing when a connection has failed. Suppose a client establishes an SSH connection, and sometime later, the client host crashes abruptly. If the SSH server

---

* Never use the –*R* option to start *sshd*; it's really part of the protocol for communication between the parent and the (restarted) child server processes.

has no reason to send unsolicited messages to the client, it may never notice the half-dead TCP connection to its partner, and the *sshd* remains around indefinitely, using up system resources such as memory and a process slot (and making the sysadmin's *ps* output messy).

The `TCPKeepAlive` or `KeepAlive` keyword instructs *sshd* how to proceed if a connection problem occurs, such as a prolonged network outage or a client machine crash:

```
# OpenSSH
TCPKeepAlive yes
# Tectia
KeepAlive yes
```

The value yes (the default) tells the server to set the TCP keepalive option on its connection to the client. This causes TCP to transmit and expect periodic keepalive messages. If it doesn't receive responses to these messages for a while, it returns an error to *sshd*, which then shuts down the connection.

The value no means not to use keepalive messages. Note that SSH clients can also enable keepalive messages from their side of the connections, so it's important to disable those too if you want to avoid keepalive traffic completely. [7.4.5.4]

The TCP keepalive feature is intended to prevent half-dead connections from building up over time. The keepalive message interval and timeout period reflect this: they are quite long, typically on the order of hours. This is to minimize the network load imposed by the keepalive messages and also to prevent connections from being unnecessarily torn down because of transient problems, such as a temporary network outage or routing flap. These timers aren't set in SSH; they are properties of the host's TCP stack. They shouldn't be altered lightly, since they affect every TCP connection using keepalives on that host.

This feature isn't intended to prevent lost connections due to firewall, proxying, NAT, or IP masquerading timeouts. For instance, when your SSH connection is going across a firewall but has been idle for a while, the firewall can decide to tear down the connection. Since this is done to conserve shared resources (such as a limited pool of external, routable IP addresses), these timeouts are typically quite short, perhaps a few minutes to an hour or so. The name "keepalive" suggests that it might be the right thing to use, since that's what you want to do—keep your connection alive. But really, "keepalive" is the wrong name for it; it would be better named "detect dead" (but that sounds like a second-level cleric spell to avoid being eaten by zombies). To deal with this problem, you'd have to shorten the TCP keepalive interval dramatically on the SSH host. This is contrary to its purpose and unwise because it affects not only SSH connections, but also every other TCP connection using keepalives, even those that don't need it. Doing this on the server side is an especially bad idea as a general principle, since a busy server may be using lots of TCP connections, and enabling keepalives on many of them since it's supposed to be an inexpensive feature. This can impose an unnecessary and damaging additional network load, especially if it becomes a widespread practice.

It's good to remember that the timeout annoying you so much is there for a reason. You might like to leave an unused SSH connection up for a long time, but if it's occupying one of a limited number of simultaneous outbound Internet TCP connections for your company, perhaps it's better if you just suck it up for the common good. Typing ssh again once in a while is really not that hard; use your shell's alias feature if you find the number of keystrokes onerous. If you genuinely think the timeout is inappropriate or unnecessary, argue the case with the network administrator, and try to get it changed.

For the occasions when it's really necessary, the right way to accomplish this sort of keepalive behavior is with an application-level mechanism implemented in SSH—having it periodically send SSH protocol messages over the connection to make it appear nonidle. This is exactly what OpenSSH does with its ClientAliveInterval and ClientAliveCountMax keywords. ClientAliveInterval controls how the server sends client-alive messages.* Its argument is a length of time in seconds:

```
# OpenSSH
ClientAliveInterval 300     Send client-alive every 300 seconds, or five minutes
```

or a time value with optional units:

```
# OpenSSH
ClientAliveInterval 5m      Send client-alive every five minutes
```

If your server hasn't heard from the client within the given amount of time, the server will send a client-alive message to the client. It will continue sending these messages at the given interval (in this case, every five minutes) until it receives a response or gives up. You control how it gives up with the third keyword, ClientAliveCountMax, representing the maximum number of consecutive client-alive messages the server will send:

```
# OpenSSH
ClientAliveCountMax 8       Try eight times, then give up. The default is three times.
```

Once this maximum is reached, the server considers the SSH connection inactive and terminates it. If you don't want the server to send client-alive messages, set ClientAliveInterval to zero.

If your SSH implementation has no similar feature (Tectia doesn't), we recommend simply sending characters over your connection once in a while. Run Emacs with a clock in its mode line. Run a program in the background that prints "Boo!" to your terminal if it's been idle for 20 minutes. You get the idea.

---

* OpenSSH clients have analogous ServerAliveInterval and ServerAliveCountMax keywords. [7.4.5.4]

Time Values in Configuration Files

Some keywords specify intervals of time. By default, the values are numbers of seconds, but both OpenSSH and Tectia recognize single-character suffixes for units, in either lowercase or uppercase: s for seconds, m for minutes, h for hours, d for days, and w for weeks. For example, one day could be represented as 1d or 24H or 1440m.

OpenSSH adds sequences of time values, so a 90-minute interval can be specified as 1h30m. Tectia allows only a single time-unit suffix.

OpenSSH recognizes time values with units for the keywords ClientAliveInterval, LoginGraceTime, and KeyRegenerationTime.

Unfortunately, Tectia handles time values rather inconsistently. Units are recognized only for the keywords IdleTimeout, HostkeyEKTimeOut, and ExternalMapperTimeout. Other keywords that specify intervals accept only numbers of seconds, without units: LoginGraceTime, AuthInteractiveFailureTimeout, and RekeyIntervalSeconds (which is especially unusual, since the time unit "seconds" is in the keyword name).

5.3.3.5 Idle connections

Keepalive messages are concerned with recognizing that a connection has failed. A related feature is recognizing when a healthy connection is unused and should be terminated. Tectia supports the IdleTimeout keyword for this purpose. If an SSH connection is established between a server and a client, but no data passes over the connection for a long time, what should the server do: keep the connection, or terminate it?

The IdleTimeout keyword tells the server what to do if a connection is idle, i.e., if the user doesn't transmit any data in a given period. If IdleTimeout is zero (the default), the server does nothing, leaving idle connections intact:

```
# Tectia
IdleTimeout 0
```

Otherwise, the server terminates the connection after a specified interval of idleness. The time value can specify units, e.g., three hours:

```
# Tectia
IdleTimeout 3H
```

See the sidebar "Time Values in Configuration Files" for more syntax details.

The idle timeout can also be set for a given key in a user's *authorized_keys* file using the idle-timeout option. [8.2.7] Notably, this option overrides the server's IdleTimeout value but only for that key. This is a rare instance of a per-account option overriding a serverwide option; however, the server will only allow a client to *decrease* the timeout.

5.3.3.6   Failed logins

Suppose a user attempts to log in via SSH but fails to authenticate. What should the server do? The keywords `LoginGraceTime`, `MaxAuthTries` (OpenSSH), and `PasswordGuesses` (Tectia) control the server's response.

Users are given a limited time to authenticate successfully. The default is 120 seconds (2 minutes) for OpenSSH or 600 seconds (10 minutes) for Tectia. This timeout is controlled by the `LoginGraceTime` keyword, given a value in seconds:

```
LoginGraceTime 60
```

or the –g command-line option:

```
$ sshd -g 60
```

OpenSSH allows time units to be used in the configuration file or on the command line:

```
# OpenSSH
LoginGraceTime 5m
```

```
# OpenSSH
$ sshd -g 5m
```

To disable this feature, provide a `LoginGraceTime` value of zero:

```
LoginGraceTime 0
```

or by command-line option:

```
$ sshd -g 0
```

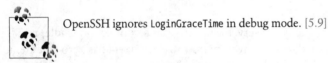 OpenSSH ignores `LoginGraceTime` in debug mode. [5.9]

OpenSSH limits the number of times (six by default) that a user can attempt to authenticate in a single SSH connection:

```
# OpenSSH
MaxAuthTries 4            Permit four attempts, and log the third and fourth failures if they occur
```

If authentication fails half the number of times specified (in this example, two times, half of four), then failures are logged by *sshd*. In other words, *sshd* gives you the benefit of the doubt at first, then considers you suspicious. By default, you have six chances to authenticate in one connection.

If password authentication is used for a connection request, Tectia's *sshd* permits a client three tries to authenticate before dropping the connection. This restriction may be modified with the `PasswordGuesses` keyword for Tectia:

```
# Tectia
PasswordGuesses 5
```

There are two sorts of requests a client can make in this regard: a query whether a particular public key is authorized to log into the target account, and an actual authentication attempt including a signature by the corresponding private key. As Tectia does not limit the number of public-key authentication requests, there's no issue with it. The OpenSSH MaxAuthTries setting, however, limits the number of failed authentication requests overall, of any type, and OpenSSH counts a "no" answer to a public-key query as a failure. A common side effect is an unexpected limit to the number of keys you can usefully have in an agent! If you have five keys in your agent, and it happens to be the fifth one that would let you in, you're out of luck: the server will disconnect you after the client tries the fourth key. And that's assuming the client didn't try and fail some other methods first, e.g., GSSAPI or host-based; then even fewer keys could be tried. (See [7.4.2.1] for a workaround.)

There are various security arguments to made here, of course. The server can't distinguish between a legitimate user trying keys and an attacker knocking on the door, so it measures all attempts against the repeated-authentication limit. In fact, one can argue that the server shouldn't honor public-key queries because they reveal information to an attacker: which key to try to steal, or whether an account can be accessed at all. These are all trade-offs of convenience versus security, and different server implementations take different approaches.

You can work around this issue by listing your most relevant keys in your client configuration file, ~/.ssh/config, with the IdentityFile keyword. [7.4.2] Keys that are in both the agent and the configuration file are tried first by the client. Therefore, you can associate particular keys with a particular host so that they're tried first for authentication.

5.3.3.7   Limiting simultaneous connections

sshd can handle an arbitrary number of simultaneous connections by default. Both OpenSSH and Tectia provide keywords to limit the maximum number, if you want to conserve resources on your server machine or reduce the risk of denial-of-service attacks. For OpenSSH it is MaxStartups, and for Tectia it is MaxConnections:

```
# OpenSSH
MaxStartups 32

# Tectia
MaxConnections 32
```

To specify an unlimited number of connections, provide a value of zero:

```
# OpenSSH
MaxStartups 0

# Tectia
MaxConnections 0
```

Of course, the number of connections is also limited by available memory or other operating system resources. These keywords have no effect on these other factors. (Sorry, you can't increase your CPU speed by setting a keyword!)

OpenSSH's MaxStartups keyword has one additional bit of functionality. If you provide a triple of integers separated by colons, of the form $A:B:C$, this tells the server to refuse connections based on probabilities. Specifically, if the number of connections is A or greater, *sshd* will begin rejecting connections. When there are A connections, the probability of rejection is $B\%$. When there are C connections, the probability of rejection is 100% (every attempt is rejected). Between A and C connections, the probability increases linearly from $B\%$ to 100%. So, for example, if you have:

```
# OpenSSH
MaxStartups 10:50:20
```

then at a load of 10 connections, the probably of rejection is 50%; at 15 connections (halfway between 10 and 20) it's 75% (halfway between 50% and 100%), and at 20 connections it's 100%.

Tectia's behavior is simpler. After the maximum number of connections have been accepted, new connection attempts are rejected, and the server sends a "Too many connections" error message back to the client before it disconnects. Tectia can also limit the number of connections at compile time via the --with-ssh-connection-limit option. [4.3.5.3]

If *sshd* is launched by *xinetd*, then you can control server resources much more precisely: the rate of incoming connections, server memory, and more. [5.3.3.2]

5.3.3.8 Reverse IP mappings

The SSH server optionally does a reverse DNS lookup on a client's IP address. That is, it looks up the name associated with the address, then looks up the addresses for that name and makes sure that the client's address is among them. If this check fails, the server refuses the connection. This feature uses standard system services like gethostbyname( ) and gethostbyaddr( ) to perform these mappings, so the databases that are consulted depend on the host operating system configuration. It might use the DNS, the Network Information Service (NIS or YP), static files on a server machine, or some combination.

To enable this check for OpenSSH, provide the UseDNS keyword with a value of yes or no:[*]

```
# OpenSSH
UseDNS yes
```

---

[*] Tectia has a similar-sounding keyword, RequireReverseMapping, but it applies only to the AllowHosts and DenyHosts features. [5.5.3]

This feature is a bit of security-oriented consistency checking. SSH uses cryptographic signatures to determine a peer's identity, but the list of peer public keys (the known hosts database) is often indexed by hostname, so SSH must translate the address to a name in order to check the peer's identity. Reverse mapping tries to ensure that someone isn't playing games with the naming service in a cracking attempt. There is a trade-off, however, since in today's Internet, the DNS reverse-address mappings aren't always kept up to date. The SSH server might reject legitimate connection attempts because of poorly maintained reverse-address mappings over which you have no control. In general, we recommend turning off this feature; it isn't usually worth the hassle, and you avoid long reverse-lookup delays at times when DNS is down.

5.3.3.9 Controlling the Nagle Algorithm

TCP/IP has a feature called the Nagle Algorithm, which is designed to reduce the number of TCP segments sent with very small amounts of data (e.g., one byte), usually as part of an interactive terminal session. Over fast links such as Ethernet, the Nagle Algorithm generally isn't needed. Over a wide-area network, however, it can cause noticeable delays in the responsiveness of X clients and character terminal displays, as multibyte terminal control sequences may be transmitted inconveniently by the algorithm. In such cases, you should turn off the Nagle Algorithm using the NoDelay keyword:

```
# Tectia
NoDelay yes
```

NoDelay disables the Nagle Algorithm by toggling the TCP_NODELAY bit when requesting a TCP connection from the Unix kernel. Legal values are yes (to disable) and no (to enable; the default).

NoDelay can be enabled or disabled by the Tectia client, rather than serverwide, using the client configuration keyword NoDelay. [7.4.5.5] It usually makes more sense to use NoDelay for a single client connection than to control the Nagle Algorithm globally for all connections on the server side.

5.3.3.10 Discovering other servers

Tectia can seek out and discover other Tectia servers automatically. The keyword MaxBroadcastsPerSecond, when given an integer value greater than zero, causes a Tectia server to respond to UDP broadcasts sent to port 22:

```
# Tectia
MaxBroadcastsPerSecond 10
```

The server responds to only this many queries per second; any excess broadcasts are silently ignored. All UDP broadcasts received on port 22 apply to this limit, including unrecognized or malformed packets. The rate limiting prevents a denial-of-service attack that floods the server with queries, causing it to spend all its time replying to them.

By default, Tectia servers do not respond to UDP broadcasts. This behavior can be specified explicitly by setting MaxBroadcastsPerSecond to zero:

```
# Tectia
MaxBroadcastsPerSecond 0
```

No mechanism is provided to use a UDP port other than 22, and the UDP port is completely independent of the TCP port(s) used for ordinary SSH connections.

A program supplied with Tectia, *ssh-probe*, sends queries to one or more specified broadcast addresses. It listens for replies, and prints the locations (IP addresses and ports) along with the versions of any Tectia servers that it finds:

```
# Tectia
$ ssh-probe 10.1.2.255
10.1.2.3:22:SSH Tectia Server 4.1.3.2
10.1.2.5:22:SSH Tectia Server 4.1.3.2
10.1.2.5:2222:SSH Tectia Server 4.1.3.2
10.1.2.5:3333:SSH Tectia Server 4.1.3.2
10.1.2.9:22:SSH Tectia Server 4.1.3.2
...
```

Directed broadcasts (i.e., those on different networks) can be used if intervening gateways are willing to forward them. IP addresses of specific hosts (but not host-names) can also be used.

 UDP datagrams received on non-broadcast addresses are usually delivered only to a single process, so if several Tectia servers are running on a target host, then only one will respond. Use broadcast addresses to detect multiple servers.

ssh-probe does *not* use the ProtocolVersionString to determine the version: this string is part of the initial negotiation between SSH servers and clients for TCP connections. [5.3.7] Tectia servers always supply their actual version string in response to UDP queries by *ssh-probe*.

The default output format is intended to be parsed easily by programs. The *–r* option prints results in a more human-readable format:

```
# Tectia
$ ssh-probe -r 10.1.2.255
Server address = "10.1.2.3"
Server port = "22"
Server version = "SSH Tectia Server 4.1.3.2"
...
12 servers detected.
```

The *–s* option causes *ssh-probe* to operate silently, returning only an exit value of 0 to indicate that at least one server was found, 1 if no replies were received, or -1 if some other error occurred:

```
# Tectia
$ ssh-probe -s 10.1.2.255
$ case $? in
>       0) echo "Tectia found.";;
>       1) echo "Tectia missing.";;
>       *) echo "Something bad happened to ssh-probe!";;
> esac
Tectia found.
```

By default, *ssh-probe* waits one second for replies. The *–t* option specifies a longer timeout, e.g., for slow or distant servers:

```
# Tectia
$ ssh-probe -t 5 10.1.2.255
```

ssh-probe supports the *–d* option for debug output. [5.9] The program uses the module names SshProbe and SshServerProbe.

Port-scanning programs such as *nmap* provide a more general way to locate SSH servers, including other implementations like OpenSSH, even though port scans typically don't provide version information as *ssh-probe* does for Tectia servers. For example, to use *nmap* to scan a range of network addresses for any kinds of SSH servers listening on (TCP) port 22:

```
$ nmap -v -p 22 10.1.2.0/24
```

The ScanSSH program* scans ranges of network addresses, identifying SSH servers (along with open proxies and other interesting servers, such as HTTP and SMTP). It attempts to determine the version for each. For example, to scan the same network address range:

```
$ scanssh -s ssh 10.1.2.0/24
```

MaxBroadcastsPerSecond and *ssh-probe* are a rather ad hoc solution for locating Tectia servers, and port scans are questionable, since authorized users typically know the identity of specific servers to which they have been granted access. Probes often don't work across firewalls, and they might be mistaken for attacks by people and programs that monitor network activity.

Better techniques are available to enumerate servers for administrative tasks, e.g., maintaining a list of servers in a netgroup or other database. Dynamic DNS and SRV records are alternatives, although this nameserver functionality is still not widely used.

5.3.4 Key Regeneration

All SSH servers maintain a persistent host key. It is generated by the system administrator when installing SSH and identifies the host for authentication purposes. [5.3.1.1]

---

* *http://www.monkey.org/~provos/scanssh/*

Additionally, SSH-2 clients and servers exchange keys for data encryption and integrity. By default, the Tectia client and server perform this key exchange every hour (3600 seconds) but you can set this with the RekeyIntervalSeconds keyword. A value of zero disables rekeying.

```
# Tectia
RekeyIntervalSeconds 7200
```

This keyword only controls the automatic, periodic session rekeying that is initiated by the server. An SSH client can still request session rekeying at any time.

You can make the *ssh* client force rekeying with the escape sequence ~R (OpenSSH) or ~r (for Tectia). [7.4.6.8]

5.3.5 Encryption Algorithms

The SSH server can use a number of data-encryption algorithms for its secure connection; the client chooses a cipher from the list the server allows. The Ciphers keyword describes the subset of allowable ciphers, selected from those the server software supports. Its value is a comma-separated list of algorithm names (strings), case-sensitive,* indicating which algorithms are permissible. For example:

```
Ciphers 3des-cbc
Ciphers 3des-cbc,blowfish-cbc,arcfour
```

The order of the values is not significant, since the client drives the choice of the cipher.

If multiple Ciphers keywords are specified, the values are not accumulated into a single list. Instead, OpenSSH uses the list for the first Ciphers keyword, and Tectia uses the last.

OpenSSH treats unrecognized cipher names as fatal errors, but Tectia silently ignores them, which makes typos hard to detect. For troubleshooting, use the *sshd -d* command-line option [5.9] with the SshConfigParse module and a high debug level:

```
# Tectia
sshd -d SshConfigParse=9
```

Look for "ssh_config_set_param_algs" in the output to see the actual list of cipher names that were used.

The Ciphers keyword is useful for quickly disabling individual encryption algorithms—say, if a security hole is discovered in one of them. Just omit that algorithm from the Ciphers list and restart the server.

---

* Older versions of OpenSSH treat the algorithm names as case-insensitive.

Both OpenSSH and Tectia support the following standard ciphers that are defined by the IETF SECSH draft:

    3des-cbc
    aes128-cbc
    aes192-cbc
    aes256-cbc
    arcfour
    blowfish-cbc
    cast128-cbc

In addition, Tectia implements the following standard ciphers:*

    none
    twofish-cbc
    twofish128-cbc
    twofish192-cbc
    twofish256-cbc

The "none" cipher means that no encryption is used. This is unsuitable for production use, but it might occasionally be convenient for testing, e.g., if you are watching SSH traffic using a network sniffer for diagnostic purposes. Subconfiguration files can restrict insecure ciphers like "none" to specific hosts or users. [11.6.2]

OpenSSH also implements a number of nonstandard ciphers:

    acss@openssh.org†
    aes128-ctr
    aes192-ctr
    aes256-ctr
    rijndael-cbc@lysator.liu.se

By default, all ciphers supported by the OpenSSH server (both standard and nonstandard) are allowed.

Tectia supports a different set of recommended, nonstandard ciphers:

    cast128-12-cbc@ssh.com
    des-cbc@ssh.com
    rc2-cbc@ssh.com
    rc2-128-cbc@ssh.com
    rijndael-cbc@ssh.com

Tectia also recognizes special values for the Cipher keyword indicating sets of algorithms:

---

* A few standard ciphers aren't supported by either OpenSSH or Tectia: idea-cbc, serpent128-cbc, serpent192-cbc, and serpent256-cbc. These are all considered optional by the IETF SECSH draft.

† Cipher acss@openssh.org is not allowed by default; it must be explicitly enabled.

Tectia FIPS Mode

The FIPS 140-2 standard defines strict requirements for performing cryptographic operations, including allowable ciphers. Tectia servers can use a special cryptographic library that is certified to be FIPS 140-2 compliant. In FIPS mode, the server supports *only* the following ciphers:

```
3des-cbc
aes128-cbc
aes192-cbc
aes256-cbc
des-cbc@ssh.com
```

To enable FIPS mode, run the *ssh-crypto-library-chooser* command:

```
# Tectia
$ ssh-crypto-library-chooser fips
```

To use the standard cryptographic library that supports all of the ciphers:

```
# Tectia
$ ssh-crypto-library-chooser std
```

With no command-line argument, the *ssh-crypto-library-chooser* command just prints the currently used library.

The server must be restarted whenever the library is changed.

AnyStd
> Any standard algorithm implemented by Tectia, including none

AnyStdCipher
> Same as AnyStd, but excluding none

Any
> Any standard or recommended, nonstandard algorithm implemented by Tectia, including none

AnyCipher
> Same as Any, but excluding none

These special values are case-insensitive, in contrast to the other values for cipher names. We recommend using the capitalization shown earlier, but you may see lowercase values in older Tectia configuration files or documentation.

An important and unfortunate restriction is that the special values for cipher sets cannot be mixed with other cipher names:

```
# Tectia: This is ILLEGAL
Ciphers 3des-cbc,AnyStd
```

The default for Tectia is AnyStdCipher.

Cipher Naming Conventions

Ciphers use a conventional naming scheme that encodes the algorithm and any variable parameters. We illustrate the conventions by dissecting a sample cipher name: *cast128-12-cbc@ssh.com*. Here is the meaning of each part:

cast

> The name of the algorithm in lowercase. [3.8]

128

> Many algorithms can use different key lengths. For these, the number of bits in the key immediately follows the algorithm name. If the algorithm name ends in a digit, then a hyphen is added between the name and the key size (e.g., *rc2-128* for the RC2 algorithm using 128-bit keys).

-12

> A few algorithms are defined in terms of other parameters. If needed, these are specified next, each with a leading hyphen. For example, the CAST algorithm can use different numbers of rounds of encryption instead of the default 16.

-cbc

> Block cipher algorithms can be run in a variety of modes of operation:
>
> *ECB*
>> Electronic code book
>
> *CBC*
>> Cipher block chaining
>
> *CFB*
>> Cipher feedback
>
> *OFB*
>> Output feedback
>
> *CTR*
>> Counter
>
> The mode is appended to the cipher name, again translated to lowercase, with a hyphen.

@ssh.com:

> Finally, the IETF SECSH draft specifies that nonstandard ciphers must have a suffix with a leading @ character indicating the domain that defined the cipher.

Tectia's extensive but poorly documented cryptographic library actually supports a much wider range of ciphers, including:

    3des-ecb@ssh.com
    3des-cfb@ssh.com
    3des-ofb@ssh.com
    aes-ecb@ssh.com
    aes-cbc@ssh.com

aes-cfb@ssh.com
aes-ofb@ssh.com
aes-ctr@ssh.com
blowfish-ecb@ssh.com
blowfish-cfb@ssh.com
blowfish-ofb@ssh.com
cast128-ecb@ssh.com
cast128-cfb@ssh.com
cast128-ofb@ssh.com
cast128-12-ecb@ssh.com
cast128-12-cfb@ssh.com
cast128-12-ofb@ssh.com
des-ecb@ssh.com
des-cfb@ssh.com
des-ofb@ssh.com
rc2-ecb@ssh.com
rc2-cfb@ssh.com
rc2-ofb@ssh.com
rc2-128-ecb@ssh.com
rc2-128-cfb@ssh.com
rc2-128-ofb@ssh.com
rijndael-ecb@ssh.com
rijndael-cfb@ssh.com
rijndael-ofb@ssh.com
rijndael-ctr@ssh.com
twofish-ecb@ssh.com
twofish-cfb@ssh.com
twofish-ofb@ssh.com

These are not included in the sets for Any or AnyCipher. In some cases, this is because the ciphers are considered experimental or inferior. For example, DES is usually not recommended because of its short key length, and block ciphers in ECB mode are considered vulnerable to replay attacks. Other modes such as CFB, OFB, and CTR are plausible alternatives to the default CBC, however.

Finally, Tectia recognizes a small number of convenient aliases for sets of ciphers:

Value	Meaning
aes-cbc	aes128-cbc, aes192-cbc aes256-cbc
cast	cast128-cbc
twofish	twofish-cbc, twofish128-cbc, twofish192-cbc, twofish256-cbc

In most cases, the names of block ciphers in CBC mode are also recognized by Tectia without "-cbc", since CBC is considered the default mode. There are exceptions, however, that don't follow any obvious pattern:

- aes-cbc@ssh.com
- cast128-cbc
- cast128-12-cbc@ssh.com
- rc2-cbc@ssh.com
- rc2-128-cbc@ssh.com
- twofish-cbc

We therefore recommend explicitly specifying -cbc in cipher names.

Tectia is rather forgiving (or sloppy, depending on your point of view) about the @ssh.com suffix for cipher names, which is supposed to be used consistently for nonstandard ciphers.

Most standard cipher names are also recognized with this suffix. The exceptions are:

- aes128-cbc
- aes192-cbc
- aes256-cbc
- twofish128-cbc
- twofish192-cbc
- twofish256-cbc

Similarly, the suffix can be omitted from most nonstandard cipher names. The lone exception is *aes-cbc@ssh.com*, because the name without the suffix is used as an alias for all AES ciphers in CBC mode with any key length, as described earlier.

Misusing the @ssh.com suffix in this way is inadvisable, because it violates the IETF SECSH draft.

5.3.6   Integrity-Checking (MAC) Algorithms

The MACs keyword selects the allowable integrity-checking algorithms, known as the message authentication code (MAC), used by *sshd*. [3.4.2.3] Except as described below, the MACs keyword behaves exactly like the Ciphers keyword. [5.3.5] Here are some examples:

```
MACs hmac-sha1
MACs hmac-sha1,hmac-md5
```

Both OpenSSH and Tectia support the following standard MAC algorithms defined by the IETF SECSH draft:

hmac-sha1
hmac-sha1-96
hmac-md5
hmac-md5-96

In addition, Tectia implements the standard "none" MAC, meaning that no integrity checking is performed. This is intended only for testing.

 In Tectia's FIPS mode, *only* the hmac-sha1 MAC is supported.

OpenSSH also implements a nonstandard MAC algorithm, hmac-ripemd160@openssh.com. The name hmac-ripemd160 is also recognized without the @openssh.com suffix, but this is deprecated, since all nonstandard names are supposed to use a domain suffix. Tectia also supports some nonstandard MAC algorithms:

hmac-ripemd160@ssh.com
hmac-ripemd160-96@ssh.com
hmac-sha256@ssh.com
hmac-sha256-96@ssh.com
hmac-tiger128@ssh.com
hmac-tiger128-96@ssh.com
hmac-tiger160@ssh.com
hmac-tiger160-96@ssh.com
hmac-tiger192@ssh.com
hmac-tiger192-96@ssh.com
ssl3-md5@ssh.com
ssl3-sha1@ssh.com

Tectia recognizes special values for the Macs keyword to describe sets of algorithms:

AnyStd
> Any standard algorithm implemented by Tectia, including none

AnyStdMac
> Same as AnyStd, but excluding none

Any
> Any standard or nonstandard algorithm implemented by Tectia, including none

AnyMac
> Same as Any, but excluding none

MAC names encode the algorithm and parameters, as for cipher names. To demonstrate, let's decode a sample name: hmac-ripemd160-96@ssh.com:

hmac-

> Algorithms are prefixed by the name of the scheme that is used to combine a shared secret key with the contents of each packet. The most common is HMAC, the keyed hashing technique described by RFC-2104. Tectia also supports an early HMAC variant used by SSL Version 3, denoted by the prefix "ssl3-".

ripemd160

> The name of MAC hash algorithm is next, which often contains digits that indicate either a version (e.g., sha1 and md5) or the number of bits produced by the hash. [3.8.3] The names are translated to lowercase, and any hyphens are removed.

-96

> Some MAC algorithms have variants that truncate a larger message digest to a smaller number of bits. These are appended to the name, preceded by a hyphen.

@ssh.com

> A suffix is required by the IETF SECSH draft for nonstandard ciphers, describing the domain that defined the MAC algorithm, preceded by an @ character.

By default, Tectia allows algorithms in the `AnyStdMac` set. (The `Any` value includes *all* supported MAC algorithms, unlike the `Ciphers` keyword.) OpenSSH allows all its available MACs by default.

> Tectia also recognizes standard MAC names with the @ssh.com suffix. The suffix cannot be omitted for nonstandard MAC names, however, in contrast to the `Ciphers` keyword.
>
> It's best to use the suffix consistently according to the IETF SECSH draft, only for nonstandard names.

5.3.7   SSH Protocol Settings

OpenSSH lets you limit its protocol support to SSH-1, SSH-2, or both, using the `Protocol` keyword. Permissible values are 1 (for SSH-1), 2 (for SSH-2), or both 1 and 2 separated by a comma (the default):

```
# OpenSSH
Protocol 2,1
```

If you specify both protocols, the order doesn't matter since the client, not the server, drives the authentication process. And as we've said before, the SSH-1 protocol is less secure and we recommend avoiding it. [3.5]

5.3.7.1 Protocol version string

SSH servers and clients exchange protocol version information as part of their initial negotiations, to agree on a protocol. [3.4.4.2] You can see the protocol version string used by the server by connecting to the SSH port:

```
$ telnet localhost 22
Trying 127.0.0.1...
Connected to localhost.
Escape character is '^]'.
SSH-2.0-4.1.3.2 SSH Secure Shell
```

By default, Tectia servers use a string like "4.1.3.2 SSH Secure Shell" for the comment part (after the second hyphen) of the protocol version. This can be changed using the undocumented ProtocolVersionString keyword:

```
# Tectia
ProtocolVersionString Generic SSH Implementation
```

Port-scanning tools that connect to the SSH port and observe the protocol version string will not see the detailed information about the specific installed version of Tectia if the string is changed:

```
$ telnet localhost 22
Trying 127.0.0.1...
Connected to localhost.
Escape character is '^]'.
SSH-2.0-Generic SSH Implementation
```

> ProtocolVersionString changes only the comment part of the version string. The initial parts (e.g., SSH-2.0) always specify the protocol(s) that the server is willing to use, according to the SSH protocol standard.

Although an obscured ProtocolVersionString might thwart very simplistic port-scanning tools, in practice it doesn't help much, since many attacks try to exploit bugs regardless of the version string, and determined attackers can probably figure out the implementation by noticing specific behavioral quirks of the server anyway. If the Tectia server is configured to respond to UDP queries by *ssh-probe* [5.3.3.10], then it always will respond to such queries with the actual version information, not the changed ProtocolVersionString. Furthermore, changing ProtocolVersionString might prevent workarounds by clients for known server incompatibilities or bugs.

The OpenSSH server always uses a string like "OpenSSH_3.9p1" for its protocol version string. This cannot be changed except by modifying the source code.

5.3.8 Compression

The data flowing between the SSH client and server may optionally be compressed to save bandwidth. Often this option is set by the client [7.4.14], but OpenSSH gives the server the ultimate authority on whether data compression is permitted, using the `Compression` keyword:

```
# OpenSSH
Compression no
```

The default value is yes.

5.4   Authentication: Verifying Identities

A large part of the SSH server's job is to grant or deny connection requests from clients. This is done at two levels: *authentication* and *access control* (a.k.a. *authorization*). We discuss the former here and the latter in the section "Access Control: Letting People In." [5.5] Authentication, as we've seen, means verifying the identity of the user requesting a connection.

5.4.1   Authentication Syntax

sshd supports several different techniques for authentication that may be enabled or disabled. [3.1.3] [3.4.3] For example, if you don't trust password authentication, you can turn it off serverwide but still permit public-key authentication.

As SSH has evolved, the syntax for configuring authentication has changed several times, and OpenSSH and Tectia use entirely different syntaxes. In OpenSSH, different authentication techniques are turned on and off with keywords of the form:

```
<Name_Of_Technique>Authentication
```

For example, password authentication is controlled by the keyword `PasswordAuthentication`, public-key authentication by `PubKeyAuthentication`, and so forth, one keyword per technique. Values may be yes or no, as in:

```
# OpenSSH
PubKeyAuthentication yes
```

Table 5-1 lists all the authentication techniques supported by OpenSSH, and each is described in detail later.

Table 5-1. OpenSSH authentication keywords

Keyword	Meaning
`ChallengeResponseAuthentication`	One-time passwords.
`GSSAPIAuthentication`	Typically used for Kerberos.
`HostbasedAuthentication`	Host-based authentication.
`PasswordAuthentication`	Password authentication. Exactly what this means is determined by the `UsePAM` and `KerberosAuthentication` keywords.
`PubKeyAuthentication`	Public-key authentication.

Table 5-1. OpenSSH authentication keywords (continued)

Keyword	Meaning
RhostsRSAAuthentication	SSH-1 protocol only: avoid.
RSAAuthentication	SSH-1 protocol only: avoid.

Tectia has a more extensible syntax. Instead of creating a new keyword for each technique, you use only two keywords, `AllowedAuthentications` and `RequiredAuthentications`. Each is followed by the names of one or more authentication techniques, separated by commas. For example:

```
# Tectia
AllowedAuthentications password,hostbased,publickey
```

`AllowedAuthentications` means that *any* of the given techniques *can* be used. In contrast, `RequiredAuthentications` means that *all* of the listed techniques *must* be used. If both keywords are present, then `RequiredAuthentications` is used, and `AllowedAuthentications` is ignored.* Table 5-2 lists the supported values for these keywords. The first four techniques are specified by the IETF SECSH draft, while the ones with the @ssh.com suffix are nonstandard. It doesn't matter in what order you list the values because the SSH client, not the server, drives the authentication process. By default, Tectia's *sshd* allows only password and public-key authentication.

Table 5-2. Tectia authentication techniques for AllowedAuthentications and RequiredAuthentications

Value	Meaning
password	Password authentication.
publickey	Public-key authentication.
hostbased	Host-based authentication.
keyboard-interactive	Extensible, general-purpose, interactive authentication.
gssapi-with-mic	GSSAPI authentication with Message Integrity Code (MIC).
gssapi	GSSAPI authentication (deprecated in favor of `gssapi-with-mic`).
kerberos-2@ssh.com	Kerberos. Unsupported. Not available by default: requires recompilation.
kerberos-tgt-2@ssh.com	Kerberos authentication with TGT (passed to server). Unsupported. Not available by default: requires recompilation.
pam-1@ssh.com	Mostly obsolete: replaced by `keyboard-interactive`. Used only for old clients.
securid-1@ssh.com	Mostly obsolete: replaced by `keyboard-interactive`. Used only for old clients.

---

* This behavior, with `RequiredAuthentications` overriding `AllowedAuthentications`, began in Version 3.1.0 of Tectia's *sshd*. In previous versions, the two keywords were used together, but in practice this forced the two lists of techniques to be identical: a required technique must also be allowed, and an allowed technique that is not required is pointless, since it would be insufficient for authentication.

We now describe how to enable and disable each type of authentication except the deprecated SSH-1 keywords, which are in Appendix D.

5.4.2 Password Authentication

Password authentication accepts your login password as proof of identity. [3.4.3.5] OpenSSH allows or disallows password authentication with the `PasswordAuthentication` keyword, given the value yes (the default) or no:

```
# OpenSSH
PasswordAuthentication yes
```

Normally, OpenSSH password authentication requires your ordinary login password. However, this may be changed via PAM [5.4.8], Kerberos [5.4.7], or other features.

For Tectia, you can allow or require password authentication by adding the value password to the lists for `AllowedAuthentications` or `RequiredAuthentications`, respectively:

```
# Tectia
AllowedAuthentications password
```

5.4.2.1 Failed password attempts

Tectia servers wait two seconds by default after each failed password authentication attempt, to thwart brute-force password-guessing attacks. The `AuthInteractiveFailureTimeout` keyword controls this delay:

```
# Tectia
AuthInteractiveFailureTimeout 5
```

5.4.2.2 Empty passwords

If an account has an empty password, both the OpenSSH and Tectia servers may refuse access to the account. This feature is controlled by the keyword `PermitEmptyPasswords` with a value of yes (the default) or no. If enabled:

```
PermitEmptyPasswords yes
```

empty passwords are permissible; otherwise, they are not.

5.4.2.3 Expired passwords

Some operating systems support expiration dates for passwords. For those that do, OpenSSH and Tectia allow expired passwords to be changed during authentication.

If the OpenSSH server detects an expired password, it runs the system *passwd* command to change it once the user has logged in. It then closes the connection so that the user must log in again:

```
$ ssh -oPubKeyAuthentication=no -l smith server.example.com
smith@server.example.com's password:
```

```
Last login: Sat Jan 22 17:07:27 2005 from client.example.com
WARNING: Your password has expired.
You must change your password now and login again!
Changing local password for smith.
Old password:
New password:
Retype new password:
Connection to server.example.com closed.
```

For Tectia, by default, after the server verifies the user's password, if the password is found to be expired, then the system's password-change program (e.g., *passwd*) is run as a forced command. [8.2.3] An alternate password-change program (e.g., one that enforces policies for choosing good passwords) can be specified by the PasswdPath keyword:

```
# Tectia
PasswdPath /usr/local/bin/goodpasswd
```

The password-change program runs with the privileges of the user, not those of the server (typically root). Here's an example of a password change during authentication, from the client's perspective:

```
$ ssh server.example.com
rebecca's password: < ... old, expired password ... >
Authentication successful.
< ... the following output is from running the passwd forced command ... >
Changing password for user rebecca.
Changing password for rebecca
(current) UNIX password: < ... old, expired password, again ... >
New password: < ... new password ... >
Retype new password: < ... new password, again ... >
passwd: all authentication tokens updated successfully.
Connection to server.example.com closed.
```

We discuss more powerful alternatives to this technique in a later case study. [11.7.1]

5.4.3   Public-Key Authentication

Public-key authentication verifies a user's identity by cryptographic key. [2.4] In OpenSSH, public-key authentication is permitted or forbidden with the PubKeyAuthentication keyword which may have the value yes (the default) or no:*

```
#  OpenSSH
PubKeyAuthentication yes
```

For Tectia, you allow or require public-key authentication by adding the value publickey to the lists for AllowedAuthentications or RequiredAuthentications, respectively:

```
# Tectia
AllowedAuthentications publickey
```

---

* For SSH-1 protocol connections in OpenSSH, use the keyword RSAAuthentication instead.

Tectia provides keywords that restrict the minimum and maximum sizes for public keys:

```
# Tectia
AuthPublicKey.MinSize 1024
AuthPublicKey.MaxSize 2048
```

You might want to require a minimum key size for improved security, but reject huge keys because they slow down authentication. A value of zero (the default) disables the key-size checks.

Public-key authentication is marvelously configurable for most SSH implementations. See Chapter 8 for details on tailoring authentication for individual accounts.

5.4.4   Hostbased Authentication

Hostbased authentication verifies an SSH client's identity by checking the remote hostname and username associated with it. [3.4.3.6] This mimics the behavior of the insecure Berkeley r-commands (*rsh*, *rlogin*, *rcp*) which check the server files */etc/hosts.equiv* and *~/.rhosts* for permission to authenticate. SSH's hostbased authentication is more secure, however: instead of relying on a potentially compromised network naming service (e.g., DNS, NIS) and a privileged TCP source port, the SSH server uses secure, cryptographic tests of host keys to verify the client host's identity.

OpenSSH has the keyword HostbasedAuthentication (surprise!) to enable or disable this type of authentication:*

```
# OpenSSH
HostbasedAuthentication yes
```

For Tectia, you allow or require hostbased authentication by adding the value hostbased to the lists for AllowedAuthentications or RequiredAuthentications, respectively:

```
# Tectia
AllowedAuthentications hostbased
```

Hostbased authentication is useful but unfortunately also enables connections via the insecure r-commands, since it obeys the same permission files. To eliminate this potential security risk, use the SSH-specific files */etc/shosts.equiv* and *~/.shosts* instead of */etc/hosts.equiv* and *~/.rhosts*. In fact, we recommend you delete */etc/hosts.equiv* and forbid your users to create *~/.rhosts* files. (An even better approach is to disable the services for insecure protocols like the r-commands; these services are usually started by *inetd* or *xinetd*.)

You can also tell the SSH server to ignore all users' *.rhosts* and *.shosts* files with the keyword IgnoreRhosts. (This keyword does not impact the system files */etc/shosts.equiv*

---

* OpenSSH has another keyword, RhostsRSAAuthentication, that applies only to SSH-1 protocol connections.

and *etc/hosts.equiv*, however.) Permissible values are yes (to ignore them) or no (the default):

```
IgnoreRhosts yes
```

Ignoring users' files might be appropriate in an environment of centralized control, where only sysadmins are authorized to decide which hosts are trusted for authentication.

Tectia permits separate control over hostbased authentication for root. The keyword IgnoreRootRhosts permits or prevents use of the superuser's *.rhosts* and *.shosts* files, overriding IgnoreRhosts:

```
# Tectia
IgnoreRootRhosts yes
```

Values of yes (ignore the files) and no (don't ignore) are permitted. If not specified, the value of IgnoreRootRhosts defaults to that of IgnoreRhosts. For example, you can permit all *.rhosts* and *.shosts* files except root's:

```
# Tectia
IgnoreRhosts no
IgnoreRootRhosts yes
```

or ignore all *.rhosts* files except root's:

```
# Tectia
IgnoreRhosts yes
IgnoreRootRhosts no
```

Again, IgnoreRootRhosts doesn't stop the server from considering *etc/hosts.equiv* and *etc/shosts.equiv*. For stronger security, it's best to disable hostbased access entirely.

The SSH server needs the public keys of all hosts from which it accepts connections via hostbased authentication. These keys are kept in a single file, *etc/ssh/ssh_known_hosts* (for OpenSSH), or in separate files in the directory *etc/ssh2/knownhosts* (for Tectia). A host's public key is fetched from these locations whenever that host requests a connection. Optionally, the server also searches the file *~/.ssh/known_hosts* (for OpenSSH) or separate files in the directory *~/.ssh2/knownhosts* in the target user's account.

This optional feature (which is enabled by default) can be controlled with the keywords IgnoreUserKnownHosts (for OpenSSH):

```
# OpenSSH
IgnoreUserKnownHosts yes
```

or UserKnownHosts (for Tectia):

```
# Tectia
UserKnownHosts no
```

Having *sshd* consult the user's known hosts database might be unacceptable in a security-conscious environment. Since hostbased authentication relies on the integrity and correct administration of the client host, the system administrator usually grants hostbased authentication privileges to only a limited set of audited hosts. If the user's file is respected, however, a user can extend this trust to a possibly insecure remote host. An attacker can then:

- Compromise the insecure, remote host
- Impersonate the user on the remote host
- Access the user's local account via SSH, without needing a key passphrase or the local account password

Hostbased authentication can be complicated by other aspects of your server machine's environment, such as DNS, NIS, and the ordering of entries in static host files. It may also open new avenues for attack on a system. [3.4.3.6]

Tectia servers can require that the hostname provided by the client must match the one found in DNS, using the keyword HostbasedAuthForceClientHostnameDNSMatch:

```
# Tectia
HostbasedAuthForceClientHostnameDNSMatch yes
```

By default, no such check is performed, and in practice, this feature provides only a moderate level of protection against spoofing, since the DNS server(s) can still be attacked. [3.6.2]

5.4.5   Keyboard-Interactive Authentication

Keyboard-interactive authentication is an extensible, general-purpose mechanism for implementing a variety of authentication techniques that require interaction with the remote user, such as one-time passwords and challenge-response schemes. Clients must implement the keyboard-interactive protocol (described in an IETF SECSH draft, and tunneled securely over the SSH transport layer) but need no other modifications as new authentication techniques are added.

An example of a keyboard-interactive authentication technique is *one-time passwords*, found in systems like Bellcore's S/Key. "One-time" means that each time you authenticate, you provide a different password, helping to guard against attacks, since a captured password will likely be useless. Here's how it works:

1. When you connect to a remote service, it provides you with an integer and a string, called the *sequence number* and the *key*, respectively.
2. You enter the sequence number and key into an *S/Key calculator* program on your local machine.
3. You also enter a secret passphrase into the calculator, known only to yourself. This passphrase isn't transmitted over the network, only into the calculator on your local machine, so security is maintained.
4. Based on the three inputs you provided, the calculator produces your one-time password.
5. You enter the password to authenticate to the remote service.

More information on one-time passwords is available at:

http://www.ietf.org/html.charters/otp-charter.html

5.4.5.1   OpenSSH keyboard-interactive authentication

In OpenSSH, you enable keyboard-interactive authentication with the keyword
ChallengeResponseAuthentication:

```
# sshd_config
ChallengeResponseAuthentication yes
```

OpenSSH supports three challenge/response methods, called "devices," listed in
Table 5-3. Since these methods are dependent on external software, you have to configure OpenSSH at compile time to support them.

Table 5-3. OpenSSH keyboard-interactive (challenge/response) authentication methods

Method	Device name	Compilation option
BSD authentication	bsdauth	--with-bsd-auth
PAM	pam	--with-pam
S/Key	skey	--with-skey

PAM is widely available and hence often included in compiled OpenSSH packages.
Just make sure the server configuration keyword UsePAM is set: [5.4.8]

```
# OpenSSH
UsePAM yes
```

BSD authentication will likely be available only if running on a BSD platform (e.g.,
OpenBSD); see the manpage for *login.conf* for details on its operation. If you want
S/Key support, you have two options: obtain a PAM library that supports it, such as
libpam_opie or *libpam_skey*, or build OpenSSH yourself to get direct S/Key support. We recommend the PAM library approach.

In conducting keyboard-interactive authentication, the client by default specifies no
device, which means the server will try all. There's an undocumented client-side
option, KbdInteractiveDevices, however, whose value is the list of devices to try:

```
# OpenSSH
KbdInteractiveDevices pam,skey,bsdauth
```

5.4.5.2   Tectia's keyboard-interactive authentication

For Tectia, you can allow or require keyboard-interactive authentication by adding
the value keyboard-interactive to the lists for AllowedAuthentications or
RequiredAuthentications, respectively:

```
# Tectia
AllowedAuthentications keyboard-interactive
```

Tectia servers support the following keyboard-interactive authentication techniques:

password
> Standard password authentication [5.4.2]

pam
> Pluggable Authentication Modules [5.4.8]

securid
> SecurID hardware-based authentication

plugin
> Programmatic authentication [11.7.2]

Keyboard-interactive authentication techniques can be either optional or required (or both), and are specified using the keywords `AuthKbdInt.Optional` or `AuthKbdInt.Required`. Multiple authentication techniques are separated by commas:

```
# Tectia
AuthKbdInt.Optional pam,securid,password
AuthKbdInt.Required plugin,password
```

The order of the authentication techniques is not significant for either keyword, since the client drives the authentication process.

> Beware of typographic errors in the values of `AuthKbdInt.Optional` and `AuthKbdInt.Required`: they are not checked when the server reads them from configuration files. Invalid or unrecognized techniques are detected only when keyboard-interactive authentication is attempted, which can be long after the server starts.

Authentication succeeds if *all* of the required authentication techniques succeed, as well as a number of optional authentication techniques specified by the `AuthKbdInt.NumOptional` keyword:

```
# Tectia
AuthKbdInt.NumOptional 2
```

The default for `AuthKbdInt.NumOptional` is zero if there are any required authentication techniques, or one otherwise.

The `AuthKbdInt.Retries` keyword determines how many attempts are allowed for keyboard-interactive authentication:

```
# Tectia
AuthKbdInt.Retries 5
```

By default, three retries are allowed.

The Tectia server waits after each failed keyword-interactive authentication attempt, as for password authentication; the `AuthInteractiveFailureTimeout` keyword applies to this delay. [5.4.2.1]

The keyboard-interactive password authentication technique is functionally identical to standard password authentication. [5.4.2]

PAM authentication is supported by binary distributions of Tectia on systems that provide PAM (e.g., Linux, Solaris). On other systems, support for PAM requires recompiling the SSH server with the appropriate PAM headers and libraries. [5.4.8]

SecurID from Security Dynamics is a hardware-based authentication technique. Users need a physical card, called a SecurID card, in order to authenticate. The card contains a microchip that displays (on a little LCD) an integer that changes at regular intervals. To authenticate, provide this integer along with your password. Some versions of the SecurID card also have a keypad that supports entering a password, for two-factor authentication. Users must provide the current integer from their card in order to authenticate.

By default, Tectia allows three attempts to enter the SecurID password. This can be changed with the SecurIdGuesses keyword:

```
# Tectia
SecurIdGuesses 5
```

SecurID support is included in binary distributions of Tectia. The securid keyboard-interactive authentication technique mentioned previously refers to code incorporated into the server. Alternately, separate plugins called *ssh-securidv5-plugin* and *ssh-securidv4-plugin* are provided for different RSA ACE versions on some platforms.* In either case, recompiling the server or plugins requires special SecurID headers and libraries. SecurID must also be configured by setting the environment variable VAR_ACE to the pathname of the ACE data directory before the server is started: consult the SecurID documentation for details.

New authentication techniques can be added using keyboard-interactive plugins. If plugin is specified as either an optional or required keyboard-interactive authentication technique, then the AuthKbdInt.Plugin keyword must be used to identify a program that controls the interactive authentication steps:†

```
# Tectia
AuthKbdInt.Plugin /usr/local/sbin/ssh-keyboard-interactive-plugin
```

The server communicates with the plugin program using the Tectia plugin protocol, which we'll describe in a later case study. [11.7.2]

---

* If SecurID plugins are used, specify plugin instead of securid as the value of AuthKbdInt.Optional or AuthKbdInt.Required, and set AuthKbdInt.Plugin to the pathname for the appropriate plugin.

† If no plugin program is specified, or the specified program cannot be run, then keyboard-interactive plugin authentication will always fail.

5.4.6   PGP Authentication

Tectia can authenticate users via the PGP key. We cover this topic in Chapter 6. [6.5]

5.4.7   Kerberos Authentication

Kerberos, the well-known secure authentication system, can be used by OpenSSH and Tectia. We summarize the Kerberos-related configuration keywords here and defer a more detailed treatment of the topic. [11.4]

5.4.7.1   Kerberos and OpenSSH

Kerberos authentication is supported only if enabled at compile time by the configuration option --with-kerberos5. Assuming the SSH server was built in this manner, Kerberos authentication can be used in two ways: directly, and as a verifier for password authentication.

Direct Kerberos authentication is enabled by the GSSAPIAuthentication keyword:

```
# OpenSSH
GSSAPIAuthentication yes
```

This allows normal, ticket-based Kerberos user authentication: it requires that the usual service principal *host/server@REALM* be added to the Kerberos KDC, and that principal's key added to the server host *keytab*, usually */etc/krb5.keytab*. By default, the Kerberos principal *foo@REALM* will be allowed access to server account "foo"; you can allow others by adding them to *~foo/.k5login* (along with *foo@REALM* itself, which would otherwise lose access!). There is also the default:

```
# OpenSSH
GSSAPICleanupCredentials yes
```

which means *sshd* will delete a user's forwarded Kerberos credentials on logout; this is usually a good idea and should be left on. [11.5.2]

The second method, password verification, is indirect. It does not require any Kerberos support on the client at all: it simply means that for regular SSH password authentication, *sshd* will verify a user's password against Kerberos. This mode is enabled or disabled by the keyword KerberosAuthentication with the value yes or no:

```
# OpenSSH
KerberosAuthentication yes
```

Instead of checking against the local login password, *sshd* requests a Kerberos ticket-granting ticket (TGT) for the user and allows login if the ticket matches the password.* It also stores that TGT in the user's credentials cache, eliminating the need to do a separate *kinit*. Note that for technical reasons, the server also requires a service

---

* It also requires a successful granting of a host ticket for the local host as an antispoofing measure.

principal in this case, even though it might not seem necessary: there's an extra step involved that protects against a KDC spoofing attack.

If Kerberos fails to validate a password, the server optionally validates the same password by ordinary password authentication. This is convenient in an environment where not everyone uses Kerberos. To enable this option, use the keyword KerberosOrLocalPasswd with a value of yes; the default is no:

```
# OpenSSH
KerberosOrLocalPasswd yes
```

Finally, since password authentication via Kerberos may also result in stored Kerberos user credentials, there's a KerberosTicketCleanup keyword:

```
# OpenSSH
KerberosTicketCleanup yes
```

Similar to GSSAPICleanupCredentials, this has the server delete such credentials upon logout.

OpenSSH also used to support Kerberos TGT passing via the KerberosTgtPassing keyword, but at press time the support has been removed.

5.4.7.2 Kerberos and Tectia

Kerberos is used with Tectia via GSSAPI authentication. You can allow or require GSSAPI authentication by adding the value gssapi to the lists for AllowedAuthentications or RequiredAuthentications, respectively:

```
# Tectia
AllowedAuthentications gssapi
```

 GSSAPI authentication was added in Tectia Version 4.2. The older kerberos-2@ssh.com and kerberos-tgt-2@ssh.com authentication methods are still available if they were enabled when Tectia was configured, but they are unsupported.

The GSSAPI.AllowedMethods keyword specifies a list of allowed GSSAPI methods. Currently, only kerberos is supported:

```
# Tectia
GSSAPI.AllowedMethods kerberos
```

The kerberos GSSAPI method is allowed by default, so there is currently no reason to use the GSSAPI.AllowedMethods keyword, unless you want to be explicit.

Tectia's GSSAPI authentication attempts to use the MIC. If the keyword GSSAPI.AllowOldMethodWhichIsInsecure is enabled, then Tectia is willing to fall back to using GSSAPI without MIC:

```
# Tectia
GSSAPI.AllowOldMethodWhichIsInsecure yes
```

The default is yes, since GSSAPI with MIC is not yet widely supported. If the value no is used, then GSSAPI authentication requires MIC: another way to specify this is to use gssapi-with-mic instead of gssapi as the authentication method.

The GSSAPI.Dlls keyword identifies the location of the GSSAPI libraries, as a comma-separated list of full pathnames:

```
# Tectia
GSSAPI.Dlls /usr/local/gssapi/lib/libgssapi.so
```

By default, Tectia searches a list of common locations for the libraries, including:

*   */usr/lib/libgssapi_krb5.so*
*   */usr/lib/libkrb5.so*
*   */usr/lib/libgss.so*
*   */usr/local/gss/gl/mech_krb5.so*
*   */usr/local/lib/libgssapi_krb5.so*
*   */usr/local/lib/libkrb5.so*
*   */usr/kerberos/lib/libgssapi_krb5.so*
*   */usr/kerberos/lib/libkrb5.so*
*   */usr/lib/gss/libgssapi_krb5.so*

The *.so* suffix varies for different Unix platforms.

5.4.8   PAM Authentication

The Pluggable Authentication Modules system (PAM) by Sun Microsystems is an infrastructure for supporting multiple authentication methods; it's found on Solaris and most Linux systems. Ordinarily when a new authentication mechanism comes along, programs need to be rewritten to accommodate it. PAM eliminates this hassle. Programs are written to support PAM, and new authentication mechanisms may be plugged in at runtime without further source-code modification. More PAM information is found at:

http://www.sun.com/software/solaris/pam/

OpenSSH includes support for PAM, enabled with the UsePAM keyword, which defaults to no:

```
# OpenSSH
UsePAM yes
```

Tectia supports PAM as a keyboard-interactive authentication technique. [5.4.5]

5.4.9   Privilege Separation

OpenSSH supports privilege separation, a security feature that isolates the code that requires root privileges. [3.6.5] You can enable and disable it with the keyword UsePrivilegeSeparation with the value yes (the default) or no.

```
# OpenSSH
UsePrivilegeSeparation yes
```

5.4.10   Selecting a Login Program

Most Unix systems have a program called *login* for setting up a new user login process. It can be called by the *getty* process, for instance, when processing logins on a terminal line, or by a Telnet server. By default, OpenSSH does not use the system's *login* program. You can make it do so with the UseLogin keyword:

```
# OpenSSH
UseLogin yes
```

You might need to do this if your system has a *login* program that performs some specialized processing missing from OpenSSH. However, there are drawbacks to UseLogin yes:

* X forwarding is turned off, since *sshd* loses the chance to specially handle its *xauth* cookies for X authentication.

* Privilege separation is turned off after user authentication, in order to allow *login* to function correctly.

The behavior of a login program versus a login shell is entirely implementation- and operating-system-specific, so we won't cover the intricacies. If you need to muck about with UseLogin, you first need to understand the features of your operating system and your *login* program in detail.

5.5   Access Control: Letting People In

Serverwide access control permits or denies connections from particular hosts or Internet domains, or to specific user accounts on the server machine. It's applied separately from authentication: for example, even if a user's identity is legitimate, you might still want to reject connections from her computer. Similarly, if a particular computer or Internet domain has poor security policies, you might want to reject all SSH connection attempts from that domain.

SSH access control is scantily documented and has many subtleties and "gotchas." The configuration keywords look obvious in meaning, but they aren't. Our primary goal in this section is to illuminate the murky corners so that you can develop a correct and effective access-control configuration.

Keep in mind that SSH access to an account is permitted only if both the server and the account are configured to allow it. If a server accepts SSH connections to all accounts it serves, individual users may still deny connections to their accounts. [8.2] Likewise, if an account is configured to permit SSH access, the SSH server on its host can nonetheless forbid access. This two-level system applies to all SSH access control, so we won't state it repeatedly. Figure 5-2 summarizes the two-level access control system.*

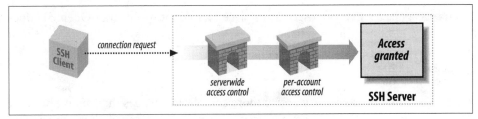

Figure 5-2. Access control levels

5.5.1   Account Access Control

Ordinarily, any account may receive SSH connections as long as it is set up correctly. This access may be overridden by the server keywords AllowUsers and DenyUsers. AllowUsers specifies that only a limited set of local accounts may receive SSH connections. For example, the line:

```
AllowUsers smith
```

permits the local smith account, and *only* the smith account, to receive SSH connections. The configuration file may have multiple AllowUsers lines:

```
AllowUsers smith
AllowUsers jones
AllowUsers oreilly
```

in which case the results are cumulative: the local accounts smith, jones, and oreilly, and only those accounts, may receive SSH connections. The SSH server maintains a list of all AllowUsers values, and when a connection request arrives, it does a string comparison (really a pattern match, as we'll see in a moment) against the list. If a match occurs, the connection is permitted; otherwise, it's rejected.

 A single AllowUsers keyword in the configuration file cuts off SSH access for all other accounts not mentioned. If the configuration file has no AllowUsers keywords, the server's AllowUsers list is empty, and connections are permissible to all accounts.

---

* This concept is true for the configuration keywords discussed in this section but not for hostbased control files, e.g., ~/.rhosts and /etc/hosts.equiv. Each of these may in fact override the other. [3.4.3.6]

`DenyUsers` is the opposite of `AllowUsers`: it shuts off SSH access to particular accounts. For example:

```
DenyUsers smith
```

states that the smith account may not receive SSH connections. `DenyUsers` keywords may appear multiple times, just like `AllowUsers`, and the effects are again cumulative. As for `AllowUsers`, the server maintains a list of all `DenyUsers` values and compares incoming connection requests against them.

Tectia recognizes numerical user IDs in place of account names (but OpenSSH does not):

```
# Tectia
AllowUsers 123
DenyUsers 456
```

Both `AllowUsers` and `DenyUsers` accept more complicated values than simple account names. An interesting but potentially confusing syntax is to specify both an account name and a hostname (or numeric IP address), separated by an @ symbol:

```
AllowUsers jones@example.com
```

Despite its appearance, this string isn't an email address, and it doesn't mean "the user jones on the machine *example.com*." Rather, it describes a relationship between a *local* account, jones, and a *remote* client machine, *example.com*. The meaning is: "clients on *example.com* may connect to the server's jones account." Although this meaning is surprising, it would be even stranger if jones were a remote account, since the SSH server has no way to verify account names on remote client machines (except when using hostbased authentication).

For OpenSSH, wildcard characters are acceptable in `AllowUsers` and `DenyUsers` arguments. The ? symbol represents any single character except @, and the * represents any sequence of characters, again not including @. For Tectia, the patterns use the regular-expression syntax that is specified by the `REGEX-SYNTAX` metaconfiguration parameter; see Appendix B.*

 The default *egrep* regex syntax used by Tectia treats "." as a wildcard that matches any character, so a hostname pattern like *example.com* will also match unqualified hostnames like *examplexcom*. If you are using the *egrep* regex syntax, be sure to escape literal "." characters in hostnames, IP addresses, etc., with a backslash character:

```
# Tectia (egrep regex syntax)
AllowUsers jones@example\.com
```

Alternatively, use the `zsh_fileglob` or traditional regex syntax, which treats "." characters literally. See Appendix B for more detailed information about the different regex syntaxes supported by Tectia.

---

* Our general discussion of metaconfiguration might also be of help. [11.6.1]

Here are some examples. SSH connections are permitted only to accounts with five-character names ending in "mith":

```
# OpenSSH, and Tectia with zsh_fileglob or traditional regex syntax
AllowUsers ?mith

# Tectia with egrep regex syntax
AllowUsers .mith
```

SSH connections are permitted only to accounts with names beginning with the letter "s", coming from hosts whose names end in ".edu":

```
# OpenSSH, and Tectia with zsh_fileglob or traditional regex syntax
AllowUsers s*@*.edu

# Tectia with egrep regex syntax
AllowUsers s.*@.*\.edu
```

Tectia connections are permitted only to account names of the form "testN" where N is a number, e.g., "test123".

```
# Tectia with zsh_fileglob or traditional regex syntax
AllowUsers test[[:digit:]]##

# Tectia with egrep regex syntax
AllowUsers test[[:digit:]]+
```

Tectia connections are permitted only to accounts with numerical user IDs in the range 3000–6999:

```
# Tectia with zsh_fileglob or traditional regex syntax
AllowUsers [3-6][[:digit:]][[:digit:]][[:digit:]]

# Tectia with egrep regex syntax
AllowUsers [3-6][[:digit:]]{3}
```

IP addresses can be used instead of hostnames. For example, to allow access to any user from the network 10.1.1.0/24:[*]

```
# OpenSSH, and Tectia with zsh_fileglob or traditional regex syntax
AllowUsers *@10.1.1.*
# Tectia  with egrep regex syntax
AllowUsers .*@10\.1\.1\..*
```

Tectia also recognizes netmasks preceded by the \m prefix:

```
# Tectia with zsh_fileglob or traditional regex syntax
AllowUsers *@\m10.1.1.0/28

# Tectia with egrep regex syntax
AllowUsers .*@\m10.1.1.0/28
```

---

[*] In this notation, the mask specifies the number of 1 bits in the most-significant portion of the netmask. You might be more familiar with the older, equivalent notation giving the entire netmask, e.g., 10.1.1.0/255.255.255.0.

Wildcards and regular-expression metacharacters are not used in netmasks, so netmasks are independent of the regex syntax, and "." characters are not escaped with backslashes as usual for the *egrep* regex syntax. Netmasks are always interpreted IP address ranges, without hostname lookups, so \mexample.com/28 does not work.

Netmasks are often more concise than other patterns for expressing IP address ranges, especially those that don't coincide with an octet boundary. For example, 10.1.1.0/28 is equivalent to the range of addresses 10.1.1.0 through 10.1.1.15, which is expressed as:

```
# Tectia with zsh_fileglob or traditional regex syntax
AllowUsers *@10.1.1.([[:digit:]]|1[0-5])

# Tectia with egrep regex syntax
AllowUsers .*@10\.1\.1\.([[:digit:]]|1[0-5])
```

The specification of address ranges is even more of a struggle using OpenSSH's limited wildcards, and it is frequently necessary to enumerate individual addresses:

```
# OpenSSH
AllowUsers *@10.1.1.?
AllowUsers *@10.1.1.10 *@10.1.1.11 *@10.1.1.12 *@10.1.1.13 *@10.1.1.14 *@10.1.1.15
```

By default, a reverse lookup is first attempted to convert the client's IP address to a canonical hostname, and if the lookup succeeds, then the hostname is used for pattern matches. Next, the IP address is checked using the same patterns.

Access control using IP addresses can avoid some attacks on hostname lookup mechanisms, such as compromised nameservers, but we need to be careful. For example, our previous example that intended to limit access to the network 10.1.1.0/24 would actually also allow connections from a machine on some remote network named 10.1.1. evil.org!

Tectia provides several ways to fix this. We can use a more precise pattern that matches only digits, to reject arbitrary domains like *evil.org*.

```
# Tectia with zsh_fileglob or traditional regex syntax
AllowUsers *@10.1.1.[[:digit:]]##

# Tectia with egrep regex syntax
AllowUsers .*@10\.1\.1\.[[:digit:]]+
```

An even better approach is to add the \i prefix to force the pattern to be interpreted only as an IP address. This avoids the hostname lookup entirely, and allows us to use simpler patterns safely:

```
# Tectia with zsh_fileglob or traditional regex syntax
AllowUsers *@\i10.1.1.*

# Tectia with egrep regex syntax
AllowUsers .*@\i10\.1\.1\..*
```

Even this isn't foolproof: source IP addresses can be easily spoofed. Address-based access controls are most appropriate for trusted internal networks protected by an external firewall.

Tectia allows some control of the hostname lookups performed for all of the access control patterns. To disable hostname lookups completely, use the Resolve-ClientHostName keyword:

```
# Tectia
ResolveClientHostName no
```

This is appropriate if only IP address matching is desired. It can also be useful if hostname lookups would cause unnecessary delays, e.g., if some nameservers aren't available.

Conversely, to insist that hostname lookups must succeed, rejecting connections instead of resorting to IP address matching whenever the hostname lookups fail, use the RequireReverseMapping keyword:

```
# Tectia
RequireReverseMapping yes
```

This is appropriate if only hostname address matching is desired. It also provides some limited protection against connections from unrecognized machines.

Of course, hostname lookups should not be disabled by ResolveClientHostName if they are forced by RequireReverseMapping.

Keep in mind that hostname-based access controls are even more inherently weak restrictions than address-based controls, and both should be used only as an adjunct to other strong authentication methods.

Multiple strings may appear on a single AllowUsers line, but the syntax differs for OpenSSH and Tectia. OpenSSH separates strings with whitespace:

```
# OpenSSH
AllowUsers smith jones
```

and Tectia separates them with commas:

```
# Tectia
AllowUsers smith,jones
AllowUsers rebecca, katie, sarah   Whitespace after commas is undocumented but works
```

 Commas must be escaped with backslashes within regular expressions, to prevent misinterpretation as list separators. For example, to allow access by usernames that begin with "elf" and are followed by one to three digits, plus elvis:

```
# Tectia with egrep regex syntax
AllowUsers elf[[:digit:]]{1\,3},elvis
```

AllowUsers and DenyUsers may be combined effectively. Suppose you're teaching a course and want your students to be the only users with SSH access to your server. It happens that only student usernames begin with "stu", so you specify:

```
# OpenSSH, and Tectia with zsh_fileglob or traditional regex syntax
AllowUsers stu*

# Tectia with egrep regex syntax
AllowUsers stu.*
```

Later, one of your students, stu563, drops the course, so you want to disable her SSH access. Simply add the following to the configuration:

```
DenyUsers stu563
```

Hmm...this seems strange. The AllowUsers and DenyUsers lines appear to conflict because the first permits stu563 but the second rejects it. The server handles this in the following way: if any line prevents access to an account, the account can't be accessed. So, in the preceding example, stu563 is denied access by the second line.

Consider another example with this AllowUsers line:

```
# OpenSSH, Tectia
AllowUsers smith
```

followed by a DenyUsers line (appropriate to your SSH implementation):

```
# OpenSSH, Tectia with zsh_fileglob or traditional regex syntax
DenyUsers s*

# Tectia with egrep regex syntax
DenyUsers s.*
```

The pair of lines permits SSH connections to the smith account but denies connections to any account beginning with "s". What does the server do with this clear contradiction? It rejects connections to the smith account, following the same rule: if any restriction prevents access, such as the DenyUsers line shown, access is denied. Access is granted only if there are no restrictions against it.

Finally, here is a useful configuration example:

```
# OpenSSH
AllowUsers walrus@* carpenter@* *@*.beach.net

# Tectia with zsh_fileglob or traditional regex syntax
AllowUsers walrus@*,carpenter@*,*@*.beach.net

# Tectia with egrep regex syntax
AllowUsers walrus@.*,carpenter@.*,.*@.*\.beach\.net
```

This restricts access for most accounts to connections originating inside the domain *beach.net*—except for the accounts walrus and carpenter, which may be accessed from anywhere. The hostname qualifiers following walrus and carpenter aren't strictly necessary but help make clear the intent of the line.

5.5.1.1 Restricting all logins

AllowUsers and DenyUsers operate on individual accounts, but you can also deny access to all users in a pinch. If the file */etc/nologin* exists, *sshd* allows only root to log in; no other accounts are allowed access. Thus, *touch /etc/nologin* is a quick way to restrict access to the system administrator only, without having to reconfigure or shut down SSH.

Tectia also checks */etc/nologin_<hostname>*, where *<hostname>* should match the output from the *hostname* command. This is useful if the */etc* directory is shared among several machines in a cluster.

5.5.2   Group Access Control

sshd may permit or deny SSH access to all accounts in a Unix group on the server machine. The keywords AllowGroups and DenyGroups serve this purpose:

```
AllowGroups faculty
DenyGroups students
```

These keywords operate much like AllowUsers and DenyUsers. OpenSSH accepts the wildcards * and ? within group names, and separates multiple groups with whitespace. Tectia accepts patterns according to the regular-expression syntax determined by the metaconfiguration information [11.6.1], and separates groups with commas:

```
# OpenSSH
AllowGroups good* better
DenyGroups bad* worse

# Tectia with zsh_fileglob or traditional regex syntax
AllowGroups good*,better
DenyGroups bad*, worse

# Tectia with egrep regex syntax
AllowGroups good.*,better
DenyGroups bad.*, worse
```

Tectia recognizes numerical group IDs as well (but OpenSSH does not):

```
# Tectia
AllowGroups 513
DenyGroups 781
```

By default, access is allowed to all groups. If any AllowGroups keyword appears, access is permitted only to the groups specified (and may be further restricted with DenyGroups).

These directives apply to both the primary group (typically listed in */etc/passwd* or the corresponding NIS map) and all supplementary groups (in */etc/group* or an NIS map). If a user is a member of any group that matches a pattern listed by AllowGroups or DenyGroups, then access is restricted accordingly.

Group access control is often more convenient than restricting specific users, since group memberships can be changed without updating the configuration of the SSH server.

AllowGroups and DenyGroups do not accept hostname qualifiers, however, in contrast to AllowUsers and DenyUsers. This is a surprising and unfortunate inconsistency: if hostname (or IP address) restrictions are useful for controlling access by specific users, then those same restrictions could be even more useful for controling access for entire groups.

As was the case for AllowUsers and DenyUsers, conflicts are resolved in the most restrictive way. If any AllowGroups or DenyGroups line prevents access to a given group, access is denied to that group even if another line appears to permit it.

5.5.3   Hostname Access Control

We've described previously how to use hostname qualifiers with AllowUsers and DenyUsers. [5.5.1] For the common case when you don't need to restrict username, Tectia provides the keywords AllowHosts and DenyHosts to restrict access by hostname (or IP address) more concisely, without wildcards to match usernames:[*]

```
# Tectia with zsh_fileglob or traditional regex syntax
AllowHosts good.example.com,\i10.1.2.3
DenyHosts bad.example.com, \m10.1.1.0/24

# Tectia with egrep regex syntax
AllowHosts good\.example\.com,\i10\.1\.2\.3
DenyHosts bad\.example\.com, \m10.1.1.0/24
```

As with AllowUsers and DenyUsers:

- Patterns are interpreted according to the regular-expression syntax determined by the metaconfiguration information (Appendix B).
- Values may contain multiple strings separated by commas, plus optional whitespace.
- Keywords may appear multiple times in the configuration file, and the results are cumulative.
- Hostnames or IP addresses may be used, with optional \i or \m prefixes.
- By default, access is allowed to all hosts, and if any AllowHosts keyword appears, access is permitted only to the hosts specified (and may be further restricted with DenyHosts).

---

[*] Finer-grained control is provided by the from option in *authorized_keys*. [8.2.4] Each public key may be tagged with a list of acceptable hosts that may connect via that key.

You can also make `AllowHosts` and `DenyHosts` do reverse DNS lookups (or not) with the `RequireReverseMapping` keyword, providing a value of yes or no:

```
# Tectia
RequireReverseMapping yes
```

5.5.4   shosts Access Control

`AllowHosts` and `DenyHosts` offer total hostname-based access control, regardless of the type of authentication requested. A similar but less restrictive access control is specific to hostbased authentication. The Tectia server can deny access to hosts that are named in *.rhosts*, *.shosts*, */etc/hosts.equiv*, and */etc/shosts.equiv* files. This is accomplished with the keywords `AllowSHosts` and `DenySHosts`:[*]

For example, the line:

```
# Tectia with zsh_fileglob or traditional regex syntax
DenySHosts *.badguy.com
```

```
# Tectia with egrep regex syntax
DenySHosts .*\.badguy\.com
```

forbids access by connections from hosts in the *badguy.com* domain, but only when hostbased authentication is being attempted. Likewise, `AllowSHosts` permits access only to given hosts when hostbased authentication is used. Values follow the same syntax as for `AllowHosts` and `DenyHosts`. As a result, system administrators can override values in users' *.rhosts* and *.shosts* files (which is good, because this can't be done via the */etc/hosts.equiv* or */etc/shosts.equiv* files).

`AllowSHosts` and `DenySHosts` have caveats similar to those of `AllowHosts` and `DenyHosts`:

- Patterns are interpreted according to the regular-expression syntax determined by the metaconfiguration information (Appendix B).
- Values may contain multiple patterns separated by commas, plus optional whitespace.
- Keywords may appear multiple times in the configuration file, and the results are cumulative.
- Hostnames or IP addresses may be used, with optional \i or \m prefixes.
- By default, access is allowed to all hosts, and if any `AllowSHosts` keyword appears, access is permitted only to the hosts specified (and may be further restricted with `DenySHosts`).

---

[*] Even though the keywords have "SHosts" in their names, they apply also to *.rhosts* and */etc/hosts.equiv* files.

5.5.5   Root Access Control

sshd has a separate access-control mechanism for the superuser. The keyword PermitRootLogin allows or denies access to the root account by SSH:

```
PermitRootLogin no
```

Permissible values for this keyword are yes (the default) to allow access to the root account by SSH; no to deny all such access; and without-password (OpenSSH) or nopwd (Tectia) to allow access except by password authentication.

In addition, OpenSSH recognizes the value forced-commands-only to allow access only for forced commands specified in *authorized_keys* [8.2.3]; Tectia always allows such access for all values of PermitRootLogin. OpenSSH's level of control is useful, for example, if root's *authorized_keys* file contains a line beginning with:

```
command="/bin/dump" ....
```

Then the root account may be accessed by SSH to run the *dump* command. This capability lets remote clients run superuser processes, such as backups or filesystem checks, but not unrestricted login sessions.

The server checks PermitRootLogin after authentication is complete. In other words, if PermitRootLogin is no, a client is offered the opportunity to authenticate (e.g., is prompted for a password or passphrase) but is shut down afterward regardless.

We've previously seen a similar keyword, IgnoreRootRhosts, that controls access to the root account by hostbased authentication. [5.4.4] It prevents entries in *~root/.rhosts* and *~root/.shosts* from being used to authenticate root. Because *sshd* checks PermitRootLogin after authentication is complete, it overrides any value of IgnoreRootRhosts. Table 5-4 illustrates the interaction of these two keywords.

Table 5-4. Can root log in?

	IgnoreRootRhosts yes	IgnoreRootRhosts no
PermitRootLogin yes	Yes, except by hostbased	Yes
PermitRootLogin no	No	No
PermitRootLogin without-password (OpenSSH); PermitRootLogin nopwd (Tectia)	Yes, except by hostbased or password	Yes, except by password

5.5.6   External Access Control

Tectia allows access control (authorization) decisions to be made by an external program, which is identified by the ExternalAuthorizationProgram keyword:[*]

```
# Tectia
ExternalAuthorizationProgram /usr/local/sbin/ssh-external-authorization-program
```

---

[*] If the specified program cannot be run, then access is denied.

The program can be used to implement arbitrary access control logic, extending the mechanisms that are supported directly by the Tectia server.* The server communicates with the program using the Tectia plugin protocol, and we'll go into more detail in a later case study. [11.7.3]

 The external authorization program can only veto access controls applied by other keywords in the server's configuration. This follows the same policy that we have seen earlier: conflicts are always resolved using the most restrictive interpretation.

5.5.7 Restricting Directory Access with chroot

The Unix system call chroot causes a process (and any subprocesses) to treat a given directory as the root directory. After chroot, absolute filenames beginning with "/" actually refer to subdirectories of the given directory. Access is effectively restricted to the given directory, because it is impossible to name files outside. This is useful for restricting a user or process to a subset of a filesystem for security reasons.

Tectia provides two keywords for imposing this restriction on incoming SSH clients. ChRootUsers specifies that SSH clients, when accessing a given account, are restricted to the account's home directory and its subdirectories:

```
# Tectia
ChRootUsers guest
```

Values for ChRootUsers use the same syntax as for AllowUsers: [5.5.1]

```
# Tectia with zsh_fileglob or traditional regex syntax
ChRootUsers guest*,backup,300[[:digit:]],visitor@*.friendly.org

# Tectia with egrep regex syntax
ChRootUsers guest.*,backup,300[[:digit:]],visitor@.*\.friendly\.org
```

The other keyword, ChRootGroups, works similarly but applies to all accounts that belong to a group that matches any of the specified patterns:

```
# Tectia
ChRootGroups guest[a-z],ops,999[[:digit:]]
```

Values for ChRootGroups use the same syntax as for AllowGroups. [5.5.2]

ChRootUsers and ChRootGroups can be specified multiple times in configuration files; the values are accumulated into a single list for each keyword. Each account that matches a pattern from either ChRootUsers or ChRootGroups is individually restricted when accessed via Tectia.

---

* The external authorization program is similar in function to a keyboard-interactive plugin that is used for authentication, except that access control does not need interaction with the remote user, because the user has already authenticated successfully before the program is run.

Files Used by the Tectia Server After chroot

After chroot, the Tectia server needs only minimal access to files. All its configuration files (and subconfiguration files, if any) have already been read, and all authentication and authorization steps completed, before chroot is done. The server therefore needn't access devices, shared libraries, system configuration files, etc., used during these earlier operations. The only files accessed after chroot are related to starting a user session:

- Setting up the environment: [5.6.2]

  /etc/environment
  $HOME/.ssh2/environment

- The user *rc* file(s) [5.6.3], plus any programs and files used by the scripts:

  $HOME/.ssh2/rc
  /etc/ssh2/sshrc (if *$HOME/.ssh2/rc* doesn't exist)

- X authentication, if no user *rc* files are found [9.4.5.2], plus any shared libraries, files, etc., used by *xauth*:

  /usr/X11R6/bin/xauth (or a similar location, possibly determined by XauthPath)

- Suppressing login messages: [5.6.1]

  $HOME/.hushlogin

- Message of the day: [5.6.1]

  /etc/motd

- Checking for mail: [5.6.1]

  /var/spool/mail/$USER (or a similar location)

In most cases, accounts using chroot are heavily restricted and wouldn't use these features anyway, so this is rarely a problem.

Sometimes the Tectia server uses the original pathname from the *passwd* database for *$HOME* after chroot, even though it really should use "/" instead. This can be fixed by a symbolic link in the user's home directory (after any necessary parent directories are created):

```
$ mkdir -p "$HOME$HOME"
$ rmdir    "$HOME$HOME"
$ ln -s  / "$HOME$HOME"
```

If, for example, $HOME is */home/elvis* according to the *passwd* database, then this sets up a symbolic link:

```
/home/elvis/home/elvis -> /
```

After chroot("/home/elvis"), the symbolic link will cause the original */home/elvis* pathname to be equivalent to the new root directory, as it should be. Crude but effective!

To make chroot functionality work, all system files used by any programs run via the Tectia server must be copied into the home directory for each restricted account.

Such files can include special device files like */dev/null* or */dev/zero*, shared libraries from */lib* or */usr/lib*, configuration files like */etc/termcap*, etc.

The permissions for the copied system files (and the directories in which they live) need to be carefully controlled. Typically they should *not* be writable by the owner of the restricted account.

Discovering all of the system files needed for all of the programs used by an account can be challenging, and may require considerable experimentation and debugging: tools that monitor filesystem usage (like *lsof*, *strace*, and *ldd*) can help.* Dependencies on shared libraries can be eliminated by statically linking the programs.

Maintenance costs for restricted accounts are minimized if the accounts are further restricted to run only a very limited set of carefully controlled commands. The login shell is typically set to a special-purpose program, or access is allowed only to a collection of forced commands. [8.2.3]

5.5.8 Summary of Authentication and Access Control

SSH provides several ways to permit or restrict connections to particular accounts or from particular hosts. Tables 5-5 and 5-6 summarize the available options.

Table 5-5. OpenSSH summary of authentication and access control

If you are...	And you want to allow or restrict...	Then use...
User	Connections to your account by public-key authentication	*authorized_keys* [8.2.1]
Administrator	Connections to an account	AllowUsers, DenyUsers
User	Connections by a host	from option in *authorized_keys* [8.2.4.1]
Administrator	Connections by a host	AllowUsers, DenyUsers
User	Connections to your account by host-based authentication	*.shosts*
Administrator	Hostbased authentication	HostbasedAuthentication, IgnoreRhosts
Administrator	Root logins	PermitRootLogin

Table 5-6. Tectia summary of authentication and access control

If you are...	And you want to allow or restrict...	Then use...
User	Connections to your account by public-key authentication	*authorization* file [8.2.2]
Administrator	Connections to an account	AllowUsers, DenyUsers
User	Connections by a host	allow-from, deny-from options in the *authorization* file [8.2.4.2]

---

* We discuss this in more detail in our other O'Reilly book, *Linux Security Cookbook*.

Table 5-6. Tectia summary of authentication and access control (continued)

If you are...	And you want to allow or restrict...	Then use...
Administrator	Connections by a host	AllowHosts, DenyHosts (or AllowUsers, DenyUsers)
User	Connections to your account by hostbased authentication	*.shosts*
Administrator	Hostbased authentication	AllowedAuthentications, AllowSHosts, DenySHosts, IgnoreRhosts
Administrator	Root logins	PermitRootLogin, IgnoreRootRhosts

5.6   User Logins and Accounts

When a login occurs, the SSH server can take special actions. Here, we discuss:

- Printing welcome messages for the user
- Setting environment variables
- Taking arbitrary actions with initialization scripts

5.6.1   Welcome Messages for the User

sshd can display custom messages for the user before and after authentication. Before authentication, the SSH server can optionally display the contents of any file you select with the Banner keyword (OpenSSH) or BannerMessageFile keyword (Tectia):

```
# OpenSSH
Banner /usr/local/etc/warning.txt

# Tectia
BannerMessageFile  /usr/local/etc/warning.txt
```

By default, OpenSSH displays no banner message, whereas Tectia displays the contents of */etc/ssh2/ssh_banner_message* if the file exists.* The banner message is often used for legal statements that forbid unauthorized access. Since the file is sent before authentication, be careful that it doesn't reveal sensitive information.

After authentication, both OpenSSH's and Tectia's *sshd* optionally prints the standard Unix "message of the day" file (*/etc/motd*). This output may be turned on and off with the PrintMotd keyword with the value yes (the default) or no:

```
PrintMotd no
```

Since most Unix shells print */etc/motd* on login, this SSH feature is often redundant and turned off.

---

* SSH clients are not required (by the SSH-2 protocol) to display the message.

For Tectia, a message about email (e.g., "You have mail") is printed on login if the CheckMail keyword has the value of yes (the default), or the message is skipped if the value is no:

```
# Tectia
CheckMail yes
```

In OpenSSH, the last login time is also printed if the PrintLastLog keyword has the value of yes (the default), or the message is skipped if the value is no:

```
# OpenSSH
PrintLastLog yes
```

Tectia has no separate keyword to control printing the last login time—it's always printed, if available.

The SSH server also obeys the Unix hushlogin convention, which allows each user to control whether these welcome messages are printed. If the file *~/.hushlogin* exists, then the message of the day, the mail notification message (for Tectia), and the last login time are all omitted.

5.6.2   Setting Environment Variables

As we'll see later, SSH clients have several ways to set environment variables in the server before the login shell is invoked,* such as the *environment* file [7.1.3], the SendEnv (OpenSSH) or SetRemoteEnv (Tectia) configuration keywords [7.4.4.3], and the environment option in the *authorized_keys* (OpenSSH) or *authorization* (Tectia) file [8.2.5]. However, these changes happen only with the server's permission; otherwise, SSH clients could circumvent server security policies.

The OpenSSH server grants or denies permission for clients to modify the environment in this manner, using the PermitUserEnvironment and AcceptEnv keywords. PermitUserEnvironment controls whether the server pays attention to the user's *~/.ssh/environment* file and *authorized_keys* files, with a value of yes or no (the default):

```
# OpenSSH
PermitUserEnvironment yes
```

AcceptEnv controls how the server accepts or rejects environment variables that are sent from the SSH client according to the SendEnv (OpenSSH) or SetRemoteEnv (Tectia) keywords. Normally the SSH server pays no attention to such environment variables, but you can use the AcceptEnv keyword to allow specific variables to be copied, with their values, into SSH sessions on the server machine.

The AcceptEnv keyword lists the environment variables that are accepted, either separated by whitespace or specified by multiple keywords. Wildcard characters * and ? will match classes of environment variables.

* And also before the user *rc* script, *~/.ssh/rc* (OpenSSH) or *~/.ssh2/rc* (Tectia). [5.6.3]

```
# OpenSSH
AcceptEnv LANG LC_*
AcceptEnv PATH TERM TZ
```

Likewise, the Tectia SSH server permits or denies permission for clients to modify the environment prior to login. Its `SettableEnvironmentVars` keyword lists environment variables that can be set by any of the methods, separated by commas (and optional whitespace), or specified by multiple keywords. The environment variables are matched against patterns. [11.6.1]

```
# Tectia
SettableEnvironmentVars LANG,LC_(ALL|COLLATE|CTYPE|MONETARY|NUMERIC|TIME)
SettableEnvironmentVars PATH, TERM, TZ
```

The `SettableEnvironmentVars` keyword applies only to user-configurable environment variables. Files like */etc/environment* controlled by the server administrator are not affected.

In all these cases, users are still free to set any environment variables after their login shells are invoked. The restrictions apply only to the mechanisms for initializing the environment of the login shell.

5.6.3   Initialization Scripts

When a user logs in, her Unix shell runs one or more initialization scripts, such as */etc/ profile*. In addition, *sshd* runs the script */etc/ssh/sshrc* (OpenSSH) or */etc/ssh2/sshrc* (Tectia) for each SSH-based login. This feature lets the system administrator run special commands for SSH logins that don't occur for ordinary logins. For example, you can do some additional logging of SSH connections, print welcome messages for SSH users only, etc.

The */etc/ssh/sshrc* or */etc/ssh2/sshrc* script is always processed by the Bourne shell (*/bin/ sh*), rather than the user's shell, so it can run reliably for all accounts regardless of their various shells. It is run for logins (e.g., *ssh my-host*) and remote commands (*ssh my-host /bin/who*), just before the user's shell or command is invoked but after environment variables are initialized. The script runs in a separate shell, which exits after the script finishes, so it cannot initialize environment variables for the session. The script runs under the target account's uid, so it can't take privileged actions. If the script exits due to an error (say, a syntax error), the SSH session continues normally.

Note that this file is run as input to the Bourne shell: *sshd* runs */bin/sh /etc/ssh/sshrc*, not */bin/sh –c /etc/ssh/sshrc*. This means that it can't be an arbitrary program; it must be a file containing Bourne-shell commands (and it doesn't need the execute mode bit set).

/etc/ssh/sshrc or */etc/ssh2/sshrc* operates machinewide: it is run for every incoming SSH connection. For more fine-grained control, users may create the script *~/.ssh/ rc* (OpenSSH) or *~/.ssh2/rc* (Tectia) to be run instead of the machinewide script */etc/ssh/sshrc* or */etc/ssh2/sshrc*, respectively. [8.4] The machinewide script isn't executed if the user-specific script exists in the target account, but a user script can run the machinewide script directly. OpenSSH always runs *~/.ssh/rc* using the

Bourne shell (like */etc/ssh/sshrc*), but Tectia runs *~/.ssh2/rc* using each user's shell (in contrast to */etc/ssh2/sshrc*). OpenSSH ignores user scripts if a subsystem is used, but Tectia does not. [5.8]

Note that SSH *rc* files interact with X authentication. [9.4.5.2]

5.7   Forwarding

Forwarding (or tunneling) is the use of SSH to protect another network service. We discuss it in detail in Chapter 9, but here we describe the available serverwide configuration options.

5.7.1   Port Forwarding

SSH's forwarding (or tunneling) features protect other TCP/IP-based applications by encrypting their connections. We cover forwarding in great detail in Chapter 9, but we introduce here the serverwide configuration keywords for controlling it.

TCP port forwarding can be enabled or disabled by the keyword `AllowTcpForwarding`, with the value yes (the default) or no:

```
AllowTcpForwarding no
```

Tectia can specify this more selectively for particular users or Unix groups, with the keywords `AllowTcpForwardingForUsers`, `AllowTcpForwardingForGroups`, `DenyTcp-ForwardingForUsers`, and `DenyTcpForwardingForGroups`:

```
# Tectia
AllowTcpForwardingForUsers smith
AllowTcpForwardingForGroups students
DenyTcpForwardingForUsers evildoer
DenyTcpForwardingForGroups badguys
```

The values for these keywords use the same syntax as for `AllowUsers`, `AllowGroups`, `DenyUsers`, and `DenyGroups`, respectively: [5.5.1] [5.5.2]

```
# Tectia with zsh_fileglob or traditional regex syntax
AllowTcpForwardingForUsers good*@*.friendly.org,*@\i10.1.2.*,12[[:digit:]]
DenyTcpForwardingForGroups bad*,33[[:digit:]]

# Tectia with egrep regex syntax
AllowTcpForwardingForUsers good.*@.*\.friendly\.org,.*@\i10\.1\.2\.*,12[[:digit:]]
DenyTcpForwardingForGroups bad.*,33[[:digit:]]
```

Tectia's `ForwardACL` keyword provides the most precise access control for specific forwardings.* Its use is complicated but it provides great flexibility. It uses multiple values (separated by whitespace), with the general format:

```
# Tectia
ForwardACL access direction client forward [originator]
```

---

* ACL stands for "access control list."

The values stand for:

access

Either `allow` or `deny`, indicating the type of control to be applied.

direction

Either `local` or `remote`, specifying the kind of forwarding being controlled.*

client

A pattern describing the SSH client, with the same syntax as the `UserSpecificConfig` keyword, with the components *user*[%*group*][@*chost*]: [11.6.2]

    user

        Matches the username requested by the client

    group

        (Optional) Matches any of the groups that claim the user as a member

    chost

        (Optional) Matches the machine from which the SSH connection originates, i.e., where the SSH client program runs

forward

For local forwardings, a pattern that matches the forwarding target, where the application server runs, as shown in Figure 5-3, which illustrates the result of running the command:†

```
chost$ ssh -L[faddr:]fport:thost:tport shost
```

The local forward value has the form *thost*[%*tport*], where the *thost* component uses the same syntax as the `AllowHost` keyword, and matches either the hostname provided by the SSH client, or the address resulting from the hostname lookup that is performed by the SSH server for the forwarding. The optional *tport* is a pattern matching the numeric value of the port on which the application server is listening, and to which the SSH server connects for the forwarding. If the port is not specified, then the access control applies to all ports.

For remote forwardings, the forward value matches the address and (optionally) the port on which the SSH server listens for forwarded connections, as shown in Figure 5-4, which illustrates the result of running the command:

```
chost$ ssh -R[faddr:]fport:thost:tport shost
```

The remote forward value uses the same syntax as for local forwardings, with the components *faddr*[%*fport*].

---

* These keywords are case-insensitive, but the documentation mentions only lowercase, so we recommend it.

† Only Tectia SSH clients allow the listening address *faddr* to be specified with the forwarding command-line options -L and -R.

---

originator

(Optional) A pattern that matches the source address used by the application client to connect to the forwarded port, labeled ohost in Figures 5-3 and 5-4. This is most useful for remote forwarding, since the source address can be directly determined by the SSH server when it accepts the forwarded connection.

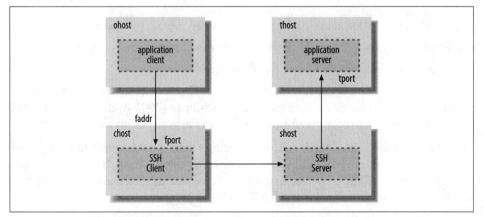

Figure 5-3. Local forwarding with the Tectia ForwardACL keyword

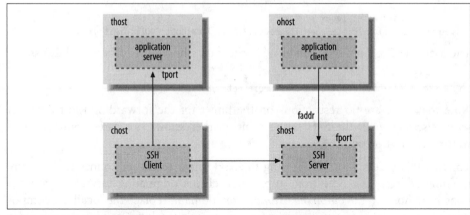

Figure 5-4. Remote forwarding with the Tectia ForwardACL keyword

For local forwarding, the SSH server must rely on the SSH client to provide the source address, and a malicious client might forge the address, so it really can't be trusted as a basis for granting access. In addition, the source address reported by the SSH client might belong to private address space that is not meaningful to the SSH server, e.g., if network address translation (NAT) is used.

The ForwardACL keyword is one of the most complex keywords available for configuring Tectia, because so many parameters are needed to describe forwarded connections fully. The reward for conquering this complexity is precision. For example, to allow any user in the trusted group to use local forwarding when initiating SSH connections from any machine in the *friendly.org* domain, but only to forward IMAP connections (port 143) to the internal server *mail.example.com*, use:

```
# Tectia with zsh_fileglob or traditional regex syntax
ForwardACL allow local *%trusted@*.friendly.org mail.example.com%143

# Tectia with egrep regex syntax
ForwardACL allow local .*%trusted@.*\.friendly\.org mail\.example\.com%143
```

A trusted user could then run her SSH client on *somewhere.friendly.org* as:

```
$ ssh -L2001:mail.example.com:143 ssh.example.com
```

where *ssh.example.com* is the host that runs the SSH server. Note that no restrictions are imposed on the listening port for local forwardings (2001 in this case); the SSH server has no reason to care about that, and no way to verify it anyway.

To allow guest users (i.e., those whose usernames start with "guest") initiating SSH connections from a range of addresses described by the netmask 10.1.2.0/24 to use remote forwarding, but only listening on the localhost interface and accepting forwarded connections on a range of ports 7000-7009:

```
# Tectia with zsh_fileglob or traditional regex syntax
ForwardACL allow remote guest*@\m10.1.2.0/24 localhost:700[[:digit:]]

# Tectia with egrep regex syntax
ForwardACL allow remote guest.*@\m10.1.2.0/24 localhost:700[[:digit:]]
```

The user guest33 could then run his SSH client on a host with address 10.1.2.3 as:

```
# Tectia
$ ssh -Rlocalhost:7005:server.elsewhere.net:8080 ssh.example.com
```

Note that there are no restrictions on the target for the forwarding (port 8080 on *server.elsewhere.net*); the SSH server again neither knows nor cares about the forwarded connection on the SSH client side.

To relax this access control, allowing the SSH server to accept connections on any listening address, but only from application clients originating forwarded connections from hosts in the *outbound.example.com* domain, replace the localhost component in the previous forward pattern with a "match anything" wildcard, and add a fifth *originator* pattern:

```
# Tectia with zsh_fileglob or traditional regex syntax
ForwardACL allow remote guest*@\m10.1.2.0/24 *:700[[:digit:]] *.outbound.example.com

# Tectia with egrep regex syntax
ForwardACL allow remote guest.*@\m10.1.2.0/24 .*:700[[:digit:]] .*\.outbound\.
example\.com
```

ForwardACL restrictions for local and remote forwardings are completely independent. If any ForwardACL keywords allow specific, limited access for either kind of forwarding, then all other access for that kind of forwarding will be denied.

Tectia uses the most restrictive interpretation for forwarding access control: if multiple `ForwardACL` keywords match a requested forwarding, and any of them deny access, then the forwarding is rejected. This can be useful for creating exceptions. For example, to allow local forwarding to any port on any target host in the *example.com* domain, but not to any port on the database server *db.example.com*, or to http servers (port 80) on any *example.com* hosts:

```
# Tectia with zsh_fileglob or traditional regex syntax
ForwardACL allow local  *  *.example.com
ForwardACL deny  local  *  db.example.com
ForwardACL deny  local  *  *.example.com%80

# Tectia with egrep regex syntax
ForwardACL allow local .*  .*\.example\.com
ForwardACL deny  local .*  db\.example\.com
ForwardACL deny  local .*  .*\.example\.com%80
```

Furthermore, `ForwardACL` keywords cannot override restrictions imposed by the other forwarding access control keywords (`AllowTcpForwardingForUsers`, `AllowTcpForwardingForGroups`, `DenyTcpForwardingForUsers`, `DenyTcpForwardingForGroups`, or `AllowTcpForwarding`): if any of these applicable keywords deny access for a requested forwarding, then the forwarding is forbidden.

5.7.2   X Forwarding

Forwarding for X, the popular Window System, can be separately enabled or disabled with the keyword `X11Forwarding`:*

```
X11Forwarding no
```

OpenSSH automatically disables `X11Forwarding` if `UseLogin` is enabled. [5.4.10]

Administrators may wish to disable forwarding for users who are not trusted to have forwarding securely configured on the client side. For example, it is usually desirable to avoid SSH clients that indiscriminately accept connections from anywhere, and then forward them across SSH tunnels to trusted servers. Similarly, misconfigured X servers (which run on the SSH client side) can expose X client programs running on the SSH server side to attack, if the X server access is overly permissive.

Disabling forwarding isn't effective for users who are granted shell access to run arbitrary commands, because such users can use their own programs to set up equivalent forwarding functionality. For better control, set up special-purpose accounts that use carefully written, restricted programs instead of standard shells, and consider using subsystems. [5.8]

---

* Tectia supports the keywords `ForwardX11` and `AllowX11Forwarding` as synonyms for `X11Forwarding`.

5.7.3 Agent Forwarding

Agent forwarding permits a series of SSH connections (from one machine to another to another, ...) to operate seamlessly using a single agent. [6.3.5] Agent forwarding may be enabled or disabled in the Tectia server using the keyword AllowAgentForwarding with a value of yes (the default) or no:*

```
# Tectia
AllowAgentForwarding no
```

It may also be enabled or disabled by OpenSSH and Tectia clients. [6.3.5.3]

Agent forwarding is convenient, but in a security-sensitive environment, it might be appropriate to disable this feature. Because forwarded agent connections are implemented as Unix domain sockets, an attacker can conceivably gain access to them. These sockets are just nodes in the filesystem, protected only by file permissions that can be compromised.

For example, suppose you maintain a network of exposed, untrusted machines that you access from a more secure network using SSH. You might consider disabling agent forwarding on the untrusted machines. Otherwise, an attacker can compromise an untrusted machine; take control of a forwarded agent from a legitimate, incoming SSH connection; and use the agent's loaded keys to gain access to the secure network via SSH. (The attacker can't retrieve the keys themselves in this way, however.)

5.8 Subsystems

Subsystems are a layer of abstraction for defining and running remote commands via SSH.† Normally remote commands are specified ad hoc on the client command line. For example, the following command runs a script to perform tape backups:

```
$ ssh server.example.com /usr/local/sbin/tape-backups
```

Subsystems are a set of remote commands predefined on the server machine, with simple names so that they can be executed conveniently.

The syntax to define subsystems in the server configuration file is slightly different for OpenSSH and Tectia. A subsystem for the preceding backup command is:

```
# OpenSSH
Subsystem backups    /usr/local/sbin/tape-backups

# Tectia
Subsystem-backups    /usr/local/sbin/tape-backups
```

---

* The keyword ForwardAgent is also supported as a synonym for backward compatibility.

† Subsystems are supported only by the SSH-2 protocol.

Note that OpenSSH uses the keyword Subsystem with a separate value for the subsystem name, whereas Tectia uses a keyword of the form Subsystem-*name*. This Tectia syntax is quite odd and unlike anything else in its configuration language; we don't know how it ended up that way.

To run this tape backup script on the server machine, use the *ssh -s* option:

```
$ ssh server.example.com -s backups
```

This command behaves identically to the previous one in which the script was specified explicitly.

Subsystems are mainly a convenience feature to predefine commands for SSH clients to invoke easily. The additional level of abstraction is useful for system administrators, who can hide (and therefore easily change) details for the subsystem commands. For example, the backups subsystem could be changed to use a completely different script, without any changes in the *ssh* client command that operators run to perform tape backups.

System administrators can also define and advertise more generally useful subsystems. Suppose your users run the Pine email reader to connect to your IMAP server to secure the connection. [11.3] Instead of telling everyone to use the command:

```
$ ssh server.example.com /usr/sbin/imapd
```

and revealing the path to the IMAP daemon, *imapd*, you can define an imap subsystem to hide the path in case it changes in the future:

```
# OpenSSH
Subsystem imap  /usr/sbin/imapd

# Tectia
Subsystem-imap  /usr/sbin/imapd
```

Now users can run the command:

```
$ ssh server.example.com -s imap
```

to establish secure IMAP connections via the subsystem.

Subsystems are especially useful for tunneling other protocols. If clients refer only to a subsystem, the corresponding server implementation can be changed without modifying (and redeploying) the clients, which might be numerous and widely scattered.

The best example is the *sftp* subsystem, which provides secure file transfers. [2.7.1] The *sftp* client runs *ssh -s sftp* to launch an *sftp-server* program and set up a secure tunnel for communication between the client and server.* The default server configuration file for both OpenSSH and Tectia contains a definition of the *sftp* subsystem, with the correct, absolute pathname for *sftp-server*. Tectia also provides an internal

---

* Tectia's *scp* client also uses the sftp subsystem.

implementation of the sftp subsystem that is built into the SSH server itself. This can be selected by using a special syntax for the command:

```
# Tectia
Subsystem-sftp  internal://sftp-server
```

The internal sftp subsystem is much more convenient than the default (external) *sftp-server* command for accounts that are subject to chroot restrictions. [5.5.7]

Subsystem commands are executed by each user's shell, and they can be affected by environment variables set by the user (if permitted by the server [5.6.2]), shell start-up scripts, etc. OpenSSH avoids running the ~/.ssh/rc script for subsystems, but Tectia always runs ~/.ssh2/rc. If a subsystem server command uses a special token to mark the start of its output, clients can ignore unexpected output from user scripts. Of course, the token must be defined as part of the protocol that's understood and used by the client and server.

OpenSSH requires that subsystem commands use absolute filenames, since no PATH search is performed. If a relative filename is used, e.g.:

```
# OpenSSH: this does not work
Subsystem backups   tape-backups
```

then no error occurs when the server configuration file is read, but on subsequent attempts to use the subsystem, clients fail silently, and the server emits syslog warnings:

```
Dec 20 14:14:47 server.example.com sshd[1554]: error: subsystem: cannot stat tape-
backups: No such file or directory
```

Furthermore, OpenSSH doesn't permit command-line arguments for subsystem commands:

```
# OpenSSH: this does not work
Subsystem backups   /usr/local/sbin/tape-backups --full --filesystem=/home
```

This restriction is enforced when the server configuration file is read:

```
/etc/ssh/sshd_config line 99: garbage at end of line; "--full".
```

Tectia is more permissive. The server searches for simple commands (i.e., relative filenames and no command-line arguments) in the *libexec* and *bin* subdirectories of the Tectia *install* directory, and then searches each directory in the PATH. Absolute filenames are still recommended, however, since the PATH can be redefined or modified by each user, and (if not set explicitly) defaults to the value inherited when the server was started.

Tectia also allows extra arguments or even shell metacharacters in subsystem commands:

```
# Tectia
Subsystem-backups   /usr/local/sbin/tape-backups --full 2>&1 | tee /var/log/backups
```

This is usually a bad idea, because various shells for individual users differ in their interpretation of metacharacters (e.g., the 2>&1 notation in the previous example is understood only by Bourne-style shells). The SSH server configuration file is the wrong place for this complexity: a better approach is to wrap the details in a separate script, and use the name of that script as the subsystem command.

Subsystem keywords can be repeated to define multiple, independent subsystems. OpenSSH can define a maximum of 256 subsystems; there is no limit for Tectia. OpenSSH refuses to allow subsystem names to be reused:

```
/etc/ssh/sshd_config line 98: Subsystem 'backups' already defined.
```

Tectia uses later subsystem definitions with the same name to override the commands from earlier definitions. This can be useful in conjunction with subconfiguration files. [11.6.2]

OpenSSH subsystem names are case-sensitive. In contrast, Tectia maps subsystem names to lowercase when the configuration file is read, but then uses case-sensitive comparisons to look up the subsystems specified by clients. This unfortunate and confusing behavior effectively restricts Tectia subsystem names to be all lowercase.*

The IETF SECSH draft only defines the "sftp" subsystem name and mandates that other, nonstandard names use an @ suffix to identify the domain that defined the subsystem:

```
# OpenSSH
Subsystem smail@example.com     /usr/local/sbin/secure-mail-server

# Tectia
Subsystem-smail@example.com     /usr/local/sbin/secure-mail-server
```

This convention should be followed to avoid name clashes for software that is widely used, but the domain suffix is commonly omitted for subsystems that are used only within a single organization, and the convention is not enforced.

5.9   Logging and Debugging

As an SSH server runs, it optionally produces log messages to describe what it's doing. Log messages aid the system administrator in tracking the server's behavior and detecting and diagnosing problems. For example, if a server is mysteriously rejecting connections, one of the first places to look is the server's log output.

---

* We suspect this is a consequence of Tectia's peculiar syntax for the Subsystem keyword in server configuration files. Keywords are case-insensitive, and it's therefore consistent to ignore the case of the subsystem name when the name is appended to the keyword.

By default, the SSH server writes log messages to *syslog*, the standard Unix logging service (see the sidebar, "The Syslog Logging Service"). For example, an SSH server typically announces its startup with log messages like:*

```
Server listening on 0.0.0.0 port 22.
Generating 768 bit RSA key.
RSA key generation complete.
```

and a connection from a client is recorded with log messages like:

```
session opened for user rebecca by (uid=9005)
Accepted publickey for rebecca from 10.1.2.3 port 1265
ssh2 session closed for user rebecca
```

The SyslogFacility keyword specifies how the SSH server tags log messages:

```
SyslogFacility LOCAL3
```

The value is one of the (case-insensitive) syslog facility codes, and the default is AUTH.

The Syslog Logging Service

Syslog is the standard Unix logging service. Programs send their log messages to the syslog daemon, *syslogd*, which forwards them to other destinations such as files, the system console, or even other machines. Destinations are specified in the syslog configuration file, */etc/syslog.conf*.

Messages received by *syslogd* are processed according to their *facility*, which indicates their origin. Standard syslog facilities include AUTH (security and authorization), AUTHPRIV (similar, but for sensitive information), DAEMON (system daemons), LOCAL0 through LOCAL7 (reserved for local use), and USER (user processes).

Log messages are also assigned a *priority level*, which indicates their importance. The standard syslog priorities are, in order from most to least important, EMERG, ALERT, CRIT, ERR, WARNING, NOTICE, INFO, and DEBUG.

See the manpages for *syslog*, *syslogd*, and *syslog.conf* for more information about this logging service.

 Tectia confusingly interprets AUTH to actually mean AUTHPRIV (this also applies to the default behavior), and does not recognize AUTHPRIV as a syslog facility code. On systems that do not support a separate AUTHPRIV facility, Tectia resorts to AUTH. Otherwise, Tectia provides no way to specify the AUTH facility explicitly.

---

* The system logger adds other information to each log message, such as a timestamp, the name of the machine, and the process ID of the SSH server, so lines in the log files will actually look like:

```
Aug 30 17:41:47 graceland sshd[731]: Illegal user elvis from 10.11.12.13
```

For Tectia, a separate syslog facility code is used for the *sftp* subsystem. [5.8] This is specified by the SftpSysLogFacility keyword:

```
# Tectia
SftpSysLogFacility LOCAL7
```

By default, no logging is performed for *sftp*.

 If the *sftp* subsystem is implemented by an external program, then the Tectia server passes the *sftp* syslog facility code via the environment variable SSH2_SFTP_LOG_FACILITY. Otherwise, if the internal *sftp* subsystem that is built into the server is used, then the value for the SftpSysLogFacility keyword is consulted directly.

SSH servers use a range of syslog priority levels, depending on the types of log messages that are sent. These priority levels aren't directly controllable, but the syslog configuration determines where and how they are recorded (or discarded).

The amount of detail provided by log messages can be specified in a variety of ways, however. OpenSSH uses the keyword LogLevel to control the verbosity level:

```
# OpenSSH
LogLevel VERBOSE
```

The permitted values (in order of increasing verbosity) are QUIET, FATAL, ERROR, INFO, VERBOSE, DEBUG, and DEBUG1 through DEBUG3.*

The QUIET level sends nothing whatsoever to the system log (although some messages resulting from OpenSSH activity may still be recorded by other programs and libraries, such as PAM). Tectia uses a separate keyword, QuietMode, to suppress all log messages (except fatal errors), with the values yes or no (the default):

```
# Tectia
QuietMode yes
```

The *–q* command-line option also selects quiet operation:

```
$ sshd -q
```

5.9.1   OpenSSH Logging and Debugging

For OpenSSH, the LogLevel values DEBUG1 through DEBUG3 produce voluminous information useful only for diagnostic purposes.† These levels are sufficiently verbose to reveal sensitive personal information that should not normally be recorded, so avoid them for routine operation. Debugging output is usually requested on the command line:

```
# OpenSSH
$ sshd -o "LogLevel DEBUG2"
```

---

* These names are *not* syslog priority levels, although some of the names are similar.

† DEBUG is a synonym for DEBUG1.

More concisely, the –*d* command-line option can be specified one to three times, to set the LogLevel to DEBUG1 through DEBUG3, respectively:

```
# OpenSSH
$ sshd -d -d              DEBUG2 level
```

The –*t* (test) option causes the OpenSSH server to start up, check the validity of its host keys and the server configuration file, and exit. [5.2.2] Combine it with –*d* to see more details about successful operation:

```
# OpenSSH
$ sshd -d -t
debug1: sshd version OpenSSH_3.9p1
debug1: read PEM private key done: type RSA
debug1: private host key: #0 type 1 RSA
debug1: read PEM private key done: type DSA
debug1: private host key: #1 type 2 DSA
```

For OpenSSH, the –*d* command-line option also causes the server to run in "debug mode," which alters its behavior to support debugging. The LogLevel keyword does *not* enable debug mode—it only sets the verbosity level.

In debug mode, the OpenSSH server runs in the foreground, without forking, instead of running detached as a daemon. Normally, the server forks again after it accepts each connection from a client, and continues further work for the session in a separate child process, while the parent process resumes listening for more connection requests. In debug mode, however, the OpenSSH server handles only a single connection, again without forking, and then exits. This is usually convenient for debugging, when forking and multiple processes are unwelcome complications; it's often easier to determine what's happening if all actions are performed by a single process.

OpenSSH doesn't bother to record its process ID in the PidFile [5.3.1.3] when it runs in debug mode, since no forking occurs, and it's easy to determine the process ID if the server needs to be signaled.

OpenSSH can also be prevented from running as a daemon by using the –*D* command-line option:

```
# OpenSSH
$ sshd -D
```

The –*D* option does not change the LogLevel or enable any of the other side effects of debug mode. The OpenSSH server still forks to handle multiple client connections, even when –*D* is specified.

The –*D* option is handy in special circumstances when some other process needs to monitor the OpenSSH server, and would incorrectly conclude that *sshd* had exited if it forked and ran in the background. For example, the Cygwin program *cygrunsrv* uses *sshd -D* to launch OpenSSH as a Windows service. [14.1]

In debug mode, the OpenSSH server prints log messages to the standard error, instead of sending them to syslog. For example, we can use the *–p* option to test the server without disturbing normal operation on the standard port: [5.3.3.1]

```
# OpenSSH
$ sshd -d -p 2222
debug1: sshd version OpenSSH_3.5p1
debug1: private host key: #0 type 0 RSA1
debug1: read PEM private key done: type RSA
debug1: private host key: #1 type 1 RSA
debug1: read PEM private key done: type DSA
debug1: private host key: #2 type 2 DSA
debug1: rexec_argv[0]='/usr/sbin/sshd'
debug1: rexec_argv[1]='-d'
debug1: rexec_argv[2]='-p'
debug1: rexec_argv[3]='2222'
debug1: Bind to port 2222 on 0.0.0.0.
Server listening on 0.0.0.0 port 2222.
Generating 768 bit RSA key.
RSA key generation complete.
... The server waits for an incoming connection request, and then ...
debug1: Server will not fork when running in debugging mode.
debug1: rexec start in 4 out 4 newsock 4 pipe -1 sock 7
... Further debug output is sent to syslog: see below ...
```

Log messages that would have been sent to syslog are printed directly. Extra debug messages are printed with the debug1 prefix (or debug2 or debug3 if more verbose debugging log levels are used). Lots of sample output from *sshd -d* can be found in Chapter 3.

The *–e* option causes the OpenSSH server to independently redirect syslog output to the standard error, without all of the other side effects of debug mode. For example:

```
# OpenSSH
$ sshd -D -e -p 2222
Server listening on 0.0.0.0 port 2222.
Accepted publickey for rebecca from 10.1.2.3 port 32788 ssh2
...
```

When debugging OpenSSH, it's usually a good idea to disable server restarts with the undocumented *–r* option, again to confine all activity to a single process for simplicity, and to prevent debug output from being diverted from stderr to syslog after the restart. [5.3.3.3] In the previous example for *sshd -d*, debug output lines that mention *rexec* refer to server restarts, and debug output sent to stderr abruptly ends after the *rexec* start line. If we repeat the example with the *–r* option, we see much more debugging information sent to stderr, without any of the *rexec* clutter:

```
# OpenSSH
$ sshd -d -r -p 2222
debug1: sshd version OpenSSH_3.9p1
debug1: private host key: #0 type 0 RSA1
debug1: read PEM private key done: type RSA
debug1: private host key: #1 type 1 RSA
```

```
debug1: read PEM private key done: type DSA
debug1: private host key: #2 type 2 DSA
debug1: Bind to port 2222 on 0.0.0.0.
Server listening on 0.0.0.0 port 2222.
Generating 768 bit RSA key.
RSA key generation complete.
... The server waits for an incoming connection request, and then ...
debug1: Server will not fork when running in debugging mode.
Connection from 10.1.2.3 port 32777
debug1: Client protocol version 2.0; client software version OpenSSH_3.9p1
debug1: match: OpenSSH_3.9p1 pat OpenSSH*
debug1: Enabling compatibility mode for protocol 2.0
debug1: Local version string SSH-1.99-OpenSSH_3.9p1
... Lots more output follows ...
```

Alternately, if the restart mechanism itself is being debugged, the *–e* option can be used to prevent the diversion of debug output from syslog to stderr after the server restarts:

```
# OpenSSH
$ sshd -d -e -p 2222
debug1: sshd version OpenSSH_3.9p1
debug1: private host key: #0 type 0 RSA1
debug1: read PEM private key done: type RSA
debug1: private host key: #1 type 1 RSA
debug1: read PEM private key done: type DSA
debug1: private host key: #2 type 2 DSA
debug1: rexec_argv[0]='/usr/sbin/sshd'
debug1: rexec_argv[1]='-d'
debug1: rexec_argv[2]='-e'
debug1: rexec_argv[3]='-p'
debug1: rexec_argv[4]='2222'
debug1: Bind to port 2222 on 0.0.0.0.
Server listening on 0.0.0.0 port 2222.
Generating 768 bit RSA key.
RSA key generation complete.
... The server waits for an incoming connection request, and then ...
debug1: Server will not fork when running in debugging mode.
debug1: rexec start in 4 out 4 newsock 4 pipe -1 sock 7
... The restarted process rereads the host keys as it repeats all of the initializations ...
debug1: sshd version OpenSSH_3.9p1
debug1: private host key: #0 type 0 RSA1
debug1: read PEM private key done: type RSA
debug1: private host key: #1 type 1 RSA
debug1: read PEM private key done: type DSA
debug1: private host key: #2 type 2 DSA
... The restarted process uses the SSH socket accepted by the original process ...
debug1: inetd sockets after dupping: 3, 3
... Finally, the server continues to handle the session, as before ...
Connection from 10.1.2.3 port 32778
debug1: Client protocol version 2.0; client software version OpenSSH_3.9p1
debug1: match: OpenSSH_3.9p1 pat OpenSSH*
debug1: Enabling compatibility mode for protocol 2.0
debug1: Local version string SSH-1.99-OpenSSH_3.9p1
... Lots more output follows ...
```

When the OpenSSH server is running in debug mode, extra information is also sent to (and displayed by) the client, such as environment variables, initialization scripts, *xauth* actions, etc., which aid in debugging connection problems.

For example, a connection to the server on the alternate port shown earlier produces diagnostic output like this:

```
$ ssh -p 2222 server.example.com
Environment:
 USER=elvis
 LOGNAME=elvis
 HOME=/u/elvis
 PATH=/usr/local/bin:/bin:/usr/bin
 MAIL=/var/mail/elvis
 SHELL=/bin/tcsh
 SSH_CLIENT=10.1.2.3 1059 2222
 SSH_CONNECTION=10.1.2.3 1059 10.4.5.6 2222
 SSH_TTY=/dev/pts/2
 TERM=xterm
 DISPLAY=localhost:10.0
 SSH_AUTH_SOCK=/tmp/ssh-XXgOcfvG/agent.1989
Running /bin/tcsh -c '/bin/sh .ssh/rc'
... or ...
Running /bin/sh /etc/ssh/sshrc
... or ...
Running /usr/X11R6/bin/xauth remove unix:13.0
/usr/X11R6/bin/xauth add unix:13.0 MIT-MAGIC-COOKIE-1
007ab9e94cf72f081390f46ab0d92f1f
```

The OpenSSH server ignores the `LoginGraceTime` keyword [5.3.3.6] when it runs in debug mode, since debugging sessions often last much longer!

5.9.2   Tectia Logging and Debugging

Debug mode for Tectia is also controlled by the *–d* command-line option,[*] but the option requires an argument indicating the debug level.

 We strongly recommend compiling Tectia with heavy debugging turned on, using the `--enable-debug-heavy` configure option. [4.3.5.9] The resulting log messages are far more detailed than those printed by default.

Debug levels may be indicated in a variety of ways. The simplest is a nonnegative integer:

```
# Tectia
$ sshd -d 2
```

---

[*] The *–d* option has no corresponding keyword.

Specifying a debug level means that messages for all lower levels will be printed as well. Higher numbers indicate increased verbosity. The approximate meanings of the integer debug levels are:

Level	Approximate meaning
0–2	Software malfunctions
3	Non-fatal, high-level errors caused by data received from the network
4	Successful, high-level operations
5	Start of high-level operations
6	Uncommon situations that might indicate bugs
7	Successful, mid-level operations
8	Data block dumps
9	Protocol packet dumps
10	Successful, low-level operations
11–15	Miscellaneous, extremely low-level operations

The *–v* command line option is equivalent to -d 2:

```
# Tectia
$ sshd -v
```

Alternatively, the VerboseMode keyword (or the abbreviated synonym Verbose) is equivalent to the *–v* option:

```
# Tectia
VerboseMode yes
```

Since debug logging isn't recommended for normal operation, the VerboseMode keyword is useful primarily in alternate configuration files that are specified with the *–f* command-line option [5.2.1], or in subconfiguration files. [11.6.2]

The integer debug levels affect all aspects of Tectia's operation. Debug levels can also be set differently for each module in the Tectia source distribution. This permits much finer-grained control over logging.

To use module-based debugging effectively, you should have some understanding of C programming, and consult the source code (especially the header file *lib/sshutil/sshcore/sshdebug.h*). Each source file is considered to be a "module" for debugging purposes, as determined by the definition of SSH_DEBUG_MODULE within the file. For example, the file *apps/ssh/authspasswd.c* has the module name Ssh2AuthPasswdServer because it contains the line:

```
#define SSH_DEBUG_MODULE "Ssh2AuthPasswdServer"
```

The complete set of module names for Tectia at press time is found in Appendix C. To extract the current set of module names from the source code, search for SSH_ DEBUG_MODULE definitions in all source files from within the Tectia distribution:

```
$ find . -type f -print | xargs grep "define.*SSH_DEBUG_MODULE"
```

Module names are case-sensitive. Once you have identified the name of your desired module, run the server in debug mode, providing the module's name and debug level. For example, to cause the Ssh2AuthPasswdServer module to log at debug level 2:

```
# Tectia
$ sshd -d "Ssh2AuthPasswdServer=2"
```

If the debug level is omitted (i.e., only the module name is specified), then the debug level is taken to be zero, so either of the following forms can be used:

```
# Tectia
$ sshd -d "Ssh2AuthPasswdServer"
$ sshd -d "Ssh2AuthPasswdServer=0"
```

The special module name global refers to all modules, and is equivalent to specifying an integer debug level. For example, the following two commands function identically:

```
# Tectia
$ sshd -d "global=2"
$ sshd -d 2
```

The default global debug level is zero.

Multiple modules may be specified, separated by commas, each set to individual debug levels:

```
# Tectia
$ sshd -d "Ssh2AuthPasswdServer=2,SshAdd=3,SshSftpServer=5"
```

Add whitespace to improve readability:

```
# Tectia
$ sshd -d "Ssh2AuthPasswdServer = 2, SshAdd = 3, SshSftpServer = 5"
```

If the −d option is repeated, the debug levels are concatenated. This is an alternative to comma-separated lists:

```
# Tectia
$ sshd -d "Ssh2AuthPasswdServer=2" -d "SshAdd=3" -d "SshSftpServer=5"
```

More generally, module names are patterns that can contain the wildcards * and ? to match multiple modules:

```
# Tectia
$ sshd -d "Ssh2Auth*=3"
```

 These two wildcards have the same meaning as for zsh_fileglob or traditional regex syntax, but debug module patterns are not full regular expressions: no other wildcards or regex syntax is recognized.

Remember to enclose wildcards for the patterns in quotes to prevent their expansion by the Unix shell.

Wildcards cannot match the special global module name, so the following does not work:

```
# Tectia: does not work
$ sshd -d "glo*=2"
```

Setting the global debug level (using either a simple integer or the special global module name) causes all earlier module debug level assignments to be ignored, so global assignments should always be specified first:

```
# Tectia
$ sshd -d 1 -d "Ssh2AuthPasswdServer=2,SshAdd=3,SshSftpServer=5"
$ sshd -d "global=1, Ssh2AuthPasswdServer=2,SshAdd=3,SshSftpServer=5"
```

The global debug level is used as the default for all modules; otherwise, the debug level for a specific module is determined by the *last* match in the list. This rule, when combined with wildcards, can be used to conveniently set debug levels for entire categories of modules, by overriding earlier, more general assignments with a sequence of increasingly specific patterns. For example:

```
# Tectia
$ sshd -d "global = 1, Ssh2* = 2, Ssh2Auth* = 3, Ssh2AuthPasswd* = 4"
```

The "match anything" pattern * functions similarly to the global debug level:

```
# Tectia
$ sshd -d "* = 1, Ssh2* = 2, Ssh2Auth* = 3, Ssh2AuthPasswd* = 4"
```

Debug output lines always start with the word "debug," followed by the process ID in square brackets. Messages for specific modules mention the module name, and provide the name of the source file (with a line number) in which the code is found, plus the name of the function in which they occur. For example:

```
# Tectia
$ sshd -d "Ssh2AuthPasswdServer=2"
...
debug[2665]: Ssh2AuthPasswdServer/auths-passwd.c:136/ssh_server_auth_passwd: password
auth.
debug[2665]: Ssh2AuthPasswdServer/auths-passwd.c:138/ssh_server_auth_passwd: op = 0
user = elvis
...
debug[2665]: Ssh2AuthPasswdServer/auths-passwd.c:250/ssh_server_auth_passwd: ssh_
server_auth_passwd: accepted by local passwd
...
```

Some debug output isn't associated with any module, and is printed for all debug levels. In addition, some modules produce output even for debug level 0:

```
# Tectia
$ sshd -d 0
debug[3320]: Host key pair is not specified, trying to use default 'hostkey'.
debug[3320]: Becoming server.
```

```
debug[3320]: Creating listener(s)
...
debug[3320]: Listeners created
debug[3320]: no udp listener created.
...
debug[3320]: Running event loop
...
debug[3320]: Ssh2Common/sshcommon.c:510/ssh_common_wrap: local ip = 10.1.2.3, local
port = 22
debug[3320]: Ssh2Common/sshcommon.c:512/ssh_common_wrap: remote ip = 10.1.2.3, remote
port = 32793
...
debug[3320]: Sshd2/sshd2.c:334/server_disconnect: locally_generated = TRUE
```

> Just because a source code file has a debugging module name associ-
> ated with it doesn't mean it actually logs any information that way.
> You may find that turning on debugging for specific modules doesn't
> produce any extra debugging output.

The *sshd-check-conf* program [5.2.2] also accepts the debug options –*d* and –*v*. Use
the module names SshdCheckConf, SshConfigParse, or SshConfig to see more details
about parsing of configuration files:

```
# Tectia
$ sshd-check-conf -d "SshConfigParse=9"
debug: SshConfigParse/sshconfig_parse.c:224/ssh_parse_config_ext: Got metaconfig line
`## REGEX-SYNTAX egrep'.
debug: SshConfigParse/sshconfig_parse.c:246/ssh_parse_config_ext: Metaconfig
specifies regex style 'EGREP'.
debug: SshConfigParse/sshconfig_parse.c:252/ssh_parse_config_ext: Metaconfig parsing
stopped at line 3.
debug: SshConfigParse/sshconfig_parse.c:464/ssh_config_parse_line: n_var = `Port', n_
val = `22'
debug: SshConfigParse/sshconfig_parse.c:464/ssh_config_parse_line: n_var =
`SettableEnvironmentVars', n_val = `LANG,LC_
(ALL|COLLATE|CTYPE|MONETARY|NUMERIC|TIME),PATH,TERM,TZ'
debug: SshConfigParse/sshconfig_parse.c:464/ssh_config_parse_line: n_var =
`subsystem-sftp', n_val = `sftp-server'
...
```

As for OpenSSH, the –*d* command-line option causes the Tectia server to run in the
foreground, processing a single connection, and then exiting.

> Although the VerboseMode keyword is equivalent to the –*v* option,
> which in turn means the same as -d 2, the keyword cannot prevent
> forking if it is used in a subconfiguration file [11.6.2], because forking
> will have already occurred when the subconfiguration file is read.
> Therefore, VerboseMode in a subconfiguration file only determines the
> debug level. In the main configuration file, the keyword controls fork-
> ing too.

To continue listening for more connections, use the –D option instead of –d:

```
# Tectia
$ sshd -D "Ssh*TCP*=8"
```

When the Tectia server is started with the –D option, it runs in the foreground, but subsequently forks to spawn a separate child process to handle the session for each client connection. In all other respects, the –D and –d options function identically.

Tectia doesn't provide any means to run the server in the foreground without enabling debug mode. However, debug output can be minimized by using the –D option with a debug level of zero, and the relatively small amount of unneeded debug information can be discarded:

```
# Tectia
$ sshd -D 0 2> /dev/null
```

If you need this quieter mode of operation frequently, consider rebuilding the server without debugging support. [4.3.5.9]

 When specifying debug options (–d, –D, or –v) on the *sshd* command line, list them first so that debugging output starts as early as possible. This is especially important if you are investigating the parsing of command-line options or configuration files.

Tectia always sends debug output to the standard error, distinct from the messages sent to syslog. In debug mode, messages continue to be sent to syslog as they are for normal operation, but these messages are also copied to the standard error, and intermingled with the debug output. The copied syslog messages are annotated with the name of the Tectia server program (usually "sshd2") instead of "debug," and they are unaffected by the debug level:

```
# Tectia
$ sshd -d 0
sshd2[3320]: Listener created on  *** SSH_IPADDR_ANY ***:22.
sshd2[3320]: Daemon is running.
sshd2[3320]: connection from "10.1.2.3" (listen iface: *** SSH_IPADDR_ANY ***:22)
...
sshd2[3320]: Destroying session channel 0
sshd2[3320]: Local disconnected: Connection closed.
sshd2[3320]: connection lost: 'Connection closed.'
sshd2[3320]: Logout for user elvis.
```

If syslog output is not desired when debugging Tectia, it can be directed to some syslog facility that is discarded by *syslogd*:

```
# Tectia
$ sshd -d 0 -o "SysLogFacility LOCAL3"
```

The Tectia server catches the signal SIGUSR1 after it accepts a connection from a client, and finishes authentication and authorization. When SIGUSR1 is received, the server prints detailed information about the connection to its standard error stream. This is useful only when the server is running in the foreground (i.e., with the *–d* or *–D* options), since output to stderr is discarded when *sshd* is running in the background, as a daemon.

If the *–d* option is used, no forking occurs, and SIGUSR1 can be sent to the single server process anytime after the single session starts. For the -D option, however, a separate child process is used for each connection, and SIGUSR1 must be sent to children, not the original parent process that continues to listen for connections:[*]

```
# Tectia
$ sshd -D 0 -p 2222
...
debug[1234]: Becoming server.
debug[1234]: Creating listener(s)
sshd2[1234]: Listener created on  *** SSH_IPADDR_ANY ***:2222.
debug[1234]: Listeners created
debug[1234]: no udp listener created.
sshd2[1234]: Daemon is running.
...
sshd2[5678]: Public key authentication for user elvis accepted.
sshd2[5678]: User elvis (uid 501), coming from client.friendly.org, authenticated.
sshd2[5678]: Received a channel open request, type session, channel id 0
sshd2[5678]: Received a session channel extension request of type x11-req for channel
number 0
sshd2[5678]: Received a session channel extension request of type exec for channel
number 0
...
```

Here the parent process that is listening for connections is 1234, while the child that accepted the connection is 5678. If we send SIGUSR1 to the latter:

```
$ kill -USR1 5678
```

then the server responds with the requested information:

```
*** Config Data ***
Server Protocol Version String: 4.1.0.34 SSH Secure Shell

*** Connection Data ***
Server on host: client.friendly.org (10.1.2.3)
Server listening on port: 2222
Connection from 10.1.2.3
Client hostname: client.friendly.org

*** Algorithm Data ***
Chosen Hostkey Algorithm: ssh-dss

Client to Server Algorithms:
Chosen Cipher: aes128-cbc
Chosen MAC: hmac-sha1
Chosen Compression: none
```

[*] If SIGUSR1 is sent to the parent, it will die, since it has not arranged to catch the signal.

```
Server to Client Algorithms:
Chosen Cipher: aes128-cbc
Chosen MAC: hmac-sha1
Chosen Compression: none

*** Channel Data ***
Number of Channels: 1
 Channel 0 (session):
   Sent bytes: 0
   Received bytes: 0

   Incoming window size: 100000
   Incoming window left: 100000
   Outgoing window left: 99249

*** Connection Statistics ***
compressed bytes in: 3918
uncompressed bytes in: 3918
compressed bytes out: 5418
uncompressed bytes out: 5418
packets in: 22
packets out: 22
rekeys: 0

*** User Data ***
Username: elvis
User's uid: 501
User belongs to the following groups:
Group: memphis, gid: 501
User's home directory: /u/elvis
User's shell: /bin/tcsh

*** Local/Remote Tunnel Data ***
No active local forwards.
No active remote forwards.
```

In debug mode, the Tectia server sends extra information to the client. The content and format are similar to information sent by the OpenSSH server, except for Tectia's annotations identifying debug and (copied) syslog messages, with the process ID of the server after it forks to launch the user's shell:

```
# Tectia
$ ssh -p 2222 server.example.com
debug[2045]: /etc/nologin_server.example.com does not exist.
sshd2[2045]: Now running on elvis's privileges.
debug[2045]: Environment:
debug[2045]:   HOME=/u/elvis
debug[2045]:   USER=elvis
debug[2045]:   LOGNAME=elvis
debug[2045]:   PATH=/usr/local/bin:/bin:/usr/bin:/usr/X11R6/bin
debug[2045]:   MAIL=/var/spool/mail/elvis
debug[2045]:   SHELL=/bin/tcsh
debug[2045]:   SSH2_CLIENT=10.1.2.3 32781 10.1.2.3 2222
debug[2045]:   DISPLAY=server.example.com:10.0
```

```
debug[2045]:   SSH2_SFTP_LOG_FACILITY=-1
debug[2045]: Running /bin/tcsh /u/elvis/.ssh2/rc
... or ...
debug[2045]: Running /bin/sh /etc/ssh2/sshrc
... or ...
debug[2045]: Running /usr/X11R6/bin/xauth add server.example.com:10.0 MIT-MAGIC-
COOKIE-1 81e51d2ccefaf62b288e9f772cdaa21d
debug[2045]: Running /usr/X11R6/bin/xauth add 10.1.2.3:10.0 MIT-MAGIC-COOKIE-1
81e51d2ccefaf62b288e9f772cdaa21d
```

5.9.3   Debugging Under inetd or xinetd

If you run the SSH server from *inetd* or *xinetd* using the –*i* command-line option [5. 3.3.2], debugging can be tricky. It is necessary for *sshd* to avoid sending any extra debugging output to the standard error, since it would be relayed by *inetd* or *xinetd* to the SSH client along with the normal SSH protocol conversation, messing it up and causing the connection to fail.

OpenSSH forces all debug output to be sent to syslog if the –*i* option is used, which neatly solves the problem. For Tectia, however, the easiest approach is to redirect the debug output from the standard error to a file. Because many versions of *inetd* or *xinetd* do not support shell metacharacters in their configuration files, it's best to use a short shell script to invoke *sshd* with the redirected output:

```
#!/bin/sh
# redirect Tectia sshd standard error to a file
exec /usr/local/sbin/sshd -d 2 -i 2> /tmp/sshd2.debug
```

Simply specify this shell script in place of *sshd* in the *inetd* or *xinetd* configuration files.

Alternately, you can send debug output to syslog using the *logger* program:

```
#!/bin/sh
# send Tectia sshd debug output to syslog
exec /usr/local/sbin/sshd -d 2 -i 2>&1 | grep "^debug" | logger -p local3.debug
```

grep selects only the debug output, discarding the duplicate syslog messages that are also sent to the standard error in debug mode.

5.10   Compatibility Between SSH-1 and SSH-2 Servers

OpenSSH supports both the SSH-1 and SSH-2 protocols within a single daemon accepting both types of connections. The Protocol keyword can be used to limit the support to either protocol exclusively. [5.3.7]

For Tectia, however, the story is more complicated. The Tectia server itself only supports the SSH-2 protocol, but it can accept connections from clients that request the older SSH-1 protocol. This backward compatibility is achieved by having the Tectia server run some other server program for the SSH-1 protocol instead, whenever an SSH-1 connection is requested. This feature is enabled and disabled with the Tectia Ssh1Compatibility keyword, given a value of yes or no (the default):

```
# Tectia
Ssh1Compatibility yes
```

When Ssh1Compatibility is enabled, and an SSH-1 client connects to the Tectia server, the two programs exchange strings indicating their versions. [3.6.3] *sshd* (also known as *sshd2*, see the sidebar "Tectia's File-Naming Conventions" [5.1]) then locates the *sshd1* executable by examining the value of the Sshd1Path keyword:

```
# Tectia
Sshd1Path /usr/local/sbin/sshd1
```

and invokes *sshd1*. The Tectia server adds the *–i* option [5.3.3.2] to the *sshd1* command line to indicate that the client connection has already been accepted by Tectia, and *sshd1* should expect the socket to be attached to its standard input, output, and error streams. In addition, the Tectia server passes the client's version string using the (mostly undocumented) *–V* command-line option:

```
# Tectia, invoked automatically by sshd
/usr/local/sbin/sshd1 -i -V "client version string" <other arguments>
```

Although *sshd2* can accept and reroute SSH-1 client connections, the reverse isn't true: *sshd1* can't accept SSH-2 connections.

The *–V* command-line option is supported by *sshd1* implementations for internal use only by *sshd2*. It is necessary because when *sshd1* starts this way, the client has already sent its initial version announcement, which *sshd1* needs to get somehow. We can't think of any practical reason to use this option manually, but we mention it here for completeness.

The OpenSSH server also implements the *–V* option, so you could use OpenSSH to handle SSH-1 protocol connections that are delegated from Tectia in its backward-compatibility mode. Be sure to set OpenSSH's Protocol keyword value to 1 to force protocol SSH-1.

Unfortunately, Tectia's SSH-1 compatibility mode is scarcely supported by other SSH implementations. Only OpenSSH versions earlier than 3.7 understand the *–V* option. An alternative is to use the latest implementation of SSH1—the original SSH product—which is still available from *ftp://ftp.ssh.com/pub/ssh/*, but it is ancient and no longer actively maintained.

Most other command-line options are passed on from *sshd2* to *sshd1* without modification. Specifically, the Tectia server leaves the following options untouched: *–b*, *–g*, *–h*, *–k*, *–p*, *–q*, and *–i*. The *–d* option [5.9] is passed to *sshd1*, but the debug level argument is removed, since it is Tectia-specific. Similarly, the argument for the *–f* option is unsuitable for *sshd1*, since it specifies an alternate configuration file, and the syntax for *sshd2* and *sshd1* configuration files isn't compatible. Therefore, if an *sshd2 -f* option is specified, then Tectia uses the Sshd1ConfigFile keyword to modify the argument for the *–f* option that is used for the *sshd1* invocation:

```
# Tectia
Sshd1ConfigFile /usr/local/etc/sshd1_config
```

The Sshd1ConfigFile is only used if *sshd2* was invoked with an explicit *–f* command-line option. Otherwise, no *–f* option is passed on the *sshd1*, and *sshd1* uses its own default configuration file, just like *sshd2*.

All other *sshd2* options are removed from the command line that is passed to *sshd1*.

 Other command-line options besides *–f* can cause compatibility problems when they are passed on from *sshd2* to *sshd1*. Some *sshd2* options are not supported by all *sshd1* implementations, and (even worse) some options with the same names have different interpretations. Be sure to carefully compare the *sshd2* and *sshd1* documentation for any options that are used. It is usually best to use keywords in different configuration files for *sshd2* and *sshd1* instead of command-line options in SSH-1 compatibility mode.

If SSH-1 compatibility mode is used, only the Tectia server should be started at boot time. *sshd1* is then launched by *sshd2* only when needed for SSH-1 connections.

5.10.1   Security Issues with Tectia's SSH-1 Compatibility Mode

There's one vital thing to keep in mind if you're using the SSH-1 compatibility feature in Tectia: you must maintain two separate SSH server configurations. When *sshd2* starts *sshd1*, it is an entirely new process, with its own SSH-1 server configuration file. No restrictions set in your *sshd2* server configuration apply to it. Even restrictions that could apply, such as AllowHosts, don't, because *sshd2* invokes *sshd1* before performing such checks.

This means you must keep the two configurations synchronized with respect to your security intent. Otherwise, an attacker can circumvent your carefully crafted *sshd2* configuration simply by connecting with an SSH-1 client.

A good strategy for automating the synchronization of *sshd2* and *sshd1* configurations is to derive the configuration files from a common template file, using a general-purpose macro preprocessor like *m4*. The following list describes the basic idea.

1. Invent symbols like `TECTIA` and `OPENSSH` to label the implementations for the *sshd2* and *sshd1* configurations.

2. Construct the template file using *m4* preprocessor conditionals like `ifdef` to handle incompatibilities between *sshd2* and *sshd1*, such as syntax differences:

```
ifdef(TECTIA, 'DenyGroups bad.*, worse')
ifdef(OPENSSH,'DenyGroups bad* worse')
```

   The template file helps to maintain the configurations because similar constructs are kept together, and duplicate information is minimized. Any common keywords and values can be specified in the template file without conditionals.

3. Generate the *sshd2* and *sshd1* configurations from the template by defining the appropriate implementation symbols on the command line using the *m4* preprocessor:

```
m4 -DTECTIA sshd_config_template > sshd2_config
m4 -DOPENSSH sshd_config_template > sshd1_config
```

4. For even more automation, set up a *Makefile* containing targets for the *sshd2* and *sshd1* configuration files, with *m4* preprocessor commands for each:

```
all: sshd2_config sshd1_config
sshd2_config: sshd_config_template
        m4 -DTECTIA $< > $@
sshd1_config: sshd_config_template
        m4 -DOPENSSH $< > $@
```

5. To ensure that the real *sshd2* and *sshd1* configuration files are up to date whenever the template file changes, regenerating the configuration files if necessary, simply use the command *make*. This can be done at boot time before the Tectia server is started, or subsequently when the configuration file is reread using SIGHUP. [5.2.4]

5.11 Summary

As you can see, SSH servers have a tremendous number of configuration options, and in some cases, multiple ways to achieve the same results. All this power comes at a price, however. When setting up a secure system, it is vital to consider each option carefully and select appropriate values. Don't skimp on understanding: the security of your systems may depend on it. Chapter 10 lists configurations for OpenSSH and Tectia. In addition, all the keywords and options in this chapter appear in Appendix E.

Remember that serverwide configuration is only one avenue for affecting server behavior. We discuss compile-time configuration in Chapter 4 and per-account configuration in Chapter 8.

## CHAPTER 6

Key Management and Agents

Your SSH private key is a precious thing. When you use public-key authentication, your key proves your identity to SSH servers. We've encountered several programs related to keys:

ssh-keygen
Creates key pairs

ssh-agent
Holds private keys in memory, saving you from typing your passphrase repeatedly

ssh-add
Loads private keys into the agent

However, we haven't gone into much depth, covering only the most basic operations with keys. Now it's time to examine these concepts and programs in detail.

We begin with an overview of SSH *identities* and the keys that represent them. After that, we thoroughly cover SSH agents and their many features. Finally, we extol the virtues of having multiple SSH identities. If you've been getting by with a single key and only light agent use, we have a lot of cool stuff in store for you. Figure 6-1 summarizes the role of key management in the overall configuration process.

This chapter is the first in a sequence on advanced SSH for end users, as opposed to system administrators. Once you've covered key management in this chapter, we'll take you through client configuration, server configuration, and forwarding in Chapters 7–9.

6.1 What Is an Identity?

An SSH identity is a sequence of bits that says, "I am really me." It is a mathematical construct that permits an SSH client to prove itself to an SSH server, so the SSH server says, "Ah, I see, it's really you. You are hereby authenticated. Come in."

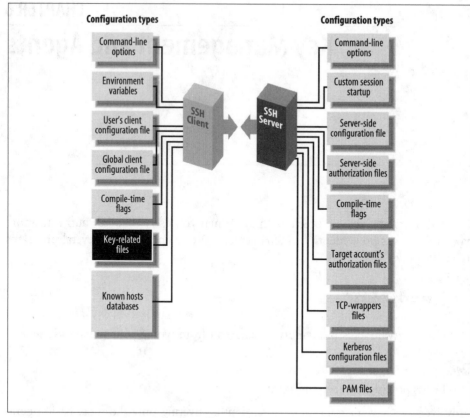

Figure 6-1. SSH user key and agent configuration (highlighted parts)

An identity consists of two parts, called the private key and the public key. Together, they are known as a *key pair*.

The private key represents your identity for *outgoing* SSH connections. When you run an SSH client in your account, such as *ssh* or *scp*, and it requests a connection with an SSH server, the client uses this private key to prove your identity to the server.

> *Private keys must be kept secret.* An intruder with your private key can access your account as easily as you can.

The public key represents your identity for *incoming* connections to your account. When an SSH client requests access to your account, using a private key as proof of identity, the SSH server examines the corresponding public key. If the keys "match" (according to a cryptographic test), authentication succeeds and the connection proceeds. Public keys don't need to be secret; they can't be used to break into an account.

A key pair is typically stored in a pair of files with related names. In SSH, the public-key filename is the same as the private one, but with the suffix *.pub* added. For example, if the file *mykey* holds a private key, its corresponding public key is found in *mykey.pub*.

You may have as many SSH identities as you like. Most SSH implementations let you specify a *default identity* clients use unless told otherwise. To use an alternative identity, you must change a setting by command-line argument, configuration file, or some other configuration tool.

The structure of identity files differs for OpenSSH and Tectia, so we explain them separately. Their locations in the filesystem are shown in Figures 6-2 (private keys) and 6-3 (public keys).

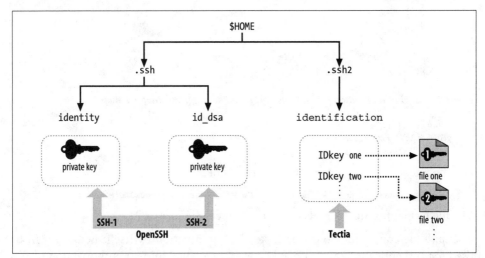

Figure 6-2. SSH identity files (private keys) and the programs that use them

6.1.1 OpenSSH Identities

An OpenSSH identity is stored in two files. By default, the private key is stored in the file *id_dsa*, and the public key in *id_dsa.pub*.* This key pair, which is kept in your *~/.ssh* directory, is your default identity that clients use unless told otherwise. The private key looks something like this:

```
-----BEGIN DSA PRIVATE KEY-----          Or "BEGIN RSA" for RSA keys
Proc-Type: 4,ENCRYPTED
DEK-Info: DES-EDE3-CBC,89C3AE51BC5876FD

MXZJgnkYE+1+eff3yt9j/aCCABz75egbGJfAbWrseiuOk3Dim9Teu2Ob1Xjdv4U9
II1hVYOkgQYuhdJbzrLMpJOW1+N5ujI8akJ6jOESeGTwJbhGyst71Y3A2+w4m1iv
```

---

* If your default key is an RSA key, the filenames are *id_rsa* and *id_rsa.pub*.

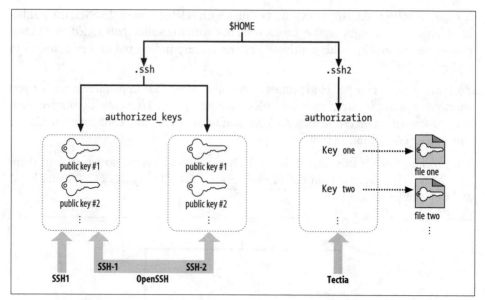

Figure 6-3. SSH authorization files (public keys) and the programs that use them

```
... lines omitted ...
gMtQSdL26V1+EmGiPfio8Q==
-----END DSA PRIVATE KEY-----
```

and the public key file contains a long, single line:

```
ssh-dss AAAAB3NzaC1kc3MAAACBAM4a2KKBE6zhPBgR ...more... smith@example.com
```

The file format for these keys is known as "OpenSSH format."

The *.pub* file containing your public key has no function by itself. Before it can be used for authentication, this public key must be copied into an authorization file on an SSH server machine, *~/.ssh/authorized_keys*. Thereafter, when an SSH client requests a connection to your server account using a private key as proof of identity, the OpenSSH server consults your *authorized_keys* file to find the matching public key.

6.1.2   Tectia Identities

A Tectia key pair is also stored in two files with related names (i.e., the private-key filename plus *.pub* yields the public-key filename). Tectia key files are often named based on the key's cryptographic properties. For example, a 2048-bit, DSA-encrypted key is generated by default in the Tectia files *id_dsa_2048_a* and *id_dsa_2048_a.pub*. These files are in a format known as "SECSH public-key file format" and sometimes "SSH2 format." The encrypted private key looks like this:

```
---- BEGIN SSH2 ENCRYPTED PRIVATE KEY ----
Subject: smith
Comment: "2048-bit dsa, smith@example.com, Sat Feb 12 2005 15:17:53 -0200"
```

Converting SSH-1 Keys to SSH-2 with ssh-keyconverter

OpenSSH includes the program *ssh-keyconverter*, which converts old SSH-1 RSA keys into a format suitable for SSH-2 authentication. If you used SSH-1 in the early days but are just getting around to upgrading, *ssh-keyconverter* might save you the time of generating and installing new keys. There are two uses:

Converting key files

Run *ssh-keyconverter* with the *–k* option to convert a single SSH-1 RSA key file to SSH-2 format. If your private key file is *mykey*, run:

```
$ ssh-keyconverter -k -o newfile mykey
Creates newfile and newfile.pub
```

Converting your entire authorized_keys file

Run *ssh-keyconverter* with the *–a* option to convert all SSH-1 RSA keys in your *authorized_keys* file to SSH-2 format:

```
$ cd ~/.ssh
$ ssh-keyconverter -a -o newfile authorized_keys
...Check that file newfile looks correct, and then...
$ mv newfile authorized_keys
$ chmod 600 authorized_keys
```

Existing SSH-2 format keys are ignored.

See the manpage for *ssh-keyconverter* for more details.

```
P2/56wAAA4oAAAAmZGwtbW9kcHtzaWdue2RzYS1uaXN5LXNoYTF9LGRoe3BsYWlufX0AAA
AIM2Rlcy1jYmMAAANIEYkNTUySnPZlYsNh15lkVfzRk6dPx4XYcXe+4f45XHIxwqcUo2Cd
... lines omitted ...
RFIORQxDhgWS/SXlFF
---- END SSH2 ENCRYPTED PRIVATE KEY ----
```

and the public key like this:

```
---- BEGIN SSH2 PUBLIC KEY ----
Subject: smith
AAAAB3NzaC1kc3MAAAEBAP3QfkjOBm1+aPgEUG39j5va13CRrPSedFYtv/52VqIgrBzRV8
Es1KHPIwmB1FOn5ejO2FATNGtaR/fg6K4DVoWscIHGZk95OjLgAz+JeBq7lxYwQOEzpsTQ
... lines omitted ...
mQ1et1r4WrOfjOF/2tXf+o71P2HfNw1M6IOB/54eI=
---- END SSH2 PUBLIC KEY ----
```

Unlike OpenSSH, however, a Tectia identity is not a single key but a *collection* of keys. When a Tectia client tries to authenticate, it may use all keys in the collection. If the first key fails to authenticate, the Tectia client automatically tries the second, and so forth, until it succeeds or fails completely.

To create an identity in Tectia, private keys must be listed in a file called an *identification file*. Your default identity file is *~/.ssh2/identification.*[*] Inside the file, private keys are listed one per line. For public-key authentication, a line begins with the keyword IdKey, followed by the name of the private-key file:

```
# Tectia identification file
# The following names are relative to ~/.ssh2
IdKey id_dsa_2048_a
IdKey my-other-tectia-key
# This key uses an absolute path
IdKey /usr/local/etc/third-key
```

The identification file may also contain PGP-related keywords: [6.5]

```
# Tectia identification file
PgpSecretKeyFile my-file.pgp
IdPgpKeyName my-key-name
```

Like OpenSSH, Tectia has an authorization file for incoming connections, but with a difference. Instead of containing copies of the public keys, the Tectia authorization file merely lists the public-key filenames using the Key keyword:

```
# Tectia authorization file
Key id_dsa_2048_a.pub
Key something-else.pub
```

Notice you have only one copy of each public key. This is slightly easier to maintain than OpenSSH's system, which has separate copies in the *.pub* file and *authorized_keys* file. [8.2.1]

Tectia's identification file can group multiple keys as a single identity. You can approximate this behavior in OpenSSH with the IdentityFile keyword. [7.4.2] To set up a default "identity" with multiple keys, add the following section to the end of your *~/.ssh/config* file:

```
Host *
IdentityFile key1
IdentityFile key2
IdentityFile key3
```

Now this multiple-key "identity" is available for all SSH connections. Similarly, you can place multiple IdentityFile values in any other section of the configuration file to associate a multikey identity with a particular host or set of hosts.

---

[*] This default may be changed with the IdentityFile keyword. [7.4.2]

6.2   Creating an Identity

Most SSH implementations include a program for creating key pairs. We cover *ssh-keygen* from OpenSSH and Tectia.

6.2.1   Generating Keys for OpenSSH

OpenSSH uses the program *ssh-keygen* to create key pairs. [2.4.2] Let's go into more detail about this program for creating new keys or modifying existing keys.

6.2.1.1   Creating OpenSSH keys

When creating a new key, you *must* indicate the key type (DSA or RSA) using the *–t* flag:

```
$ ssh-keygen -t dsa
```

You may also specify these options for creating keys:

- The number of bits in the key, using *–b*; the default is 1024 bits:

    ```
    $ ssh-keygen -t dsa -b 2048
    ```

- The name of the private-key file to be generated, using *–f*. The name is relative to your current directory. Recall that the public-key file is named after the private one with *.pub* appended.

    ```
    $ ssh-keygen -t dsa -f mykey        Creates mykey and mykey.pub
    ```

    If you omit the *–f* option, you are prompted for the information:

    ```
    $ ssh-keygen -t dsa
    ...
    Enter file in which to save the key (/home/barrett/.ssh/id_dsa): mykey
    ```

    The default filename for DSA keys is *~/.ssh/id_dsa*, and for RSA keys it's *~/.ssh/id_rsa*.

- The passphrase to decode the key, using *–N*:

    ```
    $ ssh-keygen -t dsa -N secretword
    ```

    If you omit this option, you'll be prompted for the information:

    ```
    $ ssh-keygen -t dsa
    ...
    Enter passphrase: [nothing is echoed]
    Enter the same passphrase again: [nothing is echoed]
    ```

- A textual comment associated with the key, using *–C*. If you omit this option, the comment is *username@host*, where *username* is your username and *host* is the local hostname:

    ```
    $ ssh-keygen ... -C "my favorite key"
    ```

Before using any option that places your passphrase on the shell command line, such as the *–N* or *–P* options of *ssh-keygen*, carefully consider the security implications. Because the passphrase appears on your screen, it may be visible to onlookers, and while running, it may be visible to other users viewing the machine's process list via the *ps* command. In addition, if your shell creates history files of the commands you type, the passphrase is inserted into a history file where it can be read by a third party.

Also, if you think you have a good reason just to type Return and give your key no passphrase, think again. That is essentially equivalent to putting your password in a file in your home directory named *MY-PASSWORD.PLEASE-STEAL-ME*. If you don't want to have to type a passphrase, the right thing to do is to use *ssh-agent*, hostbased authentication, or Kerberos. There are very limited circumstances having to do with unattended usage (e.g., *cron* jobs) where a plaintext, passphrase-less client key might be acceptable. [11.1]

If you use both *–f* (specify output file) and *–N* (specify passphrase), *ssh-keygen* issues no prompts. Therefore, you can automate key generation using these options (and perhaps redirecting output to */dev/null*):

```
$ ssh-keygen -f mykey -N secretword
```

You might use this technique to automate generation of a large number of keys for some purpose. Use it carefully, though, and always on a secure machine. The password on the command line is probably visible to other users on the same machine via *ps* or similar programs; and if you're scripting with this technique, obviously the passphrases shouldn't be kept in files for long.

6.2.1.2 Working with OpenSSH keys

In addition to creating keys, *ssh-keygen* can manipulate existing keys in the following ways:

- Changing the passphrase of an existing key, using *-p*. You can specify the filename with *–f* and the old and new passphrases with *–P* and *–N*, respectively:

```
$ ssh-keygen -t dsa -p -f mykey -P secretword -N newword
Your identification has been saved with the new passphrase.
```

  But if you omit them, you are prompted:

```
$ ssh-keygen -t dsa -p
Enter file in which the key is (/home/barrett/.ssh/id_rsa): mykey
Enter old passphrase: [nothing is echoed]
Key has comment 'my favorite key'
Enter new passphrase (empty for no passphrase): [nothing is echoed]
Enter the same passphrase again:
Your identification has been saved with the new passphrase.
```

  Note that this changes the passphrase but *doesn't change the key*, it just re-encrypts the key with the new passphrase. So, the corresponding public-key file on remote machines doesn't change or need to be replaced.

- Printing the *fingerprint* of a given key file, with *–l*. See the sidebar "Key Fingerprints" for more information. The fingerprint can be calculated from the public key:

```
$ ssh-keygen -l -f stevekey.pub
1024 5c:f6:e2:15:39:14:1a:8b:4c:93:44:57:6b:c6:f4:17 steve@snailbook.com
$ ssh-keygen -B -f stevekey.pub
1024 xitot-larit-gumet-fyfim-sozev-vyned-cigeb-sariv-tekuk-badus-bexax
Steve@snailbook.com
```

- Printing a DNS resource record with *–r*, and using DNS resource record format with *–g*. These options produce key fingerprints in a format suitable for a BIND nameserver, for the purposes of verifying SSH host keys via the DNS. [7.4.3.2]
- Converting between SECSH (Tectia) and OpenSSH key-storage formats, with *–e*, *–i*, and *–y*.

Option	Extract/convert from...	To...
-e	OpenSSH private-key file ("export")	SECSH public key (Tectia format)
-i	SECSH public-key file ("import")	OpenSSH public key
-y	OpenSSH private-key file	OpenSSH public key

An OpenSSH "private" key file actually contains both the public and private keys of a pair, so the *–e* and *–y* options simply extract the public key and print it out in the desired format. Use *–e* to convert an OpenSSH public key for your *~/.ssh2/ authorization* file on a Tectia server host, and -i to do the opposite. The *–y* option is useful if you accidentally delete your OpenSSH public-key file and need to restore it. Tectia keys are in a format called SECSH Public Key File Format or SSH2 format, also used by other SSH implementations whose keys you may import and export.

A function that's missing is converting the *private* keys as well. This is useful if you have an OpenSSH server host on which you also want to run Tectia, and you want the two SSH servers to share a host key.

When you make changes to a key, such as its passphrase or comment, the changes are applied to the key file only. If you have keys loaded in an SSH agent, the copies in the agent don't get changed. For instance, if you list the keys in the agent with *ssh-add -l* (lowercase L) after changing the comment, you still see the old comment in the agent. To make the changes take effect in the agent, unload and reload the affected keys.

6.2.2 Generating Keys for Tectia

Tectia also uses a program named *ssh-keygen* to create key pairs and manipulate existing keys.

Key Fingerprints

Fingerprints are a common cryptographic feature for checking that two keys in different places are the same, when comparing them literally—bit by bit—is infeasible. OpenSSH and Tectia can compute fingerprints.

Suppose Steve wants SSH access to Judy's account. He sends his public key to Judy by email, and she installs it in her SSH authorization file. While this key exchange seems straightforward, it is insecure: a hostile third party could intercept Steve's key and substitute his own, gaining access to Judy's account.

To prevent this risk, Judy needs some way to verify that the key she receives is Steve's. She can call Steve on the telephone and check, but reading a 500-byte encrypted public key over the phone is annoying and error-prone. This is why fingerprints exist.

A *fingerprint* is a short value computed from a key. It's analogous to a checksum, verifying that a string of data is unaltered—in our case, a key. To check the validity of a key using fingerprints, Steve and Judy could do the following:

1. Judy receives a public key that is supposed to be Steve's, storing it in the file *stevekey.pub*.

2. Separately, Judy and Steve view the fingerprint of the key:

   ```
   # OpenSSH
   $ ssh-keygen -l -f stevekey.pub
   1024 5c:f6:e2:15:39:14:1a:8b:4c:93:44:57:6b:c6:f4:17 Steve@snailbook.com
   $ ssh-keygen -B -f stevekey.pub
   1024 xitot-larit-gumet-fyfim-sozev-vyned-cigeb-sariv-tekuk-badus-bexax
   Steve@snailbook.com


   # Tectia
   $ ssh-keygen -F stevekey.pub
   Fingerprint for key:
   xitot-larit-gumet-fyfim-sozev-vyned-cigeb-sariv-tekuk-badus-bexax
   ```

3. Judy calls Steve on the telephone and asks him to read the fingerprint over the phone. Judy verifies that it matches the fingerprint of the key she received. Fingerprints are not unique, but for any two keys, the probability that their fingerprints are identical is extremely small. Therefore, fingerprints are a quick and convenient method for checking that a key is unaltered.

As you can see, OpenSSH and Tectia use different output formats for fingerprints. OpenSSH supports both a numeric format which is more traditional and should be familiar to users of PGP, and a textual format called "Bubble Babble" which is claimed to be easier to read and remember. Tectia supports only Bubble Babble fingerprints.

Fingerprints also surface when you connect to an SSH server whose host key has changed. In this case, OpenSSH prints a warning message and the fingerprint of the new key, which may be conveniently compared with the fingerprint of the real host key, should you have it.

6.2.2.1 Creating Tectia keys

When creating a new key, you may choose the name of the private-key file to be generated, by specifying the name at the end of the command line:

```
$ ssh-keygen mykey        creates mykey and mykey.pub
```

The name is relative to your current directory, and as usual, the public key file is named after the private one with *.pub* appended. The key is saved in the directory *~/.ssh2* in a file whose name indicates the key type and number of bits. An example is *id_dsa_2048_a*, which was generated by the DSA algorithm with 2048 bits.

You also may indicate the following with command-line options:

- The number of bits in the key, using *–b*; the default is 2048 bits:

```
$ ssh-keygen -b 4096
```

- The key type, such as DSA or RSA, using *–t*:

```
$ ssh-keygen -t dsa
```

- A textual comment associated with the key, using *–c*:

```
$ ssh-keygen -c "my favorite Tectia key"
```

  If you omit this option, the generated comment describes how and by whom the key was generated. For example:

```
"2048-bit dsa, barrett@server.example.com, Tue Feb 22 2000 02:03:36"
```

- The passphrase to decode the key, using *–p*. If you omit this option, you are prompted after generation.

```
$ ssh-keygen -p secretword
```

  You can also designate an empty password using *–P*. This shouldn't be done in general but is appropriate in some special cases: [11.1.2.2]

```
$ ssh-keygen -P
```

- Whether or not to overwrite the key file, if it already exists, with --overwrite and the value yes (the default) or no:

```
$ ssh-keygen --overwrite no mykeyfile
```

6.2.2.2 Working with Tectia keys

In addition to creating keys, *ssh-keygen* can operate on keys in the following ways:

- By changing the passphrase and comment of an existing key, using *–e*. This option causes *ssh-keygen* to become interactive, prompting for the new information. This interactive mode is primitive and annoying, requiring nearly 10 user responses to change the passphrase and comment, but it does the job:

```
$ ssh-keygen -e mykey
Passphrase needed for key "my favorite Tectia key"
Passphrase : [nothing is echoed]
Do you want to edit key "my favorite Tectia key" (yes or no)? yes
Your key comment is "my favorite Tectia key".
 Do you want to edit it (yes or no)? yes
```

```
New key comment: this is tedious
Do you want to edit passphrase (yes or no)? yes
New passphrase : [nothing is echoed]
Again        : [nothing is echoed]
Do you want to continue editing key "this is tedious" (yes or no)? god no
(yes or no)? no
Do you want to save key "this is tedious" to file mykey (yes or no)? yes
```

Changes are applied to the key files but not propagated to any copies currently loaded in an agent. (So, if you run *ssh-add -l* to list the keys in your agent, for example, you still see the old comment.)

- By converting between various key-storage formats, with the following options:

Option	Extract/convert from...	To...
-1	SSH1 key	SECSH key
--import-public-key	OpenSSH public key	SECSH public key
--import-private-key	OpenSSH private key, unencrypted only	SECSH private key
--import-ssh1-authorized-keys	An OpenSSH or SSH1 *authorized_keys* file	Tectia *authorization* file, plus an individual file for each referenced public key
-D	SECSH private key	SECSH public key[a]
-x	X.509 private key	SECSH private key
-k	PKCS 12 file	SECSH certificate and private key
-7	PKCS 7 file	Certificates from that file

[a] Handy if you ever lose your public-key file.

ssh-keygen also gives you some control over input, output, and diagnostics:

- By printing the *fingerprint* of a given key file, with *–F*. See the sidebar "Key Fingerprints" for more information. [6.2] The fingerprint is calculated from the public key:

```
$ ssh-keygen -F stevekey.pub
Fingerprint for key:
xitot-larit-gumet-fyfim-sozev-vyned-cigeb-sariv-tekuk-badus-bexax
```

- By printing cryptographic information about a key, with *–i*:

```
$ ssh-keygen -i stevekey.pub
DSA Public Key
[Strength estimation as of July, 2000 considering NFS and Pollard rho: Attack
requires O(2^80) steps, which is roughly equivalent to 6.7 * 10^7 years of effort
with 1GHz machine.]
  p = [Large prime, characteristic of the finite field]
182571555106806347080918139014450793135545573296373374132720333695050536932225483
299495917909533800218421270640772516559765425500541195802496899654480395549685.
...
```

You can display this information in different bases with $-B$; the default is base 10:

```
$ ssh-keygen -i -B 16 stevekey.pub    Base 16, hexadecimal
...
0x909fe130f9fa7192dc2a28591a53c0687...
```

- By printing the program version number, with $-V$:

```
$ ssh-keygen -V
ssh-keygen: SSH Tectia Server 4.2.1 on i686-pc-linux-gnu
Build: 1
Crypto library version: SSH Cryptographic Library, version 1.2.4
```

- By printing a help message, with $-h$ or $-?$; most Unix shells require you to escape the question mark to prevent the shell from interpreting it as a wildcard:

```
$ ssh-keygen -h
$ ssh-keygen -\?       escaping the question mark
```

- By printing debug information, with $-d$, as for Tectia's *sshd*. [5.9]

- By suppressing the progress indicator, using $-q$. The progress indicator is a sequence of O's and periods that displays while *ssh-keygen* runs, like this: .oOo. oOo.oOo.oOo:

```
$ ssh-keygen
Generating 2048-bit dsa key pair
.oOo.oOo.oOo.oOo
Key generated.

$ ssh-keygen -q
Generating 2048-bit dsa key pair
Key generated.
```

Finally, *ssh-keygen* has one guru-level advanced option, $-r$, for affecting the random numbers used for key generation. It causes *ssh-keygen* to modify *~/.ssh2/random_seed* using data you enter on standard input. [3.6.4] The Tectia manpages call this "stirring data into the random pool." Note that the program doesn't prompt you to enter data, it just sits there looking like it's hung. When this occurs, type as much data as you like and press the EOF character (Control-D in most shells):

```
$ ssh-keygen -r
I am stirring the random pool.
blah blah blah
^D
Stirred in 46 bytes.
```

See Table 6-1 for a description of *ssh-keygen* options.

Table 6-1. ssh-keygen options

ssh-keygen feature	OpenSSH	Tectia
Set number of bits	$-b$ *bits*	$-b$ *bits*
Set output file	$-f$ *file*	final argument of the command
Overwrite output file if present		*--overwrite* [*yes|no*]

Table 6-1. ssh-keygen options (continued)

ssh-keygen feature	OpenSSH	Tectia
Set comment string	−C *comment*	−c *comment*
Change comment string	−c	−e *file*
Set (new) passphrase	−N *phrase*	−p *phrase*
Set empty passphrase	−N "	−P
Specify current passphrase	−P	
Change passphrase	−p	−e *file*
Set encryption algorithm	−t *algorithm*	−t *algorithm*
Change encryption algorithm	−u	
Derive public key from private		−D *file*
Quieter output	−q	−q
Describe key		−i *file*
Set numeric base for printing key information		−B *base*
Print version number	−V	−V
Print help message	−h [a]	−h, −? [b]
Print debugging information		−d *debug_spec*
Use data from stdin for randomness		−r
Print a key's fingerprint	− l or −B	−F *file*
Convert from SSH-1 to SSH-2 format		−1 *file*
Convert OpenSSH private to Tectia public	−e	
Convert OpenSSH private to Tectia private		--import-private-key
Convert Tectia public to OpenSSH public	−i	--import-public-key
Extract OpenSSH private to public	−y	
Convert *authorized_keys* to *authorization* file		--import-ssh1-authorized-keys
Convert X.509 key to SECSH format[c]		−x *file*
Convert PKCS 12 file to SECSH format		−k *file*
Convert PKCS 7 file to SECSH format		−7 *file*

[a] Any illegal argument, such as −h, causes a help message to print.
[b] You might need to escape the question mark in your shell, e.g., -\?.
[c] The key file format used by SSH Tectia and several other implementations, but not OpenSSH.

6.2.3   Selecting a Passphrase

Choose your passphrases carefully. Make them at least 10 characters long, containing a mix of uppercase and lowercase letters, digits, and nonalphanumeric symbols. At the same time, you want the passphrase to be easy to remember, but hard for others to guess. Don't use your name, username, phone number, or other easily guessed information in the passphrase. Coming up with an effective passphrase can be a chore, but the added security is worth it.

If you forget a passphrase, you are out of luck: the corresponding SSH private key becomes unusable because you can't decrypt it. The same encryption that makes SSH so secure also makes passphrases impossible to recover. You have to abandon your SSH key, generate a new one, and choose a new passphrase for it. You must also install the new public key on every machine that holds the original one.

Smartcard Support in OpenSSH

OpenSSH includes experimental support for hardware devices (smartcards) that can hold private user keys. This includes:

ssh-keygen
> The *–D* (download) and *–U* (upload) options

ssh-add
> The *–s* (add key) and *–e* (remove key) options

ssh
> The *–I* option and the `SmartCardDevice` configuration keyword, to choose a smart-card device

At press time, smartcard support in OpenSSH is still experimental, so we don't cover it. We mention it only for completeness.

6.2.4   Generating New Groups for Diffie-Hellman Key Exchange

As we saw in Chapter 3, the SSH Transport Protocol uses the Diffie-Hellman key-agreement algorithm to generate cryptographic session keys for the SSH connection. [3.8.1.3] One parameter to this algorithm is a mathematical structure from algebra known as a "group"; specifically, a finite integer group with respect to multiplication modulo a prime. In the initial SSH protocol, a single fixed group was used for the key exchange. Due to concern over possible future attacks against this fixed parameter, an extension was created to allow the group to be negotiated, and this extension is now widely implemented.

The OpenSSH server selects the groups to be offered the client from the file */etc/moduli*. OpenSSH comes with a *moduli* file defining a set of suitable groups, and for most people this is sufficient; there is no pressing need to regenerate them. On particularly slow systems, you might edit this file to select groups with a smaller prime modulus, to speed up the key exchange.

If you like, you can generate your own set of key-exchange groups using *ssh-keygen -G*. This usage is quite technical and infrequently used, so we won't delve further into it here; refer to the *ssh-keygen* manpage, in the section "MODULI GENERATION," for details. You can also see an example in OpenBSD's *usr/src/etc/Makefile* for OpenSSH, e.g.:

> *http://www.openbsd.org/cgi-bin/cvsweb/src/etc/Makefile?*
> *rev=1.215&content-type=text/x-cvsweb-markup*

6.3   SSH Agents

An SSH agent is a program that caches private keys and responds to authentication-related queries from SSH clients. [2.5] They are terrific labor-saving devices, handling all key-related operations and eliminating the need to retype your passphrase.

The programs related to agents are *ssh-agent* and *ssh-add*. *ssh-agent* runs an agent, and *ssh-add* inserts and removes keys from the agent's key cache. A typical use might look like this:

```
# Start the agent
$ ssh-agent $SHELL
# Load your default identity
$ ssh-add
Need passphrase for /home/barrett/.ssh/identity (barrett@example.com).
Enter passphrase: ********
```

By typing your passphrase a single time, you decrypt the private key which is then stored in memory by the agent. From now on, until you terminate the agent or log out, SSH clients automatically contact the agent for all key-related operations. You needn't type your passphrase again.

We now briefly discuss how agents work. After that we get practical and illustrate different ways to start an agent, various configuration options, and several techniques for automatically loading your keys into the agent. Finally, we cover agent security and agent forwarding.

6.3.1   Agents Do Not Expose Keys

Agents perform two tasks:

- Store your private keys in memory
- Answer questions (from SSH clients) about those keys

Agents don't, however, send your private keys anywhere. This is important to understand. Once loaded, private keys remain within an agent, unseen by SSH clients. To access a key, a client says, "Hey agent! I need your help. Please perform a key-related operation for me." The agent obeys and sends the results to the client, as in Figure 6-4.

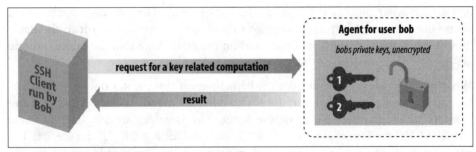

Figure 6-4. How an SSH agent works with its clients

For example, if *ssh* needs to sign an authenticator, it sends the agent a signing request containing the authenticator data and an indication of which key to use. The agent performs the cryptographic operation itself and returns the signature.

In this manner, SSH clients use the agent without seeing its private keys. This technique is more secure than handing out keys to clients. The fewer places that private keys get stored or sent, the harder it is to steal them.*

6.3.2 Starting an Agent

There are two ways to invoke an agent in your login account:

- The *single-shell* method that uses your current login shell
- The *subshell* method that forks a subshell to facilitate the inheritance of some environment variables

 Don't invoke an agent with the "obvious" but wrong command:

```
$ ssh-agent
```

Although the agent runs without complaint, SSH clients can't contact it, and the termination command (*ssh-agent -k*) doesn't kill it, because some environment variables aren't properly set.

6.3.2.1 Single-shell method

The single-shell method runs an agent in your current login shell. This is most convenient if you're running a login shell on a single terminal, as opposed to a Unix Window system such as X. Type:

```
$ eval `ssh-agent`
```

---

* This design also fits well with *token-based key storage*, in which your keys are kept on a smart card carried with you. Like agents, smart cards respond to key-related requests but don't give out keys, so integration with SSH would be straightforward. Though adoption of tokens has been slow, we believe it will be commonplace in the future.

and an *ssh-agent* process is forked in the background. The process detaches itself from your terminal, returning a prompt to you, so you needn't run it in the background manually (i.e., with an ampersand on the end). Note that the quotes around *ssh-agent* are backquotes, not apostrophes.

What purpose does *eval* serve? Well, when *ssh-agent* runs, it not only forks itself in the background, but it also outputs some shell commands to set several environment variables necessary for using the agent. The variables are SSH_AUTH_SOCK and SSH_AGENT_PID for OpenSSH, or SSH2_AUTH_SOCK and SSH2_AGENT_PID for Tectia. The *eval* command causes the current shell to interpret the commands output by *ssh-agent*, setting the environment variables. If you omit the *eval*, the following commands are printed on standard output as *ssh-agent* is invoked. For example:

```
# OpenSSH
$ ssh-agent
SSH_AUTH_SOCK=/tmp/ssh-barrett/ssh-22841-agent; export SSH_AUTH_SOCK;
SSH_AGENT_PID=22842; export SSH_AGENT_PID;
echo Agent pid 22842;

# Tectia
SSH2_AUTH_SOCK=/tmp/ssh-barrett/ssh2-22842-agent; export SSH2_AUTH_SOCK;
SSH2_AGENT_PID=22842; export SSH2_AGENT_PID;
echo Agent pid 22842;
```

Now you've got an agent running, but inaccessible to the shell. You can either kill it using the pid printed in the previous output:

```
$ kill 22842
```

or point your shell manually to the agent by setting the environment variables exactly as given:*

```
# OpenSSH
$ SSH_AUTH_SOCK=/tmp/ssh-barrett/ssh-22841-agent; export SSH_AUTH_SOCK
$ SSH_AGENT_PID=22842; export SSH_AGENT_PID

# Tectia
$ SSH2_AUTH_SOCK=/tmp/ssh-barrett/ssh2-22842-agent; export SSH2_AUTH_SOCK
$ SSH2_AGENT_PID=22842; export SSH2_AGENT_PID
```

Nevertheless, it's easier to use *eval*, so everything is set up for you.†

To terminate the agent, kill its pid:

```
$ kill 22842
```

and unset the environment variables:

```
# OpenSSH
$ unset SSH_AUTH_SOCK
```

---

* This is Bourne shell syntax. If your shell is *csh* or *tcsh*, use the appropriate syntax. [6.3.2.3]

† Why can't *ssh-agent* set its environment variables without all this trickery? Because under Unix, a program can't set environment variables in its parent shell.

```
$ unset SSH_AGENT_PID

# Tectia
$ unset SSH2_AUTH_SOCK
$ unset SSH2_AGENT_PID
```

Or for OpenSSH, use the more convenient *–k* command-line option:

```
# OpenSSH
$ eval `ssh-agent -k`
```

This prints termination commands on standard output so that *eval* can invoke them. If you forget *eval*, the agent is still killed, but your environment variables don't get unset automatically:

```
# OpenSSH
$ ssh-agent -k
unset SSH_AUTH_SOCK;        # This won't get unset,
unset SSH_AGENT_PID         # and neither will this,
echo Agent pid 22848 killed # but the agent gets killed.
```

Running an agent in a single shell, as opposed to the method we cover next (spawning a subshell), has one problem. When your login session ends, the *ssh-agent* process doesn't die. After several logins, you see many agents running, serving no purpose:[*]

```
$ ps uax | grep ssh-agent
barrett   7833  0.4  0.4   828  608 pts/1   S  21:06:10  0:00 grep agent
barrett   4189  0.0  0.6  1460  844 ?        S  Feb 21   0:06 ssh-agent
barrett   6134  0.0  0.6  1448  828 ?        S  23:11:41  0:00 ssh-agent
barrett   6167  0.0  0.6  1448  828 ?        S  23:24:19  0:00 ssh-agent
barrett   7719  0.0  0.6  1456  840 ?        S  20:42:25  0:02 ssh-agent
```

You can get around this problem by running *ssh-agent -k* automatically when you log out. In Bourne-style shells (*sh*, *ksh*, *bash*), this may be done with a trap of Unix signal 0 at the top of *~/.profile*:

```
# ~/.profile
trap '
  test -n "$SSH_AGENT_PID"  && eval `ssh-agent -k` ;
  test -n "$SSH2_AGENT_PID" && kill $SSH2_AGENT_PID
' 0
```

For C shells and for *tcsh*, terminate the agent in your *~/.logout* file:

```
# ~/.logout
if ( "$SSH_AGENT_PID" != "" ) then
  eval `ssh-agent -k`
endif
if ( "$SSH2_AGENT_PID" != "" ) then
  kill $SSH2_AGENT_PID
endif
```

---

[*] Actually, you can reconnect to an agent launched in a previous login, by modifying your SSH_AUTH_SOCK variable to point to the old socket.

Once this trap is set, your *ssh-agent* process is killed automatically when you log out, printing a message like:

```
Agent pid 8090 killed
```

6.3.2.2 Subshell method

The second way to invoke an agent spawns a *subshell*. You provide an argument to *ssh-agent*, which is a path to a shell or shell script. Examples are:

```
$ ssh-agent /bin/sh
$ ssh-agent /bin/csh
$ ssh-agent $SHELL
$ ssh-agent my-shell-script # Run a shell script instead of a shell
```

This time, instead of forking a background process, *ssh-agent* runs in the foreground, spawning a subshell and setting the aforementioned environment variables automatically. The rest of your login session runs within this subshell, and when you terminate it, *ssh-agent* terminates as well. This method, as you will see later, is most convenient if you run a Window System such as X and invoke the agent in your initialization file (e.g., *~/.xsession*).* However, the method is also perfectly reasonable for single-terminal logins.

When using the subshell method, invoke it at an appropriate time. We recommend the last line of your login initialization file (e.g., *~/.profile* or *~/.login*) or the first typed command after you log in. Otherwise, if you first run some background processes in your shell and then invoke the agent, those initial background processes become inaccessible until you terminate the agent's subshell. For example, if you run the *vi* editor, suspend it, and then run the agent, you lose access to the editor session until you terminate the agent:

```
$ vi myfile                    # Run your editor.
^Z                             # Suspend it.
$ jobs                         # View your background processes.
[1] + Stopped (SIGTSTP) vi
$ ssh-agent $SHELL             # Run a subshell.
$ jobs                         # No jobs here! They're in the parent shell.
$ exit                         # Terminate the agent's subshell.
$ jobs                         # Now we can see our processes again.
[1] + Stopped (SIGTSTP) vi
```

The advantages and disadvantages of the two methods are shown in Table 6-2.

---

* In fact, many Linux distributions set this up for you, automatically launching *ssh-agent* when you log in via KDE or GNOME. Red Hat Linux and SUSE Linux are two examples. After logging in, run a *ps* command and grep for "agent" to see this in action.

Table 6-2. Pros and cons of invoking an agent

Method	Pros	Cons
`eval ``ssh-agent```	Simple, intuitive.	Must be terminated manually.
`ssh-agent $SHELL`	Agent's environment variables are propagated automatically; terminates on logout. Conveniently set up by many Linux distributions.	Your login shell becomes dependent on the agent's health; if the agent dies, your login shell may die.

6.3.2.3   Format of environment variable commands

As we've said, *ssh-agent* prints a sequence of shell commands to set several environment variables. The syntax of these commands differs depending on which shell is being used. You can force the commands to use Bourne-style or C-shell-style syntax with the *–s* and *–c* options, respectively:

```
# Bourne-shell style commands
$ ssh-agent -s
SSH_AUTH_SOCK=/tmp/ssh-barrett/ssh-3654-agent; export SSH_AUTH_SOCK;
SSH_AGENT_PID=3655; export SSH_AGENT_PID;
echo Agent pid 3655;

# C-shell style commands
$ ssh-agent -c
setenv SSH_AUTH_SOCK /tmp/ssh-barrett/ssh-3654-agent;
setenv SSH_AGENT_PID 3655;
echo Agent pid 3655;
```

Normally *ssh-agent* detects your login shell and prints the appropriate lines, so you don't need *–c* or *–s*. One situation where you need these options is if you invoke *ssh-agent* within a shell script, but the script's shell is not the same type as your login shell. For example, if your login shell is */bin/csh*, and you invoke this script:

```
#!/bin/sh
`ssh-agent`
```

ssh-agent outputs C-shell-style commands, which fails. So, you should use:

```
#!/bin/sh
`ssh-agent -s`
```

This is particularly important if you run an agent under X, and your *~/.xsession* file (or other startup file) is executed by a shell different from your login shell.

6.3.3   Loading Keys with ssh-add

The program *ssh-add* is your personal communication channel to an *ssh-agent* process. When you first invoke an SSH agent, it contains no keys. *ssh-add*, as you might guess from its name, can *add* private keys to an SSH agent. But the name is misleading because *ssh-add* also controls the agent in other ways, such as listing keys, deleting keys, and locking the agent from accepting further keys.

If you invoke *ssh-add* with no arguments, your default SSH keys are loaded into the agent, once you have typed their passphrases.[*] For example:

```
# Output shown for OpenSSH
$ ssh-add
Enter passphrase for /home/smith/.ssh/id_dsa: ********
Identity added: /home/smith/.ssh/id_dsa
```

Normally, *ssh-add* reads the passphrase from the user's terminal. If the standard input isn't a terminal, however, and the DISPLAY environment variable is set, *ssh-add* instead invokes an X Window graphical program called *ssh-askpass* or *x11-ssh-askpass* that pops up a window to read your passphrase. This is especially convenient in *xdm* startup scripts.[†]

 If you don't like *ssh-askpass*, set your environment variable SSH_ASKPASS to the full path to an alternative program (say, */usr/local/bin/ my-ask-pass*). Then this other program, rahter than *ssh-askpass*, runs automatically to gather your passphrase. (OpenSSH only.)

ssh-add supports the following command-line options for listing and deleting keys, and for reading the passphrase:

- List all identities loaded in the agent. OpenSSH lists the key fingerprints with *–l* (see the earlier sidebar "Key Fingerprints" for more detail):

```
# OpenSSH
$ ssh-add -l
1024 e9:39:50:f0:b4:65:ba:b9:d7:d3:69:10:d0:23:a7:88 a (DSA)
1024 7c:91:07:29:46:a8:61:b4:7c:95:69:fc:47:1e:3c:ff b (RSA)
```

  To print the public keys held in the OpenSSH agent, use *–L*:

```
# OpenSSH
$ ssh-add -L
ssh-dss AAAAB3NzaC1kc3MAAACBAK5ArDaZyPXa5Iz... and so forth
ssh-rsa AAAAB3NzaC1yc2EAAAABIwAAAIEAtIgHblLp1i... and so forth
```

  Tectia lists brief information about the loaded keys with *–l*:

```
# Tectia
$ ssh-add -l
Listing identities.
The authorization agent has two keys:
id_dsa_2048_a: my main key
id_dsa_2048_b: another key
```

- Delete an identity from the agent, with *–d*:

```
$ ssh-add -d ~/.ssh/second_id
Identity removed: /home/smith/.ssh/second_id (second_id.pub)
```

---

[*] OpenSSH's *ssh-add* tries to reuse a passphrase to load subsequent keys.

[†] X has its own security problems, of course. If someone can connect to your X server, they can monitor all your keystrokes, including your passphrase. Whether this is an issue in using *ssh-askpass* depends on your system and security needs.

If you don't specify a key file, *ssh-add* deletes your default identity from the agent:

```
$ ssh-add -d
Identity removed: /home/smith/.ssh/id_dsa (/home/smith/.ssh/id_dsa.pub)
```

- Delete all identities from the agent, with *–D*; this unloads every currently loaded key but leaves the agent running:

```
# OpenSSH
$ ssh-add -D
All identities removed.


# Tectia
$ ssh-add -D
Deleting all identities.
```

- Set a timeout for a key, with *–t*. Normally when you add a key, it remains loaded in the agent indefinitely, until the agent terminates or you unload the key manually. The *–t* option assigns a lifetime to a key, measured in seconds (OpenSSH) or minutes (Tectia). After this time has passed, the agent automatically unloads the key:

```
$ ssh-add -t 30 mykey
```

OpenSSH has a richer syntax for specifying times that may also be used here; see the sidebar "Time Values in Configuration Files" in Chapter 5:

```
# OpenSSH
$ ssh-add -t 3W mykey          Set a key lifetime of three weeks
```

You can also specify the maximum lifetime for all keys in the agent:

```
# OpenSSH
$ eval 'ssh-agent -t 3W'       All keys in the agent have a lifetime of three weeks or less
```

- Lock and unlock the agent with a password, using *–x* and *–X* (OpenSSH) or *–L* and *–U* (Tectia). A locked agent refuses all *ssh-add* operations except an unlock request. If you try to modify the state of the agent (adding or deleting keys, etc.), the operation is rejected, and if you try to list the agent's keys, you are told the agent has no keys.

To lock:

```
# OpenSSH
$ ssh-add -x
Enter lock password: ****
Again: ****
Agent locked

# Tectia
$ ssh-add -L
Enter lock password: ****
Again: ****
```

and to unlock:

```
# OpenSSH
ssh-add -X
```

```
Enter lock password: ****
Agent unlocked

# Tectia
$ ssh-add -U
Enter lock password: ****
```

Locking is a convenient way to protect the agent if you step away from your computer but leave yourself logged in. You can instead unload all your keys with *ssh-add -D*, but then you have to reload them again when you return. If you have only one key there's no difference, but if you use several it's a pain. Unfortunately, both OpenSSH and Tectia's locking mechanism aren't tremendously secure. *ssh-agent* simply stores the lock password in memory, refusing to honor any more requests until it receives an unlock message containing the same password. The locked agent is still vulnerable to attack: if an intruder gains access to your account (or the root account), he can dump the agent's process address space and extract your keys. The lock feature certainly deters casual misuse, but the potential for an attack is real. If you're seriously concerned about key disclosure, think twice before relying on locking. We prefer to see this feature implemented by encrypting all the agent's loaded keys with the lock password. This gives the same user convenience and provides better protection.

OpenSSH's *ssh-add* program can also be forced to confirm identities via *ssh-askpass* before using them, with *-c*. [6.3.3]

Tectia's *ssh-add* program has additional features controlled by command-line options:

*   Place limits on agent forwarding with *-f* and *-F*. (Agent forwarding, which we'll cover soon, transmits agent requests between hosts.) The *-f* option lets you limit, for a given key, the distance that requests for this key may traverse. If a request is made from too far away, measured in hops from machine to machine, the request fails. A hop count of zero disables forwarding for this key alone.

```
# Tectia
$ ssh-add -f 0 mykey          Load a key that may be used only locally
$ ssh-add -f 3 mykey          Load a key and accept requests from up to three hops
                              away
```

The *-F* option lets you limit the set of hosts that may make requests relating to this key. It takes as an argument a set of hostnames, domains, and IP addresses that may make or forward requests. The argument is a comma-separated list of wildcard patterns, as for the serverwide configuration keywords AllowHosts and DenyHosts. [5.5.3]

```
# Tectia
$ ssh-add -F '*.example.com' mykey   Permit forwarding only in the example.com domain
$ ssh-add -F 'server.example.com,*.harvard.edu' mykey Permit forwarding from server
     example.com and the harvard.edu domain
    $ ssh-add -F 'server.example.com,*.harvard.edu' -f 2 mykey Same as the preceding
     command, but limit forwarding to two hops
```

- Reading your passphrase from standard input, with –*p*, to provide it by a pipe or similar means. So, if you had a program *passphraser* that produces the passphrase, you could feed the passphrase to *ssh-add*:

  ```
  # Tectia
  $ passphraser | ssh-add
  ```

- Read keys from a URL rather than a file, with –*u*:

  ```
  # Tectia
  $ ssh-add -u http://server.example.com/mykey
  ```

- Prohibit keys from being used for SSH-1 protocol connections, with -*1*:

  ```
  # Tectia
  $ ssh-add -1 my-ssh2-only-key
  ```

- Perform PGP key operations. Tectia's *ssh-add2* manpage documents the options –*R*, –*N*, –*P*, and –*I* for OpenPGP keyring operations, but they aren't officially supported.

- Print the program version number, with –*V*:

  ```
  # Tectia
  $ ssh-add -V
  ssh-add2 SSH Tectia Server 4.2.1 on i686-pc-linux-gnu
  Build: 1
  Released 2004-11-30 (YYYY-MM-DD).
  ```

6.3.3.1 Automatic agent loading (single-shell method)

It's a pain to invoke *ssh-agent* and/or *ssh-add* manually each time you log in. With some clever lines in your login initialization file, you can automatically invoke an agent and load your default identity. We'll demonstrate this with both methods of agent invocation, single-shell and subshell.

With the single-shell method, here are the major steps:

1. Make sure you're not already running an agent, by testing the environment variable SSH_AUTH_SOCK or SSH2_AUTH_SOCK.

2. Run *ssh-agent* using *eval*.

3. If your shell is attached to a tty, load your default identity with *ssh-add*.

For the Bourne shell and its derivatives (*ksh*, *bash*), the following lines can be placed into ~/.*profile*:

```
# Make sure ssh-agent dies on logout
trap '
  test -n "$SSH_AGENT_PID"  && eval `ssh-agent -k` ;
  test -n "$SSH2_AGENT_PID" && kill $SSH2_AGENT_PID
' 0

# If no agent is running and we have a terminal, run ssh-agent and ssh-add.
# (For Tectia, change this to use SSH2_AUTH_SOCK.)
if [ "$SSH_AUTH_SOCK" = "" ]
then
```

```
   eval `ssh-agent`
   /usr/bin/tty > /dev/null && ssh-add
fi
```

For the C shell and *tcsh*, the following lines can be placed into *~/.login*:

```
# Use SSH2_AUTH_SOCK instead for Tectia
if ( ! $?SSH_AUTH_SOCK  ) then
  eval `ssh-agent`
  /usr/bin/tty > /dev/null && ssh-add
endif
```

and termination code in *~/.logout*:

```
# ~/.logout
if ( "$SSH_AGENT_PID" != "" ) eval `ssh-agent -k`
if ( "$SSH2_AGENT_PID" != "" ) kill $SSH2_AGENT_PID
```

> Another single-shell technique to make your clients aware of the agent
> is to use OpenSSH's *ssh-agent -a* option. (This does not work with
> Tectia's agent.) With this approach, you choose your own socket in
> advance—say, *~/.ssh/mysocket*—and make decisions based on its
> existence. For example, in your *~/.profile* you could have:
>
> ```
> #!/bin/bash
> SOCKETFILE=~/.ssh/mysocket
> if [ ! -S "$SOCKETFILE" ]
> then
>     eval `ssh-agent -a $SOCKETFILE`
> fi
> ```
>
> Since you know the socket path, you can direct SSH clients to it by set-
> ting *SSH_AUTH_SOCK=~/.ssh/mysocket* as needed. When you termi-
> nate the OpenSSH agent with *ssh-agent -k*, the socket file is deleted
> automatically.

6.3.3.2 Automatic agent loading (subshell method)

The second way to load an agent on login uses the subshell method to invoke the
agent, and is described in the following list. This time, you add lines to both your login
initialization file (*~/.profile* or *~/.login*), an optional second file of your choice, and your
shell initialization file (*~/.cshrc*, *~/.bashrc*, etc.). This method doesn't work for the
Bourne shell, which has no shell initialization file.

1. In your *login* initialization file, make sure you're not already running an agent,
   by testing the environment variable SSH_AUTH_SOCK or SSH2_AUTH_SOCK.

2. As the last line of your login initialization file, exec *ssh-agent*, which spawns a
   subshell. Optionally run a *second* initialization file to configure aspects of the
   subshell.

3. In your *shell* initialization file, check whether the shell is attached to a tty and the
   agent has no identities loaded yet. If so, load your default identity with *ssh-add*.

Now let's see how to do this with Bourne-shell and C-shell families. For derivatives of the Bourne shell (*ksh*, *bash*), put the following line at the end of *~/.profile*:

```
test -n "$SSH_AUTH_SOCK" && exec ssh-agent $SHELL
```

This runs the agent, spawning a subshell. If you want to tailor the environment of the subshell, create a script (say, *~/.profile2*) to do so, and use this instead:

```
test -n "$SSH_AUTH_SOCK" && exec ssh-agent $SHELL $HOME/.profile2
```

Next, in your shell initialization file (*$ENV* for *ksh*, or *~/.bashrc* for *bash*), place the following lines to load your default identity only if it's not loaded already:

```
# Make sure we are attached to a tty
if /usr/bin/tty > /dev/null
then
  # Check the output of "ssh-add -l" for identities.
  ssh-add -l | grep 'no identities' > /dev/null
  if [ $? -eq 0 ]
  then
    # Load your default identity.
    ssh-add
  fi
fi
```

6.3.3.3 Automatic agent loading (X Window System)

If you're using X and want to run an agent and load your default identity automatically, it's simple. Just use the single-shell method. For example, in your X startup file, usually *~/.xsession*, you can use these two lines:

```
eval `ssh-agent`
ssh-add
```

However, first check if your window environment (e.g., GNOME or KDE) is already running an SSH agent for you, in which case you needn't do it yourself. This setup is commonly found in Linux distributions.

6.3.4   Agents and Security

As we mentioned earlier, agents don't expose private keys to SSH clients. Instead, they answer requests from clients *using* the keys. This approach is more secure than passing keys around, but it still has security concerns. It is important to understand these concerns before completely trusting the agent model:

- Agents rely on external access control mechanisms.
- Agents can be cracked.

6.3.4.1   Access control

When your agent is loaded with private keys, a potential security issue arises. How does your agent distinguish between legitimate requests from your SSH clients and illegitimate requests from unauthorized sources? Since the agent speaks only to other processes on the same host, it uses the host's existing security mechanisms. These vary from one operating system to another, but the four main mechanisms are:

- File permissions
- Client identification
- Protected memory
- Prompt-on-use

File permissions. Under Unix, the agent communicates with users via a named pipe (Unix-domain socket) in the filesystem, so the first line of defense is the file permissions on the socket. OpenSSH and Tectia keep agent sockets in a protected directory. OpenSSH's socket is named */tmp/ssh-STRING/agent.N*, where *STRING* is random text based on the agent's process ID, and *N* is a number:

```
# OpenSSH
$ ls -la /tmp/ssh-alHMKX4537
drwx------   2 smith    smith        4096 Feb  4 13:40 .
drwxrwxrwt   7 root     root         4096 Feb  4 13:40 ..
srwxr-xr-x   1 smith    smith           0 Feb  4 13:40 agent.4537
```

while Tectia's is named */tmp/ssh-USERNAME/ssh2-N-agent*, where *USERNAME* is your username and *N* is again a number:

```
# Tectia
$ ls -la /tmp/ssh-smith/
drwx------   2 smith    smith        4096 Feb  4 13:40 .
drwxrwxrwt   7 root     root         4096 Feb  4 13:40 ..
srw-------   1 smith    smith           0 Feb  4 13:40 ssh2-4537-agent
```

The number *N* is usually one less than the process ID (pid) of the agent itself. This is because *ssh-agent* first creates the socket using its pid, then later starts another process that actually persists as the agent. In these examples, user smith has a socket for an agent which probably has PID 4536. The containing directory itself has mode 0700.

This organization of a user's sockets into a single directory is not only for neatness but also for security and portability, because different operating systems treat socket permissions in different ways. For example, Solaris appears to ignore them completely; even a socket with permission 000 (no access for anyone) accepts all connections. Linux respects socket permissions, but a write-only socket permits both reading and writing. To deal with such diverse implementations, SSH keeps your sockets in a directory owned by you, with directory permissions that forbid anyone else to access the sockets inside.

Using a subdirectory of */tmp*, rather than */tmp* itself, also prevents a class of attacks called *temp races*. A temp-race attack takes advantage of race conditions inherent in the common setting of the "sticky" mode bit on the Unix */tmp* directory, allowing anyone to create a file there, but only allowing deletion of files owned by the same uid as the deleting process.

If you want to move the socket out of the default */tmp* directory, use the *–a* option: [6.3.3.1]

```
# OpenSSH
ssh-agent -a /private/ssh/mysocket
SSH_AUTH_SOCK=/private/ssh/mysocket; export SSH_AUTH_SOCK;
echo Agent pid 28320;
```

Client identification. Some flavors of Unix allow one process to find out who's on the other end of a named pipe: the peer's process ID, user ID, etc. If this feature is available, an agent can verify that the client's user ID matches its own.

Protected memory. The *ssh-agent* process won't reveal keys via the agent protocol, but those keys are in its memory. A privileged user might be able to attach to the agent process and read the keys from its memory space, bypassing the usual Unix process separation. Some Unixes allow a process to limit or prevent this kind of external interference, so some agents make use of this feature.

Prompt-on-use. Some agents can query the user for permission each time a request comes in over the agent socket (e.g., OpenSSH *ssh-add -c*). If you use this feature and a window pops up unexpectedly asking about your agent, something's wrong!

6.3.4.2   Cracking an agent

If the machine running your agent is compromised, an attacker can easily gain access to the IPC channel and thus to your agent. This permits the interloper to make requests of the agent, at least for a time. Once you log out or unload your keys from the agent, the security hole is closed. Therefore, you should run agents only on trusted machines, perhaps unloading your keys (*ssh-agent -D*) if you're away from the computer for an extended time, such as overnight.

Since agents don't give out keys, your keys seem safe from theft if the machine is compromised. Alas, that's not the case. An enterprising cracker, once logged into the machine, has other means for getting your keys, such as:

* Stealing your private-key file and attempting to guess your passphrase
* Tracing processes that you're running, and catching your passphrase while you type it
* Trojan horse attacks: installing modified versions of system programs, such as the login program, shells, or the SSH implementation itself, that steal your passphrase
* Obtaining a copy of the memory space of your running agent and picking the keys out of it directly (this is a bit harder than the others)

The bottom line is this: run agents only on trusted machines. SSH does not excuse you from securing other aspects of your system.

6.3.5 Agent Forwarding

So far, our SSH clients have conversed with an SSH agent on the same machine. Using a feature called *agent forwarding*, clients can also communicate with agents on remote machines. This is both a convenience feature—permitting your clients on multiple machines to work with a single agent—and a means for avoiding some firewall-related problems.

6.3.5.1 A firewall example

Suppose you want to connect from your home computer, H, to a computer at work, W. Like many corporate computers, W is behind a network firewall and not directly accessible from the Internet, so you can't create an SSH connection from H to W. Hmm...what can you do? You call technical support and for once, they have good news. They say that your company maintains a gateway or "bastion" host, B, that is accessible from the Internet and runs an SSH server. This means you *should* be able to reach W by opening an SSH connection from H to B, and then from B to W, since the firewall permits SSH traffic. Tech support gives you an account on the bastion host B, and the problem seems to be solved...or is it?

For security reasons, the company permits access to its computers only by public-key authentication. So, using your private key on home machine H, you successfully connect to bastion host B. And now you run into a roadblock: also for security reasons, the company prohibits users from storing SSH keys on the exposed bastion host B, since they can be stolen if B is hacked. That's bad news, since the SSH client on B needs a key to connect to your work account on W. Your key is at home on H. (Figure 6-5 illustrates the problem.) What now? Use SSH agent forwarding.

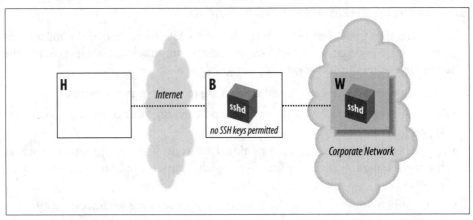

Figure 6-5. Bastion host scenario

SSH agent forwarding allows a program running on a remote host, such as B, to access your *ssh-agent* on H transparently, as if the agent were running on B. Thus, a remote SSH client running on *B* can now sign and decrypt data using your key on H, as shown in Figure 6-6. As a result, you can invoke an SSH session from B to your work machine W, solving the problem.

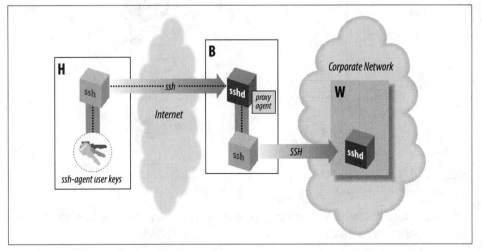

Figure 6-6. Solution with SSH agent forwarding

6.3.5.2 How agent forwarding works

Agent forwarding, like all SSH forwarding (Chapter 9), works "behind the scenes." In this case, the key-related requests of an SSH client are forwarded across a separate, previously established SSH session to an agent holding the needed keys, shown in Figure 6-7. Let's examine in detail the steps that occur.

1. Suppose you're logged onto machine X, and you invoke ssh to establish a remote terminal session on machine Y.

   ```
   # On machine X:
   $ ssh Y
   ```

2. Assuming that agent forwarding is turned on, the client says to the SSH server, "I would like to request agent forwarding, please," when establishing the connection.

3. *sshd* on machine *Y* checks its configuration to see if it permits agent forwarding. Let's assume that it's enabled.

4. *sshd* on machine Y sets up an interprocess communication (IPC) channel local to Y by creating some Unix domain sockets and setting some environment variables. [6.3.2.1] The resulting IPC mechanism is just like the one *ssh-agent* sets up. As a result, *sshd* is now prepared to pose as an SSH agent.

5. Your SSH session is now established between X and Y.

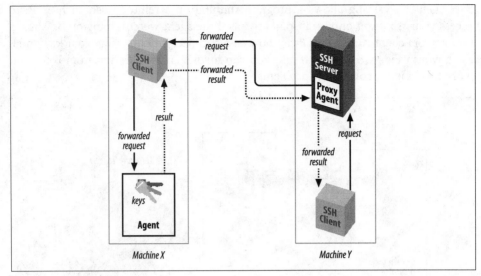

Figure 6-7. Agent forwarding

6. Next, from machine Y, you run another *ssh* command to establish an SSH session with a third machine, Z:

```
# On machine Y:
$ ssh Z
```

7. This new *ssh* client now needs a key to make the connection to Z. It believes there's an agent running on machine Y, because *sshd* on Y is posing as one. So, the client makes an authentication request over the agent IPC channel.

8. *sshd* intercepts the request, masquerading as an agent, and says, "Hello, I'm the agent. What would you like to do?" The process is transparent: the client believes it's talking to an agent.

9. *sshd* then forwards the agent-related request back to the original machine, X, over the secure connection between X and Y. The agent on machine X receives the request and accesses your local key, and its response is forwarded back to *sshd* on machine *Y*.

10. *sshd* on Y passes the response on to the client, and the connection to machine Z proceeds.

Thanks to agent forwarding, you have transparent access from machine Y to any SSH keys back on machine X. Thus, any SSH clients on Y can access any hosts permitted by your keys on X. To test this, run this command on machine Y to list your keys:

```
# On machine Y:
$ ssh-add -l
```

You see all keys that are loaded in your agent on machine *X*.

It's worth noting that the agent-forwarding relationship is transitive: if you repeat this process, making a chain of SSH connections from machine to machine, then clients on the final host still have access to your keys on the first host (X). (This assumes agent forwarding is permitted by *sshd* on each intermediate host.)

6.3.5.3 Enabling agent forwarding

Before an SSH client can take advantage of agent forwarding, the feature must be turned on. SSH implementations vary in their default settings of this feature, and of course the system administrator can change it. If necessary, you can turn it on manually with the configuration keyword ForwardAgent in the client configuration file *~/.ssh/config*, giving a value of yes (the default) or no:[*]

```
ForwardAgent yes
```

Likewise, you can use command-line options. In addition to the –o command-line option, which accepts any configuration keyword and its value:

```
$ ssh -o "ForwardAgent yes" ...
```

ssh accepts command-line options to turn on agent forwarding, even though it's on by default:

```
# OpenSSH
$ ssh -A ...

# Tectia
$ ssh +a ...
```

The option –a turns off agent forwarding:

```
$ ssh -a ...
```

6.3.6 Agent CPU Usage

Before we leave our discussion of agents, we'll make one final note about performance. Agents carry out all cryptographic work that is otherwise done by SSH clients. This means an agent can accumulate substantial CPU time. In one case we saw, some friends of ours were using SSH for a great deal of automation, running hundreds of short-lived sessions in a row. Our friends were quite puzzled to find that the single *ssh-agent* used by all these processes was eating the lion's share of CPU on that machine!

6.3.7 Debugging the Agent

OpenSSH's *ssh-agent* has a primitive debugging mode that's enabled with the –d option:

```
# OpenSSH
ssh-agent -d
```

---

[*] Tectia supports the keyword AllowAgentForwarding as a synonym for ForwardAgent.

```
SSH_AUTH_SOCK=/tmp/ssh-nQxHO27500/agent.27500; export SSH_AUTH_SOCK;
echo Agent pid 27500;
```

In debug mode, the agent runs in the foreground instead of putting itself into the background (forking). To communicate with the agent and watch it print debug messages, open a second shell (e.g., in a separate X terminal window) and run the variable-setting command that *ssh-agent* printed on invocation:

```
$ SSH_AUTH_SOCK=/tmp/ssh-nQxHO27500/agent.27500; export SSH_AUTH_SOCK;
```

Then try some *ssh-add* commands and see what the agent does. For example, if you run this in your second shell:

```
$ ssh-add -l
The agent has no identities.
```

then the agent in the original shell prints:

```
debug1: type 1
debug1: type 11
```

The type output indicates the type of message that *ssh-agent* has received. Types 1 and 11 are requests for identities (SSH-1 and SSH-2, respectively), which makes perfect sense because that's what *ssh-add -l* does. A few other message codes are 17 to load an identity, 18 to delete one, and 19 to delete all identities. You can learn more message types by reading the C header file *authfd.h* in the OpenSSH source code.

6.4   Multiple Identities

Until now, we've assumed you have a single SSH identity that uniquely identifies you to an SSH server. You do have a default identity—our earlier *ssh-add* examples operated on it—but you may create as many other identities as you like.

Why use several identities? After all, with a single SSH identity, you can connect to remote machines with a single passphrase. That's very simple and convenient. In fact, most people can survive perfectly well with just one identity. Multiple identities have important uses, however:

Additional security
> If you use different SSH keys for different remote accounts, and one of your keys is cracked, only some of your remote accounts are vulnerable.

Secure batch processes
> Using an SSH key with an empty passphrase, you can create secure, automated processes between interacting computers, such as unattended backups. [11.1.2.2] However, you definitely don't want your regular logins to use an unencrypted private key, so you should create a second key for this purpose.

Different account settings
> You can configure your remote account to respond differently based on which key is used for connecting. For example, you can make your Unix login session run different startup files depending on which key is used.

Triggering remote programs

Your remote account can be set up to run specific programs when an alternative key is used, via forced commands. [8.2.3]

In order to use multiple identities, you need to know how to switch between them. There are two ways: manually, and automatically with an agent.

6.4.1   Switching Identities Manually

ssh and *scp* let you switch your identity with the *–i* command-line option and the IdentityFile configuration keyword. For either of these techniques, you provide the name of your desired private-key file (OpenSSH) or identification file (Tectia). [7.4.2] Table 6-3 displays a summary of the syntax.

Table 6-3. Specifying an alternate identity

Version	ssh	scp	IdentityFile keyword
OpenSSH	ssh -i *key_file* ...	scp -i *key_file* ...	IdentityFile *key_file*
Tectia	ssh -i *id_file* ...	scp -i *id_file* ...	IdentityFile *id_file*

6.4.2   Switching Identities with an Agent

If you use an SSH agent, identity switching is handled automatically. Simply load all the desired identities into the agent using *ssh-add*. Thereafter, when you attempt a connection, your SSH client requests and receives a list of all your identities from the agent. The client then tries each identity in turn until one authenticates successfully, or they all fail. Even if you have 10 different identities for 10 different SSH servers, a single agent (containing these keys) provides appropriate key information to your SSH clients for seamless authentication with all 10 servers.

All of this happens transparently with no effort on your part. Well, almost no effort. If you have several identities loaded in the agent, and more than one can apply in a given situation, the agent might pick the wrong one. For example, suppose you have two OpenSSH identities stored in the files *id-normal* and *id-backups*. You use *id-normal* for terminal sessions, and *id-backups* for invoking a remote backup program on the same server machine (e.g., using a forced command [8.2.3]). Each day when you log in, you load both keys into an agent, using a clever script that locates and loads all key files in a given directory:

```
#!/bin/csh
cd ~/.ssh/my-keys          # An example directory
foreach keyfile (*)
  ssh-add $keyfile
end
```

What happens when you invoke an SSH client?

```
$ ssh server.example.com
```

In this case, the remote backup program gets run, authenticating with the key in file *id-backups*. You see, the wildcard in your script returns a list of key files in alphabetical order, so *id-backups* is added before *id-normal*, as if you'd typed:

```
$ ssh-add id-backups
$ ssh-add id-normal
```

Therefore, your SSH clients *always* use the key `id-backups` when connecting to *server.example.com* because the agent provides it first in response to a client request. This might not be what you intended. In this case you could specify the right key on the command line using the *–i* option:

```
$ ssh -i id-normal server.example.com
```

or use the `IdentityFile` configuration keyword in *~/.ssh/config*. [7.4.2]

6.4.3 Tailoring Sessions Based on Identity

Multiple identities can be extremely useful. In particular, you can configure your remote accounts to respond differently to different identities. This is a three-step process:

1. Generate a new SSH identity, as we have discussed in this chapter.

2. Set up a detailed client configuration that does what you want, using your new identity. This is the subject of Chapter 7.

3. Set up your account on the SSH server machine to respond to your new identity in a desired manner. This is covered in detail in Chapter 8.

We *strongly* encourage you to experiment with this technique. You can do some really powerful and interesting things with SSH this way. If you're just running simple terminal sessions with SSH, you are missing half the fun.

6.5 PGP Authentication in Tectia

Pretty Good Privacy (PGP) is another security product employing public-key authentication. [1.6.2] PGP keys and SSH keys are implemented differently and aren't interchangeable, however, Tectia can perform authentication by PGP key, following the OpenPGP standard.* Yes, you can use your favorite PGP key to prove your identity to a Tectia server (as long as the key file is OpenPGP-compatible; some PGP keys, especially those produced by older software versions, aren't). At press time, this feature is only sketchily documented. Here's how to make it work.

---

* According to SSH Communications Security, PGP authentication in Tectia is not officially supported, nor is any other feature that is enabled by recompiling the source code.

First, you need Tectia installed on both the client and server machines. Also, both implementations must be compiled with PGP support included, using the compile-time flag --with-pgp. [4.3.5.7]

On the client machine, you need to make your PGP secret key ring and the desired secret key for authentication available to Tectia clients. Here's how:

1. Copy your PGP secret key ring to your account's Tectia directory, ~/.ssh2. Suppose it is called *secring.pgp*.

2. In an identification file, either ~/.ssh2/identification or another of your choice, indicate the secret key ring with the keyword PgpSecretKeyFile:

   ```
   # Tectia
   PgpSecretKeyFile secring.pgp
   ```

3. Identify the PGP key you wish to use for authentication. This may be done with any of three keywords:

   - To identify the key by name, use IdPgpKeyName:

     ```
     # Tectia
     IdPgpKeyName mykey
     ```

   - To identify the key by its PGP fingerprint, use IdPgpKeyFingerprint:

     ```
     # Tectia
     IdPgpKeyFingerprint 48 B5 EA 28 80 5E 29 4D 03 33 7D 17 5E 2E CD 20
     ```

   - To identify the key by its key ID, use IdPgpKeyId:

     ```
     # Tectia
     IdPgpKeyId 0xD914738D
     ```

For IdPgpKeyId, the leading 0x is necessary, indicating that the value is in hexadecimal. You can give the value in decimal instead, without the leading 0x, but since PGP displays the value in hex already, it's unlikely you'd want to do this.

On the server machine, you need to make your PGP public-key ring and the desired public key for authentication available to the Tectia server:

1. Copy your public-key ring from the client machine to the server machine. (Note that this is a key ring, not a lone public key.) Place the ring into your ~/.ssh2 directory on the server. Suppose it is called *pubring.pgp*.

2. In your authorization file, ~/.ssh2/authorization, identify the public-key ring with the keyword PgpPublicKeyFile:

   ```
   # Tectia
   PgpPublicKeyFile pubring.pgp
   ```

3. Identify the public key by name, fingerprint, or key ID, as in the client's identification file. The relevant keywords are slightly different: PgpKeyName, PgpKeyFingerprint, and PgpKeyId, respectively. (The keywords for the identification file begin with "Id".)

   ```
   # Tectia: use any ONE of these
   PgpKeyName mykey
   ```

```
PgpKeyFingerprint 48 B5 EA 28 80 5E 29 4D 03 33 7D 17 5E 2E CD 20
PgpKeyId 0xD914738D
```

You are done! From the client, initiate a Tectia SSH session. Suppose you create an alternative identification file to use PGP authentication, called *~/.ssh2/idpgp*, containing your `PgpSecretKeyFile` and other lines. Use the *–i* flag to indicate this file, and initiate a connection:

```
# Tectia
$ ssh -i idpgp server.example.com
```

If everything is set up properly, you are prompted for your PGP passphrase:

```
Passphrase for pgp key "mykey":
```

Enter your PGP passphrase, and authentication should succeed.

6.6   Tectia External Keys

Tectia clients can use external key providers that distribute keys, somewhat like authentication agents. These are typically part of a more general solution for PKI (Public Key Infrastructure). The *ssh -E* command-line option identifies the name of the provider, and Tectia currently supports two of them:

entrust

> Entrust products, such as the Entrust Authority Security Manager; see *http://www.entrust.com/authority*.

pkcs11

> PKCS#11-compliant dynamic libraries.

An initialization string must be sent to the external key provider using the *–I* option. The format of this string depends on the provider. It typically includes authentication information and identifies the desired key. Sometimes you also need a DLL supplied by the provider. Consult the documentation for specific providers, and the *ssh-externalkeys* manpage, for details about the initialization string.

```
# Tectia
$ ENTRUST_INIT="dll(libentrust.so)"
$ ENTRUST_INIT="$ENTRUST_INIT password(blartz)"
$ ENTRUST_INIT="$ENTRUST_INIT ini-file($HOME/solo.ini)"
$ ENTRUST_INIT="$ENTRUST_INIT profile-file($HOME/solo_user.epf)"
$ ENTRUST_INIT="$ENTRUST_INIT login-options(entrust)""
$ ssh -E entrust -I "$ENTRUST_INIT"
```

The external key provider and initialization string can also be specified in the client configuration file, using the keywords `EkProvider` and `EkInitString`, respectively:

```
# Tectia
EkProvider      pkcs11
EkInitString    "lib=libpcks11.so password=blurfl key=laptop"
```

The keywords are usually more convenient than the command-line options, especially for long initialization strings, but beware of storing sensitive authentication information in configuration files. Be sure to quote the initialization string if it contains characters with special meaning to the shell (e.g., wildcards) or to the configuration file itself.

6.7 Summary

In this chapter, we've seen how to create and use SSH identities, represented by key pairs, either individually (OpenSSH) or in collections (Tectia). Keys are created by *ssh-keygen* and are accessed by clients as needed. Tectia provides an additional layer of configuration, the identification file, which lets you use a set of identities as a single identity. You may have as many identities as you like. Be sure to read our case study on PKI and scalable authentication for another detailed look at identities. [11.5]

SSH agents are useful timesavers to avoid retyping passphrases. Their operation has numerous subtleties, but once you get the hang of it, running an agent should become second nature.

CHAPTER 7

Advanced Client Use

SSH clients are marvelously configurable. Chapter 2 introduced remote logins and file copying but covered only the tip of the iceberg. You can also connect with multiple SSH identities, use a variety of authentication and encryption techniques, exercise control over TCP/IP settings, and generally tailor the feel and operation of SSH clients to your liking. You can even save common collections of SSH settings in configuration files for ease of use.

We'll be focusing on *outgoing* SSH use, running SSH clients to connect to remote hosts, using the components highlighted in Figure 7-1. A related topic, not covered in this chapter, is how to control incoming SSH connections to your account. That sort of access control is a function of the SSH server, not the clients, and is covered in Chapter 8.

7.1   How to Configure Clients

The clients *ssh* and *scp* are quite configurable, with many settings that can be changed to suit your whim. If you want to modify the behavior of these clients, three general techniques are at your disposal:

Command-line options
: For changing the behavior of *ssh* or *scp* for a single invocation

Configuration keywords
: For changes that remain in force until you change them again; these are stored in a client configuration file

Environment variables
: For a few miscellaneous features

We now present a general overview of these three methods.

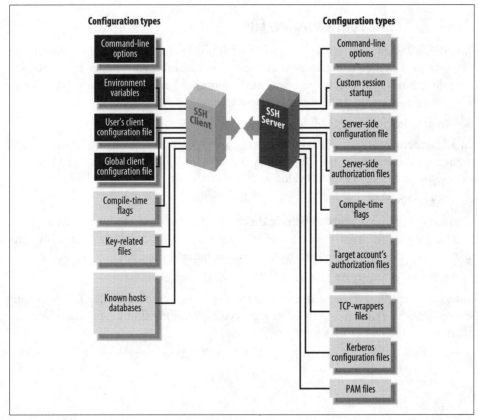

Figure 7-1. Client configuration (highlighted parts)

7.1.1 Command-Line Options

Command-line options let you change a client's behavior just once, at invocation. For example, if you're using *ssh* over a slow modem connection, you can tell it to compress the data with the *–C* command-line option:

```
$ ssh -C server.example.com
```

ssh, *scp*, and most of their support programs, when invoked with the *--help* option, will print a helpful summary describing all their command-line options.[*] For example:

```
$ ssh --help
$ scp --help
$ ssh-keygen -help
```

---

[*] Tectia recognizes *–h* as an abbreviation of *--help*.

7.1.2 Client Configuration Files

If you don't want to retype command-line options continually, configuration files let you change a client's behavior now and in the future, until you change the configuration file again. For example, you can enable compression for all clients you invoke by inserting this line into a client configuration file:

```
Compression yes
```

In a client configuration file, client settings are changed by specifying keywords and values. In the example, the keyword is Compression and the value is yes. You may also separate the keyword and value with an equals sign, with optional whitespace:

```
Compression = yes
```

You may configure clients to behave differently for each remote host you visit. This can be done on the fly with command-line options, but for anything reasonably complex, you'll end up typing long, inconvenient command lines like:

```
$ ssh -a -p 220 -c blowfish -l sally -i myself server.example.com
```

Alternatively, you can set these options within a configuration file. The following entry duplicates the function of the preceding command-line options, collecting them under the name "myserver":

```
# OpenSSH (Tectia's syntax differs slightly as we'll see later)
Host myserver
 ForwardAgent no
 Port 220
 Cipher blowfish
 User sally
 IdentityFile myself
 HostName server.example.com
```

Now, to run a client with these options enabled, simply type:

```
$ ssh myserver
```

Configuration files take some time to set up, but in the long run they are significant timesavers. We now discuss the general structure of these files (host specifications followed by keyword/value pairs), then dive into specific keywords.

7.1.2.1 Keywords versus command-line options

Configuration files and command-line options have two important relationships:

- Every configuration keyword can appear on the command line with the *–o* option.
- Alternative configuration files are referenced with the *–F* option.

For any configuration line of the form:

```
Keyword Value
```

you may type:

```
$ ssh -o "Keyword Value" ...
```

For example, the configuration file lines:

```
User sally
Port 220
```

can be specified on the command line as:

```
$ ssh -o "User sally" -o "Port 220" server.example.com
```

As in the configuration file, an equals sign (with optional whitespace) is permitted between the keyword and the value:

```
$ ssh -o User=sally -o Port=220 server.example.com
```

If you use an equals sign, and the value for the keyword contains special characters that would be misinterpreted by the shell, surround the value with quotes.

The *–o* option may appear multiple times on the same command line, for both *ssh* and *scp*:

```
# OpenSSH
$ scp -o "User sally" -o "Port 220" myfile server.example.com:
```

The other relationship between command-line options and configuration keywords is found in the *–F* option, which instructs a client to use a different configuration file instead of the default. For example:

```
$ ssh -F /usr/local/ssh/other_config
```

 OpenSSH and Tectia treat the *–F* option differently. OpenSSH will ignore the default configuration file (*/etc/ssh/ssh_config*) and use only the one you provide. Tectia, on the other hand, will still process its default configuration file (*/etc/ssh2/ssh2_config*), and then your provided file can override those settings.

7.1.2.2   Global and local files

Client configuration files come in two flavors. A single, *global* client configuration file, usually created by a system administrator, governs client behavior for an entire computer. The file is traditionally */etc/ssh/ssh_config* (OpenSSH) or */etc/ssh2/ssh2_config* (Tectia). (Don't confuse these with the *server* configuration files in the same directories.) Each user may also create a *local* client configuration file within his or her account, usually *~/.ssh/config* (OpenSSH) or *~/.ssh2/ssh2_config* (Tectia). This file controls the behavior of clients run in the user's login session.*

---

* The system administrator may change the locations of client configuration files via the compile-time flag *--with-etcdir* [4.3.5.1] or the serverwide keyword UserConfigDirectory. [5.3.1.5] If the files aren't in their default locations on your computer, contact your system administrator.

Values in a user's local file take precedence over those in the global file. For instance, if the global file turns on data compression, and your local file turns it off, the local file wins for clients run in your account. We cover precedence in more detail later. [7.2]

7.1.2.3 Configuration-file sections

Client configuration files are divided into *sections*. Each section contains settings for one remote host or for a set of related remote hosts, such as all hosts in a given domain.

The beginning of a section is marked differently in different SSH implementations. For OpenSSH, the keyword Host begins a new section, followed by a string called a *host specification*. The string may be a hostname:

```
Host server.example.com
```

an IP address:

```
Host 123.61.4.10
```

a nickname for a host: [7.1.2.5]

```
Host my-nickname
```

or a wildcard pattern representing a set of hosts, where ? matches any single character and * any sequence of characters (just like filename wildcards in your favorite Unix shell):

```
Host *.example.com
Host 128.220.19.*
```

Some further examples of wildcards:

```
Host *.edu        Any hostname in the edu domain
Host a*           Any hostname whose name begins with "a"
Host *1*          Any hostname (or IP address!) with 1 in it
Host *            Any hostname or IP address
```

Tectia, in contrast, does not use a Host keyword. A new section is marked by a host specification string followed by a colon. This string may likewise be a computer name:

```
server.example.com:
```

an IP address:

```
123.61.4.10:
```

a nickname:

```
my-nickname:
```

or a wildcard pattern:

```
*.example.com:
128.220.19.*:
```

You then follow the host-specification line with one or more settings, i.e., configuration keywords and values, as in the example we saw earlier. The following table contrasts OpenSSH and Tectia configuration files:

OpenSSH	Tectia
Host myserver	myserver:
User sally	User sally
IdentityFile myself	IdentityFile myself
ForwardAgent no	ForwardAgent no
Port 220	Port 220
Cipher blowfish	Ciphers blowfish

The settings apply only to the hosts named in the host specification. The section ends at the next host specification or the end of the file, whichever comes first.

7.1.2.4   Multiple matches

Because wildcards are permitted in host specifications, a single hostname might match two or more sections in the configuration file. For example, if one section begins:*

```
Host *.edu
```

and another begins:

```
Host *.harvard.edu
```

and you connect to *server.harvard.edu*, which section applies? Believe it or not, they both do. Every matching section applies, and if a keyword is set more than once with different values, only one value applies. For OpenSSH, the earliest value takes precedence, whereas for Tectia the latest value wins.

Suppose your client configuration file contains two sections to control data compression, password authentication, and the *ssh* escape character:

```
Host *.edu
  Compression yes
  PasswordAuthentication yes

Host *.harvard.edu
  Compression no
  EscapeChar %
```

and you connect to *server.harvard.edu*:

```
$ ssh server.harvard.edu
```

Notice that the string server.harvard.edu matches both Host patterns, *.edu and *.harvard.edu. As we've said, the keywords in both sections apply to your connection.

---

* We use only the OpenSSH file syntax here to keep things tidy, but the explanation is true of Tectia as well.

Therefore, the preceding *ssh* command sets values for the keywords `Compression`, `PasswordAuthentication`, and `EscapeChar`.

But notice, in the example, that the two sections set different values for `Compression`. What happens? The rule is that the first value prevails—in this case, yes. So, in the previous example, the values used for *server.harvard.edu* are:

```
Compression yes             The first of the Compression lines
PasswordAuthentication yes  Unique to first section
EscapeChar %                Unique to second section
```

and as shown in Figure 7-2. `Compression no` is ignored because it is the second `Compression` line encountered. Likewise, if 10 different `Host` lines match *server.harvard. edu,* all 10 of those sections apply, and if a particular keyword is set multiple times, only the first value is used.

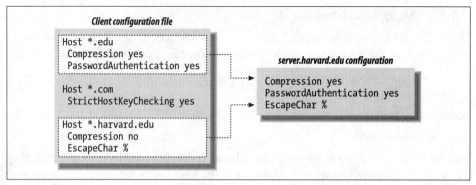

Figure 7-2. OpenSSH client configuration file with multiple matches (Tectia not shown)

While this feature might seem confusing, it has useful properties. Suppose you want some settings applied to all remote hosts. Simply create a section beginning with:

```
Host *
```

and place the common settings within it. This section should be either the first or the last in the file. If first, its settings take precedence over any others. This can be used to guard against your own errors. For example, if you want to make sure you never, ever, accidentally use the old SSH-1 protocol, at the beginning of your configuration file put:

```
# First section of file
Host *
  Protocol 2
```

Alternatively, if you place `Host *` as the last section in the configuration file, its settings are used only if no other section overrides them. This is useful for changing SSH's default behavior, while still permitting overrides. For example, by default, data compression is disabled. You can make it enabled by default by ending your configuration file with:

```
# Last section of file
Host *
 Compression yes
```

Voilá, you have changed the default behavior of *ssh* and *scp* for your account! Any other section, earlier in the configuration file, can override this default simply by setting Compression to no.

 The precedence rule is different for keywords that can apply multiple times in a section. For example, you can legitimately have more than one IdentityFile keyword in a section of *~/.ssh/config* (OpenSSH), meaning to try all the listed keys in turn. [7.4.2] Likewise, if more than one section applies to a host, and they each contain IdentityFile lines, then the union of all the named keys will be tried for authentication. In other words, IdentityFile values *accumulate* rather than override each other.

7.1.2.5 Making nicknames for hosts

Suppose your client configuration file contains a section for the remote host *myserver.example.com*:

```
Host myserver.example.com
 ...
```

One day, while logged onto *ourclient.example.com*, you decide to establish an SSH connection to *myserver.example.com*. Since both computers are in the same domain, *example.com*, you can omit the domain name on the command line and simply type:

```
$ ssh myserver
```

This does establish the SSH connection, but you run into an unexpected nuance of configuration files. *ssh* compares the command-line string "myserver" to the Host string "myserver.example.com", determines that they don't match, and doesn't apply the section of the configuration file. Yes, the software requires an exact textual match between the hostnames on the command line and in the configuration file.

You can get around this limitation by declaring myserver to be a nickname for *myserver.example.com*. In OpenSSH, this is done with the Host and HostName keywords. Simply use Host with the nickname and HostName with the fully qualified hostname:

```
# OpenSSH
Host myserver
 HostName myserver.example.com
 ...
```

ssh will now recognize that this section applies to your command *ssh myserver*. You may define any nickname you like for a given computer, even if it isn't related to the original hostname:

```
# OpenSSH
Host simple
 HostName myserver.example.com
 ...
```

Then you can use the nickname on the command line:

```
$ ssh simple
```

For Tectia, the syntax is different but the effect is the same. Use the nickname in the host specification, and provide the full name to the Host keyword:

```
# Tectia
simple:
 Host myserver.example.com
 ...
```

Then type:

```
$ ssh simple
```

Nicknames are convenient for testing new client settings. Suppose you have an OpenSSH configuration for *server.example.com*:

```
Host server.example.com
 ...
```

and you want to experiment with different settings. You could just modify the settings in place, but if they don't work, you'd have to waste time changing them back. The following steps demonstrate a more convenient way:

1. Within the configuration file, make a copy of the section you want to change:

   ```
   # Original
   Host server.example.com
    ...
   # Copy for testing
   Host server.example.com
    ...
   ```

2. In the copy, change "Host" to "HostName":

   ```
   # Original
   Host server.example.com
    ...
   # Copy for testing
   HostName server.example.com
    ...
   ```

3. Add a new Host line at the beginning of the copy, using a phony name; for example, "Host my-test":

   ```
   # Original
   Host server.example.com
   ```

```
...
# Copy for testing
Host my-test
 HostName server.example.com
 ...
```

4. Setup is done. In the copy (my-test), make all the changes you want and connect using *ssh my-test*. You can conveniently compare the old and new behavior
by running *ssh server.example.com* versus *ssh my-test*. If you decide against the
changes, simply delete the my-test section. If you like the changes, copy them to
the original section (or delete the original and keep the copy).

You can do the same with Tectia:

```
# Original
server.example.com:
 ...
# Copy for testing
my-test:
 Host server.example.com
 ...
```

7.1.2.6 Comments, indenting, and style

You probably noticed in the previous examples that we use the # symbol to represent comments:

```
# This is a comment
```

In fact, any line beginning with # in the configuration file is treated as a comment
and ignored. Likewise, blank lines (empty or containing only whitespace) are also
ignored.

You might also have noticed that the lines following a host specification are
indented:

```
# OpenSSH
Host server.example.com
 Keyword1 value1
 Keyword2 value2

# Tectia
server.example.com:
 Keyword1 value1
 Keyword2 value2
```

Indenting is considered good style because it visually indicates the beginning of a
new section. It isn't required, but we recommend it.

7.1.3 Environment Variables

SSH clients set a number of environment variables, and a few miscellaneous features
are controlled by variables you can set. We'll point out these variables as we

encounter them from time to time. Environment variables may be set in your current shell by the standard methods:

```
# C shell family (csh, tcsh)
$ setenv MY_VARIABLE 1

# Bourne shell family (sh, ksh, bash)
$ MY_VARIABLE=1
$ export MY_VARIABLE
```

Alternatively, environment variables and values may be specified in a file. System administrators can set environment variables for all users in */etc/environment*, and users can set them in *~/.ssh/environment* (OpenSSH) and *~/.ssh2/environment* (Tectia). These files contain lines of the format:

```
NAME=VALUE
```

where *NAME* is the name of an environment variable, and *VALUE* is its value. The value is taken literally, read from the equals sign to the end of the line. Don't enclose the value in quotes, even if it contains whitespace, unless you want the quotes to be part of the value.

7.2 Precedence

Perhaps you are wondering: what happens if some configuration settings conflict? For instance, if you use the Compression keyword to turn compression off, and also the –C command-line option to turn it on, who wins? In other words, who has *precedence*?

For OpenSSH and Tectia clients, the order of precedence is, from strongest to weakest:

1. Command-line options
2. The user's local client configuration file
3. The global client configuration file*

Command-line options have the highest precedence, overriding any client configuration files. The user's local file has next highest precedence, and the global file has lowest precedence. So, in our compression example, –C takes precedence over the Compression keyword, and compression is enabled. If a setting isn't changed by any keyword or command-line option, the client's default setting is used.

Remember that we're speaking only of outgoing connections initiated by clients. Incoming connections, controlled by the SSH server, have other precedence rules. For servers, the user's local configuration file definitely does *not* override the global

---

* We don't mention environment variables in this list because they don't compete for precedence. Environment variables control different features that don't overlap with command-line options and configuration files.

file; otherwise, users could override global server settings, creating security holes and wreaking other havoc. [8.1.1]

7.3 Introduction to Verbose Mode

Now that we've covered the generalities of command-line options and configuration files, we're about to launch into an extended discussion of configuration. Before we begin, let's practice some defense. As you try these options, occasionally you might see behavior that's not what you expected. Whenever this occurs, your first instinct should be: turn on verbose mode with the *-v* command-line option to track down the problem:

```
$ ssh -v server.example.com
```

In verbose mode, the client prints messages as it proceeds, providing clues to the problem. New SSH users (and quite a few experienced ones) frequently forget or neglect to use verbose mode when problems arise. Don't hesitate! Many questions we've seen in the Usenet SSH newsgroup, *comp.security.ssh* [12.3], could have been answered immediately by running *ssh -v* and examining the output.

Suppose you just installed your public key on *server.example.com* and are trying to authenticate with it. Strangely, you are prompted for your login password instead of your public-key passphrase:

```
$ ssh server.example.com
barrett@server.example.com's password:
```

Don't just sit there scratching your head in wonder. Let verbose mode come to the rescue:

```
$ ssh -v server.example.com
OpenSSH_3.8p1, SSH protocols 1.5/2.0, OpenSSL 0.9.7d 17 Mar 2004
debug1: Reading configuration data /etc/ssh/ssh_config
debug1: Applying options for *
debug1: Connecting to server.example.com [192.168.0.10] port 22.
debug1: Connection established.
debug1:  Remote: Bad file modes for /users/barrett/.ssh         Uh oh!
debug1: Server refused our key.
debug1: Doing password authentication.
barrett@server.example.com's password:
```

These messages (which are abbreviated for this example) confirm that the SSH connection is succeeding, but public-key authentication is failing. The reason is "bad file modes": the remote SSH directory, */home/barrett/.ssh*, has incorrect permissions. A quick trip to the server and a well-placed *chmod* command later, the problem is solved:

```
# On the server
$ chmod 700 ~/.ssh
```

Repeating the *–v* option causes OpenSSH clients to produce even more detailed information:

```
# OpenSSH
$ ssh -v -v -v server.example.com
```

whereas for Tectia, use its *–d* option, as we saw in detail for *sshd*: [5.9]

```
# Tectia
$ ssh -d3 server.example.com
```

And of course, verbose mode also works for *scp*:

```
$ scp -v myfile server.example.com:
Executing: program /usr/bin/ssh host server.example.com, user (unspecified), command
scp -v -t .
OpenSSH_3.9p1, SSH protocols 1.5/2.0, OpenSSL 0.9.7e 24 Oct 2004
...
```

except that Tectia's *scp* uses *–D* instead of *–d:**

```
# Tectia
$ scp -D3 myfile server.example.com:
```

scp also supports the *–q* option for no output at all:

```
# Tectia
$ scp -q myfile server.example.com: Be completely quiet
```

Verbose mode is your friend. Use it liberally. Now we're ready to learn those dozens of options.

7.4   Client Configuration in Depth

ssh and *scp* take their cues from command-line options, configuration-file keywords, and environment variables. OpenSSH and Tectia clients behave differently and obey different settings, but as usual, we cover them simultaneously. When a setting is supported by only some of these products, we'll say so.

Both OpenSSH and Tectia *ssh* will print a usage message briefly describing all its options:

```
$ ssh --help
```

You can get the same effect if you omit all arguments (OpenSSH) or use *–h* (Tectia). Tectia will also print its version number on request, with the *–V* option:

```
# Tectia
$ ssh -V
ssh: SSH Tectia Server 4.2.1 on i686-pc-linux-gnu
Build: 1
Released 2004-11-30 (YYYY-MM-DD).
Crypto library version: SSH Cryptographic Library, version 1.2.4
```

---

* Tectia's *–v* option is equivalent to *–D2*, and can also be written as *--verbose*.

```
FIPS certification mode: DISABLED
Product: SSH Tectia Server (T)
License type: commercial
```

7.4.1   Remote Account Name

ssh and *scp* assume that your local and remote usernames are the same. If your local username is henry and you run:

```
$ ssh server.example.com
```

ssh assumes your remote username is also henry and requests a connection to that account on *server.example.com*. If your remote account name differs from the local one, you must tell the SSH client your remote account name. For henry to connect to a remote account called sally, he can use the *–l* command-line option:

```
$ ssh -l sally server.example.com
```

If copying files with *scp*, the syntax is different for specifying the remote account name, looking more like an email address. [7.5.1] To copy the file *myfile* to the remote account sally on *server.example.com*:

```
$ scp myfile sally@server.example.com:
```

If you frequently connect to a remote machine using a different username, instead of monkeying with command-line options specify the remote username in your client configuration file. The User keyword serves this purpose, and both *ssh* and *scp* pay attention to it. Here's how to declare that your remote username is sally on a given remote host:

OpenSSH	Tectia

Host server.example.com
  User sally
	server.example.com:
	  User sally

Now, when connecting to *server.example.com*, you don't have to specify that your remote username is sally:

```
# The remote username sally will be used automatically
$ ssh server.example.com
```

7.4.1.1   Tricks with remote account names

With User and nicknames, you can significantly shorten the command lines you type for *ssh* and *scp*. Continuing the preceding example with sally, if you have the configuration shown:

OpenSSH	Tectia

Host simple
  HostName server.example.com
  User sally
	simple:
	  Host server.example.com
	  User sally

then these long commands:

```
$ ssh server.example.com -l sally
$ scp myfile sally@server.example.com:
```

may be reduced to:

```
$ ssh simple
$ scp myfile simple:
```

Here's how to specify separately several different account names on different hosts, each in its own section of the configuration file:

OpenSSH	Tectia

`Host server.example.com`
`  User sally`
`  ...`
`Host another.example.com`
`  User sharon`
`  ...`
	`server.example.com:`
	`  User sally`
	`  ...`
	`another.example.com:`
	`  User sharon`
	`  ...`

This technique is convenient if you have only one account on each remote machine. But suppose you have two accounts on *server.example.com*, called sally and sally2. Is there some way to specify both in the configuration file? The following attempt *doesn't* work (we show OpenSSH syntax only):

```
# THIS WILL NOT WORK PROPERLY!!!
Host server.example.com
  User sally
  User sally2
  Compression yes
```

because only the first value (`sally`) prevails. To get around this limitation, you can use nicknames to create two sections for the same machine in your configuration file, each with a different `User`:

```
# OpenSSH
# Section 1: Convenient access to the sally account
Host sally-account
  HostName server.example.com
  User sally
  Compression yes

# Section 2: Convenient access to the sally2 account
Host sally2-account
  HostName server.example.com
  User sally2
  Compression yes
```

Now you can access the two accounts easily by nickname:

```
$ ssh sally-account
$ ssh sally2-account
```

This works, but it isn't ideal. You've duplicated your settings (`HostName` and `Compression`) in each section. Duplication makes a configuration file harder to maintain, since any future changes need to be applied twice. (In general, duplication isn't good software engineering.) Are you doomed to duplicate? No, there's a better solution. Immediately after the two sections, create a third section with a `Host` wildcard that matches both `sally-account` and `sally2-account`. Suppose you use `sally*-account` and move all duplicated settings into this new section:

```
# OpenSSH
Host sally*-account
  HostName server.example.com
  Compression yes
```

The end result is:

OpenSSH	Tectia

`Host sally-account`
`  User sally`
`Host sally2-account`
`  User sally2`
`Host sally*-account`
`  HostName server.example.com`
`  Compression yes`
	`sally-account:`
	`  User sally`
	`sally2-account:`
	`  User sally2`
	`sally*-account:`
	`  Host server.example.com`
	`  Compression yes`

Since `sally*-account` matches both previous sections, its full name and compression settings apply to both `sally-account` and `sally2-account`. Any settings that differ between `sally-account` and `sally2-account` (in this case, `User`) are kept in their respective sections. You've now achieved the same effect as in the previous example—two accounts with different settings on the same remote machine—but with no duplication of settings.

7.4.2 User Identity

SSH identifies you by an *identity* represented by a key pair (OpenSSH) or a collection of key pairs (Tectia). [6.1] Normally, SSH clients use your default key file (OpenSSH) or default identification file (Tectia) to establish an authenticated connection. However, if you've created other keys, you may instruct SSH clients to use them to establish your identity. A command-line option (*–i*) and configuration keyword (`IdentityFile`) are available for this purpose.

In OpenSSH, for example, if you have a private-key file called *my-key*, you can make clients use it with the commands:

```
$ ssh -i my-key server.example.com
$ scp -i my-key myfile server.example.com:
```

or with the configuration keyword:

```
IdentityFile my-key
```

The file location is assumed to be relative to the current directory, i.e., in these cases the file is *./my-key*.

Tectia also has *–i* and IdentityFile, but their meanings are slightly different from those of OpenSSH. Instead of a key file, you supply the name of an identification file:

```
# Tectia
$ ssh -i my-id-file server.example.com

# Tectia configuration file
IdentityFile my-id-file
```

 If Tectia complains about your identity file:

```
warning: /home/smith/.ssh2/id_dsa_2048_a: 4: parsing line
failed.
```

you probably handed *ssh* a key file (*id_dsa_2048_a*) instead of an identity file like *~/.ssh2/identification*.

Multiple identities can be quite useful. [6.4] For example, you can set up your remote account to run specific programs when a second key is used. The ordinary command:

```
$ ssh server.example.com
```

initiates a regular login session, but:

```
$ ssh -i other_identity server.example.com
```

can run a complex batch process on *server.example.com*. Using configuration keywords, you can accomplish the same effect by specifying an alternative identity, as shown in this table:

OpenSSH	Tectia
Host SomeComplexAction HostName server.example.com IdentityFile other_identity ...	SomeComplexAction: Host server.example.com IdentityFile other_identity ...

You can then invoke:

```
$ ssh SomeComplexAction
```

OpenSSH can specify multiple identities in a single command:*

```
# OpenSSH
$ ssh -i id1 -i id2 -i id3 server.example.com
```

or:

```
# OpenSSH
Host server.example.com
 IdentityFile id1
```

---

* Tectia accomplishes the same thing with identification files, which may contain multiple keys.

```
IdentityFile id2
IdentityFile id3
```

Multiple identities are tried in order until one successfully authenticates. However, OpenSSH limits you to 100 identities per command.*

If you plan to use multiple identities frequently, remember that an SSH agent can eliminate hassle. Simply load each identity's key into the agent using *ssh-add*, and you won't have to remember multiple passphrases while you work.

7.4.2.1 Using identities

IdentityFile specifies an identity you'd like to use for authentication, but it does not *restrict* authentication to that identity. Suppose your client configuration file says:

```
# OpenSSH
Host server.example.com
 IdentityFile wendy
 IdentityFile abby
```

and you run:

```
# OpenSSH
$ ssh server.example.com
```

ssh will dutifully try to authenticate using identities *wendy* and *abby*; but if it fails, *ssh* will try other identities held in your SSH agent, in case one of them might succeed. You can change this behavior with the IdentitiesOnly keyword:

```
# OpenSSH
Host server.example.com
 IdentityFile wendy
 IdentityFile abby
 IdentitiesOnly yes    Restrict authentication only to listed identity files
```

Now if *ssh* fails to authenticate by identities *wendy* and *abby*, it will stop trying (and move on to other non-public-key techniques, if configured to do so).

This feature is particularly useful with a server that limits the number of public-key authentication attempts, such as OpenSSH. If you have many keys in your agent, only a few can be tried before the server disconnects you for "too many failures." The configuration shown avoids this problem by indicating exactly which keys to use for a given host. Even though the IdentityFile keyword refers to files, the OpenSSH client will try those keys from the agent if they've been loaded. You are prompted for a passphrase only if the needed key isn't in the agent and is encrypted on disk.

---

* Per the constant SSH_MAX_IDENTITY_FILES in the source code.

7.4.3   Host Keys and Known-Hosts Databases

Every SSH server has a host key [3.3] that uniquely identifies the server to clients. This key helps prevent spoofing attacks. When an SSH client requests a connection and receives the server's host key, the client checks it against a local database of known host keys. If the keys match, the connection proceeds. If they don't, the client behaves according to several options you can control.

In OpenSSH, the host key database is maintained partly in a serverwide location (*/etc/ssh/ssh_known_hosts*) and partly in the user's SSH directory (*~/.ssh/known_hosts*). In Tectia, there are two databases of host keys for authenticating server hosts (the "host-keys" map in */etc/ssh2/hostkeys*) and client hosts (the "knownhosts" map); in this section we are concerned only with the former. Similar to its OpenSSH counterpart, the Tectia hostkeys map is maintained in a serverwide directory (*/etc/ssh2/hostkeys/*) and a per-account directory (*~/.ssh2/hostkeys/*). In this section, we refer to the OpenSSH and Tectia map simply as the *host key database*.

7.4.3.1   Strict host-key checking

Suppose you request an SSH connection with *server.example.com,* which sends its host key in response. Your client looks up *server.example.com* in its host key database. Ideally, a match is found and the connection proceeds. But what if this doesn't happen? Two scenarios may arise:

SCENARIO 1: *Mismatched key*

> A host key is found for *server.example.com* in the database, but it doesn't match the incoming key. This can indicate a security hazard, or it can mean that *server.example.com* has changed its host key, which can happen legitimately. [3.9.4]

SCENARIO 2: *No key*

> No host key for *server.example.com* exists in the database. In this case, the SSH client is encountering *server.example.com* for the first time.

In each scenario, should the client proceed or fail? Should it store the new host key in the database, or not? These decisions are controlled by the keyword StrictHostKeyChecking, which may have three values:

yes

> Be strict. If a key is unknown or has changed, the connection fails. This is the most secure value, but it can be inconvenient or annoying if you connect to new hosts regularly or if your remote host keys change frequently.

no

> Not strict. If a key is unknown, automatically add it to the user's database and proceed. If a key has changed, leave the known hosts entry intact, print a warning, and permit the connection to proceed. This is the least secure value.

ask

> Prompt the user. If a key is unknown, ask whether it should be added to the user's database and whether to connect. If a key has changed, ask whether to connect. This is the default and a sensible value for knowledgeable users. (Less-experienced users might misunderstand what they're being asked and make the wrong decision.)

Here's an example:

```
StrictHostKeyChecking yes
```

Table 7-1 summarizes SSH's StrictHostKeyChecking's behavior.

Table 7-1. StrictHostKeyChecking behavior

Key found?	Match?	Strict?	Action
Yes	Yes	–	Connect
Yes	No	Yes	Warn and fail
Yes	No	No	Warn and connect
Yes	No	Ask	Warn and ask whether to connect
No	–	Yes	Warn and fail
No	–	No	Add key and connect
No	–	Ask	Ask whether to add key and to connect

OpenSSH has an additional keyword, CheckHostIP, to make a client verify the IP address of an SSH server in the database. Its values may be yes (the default, to verify the address) or no. The value yes provides security against name service spoofing attacks: [3.9.2]

```
# OpenSSH
CheckHostIP no
```

7.4.3.2   Verifying host keys by DNS

The known-hosts mechanism for verifying hostkeys is fine when dealing with a handful of hosts, but quickly becomes unwieldy for larger numbers. Later we discuss overarching authentication systems such as PKI or Kerberos to address this problem. [11.5] Another method is to use the DNS: if we could attach hostkeys to domain names, then SSH could verify the server by looking up its keys in the DNS. The method is documented in draft-ietf-secsh-dns. It uses DNS resource records with the following format:

```
IN SSHFP <key type> <fingerprint type> <fingerprint>
```

where the key types can be 1 (for RSA) or 2 (DSS), and the fingerprint type can be 1 (for SHA-1).

ssh-keygen can generate these DNS records in a form ready to be included in a zone file for the BIND nameserver:

```
# OpenSSH
$ ssh-keygen -r host.domain.net -f /etc/ssh/ssh_host_dsa_key.pub
host.domain.net IN SSHFP 2 1 7ae79057cbff7de6d61b30fba02d936d6a0f5b5f

$ ssh-keygen -r host.domain.net -f /etc/ssh/ssh_host_dsa_key.pub -g
host.domain.net IN TYPE44 \# 22 02 01 7ae79057cbff7de6d61b30fba02d936d6a0f5b5f
```

The *–g* form is for nameservers that don't understand the SSHFP RR type.

To have OpenSSH use these DNS records, set the `VerifyHostDNS` keyword to yes, no, or ask:

```
# ~/ssh/config
VerifyHostKeyDNS=yes
```

It's vitally important to remember that the DNS itself is usually not secure! There is a standard for DNS security (DNSSEC, RFC-2535), but it is not much used yet. Without DNSSEC, DNS queries and replies can be easily intercepted and forged by attackers, so this level of hostkey verification may not be acceptable.

If `VerifyHostKeyDNS` is ask, and `StrictHostKeyChecking` is yes or ask, OpenSSH will indicate whether it found a matching hostkey in the DNS, but still obey the usual semantics of `StrictHostKeyChecking` in deciding whether to approve the server. `VerifyHostKeyDNS` yes is the same, except that matching fingerprints obtained via secure DNS are considered just as trustworthy as those stored in the known-hosts list. If `StrictHostKeyChecking` is no, then `VerifyHostKeyDNS` makes no difference.

7.4.3.3 Host key aliasing

OpenSSH uses a simple method to find the host key for server authentication: it simply looks up in the known-hosts list exactly what you type on the command line for the remote server name. Sometimes, the situation is more complicated; you know which host you're actually contacting, but OpenSSH doesn't. For instance, you might be using SSH-over-SSH to contact a remote host through a second SSH port forwarding, like so:

```
$ ssh -L 2001:david:22 goliath
$ ssh -p 2001 localhost
```

The second command will connect to the SSH server *david* through another one, *goliath*. However, the second *ssh* may complain about a host-key mismatch. It has no way of knowing about the port-forwarding indirection; it thinks you are connecting to an SSH server which is actually running on the local host, compares *goliath*'s host-key to that of the local host, and finds they do not match. In this situation, you can tell OpenSSH which key to use with `HostKeyAlias`:

```
# OpenSSH
$ ssh -p 2001 -o HostKeyAlias=david localhost
```

7.4.3.4 Ignoring host keys for localhost

In many computing environments, users' home directories are shared across many machines. As a result, users' *~/.ssh* configuration files are shared in this manner. This is useful but has one little glitch: the idiom *ssh localhost*.

The problem is that "localhost" means something different on every host! The first time you run this command, *ssh* will add a key for "localhost" to your known-hosts file—but the next time you do it on a different machine, SSH will complain about a host-key mismatch! You could get around this by adding multiple "localhost" lines to the known-hosts list, expanding the set of keys acceptable for that destination. However, since there's little security to be gained in verifying the identity of the host you're already logged into, OpenSSH has a special option, NoHostAuthentication-ForLocalhost, to disable server authentication for the connections to the loopback address:

```
# ~/.ssh/config
NoHostAuthenticationForLocalhost yes
```

7.4.3.5 Moving the known hosts files

OpenSSH permits the locations of the host key database, both the serverwide and per-account parts, to be changed using configuration keywords. GlobalKnown-HostsFile defines an alternative location for the serverwide file. It doesn't actually move the file—only the system administrator can do that—but it does force your clients to use another file in its place. This keyword is useful if the default file is outdated and you want your clients to ignore the serverwide file, particularly if you're tired of seeing warning messages from your clients about changed keys:

```
# OpenSSH
GlobalKnownHostsFile /users/smith/.ssh/my_global_hosts_file
```

Similarly, you can change the location of your per-user part of the database with the keyword UserKnownHostsFile:

```
# OpenSSH
UserKnownHostsFile /users/smith/.ssh/my_local_hosts_file
```

7.4.4 SSH Protocol Settings

OpenSSH lets the client control a number of features relating to the SSH protocol itself.

7.4.4.1 Choosing a protocol version

OpenSSH supports protocols SSH-1 and SSH-2. By default, the client and server will try to negotiate an SSH-2 connection first, then fall back to an SSH-1 connection if unsuccessful. You can control which protocols are tried by the client, and in what order, with the Protocol keyword, just as for the server: [5.3.7]

```
# OpenSSH
Protocol 2,1          Comma-separated list of protocol versions
```

You should always use SSH-2 for maximum security, if your software supports it, so it's a good idea to instruct your clients to avoid SSH-1 servers. You can do this for all hosts by placing a Protocol line at the bottom of your *~/.ssh/config* file:

```
# OpenSSH
Host *
 Protocol 2
```

or by the command-line arguments *–1* and *–2*, for protocols SSH-1 and SSH-2, respectively:

```
# OpenSSH
$ ssh -2 server.example.com   Require an SSH-2 connection
```

Tectia supports the *–1* option, with required qualifiers t and i to control how the SSH-1 support is accomplished:

```
# Tectia
$ ssh-1t server.example.com   "traditional": invoke an external ssh1 program
$ ssh-1i server.example.com   "internal": do SSH-1 protocol internally
```

7.4.4.2   Connection sharing

A single SSH connection can have multiple *channels* simultaneously supporting a variety of services: interactive terminals, remote program execution, file transfer, agent forwarding, etc. [3.4.4.1] Setting up an SSH connection is a computationally expensive process, and can take a few seconds. That's no big deal if you do it once in a while, but if you have a procedure that makes many connections, the delay can get pretty annoying or problematic. The Unix "style" promotes this problem: for instance, you can use CVS over SSH by setting the environment variable CVS_RSH=ssh. If you're running a lot of CVS commands, however, each will now take an extra five seconds or so, and computer users are notoriously impatient. Given that SSH can use channels, wouldn't it be better to set up one SSH connection to a given host, and then somehow issue our various commands over that one session?

Well, yes it would, and OpenSSH has this feature in its ControlMaster and ControlPath keywords, and the *–M* and *–S* options of *ssh*. This command:

```
# OpenSSH
$ ssh -S /tmp/ssh-snowcrash -Mfn snowcrash.neal.org
```

opens an SSH connection to the server *snowcrash.neal.org*, placing it in the background. It also tells this SSH process to act as a "master" process, allowing other *ssh* invocations (its "slaves") to open channels to this server through it. Master and slave communicate via the Unix socket */tmp/ssh-snowcrash*. So this:

```
# OpenSSH
$ ssh -S /tmp/ssh-snowcrash snowcrash.neal.org
```

will open a remote terminal on *snowcrash*, and will do it quickly because no new SSH connection is set up; it goes through the existing connection. You can make this more convenient with custom configuration:

```
# ~/.ssh/config
host snowcrash-master
  hostname snowcrash.neal.org
  ControlPath /tmp/ssh-snowcrash
  ControlMaster

host snowcrash-slave
  hostname snowcrash.neal.org
  ControlPath /tmp/ssh-snowcrash
```

And thus you can efficiently run:

```
# OpenSSH
$ ssh -fn snowcrash-master
$ ssh snowcrash-slave
```

7.4.4.3 Setting environment variables in the server

SSH clients can set environment variables in their remote SSH sessions. This mechanism is supported only by the SSH-2 protocol, and works only if it is permitted by the server, according to the keywords AcceptEnv (OpenSSH) or SettableEnvironmentVars (Tectia). [5.6.2]

OpenSSH clients use the SendEnv keyword to specify the names of environment variables that are sent to the server:

```
# OpenSSH
SendEnv COLOR
```

Multiple variables can be listed, separated by whitespace, or specified by multiple keywords. Wildcard characters * and ? send all variables in the client's environment whose name matches the pattern:

```
# OpenSSH
SendEnv LANG LC_*
SendEnv PATH TERM TZ
```

The value for each variable is copied from the environment of the OpenSSH client.

Tectia clients use the SetRemoteEnv keyword to specify both the name and the value, separated by an equals sign (with no whitespace):

```
# Tectia
SetRemoteEnv COLOR=blue
```

Use multiple keywords to send several variables to the server. Each variable must be named explicitly: no wildcards or patterns are used. The value can be omitted (to indicate an empty string), but the equals sign is required. Whitespace is permitted within the value, and is copied verbatim:

```
# Tectia
SetRemoteEnv GRANDDAUGHTERS=katie rebecca sarah
```

Note that the Tectia client's environment is not consulted at all, and the variables that are sent to the server need not even be present in the environment of the client.

7.4.5   TCP/IP Settings

SSH uses TCP/IP as its transport mechanism. Most times you don't need to change the default TCP settings, but in some situations it's necessary:

- Connecting to SSH servers on other TCP ports
- Connecting via a particular network interface
- Using privileged versus nonprivileged ports
- Keeping an idle connection open by sending keepalive messages
- Enabling the Nagle Algorithm (TCP_NODELAY)
- Requiring IP addresses to be Version 4 or 6

7.4.5.1   Selecting a remote port

Most SSH servers listen on TCP port 22, so clients connect to this port by default. Nevertheless, sometimes you need to connect to an SSH server on a different port number. For example, if you are a system administrator testing a new SSH server, you might run it on a different port to avoid interference with an existing server. Then your clients need to connect to this alternate port. This can be done with the client's Port keyword, followed by a port number:

```
Port 2035
```

or the *-p* command-line option, followed by the port number:

```
$ ssh -p 2035 server.example.com
```

You can also specify an alternative port for *scp*, but the command-line option is *-P* instead of *-p*:[*]

```
$ scp -P 2035 myfile server.example.com:
```

Tectia also accepts a port number as part of the user and host specification, preceded by a hash sign. For example, the commands:

```
# Tectia
$ ssh server.example.com#2035
$ ssh smith@server.example.com#2035
$ scp smith@server.example.com#2035:myfile localfile
```

each connect to remote port 2035. (We don't see much use for this syntax, but it's available.)

After connecting to the server, *ssh* sets an environment variable in the remote shell to hold the port information. For OpenSSH, the variable is called SSH_CLIENT, and for Tectia it is SSH2_CLIENT. The variable contains a string with three values, separated by a space character: the client's IP address, the client's TCP port, and the

---

[*] *scp* already has a lowercase *-p* option that means "preserve file permissions." [7.5.4]

server's TCP port. For example, if your client originates from port 1016 on IP address 24.128.23.102, connecting to the server's port 22, the value is:

```
# OpenSSH
$ echo $SSH_CLIENT
::ffff:24.128.23.102 1016 22

# Tectia
$ echo $SSH2_CLIENT
24.128.23.102 1016 22
```

OpenSSH also sets an environment variable, SSH_CONNECTION, with slightly extended port information, appending the server's IP address and port:

```
# OpenSSH
$ echo $SSH_CONNECTION
::ffff:24.128.23.102 10969 ::ffff:128.220.67.30 22
```

These variables are useful for scripting. In your shell's startup file (e.g., *~/.profile*, *~/.login*), you can test for the variable and, if it exists, take actions. For example:

```
#!/bin/sh
# Test for an SSH_CLIENT value of nonzero length
if [ -n "$SSH_CLIENT" ]
then
# We logged in via SSH.
  echo 'Welcome, OpenSSH user!'
  # Extract the IP address from SSH_CLIENT
  IP=`echo $SSH_CLIENT | awk '{print $1}'`
  # Translate it to a hostname.
  HOSTNAME=`host $IP | grep Name: | awk '{print $2}'`
  echo "I see you are connecting from $HOSTNAME."
else
  # We logged in not by SSH, but by some other means.
  echo 'Welcome, O clueless one. Feeling insecure today?'
fi
```

7.4.5.2   Connecting via a given network interface

If your client machine has more than one network interface or IP address, OpenSSH clients can connect through a particular one with the BindAddress keyword:

```
# OpenSSH
BindAddress 192.168.10.235
```

or the *–b* command-line option:

```
# OpenSSH
$ ssh -b 192.168.10.235 server.example.com
```

7.4.5.3   Forcing a nonprivileged local port

SSH connections get locally bound to a privileged TCP port, one whose port number is below 1024. If you ever need to override this feature—say, if your connection must pass through a firewall that doesn't permit privileged source ports—use the configuration keyword UsePrivilegedPort. Its values are yes (use a privileged port) and no (use a nonprivileged port, the default):

```
# OpenSSH
UsePrivilegedPort no
```

Hostbased authentication requires a privileged port.

7.4.5.4 Keepalive messages

The TCPKeepAlive (OpenSSH) and KeepAlive (Tectia) keywords instruct the client how to proceed if a TCP connection problem occurs, such as a prolonged network outage or a server machine crash:

```
# OpenSSH
TCPKeepAlive yes
```

```
# Tectia
KeepAlive yes
```

The value yes (the default) tells the client to transmit and expect periodic *keepalive messages*. If the client detects a lack of responses to these messages, it shuts down the connection. The value no means not to use keepalive messages.

Keepalive messages represent a trade-off. If they are enabled, a faulty connection is shut down even if the problem is transient. However, the TCP keepalive timeout on which this feature is based is typically several hours, so this shouldn't be a big problem. If keepalive messages are disabled, an unused faulty connection can persist indefinitely.

TCP keepalive messages are generally more useful in the SSH server, since a user sitting on the client side will certainly notice if the connection becomes unresponsive. However, SSH can connect two programs together, with the one running the SSH client waiting for input from the other side. In such a situation, it may be necessary to detect dead connections eventually.

TCPKeepAlive and KeepAlive aren't intended to deal with the problem of SSH sessions being torn down because of firewall, proxying, NAT, or IP masquerading timeouts. [5.3.3.4] In these cases, if you don't send any data for some period of time, the firewall (or whatever) closes the TCP connection. Additionally, TCP keepalive messages are not secure, as they don't use any real authentication technique.

OpenSSH provides a robust and secure solution to keep the connection up, called *client-alive* and *server-alive* messages. OpenSSH clients can send client-alive messages to the server, indicating the client is up. The client also detects server-alive messages sent by the OpenSSH server. [5.3.3.4]

If certain criteria are met, the client or server will tear down the connection. You can control this at three levels. First, the client's initial connection to the server can obey a timeout. If the server hasn't responded at all within a certain number of seconds, the client will give up. This is controlled by the ConnectTimeout keyword:

```
# OpenSSH
ConnectTimeout 60          If no connection with the server within one minute, give up
```

Next, the ServerAliveInterval keyword controls how the client sends server-alive messages. Its argument is a length of time in seconds:

```
# OpenSSH
ServerAliveInterval 300    Send server-alive every 300 seconds, or five minutes
```

If your client hasn't heard from the server within the given amount of time, the client will send a server-alive message to the server. It will continue sending these messages at the given interval (in this case, every five minutes) until it receives a response or gives up. You control how it gives up with the third keyword, ServerAliveCountMax, representing the maximum number of consecutive server-alive messages the client will send:

```
# OpenSSH
ServerAliveCountMax 8      Try eight times, then give up. The default is three times.
```

Once this maximum is reached, the client says, "Oh well, I guess the server has gone out for a walk," and terminates the SSH connection. If you don't want the client to send server-alive messages, set ServerAliveInterval to zero.

7.4.5.5   Controlling TCP_NODELAY

TCP/IP has a feature called the Nagle Algorithm, an optimization for reducing the number of TCP segments sent with very small amounts of data. [5.3.3.9] Tectia clients may also enable or disable the Nagle Algorithm using the NoDelay keyword:

```
# Tectia
NoDelay yes
```

Legal values are yes (to disable the algorithm) and no (to enable it; the default).

7.4.5.6   Requiring IPv4 and IPv6

OpenSSH can force its clients to use Internet Protocol Version 4 (IPv4) or 6 (IPv6) addresses. IPv4 is the current version of IP used on the Internet; IPv6 is the future version, permitting far more addresses than IPv4 can support. For more information on these address formats, visit:

http://www.ipv6.org/

To force IPv4 addressing, use the *–4* flag:

```
# OpenSSH
$ ssh -4 server.example.com
```

or likewise for IPv6, use −6:

```
# OpenSSH
$ ssh -6 server.example.com
```

You can also control these settings with the `AddressFamily` keyword, with the values inet (IPv4 only), inet6 (IPv6 only), or any:

```
# OpenSSH
AddressFamily inet6          Use IPv6 only
```

7.4.6   Making Connections

Under the best conditions, an SSH client attempts a secure connection, succeeds, obtains your authentication credentials, and executes whatever command you've requested, be it a shell or otherwise. Various steps in this process are configurable, including:

- The number of times the client attempts the connection
- The look and behavior of the password prompt (for password authentication only)
- Suppressing all prompting
- Running remote commands interactively with a tty
- Running remote commands in the background
- Whether or not to fall back to an insecure connection, if a secure one can't be established
- The escape character for interrupting and resuming an SSH session

7.4.6.1   Number of connection attempts

If you run an OpenSSH client and it can't establish a secure connection, it will retry. By default, it tries once. You can change this behavior with the keyword `ConnectionAttempts`:

```
# OpenSSH
ConnectionAttempts 10
```

In this example, *ssh* tries 10 times before admitting defeat. Most people don't have much use for this keyword, but it might be helpful if your network is unreliable. Just for fun, you can force *ssh* to give up immediately by setting `ConnectionAttempts` equal to zero:

```
# OpenSSH
$ ssh -o ConnectionAttempts=0 server.example.com
ssh: connect to host server.example.com port 22: Success
$                                  ssh has exited: no connection was made
```

7.4.6.2 Password prompting in OpenSSH

If you're using password authentication in OpenSSH, you may control the number of times you are prompted for your password if mistyped. By default, you're prompted three times, and if you mistype the password repeatedly, the client exits. You can change this number with the keyword `NumberOfPasswordPrompts`:[*]

```
# OpenSSH
NumberOfPasswordPrompts 2
```

Now your SSH client provides only two chances to type your password correctly.

7.4.6.3 Password prompting in Tectia

Tectia adds flexibility to password prompting. Instead of preset prompt strings, you can design your own with the `PasswordPrompt` keyword:

```
# Tectia
PasswordPrompt Enter your password right now, infidel:
```

You can insert the remote username or hostname with the symbols `%U` (remote username) or `%H` (remote hostname). For a typical username@hostname prompt you could use:

```
# Tectia
PasswordPrompt "%U@%H's password:"
```

Or you can be fancier:

```
# Tectia
PasswordPrompt "Welcome %U! Please enter your %H password:"
```

7.4.6.4 Batch mode: suppressing prompts

In some cases, you don't want to be prompted for your password or passphrase. If *ssh* is invoked by an unattended shell script, for example, nobody will be at the keyboard to type a password. This is why SSH *batch mode* exists. In batch mode, all prompting for authentication credentials is suppressed. The keyword `BatchMode` can have a value of yes (disable prompting) or no (the default, with prompting enabled):

```
BatchMode yes
```

Batch mode may be enabled for *scp* also with the *–B* option, for OpenSSH:

```
# OpenSSH
$ scp -B myfile server.example.com:
```

Batch mode doesn't replace authentication. If a password or passphrase is required, you can't magically log in without it by suppressing the prompt. If you try, your client exits with an error message such as "permission denied." In order for batch mode to

---

[*] Although this is a client setting, the SSH server ultimately controls how many authentication attempts to accept.

work, you must arrange for authentication to work without a password/passphrase—say, with hostbased authentication or an SSH agent. [11.1]

7.4.6.5   Pseudo-terminal allocation (TTY/PTY/PTTY)

A Unix *tty* (pronounced as it's spelled, T-T-Y) is a software abstraction representing a computer terminal, originally an abbreviation for "teletype." As part of an interactive session with a Unix machine, a tty is allocated to process keyboard input, limit screen output to a given number of rows and columns, and handle other terminal-related activities. Since most terminal-like connections don't involve an actual hardware terminal, but rather a window, a software construct called a *pseudo-tty* (or *pty,* pronounced P-T-Y) handles this sort of connection.

When a client requests an SSH connection, the server doesn't necessarily allocate a pty for the client. It does so, of course, if the client requests an interactive terminal session, e.g., just *ssh host.* But if you ask *ssh* to run a simple command on a remote server, such as *ls*:

```
$ ssh remote.server.com /bin/ls
```

no interactive terminal session is needed, just a quick dump of the output of *ls.* In fact, by default *sshd* doesn't allocate a pty for such a command. On the other hand, if you try running an interactive command like the text editor Emacs in this manner, you get an error message:

```
$ ssh remote.server.com emacs -nw
emacs: standard input is not a tty
```

because Emacs is a screen-based program intended for a terminal. In such cases, you can request that SSH allocate a pty using the *–t* option:

```
$ ssh -t server.example.com emacs
```

Tectia also has the keyword ForcePTTYAllocation, which does the same thing as *–t.**

```
# Tectia
ForcePTTYAllocation yes
```

Also, OpenSSH can request *not* to use a pty with the *–T* option, though most of the time this isn't needed:

```
# OpenSSH
$ ssh -T server.example.com who
barrett      :0        Aug 25 21:51  (console)
byrnes       pts/1     Aug 25 15:19  (yoyodyne.org)
silverman    pts/2     Aug 22 09:42  (client.example.com)
```

If SSH allocates a pty, it also automatically defines an environment variable in the remote shell. The variable is SSH_TTY (for OpenSSH) or SSH2_TTY (for Tectia) and contains the name of the character device file connected to the "slave" side of the pty,

---

* The no-pty option in the authorization file can override this request for a tty. [8.2.8]

the side that emulates a real tty. We can see this in action with a few simple commands. Try printing the value of SSH_TTY on a remote machine. If no tty is allocated, the result is blank:

```
$ ssh server.example.com 'echo $SSH_TTY$SSH_TTY2'
[no output]
```

If you force allocation, the result is the name of the tty:

```
$ ssh -t server.example.com 'echo $SSH_TTY$SSH_TTY2'
/dev/pts/1
```

Thanks to this variable, you can run shell scripts on the remote machine that use this information. For example, here's a script that runs your default editor only if a terminal is available:

```
#!/bin/sh
if [ -n $SSH_TTY -o -n $SSH2_TTY ]; then
    echo 'Success!'
    exec $EDITOR
else
    echo "Sorry, interactive commands require a tty"
fi
```

Place this script in your remote account, calling it *myscript* (or whatever), and run:

```
$ ssh server.example.com myscript
Sorry, interactive commands require a tty
$ ssh -t server.example.com myscript
Success!
...Emacs runs...
```

7.4.6.6 Backgrounding a remote command

If you try running an SSH remote command in the background, you might be surprised by the result. After the remote command runs to completion, the client automatically suspends before the output is printed:

```
$ ssh server.example.com ls &
[1]   11910
$
... time passes ...
[1] + Stopped (SIGTTIN)         ssh server.example.com ls &
```

This happens because *ssh* is attempting to read from standard input while in the background, which causes the shell to suspend *ssh*. To see the resulting output, you must bring *ssh* into the foreground:

```
$ fg
README
myfile
myfile2
```

ssh provides the *–n* command-line option to get around this problem. It redirects standard input to come from */dev/null*, which prevents *ssh* from blocking for input. Now when the remote command finishes, the output is printed immediately:

```
$ ssh -n server.example.com ls &
[1] 11912
$
... time passes ...
README
myfile
myfile2
```

Tectia has a keyword, DontReadStdin, that does the same thing as *–n*, accepting the values yes or no (the default is no):

```
# Tectia
DontReadStdin yes
```

7.4.6.7   Backgrounding a remote command, take two

The preceding section assumed you didn't need to type a password or passphrase, e.g., that you're running an SSH agent. What happens if you use *–n* or Tectia's DontReadStdin but the SSH client needs to read a password or passphrase from you?

```
$ ssh -n server.example.com ls &
$
Enter passphrase for RSA key 'smith@client':
```

 STOP! Don't type your passphrase! Because the command is run in the background with *–n*, the prompt is also printed in the background. If you respond, your password will be visible! This is because you will be typing to the shell, not the *ssh* prompt.

You need a solution that not only disables input and sends the process into the background, but also permits *ssh* to prompt you. This is the purpose of the *–f* command-line option, which instructs *ssh* to do the following, in order:

1. Perform authentication, including any prompting

2. Cause the process to read from */dev/null*, exactly like *–n*

3. Put the process into the background: no "&" is needed

Here's an example:

```
$ ssh -f server.example.com ls
Enter passphrase for RSA key 'smith@client': ********
$
... time passes...
README
myfile
myfile2
```

Tectia has a keyword, GoBackground, that does the same thing, accepting the values yes or no (the default):

```
# Tectia
GoBackground yes
```

GoBackground and –*f* also set up any port forwardings you may have specified on the command line. [9.2.6] The setup occurs after authentication but before backgrounding.

7.4.6.8 Escaping

Recall that the *ssh* client has an *escape sequence* feature. [2.3.2] By typing a particular character, normally a tilde (~), immediately after a newline or carriage return, you can send special commands to *ssh*: terminate the connection, suspend the connection, and so forth. Table 7-2 summarizes the supported escape sequences. It's followed by a list that describes each sequence's meaning.

> If the next character following the escape character isn't in Table 7-2, then OpenSSH sends the entire (unrecognized) escape sequence to the server verbatim, whereas Tectia discards the escape sequence and sends nothing.

Table 7-2. ssh escape sequences

Sequence	Example with <ESC> = ~	Meaning
<ESC> ^Z	~ ^Z	Suspend the connection (^Z means Control-Z)
<ESC> .	~ .	Terminate the connection
<ESC> #	~ #	List all forwarded connections
<ESC><ESC>	~ ~	Send the escape character (by typing it twice)
<ESC> ?	~ ?	Print a help message
OpenSSH only:		
<ESC> &	~ &	Send *ssh* into the background when waiting for connections to terminate
<ESC> B	~ B	Send a break to the server)
<ESC> C	~ C	Open a command line to add or remove a port forwarding
<ESC> R	~R	Request rekeying immediately
Tectia only:		
<ESC> -	~ -	Disable the escape character
<ESC> c	~ c	Print statistics for individual channels
<ESC> l	~ l	Switch to line mode
<ESC> r	~r	Request rekeying immediately
<ESC> s	~ s	Print statistics about this session
<ESC> V	~ V	Print version information

- "Suspend the connection" puts *ssh* into the background, suspended, returning control of the terminal to the local shell. To return to *ssh*, use the appropriate job control command of your shell, typically *fg*. While suspended, *ssh* doesn't run, and if left suspended long enough, the connection may terminate since the client isn't responding to the server. Also, any forwarded connections are similarly blocked while *ssh* is suspended. [9.2.9]

- "Terminate the connection" ends the SSH session immediately. This is most useful if you have lost control of the session: for instance, if a shell command on the remote host has hung and become unkillable, or if you tried exiting while a tunnel (forwarding) is still active. Any X or TCP port forwardings are terminated immediately as well. [9.2.9]

- "List all forwarded connections" prints a list of each X forwarding or TCP port forwarding connection currently established. This lists only active instances of forwarding; if forwarding services are available but not currently in use, nothing is listed here.

- "Send *ssh* into the background," like the "suspend connection" command, reconnects your terminal to the shell that started *ssh*, but it doesn't suspend the *ssh* process. Instead, *ssh* continues to run. This isn't ordinarily useful, since the backgrounded *ssh* process immediately encounters an error.* This escape sequence becomes useful if your *ssh* session has active, forwarded connections when you log out. Normally in this situation, the client prints a message about waiting for forwarded connections to terminate. The client typically waits (silently) in the foreground for the forwarded connections to close before it exits: you can detect this by using the "list all forwarded connections" escape. While the client is in this state, the "send *ssh* into the background" escape sequence returns you to the local shell prompt.

- "Request rekeying immediately" causes the SSH client and server to generate and use some new internal keys for encryption and integrity. Normally, the client and server agree to rekey automatically at regular intervals. [5.3.4]

- "Send the escape character" tells the client to send a real tilde (or whatever the escape character is) to the SSH server as plaintext, not to interpret it as an escape.

- "Disable the escape character" prevents further escape sequences from having any effect, and is therefore irrevocable.

- "Open a command line to add or remove a port forwarding" prompts for –L or –R options to create a new local or remote port forwarding, respectively. [9.2] An existing remote forwarding can be canceled using -KR, followed by the target port number.† To obtain a help message, type –h or ?.

---

* The error occurs as *ssh* attempts to read input from the now disconnected pseudo-terminal.

† Local forwardings cannot be canceled.

- "Switch to line mode" causes characters to be collected by the client and then sent together to the server after a newline has been entered. This allows line-editing features that are available on the client machine to be used, even in situations when similar features are not available on the server machine. Line mode is temporary: after a single line has been sent, the client resumes its normal operation of sending each character to the server as soon as it has been entered.

The rest of the escape sequences are self-explanatory.

Sometimes the default escape character can cause a problem. Suppose you connect by *ssh* from host A to host B, then from host B to host C, and finally from host C to host D, making a chain of *ssh* connections (we represent the machines' shell prompts as A$, B$, C$, and D$):

```
A$ ssh B
...
  B$ ssh C
  ...
    C$ ssh D
    ...
      D$
```

While logged onto host D, you press the Return key, then ~ ^Z (tilde followed by Control-Z) to suspend the connection temporarily. Well, you've got three *ssh* connections active, so which one gets suspended? The first one does, and this escape sequence brings you back to the host A prompt. Well, what if you want to escape back to host B or C? There are two methods, one with forethought and one on the spur of the moment.

If you prepare in advance, you may change the escape character for each connection with the configuration keyword EscapeChar, followed by a character:

```
EscapeChar %
```

or the *–e* command-line option, followed again by the desired character (quoted if necessary to protect it from expansion by the shell):

```
$ ssh -e '%' server.example.com
```

OpenSSH supports the value none to mean no escape character:

```
# OpenSSH
EscapeChar none
```

So, going back to our example of hosts *A* through *D*, you want a different escape character for each segment of this chain of connections. For example:

```
A$ ssh B
...
  B$ ssh -e '$' C
  ...
    C$ ssh -e '%' D
    ...
      D$
```

Now, while logged onto host *D*, a tilde still brings you back to host A, but a dollar sign brings you back to host B and a percent sign back to host C. The same effect can be achieved with the EscapeChar keyword, but the following table shows that more forethought is required to set up configuration files on three hosts.

OpenSSH	Tectia
# Host A configuration file Host B EscapeChar ~	# Host A configuration file B: EscapeChar ~
# Host B configuration file Host C EscapeChar ^	# Host B configuration file C: EscapeChar ^
# Host C configuration file Host D EscapeChar %	# Host C configuration file D: EscapeChar %

Even if you don't normally make chains of SSH connections, you might still want to change the escape character. For example, your work might require you to type a lot of tildes for other reasons, and you might accidentally type an escape sequence such as ~. (tilde period) and disconnect your session. Oops!

There's a second method that requires no forethought: type the escape character multiple times. Typing it twice sends the character literally across the SSH connection. [7.4.6.8] Therefore, you can suspend the second SSH connection by typing two escapes, the third by typing three escapes, and so on. Remember, you must precede your escape characters by pressing the Return key. While logged onto host D, you could escape back to host B, for example, by hitting the Return key, then typing two tildes, and Control-Z.

7.4.7   Proxies and SOCKS

SOCKS is an application-layer network proxying system supported by various SSH implementations. Proxying in general provides a way to connect two networks at the application level, without allowing direct network-level connectivity between them. Figure 7-3 shows a typical SOCKS installation.

The figure shows a private network and the Internet. The gateway machine is connected to both, but doesn't function as a router; there's no direct IP connectivity between the two networks. If a program running on H wants to make a TCP connection to a server on S, it instead connects to the SOCKS server running on G. Using the SOCKS protocol, H requests a connection to S. The SOCKS server makes a connection from G to S on behalf of H and then steps out of the way, passing data back and forth between H and S.

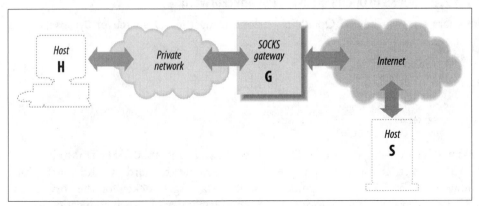

Figure 7-3. A typical SOCKS installation

A general drawback of application-level proxying is lack of transparency: only those programs written with support for the particular proxying scheme have network access. SOCKS, however, isn't specific to any higher-level protocol such as HTTP or SMTP. It provides general services: makes a TCP connection, pings a host, performs a traceroute, etc. Many of its services match the existing programming boundary between applications and network-services libraries. As a result, on modern computer systems employing dynamically linked libraries, it is often possible to extend SOCKS to non-SOCKS-aware applications, such as SSH, by replacing the right libraries with SOCKS-aware ones.

SOCKS comes in two versions, SOCKS4 and SOCKS5. There are two major added features in SOCKS5: authentication and naming support. SOCKS5 supports user authentication so that a proxy can apply access control and user logging to its service. "Naming support" refers to the fact that in SOCKS4, a proxy client expresses the socket it wants to reach as an *(IP address, port)* pair. In real-world situations, however, the client will often know only the name, not the address, of the host it wants to reach. Furthermore, it may not be able to resolve that name directly, since being behind a proxy, it is likely to be in a different naming context than the server (e.g., a corporate network with split DNS). With SOCKS5, the client can instead pass a *(name,port)* pair to the proxy server, leaving the proxy to perform the name lookup where it is mostly likely to succeed.

There are two ways in which SSH clients use SOCKS:

- As a normal SOCKS client, as described earlier.
- As a SOCKS *server*, in conjunction with port forwarding. This allows for *dynamic forwarding*, by which other SOCKS clients may reach any TCP socket on the other side of an SSH connection, through a single forwarded port.

OpenSSH supports only the second method, while Tectia supports both.

7.4.7.1   SOCKS in OpenSSH: using DynamicForward

Dynamic forwarding in OpenSSH is done using the –*D* switch or `DynamicForward` configuration statement:

```
$ ssh -D1080 server
```

or:

```
# ~/.ssh/config:
host server
  DynamicForward 1080
```

As with static (–*L*) port forwarding, this command causes the SSH client to listen for TCP connections on the given port (here 1080, the standard SOCKS port). Note, however, that there's no argument specifying a target socket for the forwarding! That's because this sort of forwarding is completely flexible: each connection to port 1080 can go to a different remote socket, given at connection time via the SOCKS protocol. Set any network client with SOCKS support to use this SSH-forwarded port as its "SOCKS server," and it will have complete TCP access to the network on the other side of the SSH connection.

Just as with static forwarding, a dynamically forwarded port by default listens only on the loopback address. Use the –g switch to have it listen on all host addresses. This option affects *all* locally forwarded ports established with this instance of *ssh*.

Unfortunately, OpenSSH does not have SOCKS *client* support built in. However, there are a number of packages around for conveniently "socksifying" existing programs on the fly; two such packages are *tsocks* and *runsocks*. They both play with the system dynamic linker to replace basic network library calls with SOCKS-aware wrappers, and they are both effective on OpenSSH.

If this sort of linking trick doesn't work, then you can use a separate program instead. You'll need a simple utility which makes the connection through your SOCKS proxy, e.g., a socksified version of *netcat* (*nc*):

> *http://www.securityfocus.com/tools/137*
> *http://netcat.sourceforge.net/*

Then simply:

```
# OpenSSH
# ssh -o ProxyCommand="nc %h %p" ...
```

7.4.7.2   SOCKS in Tectia

Tectia supports both SOCKS client and server (dynamic-forwarding) features, and both SOCKS4 and SOCKS5. However, it does not support user authentication in the SOCKS5 client.

Tectia SOCKS client.   The Tectia SOCKS client feature is controlled with a single parameter, set with the `SocksServer` configuration keyword or the `SSH_SOCKS_SERVER` environment variable. The configuration option overrides the environment variable if both are present.

The SocksServer keyword is a string with the following format:

socks://[user]@gateway[:port]/[net1/mask1,net2/mask2,...]

Here, *gateway* is the machine running the SOCKS server, *user* is the username you supply for identification to SOCKS, and *port* is the TCP port for the SOCKS server (by default, 1080). The *net/mask* entries indicate netblocks that are to be considered local; that is, *ssh* uses SOCKS only for connections lying outside the given network ranges. The mask is given as the length of the network prefix, not an explicit mask, e.g., 192.168.10.0/24 rather than 192.168.10.0/255.255.255.0.

The parts of the string enclosed in square brackets are optional. So, an SSH_SOCKS_ SERVER value can be as simple as this:

socks://laces.shoes.net

With this value, *ssh* uses SOCKS for all connections. It connects to a SOCKS server running on *laces.shoes.net*, port 1080, and it doesn't supply a username. You'll probably never want to use an SSH_SOCKS_SERVER setting as simple as this one, which uses the SOCKS server for all *ssh* connections, even those connecting back to the same machine or to a machine on the same network. A better setup is to use SOCKS only for hosts on the other side of the gateway from you. Here's a more complete example:

socks://dan@laces.shoes.net:4321/127.0.0.0/8,192.168.10.0/24

With this value, *ssh* connects directly to itself via its loopback address (127.0.0.1), or to hosts on the class C network, 192.168.10.0. It uses SOCKS for all other connections, supplying the username "dan" and looking for the SOCKS server on port 4321.

Tectia SOCKS server (dynamic port forwarding). Tectia also has dynamic port forwarding via SOCKS, as described earlier for the OpenSSH *–D* option. [7.4.7.1] It works analogously, using this syntax:

```
# Tectia
$ ssh -L socks/1080 server
```

You could then even use a separate *ssh* command as a SOCKS client of this one, to reach a second SSH server on the far side of the first one:

```
# Tectia
$ ssh -o 'SocksServer socks://localhost/' ...
```

7.4.8   Forwarding

Port forwarding and X forwarding are covered in Chapter 9 and agent forwarding in Chapter 6. We mention them here only for completeness, since forwarding can be controlled in the client configuration file and on the command line.

7.4.9   Encryption Algorithms

When establishing a connection, an SSH client and server have a little conversation about encryption. The server says, "Hello client, here are the encryption algorithms I support." In return, the client says, "Hi there server, I'd like to choose this particular algorithm, please." Normally, they reach agreement, and the connection proceeds. If they can't agree on an encryption algorithm, the connection fails.

Most users let the client and server work things out themselves. But if you like, you may instruct the client to request particular encryption algorithms in its conversation with the server. This is done with the Ciphers keyword followed by a comma-separated list of encryption algorithms of choice:

```
Ciphers blowfish,3des
```

or the *–c* command-line option, either followed by a comma-separated list (OpenSSH) or specified multiple times (Tectia):

```
# OpenSSH
$ ssh -c blowfish,3des server.example.com

# Tectia
$ ssh -c blowfish -c 3des server.example.com
```

indicating that any of these algorithms is acceptable.

All ciphers acceptable by a server may be specified for the client. [5.3.5] Check the latest SSH documentation for a current list of supported ciphers.

7.4.10   Integrity-Checking (MAC) Algorithms

The *–m* command-line option lets you select the integrity-checking algorithm, known as the message authentication code (MAC), used by the SSH-2 protocol: [3.8.3]

```
$ ssh -m hmac-sha1 server.example.com
```

You can specify multiple algorithms on the command line, either as a comma-separated list (OpenSSH) or with multiple *–m* options (Tectia):

```
# OpenSSH
$ ssh -m hmac-sha1,hmac-md5 server.example.com

# Tectia
$ ssh -m hmac-sha1 -m hmac-md5 server.example.com
```

and the SSH server selects one to use. OpenSSH supports the MACs keyword to do the same thing:

```
# OpenSSH
MACs hmac-sha1,hmac-md5
```

7.4.11   Host Key Types

OpenSSH lets you choose host key types you will accept. Provide a comma-separated list of types, from highest to lowest precedence, to the HostKeyAlgorithms keyword. See the *ssh_config* manpage for the current selection of algorithms.

```
# OpenSSH
HostKeyAlgorithms ssh-dss,ssh-rsa
```

Suppose you are about to SSH to a new server for the first time. Being security conscious, you have obtained the server's RSA hostkey through reliable means and placed it in *~/.ssh/known-hosts*. But when you connect, you find that OpenSSH uses the server's DSA key instead, and complains about an unknown hostkey. OpenSSH is not smart enough to prefer a key type it has over one it doesn't—but you can work around this by setting HostKeyAlgorithms to *ssh-rsa*.

7.4.12   Session Rekeying

The RekeyIntervalSeconds keyword specifies how often (in seconds) the Tectia client performs key exchange with the server to replace the session data-encryption and integrity keys. The default is 3600 seconds (one hour), and a zero value disables rekeying:

```
# Tectia
RekeyIntervalSeconds 7200
```

7.4.13   Authentication

In a typical SSH setup, clients try to authenticate by the strongest methods first. If a particular method fails or isn't set up, the next one is tried, and so on. This default behavior should work fine for most needs.

Nevertheless, your clients may request specific types of authentication if they need to do so. For example, you might want to use public-key authentication only, and if it fails, no other methods should be tried.

7.4.13.1 Requesting an authentication technique

OpenSSH clients can request specific authentication methods by keyword. The syntax is the same as the server's in */etc/ssh/sshd_config*, and you can specify all the same authentication methods. [5.4.1] Examples are PasswordAuthentication, PubKeyAuthentication, and KerberosAuthentication, followed by yes or no:

```
# OpenSSH
PasswordAuthentication no
PubKeyAuthentication yes
```

Additionally, you can specify the order in which the client should try these authentication methods, with the PreferredAuthentications keyword:

```
# OpenSSH
PreferredAuthentications publickey,hostbased,password
```

The *ssh_config*(5) manpage lists the currently supported methods.

For Tectia, the AllowedAuthentications keyword selects one or more authentication techniques. Again, the keyword has the same use here as for the Tectia server: [5.4.1]

```
# Tectia
AllowedAuthentications publickey, password
```

7.4.13.2 The server is the boss

When a client specifies an authentication technique, this is just a request, not a requirement. For example, the configuration:

```
PasswordAuthentication yes
```

informs the SSH server that you, the client, agree to participate in password authentication. It doesn't guarantee that you will authenticate by password, just that you are willing to do it if the server agrees. The server makes the decision and might still authenticate you by another method.

For a client to require an authentication technique, it must tell the server that one, and only one, technique is acceptable. To do this, the client must deselect every other authentication technique. For example, to try only password authentication with the server, use OpenSSH's PreferredAuthentications keyword:

```
# OpenSSH
PreferredAuthentications password
```

or Tectia's AllowedAuthentications keyword, which has the same syntax as the server keyword of the same name: [5.4.1]

```
# Tectia
AllowedAuthentications password
```

If the server doesn't support password authentication, however, this connection attempt will fail.

7.4.13.3 Detecting successful authentication

Tectia provides two keywords for reporting whether authentication is successful: AuthenticationSuccessMsg and AuthenticationNotify. Each of these causes Tectia clients to print a message after attempting authentication.

AuthenticationSuccessMsg controls the appearance of the message "Authentication successful" after authentication, which is printed on standard error. Values may be yes (the default, to display the message) or no:

```
# Tectia
$ ssh server.example.com
```

```
Authentication successful.
Last login: Sat Jun 24 2000 14:53:28 -0400
...
$ ssh -p221 -o 'AuthenticationSuccessMsg no' server.example.com
Last login: Sat Jun 24 2000 14:53:28 -0400
...
```

AuthenticationNotify, an undocumented keyword, causes Tectia's *ssh* to print a different message, this time on standard output. If the authentication is successful, the message is "AUTHENTICATED YES"; otherwise, it's "AUTHENTICATED NO". Values may be yes (print the message) or no (the default):

```
$ ssh -q -o 'AuthenticationNotify yes' server.example.com
AUTHENTICATED YES
Last login: Thu Jun 24 2004 14:53:35 -0400
...
```

The behavior of these two keywords differs in the following ways:

- AuthenticationSuccessMsg writes to stderr; AuthenticationNotify writes to std-out.

- The *–q* command-line option [7.4.17] silences AuthenticationSuccessMsg but not AuthenticationNotify. This makes AuthenticationNotify better for scripting (for example, to find out if an authentication can succeed or not). Notice that *exit* is used as a remote command so that the shell terminates immediately:

```
#!/bin/csh
# Tectia
# Get the AUTHENTICATION line
set line = `ssh -q -o 'AuthenticationNotify yes' server.example.com exit`
# Capture the second word
set result = `echo $line | awk '{print $2}'`
if ( $result == "YES" ) then
    ...
```

In fact, AuthenticationNotify is used precisely in this manner by Tectia's *scp* and *sftp*, when these programs run *ssh* in the background to connect to the remote host for file transfers. They wait for the appearance of the "AUTHENTICATED YES" message to know that the connection was successful, and they can now start speaking to the *sftp-server*.

AuthenticationSuccessMsg provides an additional safety feature: a guarantee that authentication has occurred. Suppose you invoke Tectia's *ssh* and are prompted for your passphrase:

```
# Tectia
$ ssh server.example.com
Passphrase for key "mykey": ********
```

You then see, to your surprise, a second passphrase prompt:

```
Passphrase for key "mykey":
```

You might conclude that you mistyped your passphrase the first time, and so you type it again. But what if the second prompt came not from your *ssh* client, but from the server, which has been cracked by an evil intruder? Your passphrase has just been stolen! To counteract this potential threat, *ssh* prints "Authentication successful" after authentication, so the previous session actually looks like this:

```
# Tectia
$ ssh server.example.com
Passphrase for key "mykey": ********
Authentication successful.
Passphrase for key "mykey":      Suspicious!
```

The second passphrase prompt is now revealed as a fraud.

7.4.13.4 Using ssh-keysign for hostbased authentication

Earlier we described how hostbased authentication requires a privileged program that provides SSH credentials to user processes. [3.4.3.6] In OpenSSH, this program is *ssh-keysign*. It must be installed setuid root (or any account that can read the client hostkey).

To allow a client system to perform hostbased authentication, the system administrator must set the EnableSSHKeysign keyword in */etc/ssh/ssh_config*:

```
# ssh_config
EnableSSHKeysign yes
```

Most options in *ssh_config* are for the *ssh* program itself, but this one option is read by *ssh-keysign*. Hostbased authentication relies critically on the integrity of the client host and on other administrative requirements, such as correspondence of account names across hosts. It is crucial that it not be used unless these requirements are met; this option is to make sure that it is not enabled unless the system administrator consciously chooses to do so.

7.4.14 Data Compression

SSH connections may be compressed. That is, data sent over an SSH connection may be compressed automatically before it is encrypted and sent, and automatically uncompressed after it is received and decrypted. If you're running SSH software on fast, modern processors, compression is generally a win. However, it also depends on your network speed, and whether the data you're transferring is already compressed or not (say, a large compressed *tar* file).

To enable compression for a single session, use command-line options. Unfortunately, the implementations have incompatible syntax. For OpenSSH, compression is disabled by default, and the –C command-line option turns it on:

```
# OpenSSH: turn compression ON
$ ssh -C server.example.com
$ scp -C myfile server.example.com:
```

For Tectia, however, –C means the opposite, turning compression off:

```
# Tectia: turn compression OFF
$ ssh -C server.example.com
```

and +C turns it on:

```
# Tectia: turn compression ON
$ ssh +C server.example.com
```

(There is no compression option for Tectia's *scp*.) To enable or disable compression for all sessions, use the Compression keyword, given a value of yes or no (the default):

```
Compression yes
```

7.4.15   Program Locations

The auxiliary Tectia program *ssh-signer* is normally located in Tectia's installation directory, along with the other Tectia binaries. [3.4.3.6] You can change this location with the undocumented keyword SshSignerPath:

```
# Tectia
SshSignerPath /usr/alternative/bin/ssh-signer2
```

If you use this keyword, be sure to set it to the fully qualified path of the program. If you use a relative path, hostbased authentication works only for users who have *ssh-signer2* in their search path, and *cron* jobs fail without *ssh-signer2* in their path.

7.4.16   Subsystems

Subsystems are predefined commands supported by an SSH server. [5.8] Each installed server can implement different subsystems, so check with the system administrator of the server machine for a list.*

The *–s* option of *ssh* invokes a subsystem on a remote machine. For example, if the SSH server running on *server.example.com* has a "backups" subsystem defined, you run it as:

```
$ ssh server.example.com -s backups
```

OpenSSH uses the remote command as the subsystem name: this must be specified last on the *ssh* command line. In contrast, Tectia obtains the subsystem name from the command-line argument that immediately follows the *–s* option. Therefore, our previous example works in both cases, so we highly recommend this syntax. Other orderings of the command line are possible for specific implementations:

```
# OpenSSH
$ ssh -s server.example.com backups

# Tectia
$ ssh -s backups server.example.com
```

---

* Or examine the remote machine's server configuration file yourself for lines beginning with *subsystem*.

Command-line arguments cannot be used with subsystems: neither OpenSSH nor Tectia provides any mechanism for passing them from client to server. If any extra arguments are given on the *ssh* command line, OpenSSH (mis)interprets them as part of the subsystem name:

```
# OpenSSH
$ ssh server.example.com -s backups /home
Request for subsystem 'backups /home' failed on channel 0
```

whereas Tectia simply forbids extra command-line arguments if –*s* is used:

```
# Tectia
$ ssh server.example.com -s backups /home
ssh: FATAL: No command allowed with subsystem.
```

7.4.17   Logging and Debugging

Earlier in the chapter, we introduced the –*v* command-line option which causes SSH clients to print verbose debugging messages. [7.3] Verbose mode works for *ssh* and *scp*, e.g.:

```
$ ssh -v server.example.com
```

OpenSSH also has the LogLevel keyword, which takes the following levels as an argument: QUIET, FATAL, ERROR, INFO, VERBOSE, DEBUG1, DEBUG2, and DEBUG3 (in order of increasing verbosity). The value DEBUG is equivalent to DEBUG1, and:

```
# OpenSSH
$ ssh -o LogLevel=DEBUG
```

is equivalent to *ssh –v*.

Verbose mode can also be turned on for Tectia with the (surprise!) VerboseMode keyword:

```
# Tectia
VerboseMode yes
```

If you ever encounter problems or strange behavior from SSH, your first instinct should be to turn on verbose mode.

Tectia's *ssh* has multiple levels of debug messages; verbose mode corresponds to level 2. You can specify greater or less debugging with the –*d* command-line option, followed by an integer from 0 to 99:

```
# Tectia
$ ssh -d0      No debugging messages
$ ssh -d1      Just a little debugging
$ ssh -d2      Same as -v
$ ssh -d3      A little more detailed
$ ssh -d#      And so on...
```

Tectia's −d option may also use the same module-based syntax as for serverdebugging: [5.9]

```
# Tectia
$ ssh -d Ssh2AuthPasswdServer=2 server.example.com
```

Tectia's *scp* also supports this level of debugging, but the option is −D instead of −d since *scp* −d is already used to mean something else:

```
 # Tectia
$ scp -D Ssh2AuthPasswdServer=2 myfile server.example.com
```

To disable all debug messages, use −q:

```
$ ssh -q server.example.com
```

or specify it with the LogLevel (OpenSSH) or QuietMode (Tectia) keyword:

```
# OpenSSH
LogLevel QUIET

# Tectia
QuietMode yes
```

Finally, to print the program version number, use −V:

```
$ ssh -V
```

7.4.18   Random Seeds

Tectia lets you change the location of your random seed file, which is *~/.ssh2/ random_seed* by default: [5.3.1.2]

```
# Tectia
RandomSeedFile /u/smith/.ssh2/new_seed
```

7.5   Secure Copy with scp

The secure copy program, *scp*, obeys keywords in your client configuration file just as *ssh* does. In addition, *scp* provides other features and options that we'll cover in this section. Remember that *scp* supports several options for logging and debugging, so you can watch what's going on when it runs. [7.3]

7.5.1   Full Syntax of scp

So far, we've described the syntax of *scp* only in general: [2.2.1]

```
scp name-of-source name-of-destination
```

Each of the two names, or *path specifications*, on the command line represents files or directories in the following manner (it is fairly consistent with the behavior of Unix *cp* or *rcp*):

- If *name-of-source* is a file, *name-of-destination* may be a file (existing or not) or a directory (which must exist). In other words, a single file may be copied to another file or into a directory.

- If *name-of-source* is two or more files, one or more directories, or a combination, *name-of-destination* must be an existing directory into which the copy takes place.* In other words, multiple files and directories may be copied only into a directory.

Both *name-of-source* and *name-of-destination* may have the following form from left to right:

- The *username* of the account containing the file or directory, followed by @. This part is optional, and if omitted, the value is the username of the user invoking *scp*.

- The *hostname* of the host containing the file or directory, followed by a colon. This part is optional, if the path is present, and the username isn't; if omitted, the value is *localhost*. Tectia permits an optional *TCP port number* for the SSH connection to be inserted between the hostname and the colon, preceded by a hash sign.

- The *directory path* to the file or directory. (Optional if the hostname is present.) Relative pathnames are assumed relative to the *default directory*, which is the current directory (for local paths) or the user's home directory (for remote paths). If omitted entirely, the path is assumed to be the default directory.

Although each field is optional, you can't omit them all at the same time, yielding the empty string. Either the hostname (•) or the directory path (•) must be present. Some examples:

MyFile
> The file *./MyFile* on *localhost*

MyDirectory
> The directory *./MyDirectory* on *localhost*

. (period)
> The current directory on *localhost*

server.example.com:
> The directory *~username* on *server.example.com*

---

* We say "must," but technically you *could* specify a file as a destination in some cases. However, this behavior is probably not what you want. As your multiple files get copied into a single destination file, each is overwritten by the next!

server.example.com

A local file named "server.example.com" (Oops: did you forget the trailing colon? This is a common mistake.)

server.example.com:MyFile

The file *MyFile* in the remote user's home directory on *server.example.com*

bob@server.example.com:

The directory *~bob* on *server.example.com*

bob@server.example.com

A local file named "bob@server.example.com" (oops; forgot the trailing colon again)

bob@server.example.com:MyFile

The file *~bob/MyFile* on *server.example.com*

server.example.com:dir/MyFile

The file *dir/MyFile* in the remote user's home directory on *server.example.com*

server.example.com:/dir/MyFile

The file */dir/MyFile* on *server.example.com* (note the absolute path)

bob@server.example.com:dir/MyFile

The file *~bob/dir/MyFile* on *server.example.com*

bob@server.example.com:/dir/MyFile

The file */dir/MyFile* on *server.example.com* (although you authenticate as bob, the path is absolute)

server.example.com#2000:

The remote user's home directory on *server.example.com*, via TCP port 2000 (Tectia only)

Here are a few complete examples:

```
$ scp myfile myfile2              A local copy just like cp
$ scp myfile bob@host1:           Copy ./myfile to ~bob on host1
$ scp bob@host1:myfile .          Copy ~bob/myfile on host1 to ./myfile
$ scp host1:file1 host2:file2     Copy file1 from host1 to file2 on host2
$ scp bob@host1:file1 jen@host2:file2   Same as above, but copying from bob's
                                        to jen's account
```

Table 7-3 summarizes the syntax of an *scp* path.

Table 7-3. scp path specifications

Field	Other syntax	Optional?	Default for local host	Default for remote host
Username	Followed by @	Yes	Invoking user's username	Invoking user's username
Hostname	Followed by :	Only if username is omitted and path is present	None, file is accessed locally	N/A

Table 7-3. scp path specifications (continued)

Field	Other syntax	Optional?	Default for local host	Default for remote host
Port number[a]	Preceded by #	Yes	22	22
Directory path	N/A	Only if hostname is present	Current (invoking) directory	Username's remote home directory

[a] Tectia only.

7.5.2   Handling of Wildcards

scp for OpenSSH has no special support for wildcards in filenames. It simply lets the shell expand them:

```
$ scp *.txt server.example.com:
```

Watch out for wildcards in remote file specifications, as they are evaluated on the local machine, not the remote. For example, this attempt is likely to fail:

```
$ scp server.example.com:*.txt .              Bad idea!
```

The Unix shell attempts to expand the wildcard before *scp* is invoked, but the current directory contains no filename matching "server.example.com:*.txt". The C shell and its derivatives will report "no match" and will not execute *scp*. Bourne-style shells, noticing no match in the current directory, will pass the unexpanded wildcard to *scp*, and the copy may succeed as planned, but this coincidental behavior shouldn't be relied on. Always escape your wildcards so that they are explicitly ignored by the shell and are passed to *scp*:

```
$ scp server.example.com:\*.txt .
```

Tectia's *scp* does its own regular expression matching after shell-wildcard expansion is complete. The *sshregex* manpage for Tectia (see Appendix B) describes the supported operators. Even so, escape your wildcard characters if you want your local shell to leave them alone.

7.5.3   Recursive Copy of Directories

Sometimes you want to copy not just a single file, but a directory hierarchy. In this case, use the –*r* option, which stands for *recursive*. For example, to securely copy the directory */usr/local/bin* and all its files and subdirectories to another machine:

```
$ scp -r /usr/local/bin server.example.com:
```

If you forget the –r option when copying directories, *scp* complains:

```
$ scp /usr/local/bin server.example.com:
/usr/local/bin: not a regular file
```

Although *scp* can copy directories, it isn't necessarily the best method. If your directory contains hard links or soft links, they won't be duplicated. Links are copied as plain files (the link targets). Other types of special files, such as named pipes, also aren't copied correctly.* A better solution is to use *tar*, which handles special files correctly, and send it to the remote machine to be untarred, via SSH:

```
$ tar cf - /usr/local/bin | ssh server.example.com tar xf -
```

or *rsync*, tunneled through SSH:

```
$ rsync -e ssh /usr/local/bin server.example.com:
```

7.5.4 Preserving Permissions

When *scp* copies files, the destination files are created with certain file attributes. By default, the file permissions adhere to a umask on the destination host, and the modification and last access times will be the time of the copy. Alternatively, you can tell *scp* to duplicate the permissions and timestamps of the original files. The *–p* option accomplishes this:

```
$ scp -p myfile server.example.com:
```

For example, if you transfer your entire home directory to a remote machine, you probably want to keep the file attributes the same as the original:

```
$ scp -rp $HOME server.example.com:myhome/
```

Again, *scp* does not duplicate special files and links, so consider *tar* or *rsync -a* instead:

```
$ rsync -a -e ssh /usr/local/bin server.example.com:
```

7.5.5 Automatic Removal of Original File

After copying a file, Tectia's *scp* can optionally remove the original if desired. The *–u* command-line option specifies this:

```
# Tectia
$ scp myfile server.example.com:
$ ls myfile
myfile
$ scp -u myfile server.example.com:
$ ls myfile
myfile: No such file or directory
```

If you've ever wanted a "secure move" command in addition to secure copy, you can define one in terms of *scp –u*:

```
# Tectia
$ alias smv='scp -u'
```

---

* These limitations also are true when copying single files, but at least you see the erroneous result quickly. With directories, you can copy a hierarchy incorrectly and not notice.

7.5.6   Safety Features

Tectia's *scp* has several features to protect you from running dangerous commands.

7.5.6.1   Directory confirmation

Suppose you want to copy a local file, *myfile*, to a remote directory. You type:

```
$ scp myfile server.example.com:mydir
$ rm myfile
```

Then you connect to *server.example.com* and find, to your horror, that *mydir* was a file, not a directory, and you just overwrote it! Tectia's *–d* option prevents this tragedy. If the destination isn't a directory, *scp* complains and exits without copying the file:

```
# Tectia
$ scp -d myfile server.example.com:mydir
scp: warning: Destination (example.com:mydir) is not a directory.
```

This option is necessary only if you are copying a single file. If you are copying multiple files or a directory, all the *scp* implementations check by default that the remote destination is a directory.*

7.5.6.2   No-execute mode

Another safety feature of Tectia's *scp* is the *–n* option, which instructs the program to describe its actions but not perform any copying. This is useful for verifying the behavior of *scp* before executing a potentially risky command.

```
# Tectia
$ scp -n myfile server.example.com:
Not transferring myfile -> server.example.com:./myfile  (1k)
```

7.5.6.3   Overwriting existing files

Tectia's *scp* will refuse to overwrite existing files if you desire. The *–I* or *--interactive* option will prompt you before overwriting a destination file:

```
# Tectia
$ scp -I myfile server.example.com:
Overwrite destination file './myfile' with '/home/smith/myfile' (yes/yes to all/no/no
to all/abort) [y/Y/n/N/a]:n
```

As an alternative, if you know in advance whether you'll want to overwrite existing files, use the *--overwrite* option (the default is no):

```
# Tectia
$ scp --overwrite yes myfile server.example.com:   Always overwrite
```

---

* There's one degenerate case. If your copy occurs on a single machine, e.g., *scp* *.c mydir*, the *scp* client doesn't necessarily check that *mydir* is a directory.

7.5.7 Batch Mode

If you're using *scp* in scripts with passwordless authentication [11.1], you might want to suppress all prompting of the user. That's what the *–B* option is for, which enables batch mode. When present, this option suppresses all interaction with the user. [7.4.6.4]

```
$ scp -B myfile server.example.com:
```

7.5.8 User Identity

OpenSSH provides the *–i* option for *scp*, as it does for *ssh*, to specify a particular identity file for authentication. [7.4.2]

```
# OpenSSH
$ scp -i my_favorite_key myfile server.example.com:
```

Tectia has no option like this, but you can get around this limitation with *–o*: [7.1.2.1]

```
# Tectia
$ scp -o "IdentityFile my_identity_file" myfile server.example.com:
```

7.5.9 SSH Protocol Settings

You can downgrade *scp* to use the SSH-1 protocol with the *-1* option, if you are feeling insecure:

```
$ scp -1 myfile server.example.com:
```

or redundantly specify the SSH-2 protocol, which is the default anyway:

```
# OpenSSH
$ scp -2 myfile server.example.com:
```

7.5.10 TCP/IP Settings

You can specify the remote TCP port contacted by *scp* with the *–P* option (OpenSSH):

```
# OpenSSH
$ scp -P 23456 myfile server.example.com:
```

or by appending a hash mark and port number to the file specification (Tectia):

```
# Tectia
$ scp myfile server.example.com#23456:
```

Both OpenSSH and Tectia can require the use of IP Version 4 or 6, as *ssh* does, with the *-4* and *-6* options. [7.4.5.6]

7.5.11 Encryption Algorithms

You can set the encryption cipher for *scp* with the *–c* option, exactly as for *ssh*. [7.4.9]

7.5.12   Controlling Bandwidth

The *–l* (lowercase L) option of OpenSSH's *scp* command will limit the bandwidth of the connection, in case you want to avoid saturating a slower network.

```
# OpenSSH
$ scp -l 1000 myfile server.example.com:   Limit bandwidth to 1000 kilobits per second
```

Tectia's *scp* command can limit the maximum number of concurrent requests it will issue, with the *–N* option:

```
# Tectia
$ scp -r -N 5 mydirectory server.example.com: Limit to five concurrent requests in this recursive
        directory transfer
```

Finally, Tectia's *–b* option controls the buffer size for the file transfer; the default is 32K:

```
# Tectia
$ scp -b 65536 myfile server.example.com: Set buffer size to 64K
```

7.5.13   Data Compression

OpenSSH's *scp* command can compress the data before sending it, with the *–C* option, to speed up transfers: [7.4.14]

```
# OpenSSH
$ scp -C myfile server.example.com:
```

Tectia does not provide a similar option, but you can get around this and enable compression with *–o*: [7.1.2.1]

```
$ scp -o "Compression yes" myfile server.example.com:
```

7.5.14   File Conversion

Tectia's *scp* has several options for changing the files in transit. It can change the destination filenames to all lowercase, with the *--force-lower-case* option:

```
# Tectia
$ scp --force-lower-case MyFile server.example.com:
```

The destination file on *server.example.com* will be named *myfile* rather than *MyFile*.

Another Tectia transformation involves the treatment of lines in a text file. *scp* normally transfers files literally, as binary data. You can choose to treat the files specially as text files—that is, lines of ASCII characters terminated by carriage returns and/or linefeeds—with the *–a* option. Unix, DOS, and Macintosh operating systems use different standards for terminating lines of text, and *scp* can convert between these standards.

```
# Tectia
$ scp -a my_text_file server.example.com:
```

The above command assumes that the SSH client and server can accurately communicate and agree upon the text file standards. If not, you can use a more advanced syntax for *–a* that specifies the line terminators as unix, dos, or mac. This is done by placing src: (for the source machine) and dst: (for the destination machine) after the *–a* option. Some examples:

```
# Tectia
$ scp -asrc:unix -adst:dos myfile server.example.com:  Convert from Unix to DOS/Windows
    format
$ scp -asrc:dos -adst:mac myfile server.example.com:  Convert from DOS/Windows to
    Macintosh format
$ scp -asrc:mac -adst:unix myfile server.example.com:  Convert from Macintosh to Unix
    format
```

7.5.15 Optimizations

Tectia's *scp* does a few optimizations to avoid transferring unnecessary files and data. Before coping a file, *scp* compares the file sizes. If they are different, the copy commences, but if they are the same, *scp* computes an MD5 checksum of the source and destination file. If the checksums are equal, the files are assumed to be identical and no copy takes place, and you'll see a message like this:

```
myfile: complete md5 match -> transfer skipped
```

If you always want your files copied, even if they are identical (i.e., have equal checksums), you can disable the MD5 test with the *--checksum* option, providing the value no:

```
# Tectia
$ scp --checksum no myfile server.example.com:  Don't compute checksums for files
```

Tectia's *scp* performs similar checking on individual data blocks to determine whether to transfer them or not. You can control this with the *–W* or *--whole-file* options, providing the value yes or no:

```
# Tectia
$ scp --whole-file yes myfile server.example.com:  Always transfer whole files
```

7.5.16 Statistics Display

As *scp* copies files, it prints information about its progress, including statistics about the file transfer. You can control this information with various options.

OpenSSH simply lets you suppress the statistics with its *–q* option:

```
# OpenSSH
$ scp -q myfile server.example.com:
```

Tectia can likewise suppress statistics with the *–Q* option (Tectia).

```
# Tectia
$ scp -Q myfile server.example.com:
```

but permits more control with the *--statistics* option:

```
# Tectia
$ scp --statistics no myfile server.example.com:   Same as -Q option

$ scp --statistics simple myfile server.example.com:   Minimal statistics
/home/smith/myfile |    4B |    4B/s | TOC: 00:00:01

$ scp --statistics yes myfile server.example.com:   Full statistics
myfile                                      |    4B |    4B/s | TOC: 00:00:01 | 100%
```

7.5.17   Locating the ssh Executable

To copy files securely, *scp* invokes *ssh* internally. Therefore, *scp* needs to know where the *ssh* executable resides on disk. Normally, the path to *ssh* is made known to *scp* at compile time (by the compile-time flag --prefix), but you can specify the path manually if you like. [4.3.5.1] For instance, you can test a new version of *ssh* with an old version of *scp*. The command-line option –*S* specifies the path:

```
$ scp -S /usr/alternative/bin/ssh myfile server.example.com:
```

7.5.18   Getting Help

Both OpenSSH and Tectia *scp* will print a usage message briefly describing all its options:

```
$ scp --help
```

You can get the same effect if you omit all arguments (OpenSSH) or use –*h* (Tectia). Tectia will also print its version number on request:

```
# Tectia
$ scp --version
$ scp -V
```

7.5.19   For Internal Use Only

scp for OpenSSH has two undocumented options, –*t* and –*f*, for internal use. Most likely you will never need to use them explicitly. They inform *scp* of the direction of the copy: from the local to the remote machine, or from remote to local. The –*t* option means copying to a remote machine and –*f* means copying from a remote machine.

Whenever you invoke *scp*, it invisibly runs a second *scp* process on the remote host that includes either –*t* or –*f* on its command line. You can see this if you run *scp* in verbose mode. If copying from the local to the remote machine, you see:

```
$ scp -v myfile server.example.com:
Executing: host server.example.com, ..., command scp -v -t .
...
```

On the other hand, if you copy from the remote to the local machine, you see:

```
$ scp -v server.example.com:myfile .
Executing: host server.example.com, ..., command scp -v -f .
...
```

Again, it's likely you'll never use these options, but they're useful to know when reading *scp*'s output in verbose mode.

7.5.20 Further Configuration

You can set any client configuration keywords for *scp* using the *–o* option, exactly as for *ssh*. Additionally, OpenSSH lets you specify an alternative configuration file with *–F*. [7.1.2.1]

7.6   Secure, Interactive Copy with sftp

The *sftp* client is an alternative to *scp*, though under the hood it does mostly the same thing: it copies files between SSH client and server machines securely. The main difference is that *sftp* is interactive, with an interface much like the old FTP programs. [2.7.1]

7.6.1   Interactive Commands

To get started, run *sftp* with a remote hostname:

```
$ ftp server.example.com
```

or username and hostname:

```
$ sftp smith@server.example.com
```

You'll get a prompt:

```
sftp>
```

and now may type commands to transfer files between your local and remote machine. For example:

```
sftp> cd remote_directory       Change to a particular remote directory
sftp> ls                        List the names of available files
sftp> get remotefile            Download the file "remotefile"
sftp> get remotefile newname    Same as above, but the local file will be renamed as "newname"
sftp> put localfile             Upload the file "localfile"
sftp> put localfile othername   Same as above, but the remote file will be renamed as "othername"
sftp> quit                      Quit sftp
```

The basic use of *sftp* will feel familiar to anyone who's used an FTP program. Use the *cd* command to move around the remote filesystem (or *lcd* for the local filesystem), *ls* to list the available remote files, and the *get* and *put* commands to download and upload files, respectively. Table 7-4 lists the interactive commands available during an *sftp* connection.

Table 7-4. Interactive commands for sftp, grouped by function

Command	Meaning	Support
Basic commands		
open	Open a connection to the remote machine[a]	Tectia
lopen	Open a connection to the local machine[a]	Tectia
close	Close the connection to the remote machine	Tectia
lclose	Close the connection to the local machine	Tectia
bye, quit	Quit *sftp*	OpenSSH, Tectia
exit	Quit *sftp*	OpenSSH
help	Print a help message	OpenSSH, Tectia
?	Print a help message	OpenSSH
version	Display the SFTP protocol version	OpenSSH
!	Shell escape: execute a local shell or command	OpenSSH
Directory commands		
ls	List files in a remote directory	OpenSSH, Tectia
lls	List files in a local directory	OpenSSH, Tectia
cd	Change the remote working directory	OpenSSH, Tectia
lcd	Change the local working directory	OpenSSH, Tectia
pwd	Print the name of the remote working directory	OpenSSH, Tectia
lpwd	Print the name of the local working directory	OpenSSH, Tectia
mkdir	Create a remote directory	OpenSSH, Tectia
lmkdir	Create a local directory	OpenSSH, Tectia
rmdir	Delete a remote directory	OpenSSH, Tectia
lrmdir	Delete a local directory	Tectia
lsroots	List virtual roots of a VShell SSH server [17.9]	Tectia
File commands		
get	Download a file from the remote machine	OpenSSH, Tectia[b]
mget	Download multiple files by wildcard	OpenSSH, Tectia[b]
put	Upload a file to the remote machine	OpenSSH, Tectia[b]
mput	Upload multiple files to the remote machine	OpenSSH, Tectia[b]
rename	Rename a remote file	OpenSSH, Tectia
lrename	Rename a local file	Tectia
ln, symlink	Create a symbolic link on the remote machine	OpenSSH
rm	Delete a remote file	OpenSSH, Tectia
lrm	Delete a local file	Tectia

Table 7-4. Interactive commands for sftp, grouped by function (continued)

Command	Meaning	Support
chmod	Change the permissions on a remote file	OpenSSH, Tectia
lchmod	Change the permissions on the local file	Tectia
chown	Change the owner of a remote file	OpenSSH
chgrp	Change the group ownership of a remote file	OpenSSH
Transfer settings		
binary	Transfer all files as binary	Tectia
ascii	Transfer all files as ASCII	Tectia
auto	Determine the file type using the "setext" list	Tectia
getext	Print the list of file extensions that indicate text files	Tectia
setext	Set the list of file extensions that indicate text files	Tectia
lumask	Set the umask for downloaded files	OpenSSH
progress	Toggle the display of a progress meter for file transfers	OpenSSH

a Not needed unless you run Tectia *sftp* with no arguments, so no initial connection is established.
b On Tectia, get and mget are equivalent, and so are put and mput.

7.6.2 Command-Line Options

Virtually all command-line options available to *scp* will work for *sftp*. [7.5]

7.7 Summary

SSH clients are highly configurable through environment variables, command-line options, and keywords in configuration files. Remember that command-line options have the highest precedence, followed by your local client configuration file, and finally the global client configuration file.

Client configuration files consist of sections that apply to individual hosts or groups of hosts. When you run an SSH client, remember that multiple sections can apply to it, according to the precedence rules we covered. If the same keyword is set multiple times, the earliest (OpenSSH) or latest (Tectia) value is the winner.

When experimenting with client configuration, remember verbose mode. If you experience unusual SSH behavior, your first instinct should be to add the *–v* option and run the client again, watching the debug output for clues.

CHAPTER 8
Per-Account Server Configuration

We've seen two techniques for controlling the SSH server's behavior globally: compile-time configuration (Chapter 4) and serverwide configuration (Chapter 5). These techniques affect *all* incoming SSH connections to a given server machine. Now it's time to introduce a third, finer-grained method of server control: *per-account configuration*.

As the name implies, per-account configuration controls the SSH server differently for each user account on the server machine. For example, a user account sandy can accept incoming SSH connections from any machine on the Internet, while rick permits connections only from the domain *verysafe.com*, and fraidycat refuses key-based connections. Each user configures his own account, using the facilities highlighted in Figure 8-1, without needing special privileges or assistance from the system administrator.

We have already seen a simple type of per-account configuration. A user may place a public key into her authorization file, instructing the SSH server to permit logins to her account by public-key authentication. But per-account configuration can go further, becoming a powerful tool for access control and playing some fun tricks with your account. Accepting or rejecting connections by particular keys or hosts is just the beginning. For instance, you can make an incoming SSH connection run a program of your choice, instead of the client's choice. This is called a *forced command*, and we'll cover quite a few interesting applications.

Per-account configuration may control only *incoming* SSH connections to your account. If you're interested in configuring *outgoing* SSH connections by running SSH clients, refer to Chapter 7.

8.1 Limits of This Technique

Per-account configuration can do many interesting things, but it has some restrictions that we will discuss:

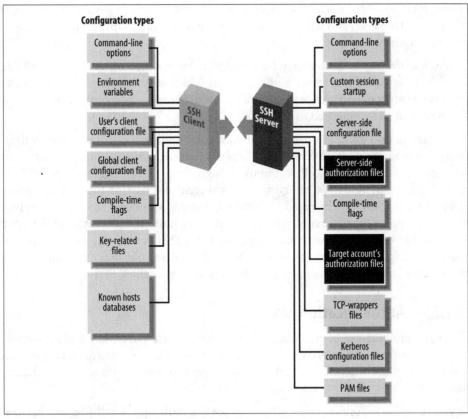

Configuration types (left)

- Command-line options
- Environment variables
- User's client configuration file
- Global client configuration file
- Compile-time flags
- Key-related files
- Known hosts databases

SSH Client

SSH Server

Configuration types (right)

- Command-line options
- Custom session startup
- Server-side configuration file
- Server-side authorization files
- Compile-time flags
- Target account's authorization files
- TCP-wrappers files
- Kerberos configuration files
- PAM files

Figure 8-1. Per-account configuration (highlighted parts)

- It can't defeat security measures put in place by compile-time or serverwide configuration. (Thank goodness.)
- It is most flexible and secure if you use public-key authentication. Hostbased and password authentication provide a much narrower range of options.

8.1.1   Overriding Serverwide Settings

SSH settings in a user's account may only *restrict* the authentication of incoming connections. They can't enable any SSH features that have been turned off more globally, and they can't permit a forbidden user or host to authenticate. For example, if your SSH server rejects all connections from the domain *evil.org*, you can't override this restriction within your account by per-account configuration.*

---

* There is one exception to this rule: hostbased authentication. A user's ~/.shosts file may override a restriction placed by the system administrator in /etc/shosts.equiv. [8.3]

This limitation makes sense. No end-user tool should be able to violate a server security policy. However, end users should be (and are) allowed to restrict incoming connections to their accounts.

A few features of the server may be overridden by per-account configuration. The most notable one is the server's idle timeout, which may be extended beyond the serverwide setting. But such features can't coerce the server to accept a connection it has been globally configured to reject.

If you are an end user, and per-account configuration doesn't provide enough flexibility, you can run your own instance of the SSH server, which you may configure to your heart's content. [5.1.2] Be cautious, though, since this is seldom the right thing to do. The restrictions you're trying to circumvent are part of the security policy defined for the machine by its administrators, and you shouldn't run a program that flouts this policy just because you can. If the machine in question is under your administrative control, simply configure the main SSH server as you wish. If not, then installing and running your own *sshd* might violate your usage agreement and/or certainly annoy your sysadmin. And that's never a wise thing to do.

8.1.2 Authentication Issues

To make the best use of per-account configuration, use public-key authentication. Password authentication is too limited, since the only way to control access is with the password itself. Hostbased authentication permits a small amount of flexibility, but not nearly as much as public-key authentication.

If you're still stuck in the password-authentication dark ages, let this be another reason to switch to public keys. Even though passwords and public-key passphrases might seem similar (you type a secret word, and *voilà*, you're logged in), public keys are far more flexible for permitting or denying access to your account. Read on and learn how.

8.2 Public-Key-Based Configuration

To set up public-key authentication in your account on an SSH server machine, you create an authorization file, typically called *authorized_keys* (OpenSSH) or *authorization* (Tectia), and list the keys that provide access to your account. [2.4] Well, we've been keeping a secret. Your authorization file can contain not only keys, but also other keywords or options to control the SSH server in powerful ways. We will discuss:

- The full format of an authorization file
- Forced commands for limiting the set of programs that the client may invoke on the server
- Restricting incoming connections from particular hosts

- Setting environment variables for remote programs
- Setting an idle timeout so that clients will be forcibly disconnected if they aren't sending data
- Disabling or placing limits on certain features of the incoming SSH connection, such as port forwarding and tty allocation

As we demonstrate how to modify your authorization file, remember that the file is consulted by the SSH server only at authentication time. Therefore, if you change your authorization file, only new connections will use the new information. Any existing connections are already authenticated and won't be affected by the change.

Also remember that an incoming connection request won't reach your authorization file if the SSH server rejects it for other reasons, namely, failing to satisfy the server-wide configuration. If a change to your authorization file doesn't seem to be having an effect, make sure it doesn't conflict with a (more powerful) serverwide configuration setting.

8.2.1   OpenSSH Authorization Files

Your OpenSSH authorization file, ~/.ssh/authorized_keys, is a secure doorway into your account via SSH. Each line of the file contains a public key and means the following: "I give permission for SSH clients to access my account, in a particular way, using this key as authentication." Notice the words "in a particular way." Until now, public keys have provided unlimited access to an account. Now we'll see the rest of the story.

Each line may contain, in order:

1. A set of authorization options for the key (optional)
2. A string indicating the key type: ssh-dss for a DSA key, or ssh-rsa for an RSA key (required)
3. The public key, represented as a long string (required)
4. A descriptive comment (optional); this can be any text, such as "Bob's public key" or "My home PC using SecureCRT 3.1"

Here's an example:

```
from="192.168.10.1" ssh-dss AAAAB3NzaC1kc3MA... My OpenSSH key
```

It contains authorization options (from="192.168.10.1"), the key type (ssh-dss), the public key itself (abbreviated here with an ellipsis), and the final comment ("My OpenSSH key").

Public keys are generated by *ssh-keygen* in *.pub* files, you may recall, and you typically insert them into *authorized_keys* by copying. [2.4.3] Options, however, are usually typed into *authorized_keys* with a text editor.*

An option may take two forms. It may be a keyword, such as:

```
# OpenSSH: Turn off port forwarding
no-port-forwarding
```

or it may be a keyword followed by an equals sign and a value, such as:

```
# OpenSSH: Allow connections only from myhost
from=myhost
```

Multiple options may be given together, separated by commas, with *no whitespace* between the options:

```
# OpenSSH
no-port-forwarding,from=myhost
```

If you mistakenly include whitespace:

```
# THIS IS ILLEGAL: whitespace between the options
no-port-forwarding, from=myhost
```

your connection by this key won't work properly. If you connect with debugging turned on (*ssh -v*), you will see a "bad options" message from the SSH server.

Many SSH users aren't aware of options or neglect to use them. This is a pity because options provide extra security and convenience. The more you know about the clients that access your account, the more options you can use to control that access.

8.2.2   Tectia Authorization Files

A Tectia authorization file, typically found in *~/.ssh2/authorization*,† has a different format than OpenSSH's. Instead of public keys, it contains keywords and values, much like other SSH configuration files we've seen. Each line of the file contains one keyword followed by its value. The most commonly used keywords are Key and Options.

Public keys are indicated using the Key keyword. Key is followed by whitespace, and then the name of a file containing a public key. Relative filenames refer to files in *~/.ssh2*. For example:

```
# Tectia
Key myself.pub
```

---

* When editing *authorized_keys*, be sure to use a text editor capable of handling long lines. The public key may be several hundred characters long. Some text editors can't display long lines, won't edit them properly, automatically insert line breaks, or wreak other sorts of havoc upon your nice public keys. (Aaargh. Don't get us started talking about brain-damaged text editors.) Use a modern editor, and turn off automatic line breaking. We use GNU Emacs.

† The name can be changed with the keyword AuthorizationFile in the serverwide configuration file. [5.3.1.6]

means that an SSH-2 public key is contained in *~/.ssh2/myself.pub.* Your *authorization* file must contain at least one Key line for public-key authentication to occur.

Each Key line may optionally be followed immediately by an Options keyword and its value, which is a comma-separated list of options:

```
# Tectia
Key myself.pub
Options no-port-forwarding, no-x11-forwarding, command="mycommand"
```

One common option is command, which specifies a *forced command*, i.e., a command to be executed whenever the key *immediately above* is used for access. We discuss forced commands later in great detail. [8.2.3] For now, all you need to know is this: a forced command begins with the keyword Options followed by command and its quoted value, a shell command line. For example:

```
# Tectia
Key somekey.pub
Options command="/bin/echo All logins are disabled"
```

Remember that an Options line by itself is an error. The following examples are illegal:

```
# Tectia
# THIS IS ILLEGAL: no Key line
Options command="/bin/echo This line is bad."
# THIS IS ILLEGAL: no Key line precedes the second Options
Key somekey.pub
Options command="/bin/echo All logins are disabled"
Options command="/bin/echo This line is bad."
```

8.2.2.1 Tectia PGP key authentication

Tectia supports authentication by PGP key. [6.5] Your *authorization* file may also include PgpPublicKeyFile, PgpKeyName, PgpKeyFingerprint, and PgpKeyId lines. An Options line may follow PgpKeyName, PgpKeyFingerprint, or PgpKeyId, just as it may follow Key.

```
# Tectia
PgpKeyName my-key
Options command="/bin/echo PGP authentication was detected"
```

8.2.3 Forced Commands

Ordinarily, an SSH connection invokes a remote command chosen by the client:

```
# Invoke a remote login shell
$ ssh server.example.com
# Invoke a remote directory listing
$ ssh server.example.com /bin/ls
```

A *forced command* transfers this control from the client to the server. Instead of the client deciding which command will run, the owner of the server account decides. In Figure 8-2, the client has requested the command */bin/ls*, but the server-side forced command runs */bin/who* instead.

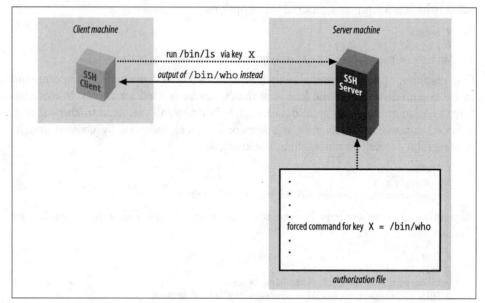

Figure 8-2. Forced command substituting /bin/who for /bin/ls

Forced commands can be quite useful. Suppose you want to give your assistant access to your account, but only to read your email. You can associate a forced command with your assistant's SSH key to run only your email program and nothing else.

In OpenSSH, a forced command may be specified in *authorized_keys* with the *command* option preceding the desired key. For example, to run the email program *pine* whenever your assistant connects:

```
# OpenSSH
command="/usr/bin/pine" ...secretary's public key...
```

In Tectia, a forced command appears on the line immediately following the desired Key, using the command option. The previous example would be represented like so:

```
# Tectia
Key secretary.pub
Options command "/usr/bin/pine"
```

You may associate, at most, one forced command with a given key. To associate multiple commands with a key, put them into a script on the remote machine and run the script as the forced command. (We will demonstrate this. [8.2.3.3])

8.2.3.1 Security issues

Before we begin in-depth examples of forced commands, let's discuss security. At first glance, a forced command seems at least as secure as a "normal" SSH connection that invokes a shell. This is because a shell can invoke any program, while a forced command can invoke only one program, the forced command itself. If a forced command is */usr/bin/pine*, only */usr/bin/pine* can be invoked.

Nevertheless, there's a caveat. A forced command, carelessly used, may lull you into a sense of false security, believing that you have limited the client's capabilities when you haven't. This occurs if the forced command unintentionally permits a *shell escape*, i.e., a way to invoke a shell from within the forced command. Using a shell escape, a client can invoke any program available to a shell. Many Unix programs have shell escapes, such as text editors (*vi*, *Emacs*), pagers (*more*, *less*), programs that invoke pagers (*man*), news readers (*rn*), mail readers (such as Pine in the previous example!), and debuggers (*gdb*). Interactive programs are the most common culprits, but even noninteractive commands may run shell commands (*find*, *xargs*, etc.).

When you define a forced command, you probably don't want its key used for arbitrary shell commands. Therefore, we propose the following safety rules for deciding whether a program is appropriate as a forced command:

* Avoid programs that have shell escapes. Read their documentation carefully. If you still aren't sure, get help.

* Avoid compilers, interpreters, or other programs that let the user generate and run arbitrary executable code.

* Treat very carefully any program that creates or deletes files on disk in user-specified locations. This includes not only applications (word processors, graphics programs, etc.), but also command-line utilities that move or copy files (*cp*, *mv*, *rm*, *scp*, *ftp*, etc.).

* Avoid programs with their setuid or setgid bits set, particularly setuid root.

* If using a script as a forced command, follow traditional rules of safe script writing. Within the script, limit the search path to relevant directories (omitting "."), invoke all programs by absolute path, don't blindly execute user-supplied strings as commands, and don't make the script setuid anything.* And again, don't invoke any program that has a shell escape.

* Consider using a restricted shell to limit what the incoming client can do. For example, the restricted shell */usr/lib/rsh* (not to be confused with the r-command also called "rsh") can limit the remote directories the client can enter.

* Associate the forced command with a separate, dedicated SSH key, not the one used for your logins, so that you can conveniently disable the key without affecting your login capability.

---

* Modern Unix implementations often ignore the setuid bit on scripts for security reasons.

- Disable unnecessary SSH features using other options we cover later. Under OpenSSH, you may disable port forwarding with `no-port-forwarding`, X forwarding with `no-x11-forwarding`, agent forwarding with `no-agent-forwarding`, and tty allocation using `no-pty`.

Any program may be used as a forced command, but some may be risky choices. In the examples that follow, we cover several of these issues as they're encountered.

8.2.3.2   Rejecting connections with a custom message

Suppose you've permitted a friend to access your account by SSH, but now you've decided to disable the access. You can simply remove his key from your authorization file, but here's something fancier. You can define a forced command to print a custom message for your friend, indicating that his access has been disabled. For example:

```
# OpenSSH
command="/bin/echo Sorry, buddy, but you've been terminated!" ...key...

# Tectia
Key friend.pub
Options command="/bin/echo Sorry, buddy, but you've been terminated!"
```

Any incoming SSH connection that successfully authenticates with this key causes the following message to be displayed on standard output:

```
Sorry, buddy, but you've been terminated!
```

and then the connection closes. If you'd like to print a longer message, which might be awkward to include in your authorization file, you can store it in a separate file (say, *~/go.away*) and display it using an appropriate program (e.g., *cat*):

```
# OpenSSH
command="/bin/cat $HOME/go.away" ...key...

# Tectia
Key friend.pub
Options command="/bin/cat $HOME/go.away"
```

Since the message is long, you might be tempted to display it one screenful at a time with a pager program such as *more* or *less*. Don't do it!

```
# OpenSSH: Don't do this!
command="/usr/bin/less $HOME/go.away" ...key...
```

This forced command opens an unwanted hole into your account: the *less* program, like most Unix pager programs, has a shell escape. Instead of restricting access to your account, this forced command permits unlimited access.[*]

---

[*] The *less* program has a secure mode that disables shell escapes. See the manpage for *less* about the environment variable LESSSECURE.

8.2.3.3 Displaying a command menu

Suppose you want to provide limited access to your account, permitting the incoming SSH client to invoke only a few, specific programs. Forced commands can accomplish this. For instance, you can write a shell script that permits a known set of programs to be executed and then run the script as a forced command. A sample script, shown in Example 8-1, permits only three programs to be chosen from a menu.

Example 8-1. Menu script

```
#!/bin/sh
/bin/echo "Welcome!
Your choices are:

1       See today's date
2       See who's logged in
3       See current processes
q       Quit"

/bin/echo "Your choice: \c"
read ans
while [ "$ans" != "q" ]
do
  case "$ans" in
    1)
        /bin/date
        ;;
    2)
        /bin/who
        ;;
    3)
        /usr/ucb/w
        ;;
    q)
        /bin/echo "Goodbye"
        exit 0
        ;;
    *)
        /bin/echo "Invalid choice '$ans': please try again"
        ;;
  esac
  /bin/echo "Your choice: \c"
  read ans
done
exit 0
```

When someone accesses your account by public key and invokes the forced command, the script displays:

```
Welcome!
Your choices are:
1       See today's date
```

```
2        See who's logged in
3        See current processes
q        Quit
```

```
Your choice:
```

The user may then type 1, 2, 3, or q to run the associated program. Any other input is ignored, so no other programs can be executed.

Such scripts must be written carefully to avoid security holes. In particular, none of the permitted programs should provide a means to escape to a shell, or else the user may execute any command in your account.

8.2.3.4 Examining the client's original command

As we've seen, a forced command gets substituted for any other command the SSH client might send. If an SSH client attempts to invoke the program *ps*:

```
$ ssh server.example.com ps
```

but a forced command is set up to execute "/bin/who" instead:

```
# OpenSSH
command="/bin/who" ...key...
```

```
# Tectia
key mykey.pub
Options command="/bin/who"
```

then *ps* is ignored and */bin/who* runs instead. Nevertheless, the SSH server does read the original command string sent by the client and stores it in an environment variable. For OpenSSH, the environment variable is SSH_ORIGINAL_COMMAND, and for Tectia, it's SSH2_ORIGINAL_COMMAND. So, in our example, the value of SSH_ORIGINAL_COMMAND would be *ps*.

A quick way to see these variables in action is to print their values with forced commands. For OpenSSH, create a forced command like the following:

```
# OpenSSH
command="/bin/echo You tried to invoke $SSH_ORIGINAL_COMMAND" ...key...
```

Then connect with an SSH client, supplying a remote command (which won't be executed), such as:

```
$ ssh server.example.com cat /etc/passwd
```

Instead of executing *cat*, the OpenSSH server simply prints:

```
You tried to invoke cat /etc/passwd
```

and exits. Similarly, for Tectia, you can set up a forced command like this:

```
# Tectia
Key mykey.pub
Options command="/bin/echo You tried to invoke $SSH2_ORIGINAL_COMMAND"
```

Then, a client command like:

```
$ ssh server.example.com cat /etc/passwd
```

produces:

```
You tried to invoke cat /etc/passwd
```

8.2.3.5   Restricting a client's original command

Let's try a slightly more complex example using the environment variable SSH_ORIGINAL_COMMAND. We create a forced command that examines the environment variable and turns a requested command into another of our choice. For example, suppose you want to permit a friend to invoke remote commands in your account, except for the *rm* (remove file) command. In other words, a command like:

```
$ ssh server.example.com rm myfile
```

is rejected. Here's a script that checks for the presence of *rm* in the command string and, if present, rejects the command:

```
#!/bin/sh
# OpenSSH.  For Tectia, use $SSH2_ORIGINAL_COMMAND.
#
case "$SSH_ORIGINAL_COMMAND" in
  *rm*)
    echo "Sorry, rejected"
    ;;
  *)
    $SSH_ORIGINAL_COMMAND
    ;;
esac
```

Save this script in *~/rm-checker*, and define a forced command to use it:

```
# OpenSSH
command="$HOME/rm-checker" ...key...

# Tectia
Key mykey.pub
Options command="$HOME/rm-checker"
```

Our script is just an example: it isn't secure. It can be easily bypassed by a clever command sequence to remove a file:

```
$ ssh server.example.com '/bin/ln -s /bin/r? ./killer && ./killer myfile'
```

which creates a link to */bin/rm* with a different name (killer) and then performs the removal. Nevertheless, the concept is still valid: you can examine SSH_ORIGINAL_COMMAND to select another command to execute instead.

8.2.3.6   Logging a client's original command

Another cool use of the "original command" environment variables is to keep a log of commands that are run using a given key. For example:

```
# OpenSSH
command="log-and-run" ...key...

# Tectia
Key mykey.pub
Options command="log-and-run"
```

where *log-and-run* is the following script. It appends a line to a log file, containing a timestamp and the command attempted:

```
#!/bin/sh
# OpenSSH.  For Tectia, use $SSH2_ORIGINAL_COMMAND.
if [ -n "$SSH_ORIGINAL_COMMAND" ]
then
    echo "`/bin/date`: $SSH_ORIGINAL_COMMAND" >> $HOME/ssh-command-log
    exec $SSH_ORIGINAL_COMMAND
fi
```

8.2.3.7   Forced commands and secure copy (scp)

We've seen what happens when *ssh* encounters a key with a forced command. But what does *scp* do in this situation? Does the forced command run, or does the copy operation take place?

In this case, the forced command executes, and the original operation (file copy) is ignored. Depending on your needs, this behavior might be good or bad. In general, we do not recommend using *scp* with any key that has a forced command. Instead, use two keys, one for ordinary logins and file copying and the other for the forced command.

Now that we've thoroughly examined forced commands, let's move on to other features of per-account configuration.

8.2.4   Restricting Access by Host or Domain

Public-key authentication requires two pieces of information: the corresponding private key and its passphrase (if any). Without either piece, authentication can't succeed. Per-account configuration lets you add a third requirement for additional security: a restriction on the client's hostname or IP address.

8.2.4.1   OpenSSH host access control

In OpenSSH, host access control is accomplished in the *authorized_keys* file with the *from* option. For example:

```
# OpenSSH
from="client.example.com" ...key...
```

enforces that any SSH connection must come from *client.example.com*, or else it is rejected. Therefore, if your private-key file is somehow stolen, and your passphrase cracked, an attacker might still be stymied if he can't connect from the authorized client machine.

If the concept of "from" sounds familiar, you've got a good memory: it's the same access control provided by the AllowUsers keyword for serverwide configuration. [5.5.1] The *authorized_keys* option, however, is set by you within your account and applies to a single key, while AllowUsers is specified by the system administrator and applies to all connections to an account. Here's an example to demonstrate the difference. Suppose you want to permit connections from *remote.org* to enter the benjamin account. As system administrator, you can configure this within */etc/ssh/sshd_config*:

```
# OpenSSH
AllowUsers benjamin@remote.org
```

Using per-account configuration, the user benjamin can configure the identical setting within his *authorized_keys* file, for a particular key only:

```
# OpenSSH
# File ~benjamin/.ssh/authorized_keys
from="remote.org" ...key...
```

Of course, the serverwide setting takes precedence. If the system administrator had denied this access using the DenyUsers keyword:

```
# OpenSSH
DenyUsers benjamin@remote.org
```

then user benjamin can't override this restriction using the from option in *authorized_keys*.

Just like AllowUsers, the from option can use the wildcard characters *, matching any string, and ?, matching any one character:

```
from="*.someplace.org"      Matches any host in the someplace.org domain
from="som?pla?e.org"        Matches somXplaYe.org but not foo.someXplaYe.org or foo.somplace.org
```

It may also match the client IP address, with or without wildcards:

```
from="192.220.18.5"
from="192.2??.18.*"
```

There can also be multiple patterns, this time separated by commas (AllowUsers employs spaces). No whitespace is allowed. You may also negate a pattern by prefixing it with an exclamation point (!). The exact matching rules are: every pattern in the list is compared to either the client's canonical hostname or its IP address. If the pattern contains only numerals, dots, and wildcards, it is matched against the address, otherwise, it is matched against the hostname.* The connection is accepted if and only if the client matches at least one positive pattern and no negated patterns. So for example, the following rule denies connections from *saruman.ring.org*, allows connections from other hosts in the domain *ring.org*, and denies everything else:

```
from="!saruman.ring.org,*.ring.org"
```

while this one again denies *saruman.ring.org* but allows all other clients:

```
from="!saruman.ring.org,*"
```

Remember that access control by hostname may be problematic, due to issues with name resolution and security. [3.4.3.6] Fortunately, the from option is just an auxiliary feature of OpenSSH public-key authentication, which provides stronger security than would an entirely hostname-based solution.

8.2.4.2   Tectia host access control

Host access control in Tectia is accomplished in the *authorization* file with the allow-from and deny-from options. For example, to permit connections to your account from the *example.com* domain:

```
# ~/.ssh2/authorization
Key mykey.pub
Options allow-from="example.com"
```

or to deny them from *very.evil.org*:

```
# ~/.ssh2/authorization
Key otherkey.pub
Options deny-from="very.evil.org"
```

These options follow the same rules as the AllowHosts and DenyHosts server configuration keywords, respectively. [5.5.3] However, allow-from and deny-from control access per key, rather than serverwide.

8.2.5   Setting Environment Variables

The environment option instructs the SSH server to set an environment variable when a client connects via the given key. For example, the OpenSSH *authorized_keys* line:

```
# OpenSSH
environment="EDITOR=emacs" ...key...
```

or Tectia *authorization* file option:

```
# Tectia
Key mykey.pub
Options environment="editor=emacs"
```

---

* OpenSSH unfortunately doesn't let you specify arbitrary IP networks using an address and mask, nor by "address / number of bits." *libwrap* does [9.5], but its restrictions apply to *all* connections, not on a per-key basis.

sets the environment variable EDITOR to the value emacs, thereby setting the client's default editor for the login session. The syntax following environment= is a quoted string containing a variable, an equals sign, and a value. All characters between the quotes are significant, i.e., the value may contain whitespace:

```
# OpenSSH
environment="MYVARIABLE=this value has whitespace in it" ...key...
```

```
# Tectia
Key mykey.pub
Options environment="MYVARIABLE=this value has whitespace in it"
```

or even a double quote, if you escape it with a forward slash:

```
# OpenSSH
environment="MYVARIABLE=I have a quote\" in my middle" ...key...
```

```
# Tectia
Key mykey.pub
Options environment="MYVARIABLE=I have a quote\" in my middle"
```

Also, a single key may have multiple environment variables set:

```
# OpenSSH
environment="EDITOR=emacs",environment="MYVARIABLE=26" ...key...
```

```
# Tectia
Key mykey.pub
environment="EDITOR=emacs",environment="MYVARIABLE=26"
```

Why set an environment variable for a key? This feature lets you tailor your account to respond differently based on which key is used. For example, suppose you create two keys, each of which sets a different value for an environment variable—say, SPECIAL:

```
# OpenSSH
environment="SPECIAL=1" ...key...
environment="SPECIAL=2" ...key...
```

```
# Tectia
Key key1.pub
Options environment="SPECIAL=1"
Key key2.pub
Options environment="SPECIAL=2"
```

Now, in your account's shell configuration file, you can examine $SPECIAL and trigger actions specific to each key:

```
# In your .login file
switch ($SPECIAL)
  case 1:
    echo 'Hello Bob!'
    set prompt = 'bob> '
    breaksw
  case 2:
```

```
        echo 'Hello Jane!'
        set prompt = jane> '
        source ~/.janerc
        breaksw
    endsw
```

Here, we print a custom welcome message for each key user, set an appropriate shell prompt, and in Jane's case, invoke a custom initialization script, *~/.janerc*. Thus, the environment option provides a convenient communication channel between a particular key and the remote shell.

8.2.5.1   Example: CVS and $LOGNAME

As a more advanced example of the environment option, suppose a team of open source software developers around the Internet is developing a computer program. The team decides to practice good software engineering and store its code with CVS, the Concurrent Versions System, a popular version control tool. Lacking the funds to set up a server machine, the team places the CVS repository into the computer account of one of the team members, Benjamin, since he has lots of available disk space. Benjamin's account is on the SSH server machine *cvs.repo.com*.

The other developers do not have accounts on *cvs.repo.com*, so Benjamin places their public keys into his *authorized_keys* file so that they can do check-ins. Now there's a problem. When a developer changes a file and checks the new version into the repository, a log entry is made by CVS, identifying the author of the change. But everyone is connecting through the benjamin account, so CVS always identifies the author as "benjamin," no matter who checked in the changes. This is bad from a software engineering standpoint: the author of each change should be clearly identified.[*]

You can eliminate this problem by modifying Benjamin's file, preceding each developer's key with an environment option. CVS examines the LOGNAME environment variable to get the author's name, so you set LOGNAME differently for each developer's key:

```
# OpenSSH
environment="LOGNAME=dan" ...key...
environment="LOGNAME=richard" ...key...
...

# Tectia
Key dan.pub
Options environment="LOGNAME=dan"
Key richard.pub
Options environment="LOGNAME=richard"
...
```

---

[*] In an industrial setting, each developer would have an account on the CVS repository machine, so the problem wouldn't exist.

Now, when a given key is used for a CVS check-in, CVS identifies the author of the change by the associated, unique LOGNAME value. Problem solved!*

8.2.6   Setting Idle Timeout

Tectia's idle-timeout option tells the SSH server to disconnect a session that has been idle for a certain time limit. This is just like Tectia's IdleTimeout keyword for serverwide configuration but is set by you within your account, instead of by the system administrator. [5.3.3.5]

Suppose you let your friend Jamie access your account by SSH. Jamie works in an untrusted environment, however, and you are worried that he might walk away from his computer while connected to your account, and someone else might come by and use his session. One way to reduce the risk is to set an *idle timeout* on Jamie's key, automatically disconnecting the SSH session after a given period of idle time. If the client stops sending output for a while, Jamie has probably walked away, and the session is terminated.

Timeouts are set with the idle-timeout option. For example, to set the idle timeout to 60 seconds:

```
# Tectia
Key mykey.pub
Options idle-timeout=60s
```

idle-timeout uses the same notation for time as the IdleTimeout server keyword. [5.3.3.5] It also *overrides* any serverwide value set with the IdleTimeout keyword. For example, if the serverwide idle timeout is five minutes:

```
# Tectia
IdleTimeout 5m
```

but your *authorization* file sets it to 10 minutes for your account:

```
# Tectia
Key mykey.pub
Options idle-timeout=10m
```

then any connection using this key has an idle timeout of 10 minutes, regardless of the serverwide setting.

This feature has more uses than disconnecting absent typists. Suppose you're using an SSH key for an automated process, such as backups. An idle timeout value kills the process automatically if it hangs due to an error.

---

* Incidentally, the authors used this technique while collaborating on this book.

8.2.7   Disabling or Limiting Forwarding

Although you're permitting SSH access to your account, you might not want your account to be used as a springboard to other machines by port forwarding. [9.2] To prevent this, use the no-port-forwarding option for that key:

```
# OpenSSH
no-port-forwarding ...key...

# Tectia
Key mykey.pub
Options no-port-forwarding
```

Rather than disable forwarding, OpenSSH can place limits on it with the permitopen option for a key. For example, to restrict port forwarding to local port 12345 connecting to remote host *server.example.com*:

```
# OpenSSH
permitopen="server.example.com:12345" ...key...
```

permitopen may have multiple values separated by commas. The syntax is *hostname*: *port* for IPv4 addresses and *hostname/port* for IPv6 addresses.

X forwarding [9.4] can be prohibited per key with the no-x11-forwarding option:

```
# OpenSSH
no-x11-forwarding ...key...

# Tectia
Key mykey.pub
Options no-x11-forwarding
```

Agent forwarding can also be disabled per key, if you don't want remote users to travel through your account and onto other computers using the given key. [6.3.5] This is done with the no-agent-forwarding option:

```
# OpenSSH
no-agent-forwarding ...key...

# Tectia
Options no-agent-forwarding
```

These aren't strong restrictions. As long as you allow shell access, just about anything can be done over the connection. The user need employ only a pair of custom programs that talk to each other across the connection and directly implement port forwarding, agent forwarding, or anything else you thought you were preventing. To be more than just a reminder or mild deterrent, these options must be used together with carefully restricted access on the server side, such as forced commands or a restricted shell on the target account.

8.2.8 Disabling TTY Allocation

Normally, when you log in via SSH, the server allocates a pseudo-terminal (henceforth, tty) for the login session: [7.4.6.5]

```
# A tty is allocated for this client
$ ssh server.example.com
```

The server even sets an environment variable, SSH_TTY for OpenSSH or SSH2_TTY for Tectia, with the name of the tty allocated. For example:

```
# After logging in via OpenSSH
$ echo $SSH_TTY            Use $SSH2_TTY for Tectia
/dev/pts/1
```

When you run a noninteractive command, however, the SSH server doesn't allocate a tty to set the environment variable, e.g.:

```
# OpenSSH: No tty is allocated
$ ssh server.example.com /bin/ls
```

Suppose you want to give someone SSH access for invoking noninteractive commands, but not for running an interactive login session. You've seen how forced commands can limit access to a particular program, but as an added safety precaution, you can also disable tty allocation with the no-pty option:

```
# OpenSSH
no-pty ...key...

# Tectia
Key mykey.pub
Options no-pty
```

Noninteractive commands will now work normally, but requests for interactive sessions are refused by the SSH server. If you try to establish an interactive session, your client may appear to hang.* Run it in verbose mode to see the reason:

```
# OpenSSH output
debug1: Remote: Pty allocation disabled.
```

Just for fun, let's observe the effect of no-pty on the environment variable with a simple experiment. Set up a public key and precede it with the following forced command:

```
# OpenSSH
command="echo SSH_TTY is [$SSH_TTY]" ...key...

# Tectia
Key mykey.pub
Options command="echo SSH2_TTY is [$SSH2_TTY]"
```

---

* If the connection hangs and your client appears to be frozen, type the *ssh* escape character followed by a period (usually ~. unless you've overridden it) to close the connection.

Now try connecting noninteractively and interactively, and watch the output. The interactive command assigns a value to the environment variable, but the noninteractive one doesn't:

```
$ ssh server.example.com
SSH_TTY is [/dev/pts/2]        For Tectia it would be SSH2_TTY

$ ssh server.example.com anything
SSH_TTY is []                  For Tectia it would be SSH2_TTY
```

Next, add the no-pty option:

```
# OpenSSH
no-pty,command="echo SSH_TTY is [$SSH_TTY]" ...key...

# Tectia
Key mykey.pub
no-pty,command="echo SSH_TTY is [$SSH_TTY]"
```

and try connecting interactively. The connection (properly) fails and the environment variable has no value:

```
$ ssh server.example.com
SSH_TTY is []                  For Tectia it would be SSH2_TTY
Connection to server.example.com closed.
```

Even if a client requests a tty specifically (with *ssh -t*), the no-pty option forbids its allocation. For instance, if you try running the Emacs editor over the SSH connection:

```
$ ssh -t server.example.com emacs
```

Emacs will fail to run or appear to hang.

8.3   Hostbased Access Control

A limited type of per-account configuration is possible in OpenSSH if you use hostbased authentication rather than public-key authentication. Specifically, you can permit SSH access to your account based on the client's remote username and hostname via the system files */etc/shosts.equiv* and */etc/hosts.equiv*, and personal files *~/.rhosts* and *~/.shosts*. A line like:

```
+client.example.com jones
```

permits hostbased SSH access by the user *jones@client.example.com*. Since we've already covered the details of these four files, we won't repeat the information in this chapter. [3.6.2]

Per-account configuration with hostbased authentication is similar to using host access control in your OpenSSH *authorized_keys* or Tectia *authorization* file. [8.2.4] Both methods may restrict SSH connections from particular hosts. The differences are shown in this table:

Feature	Hostbased access	Public-key host access
Authenticate by hostname	Yes	Yes
Authenticate by IP address	Yes	Yes
Authenticate by remote username	Yes	No
Wildcards in hostnames and IP	No	Yes
Passphrase required for logins	No	Yes
Use other public-key features	No	Yes
Security	Less	More

To use hostbased authentication for access control, all of the following conditions must be true:

- Hostbased authentication is enabled in the server, both at compile time and in the serverwide configuration file.
- Your desired client hosts aren't specifically excluded by serverwide configuration, e.g., by AllowHosts and DenyHosts.
- For OpenSSH, the server configuration keyword EnableSSHKeysign must be set to yes.*

Despite its capabilities, hostbased authentication is more complex than one might expect. For example, if your carefully crafted *.shosts* file denies access to *sandy@trusted.example.com*:

```
# ~/.shosts
-trusted.example.com sandy
```

but your *.rhosts* file inadvertently permits access:

```
# ~/.rhosts
+trusted.example.com
```

then sandy will have SSH access to your account. Worse, even if you don't have a *~/.rhosts* file, the system files */etc/hosts.equiv* and */etc/shosts.equiv* can still punch a hostbased security hole into your account against your wishes. Unfortunately, using per-account configuration, there's no way to prevent this problem. Only compile-time or serverwide configuration can disable hostbased authentication.

Because of these issues and other serious, inherent weaknesses, we recommend against using the weak form of hostbased authentication, Rhosts authentication, as a form of per-account configuration. (By default it is disabled, and we approve.) If you require the features of hostbased authentication, we recommend the stronger form, called RhostsRSAAuthentication (OpenSSH) or hostbased (Tectia), which adds cryptographic verification of host keys.

---

* In olden days, the *ssh* executable needed to be setuid root.

8.4　The User rc File

The shell script */etc/ssh/sshrc* is invoked by the SSH server for each incoming SSH connection. [5.6.3] You may define a similar script in your account, *~/.ssh/rc* (OpenSSH) or *~/.ssh2/rc* (Tectia), to be invoked for every SSH connection to your account. If this file exists, */etc/ssh/sshrc* isn't run.

The SSH *rc* file is much like a shell startup file (e.g., *~/.profile* or *~/.cshrc*), but it executes only when your account is accessed by SSH. It is run for both interactive logins and remote commands. Place any commands in this script that you would like executed when your account is accessed by SSH, rather than an ordinary login. For example, you can run and load your *ssh-agent* in this file:

```
# ~/.ssh/rc, assuming your login shell is the C shell
if ( ! $?SSH_AUTH_SOCK ) then
  eval `ssh-agent`
  /usr/bin/tty | grep 'not a tty' > /dev/null
  if ( ! $status ) then
    ssh-add
  endif
endif
```

Like */etc/ssh/sshrc*, your personal *rc* file is executed just before the shell or remote command requested by the incoming connection. OpenSSH always uses the Bourne shell (*/bin/sh*) for *~/.ssh/rc*, as it does for */etc/ssh/sshrc*. In contrast, Tectia uses your login shell for *~/.ssh2/rc*, unlike */etc/ssh2/sshrc*.

8.5　Summary

Per-account configuration lets you instruct the SSH server to treat your account differently. Using public-key authentication, you can permit or restrict connections based on a client's key, hostname, or IP address. With forced commands, you can limit the set of programs that a client may run in your account. You can also disable unwanted features of SSH, such as port forwarding, agent forwarding, and tty allocation.

Using hostbased authentication, you can permit or restrict particular hosts or remote users from accessing your account. This uses the file *~/.shosts* or (less optimally) *~/.rhosts*. However, the mechanism is less secure and less flexible than public-key authentication.

Port Forwarding and X Forwarding

One of SSH's major benefits is *transparency*. A terminal session secured by SSH behaves like an ordinary, insecure one (e.g., created by *telnet* or *rsh*) once it has been established. Behind the scenes, however, SSH keeps the session secure with strong authentication, encryption, and integrity checking.

In some situations, however, transparency is hard to achieve. A network firewall might be in the way, interfering with certain network traffic you need. Corporate security policies might prohibit you from storing SSH keys on certain machines. Or you might need to use insecure network applications in a secure environment.

In this chapter, we'll discuss an important feature of SSH, called *forwarding* or *tunneling*, that addresses several concerns about transparency:

Securing other TCP/IP applications
> SSH can transparently encrypt another application's data stream. This is called *port forwarding*.

Securing X Window applications
> Using SSH, you can invoke X programs on a remote machine and have them appear, securely, on your local display. (This feature of X is insecure ordinarily.) This is called *X forwarding*, a special case of port forwarding for which SSH has extra support.

SSH forwarding isn't completely transparent, since it occurs at the application level, not the network level. Applications must be configured to participate in forwarding, and a few protocols are problematic to forward (FTP data channels are a notable example). But in most common situations, once a secure tunnel is set up, the participating applications appear to the user to operate normally. For complete application-level transparency, you need a network-level technique, such as IPSEC [1.6.4] or a proprietary Virtual Private Network (VPN) technology available from various vendors, in host software or dedicated routers. While VPNs provide a more complete solution, they require significantly more work and expense to set up compared to SSH forwarding.

So, when we say "transparent" in this chapter, we mean "transparent to the application, once a little configuration has been done."

In this chapter, we discuss SSH forwarding techniques to allow otherwise prohibited traffic across firewalls. This can be a perfectly legitimate and adequately safe practice if done properly: the firewall prevents unauthorized traffic, while SSH forwarding allows authorized users to bypass the restriction. However, don't forget you are bypassing a security restriction that is in place for a reason. Be sure to follow the guidelines we give for safe SSH forwarding. Also, take care that you are not violating a company policy by using forwarding. Just because you *can* do something doesn't automatically mean that it's a good idea. If in doubt, consult with your system administrators.

9.1   What Is Forwarding?

Forwarding is a type of interaction with another network application, as shown in Figure 9-1. SSH intercepts a service request from some other program on one side of an SSH connection, sends it across the encrypted connection, and delivers it to the intended recipient on the other side. This process is mostly transparent to both sides of the connection: each believes it is talking directly to its partner and has no knowledge that forwarding is taking place. Even more powerfully, SSH forwarding can achieve certain types of communication that are impossible without it.

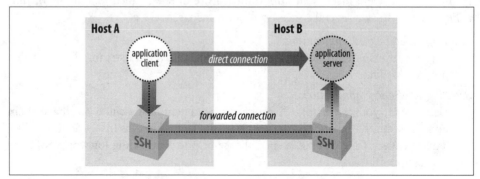

Figure 9-1. SSH forwarding

Forwarding isn't a new concept. The basic operation of a terminal connection over a network (say, using *telnet*) is also a kind of forwarding. In a *telnet* connection, you sit on one end, your remote shell is on the other, and both sides operate as if directly connected by a serial cable. Nevertheless, sitting in the middle is a cooperating *telnet* client and server, forwarding bytes back and forth. SSH forwarding is much the same, except SSH plays fancy tricks with the data to add security.

We have also seen another type of SSH forwarding, *agent forwarding*. [6.3.5] This let us create SSH connections from one computer, through a second computer, and onto a third using public-key authentication, but without installing our private key on the second machine. To accomplish this, an SSH server pretended to be an SSH agent, while transparently forwarding data to and from a remote agent. This paradigm holds true for TCP port forwarding and X forwarding, as the SSH server transparently masquerades as another network application.

9.2 Port Forwarding

SSH uses TCP/IP as its transport mechanism, usually TCP port 22 on the server machine, as it encrypts and decrypts the traffic passing over the connection. We now discuss a cool feature that encrypts and decrypts TCP/IP traffic belonging to *other* applications, on other TCP ports, using SSH. This process, called *port forwarding*, is largely transparent and quite powerful. Telnet, SMTP, NNTP, IMAP, and other insecure protocols running over TCP can be made secure by forwarding the connections through SSH. Port forwarding is sometimes called *tunneling* because the SSH connection provides a secure "tunnel" through which another TCP/IP connection may pass.

Suppose you have a home machine H that runs an IMAP-capable email reader, and you want to connect to an IMAP server on machine S to read and send mail. Normally, this connection is insecure, with your mail account password transmitted as plaintext between your mail program and the server. With SSH port forwarding, you can transparently reroute the IMAP connection (found on server S's TCP port 143) to pass through SSH, securely encrypting the data over the connection.* The IMAP server machine must be running an SSH server for port forwarding to provide real protection.

In short, with minimal configuration changes to your programs, SSH port forwarding protects arbitrary TCP/IP connections by redirecting them through an SSH session. Port forwarding can even pass a connection safely through a firewall if you configure things properly. Once you start securing your communications with port forwarding, you'll wonder how you ever got along without it. Here are examples of what you can do:

- Access various kinds of TCP servers (e.g., SMTP, IMAP, POP, LDAP, etc.) across a firewall that prevents direct access.
- Provide protection for your sessions with these same TCP servers, preventing disclosure or alteration of passwords and other content that would otherwise be sent in the clear as part of the session.

---

* Our port forwarding example protects your IMAP connection but doesn't truly protect your email messages. Before reaching your IMAP server, the messages pass through other mail servers and may be intercepted in transit. For end-to-end email security, you and your correspondent should use tools such as PGP or S/MIME to sign and/or encrypt the messages themselves.

- Tunnel the control connection of an FTP session, to encrypt your username, password, and commands. (It isn't usually possible to protect the data channels that carry the file contents, though. [11.2])

- Use your ISP's SMTP servers for sending mail, even if you're connected outside the ISP's network and the ISP forbids mail relaying from your current location. [11.3.2]

 SSH port forwarding is a general proxying mechanism for TCP only. (See the sidebar "TCP Connections" for an overview of TCP concepts.) Forwarding can't work with protocols not built on TCP, such as the UDP-based DNS, DHCP, NFS, and NetBIOS,* or with non-IP-based protocols, such as AppleTalk or Novell's SPX/IPX.

9.2.1 Local Forwarding

In our earlier example, we had an IMAP server running on machine S, and an email reader on home machine H, and we wanted to secure the IMAP connection using SSH. Let's delve into that example in more detail.

IMAP uses TCP port 143; this means that an IMAP server listens for connections on port 143 on the server machine. To tunnel the IMAP connection through SSH, we need to pick a local port on home machine H (between 1024 and 65535) and forward it to the remote socket (S,143). Suppose you randomly pick local port 2001. The following command then creates the tunnel:†

```
$ ssh -L2001:localhost:143 S
```

The –L option specifies local forwarding, in which the TCP client is on the local machine with the SSH client. The option is followed by three values separated by colons: a local port to listen on (2001), the remote machine name or IP address (S), and the remote, target port number (143).

The previous command logs you into S, just like *ssh S* does. However, this SSH session has also forwarded TCP port 2001 on H to port 143 on S; the forwarding remains in effect until you log out of the session. To make use of the tunnel, the final step is to tell your email reader to use the forwarded port. Normally, your email program connects to port 143 on the server machine—that is, the socket (S,143). Instead, it's configured to connect to port 2001 on home machine H itself, i.e., socket (localhost,2001). So the path of the connection follows the list shown next.

---

* We're being a little imprecise here. DHCP is entirely based on UDP, so SSH port forwarding can't do anything with it. The others, however, either use both TCP and UDP for different purposes or can sometimes be configured to run over TCP, though they generally use UDP. Nevertheless, in most common situations, SSH can't forward them.

† You can also use *ssh -L2001:S:143 S*, substituting "S" for localhost, but we discuss later why localhost is the better alternative when possible.

TCP Connections

To understand port forwarding, it's important to know some details about TCP, the *Transmission Control Protocol*. TCP is a fundamental building block of the Internet. Built on top of IP, it is the transport mechanism for many application-level Internet protocols such as FTP, Telnet, HTTP, SMTP, POP, IMAP, and SSH itself.

TCP comes with strong guarantees. A TCP connection is a virtual, full-duplex circuit between two communicating parties, acting like a two-way pipe. Either side may write any number of bytes at any time to the pipe, and the bytes are guaranteed to arrive unaltered and in order at the other side.[a] If an application doesn't need these strong guarantees, or doesn't want the overhead associated with them, another protocol called UDP (*User Datagram Protocol*) often suffices. It is packet-oriented, rather than connection-based, and has no guarantees of delivery or packet ordering. Some protocols that exclusively or commonly run over UDP are NFS, DNS, DHCP, NetBIOS, TFTP, Kerberos, SYSLOG, and NTP.

When a program establishes a TCP connection to a service, the program needs two pieces of information: the IP address of the destination machine, and a way to identify the desired service. TCP (and UDP) use a positive integer, called a *port number*, to identify a service. For example, SSH uses port 22, *telnet* uses port 23, and IMAP uses port 143. Port numbers allow multiple services at the same IP address.

If you combine an IP address and a port number, the pair is called a *socket*. For example, if you run *telnet* to connect to port 23 on the machine at IP address 128.220.91.4, the socket is denoted "(128.220.91.4,23)." Simply put, when you make a TCP connection, its destination is a socket. The source (client program) also has a socket on its end of the connection, and the connection as a whole is completely defined by the pair of source and destination sockets.

In order for a connection attempt to a socket to succeed, something must be "listening" on that socket. That is, a program running on the destination machine has asked TCP to accept connection requests on that port, and to pass the connections on to the program. If you've ever attempted a TCP connection and received the response "connection refused," it means that the remote machine is up and running, but nothing is listening on the target socket.

How does a client program know the target port number of a listening server? Port numbers for many protocols are standardized, being assigned by the *Internet Assigned Numbers Authority* (IANA).[b] For instance, the TCP port number assigned to the NNTP (Usenet news) protocol is 119. Therefore, news servers listen on port 119, and newsreaders (clients) connect to them via port 119. More specifically, if a newsreader is configured to talk to a news server at IP address 10.1.2.3, it requests a TCP connection to the socket (10.1.2.3,119).

—continued—

Port numbers are not always hardcoded into programs. Many operating systems let applications refer to protocols by name, instead of number, by defining a table of TCP names and port numbers. Programs can then look up port numbers by the protocol name. Under Unix, the table is often contained in the file */etc/services* or the NIS services map, and queries are performed using the library routines getservbyname, getservbyport, and related procedures. Other environments allow servers to register their listening ports dynamically via a naming service, such as the AppleTalk Name Binding Protocol or DNS's WKS and SRV records.

So far, we've discussed the port number used by a TCP server when a TCP client program wants to connect. We call this the *target* port number. The client also uses a port number, called the *source* port number, so the server can transmit to the client. If you combine the client's IP address and its source port number, you get the client's socket.

Unlike target port numbers, source port numbers are not standard. In most cases, in fact, neither the client nor the server cares which source port number is used by the client. Often a client lets TCP select an unused port number for the source.[c] If you examine the existing TCP connections on a machine with a command like *netstat -a* or *lsof -i tcp*, you'll see connections to the well-known port numbers for common services (e.g., 23 for *telnet*, 22 for SSH), with large, apparently random source port numbers on the other end. Those source ports were chosen from the range of unassigned ports by TCP on the machines initiating those connections.

Once established, a TCP connection is completely determined by the combination of its source and target sockets. Therefore, multiple TCP clients may connect to the same target socket. If the connections originate from different hosts, then the IP address portions of their source sockets differ, distinguishing the connections. If they come from two different programs running on the same host, then TCP on that host ensures they have different source port numbers.

a. The mechanisms used to implement these guarantees, though, are designed to counter transmission problems in the network, such as routing around failed links, or retransmitting data corrupted by noise or lost due to temporary network congestion. They are not very effective against deliberate attempts to steal a connection or alter data in transit part. SSH provides this protection that TCP alone lacks.

b. IANA's complete list of port numbers is found at *http://www.isi.edu/in-notes/iana/assignments/port-numbers/*.

c. The Berkeley r-commands, however, do care about source ports.

1. The email reader on home machine H sends data to local port 2001.

2. The local SSH client on H reads port 2001, encrypts the data, and sends it through the SSH connection to the SSH server on S.

3. The SSH server on S decrypts the data and sends it to the IMAP server listening on port 143 on S.

4. Data is sent back from the IMAP server to home machine H by the same process in reverse.

Port forwarding can be specified only when you create an SSH connection. You can't add a forwarding to an existing SSH connection with any SSH implementation we know of, though there's nothing intrinsic to the SSH protocol that would prevent it, and it would sometimes be a useful feature. Instead of using the –L option to establish a local forwarding, you can use the LocalForward keyword in your client configuration file:

```
# OpenSSH
LocalForward 2001 localhost:143
# Tectia
LocalForward "2001:localhost:143"
```

Note the small syntactic differences. In OpenSSH, there are two arguments: the local port number, and the remote socket expressed as *host:port*. In Tectia, the expression is just as on the command line, except that it must be enclosed in double quotes. If you forget the quotes, *ssh* doesn't complain, but it doesn't forward the port, either.

Our example with home machine H and IMAP server S can be set up like this:

```
# OpenSSH
Host local-forwarding-example
 HostName S
 LocalForward 2001 localhost:143

# Run on home machine H
$ ssh local-forwarding-example
```

9.2.1.1 Local forwarding and GatewayPorts

In OpenSSH, by default, only the host running the SSH client can connect to locally forwarded ports. This is because *ssh* listens only on the machine's loopback interface for connections to the forwarded port; that is, it binds the socket (localhost,2001), a.k.a. (127.0.0.1,2001), and not (H,2001). So, in the preceding example, only machine H can use the forwarding; attempts by other machines to connect to (H,2001) get the message "connection refused." However, *ssh* for OpenSSH has a command-line option, –g, that disables this restriction, permitting any host to connect to locally forwarded ports:

```
# OpenSSH
$ ssh -g -L<localport>:<remotehost>:<remoteport> hostname
```

The client configuration keyword GatewayPorts also controls this feature; the default value is no, whereas yes does the same thing as –g:

```
# OpenSSH
GatewayPorts yes
```

Tectia provides the +g option as the opposite of –g.

 GatewayPorts and –g are disabled by default. They are a security risk.
[9.2.4.3]

9.2.1.2 Remote forwarding

A remotely forwarded port is just like a local one, but the directions are reversed. This time the TCP client is remote, its server is local, and a forwarded connection is initiated from the remote machine.

Continuing with our example, suppose instead that you are logged into server machine S to begin with, where the IMAP server is running. You can now create a secure tunnel for remote clients to reach the IMAP server on port 143. Once again, you select a random port number to forward (say, 2001 again) and create the tunnel:

```
$ ssh -R2001:localhost:143 H
```

The –R option specifies remote forwarding. It is followed by three values, separated by colons as before but interpreted slightly differently. The *remote* port to be forwarded (2001) is now first, followed by the machine name or IP address (localhost) and port number (143). SSH can now forward connections from (localhost,143) to (H,2001).

Once this command has run, a secure tunnel has been constructed from the port 2001 on the remote machine H, to port 143 on the server machine S. Now any program on H can use the secure tunnel by connecting to (localhost,2001). As before, the command also runs an SSH terminal session on remote machine H, just as *ssh H* does.

As with local forwarding, you may establish a remote forwarding using a keyword in your client configuration file. The RemoteForward keyword is analogous to LocalForward, with the same syntactic differences between OpenSSH and Tectia:

```
# OpenSSH
RemoteForward 2001 S:143

# Tectia
RemoteForward "2001:S:143"
```

For example, here's the preceding forwarding defined in a Tectia-format configuration file:

```
# Tectia
remote-forwarding-example:
  Host H
  RemoteForward "2001:S:143"

$ ssh remote-forwarding-example
```

You might think that the GatewayPorts feature discussed in the last section applies equally well to remote port forwardings. This would make sense as a feature, but as it happens, it isn't done. There would have to be a way for the client to communicate this parameter to the server for a given forwarding, and that feature hasn't been included in the SSH protocol. In Tectia, remotely forwarded ports always listen on all network interfaces and accept connections from anywhere.

The OpenSSH server does accept the GatewayPorts configuration option, and it applies globally to all remote forwardings established by that server. This allows the server administrator to control whether users can bind to nonlocal sockets.

9.2.2 Trouble with Multiple Connections

If you use LocalForward or RemoteForward in your configuration file, you might run into a subtle problem. Suppose you have set up a section in your configuration file to forward local port 2001 to an IMAP server:

```
# OpenSSH  syntax used for illustration
Host server.example.com
 LocalForward 2001 server.example.com:143
```

This configuration works fine if you connect once:

```
$ ssh server.example.com
```

But if you try to open a second *ssh* connection to *server.example.com* at the same time—perhaps to run a different program in another window of your workstation—the attempt fails:

```
$ ssh server.example.com
Local: bind: Address already in use
```

Why does this happen? Because your configuration file section tries to forward port 2001 again but finds that port is already in use ("bound" for listening) by the first instance of *ssh*. You need some way to make the connection but omit the port forwarding.

OpenSSH provides a solution, the client configuration keyword ClearAllForwardings. From the name, you might think it terminates existing forwardings, but it doesn't. Rather, it nullifies any forwardings specified in the *current ssh command*. In the previous example, you can connect without forwardings to *server.example.com* with:

```
# OpenSSH
$ ssh -o ClearAllForwardings=yes server.example.com
```

The original tunnel, set up by the first invocation, continues to exist, but ClearAllForwardings prevents the second invocation from attempting to re-create the tunnel. To illustrate the point further, here's a rather silly command:

```
# OpenSSH
$ ssh -L2001:localhost:143 -o ClearAllForwardings=yes mymachine
```

The −L option specifies a forwarding, but ClearAllForwardings cancels it. This silly command is identical in function to:

```
$ ssh mymachine
```

ClearAllForwardings may also be placed in your client configuration file, of course. It seems more useful on the command line, however, where it can be used on the fly without editing a file.

9.2.3 · Comparing Local and Remote Port Forwarding

The differences between local and remote forwarding can be subtle. It can get a bit confusing to know which kind of forwarding to use in a given situation. The quick rule is *look for the TCP client application*.

> If the TCP client application (whose connections you want to forward) is running locally on the SSH client machine, use local forwarding. Otherwise, the client application is on the remote SSH server machine, and you use remote forwarding.

The rest of this section is devoted to dissecting the forwarding process in detail and understanding where this rule comes from.

9.2.3.1 Common elements

Local and remote forwarding can be confusing because of overloaded terminology. In a given port-forwarding situation, there are *two clients* and *two servers* lying around. We have the SSH client and server programs (e.g., *ssh* and *sshd*), plus the TCP application's client and server programs whose connection you want to protect by port forwarding.

An SSH session has a direction of establishment. That is, you run an SSH client on one machine, and it initiates a session with an SSH server on another. Likewise, a forwarded connection has a direction of establishment: you run an application client on one machine, and it initiates a session with a service on another. These two directions *may or may not match*. This is the difference between local and remote forwarding. Let's introduce some terminology and provide some diagrams to make sense of this.

To begin with, we have an application client and server running on two hosts, A and B (Figure 9-2).

The application server is listening on a well-known port W for incoming client connections. Without SSH, you can tell the application client that its server is on host B, port W. The client makes a direct connection to the server, and all application protocol data goes in the clear over the network (Figure 9-3).

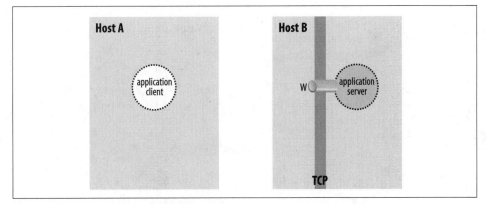

Figure 9-2. Application client and server

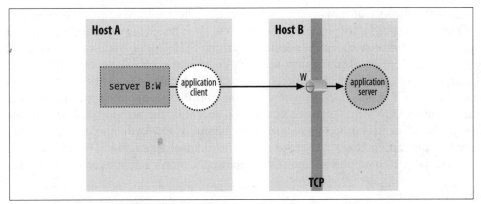

Figure 9-3. Direct client/server connection (no forwarding)

To protect the application protocol data by forwarding, you establish an SSH session between these two hosts. When setting up the SSH session, you select an unused port number P on the application client side (host A), and request SSH port forwarding from the socket (A,P) to the socket (B,W). Once the session is established, the SSH process on A is listening for incoming TCP connection requests on port P. Tell the application client that its server is on (A,P) instead of (B,W), and the stage is now set for port forwarding (Figure 9-4).

There are now two cooperating SSH processes with an established, encrypted SSH session between them; you don't distinguish between the SSH client and server. Inside that session, SSH creates multiple *channels*, or logical streams for carrying data. It uses channels to carry and distinguish the input, output, and error streams for an interactive login or remote command run via SSH, and similarly creates a new channel for each use of a port forwarding, to carry the forwarded data inside the protected SSH session.

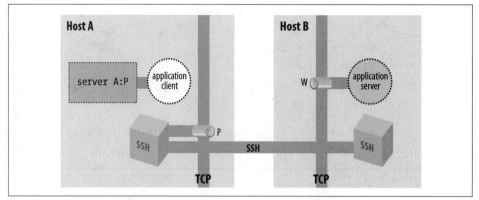

Figure 9-4. A forwarded port

Figure 9-5 shows that now, when the application client tries to connect to its server, it connects instead to the listening SSH process (1). The SSH listener notices this and accepts the connection. It then notifies its partner SSH process that a new instance of this port forwarding is starting up, and they cooperate to establish a new channel for carrying the data for this forwarding instance (2). Finally, the partner SSH process initiates a TCP connection to the target of the port forwarding: the application server listening on (B,W) (3). Once this connection succeeds, the port-forwarding instance is in place. The SSH processes cooperate to pass back and forth any data transmitted by the application client and server, over the channel inside the SSH session. This allows them to communicate and secures the application's activities on the network.

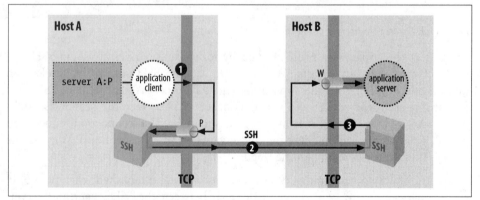

Figure 9-5. A forwarded connection

9.2.3.2   Local versus remote forwarding: the distinction

With this general framework in place, you can distinguish between local and remote forwarding. First we introduce some terms. In the generic port-forwarding description in the last section, you saw that one SSH process listens for connections, while the other is ready to initiate connections in response to connections accepted on the other side, to complete the forwarded path. We call the first side the *listening* side of the SSH session with respect to this forwarding, and the other, the *connecting* side. For example, in Figure 9-4, host A is the listening side, while host B is the connecting side. Note that these terms aren't mutually exclusive. Since a single SSH session may have multiple forwardings in place, the same side of a session may be the listening side for some forwardings, and simultaneously the connecting side for others. But with respect to any particular forwarding, it's one or the other.

Now, recall that in the last section we didn't label the SSH processes according to which was the SSH client and which was the SSH server, but simply referred to two cooperating SSH processes. We do so now and can state succinctly the local versus remote distinction:

- In a *local* forwarding (Figure 9-6), the application client and hence the listening side are located with the SSH client. The application server and connecting side are located with the SSH server.

- In a *remote* forwarding (Figure 9-7), the situation is reversed: the application client and listening side are located with the SSH server, while the application server and connecting side are located with the SSH client.

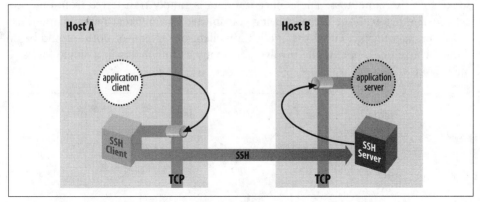

Figure 9-6. Local forwarding

So, as we said at the beginning of this section: use a local forwarding when the application client is on the local side of the SSH connection, and a remote forwarding when it's on the remote side.

9.2.4   Forwarding Off-Host

In all our discussions of port forwarding so far, the application client and server have been located on the machines on the ends of the SSH session. This is reflected in our always using "localhost" in naming the target socket of a forwarding:

```
$ ssh -L2001:localhost:143 server.example.com
```

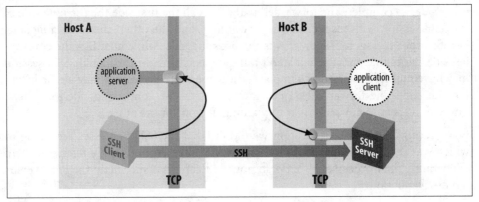

Figure 9-7. Remote forwarding

Since the application server is located on the same machine as the connecting side of the SSH port forwarding, the target host can be "localhost." But the connections between the application client and the SSH listening side, and between the application server and the SSH connecting side, are themselves TCP connections. For convenience, TCP implementations allow programs to make connections between two sockets on the same host. The connection data is simply transferred from one process to another without actually being transmitted on any real network interface. However, in principle, either the application client or server—or both—could be on different machines, potentially involving as many as four hosts in a single forwarding (Figure 9-8).

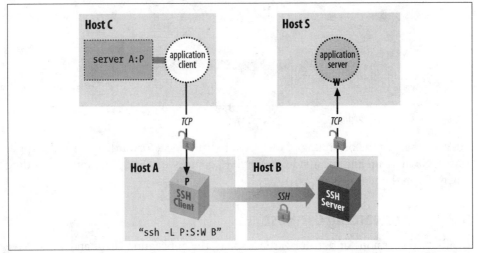

Figure 9-8. Off-host port forwarding

Although this situation is possible, you generally don't want to do it for security reasons—namely, privacy and access control.

9.2.4.1 Privacy

As shown in Figure 9-8, the complete path followed by forwarded data includes three TCP connections. But only the second connection, between the two SSH processes, is protected as a channel inside the SSH session. The other two connections are just simple TCP connections. Normally, each of these is on a single host, and is therefore protected from network snooping or interference, so the entire forwarding path is secure. But if either of these two connections is between different hosts, its data is vulnerable in transit.

9.2.4.2 Access control and the loopback address

The other security problem of off-host forwarding concerns the listening side. In short, the listening side of a forwarding has no access control, so intruders may gain access to it. To explain this problem, we must first discuss the *loopback address* of a host.

In addition to physical network interfaces, a host running IP also has a virtual interface called the *loopback* interface. This is a software construct, not corresponding to any network hardware. Nonetheless, the loopback appears and responds like a real interface. Under Unix, it is often named *lo0* and is listed by *ifconfig*:

```
$ ifconfig -a
...
lo0: flags=849<UP,LOOPBACK,RUNNING,MULTICAST> mtu 8232
        inet 127.0.0.1 netmask ff000000
```

The loopback interface leads back to the host itself. A datagram "transmitted" on the loopback interface immediately appears as an incoming packet on the loopback interface and is picked up and processed by IP as being destined for the local host.

The loopback interface is always assigned the same IP address—127.0.0.1, the *loopback address**—and the local naming service provides the name "localhost" for that address. This mechanism gives a reliable way for processes to communicate with one another on the local host via IP, regardless of what IP addresses the host may have on real connected networks, or indeed if the host has no real network connections at all. You can always refer to your local host using the well-known loopback address.

By design, a loopback address is local to its host. One machine can't contact the loopback address of another. Since the loopback address 127.0.0.1 is standard on all IP hosts, any connection to 127.0.0.1 leads a machine to talk to itself. (Plus, the loopback network isn't routed on the Internet.)

---

* Actually, the entire network 127.0.0.0/8—comprising 24 million addresses—is reserved for addresses that refer to the local host. Only the address 127.0.0.1 is commonly used, although we have seen devices use a handful of others for special purposes, such as "reject" interfaces on a terminal server or router.

9.2.4.3   Listening on ("binding") an interface

When a host listens on a TCP port, it establishes a potential endpoint for a TCP connection. But the endpoints of a TCP connection are sockets, and a socket is an (address,port) pair, not a (host,port) pair. Listening must take place on a particular socket and thus be associated with a particular address, hence a particular interface on the host. This is called *binding* the interface.* Unless otherwise specified, when asked to listen on a particular port, TCP binds all the host's interfaces and accepts connections on any of them. This is generally the right behavior for a server. It doesn't care how many network interfaces the local host has: it just accepts any connection made to its listening port, regardless of which host address was requested.

Consider, however, what this means in the case of SSH port forwarding. There is no authentication or access control at all applied to the listening side of a forwarding; it simply accepts any connection and forwards it. If the listening side binds all the host's interfaces for the forwarded port, this means that *anyone* with network connectivity to the listening host—possibly the whole Internet—can use your forwarding. This is obviously not a good situation. To address it, SSH by default binds only the loopback address for the listening side of a forwarding. This means that only other programs on the same host may connect to the forwarded socket. This makes it reasonably safe to use port forwarding on a PC or other single-user machine, but is still a security problem on multiuser hosts. On most Unix machines, for example, a knowledgeable user can connect to any listening sockets and see what's on them. Keep this in mind when using port forwarding on a Unix machine!

If you want to allow off-host connections to your forwarded ports, you can use the *–g* switch or `GatewayPorts` option to have the listening side bind all interfaces, as we did in an earlier example: [9.2.4]

```
$ ssh -g -L P:S:W B
```

But be aware of the security implications! You may want to exercise more control over the use of forwarded ports in this situation by using TCP-wrappers, which we discuss later in this chapter.

9.2.5   Bypassing a Firewall

Let's tackle a more complicated example of port forwarding. Figure 9-9 returns us to the same company situation as in Figure 6-5, when we discussed agent forwarding. [6.3.5] Your home machine H talks to work machine W via a bastion host, B, and you want to access your work email from home. Machine W runs an IMAP server, and your home machine H has an IMAP-capable email reader, but you can't hook them up. Your home IMAP client expects to make a TCP connection directly to the IMAP server on W, but unfortunately that connection is blocked by the firewall. Since host B is

---

* Named after the Berkeley sockets library routine *bind*, commonly used to establish the association.

inside the firewall, and it's running an SSH server, there *should* be some way to put all the pieces together and make the IMAP connection from H to W.

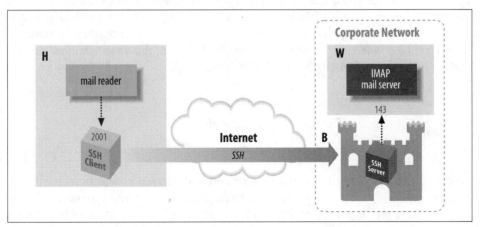

Figure 9-9. Port forwarding through a firewall

Port forwarding can solve this problem. As before, the IMAP server is on port 143, and we select a random local port number, 2001. This time, however, we use a slightly different command to set up forwarding:

```
# Executed on home machine H
$ ssh -L2001:W:143 B
```

This establishes an interactive SSH session from home machine H to bastion host B and also creates an SSH tunnel from local host H to the email server machine W. Specifically, in response to a connection on port 2001, the local SSH client directs the SSH server running on B to open a connection to port 143 on W, that is, socket W:143. The SSH server can do this because B is inside the firewall. If you configure your email reader to connect to local port 2001, as before, the communication path is now as follows:

1. The email reader on home machine H sends data to local port 2001.

2. The local SSH client reads port 2001, encrypts the data, and sends it into the tunnel.

3. The tunnel passes through the firewall, because it is an SSH connection (port 22) that the firewall accepts.

4. The SSH server on bastion host B decrypts the data and sends it to port 143 on work machine W. This transmission isn't encrypted, but it's protected behind the firewall, so encryption isn't necessary. (Assuming you're not worried about snooping on your internal network.)

5. Data is sent back from the IMAP server to home machine H by the same process in reverse.

You have now bypassed the firewall by tunneling the IMAP traffic through SSH.

9.2.6 Port Forwarding Without a Remote Login

It may happen that you'd like to forward a port via SSH but don't want an SSH login session to the remote host. For example, if you're using the IMAP forwarding example we've been harping on, you may want only to read email, not open an unnecessary terminal connection at the same time. With Tectia, this is simple: just provide the –*f* option to *ssh* in your port-forwarding command:

```
# Tectia
$ ssh -f -L2001:localhost:143 server.example.com
```

or use the GoBackground keyword for the same effect:

```
# Tectia
GoBackground yes
```

As a result, *ssh* puts itself into the background and handles connections to the forwarded port 2001, and that is all. It doesn't create an interactive terminal session with standard input, output, and error channels. The –*S* option also avoids starting a terminal session, but unlike –*f*, it doesn't put the session in the background (in other words, the –*f* option implies –*S*):

```
# Tectia
$ ssh -S -L2001:localhost:143 server.example.com
```

The –*f* option is also supported by OpenSSH, but by default it still requires a command to execute. This usage is intended more for executing remote commands that don't require terminal interaction, such as graphical programs using X. Specifically, it causes the backgrounded *ssh* to connect the local end of the terminal session to */dev/null* (that is, –*f* implies the –*n* option).

For example, if X forwarding is turned on (which we'll discuss later), the following command puts itself into the background, popping up a graphical clock on your local display, with the clock program running on the remote host *zwei.uhr.org*:

```
#  OpenSSH
$ ssh -f zwei.uhr.org xclock
```

This is similar to the background command:

```
#  OpenSSH
$ ssh -n zwei.uhr.org xclock &
```

but –*f* is better because it performs any needed user interaction—like prompting for a password—before forking into the background. If you want to background an OpenSSH session without a remote command, as with Tectia earlier, then add the –*N* switch as well:

```
$ ssh -f -L2001:localhost:143 server.example.com
```

Technically, this means the client will not create a "shell channel" in the SSH protocol. Tectia doesn't require the extra option, it just does the right thing whether you give a remote command or not; with OpenSSH, you must use the –*N* option if you don't provide a command. If you forget the option, you'll see:

```
# OpenSSH
$ ssh -f -L2001:localhost:143 server.example.com
Cannot fork into background without a command to execute.
```

The old SSH-1 protocol always requires the remote command, so as a workaround, provide one that does nothing for a long time, such as *sleep*:

```
# An SSH-1 client
$ ssh -f -L2001:localhost:143 server.example.com sleep 1000000
```

9.2.6.1 One-shot forwarding

When invoked with *–f* or GoBackground, *ssh* persists until you explicitly kill it with the Unix *kill* command. (You can find its pid with the *ps* command.) Alternatively, you can request *one-shot forwarding*, which causes the client to exit when forwarding is over with. Specifically, the client waits indefinitely for the first forwarded connection. After that, when the number of forwarded connections drops to zero, the client exits.

One-shot forwarding is accomplished easily in Tectia with the *-fo* command-line option, a variation on *–f* (the "o" stands for "one shot").

```
# Tectia
$ ssh -fo -L2001:localhost:143 server
```

One-shot forwarding isn't directly supported by OpenSSH, but you can get the same effect with the following method:

1. Set up the forwarding with *ssh -f*, and for the required remote command, use *sleep* with a short duration:

   ```
   $ ssh -f -L2001:localhost:143 server sleep 10
   ```

2. Before the sleep interval expires, use the forwarded connection:

   ```
   $ ssh -p2001 localhost
   ```

Once the *sleep* command finishes, the first *ssh* tries to exit—but it notices a forwarded connection is in use and refuses to exit, printing a warning you can ignore:

```
Waiting for forwarded connections to terminate...
The following connections are open:
  port 2001, connection from localhost port 143
```

ssh waits until that connection ends, and then terminates, providing the behavior of one-shot forwarding.

9.2.7   The Listening Port Number

Earlier, we suggested selecting any unused port for the listening side of a forwarding. Port numbers are encoded in a 16-bit field and can have any value from 1 to 65535 (port 0 is reserved). On multiuser operating systems such as Unix, ports 1 through 1023 are called *privileged* and are reserved for processes run by the superuser (user

ID zero). If a nonprivileged process tries to bind a privileged port for listening, it fails with an error message such as "insufficient permission."*

When setting up the listening side of a tunnel, you generally must select a port number between 1024 and 65535, inclusive. This is because an SSH program running under your user ID, not the superuser's, is responsible for listening on that port. If SSH reports that your chosen port is already in use, just choose another; it shouldn't be hard to find a free one.

For the target side of the tunnel, you can specify any port number, privileged or not. You are attempting to *connect to* the port, not listen on it. In fact, most of the time the target side is a privileged port, since the most common TCP services have ports in the privileged range.

If you are the superuser on a machine with SSH clients, you can perform local forwarding with a privileged port. Likewise, you can forward a remote privileged port if your remote account has superuser privileges.

Some TCP applications hardcode the server port numbers and don't permit them to be changed. These applications aren't usable with port forwarding if the operating system has a privileged port restriction. For example, suppose you have an FTP client that's hardwired to connect to the server on the standard FTP control port, 21. To set up port forwarding, you have to forward the local port 21 to the remote port 21. But since port 21 is privileged, you can't use it as a listening port number unless you are the superuser. Fortunately, most Unix TCP-based programs let you set the destination port number for connections.

9.2.8   Choosing the Target Forwarding Address

Suppose you want to forward a connection from your local machine to *remote.host. net*. Both of the following commands work:

```
$ ssh -L2001:localhost:143 remote.host.net
$ ssh -L2001:remote.host.net:143 remote.host.net
```

The forwarded connection is made from the remote machine to either the loopback address or *remote.host.net*, and in either case, the connection stays on the remote machine and doesn't go over the network. However, the two connections are perceptibly different to the server receiving the forwarded connection. This is because the *source* sockets of the connections are different. The connection to localhost appears to come from source address 127.0.0.1, whereas the connection to *remote.host.net* is from the address associated with that name.

Most of the time this difference doesn't matter, but sometimes you must take it into account. The application server (e.g., the IMAP daemon) might be doing access control based on the source address and may not be configured to accept the loop-

---

* Microsoft Windows has no privileged port restriction, so any user can listen on any free port.

back address. Or it might be running on a multihomed host, and have bound only a subset of the addresses the host has, possibly not including the loopback address. Each of these situations is usually an oversight, but you might not be able to do anything about it. If you're getting "connection refused" from the connecting side of the forwarding, but you've verified that the server appears to be running and responding to normal clients, this might be the problem. If the server machine is running Unix, the command *netstat -a -n* should list all the network connections and listeners on that machine. Look for listeners on the relevant port, and the addresses on which they are listening.

Sometimes, the problem can be more acute if the server uses the source IP address itself as part of whatever protocol it's speaking. This problem crops up when trying to forward FTP over SSH. [11.2]

In general, we recommend using localhost as the forwarding target whenever possible. This way, you are less likely to set up an insecure off-host forwarding by accident.

9.2.9 Termination

What happens to forwardings when an SSH connection terminates? The ports simply cease being forwarded; that is, SSH is no longer listening on them, and connection attempts to those ports will fail with the error "connection refused."

What happens if you try to terminate an SSH session while it still has active forwarded connections? SSH notices and waits for them to disconnect before stopping the session. The details of this behavior differ among implementations.

In Tectia, if you log out of a session that has an active forwarded connection, the session stays open but sends itself into the background:

```
remote$ logout
warning: ssh[7021]: number of forwarded channels still open, forked to background to
wait for completion.
local$
```

The *ssh* process now waits in the background until the forwarded connections terminate, and then it exits. In contrast, with OpenSSH, if you disconnect a session with active forwardings, you get a warning, but the session stays in the foreground:

```
remote$ logout
Waiting for forwarded connections to terminate...
The following connections are open:
  port 2002, connection from localhost port 1465
```

To send it into the background and return to your local shell prompt, type the escape sequence Return-tilde-ampersand: [7.4.6.8]

```
~& [backgrounded]
local$
```

and as with Tectia, the connection exits only after its forwarded connections terminate. Be careful not to use the SSH ^Z escape for this purpose. That sends *ssh* into the background, but in a suspended state, unable to accept TCP connections to its forwarded ports. If you do this accidentally, use your shell's job control commands (e.g., *fg* and *bg*) to resume the process.

9.2.9.1 The TIME_WAIT problem

Sometimes a forwarded port mysteriously hangs around after the forwarding SSH session has gone away. You try a command you've used successfully several times in a row and suddenly get an error message:

```
$ ssh -L2001:localhost:21 server.example.com
Local: bind: Address already in use
```

(This happens commonly if you're experimenting with port forwarding, trying to get something to work.) You know that you have no active SSH command listening on port 2001, so what's going on? If you use the *netstat* command to look for other listeners on that port, you may see a connection hanging around in the TIME_WAIT state:

```
$ netstat -an | grep 2001
tcp    0    0   127.0.0.1:2001   127.0.0.1:1472    TIME_WAIT
```

The TIME_WAIT state is an artifact of the TCP protocol. In certain situations, the teardown of a TCP connection can leave one of its socket endpoints unusable for a short period of time, usually only a few minutes. As a result, you can't reuse the port for TCP forwarding (or anything else) until the teardown completes. If you're impatient, choose another port for the time being (say, 2002 instead of 2001) and get on with your work, or wait a short time for the port to become usable again.

9.2.10 Configuring Port Forwarding in the Server

We've seen several keywords and command-line options for configuring SSH clients for port forwarding, such as *–L* and *–R*. In addition, the SSH *server* can be configured for port forwarding. We'll cover compile-time, serverwide, and per-account configuration.

9.2.10.1 Compile-time configuration

You can enable or disable port forwarding at compile time in Tectia with *configure*. [4.3.5.5] The Tectia flag --disable-tcp-port-forwarding disables port forwarding for both clients and servers.

9.2.10.2 Serverwide configuration

Port forwarding can be globally enabled or disabled in *sshd*. This is done with the serverwide configuration keyword AllowTcpForwarding in */etc/sshd_config*. The keyword may have the value yes (the default, enabling forwarding) or no (disabling forwarding):

```
AllowTcpForwarding no
```

In addition, Tectia has the following options:

```
# Tectia
AllowTcpForwardingForUsers
AllowTcpForwardingForGroups
```

The syntax of these is the same as for the `AllowUsers` and `AllowGroups` options. [5.5.1] They specify a list of users or groups that are allowed to use port forwarding; the server refuses to honor port-forwarding requests for anyone else. Note that these refer to the *target* account of the SSH session, not the client username (which is often not known).

9.2.10.3 Per-account configuration

In your account, you can disable port forwarding for any client that connects via a particular key. [8.2.7] For OpenSSH, locate the public key in your *authorized_keys* file and precede it with the option `no-port-forwarding`:

```
# OpenSSH
no-port-forwarding ...key...
```

or for Tectia, follow the `Key` line with an `Options` line:

```
# Tectia
Key mykey.pub
Options no-port-forwarding
```

Any SSH client that authenticates using this key can't perform port forwarding with your SSH server. Nevertheless, the earlier remarks we made about serverwide port-forwarding configuration apply here: the restriction isn't really meaningful unless you further restrict what this key is allowed to do.

9.2.11 Protocol-Specific Forwarding: FTP

SSH port forwarding works best with protocols that make simple use of TCP: those which operate over a single TCP connection and are not sensitive to its network-related details such as IP addresses or ports—in other words, they could operate just as well over a serial line or other similar path. Many common protocols fall in this category, but not all. The exceptions tend to be older protocols designed before the rise of firewalls and NAT on the Internet, which degrade true peer-to-peer connectivity and make some techniques problematic. As we have already mentioned, a prime example is FTP, which exhibits several forwarding problems all at once:

- It uses multiple TCP connections.
- They may go in different directions.

- The destination ports may be dynamically determined.
- It carries TCP port numbers and IP addresses inside the protocol.

This is all pretty disastrous from a forwarding perspective in the presence of NAT, and we'll share those gory details later. [11.2.6] Some SSH implementations, though, have an FTP-specific forwarding feature designed to work around these problems. This protocol-specific forwarding involves the SSH client watching the tunneled FTP protocol as it operates, creating dynamic forwardings to accommodate it, and possibly altering some FTP messages as they pass through in order to accommodate this hacking. Tectia has an FTP forwarding mode, while OpenSSH doesn't. The Tectia usage is:

```
# Tectia
$ ssh -L ftp/2001:localhost:21 S
```

This logs into server S, forwarding local port 2001 with the FTP workaround magic, to the FTP server running on S (the normal FTP control port is 21). To use the forwarding, point your FTP client at *localhost:2001*. FTP programs vary in syntax for this; some examples are:

```
$ ftp localhost 2001
$ ftp -P 2001 localhost
```

As long as the FTP and SSH clients are together on one host, the servers are together on another, and "localhost" is used as shown in the commands, both active and passive FTP now work. This is normally the way you want it, since if the clients or servers are split up, then FTP data transfers (which include directory listings) pass in the clear over a portion of the path, unprotected by SSH. However, in some circumstances you might be forced to split one side up. As a result of the way Tectia FTP forwarding works, the rule is:

> In active mode, the servers must be together; in passive mode, the clients must be together.

Observe that if you split up both sides so that four separate hosts (technically, addresses) are in the picture, then *neither* mode works, and FTP won't work at all beyond the initial connection and login.

This rule applies because when Tectia forwards ports to accommodate FTP data connections, the ports listen on the loopback address only, forcing both participants on one side or the other to be on the same host. Which side depends on which mode: in active mode the FTP server makes the data connections, so the SSH forwardings are remote, forcing the servers to be together. In passive mode, the FTP client makes the connections, so the SSH forwardings are local, forcing the clients to be together.

9.3 Dynamic Port Forwarding

We are often asked, "How can I tunnel my web browsing over SSH?" The usual reasons are for privacy or for browsing across a firewall. The SSH port forwarding we've described so far doesn't meet this need very well, but there is another flavor called *dynamic port forwarding* which does. We'll call the previous technique "static forwarding" in contrast.

Suppose you're at home, using your home machine H, and need to access a web server W1 at work, but your employer's internal network is behind a firewall. You might attempt to do this through a bastion server at work (say, B) which you can log into via SSH; and then from B, you can reach whatever internal web servers you want. So you create a tunnel using the following port-forwarding command on home machine H:

```
$  ssh -L 8080:W1:80 B      This runs into problems
```

and point your web browser on H at *http://localhost:8080/*. This is a reasonable try, based on forwarding as we've seen it so far, but there are lots of problems:

Problem 1: virtual hosts

Web servers can make decisions based on the hostname portion of the URL you request. For example, if the names *foo* and *bar* are aliases for the same host, then the URLs *http://foo/* and *http://bar/* may return different pages. A practical example is an ISP's web server, which could host content for dozens or hundreds of customers' web sites under different hostnames, all of which point to that same machine. This web server configuration is often called *virtual hosts*.

In our home/work example, we're trying to access web server W1 as "localhost," but it might not be configured to serve any content under this name; and even if it does, it might not be the content you want. To address this problem, you'd have to get the browser to recognize other names as aliases for localhost, e.g., by hacking */etc/hosts* on a Unix box—not exactly a smooth solution.

Problem 2: absolute links

Suppose problem 1 is a non-issue, and you see the web page you want. However, if that web page has any absolute links that directly reference the hostname W1, they might not work. For example, the absolute URL *http://W1/some_great_content.html* fails when your browser tries to follow it, because your browser knows the site only as localhost.

Problem 3: links to other secured servers

Even if problems 1 and 2 don't bite you, your luck runs out when you hit a link to *another* internal web server, W2, or even a page on the same server but on a different port (e.g., *http://W1:81/java-is-great.jsp*).

Clearly, static port forwarding is woefully inadequate for this scenario. You could get around individual problems by editing your host file or stopping now and then to forward another port, but who wants the annoyance? And such a burdensome solution isn't exactly convenient to explain to your Aunt Mae. Or your boss.

We can address problems 1 and 2 by making a realization: that we want to redirect the web browser over SSH without fussing with the URL. Most browsers have just such a feature: a *proxy*. We can set the browser's HTTP proxy to our SSH-forwarded port *localhost:8080*; this means it *always* connects to our forwarded port in response to any HTTP URL we provide. The browser assumes this port leads to a proxy server that knows how to get the content for the various web servers we seek, so the browser doesn't have to contact those servers directly.

Proxying gets us part of the way there, but doesn't solve problem 3: what happens if we hit a link to a hostname besides W1? The browser sends it to W1 anyway via its proxy setting, but W1 won't know how to handle it, so we'll get a web server error along the lines of "unrecognized URL." We can't feasibly deal with this manually; not only would we have to forward another port, but also we'd have to reset the browser to proxy through the new port, at which point it could reach the new URLs but not the old ones on W1! That's just a mess...what we really need is a way for the browser to communicate dynamically with SSH itself, telling it to forward to the correct web server for each URL the browser handles. And indeed, there is a feature to do exactly this, called *dynamic forwarding* or *SOCKS forwarding*.

SOCKS is a small protocol, defined in RFC-1928. A SOCKS client connects via TCP, and indicates via the protocol the remote socket it wants to reach; the SOCKS server makes the connection, then gets out of the way, transparently passing data back and forth. Thereafter, it is just as if the client had connected directly to the remote socket. The OpenSSH and Tectia syntax for this kind of forwarding would be:

```
# OpenSSH
$ ssh -D 1080 B

# Tectia
$ ssh -L socks/1080 B
```

We've switched to port 1080 since that's the usual SOCKS port; 8080 or any other port would do, as usual. Note that there's no destination socket in either command, just the local port to be forwarded; that's because the destination is determined dynamically, and can be different for each connection. We can use this solution only if the browser has an option to use a SOCKS proxy (as most do).

This solves the whole problem neatly! The process goes like so:

1. The user types URL *scheme://foo:1234/* into the browser. The port 1234 might be implicit, as in 80 for HTTP or 443 for HTTPS.

2. The browser connects to the SSH SOCKS proxy on *localhost:1080*, and asks for a connection to *foo:1234* using the SOCKS protocol.

3. In response, the SSH client associates the browser's connection with a new *direct-tcpip* channel in the existing SSH session [3.4.4.1], connected to *foo:1234* via another TCP connection established by the SSH server.

4. The SSH client and server "get out of the way," and the browser is connected to the desired web server. Note that there is nothing here specific to HTTP; the browser can next build an SSL session if the scheme is HTTPS, or use any protocol at all over the proxied connection.

Each time a new connection arrives on port 1080, it can be forwarded to a different socket. This might seem odd if you have static forwarding firmly in mind, but it's just an extension of what you already know. With static forwarding, the SSH client still creates a new channel for each connection; it just sends them all to the same place. With dynamic forwarding, SOCKS allows each connection to indicate its own destination, and SSH obliges.

No special support is required for dynamic forwarding on the SSH server, since it in fact uses the same mechanism as static forwarding. Only the client needs to support dynamic forwarding.

So, this would be a perfect lightweight solution: complete remote web browsing with just SSH. Ah, if only we lived in such a simple world....

9.3.1 SOCKS v4, SOCKS v5, and Names

There are actually two commonly used versions of the SOCKS protocol: Version 4 and Version 5. Both OpenSSH and Tectia clients can do SOCKS proxying, and recent versions implement SOCKS5 as well as SOCKS4. SOCKS5 added many features over SOCKS4—authentication, UDP support, bidirect forwarding, and more—but the germane feature here is that SOCKS4 only understands IP addresses in destination sockets, whereas SOCKS5 accepts domain names as well. This is crucial for both practical and privacy reasons. Often, the naming context on either side of the SSH connection is different: in our current example, your company's network probably has a private namespace for hosts (e.g., an internal-only DNS which isn't available to the outside world). With SOCKS4, your browser must look up the name in the URL locally, then ask the SOCKS proxy to connect to the resulting address. That won't work for us; we want to give the proxy the (name,port) to reach, and have it resolve the name on the far side of the connection, in the correct context.

The privacy aspect is, if you're proxying your browsing traffic to shield your local web traffic from prying eyes, you don't want to reveal the names of all the web servers you're hitting to anyone who can watch the DNS traffic from your browsing host.

OK, so SOCKS4 is out; that's no problem, as many browsers support SOCKS5. But there's a further complication; the ugly face of reality nosing into our elegant solution. Disappointingly, most of the major browsers, even when they support SOCKS5, don't actually use it properly: they look up names locally, even though they could be passed through the proxy. We've tried dozens of OS/browser combinations, including Firefox, Safari, Netscape, Mozilla, Internet Explorer (IE), and Opera, and the *only* one we've found so far which does the right thing is...(drum roll please...) IE 5.2 on Macintosh OS X. We guess that the main motivation for adding SOCKS5 support was authentication, and so it was added without changing the address-lookup logic—but this is an oversight that makes any use of SOCKS5 proxying much less useful than it could be. So: write your browser developers and ask for better SOCKS5 support! A switch for choosing either local or remote name resolution would be ideal.

Given the realities of browser SOCKS support, the best solution for now is usually using a static SSH port forwarding to a separate HTTP proxy server, such as Squid or Privoxy. These proxies can also provide lots of other useful features, such as pop-up blocking and cookie management—but one doesn't always have such a proxy available or the ability to set one up, so the SSH-only approach with dynamic forwarding is preferable if you can use it.

9.3.2   Other Uses of Dynamic Forwarding

The remote web-browsing problem provided a perfect setting in which to introduce dynamic forwarding, but there are certainly other uses. Any program which can use a SOCKS proxy is a candidate, and there are lots of them if you look. For instance: SSH itself! With dynamic forwarding, SSH acts as a SOCKS server, but as a completely separate feature, some SSH products can also be SOCKS *clients*. The usual use for this is for external connectivity where the local network isn't directly connected to the Internet, but provides only proxied Net access via SOCKS. However, it has a neat use in combination with dynamic forwarding:

```
# Tectia
# In one window:
$ ssh -L socks/1080 B
# In another window:
$ export SSH_SOCKS_SERVER=socks://localhost:1080/
$ ssh -o'usesocks5 yes' HOST1
```

where you're on the outside but HOST1 is on your company's *internal* network. The second *ssh* command uses the SSH/SOCKS proxy established by the first to connect through the bastion host B to HOST1, resolving the name HOST1 on the inside. This is obviously more convenient than forwarding a separate port to *host:22* for each internal host you might want to reach. It also has many advantages over the idiom *ssh B -t ssh HOST1*, including:

- It's faster, since multiple subsequent SSH commands to internal hosts use the same SSH/SOCKS connection, rather than waiting for two connections every time.

- It doesn't require an SSH client or other state (keys, known-hosts files, etc.) on bastion host B. Indeed, this technique could work were a shell login not allowed on B, only SSH connections for forwarding purposes.

- There is an SSH connection directly between home machine H and HOST1, which simplifies things immensely if you want to do X forwarding or port forwarding between them.

9.4   X Forwarding

Now that you've seen general TCP port forwarding, we move to a new topic: forwarding of X protocol connections. X is a popular window system for Unix workstations, and one of its best features is its transparency. Using X, you can run remote X applications that open their windows on your local display (and vice versa, running local applications on remote displays). Unfortunately, the inter-machine communication is insecure and wide open to snoopers. But there's good news: SSH *X forwarding* makes the communication secure by tunneling the X protocol.

X forwarding also addresses some firewall-related difficulties. Suppose you're a system administrator with a set of exposed production machines on the other side of a firewall from you. You log into one of these machines using SSH, and want to run a graphical performance-monitoring tool, such as Solaris's *perfmon*, that uses the X Window System. You can't, though, because to do that, the external machine needs to make a TCP connection back to the internal machine you started on, and the firewall blocks it (as it should, since X is quite insecure). X forwarding solves this problem, permitting X protocol connections to pass through the firewall, securely tunneled via SSH.

Our discussion begins with a brief overview, then explains the details of X forwarding. In addition to explaining how to use X forwarding, we also expose the internals of X authentication and how it interacts with SSH, as well as other technical topics.

9.4.1   The X Window System

The X Window System, or X, is the most widely used graphical display system for Unix machines. Like SSH, X has clients and servers. X clients are windowing application programs, such as terminal emulators, paint programs, graphical clocks, and so forth. An X server is the underlying display engine that processes requests from X clients, communicating via a network protocol called the *X protocol*. A machine typically runs a single X server but possibly many X clients.

Most important to our discussion, X supports sophisticated window management over a network. X clients can open windows not only on their local machine, but also on other computers on the network, whether they are down the hall or across the globe. To accomplish this, an X client makes a network connection to a remote X

VNC Forwarding: An Alternative to X Forwarding

X forwarding is problematic from a security point of view, for the same reason as X itself. As you will see, the design of X means that remote programs must make separate network connections back to the user; this requires yet another layer of authentication and authorization, complicating the situation and opening an avenue of attack. SSH X forwarding tries to secure this as much as possible, but it may still be unacceptable in some environments.

An alternative technique is to use Virtual Network Computing (VNC) over SSH. VNC is free software developed by AT&T Laboratories in the UK, which provides remote GUI access for Unix and Windows platforms. With VNC, you can open a window on your Unix machine running X, and have the desktop of a remote Windows machine appear there, so you can operate the Windows box remotely. Conversely, you can run the VNC client on a Windows machine and connect to a remote X display running on a Unix host. Since VNC involves only a single outbound connection, it is easy and safer to tunnel through SSH than X. You can find out more about VNC (and download the software) at *http://www.realvnc.com/*.

---

server and carries on a conversation, using the X protocol to draw on the remote screen, receive remote keyboard events, learn the remote mouse location, and so on. This obviously requires some type of security, which we discuss soon.

A central concept of X is the *display*, an abstraction for the screen managed by an X server. When an X client is invoked, it needs to know which display to use. Displays are named by strings of the form *HOST:n.v*, where:

- *HOST* is the name of the machine running the X server controlling the display.

- *n* is the *display* number, an integer, usually 0. X allows for multiple displays controlled by a single server; additional displays are numbered 1, 2, and so on.

- *v* is the *visual* number, another integer. A visual is a virtual display. X supports multiple virtual displays on a single, physical display. If there's only one virtual display (which is the most common scenario), you omit the ".v", and the default is visual 0.

For example, on the machine *server.example.com*, display 0, visual 1 is represented by the display string "server.example.com:0.1".

Under Unix, most X client programs let you specify the display string in two ways: the *–d* or *-display* command-line option, or the environment variable DISPLAY. For example, to run the X client program *xterm* on the only X display of the workstation *anacreon*, use the command-line option:

```
$ xterm -d anacreon:0 &
```

or the environment variable:

```
$ setenv DISPLAY anacreon:0
$ xterm &
```

X is a large, deep software product whose documentation fills a dozen O'Reilly books. We've barely scratched the surface with our explanation, but you've now seen enough to understand X forwarding.

9.4.2   How X Forwarding Works

Although X clients can communicate with remote X servers, this communication isn't secure. All interactions between the X client and server, such as keystrokes and displayed text, can be easily monitored by network snooping because the connection isn't encrypted. In addition, most X environments use primitive authentication methods for connecting to a remote display. A knowledgeable attacker can get a connection to your display, monitor your keystrokes, and control other programs you're running.

Once again, SSH comes to the rescue. An X protocol connection can be routed through an SSH connection to provide security and stronger authentication. This feature is called *X forwarding*.

X forwarding works in the following way, as illustrated in Figure 9-10. An SSH client requests X forwarding when it connects to an SSH server (assuming X forwarding is enabled in the client). If the server allows X forwarding for this connection, your login proceeds normally, but the server takes some special steps behind the scenes. In addition to handling your terminal session, it sets itself up as a proxy X server running on the remote machine and sets the DISPLAY environment variable in your remote shell to point to the proxy X display:

```
syrinx$ ssh sys1
Last login: Sat Nov 13 01:10:37 1999 from blackberry
Sun Microsystems Inc.    SunOS 5.6      Generic August 1997
You have new mail.
sys1$ echo $DISPLAY
sys1:10.0
sys1$ xeyes
The "xeyes" X client appears on the screen
```

The DISPLAY value appears to refer to X display #10 on *sys1*, but there's no such display. (In fact, there might be no true displays on *sys1* at all!) Instead, the DISPLAY value points to the X proxy established by the SSH server, i.e., the SSH server is masquerading as an X server. If you now run an X client program, it connects to the proxy. The proxy behaves just like a "real" X server, and in turn instructs the SSH client to behave as a proxy X client, connecting to the X server on your local machine. The SSH client and server then cooperate to pass X protocol information back and forth over the SSH pipe between the two X sessions, and the X client program appears on your screen just as if it had connected directly to your display. That's the general idea of X forwarding.

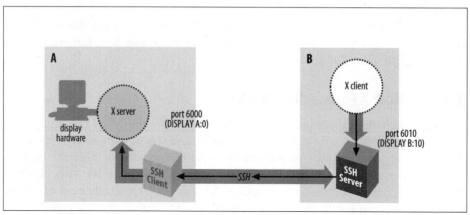

Figure 9-10. X forwarding

X forwarding can even solve the firewall problem mentioned earlier, as long as the firewall permits SSH connections to pass through. If a firewall sits between your local and remote machines, and you run an X client on the remote machine, X forwarding tunnels the X connection through the firewall's SSH port to the local machine. Therefore, the X client's windows can open on your local display. If X forwarding were not present, the firewall would block the connection.

Some aspects of X forwarding probably sound familiar from our earlier explanation of port forwarding. In fact, X forwarding is just a special case of port forwarding for which SSH has special support.

9.4.3　Enabling X Forwarding

X forwarding is on by default. If you need to enable or disable X forwarding for your clients, here's how to do it. Unlike general port forwarding, which requires you to fiddle with TCP port numbers, X forwarding has only an on/off switch. In your SSH client configuration file, use the keyword ForwardX11 with a value of yes (the default, to enable) or no (to disable):

```
ForwardX11 yes
```

On the command line, you may also use –x to disable X forwarding:

```
$ ssh -x server.example.com
```

OpenSSH and Tectia enable X forwarding with the following options:

```
# OpenSSH
$ ssh -X server.example.com

# Tectia
$ ssh +x server.example.com
```

9.4.4   Configuring X Forwarding

The behavior of X forwarding can be modified through compile-time configuration, serverwide configuration, and per-account configuration.

9.4.4.1   Compile-time configuration

Tectia can be compiled with or without X support. The compile-time flags --with-x and --without-x make this determination:

```
$ configure ... --without-x ...
```

You can also enable or disable all X forwarding by default with --enable-X11-forwarding or --disable-X11-forwarding:

```
# Tectia
$ configure ... --enable-X11-forwarding ...
```

Remember, enable/disable flags simply set the default behavior. You can override these defaults with serverwide and per-account configuration.

9.4.4.2   Serverwide configuration

The serverwide configuration keyword X11Forwarding* enables or disables X forwarding in the SSH server. By default, it is enabled.

```
X11Forwarding no
```

The X11DisplayOffset keyword lets you reserve some X11 display numbers so that *sshd* can't use them. This keyword specifies the lowest display number SSH may use, preventing *sshd* from clashing with real X servers on the lower-numbered displays. For example, if you normally run actual X servers on displays 0 and 1, set:

```
# OpenSSH
X11DisplayOffset 2
```

The XAuthLocation keyword specifies the path to the *xauth* program, which manipulates authorization records for X. We describe this keyword later, after we discuss *xauth*. [9.4.6.4]

```
# OpenSSH
XAuthLocation /usr/local/bin/xauth
```

9.4.4.3   Per-account configuration

In your authorization file for public keys, you may disallow X forwarding for incoming SSH connections that use a particular key for authentication. [8.2.7] In OpenSSH and Tectia this is done with the option no-X11-forwarding:

```
# OpenSSH
no-x11-forwarding ...key...
```

---

* And its Tectia synonyms ForwardX11 and AllowX11Forwarding.

```
# Tectia
Key mykey.pub
Options no-x11-forwarding
```

9.4.5   X Authentication

We've mentioned in passing that X performs its own authentication when X clients connect to X servers. Now we're going to dive into technical detail on the inner workings of X authentication, why it's insecure, and how SSH X forwarding builds on it to create a secure solution.

In most cases, X forwarding simply works, and you don't have to think about it. The following material is to aid your understanding and satisfy any intense cravings for tech talk (both yours and ours).

9.4.5.1   How X authentication works

When an X client requests a connection to an X server, the server authenticates the client. That is, the X server determines the client's identity to decide whether to allow a connection to the server's display. The current release of the X Window System (X11R6) provides two categories of authentication: host-based and key-based:

Host-based X authentication
> The simpler method. Using the program *xhost*, you indicate a list of hosts that may connect to your X display. Notice that connections are authenticated only by hostname, not by username. That is, *any* user on a listed host may connect to your display.

Key-based X authentication
> Uses the *xauth* program to maintain a list of X authentication keys, or *display keys*, for X clients. Keys are kept in a file, usually *~/.Xauthority*, along with other data associated with the various displays the client wants to access. When an X client connects to a server requiring authentication, the client supplies the appropriate credentials for that display from the *xauth* data. If authentication is successful, the X client can then connect to the display managed by the X server.

Display keys are obtained from the X server in various ways depending on the environment. For example, if you start the server directly on the console of a machine using *xinit* or *startx*, these programs invoke an X server and insert a copy of the server's key directly into your *xauth* data. Alternatively, if you connect to a remote machine that runs the X Display Manager (XDM), the key is sent to your remote account when establishing your XDM session.

9.4.5.2   xauth and the SSH rc files

SSH has startup files that can be set to execute on the server side when a client logs in. These are the systemwide */etc/sshrc* and the per-account *~/.ssh/rc* files. These can be shell scripts or any kind of executable program.

An important thing to note is that *sshd* runs *xauth* only to add the proxy display key if it doesn't run an *rc* program. If it does run an *rc* program, it feeds the key type and data to the program on a single line to its standard input, and it is up to the *rc* program to store the display key. This feature provides a way to customize handling the display key, in case just running *xauth* isn't the right thing to do in your situation.

9.4.5.3 Trusted X forwarding

The X Windows protocol was not designed with much security in mind. Usually, once an application has access to an X display, it pretty much has the run of it. A malicious X client can easily read all keyboard input, see all screen contents, add or modify keystrokes, and so on. This is why X forwarding is risky and should generally be turned on only when you need it, and only for hosts you trust.

There is a security extension to the X Windows protocol that allows at least some further granularity, partitioning X clients into "trusted" and "untrusted" groups. Programs like the X Window Manager must be trusted, since they have to manipulate the windows of other applications and perform other global operations on the display. Other programs may be left untrusted, though, with more limited access to the display and less opportunity for mischief.

Both OpenSSH and Tectia support this trust distinction in X forwarding. OpenSSH has the `ForwardX11Trusted` client option and Tectia has `TrustX11Applications`. Set to yes or no, these keywords control whether remote X clients accessing the local display via SSH X forwarding will be considered trusted or untrusted by the X server.

```
# OpenSSH
ForwardX11Trusted yes

# Tectia
TrustX11Applications yes
```

The default setting is no, meaning "untrusted." You can override this setting per connection with *ssh -Y* (OpenSSH) or *ssh +X* (Tectia):

```
# OpenSSH
$ ssh -Y ...            Equivalent to ssh -X -o ForwardX11Trusted=yes

# Tectia
$ ssh +X ...           Equivalent to ssh +x -o TrustX11Applications=yes
```

Technically, for trusted forwarding, the client uses the existing *xauth* key to access the display: that is, it inherits whatever trust is already in effect. For untrusted forwarding it generates a new, specifically untrusted key using the command *xauth generated ... untrusted*, and uses the new key with forwarded X connections. In either case, the local key never goes to the remote host; that is always a throwaway key used only for authenticating the connection within SSH.

9.4.5.4   Problems with X authentication

If you've used X, the authentication was probably transparent and seemed to work fine. Behind the scenes, however, the mechanism is insecure. Here are the major problems:

xhost is insecure

> Once you give permission for a remote host to connect to your display, *any user* on that host can connect. As with the r-commands, this authentication method depends on the network address of the connecting host, which can be easy for an attacker to usurp.

Key transfer may be manual and insecure

> Some remote-login protocols, such as *telnet*, don't assist with X authentication. If your display keys aren't available on a remote machine, you have to transfer them yourself, either manually or by automating the transfer, perhaps in your login script. This isn't only a nuisance but also insecure, since you're sending the key in plaintext over the network.

The most common key-based method, MIT-MAGIC-COOKIE-1, is insecure

> Although it uses a random string of bits, or *cookie*, as the *xauth* display key, this key is transmitted in plaintext at the beginning of every connection, where it can be intercepted and read.

The remote host might not support your chosen X authentication method

> X11R6 supports other, more secure authentication methods. SUN-DES-1 employs Sun's secure RPC system, XDM-AUTHORIZATION-1 uses DES, and MIT-KERBEROS-5 involves Kerberos user-to-user authentication.* Unfortunately, these methods are often not available in particular instances of the X software. Sometimes they aren't compiled into X installations due to cryptographic export restrictions; other times, the X version is too old to support the more secure methods.

If the remote host is insecure, your display key can be compromised

> In the best scenario, where the X server supports strong authentication and your key can be copied securely to the remote machine, you still have to store your sensitive display key there. If that machine is untrustworthy, your key can be at risk. (SSH doesn't have this problem, since only your public key is stored on the SSH server machine.)

9.4.5.5   SSH and authentication spoofing

Through X forwarding, SSH provides transparent, secure authentication and key transfer for X sessions. This is done by a technique called *authentication spoofing*, as

---

* See the X11R6 *Xsecurity*(1) manpage for details on these methods. Also, remember that this is authentication only, not encryption. The contents of your X connection remain unencrypted and open to snooping or modification on the network.

depicted in Figure 9-11. Authentication spoofing involves a fake display key, which we call the *proxy key*, that authenticates to the SSH X proxy server on the remote side. When relaying X traffic containing a key, SSH cleverly substitutes the real display key. Here's how it works.

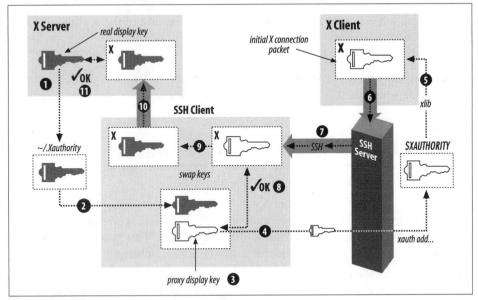

Figure 9-11. Authentication of forwarded X connections

The players begin in the following positions. You are logged into a local machine with a local display. The local machine runs an X server and SSH clients. On the other side of the network connection, an SSH server is running on a remote machine, where you invoke X clients. The goal is for the remote X clients to appear on your local display by way of SSH.

First, you run a local SSH client, asking it to set up X forwarding. The SSH client requests X forwarding from the remote SSH server, and it also reads your local display key from your *.Xauthority* file.

Next, the SSH client generates a proxy key. This is a string of random data of the same length as your local display key. The SSH client then sends the proxy key and its key type (e.g., MIT-MAGIC-COOKIE-1) to the remote machine, and the SSH server runs the *xauth* program on your behalf to associate the proxy key with your local display. The stage is now set for X forwarding.

When you start a remote X client, your local SSH client connects to your local X display. It then watches for the first X protocol message sent over the forwarded connection and treats it specially. Specifically, the SSH client parses the message, finds the X authentication key inside it, and compares it to the proxy key. If the keys don't match, the SSH client rejects and closes the connection. Otherwise, if the keys match, the SSH client substitutes the real display key in place of the proxy key and relays the modified message to your local X server. The X server, blissfully unaware that a key switch has taken place, reads the display key and proceeds normally with X authentication. The forwarded X connection is now established.

X forwarding with authentication spoofing solves all but one of the X authentication problems we raised earlier:

xhost
> X forwarding doesn't use *xhost*. (By the way, make sure to disable all *xhost* permissions when using X forwarding, or you'll undermine the X security provided by SSH.)

Key transfer
> SSH transfers the X display key automatically and runs *xauth* on your behalf to install it on the remote side. The transfer is secure since the key travels over the encrypted SSH connection.

MIT-MAGIC-COOKIE-1 insecurity
> The key transmitted at the beginning of every X session is now encrypted, along with the rest of the X traffic, inside the SSH session. This greatly increases the operational security of this common X authentication scheme.

Untrustworthy remote hosts
> With authentication spoofing, only the proxy key, not the true display key, is sent to the remote host. The proxy key is good only for connecting to your display through SSH, not for connecting to your display directly. As soon as your SSH session ends, the proxy key becomes useless. Since SSH sessions come and go, but some people leave their X sessions up (with the same key) for days, X forwarding can be a great improvement.

9.4.5.6   Improving authentication spoofing

The remaining problem with X forwarding is the possibility of unsupported X authentication mechanisms. The local side can use a more sophisticated authentication method that a remote host might not support.

In theory, SSH X forwarding can solve this problem by always installing a proxy key of type MIT-MAGIC-COOKIE-1, no matter what local authentication method is actually in use. After the SSH client has checked the X client's key against the proxy key for a match, its client could then generate and substitute whatever local authenticator is required using the true authentication type and key.

Unfortunately, SSH implementations don't go this far. The server compares keys literally as bit strings, and the SSH client substitutes keys verbatim, regardless of the key types. As a result, if you use a stronger X authentication method such as XDM-AUTHORIZATION-1, *sshd* blindly compares an encrypted authenticator with the proxy key, rightly determines that they don't match, and invalidly rejects the connection. The failure is silent and mysterious; we wish the software would detect the presence of an unsupported mode and issue a warning when setting up the connection.

If SSH knew the details of all X authentication modes, it could check the proxy authenticators on one side and generate correct ones for the X server on the other. However, this can be a significant development effort, though perhaps one could link SSH against the X11 libraries to obtain the necessary algorithms. SSH would also have to deal with differing key data lengths, constructing a new X message to hold the proxy key instead of copying it to an existing message.

It would also be useful if X forwarding could be used without authentication spoofing. Then you could arrange your own security for the connection by, say, using *xhost* to allow any connection from your local machine (and hence the SSH X proxy), while still applying key-based authentication to X connections originating from elsewhere. You can accomplish this with general port forwarding, as discussed in the next section, but direct support is more convenient.

9.4.5.7 Nonstandard X clients

X clients generally do X *xauth*-style authentication by virtue of having been linked against Xlib, the common X programming library. Occasionally, though, you run across particular X client programs that don't use Xlib and simply ignore authentication issues. Since you can't turn off SSH X authentication spoofing, you can't use such programs across SSH X forwarding; you get this message:

```
X11 connection requests different authentication protocol: 'MIT-MAGIC-COOKIE-1' vs.
''
```

You can, however, use a general port forwarding instead. For example:

```
foo% ssh -R6010:localhost:6000 bar
bar% setenv DISPLAY bar:10
```

Note that this bypasses the discipline imposed by X forwarding, of requiring *xauth* authentication on forwarded X connections. If your real X server is using *xhost* for access control, this port forwarding allows anyone on host foo to connect to your X server. Use this sort of thing with caution.

9.4.6   Further Issues

As we've said, X forwarding usually works fine without any special effort on your part. In some special situations, however, you might need to take some extra steps.

9.4.6.1   X server configuration

In order for X forwarding to work, your X server must accept the proxy X connections from your SSH client. This is sometimes not set up to begin with, because normal use doesn't require it. For example, if you're using an X server on a PC to access a remote Unix machine via XDM, you might never run local X clients at all, and they may not be allowed by default. You can use *xhost +localhost* to allow all connections from your PC, while still applying key-based authentication to connections from other sources. This allows SSH-forwarded (and authenticated) connections to be accepted.

9.4.6.2   Setting your DISPLAY environment variable

SSH sets the DISPLAY variable automatically only if X forwarding is in effect. If you don't use X forwarding but want to use X on a remote machine you logged into via SSH, remember that you have to set the DISPLAY variable yourself. You should really do this only when both machines are on the same, trusted network, as the X protocol by itself is quite insecure.

Be *careful* not to set DISPLAY unintentionally! It is common for people to set the DISPLAY variable in a login command file or by other means. If you're not careful, this can make your X connections insecure without your noticing! If you use SSH to tunnel through a firewall that blocks normal X connections, then of course you'll notice because your X clients won't work. But if normal X connections are possible but undesirable, and X forwarding isn't in effect, your X programs will work but (silently) not be secured! This is a good reason to block X traffic at the firewall if it presents a security risk or to configure your X server to accept connections only from the local host (the source of the SSH-forwarded X connections). If that's not feasible, you may want to put something like this in your login script:

```
#!/bin/csh
if ($?DISPLAY) then
    set display_host   = `expr "$DISPLAY" : '\(.*\):'`
    set display_number = `expr "$DISPLAY" : '.*:\([^.]*\)'`
    set my_host = `hostname`
    set result  = `expr '(' "$display_host" = "$my_host" ')' '&' '(' \
                   "$display_number" '>' "0" ')'`
    if ($result == 0) then
        echo "WARNING: X display $DISPLAY does not appear to be protected by SSH!"
        echo "unsetting DISPLAY variable just to be safe"
        unsetenv DISPLAY
    endif
endif
```

9.4.6.3   Shared accounts

If you share a single account among multiple people, you may have some trouble with X forwarding. For example, it is common for a group of sysadmins to share use of the root account. For each person to retain their own environment when using the root account, they may set their USER, LOGNAME, and HOME environment variables explicitly to reflect their personal accounts rather than the root account. If you use SSH to log into the root account with X forwarding turned on, though, it adds the proxy *xauth* key to root's *.Xauthority* file before the shell reads your login script and resets these environment variables. The result is that once you're logged in and try to use X, it fails: the X client looks in your *.Xauthority* file (because of the setting of your HOME variable), but the key isn't there.

You can deal with this problem by setting the XAUTHORITY variable to point to root's *.Xauthority* file, or by using code like the following in your login script to copy the needed key into your personal one:

```
if (($uid == 0) && ($?SSH_CLIENT) && ($?DISPLAY)) then
# If I do ssh -l root with X forwarding, the X proxy server's xauth key
# gets added to root's xauth db, not mine.  See if there's an entry for my
# display in root's xauth db...
  set key = `bash -c "xauth -i -f /.Xauthority list $DISPLAY 2> /dev/null"`
# ... and if so, copy it into mine.
  if ($? == 0) then
    xauth -bi add $key
    chown res ~res/.Xauthority >& /dev/null
  endif
endif
```

9.4.6.4   Location of the xauth program

Remember that *sshd* runs the *xauth* program on your behalf, to add the proxy key to your *.Xauthority* file on the remote side. The location of the *xauth* program is discovered when you configure the SSH package and compile into the *sshd* executable. If *xauth* is subsequently moved, X forwarding won't work (*ssh -v* reveals this explicitly). For OpenSSH, the system administrator on the server side can use the server-wide configuration keyword XAuthLocation to set the path to the *xauth* program without having to recompile *sshd1*:

```
# OpenSSH
XAuthLocation /usr/local/bin/xauth
```

XAuthLocation can also appear in the OpenSSH client configuration file; the client uses *xauth* to get the local X display key.

9.4.6.5   X forwarding and the GatewayPorts feature

The GatewayPorts (–g) feature discussed earlier applies only to general port forwarding, not to X forwarding. The X proxies in OpenSSH and Tectia always listen on all network interfaces and accept connections from anywhere, though those connections are then subject to X authentication as described earlier. To restrict X client source addresses, use TCP-wrappers, which we discuss in the next section.

9.5   Forwarding Security: TCP-Wrappers and libwrap

At several points in this chapter, we have talked about security issues and limitations of forwarding. So far, we've seen very little control over who can connect to a

---

forwarded port. The OpenSSH default is to allow connections only from the local host, which is reasonably secure for a single-user machine. But if you need to allow connections from elsewhere, you have a problem, since it's all or nothing: to allow connections from elsewhere (using –g or GatewayPorts yes), you must allow them from *anywhere*. And with Tectia it's worse: forwarded ports *always* accept connections from anywhere. X forwarding is in a slightly better position, since the X protocol has its own authentication, but you might still prefer to restrict access, preventing intruders from exploiting an unknown security flaw or performing a denial-of-service attack. SSH on the Unix platform provides an optional feature for access control based on the client address, called "TCP-wrappers."

The term "TCP-wrappers" refers to software written by Wietse Venema. If it isn't already installed in your Unix distribution, you can get it at:

   ftp://ftp.porcupine.org/pub/security/index.html

TCP-wrappers are a global access control mechanism that integrates with other TCP-based servers, such as *sshd* or *telnetd*. Access control is based on the source address of incoming TCP connections. That is, a TCP-wrapper permits or denies connections based on their origin, as specified in the configuration files */etc/hosts. allow* and */etc/hosts.deny*. Figure 9-12 shows where TCP-wrappers fit into the scheme of SSH configuration.

There are two ways to use TCP-wrappers. The most common method, *wrapping*, is applied to TCP servers that are normally invoked by *inetd*. You "wrap" the server by editing */etc/inetd.conf* and modifying the server's configuration line. Instead of invoking the server directly, you invoke the TCP-wrapper daemon, *tcpd*, which in turn invokes the original server. Then, you edit the TCP-wrapper configuration files to specify your desired access control. *tcpd* makes authorization decisions based on the their contents.

The *inetd* technique applies access control without having to modify the TCP server program. This is nice. However, *sshd* is usually not invoked by *inetd* [5.3.3.2], so the second method, *source code modification*, must be applied. To participate in TCP-wrapper control, the SSH server must be compiled with the flag --with-tcp-wrappers [4.2.4.5] or --with-libwrap [4.3.5.3] to enable internal support for TCP-wrappers. *sshd* then invokes TCP-wrapper library functions to do explicit access-control checks according to the rules in */etc/hosts.allow* and */etc/hosts.deny*. So, in a sense, the term "wrapper" is misleading since *sshd* is modified, not wrapped, to support TCP-wrappers. Figure 9-13 illustrates the process.

9.5.1   TCP-Wrappers Configuration

The access control language for TCP-wrappers has quite a few options and may vary depending on whose package you use and what version it is. We won't cover the language completely in this book. Consult your local documentation for a complete

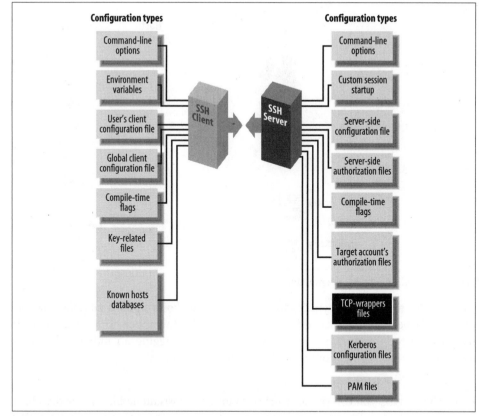

Figure 9-12. TCP-wrappers and SSH configuration (highlighted parts)

understanding: the manpages on *tcpd*, *hosts_access*, and *hosts_options*. We just indicate some simple, common configurations.

The TCP-wrapper configuration is kept in the files */etc/hosts.allow* and */etc/hosts. deny*. These files contain patterns of the form:

```
service_1 [service_2 service_3 ...] : client_1 [client_2 client_3 ...]
```

Each pattern matches some (server,client) pairs, and hence may match a particular client/server TCP connection. Specifically, a connection between client C and server S matches this rule if some service *servicei* matches S, and some *clientj* matches C. (We explain the format and matching rules for these subpatterns shortly.) The *hosts. allow* file is searched first, followed by *hosts.deny*. If a matching pattern is found in *hosts.allow*, the connection is allowed. If none is found there, but one matches in *hosts.deny*, the connection is dropped. Finally, if no patterns match in either file, the connection is allowed. Nonexistence of either file is treated as if the file existed and contained no matching patterns. Note that the default, then, is to allow everything.

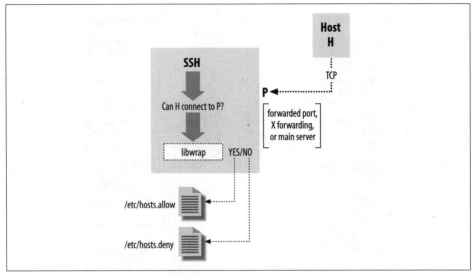

Figure 9-13. TCP-wrapper (libwrap) operation

There is also an extended syntax, documented on the *hosts_options* manpage. It may or may not be available, depending on how your TCP-wrapper library was built. It has many more options, but in particular, it allows tagging an individual rule as denying or rejecting a matching connection, for example:

```
sshd : bad.host.com : DENY
```

Using this syntax, you can put all your rules into the *hosts.allow* file, rather than having to use both files. To reject anything not explicitly allowed, just put ALL : ALL : DENY at the end of the file.

In a pattern, each *service* is a name indicating a server to which this pattern applies. SSH recognizes the following service names:

sshd
> The main SSH server. This can be *sshd*, *sshd1*, *sshd2*, or whatever name you invoke the daemon under (its argv[0] value, in C-programmer-speak).

sshdfwd-x11
> The X forwarding port.

sshdfwd-N
> Forwarded TCP port *N* (e.g., forwarded port 2001 is service sshdfwd-2001).

> The X and port -orwarding control features are available only in Tectia; OpenSSH uses *libwrap* only to control access to the main server.

Each *client* is a pattern that matches a connecting client. It can be:

- An IP address in dotted-quad notation (e.g., 192.168.10.1).

- A hostname (DNS, or whatever naming services the host is using).

- An IP network as *network-number/mask* (e.g., 192.168.10.0/255.255.255.0; note that the "*/n-mask-bits*" syntax, 192.168.10.0/24, isn't recognized).

- "ALL", matching any client source address.

Example 9-1 shows a sample */etc/hosts.allow* configuration. This setup allows connections to any service from the local host's loopback address, and from all addresses 192.168.10.x. This host is running publicly available servers for POP and IMAP, so we allow connections to these from anywhere, but SSH clients are restricted to sources in another particular range of networks.

Example 9-1. Sample /etc/hosts.allow file

```
#
# /etc/hosts.allow
#
# network access control for programs invoked by tcpd (see inetd.conf) or
# using libwrap. See the manpages hosts_access(5) and hosts_options(5).

# allow all connections from my network or localhost (loopback address)
#
ALL : 192.168.10.0/255.255.255.0 localhost

# allow connections to these services from anywhere
#
ipop3d imapd : ALL

# allow SSH connections from these eight class C networks
# 192.168.20.0, 192.168.21.0, ..., 192.168.27.0
#
sshd : 192.168.20.0/255.255.248.0

# allow connections to forwarded port 1234 from host blynken
# Tectia only
sshdfwd-1234 : blynken.sleepy.net

# restrict X forwarding access to localhost
# Tectia only
sshdfwd-x11 : localhost

# deny everything else
#
ALL : ALL : DENY
```

We allow connections to the forwarded port 1234 from a particular host, *blynken. sleepy.net*. Note that this host doesn't have to be on any of the networks listed so far but can be anywhere at all. The rules so far say what is allowed, but don't by themselves forbid any connections. So, for example, the forwarding established by the command *ssh -L1234:localhost:21 remote* is accessible only to the local host, since Tectia defaults to binding only the loopback address in any case. But *ssh -g -L1234: localhost:21 remote* is accessible to *blynken.sleepy.net* as well. The important difference is that with this use of TCP-wrappers, *sshd* rejects connections to the forwarded port, 1234, from any other address.

The `sshdfwd-x11` line restricts X-forwarding connections to the local host. This means that if *ssh* connects *to* this host with X forwarding, only local X clients can use the forwarded X connection. X authentication does this already, but this configuration provides an extra bit of protection.

The final line denies any connection that doesn't match the earlier lines, making this a default-to-closed configuration. If you wanted instead to deny some particular connections but allow all others, you would use something like this:

```
ALL : evil.mordor.net : DENY
telnetd : completely.horked.edu : DENY
ALL : ALL : ALLOW
```

The final line is technically not required, but it's a good idea to make your intentions explicit. If you don't have the *host_options* syntax available, you instead have an empty *hosts.allow* file, and the following lines in *hosts.deny*:

```
ALL : evil.mordor.net
telnetd : completely.horked.edu
```

9.5.2   Notes About TCP-Wrappers

Here are a few things to remember when using TCP-wrappers:

- You can't distinguish between ports forwarded by SSH-1 and SSH-2: the "sshdfwd" rules refer to both simultaneously. You can work around this limitation by linking each against a different *libwrap.a*, compiled with different filenames for the allow and deny files, or by patching the *ssh* and *sshd* executables directly, but then you have to keep track of these changes and extra files.

- The big drawback to TCP-wrappers is that it affects all users simultaneously. An individual user can't specify custom access rules for himself; there's just the single set of global configuration files for the machine. This limits its usefulness on multiuser machines.

- If you compile SSH with the `--with-libwrap` option, it is automatically and always turned on; there's no configuration or command-line option to disable the TCP-wrappers check. Remember that SSH does this check not only for forwarded ports and X connections, but also for connections to the main SSH server! As soon as you install a version of *sshd* with TCP-wrappers, you must ensure that the TCP-wrappers configuration allows connections to the server—for instance, with the rule `sshd : ALL` in */etc/hosts.allow*.

- Using hostnames instead of addresses in the TCP-wrappers rule set involves the usual security trade-off. Names are more convenient, and their use avoids breakage in the future if a host address changes. On the other hand, an attacker can potentially subvert the naming service and circumvent the access control. If the host machine is configured to use *only* its */etc/hosts* file for name lookup, this may be acceptable even in a highly secure environment.

- The TCP-wrappers package includes a program called *tcpdchk*. This program examines the wrapper control files and reports inconsistencies that might signal problems. Many sites run this periodically as a safety check. Unfortunately, *tcpdchk* is written only with explicit wrapping via *inetd.conf* in mind. It doesn't have any way of knowing about programs that refer to the control files via the *libwrap* routines, as does *sshd*. When *tcpdchk* reads control files with SSH rules, it finds uses of the service names "sshd1," "sshdfwd-*n*," etc., but no corresponding wrapped services in *inetd.conf*, and it generates a warning. Unfortunately, we know of no workaround.

9.6 Summary

In this chapter, we discussed SSH port forwarding and X forwarding. Port forwarding is a general TCP proxying feature that tunnels TCP connections through an SSH session. This is useful for securing otherwise insecure protocols running on top of TCP or for tunneling TCP connections through firewalls that would otherwise forbid access. X forwarding is a special case of port forwarding for X Window System connections, for which SSH has extra support. This makes it easy to secure X connections with SSH, which is good because X, while popular and useful, is notoriously insecure. Access control on forwarded ports is normally coarse, but you can achieve finer control with the TCP-wrappers feature.

CHAPTER 10

A Recommended Setup

We've just covered a pile of chapters on SSH configuration: is your head spinning yet? With so many choices, you might be wondering which options you should use. How can system administrators secure their systems most effectively with SSH?

When set up properly, SSH works well and invisibly, but sometimes a good setup takes a few tries. In addition, there are some ways to configure the software that are simply wrong. If you're not careful, you can introduce security holes into your system.

In this chapter we present a recommended set of options for compilation, server configuration, key management, and client configuration. We assume:

- You're running SSH on a Unix machine.
- You want a secure system, sometimes at the expense of flexibility. For instance, rather than tell you to maintain your *.rhosts* files carefully, we recommend disabling Rhosts authentication altogether.

Of course, no single configuration covers all the possibilities; that is, after all, the point of configuration. This is just a sample setup, more on the secure side, to give you a starting point and cover some of the issues involved.

10.1   The Basics

Before you start configuring, make sure you're running an up-to-date SSH version. Some older versions have known security holes that are easily exploited. Always run the latest stable version, and apply updates or patches in a timely manner. (The same goes for your other security software.)

Always keep important SSH-related files and directories protected. The server's host key should be readable only by root. Each user's home directory, SSH configuration directory, and *.rhosts* and *.shosts* files should be owned by the user and protected against all others.

Also, remember that SSH doesn't and can't protect against all threats. It can secure your network connections but does nothing against other types of attacks, such as dictionary attacks against your password database. SSH should be an important part, but not the only part, of a robust security policy. [3.10]

10.2 Compile-Time Configuration

In Chapter 4, we covered many compile-time flags for building SSH distributions. Several flags should be carefully set to make your server machine maximally secure:

--sysconfdir=... *(OpenSSH, Tectia)*
> Make sure your *etc* directory is on a local disk, not an NFS-mounted partition. If the SSH server reads a file via NFS, the contents are transmitted in the clear across the network, violating security. This is especially true of the host key, which is stored unencrypted in this directory.

--bindir=... *(OpenSSH, Tectia)*

--sbindir=... *(OpenSSH, Tectia)*
> Likewise, make sure your SSH executables are installed on a local disk, as they can be spoofed if loaded over NFS.*

--disable-suid-ssh-signer *(Tectia)*
> Our recommended serverwide configuration disables hostbased authentication, so there's no need for setuid permissions for *ssh-signer*.

--with-tcp-wrappers *(OpenSSH)*

--with-libwrap *(Tectia)*
> *libwrap* affords more precise control over which client machines are allowed to connect to your server. It also makes port and X forwarding more flexible, since otherwise local forwardings are available either only to the local host or from anywhere at all. With GatewayPorts (or *ssh -g*) and *libwrap*, you can limit forwarding access to specific hosts. [9.2.1.1]

10.3 Serverwide Configuration

Chapter 5 provided a detailed discussion of *sshd* and how to configure its runtime behavior. Now let's determine which configuration options are most important for security.

---

* Or use --prefix to root all SSH system directories together.

10.3.1 Disable Other Means of Access

SSH can provide a secure front door into your system, but don't forget to close the back doors. If your system allows access via the infamous r-commands, disable them. This means:

- Remove the file */etc/hosts.equiv*, or make it a read-only empty file.
- Disable *rshd*, *rlogind*, and *rexecd* by removing or commenting out their lines in the *inetd* or *xinetd* configuration file. For example, in */etc/inetd.conf* you might do:

  ```
  # turned off -- don't use!
  #shell   stream  tcp   nowait  root  /usr/sbin/in.rshd     in.rshd
  ```

  Make sure you restart *inetd* or *xinetd* after doing this so that the change takes effect.

- Educate users not to create *.rhosts* files.

You might also consider disabling *telnetd* and other insecure avenues for logging in, permitting logins only via SSH.

10.3.2 sshd_config for OpenSSH

We'll now discuss our recommended *sshd_config* settings for OpenSSH. We have omitted some keywords that aren't particularly security-related, such as `PrintMotd`, which simply prints a message after login. For any remaining keywords, use your judgment based on your system and needs.

10.3.2.1 Choice of protocol

We recommend disabling the SSH-1 protocol altogether:

```
# OpenSSH
Protocol 2
```

10.3.2.2 Important files

Important files containing your host key, PID, and so on, may be located anywhere on the machine's local disk. For security's sake, don't put them on an NFS-mounted partition. If you do, each time the files are accessed by the SSH server, their contents are transmitted in the clear over the network.

```
# OpenSSH
HostKey /etc/ssh/ssh_host_key
PidFile /var/run/sshd.pid
```

10.3.2.3 File and directory permissions

The `StrictModes` value requires users to protect their SSH-related files and directories, or else they can't authenticate.

```
# OpenSSH
StrictModes yes
```

10.3.2.4 TCP/IP settings

The Port and ListenAddress values we recommend are standard. Also, we enable keepalive messages so that connections to clients that have crashed or otherwise become unreachable will terminate rather than hang around and require manual reaping by the sysadmin.

```
# OpenSSH
Port 22
ListenAddress 0.0.0.0
TcpKeepAlive yes
```

We also disable reverse DNS lookups on incoming connections:

```
# OpenSSH
UseDNS no
```

You might think security is increased by reverse DNS lookups, but in fact, DNS isn't secure enough to guarantee accurate lookups. Also, due to other issues in your Unix and network environment, reverse DNS mappings might not even work properly. [5.3.3.8] Finally, SSH connections can be tremendously slowed down or fail altogether if the client's DNS is hosed (e.g., lots of nameservers, all unresponsive, so *sshd* times out). The IP addresses of connecting hosts end up in your logs anyway, so you can look them up later.

10.3.2.5 Login time

For logins we allow 30 seconds for a successful authentication, which should be long enough for users and automated processes:

```
# OpenSSH
LoginGraceTime 30
```

10.3.2.6 Authentication

We enable only public-key authentication. Password authentication is disabled because passwords can be stolen and used more easily than public keys. This is a fairly harsh restriction, so you might want to leave it enabled depending on your needs. Without password authentication, you have a "chicken and egg" problem: how do users upload their public keys securely the first time? As system administrator, you have to institute a process for this transfer: for example, users can generate keys on a client machine and then request that you install them on the server machine. Rhosts authentication is disabled because it can be spoofed. RhostsRSA authentication is disabled too, because overall it is a medium-security method and this configuration is on the side of higher security.

```
# OpenSSH
PubkeyAuthentication yes
```

```
PasswordAuthentication no
PermitEmptyPasswords no              Already disabled, but we're being paranoid
RSAAuthentication no
RhostsRSAAuthentication no
HostbasedAuthentication no
KerberosAuthentication no            Optional
ChallengeResponseAuthentication no   Optional
GSSAPIAuthentication no              Optional
```

We optionally disable Kerberos, keyboard-interactive, and GSSAPI authentication, even though they are quite secure, under the "keep it simple" principle: disable what you aren't using. Most SSH users aren't set up to use these techniques. Reenable them if your server needs to support them.

Although we've disabled hostbased authentication already, we still forbid *sshd* to use *.rhosts* files at all (just in case you reenable hostbased authentication):

```
# OpenSSH
IgnoreRhosts yes
IgnoreRootRhosts yes
```

10.3.2.7 Access control

If you want to restrict access to particular local accounts or Unix groups, add `AllowUsers` and `AllowGroups` lines (or `DenyUsers` and `DenyGroups`). We recommend creating a group for all your system's SSH users, called "ssh", and configuring the server with:

```
AllowGroups ssh
```

Now you've made SSH access a specific privilege to be granted or revoked, and you can easily do it for a user without changing the *sshd* configuration:

```
# usermod -G ssh,... joe      Add user joe to the SSH group
```

As a bonus, you've disallowed SSH access by system accounts like *bin*, *sys*, and *daemon* that should never use SSH anyway.

We also permit the superuser to connect via SSH but not by password authentication. This is redundant but consistent with turning off `PasswordAuthentication`.

```
# OpenSSH
PermitRootLogin without-password
```

10.3.2.8 Forwarding

We permit TCP port forwarding and X forwarding so that users can secure their other TCP connections:

```
# OpenSSH
AllowTcpForwarding yes
X11Forwarding yes
```

10.3.2.9 SFTP

Confirm that the SFTP subsystem is defined so that incoming *sftp* connections will work. (It is enabled in the default */etc/ssh/sshd_config* file for OpenSSH.)

```
# OpenSSH
Subsystem    sftp    /usr/lib/ssh/sftp-server
```

10.3.3   sshd2_config for Tectia

We now move to our recommended *sshd2_config* settings for Tectia. Again, we've omitted some keywords that are not security-related.

10.3.3.1 Choice of protocol

We recommend disabling the SSH-1 protocol altogether:

```
# Tectia
Ssh1Compatibility no
Sshd1Path /dev/null      Not strictly necessary, just our paranoia
```

10.3.3.2 Important files

As we have mentioned for OpenSSH [10.3.2.2], make sure all SSH-related files are on local disks, not remotely mounted partitions:

```
# Tectia
HostKeyFile /etc/ssh2/hostkey
PublicHostKeyFile /etc/ssh2/hostkey.pub
RandomSeedFile /etc/ssh2/random_seed
```

For the following settings, consider the pros and cons of storing user files on NFS-mounted filesystems: [10.7]

```
# Tectia
UserConfigDirectory directory
IdentityFile filename
AuthorizationFile filename
```

10.3.3.3 File and directory permissions

The StrictModes value requires users to protect their SSH-related files and directories, or else they can't authenticate:

```
# Tectia
StrictModes yes
```

10.3.3.4 TCP/IP settings

We recommend the same configuration as for OpenSSH, for the same reasons: [10.3.2.4]

```
# Tectia
Port 22
```

```
ListenAddress 0.0.0.0
KeepAlive yes
RequireReverseMapping no
```

10.3.3.5 Login time

For logins we allow 30 seconds for a successful authentication, which should be long enough for users and automated processes:

```
# Tectia
LoginGraceTime 30
```

10.3.3.6 Authentication

These settings mirror those for OpenSSH:

```
# Tectia
AllowedAuthentications publickey
RequiredAuthentications publickey      Overrides AllowedAuthentications; we're being paranoid
PermitEmptyPasswords no                Already disabled, but we're being paranoid
```

Although we've disabled hostbased authentication already, we still forbid *sshd* to use *.rhosts* files at all (just in case you reenable hostbased authentication). We also disable UserKnownHosts to prevent users from extending trust to unknown hosts for the purpose of hostbased authentication. The superuser can still specify trusted hosts in */etc/ssh2/knownhosts*.

```
# Tectia
IgnoreRhosts yes
IgnoreRootRhosts yes
UserKnownHosts no
```

10.3.3.7 Access control

We permit SSH connections only from within the local domain*:

```
# Tectia
AllowHosts fred@* *.your.domain.com               Just an example
```

except for the account fred in this example, which may receive connections from anywhere.

If you want to restrict access to particular local accounts or Unix groups, add AllowUsers and AllowGroups lines (or DenyUsers and DenyGroups). Also create an "ssh" group as we described earlier. [10.3.2.7]

We permit the superuser to connect via SSH but not by password authentication. This is redundant but consistent with turning off PasswordAuthentication.

```
# Tectia
PermitRootLogin nopwd
```

---

* The reliability of this restriction depends on the integrity of DNS. Unfortunately, due to the implementation of AllowHosts, restriction by IP address is no more secure. [5.5.1]

10.3.3.8 Forwarding

We permit TCP port forwarding and X forwarding so that users can secure their other TCP connections:

```
# Tectia
AllowTcpForwarding yes
X11Forwarding yes
```

10.3.3.9 Encryption

Use either of the following settings as fits your needs. The notable feature is that they both exclude the "none" cipher which may be a security risk.

```
# Tectia
Ciphers anycipher
Ciphers anystdcipher
```

10.3.3.10 SFTP

Confirm that the SFTP subsystem is defined so that incoming sftp connections will work. (It is enabled in the default */etc/ssh2/sshd2_config* for Tectia.)

```
# Tectia
subsystem-sftp    sftp-server
```

10.4 Per-Account Configuration

Users should be instructed not to create *.rhosts* files. If hostbased authentication is enabled in the local SSH server, advise users to create *.shosts* files instead of *.rhosts* files.

For OpenSSH, each key in *~/.ssh/authorized_keys* should be restricted by appropriate options. First, use the from option to restrict access to particular keys by particular hosts when appropriate. For example, suppose your *authorized_keys* file contains a public key for your home PC, *myhome.isp.net*. No other machine will ever authenticate using this key, so make the relationship explicit:

```
from="myhome.isp.net" ...key...
```

Also set idle timeouts for appropriate keys:

```
from="myhome.isp.net",idle-timeout=5m ...key...
```

Finally, for each key, consider whether port forwarding, agent forwarding, and tty allocation are ever necessary for incoming connections. If not, disable these features with no-port-forwarding, no-agent-forwarding, and no-pty, respectively:

```
from="myhome.isp.net",idle-timeout=5m,no-agent-forwarding ...key...
```

10.5 Key Management

We recommend creating user keys at least 1024 bits long. Protect your key with a good passphrase. Make it lengthy and use a mixture of lowercase, uppercase, numeric, and symbolic characters. Don't use words found in a dictionary.

Empty passphrases should be avoided unless you absolutely need to use one—for example, in an automated batch script. [11.1.2.2]

10.6 Client Configuration

Most SSH security pertains to the server, but SSH clients have security-related settings too. Here are a few tips:

- Whenever you leave a computer while SSH clients are running, lock the computer's display with a password-protected screen locker. This is particularly important if you're running an agent that permits an intruder to access your remote accounts without a passphrase.

- In your client configuration file, turn on some safety features as mandatory values:

```
# OpenSSH
# Put at the top of your configuration file
Host *
  GatewayPorts no
  StrictHostKeyChecking ask
 ForwardX11Trusted no

# Tectia
# Put at the bottom of your configuration file
*:
 GatewayPorts no
 StrictHostKeyChecking ask
 TrustX11Applications no
```

The GatewayPorts value forbids remote clients from connecting to locally forwarded ports. Finally, rather than blindly connect, the StrictHostKeyChecking value warns you of any changed host keys and asks what you want to do. For X11 forwarding we elect to generate a new, untrusted *xauth* key rather than inherit the trust already in effect. [9.4.5.3]

10.7 Remote Home Directories (NFS, AFS)

We've mentioned NFS several times as a potential security risk for SSH installations. Now we delve into more detail on this topic.

In today's world of ubiquitous networking, it is common for your home directory to be shared among many machines via a network file-sharing protocol, such as SMB for Windows machines or NFS and AFS for Unix. This is convenient, but it does raise some issues with SSH, both technical and security-related.

SSH examines files in the target account's home directory in order to make critical decisions about authentication and authorization. For every form of authentication except password, the various control files in your home directory (*authorized_ keys, .shosts, .k5login,* etc.) enable SSH access to your account. Two things are therefore important:

* Your home directory needs to be safe from tampering.
* SSH must have access to your home directory.

10.7.1 NFS Security Risks

The security of shared home directories is often not very high. Although the NFS protocol has versions and implementations that afford greater security, it is woefully insecure in most installations. Often, it employs no reliable form of authentication whatsoever, but rather, uses the same scheme as *rsh*: the source IP address and DNS identify clients, and a privileged source port is proof of trustworthiness. It then simply believes the uid number encoded in NFS requests and grants access as that user. Breaking into a home directory can be as simple as:

1. Discover the uid, and create an account with that uid on a laptop running Unix.
2. Connect that machine to the network, borrowing the IP address of a trusted host.
3. Issue a *mount* command, *su* to the account with the uid, and start rifling through the files.

At this point, an intruder can easily add another public key to *authorized_keys*, and the account is wide open. The moral is that when designing a system, keep in mind that the security of SSH is no stronger than that of the home directories involved. You need at least to be aware of the trade-off between security and convenience involved here. If you are using an insecure NFS and want to avoid this weakness, you can:

* Use Tectia, which has the UserConfigDirectory option to place the per-user SSH configuration files, normally in ~/.ssh2, elsewhere—say, in */var/ssh/<username>*. You can still set the permissions so their owners can control them, but they won't be shared via NFS and thus not vulnerable. You can do the same with OpenSSH, but as it lacks such a configuration option, you need to edit the source code.
* Turn off hostbased authentication, since the ~/.shosts control file is vulnerable, and you can't change its location. Or, if you want to use hostbased authentication, set the IgnoreRhosts option. This causes *sshd* to ignore ~/.shosts, relying instead solely on the systemwide */etc/shosts.equiv* file.

- If you are truly paranoid, disable swapping on your Unix machine. Otherwise, sensitive information such as server, host, and user keys, or passwords, may be written to disk as part of the normal operation of the Unix virtual memory system (should the running *sshd* be swapped out to disk). Someone with root access (and a lot of knowledge and luck) could read the swap partition and tease this information out of the mess there—though it's a difficult feat. Another option is to use an operating system that encrypts swap pages on disk, such as OpenBSD.

10.7.2 NFS Access Problems

Another problem that can arise with SSH and NFS is one of access rights. With the public-key or hostbased methods, if the per-user control files are in the usual place, *sshd* must read the target account's home directory in order to perform authentication. When that directory is on the same machine as *sshd*, this isn't a problem. *sshd* runs as root, and therefore has access to all files. However, if the directory is mounted from elsewhere via NFS, *sshd* might not have access to the directory. NFS is commonly configured so that the special access privileges accorded the root account don't extend to remote filesystems.

Now, this isn't a truly serious restriction. Since one of the root privileges is the ability to create a process with any uid, root can simply "become" the right user, and access the remote directory. Current versions of Tectia and OpenSSH handle this correctly, but you might run into older versions that do not. You can work around the problem, but to do so you must make your *authorized_keys* file world-readable; the only way to let root read it remotely is to let everyone read it. This isn't too objectionable. The *authorized_keys* file contains no secrets; though you might prefer not to reveal which keys allow access to your account, thus advertising which keys to steal. However, to grant this access, you must make your home directory and *~/.ssh* world-searchable (that is, permissions at least 711). This doesn't allow other users to steal the contents, but it does allow them to guess at filenames and have those guesses verified. It also means that you must be careful about permissions on your files, since the top-level permissions on your directory don't prevent access by others.

All this may be entirely unacceptable or no problem at all; it depends on your attitude toward your files and the other users on the machines where your home directory is accessible.

10.7.3 AFS Access Problems

The Andrew File System, or AFS, is a file-sharing protocol similar in purpose to NFS, but considerably more sophisticated. It uses Kerberos-4 for user authentication and is generally more secure than NFS. The access problem discussed previously comes up for AFS, but it's more work to solve, and this time, OpenSSH is the winner.

AFS uses its own authentication system; access to remote files is controlled by possession of an appropriate AFS *token*. There are no uid-switching games root can play; *sshd* must have the right AFS token in order to access your home directory. If you were logged into that machine, of course, you could use the usual AFS *klog* command to authenticate to AFS. However, *sshd* needs it before you've logged in, so there's a bit of a quandary.

There is one solution available, though, involving Kerberos. If Kerberos is available, AFS will usually be configured so that AFS tokens can be obtained via Kerberos, bringing AFS into the Kerberos single-signon universe. If you have protocol-2 Kerberos support enabled with ticket forwarding [11.5.2.2], then OpenSSH can use your forwarded credentials to automatically obtain the needed AFS token:

```
# ~/.ssh/config
GSSAPIAuthentication        yes
GSSAPIDelegateCredentials   yes
KerberosGetAFSToken         yes
```

Note that the older OpenSSH Kerberos-4 mechanism for this, controlled by the keyword `AFSTokenPassing`, is no longer available. The current support is only for Kerberos-5 and GSSAPI.

10.8 Summary

OpenSSH and Tectia are complex and have many options. It is vitally important to understand all options when installing and running SSH servers and clients, so their behavior will conform to your local security policy.

We have presented our recommended options for a high security setting. Your needs may vary. For instance, you might want the flexibility of other authentication methods that we have forbidden in our configuration.

Case Studies

In this chapter we'll delve deeply into some advanced topics: complex port forwarding, integration of SSH with other applications, and more. Some interesting features of SSH don't come to the surface unless examined closely, so we hope you get a lot out of these case studies. Roll up your sleeves, dive in, and have fun.

11.1   Unattended SSH: Batch or cron Jobs

SSH isn't only a great interactive tool, but also a resource for automation. Batch scripts, *cron* jobs, and other automated tasks can benefit from the security provided by SSH, but only if implemented properly. The major challenge is authentication: how can a client prove its identity when no human is available to type a password or passphrase? (We'll just write "password" from now on to mean both.) You must carefully select an authentication method, and then equally carefully make it work. Once this infrastructure is established, you must invoke *ssh* properly to avoid prompting the user. In this case study, we discuss the pros and cons of different authentication methods for operating an SSH client unattended.

Note that any kind of unattended authentication presents a security problem and requires compromise, and SSH is no exception. Without a human present when needed to provide credentials (type a password, provide a thumbprint, etc.), those credentials must be stored persistently somewhere on the host system. Therefore, an attacker who compromises the system badly enough can use those credentials to impersonate the program and gain whatever access it has. Selecting a technique is a matter of understanding the pros and cons of the available methods, and picking your preferred poison.

11.1.1   Password Authentication

Rule number 1: forget password authentication if you care about the security of your batch jobs. As we mentioned, authentication for any unattended process will require some kind of persistent secret lying around, so it might seem that a password in a protected file will do as well as anything else, and password authentication is simple. In a strict sense that's correct, but it's a bad idea both practically and securitywise. Embedding a password in a command line is unwise: it may be exposed to other users by simple commands such as *ps*, end up in shell history files (e.g. *~/.bash_history*) or system logs, etc. In fact, most SSH clients deliberately require terminal input (a "tty") for a password, precisely to discourage this. You can use a tool like Expect to get around this limitation, but that will be awkward. Another practical limitation is that more methods tend to be available on the server side to restrict logins with public-key authentication, e.g., the "command" parameters in *~/.ssh/authorized_keys* (OpenSSH) and *~/.ssh2/authorization* (Tectia). This is just an implementation detail, but it's very relevant since you definitely want to restrict unattended logins to do just what they're intended to do.

More generally, compared to other available methods, SSH password authentication is just inherently weak: passwords tend to be short and often guessable, and the client must reveal the password to the server as part of the authentication process; so if the server has been compromised, it will get your password. Public-key authentication, however, does not reveal the private key in the process.

In the real world, though, you might be stuck using password authentication anyway. Perhaps you have to automate a transaction with a server not under your control; it only supports passwords, and you can't get that changed. If you must, we suggest co-opting the "askpass" facility if it's available. [6.3.3] The *ssh-askpass* program normally displays a window prompting for the password, but it can use instead a program that provides the password from wherever you're storing it. It does so via a pipe, which is much better than letting it appear on a command line.

11.1.2 Public-Key Authentication

In public-key authentication, a private key is the client's credentials. Therefore, the batch job needs access to the key, which must be stored where the job can access it. You have three choices of location for the key, which we discuss separately:

- Store the encrypted key and its passphrase in the filesystem.
- Store a plaintext (unencrypted) private key in the filesystem, so it doesn't require a passphrase.
- Store the key in an agent, which keeps secrets out of the filesystem but requires a human to decrypt the key at system boot time.

11.1.2.1 Storing the passphrase in the filesystem

In this technique, you store an encrypted key and its passphrase in the filesystem so that a script can access them. We don't recommend this method, since you can store an unencrypted key in the filesystem with the same level of security (and considerably less complication). In either case, you rely solely on the filesystem's protections to keep the key secure. This observation is the rationale for the next technique.

11.1.2.2 Using a plaintext key

A plaintext or unencrypted key requires no passphrase. To create one, run *ssh-key-gen* and simply press the Return key when prompted for a passphrase (or similarly, remove the passphrase from an existing key using *ssh-keygen –p*). You can then supply the key filename on the *ssh* command line using the *–i* option, or in the client configuration file with the `IdentityFile` keyword. [7.4.2]

Usually plaintext keys are undesirable, equivalent to leaving your password in a file in your account. They are never a good idea for interactive logins, since the SSH agent provides the same benefits in a much more secure fashion. But a plaintext key is a viable option for automation, since the unattended aspect forces us to rely on some kind of persistent state in the machine. The filesystem is one possibility.

Plaintext keys are frightening, though. To steal the key, an attacker needs to override filesystem protections only once, and this doesn't necessarily require any fancy hacking: stealing a single backup tape will do. You can arrange to keep them off backups, but that's an additional complication. If you need your batch jobs to continue working after an unattended system restart, plaintext keys are pretty much your best option. If the situation allows for some leeway in this regard, however, consider using *ssh-agent* instead.

11.1.2.3 Using an agent

ssh-agent provides another, somewhat less vulnerable method of key storage for batch jobs. A human invokes an agent and loads the needed keys from passphrase-protected key files, just once. Thereafter, unattended jobs use this long-running agent for authentication.

In this case, the keys are still in plaintext but within the memory space of the running agent rather than in a file on disk. As a matter of practical cracking, it is more difficult to extract a data structure from the address space of a running process than to gain illicit access to a file. Also, this solution avoids the problem of an intruder walking off with a backup tape containing the plaintext key.

Security can still be compromised by other methods, though. The agent provides access to its services via a Unix-domain socket, which appears as a node in the filesystem. Anyone who can read and write that socket might be able to instruct the agent to sign authentication requests and thus gain use of the keys. Some agent implementations attempt further checks, such as ensuring the communicating process runs under the same uid, but not all flavors of Unix support this. [6.3.4.1] In any event, this compromise isn't quite so devastating since the attacker can't obtain the actual keys through the agent socket. She merely gains use of the keys for as long as the agent is running and as long as she can maintain her compromise of the host.

The agent method does have a down side: the system can't continue unattended after a reboot. When the host comes up again automatically, the batch jobs won't have their keys until someone shows up to restart the agent and provide the passphrases to load the keys. This is just a cost of the improved security, and you have a pager, right?

Another bit of complication with the agent method is that you must arrange for the batch jobs to find the agent. SSH clients locate an agent via an environment variable pointing to the agent socket, such as SSH_AUTH_SOCK for the OpenSSH agent. [6.3.2.1] When you start the agent for batch jobs, you need to record its output where the jobs can find it. For instance, if the job is a shell script, you can store the environment values in a file:

```
$ ssh-agent | head -2 > ~/agent-info
$ cat ~/agent-info
setenv SSH_AUTH_SOCK /tmp/ssh-res/ssh-12327-agent;
setenv SSH_AGENT_PID 12328;
```

You can add keys to the agent (assuming C-shell syntax here):

```
$ source ~/agent-info
$ ssh-add batch-key
Need passphrase for batch-key (batch job SSH key).
Enter passphrase: **************
```

then instrument any scripts to set the same values for the environment variables:

```
#!/bin/csh
# Source the agent-info file to get access to our ssh-agent.
set agent = ~/agent-info
if (-r $agent) then
  source $agent
else
  echo "Can't find or read agent file; exiting."
  exit 1
endif
# Now use SSH for something...
ssh -q -o 'BatchMode yes' user@remote-server my-job-command
```

You also need to ensure that the batch jobs (and nobody else!) can read and write the socket. If there's only one uid using the agent, the simplest thing to do is start the agent under that uid (e.g., as root, do *su <batch_account> ssh-agent* ...). If multiple uids are using the agent, you must adjust the permissions on the socket and its containing directory so that these uids can all access it, perhaps using group permissions.

Some operating systems behave oddly with respect to permissions on Unix-domain sockets. Some versions of Solaris, for example, completely ignore the modes on a socket, allowing any process at all full access to it. To protect a socket in such situations, set the containing directory to forbid access. For example, if the containing directory is mode 700, only the directory owner may access the socket. (This assumes there's no other shortcut to the socket located elsewhere, such as a hard link.)

Using an agent for automation is more complicated and restrictive than using a plaintext key; however, it is more resistant to attack and doesn't leave the key on disk and tape where it can be stolen. Considering that the agent is still vulnerable to being misused via the filesystem, and that it is intended to run indefinitely, the advantages of this method are debatable. Still, we recommend the agent method as the most secure and flexible strategy for automated SSH usage in a security-conscious environment.

11.1.3   Hostbased Authentication

If security concerns are relatively light, consider hostbased authentication for batch jobs. In this case, the "credentials" are the operating system's notion of a process's uid: the identity under which a process is running, which determines what rights it has over protected objects. An attacker need only manage to get control of a process running under your uid, to impersonate you to a remote SSH server. If he breaks root on the client, this is particularly simple, since root may create processes under any uid. The real crux, though, is the client host key: if the attacker gets that, he can sign bogus authentication requests presenting himself as any user at all, and *sshd* will believe them.

Hostbased authentication is in many ways the least secure SSH authentication method. [3.4.3.6] It leaves systems vulnerable to transitive compromise: if an attacker gains access to an account on host H, she immediately has access to the same account on all machines that trust H, with no further effort. Also, hostbased configuration is limited, fragile, and easy to get wrong. Public-key authentication affords both greater security and flexibility, particularly since you can restrict the commands that may be invoked and the client hosts that may connect, using its forced commands and other options in the authorization file.

Of course, if your security policy permits and you're already using hostbased for general user authentication, then you're all set for batch jobs too. However if you're using something stronger for user authentication, and you're considering the hostbased method for batch jobs, then we recommend that you:

* Restrict its use to the batch accounts *only* (via */etc/shosts.equiv* rules); continue to use stronger methods for interactive authentication.
* Use only the SSH-specific configuration files */etc/shosts.equiv* and *~/.shosts*, and not the legacy files */etc/hosts.equiv* and *~/.rhosts*. This avoids any accidental changes to the behavior of wildly insecure mechanisms like *rcmd* and *rsh*.
* Set options such as OpenSSH IgnoreRhosts and IgnoreUserKnownHosts, and Tectia AllowSHosts/DenySHosts, if possible. Since per-account hostbased configuration can override the systemwide files, it's best to disable them.

11.1.4 Kerberos

There's no reason to deploy Kerberos [11.4] solely in order to support batch jobs; it has no special overall advantage in this regard. However, if you're already using Kerberos, you might want to keep things simple by using it for batch as well as interactive jobs. Unattended Kerberos usage has similar security properties to using a plaintext SSH key as described earlier: the Kerberos principal's key is stored on disk, can be similarly strong since it does not have to be derived from a user-memorable passphrase, and is not revealed in the authentication process.

To do this, use the *kadmin* command:

```
$ kadmin -q "ktadd -k keytab principal"
```

to store the principal's key in the file *keytab*, and protect that file appropriately (e.g., so that only the Unix batch account can read it). The batch job can then call *kinit*:

```
$ kinit -k -t keytab
```

to obtain Kerberos credentials for that principal.

We suggest the following arrangement:

- Arrange that the *keytab* file does not travel insecurely over the network, e.g., on an unsecured NFS filesystem. Perhaps also arrange that it is not dumped to backup tapes.
- Create separate principals for batch jobs; do not use existing user principals.
- Create a random key for the batch principal using the *kadmin* option, addprinc -randkey.
- If feasible, periodically change these keys. An advantage of the Kerberos system is that this does not require changing corresponding authorization entries, as changing a simple SSH key would require updating the matching *authorized_ keys* files. Any running jobs will have to be restarted, though, since their credentials will become invalid.
- As always, restrict what the batch principal can do on the server side, here using the Kerberos *~/.k5login* or *~/.k5users* files.

Kerberos-5 contains support for long-running jobs with "renewable" tickets, but note that this is still intended for jobs started interactively; it just supports those that may run for a long time. It is not intended as a solution for truly unattended jobs.

11.1.5 General Precautions for Batch Jobs

Regardless of the method you choose, some extra precautions will help secure your environment.

11.1.5.1 Least-privilege accounts

The account under which the automated job runs should have only those privileges needed to run the job, and no more. Don't run every batch job as root just because it's convenient. Arrange your filesystem and other protections so that the job can run as a less-privileged user. Remember that unattended remote jobs increase the risk of account compromise, so take the extra trouble to avoid the root account whenever possible.

11.1.5.2 Separate, locked-down automation accounts

Create accounts that are used solely for automation. Try not to run system batch jobs in a user account, since you might not be able to reduce its privileges to the small set necessary to support the job. In many cases, an automation account doesn't even need to admit interactive logins. If jobs running under its uid are created directly by the batch job manager (e.g., *cron*), the account doesn't need a password and should be locked.

11.1.5.3 Restricted-use keys

As much as possible, restrict the target account to perform only the work needed for the job. With public-key authentication, automated jobs should use keys that aren't shared by interactive logins. Imagine that someday you might need to eliminate the key for security reasons, and you don't want to affect other users or jobs by this change. For maximum control, use a separate key for each automated task. Additionally, place all possible restrictions on the key by setting options in the authorization file. [8.2] The command option restricts the key to running only the needed remote command, and the from option restricts usage to appropriate client hosts. Consider always adding the following options as well, if they don't interfere with the job:

```
no-port-forwarding,no-X11-forwarding,no-agent-forwarding,no-pty
```

These make it harder to misuse the key should it be stolen.

If you're using hostbased authentication, these restrictions aren't available. In this case, it's best to use a special shell for the account, which limits the commands that may be executed. Since *sshd* uses the target account's shell to run any commands on the user's behalf, this is an effective restriction. One standard tool is the Unix "restricted shell." Confusingly, the restricted shell is usually named "rsh," but has nothing to do with the Berkeley r-command for opening a remote shell, *rsh*.

11.1.5.4 Useful ssh options

When running SSH commands in a batch job, it's a good idea to use these options:

```
ssh -q -o 'BatchMode yes'
```

The *–q* option is for quiet mode, preventing SSH from printing a variety of warnings. This is sometimes necessary if you're using SSH as a pipe from one program to another. Otherwise, the SSH warnings may be interpreted as remote program output and confuse the local program. [7.4.17]

The BatchMode keyword tells SSH not to prompt the user, who in this case doesn't exist. This makes error reporting more straightforward, eliminating some confusing SSH messages about failing to access a tty. [7.4.6.4]

11.1.6 Recommendations

Our recommended method for best security with unattended SSH operation is public-key authentication with keys stored in an agent. If that isn't feasible, hostbased or plaintext-key authentication may be used instead; your local security concerns and needs will determine which is preferable, using the foregoing discussion as a guideline.

To the extent possible, use separate accounts and keys for each job. By doing so, you limit the damage caused by compromising any one account, or stealing any one key. But of course, there is a complexity trade-off here; if you have 100 batch jobs, separate accounts or keys for each one may be too much to deal with. In that case, partition the jobs into categories according to the privileges they need, and use a separate account and/or key for each category of job.

You can ease the burden of multiple keys by applying a little automation to the business of loading them. The keys can all be stored under the same passphrase: a script prompts for the passphrase, then runs *ssh-add* multiple times to add the various keys. Or they have different passphrases, and the human inserts a diskette containing the passphrases when loading them. Perhaps the passphrase list itself is encrypted under a single password provided by the human. For that matter, the keys themselves can be kept on the key diskette and not stored on the filesystem at all: whatever fits your needs and paranoia level.

11.2 FTP and SSH

One of the most frequently asked questions about SSH is, "How can I use port forwarding to secure FTP?" If the forwarding in question is the traditional sort of static port forwarding provided by SSH clients such as OpenSSH, then the short answer is that you usually can't, at least not completely, as we will explain in detail in this section. Such port forwarding can protect your account password, but usually not the files being transferred. Still, protecting your password is a big win, since the most egregious problem with FTP is that it usually reveals your password to network snoopers.

It's worth noting that FTP can in fact be used securely on its own. Both FTP and Telnet are famously considered "insecure," but it's more accurate to say that they are simply *used* insecurely most of the time. Both protocols allow the use of strong authentication and encryption methods, such as SSL or Kerberos. However, the vast majority of FTP and Telnet servers in the world do not provide these features, and so we are left trying to secure them as best we can with other tools, such as SSH.

Before trying to figure out how to forward FTP over SSH, you should first ask yourself whether you really need to use FTP at all. If possible, it's far less trouble to simply use a file-transfer method that works easily over SSH, such as *scp*, *sftp*, *rsync*, etc. (and remember that SFTP and FTP have *nothing* to do with one another, save the acronym). If you're going to secure FTP end-to-end with SSH, then the FTP server must already be running an SSH server—which means it shouldn't be hard to make the requisite files available via SSH as well. But the real world is messy, and you might be stuck with FTP.

11.2.1 FTP-Specific Tools for SSH

As we will describe, the FTP protocol is not amenable to standard SSH port forwarding. There are SSH clients, however, with features tailored specifically for dealing with FTP. We describe two of them here.

11.2.1.1 VanDyke's SecureFX

VanDyke Software (*http://www.vandyke.com/*) has a useful Windows product, specifically designed to forward FTP over SSH, data connections and all: SecureFX. It is a specialized combination of SSH-2 and FTP clients. SecureFX acts as a GUI FTP client, first creating an SSH connection, then logging into the remote FTP server via an SSH channel. Whenever it needs an FTP data connection, it dynamically creates the needed *tcpip-direct* channels (for passive mode) or remote forwardings (active mode); to the remote FTP server, SecureFX looks like an FTP client connecting from the same host. SecureFX works very smoothly and we recommend the product.

SecureFX is a great solution if you can choose your client. However, perhaps you need to secure FTP traffic in an existing system, where you can't replace the client side. In this case, Tectia has a feature that will help.

11.2.1.2 Tectia client

The Tectia software has a special FTP-aware port-forwarding mode. In the GUI Windows client, when configuring tunneling in the Add New Outgoing Tunnel dialog box, set Type = FTP. In the command-line version, FTP forwarding works this way:

```
# Tectia
$ ssh -L ftp/1234:localhost:21 server
```

This forwards local port 1234 to an FTP server running on the standard FTP port (21), on the same machine as the SSH server. After connecting with a regular FTP client to the forwarded port, FTP data-transfer commands such as *ls*, *get*, *put*, etc., should work normally, in either FTP's "active" or "passive" mode. Tectia intercepts and alters FTP command traffic, particularly the PORT and PASV commands and their responses. It does this to "fool" the FTP client and server into using SSH-forwarded ports it creates for data channels, instead of the direct connections each side intends to make.

11.2.2   Static Port Forwarding and FTP: A Study in Pain

So far, we've described a number of alternatives for dealing with SSH and FTP. If you're particularly unlucky, though, you might be stuck having to secure FTP with SSH, without any of these options—for instance, using OpenSSH, which has no FTP-specific forwarding features. If so, this section is for you. And even if you're not stuck with this unenviable task, you may find the discussion useful for understanding the general problem and limitations. Or simply for the morbid fascination of it all.

Here, we explain in detail what you can and can't do with FTP and SSH, and why. Some difficulties are due to limitations of FTP, not only when interacting with SSH, but also in the presence of firewalls and network address translation (NAT). We will discuss each of these situations, since firewalls and NAT are common nowadays, and their presence might be the reason you're trying to forward FTP securely. If you are a system administrator responsible for both SSH and these networking components, we will try to guide you to a general understanding that will help you design and troubleshoot entire systems.

Depending on your network environment, different problems may arise when combining SSH with FTP. Since we can't cover every possible environment, we describe each problem in isolation, illustrating its symptoms and recommending solutions. If you have multiple problems occurring simultaneously, the software behavior you observe might not match the examples we've given. We recommend reading the entire case study once (at least cursorily) before experimenting with your system, so you will have an idea of the problems you might encounter. Afterward, go ahead and try the examples at your computer.

11.2.3   The FTP Protocol

To understand the problems between FTP and SSH, you need to understand a bit about the FTP protocol. Most TCP services involve a single connection from client to server on a known, server-side port. FTP, however, involves multiple connections in both directions, mostly to unpredictable port numbers:

- A single *control connection* for carrying commands from the client and responses from the server. It connects on TCP port 21 and persists for the entire FTP session.

- A number of *data connections* for transferring files and other data, such as directory listings. For each file transfer, a new data connection is opened and closed, and each one may be on a different port. These data connections may come from the client or the server.

Let's run a typical FTP client and view the control connection. We'll use debug mode (*ftp –d*) to make visible the FTP protocol commands the client sends on the control connection, since they aren't normally displayed. Debug mode prints these commands preceded by "--->". For example:

```
---> USER res
```

You'll also see responses from the server, which the client prints by default. These are preceded by a numerical code:

```
230 User res logged in.
```

Here's a session in which the user res connects to an FTP server, logs in, and attempts to change directory twice, once successfully and once not:

```
$ ftp -d aaor.lionaka.net
Connected to aaor.lionaka.net.
220 aaor.lionaka.net FTP server (SunOS 5.7) ready.
---> SYST
215 UNIX Type: L8 Version: SUNOS
Remote system type is UNIX.
Using binary mode to transfer files.
ftp> user res
---> USER res
331 Password required for res.
Password:
---> PASS XXXX
230 User res logged in.
ftp> cd rep
---> CWD rep
250 CWD command successful.
ftp> cd utopia
---> CWD utopia
550 utopia: No such file or directory.
ftp> quit
---> QUIT
221 Goodbye.
```

The control connection can be secured by standard port forwarding because it is on a known port (21). [9.2] In contrast, the destination port numbers for data connections are generally not known in advance, so setting up SSH forwarding for these connections is far more difficult. There's a second standard port number associated with FTP, the *ftp-data* port (20). But this is only the source port for data connections coming from the server; nothing ever listens on it.

Surprisingly, the data connections generally go in the opposite direction from the control one; that is, the server makes a TCP connection back to the client in order to transfer data. The ports on which these connections occur can be negotiated dynamically by the FTP client and server, and doing so involves sending explicit IP address information inside the FTP protocol. These features of usual FTP operation can cause difficulties when forwarding SSH connections and in other scenarios involving firewalls or NAT.

An alternative FTP mode, called *passive mode*, addresses one of these problems: it reverses the sense of the data connections so that they go from the client to the server. Passive mode is a matter of FTP client behavior, and so is determined by a client setting. The behavior of setting up data connections from the server to the client, which we will call *active-mode* FTP, is traditionally the default in FTP clients, although that's changing. With a command-line client, the *passive* command switches to passive mode. The internal command that the client sends the server to tell it to enter passive mode is PASV. We discuss specific problems, and how passive mode solves them, in upcoming sections. Figure 11-1 summarizes the workings of passive and active FTP.

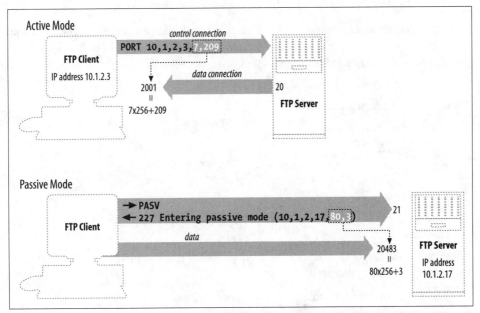

Figure 11-1. Basic FTP operation: control connection and active- versus passive-mode transfers

11.2.4 Forwarding the Control Connection

Since the FTP control connection is just a single, persistent TCP connection to a well-known port, you can forward it through SSH. As usual, the FTP server machine must be running an SSH server, and you must have an account on it that you may access via SSH (see Figure 11-2).

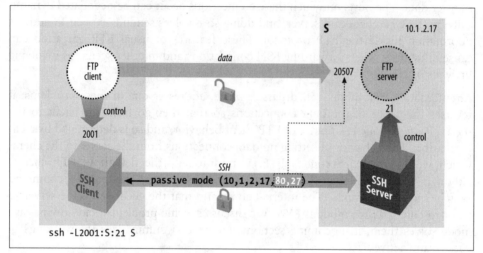

Figure 11-2. Forwarding the control connection

Suppose you are logged into the machine *client* and want to connect securely to an FTP server on the machine *server*. To forward the FTP control connection, run a port-forwarding command on *client:**

```
client% ssh -L2001:server:21 server
```

Then, to use the forwarded port:

```
client% ftp localhost 2001
Connected to localhost
220 server FTP server (SunOS 5.7) ready.
Password:
230 User res logged in.
ftp> passive
Passive mode on.
ftp> ls
...and so on
```

There are two important things to notice about the commands we just recommended. We will discuss each.

- The target of the forwarding is *server*, not *localhost*.
- The client uses passive mode.

---

* If you're using the popular *ncftp* client, run this instead: *ncftp ftp://client:2001*.

11.2.4.1 Choosing the forwarding target

We chose *server* as the target of our forwarding, not *localhost* (i.e., we didn't use *–L2001:localhost:21*). This is contrary to our previous advice, which was to use *localhost* where possible as the forwarding target. [9.2.8] Well, that technique isn't advisable here. Here's what can happen if you do:

```
client% ftp localhost 2001
Connected to client
220 client FTP server (SunOS 5.7) ready.
331 Password required for res.
Password:
230 User res logged in.
ftp> ls
200 PORT command successful.
425 Can't build data connection: Cannot assign requested address.
ftp>
```

The problem is a bit obscure but can be revealed by an execution trace of the FTP server as it responds to the *ls* command. The following output was produced by the Linux *strace* command:[*]

```
so_socket(2, 2, 0, "", 1)                     = 5
bind(5, 0x0002D614, 16, 3)                    = 0
        AF_INET  name = 127.0.0.1  port = 20
connect(5, 0x0002D5F4, 16, 1)                 Err#126 EADDRNOTAVAIL
        AF_INET  name = 192.168.10.1  port = 2845
write(1, " 4 2 5   C a n ' t   b u".., 67)    = 67
```

The FTP server is trying to make a TCP connection to the correct client address but from the wrong socket: the ftp-data port on its loopback address, 127.0.0.1. The loopback interface can talk only to other loopback addresses on the same machine. TCP knows this and responds with the error "address not available" (EADDRNOT-AVAIL). The FTP server is being careful to originate the data connection from the same address to which the client made the control connection. Here, the control connection has been forwarded through SSH; so to the FTP server, it appears to come from the local host. And because we used the loopback address as the forwarding target, the source address of that leg of the forwarded path (from *sshd* to *ftpd*) is also the loopback address. To eliminate the problem, use the server's nonloopback IP address as the target; this causes the FTP server to originate data connections from that address.

You might try to solve this problem using passive mode, since then the server wouldn't originate any connections. But if you try:

```
ftp> passive
Passive mode on.
```

---

[*] If you're on a Solaris 2 (SunOS 5) system, the corresponding operating system-supplied program is called *truss*. There is also an *strace* program with Solaris, but it is completely unrelated. Solaris 1 (SunOS 4 and earlier) has a *trace* command, and BSD has *ktrace*.

```
ftp> ls
227 Entering Passive Mode (127,0,0,1,128,133)
ftp: connect: Connection refused
ftp>
```

In this case, the failure is a slightly different manifestation of the same problem. This time, the server listens for an incoming data connection from the client, but again, it thinks the client is local, so it listens on its loopback address. It sends this socket (address 127.0.0.1, port 32901) to the client, and the client tries to connect to it. But this causes the client to try to connect to port 32901 on the client host, not the server! Nothing is listening there, of course, so the connection is refused.

11.2.4.2 Using passive mode

Note that we had to put the client into passive mode. You will see later that passive mode is beneficial for FTP in general, because it avoids some common firewall and NAT problems. Here, however, it's used because of a specific FTP/SSH problem; if you didn't, here's what happens:

```
$ ftp -d localhost 2001
Connected to localhost.
220 server FTP server (SunOS 5.7) ready.
---> USER res
331 Password required for res.
Password:
---> PASS XXXX
230 User res logged in.
ftp> ls
---> PORT 127,0,0,1,11,50
200 PORT command successful.
---> LIST
425 Can't build data connection: Connection refused.
ftp>
```

This is a mirror image of the problem we saw when localhost was the forwarding target, but this time it happens on the client side. The client supplies a socket for the server to connect to, and since it thinks the server is on the local host, that socket is on the loopback address. This causes the server to try connecting to its local host instead of the client machine.

Passive mode can't always be used: the FTP client or server might not support it, or server-side firewall/NAT considerations may prevent it (you'll see an example of that shortly). If so, you can use the GatewayPorts feature of SSH and solve this problem as we did the previous one: use the host's real IP address instead of the loopback. To wit:

```
client% ssh -g -L2001:server:21 server
```

Then connect to the client machine by name, rather than to localhost:

```
client% ftp client 2001
```

This connects to the SSH proxy on the client's nonloopback address, causing the FTP client to listen on that address for data connections. The –g option has security implications, however. [9.2.1.1]

Of course, as we mentioned earlier, it's often the case that active-mode FTP isn't usable. It's perfectly possible that your local firewall/NAT setup requires passive mode, but you can't use it. In that case, you're just out of luck. Put your data on a diskette and contribute to the local bicycle-courier economy.

The various problems we have described, while common, depend on your particular Unix flavor and FTP implementation. For example, some FTP servers fail even before connecting to a loopback socket; they see the client's PORT command and reject it, printing "illegal PORT command". If you understand the reasons for the various failure modes, however, you will learn to recognize them in different guises.

11.2.4.3 The "PASV port theft" problem

Trying to use FTP with SSH can be sort of like playing a computer dungeon game: you find yourself in a twisty maze of TCP connections, all of which look alike and none of which seem to go where you want. Even if you follow all of our advice so far, and understand and avoid the pitfalls we've mentioned, the connection might still fail:

```
ftp> passive
Passive mode on.
ftp> ls
connecting to 192.168.10.1:6670
Connected to 192.168.10.1 port 6670
425 Possible PASV port theft, cannot open data connection.
! Retrieve of folder listing failed
```

Assuming you don't decide to give up entirely and move into a less irritating career, you may want to know, "What now?" The problem here is a security feature of the FTP server, specifically the popular *wu-ftpd* from Washington University. (See *http://www.wu-ftpd.org/*. This feature might be implemented in other FTP servers, but we haven't seen it.) The server accepts an incoming data connection from the client, then notices that its source address isn't the same as that of the control connection (which was forwarded through SSH and thus comes from the server host). It concludes that an attack is in progress! The FTP server believes someone has been monitoring your FTP control connection, seen the server response to the PASV command containing the listening socket, and jumped in to connect to it before the legitimate client can do so. So, the server drops the connection and reports the suspected "port theft" (see Figure 11-3).

There's no way around this problem but to stop the server from performing this check. It's a problematic feature to begin with, since it prevents not only attacks, but also legitimate FTP operations. For example, passive-mode operation was originally intended to allow an FTP client to effect a file transfer between two remote servers

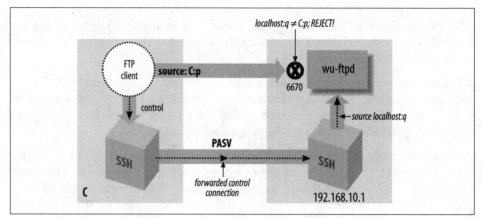

Figure 11-3. "PASV port theft"

directly, rather than first fetching the file to the client and then sending it to the second server. This isn't a common practice, but it is part of the protocol design, and the "port theft" check of *wu-ftpd* prevents its use. You can turn it off by recompiling *wu-ftpd* without FIGHT_PASV_PORT_RACE (use *configure --disable-pasvip*). You can also leave the check on but allow certain accounts to use alternate IP addresses for data connections, with the *pasv-allow* and *port-allow* configuration statements. See the *ftpaccess*(5) manpage for details. Note that these features are relatively recent additions to *wu-ftpd* and aren't in earlier versions.

11.2.5 FTP, Firewalls, and Passive Mode

Recall that in active mode, the FTP data connections go in the opposite direction than you might expect—from the server back to the client. This usual mode of operation (shown in Figure 11-4) often develops problems in the presence of a firewall. Suppose the client is behind a firewall that allows all outbound connections but restricts inbound ones. Then the client can establish a control connection to log in and issue commands, but data-transfer commands such as *ls*, *get*, and *put* will fail, because the firewall blocks the data connections coming back to the client machine. Simple packet-filtering firewalls can't be configured to allow these connections, because they appear as separate TCP destinations to random ports, with no obvious relation to the established FTP control connection.* The failure might happen

---

* More sophisticated firewalls can take care of this problem. These products are a cross between an application-level proxy and a packet filter and are often called "transparent proxies" or "stateful packet filters." Such a firewall understands the FTP protocol and watches for FTP control connections. When it sees a PORT command issued by an FTP client, it dynamically opens a temporary hole in the firewall, allowing the specified FTP data connection back through. This hole disappears automatically after a short time and can only be between the socket given in the PORT command and the server's ftp-data socket. These products often also do NAT and can transparently deal with the FTP/NAT problems we describe next.

---

quickly with the message "connection refused," or the connection might hang for a while and eventually fail. This depends on whether the firewall explicitly rejects the connection attempt with an ICMP or TCP RST message, or just silently drops the packets. Note that this problem can occur whether or not SSH is forwarding the control connection.

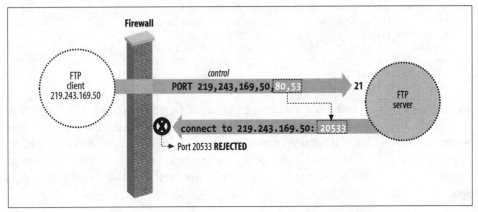

Figure 11-4. FTP client behind a firewall

Passive mode usually solves this problem, reversing the direction of data connections so they go from the client to the server. Unfortunately, not all FTP client or servers implement passive-mode transfers. Command-line FTP clients generally use the passive command to toggle passive-mode transfers on and off; if it doesn't recognize that command, it probably doesn't do passive mode. If the client supports passive mode but the server doesn't, you may see a message like "PASV: command not understood" from the server. PASV is the FTP protocol command that instructs the server to listen for data connections. Finally, even if passive mode solves the firewall problem, it doesn't help with SSH forwarding, since the ports in question are still dynamically chosen.

Here is an example of the firewall problem, blocking the return data connections:

```
$ ftp lasciate.ogni.speranza.org
Connected to lasciate.ogni.speranza.org
220 ProFTPD 1.2.0pre6 Server (Lasciate FTP Server) [lasciate.ogni.speranza.org]
331 Password required for slade.
Password:
230 User slade logged in.
Remote system type is UNIX.
Using binary mode to transfer files.
ftp> ls
200 PORT command successful.
[...long wait here...]
425 Can't build data connection: Connection timed out
```

Passive mode comes to the rescue:

```
ftp> passive
Passive mode on.
ftp> ls
227 Entering Passive Mode (10,25,15,1,12,65)
150 Opening ASCII mode data connection for file list
drwxr-x--x  21 slade    web          2048 May  8 23:29 .
drwxr-xr-x 111 root     wheel       10240 Apr 26 00:09 ..
-rw-------   1 slade    other         106 May  8 15:22 .cshrc
-rw-------   1 slade    other       31384 Aug 18  1997 .emacs
226 Transfer complete.
ftp>
```

Now, in discussing the problem of using FTP through a firewall, we didn't mention SSH at all; it is a problem inherent in the FTP protocol and firewalls. However, even when forwarding the FTP control connection through SSH, this problem still applies, since the difficulty is with the data connection, not the control, and those don't go through SSH. So, this is yet another reason why you will normally want to use passive mode with FTP and SSH.

11.2.6   FTP and Network Address Translation (NAT)

Passive-mode transfers can also work around another common problem with FTP: its difficulties with network address translation, or NAT. NAT is the practice of connecting two networks by a gateway that rewrites the source and destination addresses of packets as they pass through. One benefit is that you may connect a network to the Internet or change ISPs without having to renumber the network (that is, change all your IP addresses). It also allows sharing a limited number of routable Internet addresses among a larger number of machines on a network using private addresses not routed on the Internet. This flavor of NAT is often called *masquerading*.

Suppose your FTP client is on a machine with a private address usable only on your local network, and you connect to the Internet through a NAT gateway. The client can establish a control connection to an external FTP server. However, there will be a problem if the client attempts the usual reverse-direction data connections. The client, ignorant of the NAT gateway, tells the server (via a PORT command) to connect to a socket containing the client's private address. Since that address isn't usable on the remote side, the server generally responds "no route to host" and the connection will fail.* Figure 11-5 illustrates this situation. Passive mode gets around this problem as well, since the server never has to connect back to the client and so the client's address is irrelevant.

---

* It could be worse, too. The server could also use private addressing, and if you're unlucky, the client's private address might coincidentally match a completely different machine on the server side. It's unlikely, though, that a server-side machine would happen to listen on the random port picked by your FTP client, so this would probably just generate a "connection refused" error.

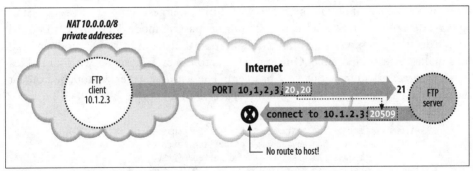

Figure 11-5. Client-side NAT prevents active-mode FTP transfers

So far, we've listed three situations requiring passive-mode FTP: control connection forwarding, client inside a firewall, and client behind NAT. Given these potential problems with active-mode FTP, and that there's no down side to passive mode that we know of, we recommend always using passive-mode FTP if you can.

11.2.6.1 Server-side NAT issues

The NAT problem we just discussed was a client-side issue. A more difficult problem can occur if the FTP server is behind a NAT gateway, and you're forwarding the FTP control connection through SSH.

First, let's understand the basic problem without SSH in the picture. If the server is behind a NAT gateway, then you have the mirror-image problem to the one discussed earlier. Before, active-mode transfers didn't work because the client supplied its internal, non-NAT'd address to the server in the PORT command, and this address wasn't reachable. In the new situation, passive-mode transfers don't work because the server supplies its internal-only address to the client in the PASV command response, and that address is unreachable to the client (see Figure 11-6).

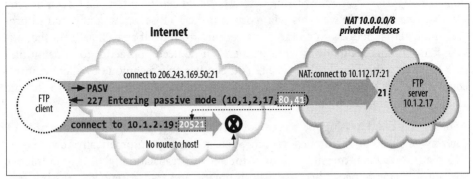

Figure 11-6. Server-side NAT prevents passive-mode FTP transfers

The earlier answer was to use passive mode; here the simplest answer is the reverse: use active mode. Unfortunately, this isn't very helpful. If the server is intended for general Net access, it should be made useful to the largest number of people. Since client-side NAT and firewall setups requiring passive-mode FTP are common, it won't do to use a server-side NAT configuration that requires active mode instead; this makes access impossible. One approach is to use an FTP server with special features designed to address this very problem. The *wu-ftpd* server we touched on earlier has such a feature. Quoting from the *ftpaccess*(5) manpage:

```
passive address <externalip> <cidr>
        Allows control of the address reported in response to
        a PASV command.  When any control connection matching
        the <cidr> requests a passive data connection (PASV),
        the <externalip> address is reported. NOTE: this
        does not change the address the daemon actually lis-
        tens on,  only  the  address reported to the client.
        This feature allows the daemon to  operate  correctly
        behind IP-renumbering firewalls.

For example:
 passive address 10.0.1.15    10.0.0.0/8
 passive address 192.168.1.5 0.0.0.0/0

Clients  connecting  from  the  class-A network 10 will be
told the passive connection  is  listening  on  IP-address
10.0.1.15  while all others will be told the connection is
listening on 192.168.1.5

Multiple passive addresses may be specified to handle com-
plex, or multi-gatewayed, networks.
```

This handles the problem quite neatly, unless you happen to be forwarding the FTP control connection through SSH. Site administrators arrange for FTP control connections originating from outside the server's private network to have external addresses reported in the PASV responses. But the forwarded control connection appears to come from the server host itself, rather than the outside network. Control connections coming from inside the private network *should* get the internal address, not the external one. The only way this will work is if the FTP server is configured to provide the external address to connections coming from itself as well as from the outside. This is actually quite workable, as there's little need in practice to transmit files by FTP from a machine back to itself. You can use this technique to allow control-connection forwarding in the presence of server-side NAT or suggest it to the site administrators if you have this problem.

Another way of addressing the server-side NAT problem is to use an intelligent NAT gateway of the type mentioned earlier. Such a gateway automatically rewrites the FTP control traffic in transit to account for address translation. This is an attractive solution in some respects, because it is automatic and transparent; there is less custom work in setting up the servers behind the gateway, and there are fewer dependencies between the server and network configurations. As it happens, though, this solution is actually worse for our purposes than the server-level one. This technique relies on the gateway's ability to recognize and alter the FTP control connection as it passes through. But such manipulation is exactly what SSH is designed to prevent! If the control connection is forwarded through SSH, the gateway doesn't know there is a control connection, because it's embedded as a channel inside the SSH session. The control connection isn't a separate TCP connection of its own; it's on the SSH port rather than the FTP port. The gateway can't read it because it's encrypted, and the gateway can't modify it even if the gateway can read it, because SSH provides integrity protection. If you're in this situation—the client must use passive-mode FTP, and the server is behind a NAT gateway doing FTP control traffic rewriting— you must convince the server administrator to use a server-level technique in addition to the gateway, specifically to allow forwarding. Otherwise, it's not going to happen, and we see trucks filled with tapes in your future, or perhaps HTTP over SSL with PUT commands.

We have now concluded our discussion of forwarding the control connection of FTP, securing your login name, password, and FTP commands. If that's all you want to do, you are done with this case study. We're going to continue, however, and delve into the murky depths of data connections. You'll need a technical background for this material as we cover minute details and little-known modes of FTP. (You might even wonder if we've accidentally inserted a portion of an FTP book into the SSH book.) Forward, brave reader!

11.2.7   All About Data Connections

Ask most SSH users about forwarding the FTP data connection, and they'll respond, "Sorry, it's not possible." Well, it *is* possible. The method we've discovered is obscure, inconvenient, and not usually worth the effort, but it works. Before we can explain it, we must first discuss the three major ways that FTP accomplishes file transfers between client and server:

- The usual method
- Passive-mode transfers
- Transfers using the default data ports

We'll just touch briefly on the first two, since we've already discussed them; we'll just amplify with a bit more detail. Then we'll discuss the third mode, which is the least known and the one you need if you really, really want to forward your FTP data connections.

11.2.7.1 The usual method of file transfer

Most FTP clients attempt data transfers in the following way. After establishing the control connection and authenticating, the user issues a command to transfer a file. Suppose the command is get fichier.txt, which asks to transfer the file *fichier.txt* from the server to the client. In response to this command, the client selects a free local TCP socket, call it C, and starts listening on it. It then issues a PORT command to the FTP server, specifying the socket C. After the server acknowledges this, the client issues the command RETR fichier.txt, which tells the server to connect to the previously given socket (C) and send the contents of that file over the new data connection. The client accepts the connection to C, reads the data, and writes it into a local file also called *fichier.txt*. When done, the data connection is closed. Here is a transcript of such a session:

```
$ ftp -d aaor.lionaka.net
Connected to aaor.lionaka.net.
220 aaor.lionaka.net FTP server (SunOS 5.7) ready.
---> USER res
331 Password required for res.
Password:
---> PASS XXXX
230 User res logged in.
---> SYST
215 UNIX Type: L8 Version: SUNOS
Remote system type is UNIX.
Using binary mode to transfer files.
ftp> get fichier.txt
local: fichier.txt remote: fichier.txt
---> TYPE I
200 Type set to I.
---> PORT 219,243,169,50,9,226
200 PORT command successful.
---> RETR fichier.txt
150 Binary data connection for fichier.txt (219.243.169.50,2530) (10876 bytes).
226 Binary Transfer complete.
10876 bytes received in 0.013 seconds (7.9e+02 Kbytes/s)
ftp> quit
```

Note the PORT command, PORT 219,243,169,50,9,226. This says the client is listening on IP address 219.243.169.50, port 2530 = (9<<8)+226; the final two integers in the comma-separated list are the 16-bit port number represented as two 8-bit bytes, most significant byte first. The server response beginning with "150" confirms establishment of the data connection to that socket. What isn't shown is that the source port of that connection is always the standard FTP data port, port 20 (remember that FTP servers listen for incoming control connections on port 21).

There are two important points to note about this process:

- The data connection socket is chosen on the fly by the client. This prevents forwarding, since you can't know the port number ahead of time to forward it with SSH. You can get around this problem by establishing the FTP process "by hand" using *telnet*. That is, choose a data socket beforehand and forward it with SSH, *telnet* to the FTP server yourself, and issue all the necessary FTP protocol commands by hand, using your forwarded port in the PORT command. But this can hardly be called convenient.

- Remember that the data connection is made in the *reverse direction* from the control connection; it goes from the server back to the client. As we discussed earlier in this chapter, the usual workaround is to use passive mode.

11.2.7.2 Passive mode in depth

Recall that in a passive-mode transfer, the client initiates a connection to the server. Specifically, instead of listening on a local socket and issuing a PORT command to the server, the client issues a PASV command. In response, the server selects a socket on its side to listen on and reveals it to the client in the response to the PASV command. The client then connects to that socket to form the data connection, and issues the file-transfer command over the control connection. With command line–based clients, the usual way to do passive-mode transfers is to use the *passive* command. Again, an example:

```
$ ftp -d aaor.lionaka.net
Connected to aaor.lionaka.net.
220 aaor.lionaka.net FTP server (SunOS 5.7) ready.
---> USER res
331 Password required for res.
Password:
---> PASS XXXX
230 User res logged in.
---> SYST
215 UNIX Type: L8 Version: SUNOS
Remote system type is UNIX.
Using binary mode to transfer files.
ftp> passive
Passive mode on.
ftp> ls
---> PASV
227 Entering Passive Mode (219,243,169,52,128,73)
---> LIST
150 ASCII data connection for /bin/ls (219.243.169.50,2538) (0 bytes).
total 360075
drwxr-xr-x98  res     500          7168 May  5 17:13 .
dr-xr-xr-x   2 root    root            2 May  5 01:47 ..
-rw-rw-r--   1 res     500           596 Apr 25  1999 .FVWM2-errors
-rw-------   1 res     500           332 Mar 24 01:36 .ICEauthority
-rw-------   1 res     500            50 May  5 01:45 .Xauthority
-rw-r--r--   1 res     500          1511 Apr 11 00:08 .Xdefaults
226 ASCII Transfer complete.
ftp> quit
---> QUIT
221 Goodbye.
```

Note that after the user gives the *ls* command, the client sends PASV instead of PORT. The server responds with the socket on which it will listen. The client issues the LIST command to list the contents of the current remote directory, and connects to the remote data socket; the server accepts and confirms the connection, then transfers the directory listing over the new connection.

An interesting historical note, which we alluded to earlier, is that the PASV command wasn't originally intended for this use; it was designed to let an FTP client direct a file transfer between two remote servers. The client makes control connections to two remote servers, issues a PASV command to one causing it to listen on a socket, issues a PORT command to the other telling it to connect to the other server on that socket, then issues the data-transfer command (STOR, RETR, etc.). These days, most people don't even know this is possible, and will pull a file from one server to the local machine, and transfer it again to get it to the second remote machine. It's so uncommon that many FTP clients don't support this mode, and some servers prevent its use for security reasons. [11.2.4.3]

11.2.7.3 FTP with the default data ports

The third file-transfer mode occurs if the client issues neither a PORT nor a PASV command. In this case, the server initiates the data connection from the well-known ftp-data port (20) to the source socket of the control connection, on which the client must be listening (these sockets are the "default data ports" for the FTP session). The usual way to use this mode is with the FTP client command *sendport*, which switches on and off the client's feature of using a PORT command for each data transfer. For this mode, we want it turned off, and it is generally on by default. So, the sequence of steps is this:

1. The client initiates the control connection from local socket C to server:21.

2. The user gives the *sendport* command, and then a data-transfer command, such as *put* or *ls*. The FTP client begins listening on socket C for an incoming TCP connection.

3. The server determines the socket C at the other end of the control connection. It doesn't need the client to send this explicitly via the FTP protocol, since it can just ask TCP for it (e.g., with the getpeername( ) sockets API routine). It then opens a connection from its ftp-data port to C, and sends or receives the requested data over that connection.

Now, this is certainly a simpler way of doing things than using a different socket for each data transfer, and so it begs the question of why PORT commands are the norm. If you try this out, you will discover why. First off, it might fail on the client side with the message "bind: Address already in use". And even if it does work, it does so only once. A second *ls* elicits another address-related error, this time from the server:

```
aaor% ftp syrinx.lionaka.net
Connected to syrinx.lionaka.net.
220 syrinx.lionaka.net FTP server (Version wu-2.5.0(1) Tue Sep 21 16:48:12 EDT
331 Password required for res.
Password:
230 User res logged in.
ftp> sendport
Use of PORT cmds off.
ftp> ls
```

```
150 Opening ASCII mode data connection for file list.
keep
fichier.txt
226 Transfer complete.
19 bytes received in 0.017 seconds (1.07 Kbytes/s)
ftp> ls
425 Can't build data connection: Cannot assign requested address.
ftp> quit
```

These problems are due to a technicality of the TCP protocol. In this scenario, every data connection is between the same two sockets, server:ftp-data and C. Since a TCP connection is fully specified by the pair of source and destination sockets, these connections are indistinguishable as far as TCP is concerned; they are different incarnations of the same connection and can't exist at the same time. In fact, to guarantee that packets belonging to two different incarnations of a connection aren't confused, there's a waiting period after one incarnation is closed, during which a new incarnation is forbidden. In the jargon of TCP, on the side that performed an "active close" of the connection, the connection remains in a state called TIME_WAIT. This state lasts for a period that is supposed to be twice the maximum possible lifetime of a packet in the network (or "2MSL," for two times the Maximum Segment Lifetime). After that, the connection becomes fully closed, and another incarnation can occur. The actual value of this timeout varies from system to system, but is generally in the range of 30 seconds to 4 minutes.*

As it happens, some TCP implementations enforce even stronger restrictions. Often, a port that is part of a socket in the TIME_WAIT state is unavailable for use, even as part of a connection to a different remote socket. We have also run into systems that disallow listening on a socket that is currently an endpoint of some connection, regardless of the connection state. These restrictions aren't required by the TCP protocol, but they are common. Such systems usually provide a way to avoid the restrictions, such as the SO_REUSEADDR option of the Berkeley sockets API. An FTP client generally uses this feature, of course, but it doesn't always work!

This address-reuse problem comes up in two places in a default-port FTP transfer. The first one is when the client must start listening on its default data port, which by definition is currently the local endpoint of its control connection. Some systems simply don't allow this, even if the program requests address reuse; that's why the attempt might fail immediately with the message, "address already in use."

The other place is on a second data transfer. When the first transfer is finished, the server closes the data connection, and that connection on the server side moves into the TIME_WAIT state. If you try another data transfer before the 2MSL period has elapsed, the server tries to set up another incarnation of the same connection, and it

---

* See *TCP/IP Illustrated, Volume 1: The Protocols*, by W. Richard Stevens (Addison Wesley), for more technical information about the TIME_WAIT state.

will fail saying "cannot assign requested address." This happens regardless of the address reuse setting, since the rules of the TCP require it. You can transfer a file again within a few minutes, of course, but most computer users aren't good at waiting a few seconds, let alone minutes. It is this problem that prompts the use of a PORT command for every transfer; since one end of the connection is different every time, the TIME_WAIT collisions don't occur.

Because of these problems, the default-port transfer mode isn't generally used. It has, however, an important property for us: it is the only mode in which the data connection destination port is fixed and knowable before the data-transfer command is given. With this knowledge, some patience, and a fair amount of luck, it is possible to forward your FTP data connections through SSH.

11.2.8 Forwarding the Data Connection

With all the foregoing discussion in mind, here we simply state the sequence of steps to set up data-connection forwarding. One caveat is that SSH must request address reuse from TCP for forwarded ports. Tectia and OpenSSH do this already, but not all SSH clients may.

Another issue is that the operating system in which the FTP client is running must allow a process to listen on a socket already in use as the endpoint of an existing connection. Some don't. To test this, try an FTP data transfer on the default data ports without SSH, just by using *ftp* as usual but giving the *sendport* command before *ls*, *get*, or whatever. If you get:

```
ftp: bind: Address already in use
```

then your operating system probably won't cooperate. There may be a way to alter this behavior; check the operating system documentation. Figure 11-7 illustrates the following steps:

1. Start an SSH connection to forward the control channel as shown earlier in this chapter, and connect with the FTP client. Make sure that passive mode is off. For OpenSSH:

   ```
   client% ssh -f -n -L2001:localhost:21 server sleep 10000 &
   ```

   or for Tectia:

   ```
   client% ssh -f -n -L2001:localhost:21 server
   ```

   Then:

   ```
   client% ftp localhost 2001
   Connected to localhost
   220 server FTP server (SunOS 5.7) ready.
   Password:
   230 User res logged in.
   ftp> sendport
   Use of PORT cmds off.
   ftp> passive
   ```

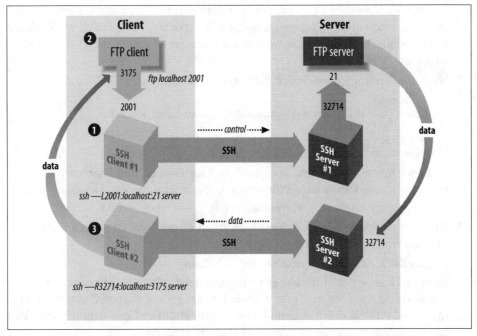

Figure 11-7. Forwarding the FTP data connection

```
Passive mode on.
ftp> passive
Passive mode off.
```

Note that we are using localhost as the forwarding target here, despite our earlier advice. That's OK, because there won't be any PORT or PASV commands with addresses that can be wrong.

2. Now, we need to determine the real and proxy default data ports for the FTP client. On the client side, you can do this with *netstat*:

```
client% netstat -n | grep 2001
tcp      0      0 client:2001 client:3175 ESTABLISHED
tcp      0      0 client:3175 client:2001 ESTABLISHED
```

This shows that the source of the control connection from the FTP client to SSH is port 3175. You can do the same thing on the server side, but this time you need to know what's connected to the FTP server port (*netstat –n | egrep '\<21\>'*), and there may be many things connected to it. If you have a tool like *lsof*, it's better to find out the pid of the *ftpd* or *sshd* serving your connection and use *lsof –p <pid>* to find the port number. If not, you can do a *netstat* before connecting via FTP and then one right afterward, and try to see which is the new connection. Let's suppose you're the only one using the FTP server, and you get it this way:

```
server% netstat | grep ftp
tcp      0      0 server:32714 server:ftp    ESTABLISHED
tcp      0      0 server:ftp    server:32714 ESTABLISHED
```

So now, we have the FTP client's default data port (3175), and the source port of the forwarded control connection to the FTP server (32714), which we'll call the proxy default data port; it is what the FTP server thinks is the client's default data port.

3. Now, forward the proxy default data port to the real one:

```
# OpenSSH
client% ssh -f -n -R32714:localhost:3175 server sleep 10000 &

# Tectia
client% ssh -f -R32714:localhost:3175 server
```

If, as we mentioned earlier, you don't replace *sshd* or run a second one, then you'd use the modified *ssh* on the server in the other direction, like this:

```
server% ./ssh -f -n -L32714:localhost:3175 client sleep 10000 &
```

4. Now, try a data-transfer command with *ftp*. If all goes well, it should work once, then fail with this message from the FTP server:

```
425 Can't build data connection: Address already in use.
```

(Some FTP servers return that error immediately; others will retry several times before giving up, so it may take a while for that error to appear.) If you wait for the server's 2MSL timeout period, you can do another single data transfer. You can use *netstat* to see the problem and track its progress:

```
server% netstat | grep 32714
127.0.0.1.32714    127.0.0.1.21       32768    0 32768    0 ESTABLISHED
127.0.0.1.21       127.0.0.1.32714    32768    0 32768    0 ESTABLISHED
127.0.0.1.20       127.0.0.1.32714    32768    0 32768    0 TIME_WAIT
```

The first two lines show the established control connection on port 21; the third one shows the old data connection to port 20, now in the TIME_WAIT state. When that disappears, you can do another data-transfer command.

And there you have it: you have forwarded an FTP data connection through SSH. You have achieved the Holy Grail of FTP with SSH, though perhaps you agree with us and Sir Gawain that "it's only a model." Still, if you're terribly concerned about your data connections, have no other way to transfer files, can afford to wait a few minutes between file transfers, and are quite lucky, then this will work. It also makes a great parlor trick at geek parties.

11.3 Pine, IMAP, and SSH

Pine is a popular, Unix-based email program from the University of Washington (*http://www.washington.edu/pine/*). In addition to handling mail stored and delivered

in local files, Pine also supports IMAP* for accessing remote mailboxes and SMTP†
for posting mail.

In this case study, we integrate Pine and SSH to solve two common problems:

IMAP authentication

In many cases, IMAP permits a password to be sent in the clear over the network. We discuss how to protect your password using SSH, but (surprisingly)
not by port forwarding.

Restricted mail relaying

Many ISPs permit their mail and news servers to be accessed only by their customers. In some circumstances, this restriction may prevent you from legitimately relaying mail through your ISP. Once again, SSH comes to the rescue.

We also discuss techniques to avoid Pine connection delays and facilitate access to
multiple servers and mailboxes, including the use of a Pine-specific SSH connection
script. This discussion will delve into more detail than the previous one on Pine/SSH
integration. [4.5.3]

11.3.1 Securing IMAP Authentication

Like SSH, IMAP is a client/server protocol. Your email program (e.g., Pine) is the client, and an IMAP server process (e.g., *imapd*) runs on a remote machine, the *IMAP
host*, to control access to your remote mailbox. Also like SSH, IMAP generally
requires you to authenticate before accessing your mailbox, typically by password.
Unfortunately, in some cases this password is sent to the IMAP host in the clear over
the network; this represents a security risk (see Figure 11-8).‡

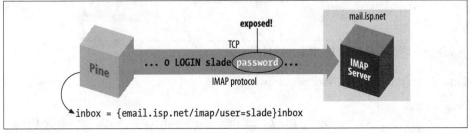

Figure 11-8. A normal IMAP connection

There's no longer any good reason for this. Years ago, security options were rarely
available in IMAP software; these days, however, they're common and should be

---

* Internet Message Access Protocol, RFC-2060.

† Simple Mail Transfer Protocol, RFC-821.

‡ IMAP does support more secure methods of authentication, but they aren't widely deployed.

used! There are standard ways to secure IMAP traffic using SSL or Kerberos. With SSL, the entire IMAP session is protected, so even plain password authentication can be used relatively securely. Kerberos can provide secure authentication and single-signon with or without session encryption; for example, the Apple Mail client implements both. Pine uses Kerberos only for authentication, not encryption—but you can combine Kerberos with SSL to get both single-signon and privacy. Note the power of having multiple independent and standards-based options available!

Nonetheless, it is still all too common to encounter IMAP servers with no security features; here, we show you how to address this problem with SSH.

If your mail server is *sealed*—that is, your only access to it is via the IMAP protocol—then there's nothing you can do to improve security using SSH. However, if you can also log into the IMAP server host via SSH, you have options. Because IMAP is a TCP/IP-based protocol, one approach is to use SSH port forwarding between the machine running Pine and the IMAP host (see Figure 11-9). [9.2.1]

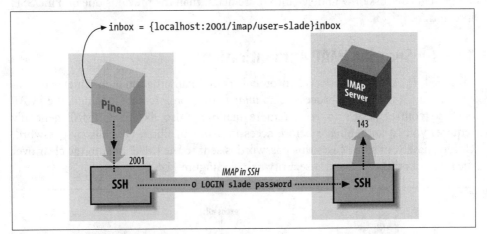

Figure 11-9. Forwarding an IMAP connection

However, this technique has two drawbacks:

Security risk

On a multiuser machine, any other user can connect to your forwarded port. [9.2.4.3] If you use forwarding only to protect your password, this isn't a big deal, since at worst, an interloper could access a separate connection to the IMAP server having nothing to do with your connection. On the other hand, if port forwarding is permitting you to access an IMAP server behind a firewall, an interloper can breach the firewall by hijacking your forwarded port, a more serious security risk.

Inconvenience

In this setup, you must authenticate twice: first to the SSH server on the IMAP host (to connect and to create the tunnel) and then to the IMAP server by password (to access your mailbox). This is redundant and annoying.

Fortunately, we can address both of these drawbacks and run Pine over SSH securely and conveniently.

11.3.1.1 Pine and preauthenticated IMAP

There are two broad types of Unix-based IMAP servers, exemplified by the University of Washington (UW) *imapd* and the Carnegie Mellon Cyrus software. Cyrus is a self-contained system: it uses an internal database to hold user mail, and the only access to it is via the IMAP protocol or particular programs for mail delivery or administration. In particular, there is no relationship between Unix accounts on the server host, and IMAP accounts; they are completely separate.

The UW *imapd*, on the other hand, is a lighter-weight affair: it simply provides an IMAP view of the traditional Unix mail store: files in */var/spool/mail* or elsewhere, owned by the Unix accounts of the mail recipients. Thus, its notion of user account and access control is tied to that of the host. If your mail is stored in a spool file owned by you, and you can log into the host via SSH, then you've already proven you have access to that file—why should you have to prove it *again* to the IMAP server? In fact, with the UW server, you don't have to. We now discuss how to do this with UW *imapd*, or another IMAP server with similar behavior.

The IMAP protocol defines two modes in which an IMAP server can start: normal and preauthenticated (see Figure 11-10). Normally, *imapd* runs with special privileges to access any user's mailbox (as when started as root by *inetd*), and hence it requires authentication from the client.

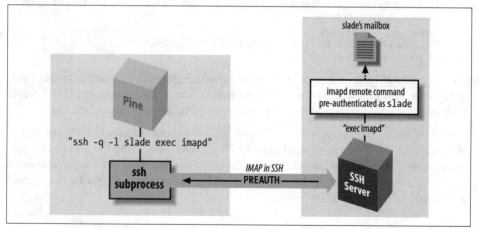

Figure 11-10. Pine/IMAP over SSH, preauthenticated

Here's a sample session that invokes an IMAP server, *imapd*, through *inetd* so that it runs as root:

```
server% telnet localhost imap
* OK localhost IMAP4rev1 v12.261 server ready
```

```
0 login res password'
1 select inbox
* 3 EXISTS
* 0 RECENT
* OK [UIDVALIDITY 964209649] UID validity status
* OK [UIDNEXT 4] Predicted next UID
* FLAGS (\Answered \Flagged \Deleted \Draft \Seen)
* OK [PERMANENTFLAGS (\* \Answered \Flagged \Deleted \Draft \Seen)] Permanent flags
1 OK [READ-WRITE] SELECT completed
2 logout
* BYE imap.example.com IMAP4rev1 server terminating connection
2 OK LOGOUT completed
```

Alternatively, in preauthenticated mode, the IMAP server assumes that authentication has already been done by the program that started the server and that it already has the necessary rights to access the user's mailbox. If you invoke *imapd* on the command line under a nonroot uid, *imapd* skips the authentication phase and simply opens the mailbox file of the current account (which must be accessible via the existing Unix permissions structure). You can then type IMAP commands and access your mailbox without authentication:

```
server% /usr/local/sbin/imapd
* PREAUTH imap.example.com IMAP4rev1 v12.261 server ready
0 select inbox
* 3 EXISTS
* 0 RECENT
* OK [UIDVALIDITY 964209649] UID validity status
* OK [UIDNEXT 4] Predicted next UID
* FLAGS (\Answered \Flagged \Deleted \Draft \Seen)
* OK [PERMANENTFLAGS (\* \Answered \Flagged \Deleted \Draft \Seen)] Permanent flags
0 OK [READ-WRITE] SELECT completed
1 logout
* BYE imap.example.com IMAP4rev1 server terminating connection
1 OK LOGOUT completed
```

Notice the PREAUTH response at the beginning of the session, indicating preauthenticated mode. It is followed by the command *select inbox*, which causes the IMAP server implicitly to open the inbox of the current user without demanding authentication.

Now, how does all this relate to Pine? Pine has a built-in feature whereby, instead of using a direct IMAP connection, it logs into the IMAP host using *ssh* and runs a preauthenticated instance of *imapd* directly. If this succeeds, Pine then converses with the IMAP server over the SSH connection, and has automatic access to the remote inbox without further authentication.

11.3.1.2 Making Pine use SSH

Pine's SSH feature is controlled by three configuration variables in the *~/.pinerc* file: ssh-path, ssh-command, and ssh-open-timeout. ssh-path stores the program name for opening a Unix remote shell connection. The default should point to a usable SSH program, but you may have to set it yourself:

```
ssh-path=/usr/bin/ssh
```

`ssh-command` represents the Unix command line for opening the SSH connection. The value is a `printf`-style format string with four "%s" conversion specifications that are automatically filled in at runtime. From first to last, these four specifications stand for:

1. The value of `ssh-path`
2. The remote hostname
3. The remote username
4. The connection method; in this case, "imap"

The default value of `ssh-command` is:

```
"%s %s -l %s exec /etc/r%sd"
```

To access the mailbox on *imap.example.com* for user smith via SSH, Pine would then run the command:

```
/usr/bin/ssh imap.example.com -l smith exec /etc/rimapd
```

This follows a convention, somewhat antiquated nowadays, of having links named */etc/r<protocol>d* that point to servers for various protocols that operate in this preauthenticated fashion. In modern systems such links are usually not available, so you may need to alter the *ssh-command* to run *imapd*. You can also use it to add other options, like so:

```
ssh-command="%s %s -l %s -o BatchMode=yes -axq exec /usr/sbin/imapd"
```

With this setting, Pine would end up running this command:

```
/usr/bin/ssh imap.example.com -l -o BatchMode=yes -axq exec /usr/sbin/imapd
```

The *–q* (Quiet) option is advisable so that *ssh* doesn't emit warning messages that may confuse Pine, which would try to interpret them as part of the IMAP protocol. The options *-ax* turns off agent and X Windows forwarding, which might be on by default but are not necessary for this connection. `BatchMode` lets *ssh* know that it can't prompt the user for a password on the terminal, since Pine is using it.

The third variable, `ssh-open-timeout`, sets the number of seconds Pine will wait for the SSH connection to succeed; its default value is 15. A value of 0 disables SSH entirely, which may be useful if the feature is on by default and you do not want to use it.

So, finally, the Pine configuration is:

```
ssh-path=/usr/bin/ssh
ssh-command="%s %s -l %s -o BatchMode=yes -axq exec /usr/sbin/imapd"
ssh-open-timeout=15
```

Generally, you want to use an SSH authentication method that doesn't require typing a password or passphrase, such as hostbased or public-key with an agent. SSH is run behind the scenes by Pine and doesn't have access to the terminal to prompt you. If you're running the X Window System, *ssh* can instead pop up an X widget—

ssh-askpass—to get input, but you probably don't want that either. Pine may make several separate IMAP connections in the course of reading your mail, even if it's all on the same server, and this will cause repeated queries for your password.

With the given settings in your *~/.pinerc* file and the right kind of SSH authentication in place, you're ready to try Pine over SSH. Just start Pine and open your remote mailbox; if all goes well, it will open without prompting for a password.

11.3.2   Mail Relaying and News Access

Pine uses IMAP to read mail but not to send it. For that, it can either call a local program (such as *sendmail*) or use an SMTP server. Pine can also be a newsreader and use NNTP (the Network News Transfer Protocol, RFC-977) to contact a news server.

An ISP commonly provides NNTP and SMTP servers for its customers, but obviously does not want to allow arbitrary people to use them. Modern extensions to the NNTP and SMTP protocols include authentication, and ISPs are starting to use and require them. Before such mechanisms were available, however, the usual method of restricting access to these services was via network address: the ISP would allow access from addresses within its own network (and hence hopefully only from its customers). Many ISPs have not yet switched to direct authentication for these services, and are still using address-based authorization; so, if you're connected to the Internet from elsewhere and try to use your ISP's mail server, the attempt might fail. Access to your usual servers might be blocked by a firewall, or the mail server might reject your mail with a message about "no relaying," and the news server rejects you with a message about "unauthorized use."

You are authorized to use the services, of course, so what do you do? Use SSH port forwarding! By forwarding your SMTP and NNTP connections over an SSH session to a machine inside the ISP's network, your connections appear to come from that machine, thus bypassing the address-based restrictions. You can use separate SSH commands to forward each port:

```
$ ssh -L2025:localhost:25 smtp-server ...
$ ssh -L2119:localhost:119 nntp-server ...
```

Alternatively, if you have a shell account on one of the ISP's machines running SSH but can't log into the mail or news servers directly, do this:

```
$ ssh -L2025:smtp-server:25 -L2119:nntp-server:119 shell-server ...
```

or neatly automate it this way:

```
[~/.ssh/config]
Host mail-news-forwarding
  Hostname shell-server
  LocalForward 2025 smtp-server:25
  LocalForward 2119 nntp-server:119

$ ssh mail-news-forwarding
```

This is an off-host forwarding, and thus the last leg of the forwarded path isn't protected by SSH. [9.2.4] But since the reason for this forwarding isn't so much protection as it is bypassing the source-address restriction, that's OK. Your mail messages and news postings are going to be transferred insecurely once you drop them off, anyway. (If you want security for them, you need to sign or encrypt them separately, e.g., with PGP or S/MIME.)

In any case, now configure Pine to use the forwarded ports by setting the smtp-server and nntp-server configuration options in your ~/.pinerc file:

```
smtp-server=localhost:2025
nntp-server=localhost:2119
```

Even if your ISP uses direct authentication, you might choose to use SSH anyway if it does so poorly. For instance, some badly deployed services require password authentication but do not provide encryption for the connection! In this case, you would forward over SSH in order to protect your password.

One possible complication: the SSH feature has a global on/off switch, applying to every remote mailbox. That is, if ssh-open-timeout is nonzero, Pine tries to use this style of access for every remote mailbox. If you have multiple mailboxes but only some of them are accessible via SSH/*imapd*, this leads to annoyance. Pine falls back to a direct TCP connection if SSH fails to get an IMAP connection, but you have to wait for it to fail. If the server in question is behind a firewall silently blocking the SSH port, this can be a lengthy delay. If you're in this situation, you can disable SSH access for specific mailboxes using the /norsh switch, like this:

```
{imap.example.com/user=smith/norsh}inbox
```

That's not a typo: the switch is /norsh rather than /nossh. This is just an historical artifact of the software: originally, Pine supported this style of mailbox access via *rsh*. In fact, there are still configuration variables—rsh-path, rsh-command, and rsh-open-timeout—that function entirely analogously; so much so, that in the first edition of this book, we described how to use SSH with older versions of Pine by simply setting rsh-command to "ssh". Anyway, /norsh turns off the use of both the *ssh* or *rsh* features of Pine for the mailbox in question.

11.3.3   Using a Connection Script

The Pine configuration option *ssh-path* can point not only to *ssh*, but also to any other program: most usefully, a script you've written providing any needed customizations. If your needs are complex, you might have to do this. For example, the ssh-path setting is global to all mailboxes, but perhaps the *imapd* executable is in different locations on different servers you want to access. You can solve this problem with a script which takes the four ssh-command arguments from Pine, and does the right thing depending on which server is specified:

```
ssh-path=/home/smith/bin/my-pine-ssh-script
ssh-command="%s %s %s %s"
```

where the script *my-pine-ssh-script* is:

```
#!/bin/sh

ssh=$1
server=$2
user=$3
method=$4

prefix="exec $ssh -qax $user@$server exec"

case $server in
    mail.work.com) $prefix /usr/sbin/imapd ;;
     imap.isp.net) $prefix /usr/local/sbin/imapd ;;
                *) exit 0
esac
```

The default action of exit will cause Pine to skip SSH access quickly for servers other than the two mentioned.

11.4   Connecting Through a Gateway Host

All along we've assumed that your outgoing connectivity is unlimited: that you can establish any outgoing TCP connection you desire. Even our discussions of firewalls have assumed that they restrict only incoming traffic. In more secure (or simply more regimented) environments, this might not be the case: in fact, you might not have direct IP connectivity at all to the outside world.

In the corporate world, companies commonly require all outgoing connections to pass through a proxy server or *gateway host*: a machine connected to both the company network and the outside. Although connected to both networks, a gateway host doesn't act as a router, and the networks remain separated. Rather, it allows limited, application-level access between the two networks.

In this case study, we discuss issues of SSH in this environment:

- Connecting transparently to external hosts using chained SSH commands
- Making *scp* connections to these hosts
- Running SSH-within-SSH by port forwarding
- Running SSH-within-SSH by `ProxyCommand`

 These gateway techniques apply equally well when the situation is reversed: you're on an *external* machine, and need to access various *internal* hosts through a single SSH gateway.

11.4.1 Making Transparent SSH Connections

Suppose your company has a gateway host, G, which is your only gateway to the Internet. You are logged into a client host, C, and want to reach a server host, S, outside the company network, as shown in Figure 11-11. We assume that all three machines have SSH installed.

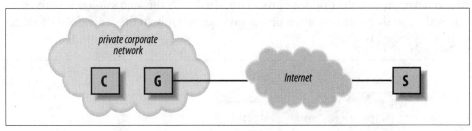

Figure 11-11. Proxy gateway

To make a connection from client C to server S now requires two steps:

1. Connect from C to gateway G:

   ```
   # Execute on client C
   $ ssh G
   ```

2. Connect from G to server S:

   ```
   # Execute on gateway G
   $ ssh S
   ```

This works, and using agent forwarding and public-key authentication on both hosts, you can avoid a second authentication prompt on gateway G.

Now, an obvious simplification would be this single command:

```
$ ssh G ssh S
```

If you do this, though, you'll have a problem: first, you'll see this warning:

```
Pseudo-terminal will not be allocated because stdin is not a terminal.
```

...and next, your shell on S will behave very strangely! You won't get a prompt, or any fancy line-editing—but if you persist and enter some commands, they will get executed. The problem is that *ssh* only creates a pseudo-terminal, needed for interactive terminal-based programs, if you explicitly request a remote shell session; to *ssh*, this means that you do *not* specify a remote program to run. By default, it assigns no terminal when running remote commands like *ssh host uname -a*. Most of the time this is a reasonable default, but sometimes you'll run a remote command that actually needs a terminal—in this case, the shell! You can fix this with the *–t* switch for force a pseudo-terminal:

```
$ ssh -t G ssh S
```

But this introduces yet another messy aspect: to reach hosts through the gateway, you not only have to use double-*ssh* commands, but furthermore, specify *–t* in some cases but not others. Not a big burden for occasional use, perhaps, but cumbersome if large numbers of hosts or automation are involved.

Fortunately, SSH configuration is flexible enough to afford a neat solution, which we now present using OpenSSH features and syntax.* We use public-key authentication to take advantage of the options of the *authorized_keys* file, and *ssh-agent* with agent forwarding so that authentication passes on transparently to the second SSH connection (see Figure 11-12).

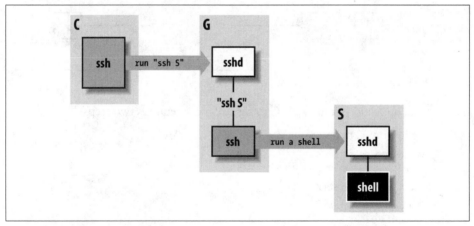

Figure 11-12. Chained SSH connections through a proxy gateway

Suppose your account on gateway G is gilligan, and on server S it is skipper. First, set up your SSH client configuration file so that the name S is a nickname for accessing your account on gateway G:

```
# ~/.ssh/config on client C
```

---

* The same method should work with Tectia: just adapt the client configuration to Tectia syntax. [7.1.2.3]

```
host S
   hostname G
   user gilligan
```

Next, on gateway G, associate a forced command with your chosen key to invoke an SSH connection to server S: [8.2.3]

```
# ~/.ssh/authorized_keys on gateway G
command="ssh -l skipper S" ...key..
```

Now, when you invoke the command *ssh S* on client C, it connects to gateway G, runs the forced command automatically, and establishes a second SSH session to server S. And thanks to agent forwarding, authentication from G to S happens automatically, assuming you've loaded the appropriate key. This can be the same key you used to access *gilligan@G* or a different one.[*]

This trick not only provides a transparent connection from client C to server S, it also sidesteps the fact that the name S might not have any meaning on client C. Often in this kind of network situation, your internal network naming scheme is cut off from the outside world (e.g., split DNS with internal roots). After all, what's the point of allowing you to name hosts you can't reach? Thanks to the Host configuration keyword for SSH clients, you can create a nickname S that instructs SSH to reach that host transparently via G. [7.1.2.5]

You'll soon notice a problem, though. Interactive logins work fine, but remote commands are ignored! And worse, the missing terminal problem rears its head again:

```
$ ssh S echo Hello
Pseudo-terminal will not be allocated because stdin is not a terminal.
```

You're left talking to a mute shell, and no "Hello" appears. The problem now is that we've done nothing to pass along any remote command to S; the forced command on G simply ignores it and always tries to start a remote-login SSH connection (hence provoking the missing terminal problem, as before). We can fix this using another OpenSSH feature:[†]

```
command="ssh -l skipper S $SSH_ORIGINAL_COMMAND" ...key...
```

If a remote command is used, *sshd* stores it in the environment variable SSH_ORIGINAL_COMMAND; we use that here to pass it along to the next *ssh* command. The variable is *not* set, however, if there is no remote command. Some shells consider this an error, so you might have to augment this in some way to accommodate the shell's predilections. For example, some shells have this syntax:

```
command="ssh -l skipper S ${SSH_ORIGINAL_COMMAND:-}" ...key...
```

---

[*] Note that if you want to use this setup for an interactive connection, you need to use the *–t* option to *ssh*, to force it to allocate a tty on G. It doesn't normally do that, because it doesn't have any way to know that the remote command—in this case, another instance of *ssh*—needs one.

[†] For Tectia use SSH2_ORIGINAL_COMMAND.

where ${foo:-bar} evaluates to "bar" if the variable foo is not set. And remember, the shell used here is the one belonging to the remote account; to be especially robust, it might be best to use a particular shell explicitly:

```
command="/bin/bash -c 'ssh -l skipper S ${SSH_ORIGINAL_COMMAND:-}'" ...key...
```

This technique also neatly solves the "missing terminal" problem at the same time!

11.4.2 Using SCP Through a Gateway

Recall that the command:

```
$ scp ... S:file ...
```

actually runs *ssh* in a subprocess to connect to S and invoke a remote *scp* server. [3.7] Now that we've gotten *ssh* working from client C to server S, you'd expect that *scp* would work between these machines with no further effort. Well, it almost does, but it wouldn't be software if there weren't a small problem to work around, in this case authentication. You can't provide a password or passphrase to the second *ssh* program, since there is no pseudo-terminal on the first *ssh* session—*ssh* requires a terminal for user input. So, you need a form of authentication that doesn't require user input: either hostbased, or public-key authentication with agent forwarding. Host-based works as is, so if you plan to use it, you can skip to the next section. Public-key authentication, however, may have a problem: some versions of *scp* run *ssh* with the *–a* switch to disable agent forwarding. [6.3.5.3] You need to reenable agent forwarding for this to work, and this is surprisingly tricky.

Normally, you could turn on agent forwarding in your client configuration file:

```
# ~/.ssh/config on client C, but this FAILS
ForwardAgent yes
```

but this doesn't help because as it happens, the *–a* on the command line takes precedence. Alternatively, you might try the *–o* option of *scp*, which can pass along options to *ssh*, such as *–o ForwardAgent yes*. But in this case, *scp* places the *–a* after any *–o* options it passes where it takes precedence, so that doesn't work either.

There is a solution, though. *scp* has a *–S* option to indicate a path to the SSH client program it should use, so you create a "wrapper" script that tweaks the SSH command line as needed, and then make *scp* use it with *–S*. Place the following script in an executable file on client C—say, *~/bin/ssh-wrapper*:

```
#!/usr/bin/perl
exec '/usr/bin/ssh', map {$_ eq '-a' ? () : $_} @ARGV;
```

This runs the real *ssh*, removing *–a* from the command line if it's there. Now, give your *scp* a command like this:

```
scp -S ~/bin/ssh-wrapper ... S:file ...
```

and it should work.

11.4.3 Another Approach: SSH-in-SSH (Port Forwarding)

Instead of using a forced command, here's another way to connect by SSH through a gateway: forward a port on client C to the SSH server on S, using an SSH session from C to G, and then run a second SSH session through the first (see Figure 11-13).

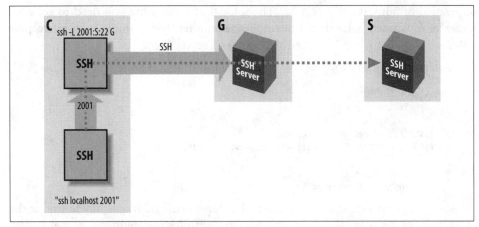

Figure 11-13. Forwarded SSH connection through a proxy gateway

That is:

```
# Execute on client C
$ ssh -L2001:S:22 G

# Execute on client C in a different shell
$ ssh -p 2001 -o HostKeyAlias=S localhost
```

This connects to server S by carrying the second SSH connection (from C to S) inside a port-forwarding channel of the first (from C to G). Note the use of HostKeyAlias, so *ssh* will look up S's host key with the name "S." Otherwise, it would try to use the key for "localhost," which would be the wrong key.

You can make this more transparent by creating a nickname S in your client configuration file:

```
# ~/.ssh/config on client C
Host S
  Hostname localhost
  Port 2001
  HostKeyAlias S
```

Now the earlier commands become:

```
# Execute on client C
$ ssh -L2001:S:22 G

# Execute on client C in a different shell
$ ssh S
```

Because this technique requires a separate, manual step to establish the port forwarding, it is less transparent than the one in [11.4.1]. However, it has some advantages. If you plan to use port or X forwarding between C and S with the first method, it's a little complicated. *scp* not only gives the *–a* switch to *ssh* to turn off agent forwarding, but also it gives *–x* and *–o* "ClearAllForwardings yes", turning off X and port forwarding. So, you need to modify the earlier wrapper script to remove these unwanted options as well. [11.4.2] Then, for port forwarding you need to set up a chain of forwarded ports that connect to one another. For example, to forward port 2017 on client C to port 143 (the IMAP port) on server S:

```
# ~/.ssh/config on client C
host S
  hostname G
  user gilligan

# ~/.ssh/authorized_keys on gateway G
command="ssh -L1234:localhost:143 skipper@S" ...key...

# Execute on client C
$ ssh -L2017:localhost:1234 S
```

This works, but it's difficult to understand, error-prone, and fragile: if you trigger the TIME_WAIT problem [9.2.9.1], you have to edit files and redo the tunnel just to pick a new ephemeral port to replace 1234.

Using the SSH-in-SSH technique instead, your port and X-forwarding options operate directly between client C and server S in the usual, straightforward manner. The preceding example becomes:

```
# ~/.ssh/config on client C
Host S
  Hostname localhost
  Port 2001
  HostKeyAlias S

# Execute on client C
$ ssh -L2001:S:22 G

# Execute on client C in a different shell
$ ssh -L2017:localhost:143 S
```

This final command connects to server S, forwarding local port 2017 to the IMAP port on S.

11.4.4   SSH-in-SSH with a Proxy Command (OpenSSH)

Here's yet another way to implement the tunneled SSH technique:

```
# ~/.ssh/config on client C
Host S
  ProxyCommand "ssh -qax G nc S 22"
```

If a `ProxyCommand` value is set, OpenSSH uses this command to get a communication channel to the remote host, rather than using the network directly. The command, in turn, can do anything at all—it could connect to an SSH server at the other end of a serial line, for example! In this case, we actually use a second *ssh* command to connect through gateway G to the SSH server TCP port on server S. The trick is that we really want a kind of connection that OpenSSH doesn't provide. Ideally, we'd like to be able to say something like *ssh --tcp S:22 G* (note: this syntax does not currently exist), the meaning of which would be: "connect to G via SSH, instruct G to make a TCP connection to host S port 22, and connect the local stdin/stdout to that stream." Making remote TCP connections is already something *sshd* can do; that's how local TCP forwarding is done. Unfortunately, no SSH clients we know of provide this useful feature. So, we must have a separate program on G, which just makes a simple TCP connection for us; here, we use *netcat (nc)*.

Expanding on this a bit...instead of a single host on the other side of the gateway, suppose you have many you want to access. If their names follow a pattern, you may be able to express this behavior very succinctly using OpenSSH. Suppose the machines in question are a cluster with hostnames beowulf-1, beowulf-1, etc. Then you can use this:

```
# ~/.ssh/config on client C
Host beowulf-*
  ProxyCommand "ssh -qax G nc %h %p"
```

This `Host` directive will match any of the cluster hostnames, and use an *ssh* subprocess to reach the host in question through the gateway: OpenSSH substitutes the %h and %p in the `ProxyCommand` with the host and port to use.

The `ProxyCommand` technique is simpler than port forwarding: there's no extra SSH command to start separately and no ad hoc port numbers to coordinate and possibly have to change. It also gains in security, since port forwarding always has the problem of unauthenticated access to the forwarded connection. And, we need no `HostKeyAlias` statements. However, we lose the speed advantage gained over chained *ssh* commands, since once again we end up waiting for two SSH connections every time. A compromise approach would be to use the `ProxyCommand` method together with an OpenSSH connection server. [7.4.4.2]

11.4.5 Comparing the Techniques

We've presented several methods of SSH access through a gateway. There are various trade-offs, but overall we think tunneling is usually the best way to go. Here's why.

11.4.5.1 Smoothness

The tunneling methods are smoother end-to-end: the interaction between client C and server S is simpler because they talk directly to one another. This is especially true if you need to request additional services via SSH, such as any kind of forwarding. On the other hand, the setup for tunneled connections using port forwarding is more cumbersome with its extra SSH process. `ProxyCommand` tunneling, though, is both smoother than chaining and at least no slower—and may be sped up if the OpenSSH connection server is available. The speedup is again at the cost of an extra SSH process, but its startup could be automated, and coordinating the control socket is easier than picking ad hoc ports and dealing with possible `TIME_WAIT` problems. Overall, tunneling via `ProxyCommand` wins.

11.4.5.2 Security

A chained connection has a serious security problem: the gateway G. All data is decrypted on G in between the two SSH sessions; if G is compromised, then all is lost. There is simply no end-to-end security in this scenario, because there is no actual SSH session from client C to server S. In contrast, a compromise of G poses no extra threat to the security of a tunneled SSH connection from C to S. The break-in simply puts the attacker on G in the position of altering or diverting the data path between C and S—but SSH already has mechanisms for countering exactly that threat. In other words, the top SSH connection does not trust the lower one at all. It treats it as it would any other connection method, and thus is no more vulnerable to attacks on it than if a simple TCP connection were in use. Tunneling in either form is the clear winner here.

11.5   Scalable Authentication for SSH

One of the main strengths of SSH is easy setup. Install an SSH server on one host and a client on another, and you immediately have secure login via password. Generate a key pair and put the public key on the server, and you immediately have even better authentication, and single-signon. This lightweight approach is one of the main reasons for the initial popularity of SSH.

No solution fits all situations, however, and this simplicity becomes a liability as the number of users and hosts grows. In large installations, managing both server and user authentication becomes difficult. Every time you add an SSH server host, or change its name, or add an alias for it, you must update the global known-hosts list. This by itself may be a practically impossible task, because there are no standards for representing these lists. OpenSSH uses one format, Tectia another; some Windows-based clients keep them in a file, some in the registry. Even if you had a means to generate lists for all your SSH clients in their various native formats, many of the actual client machines may be unreachable for updates (remote machines, laptops, etc.).

At all too many companies, the difficulty of managing SSH server keys leads to a very lax approach to server verification. Users frequently see warning messages about missing or changed keys, and the IT staff tells them to "just accept the new key." Very soon, these messages are completely ignored by everyone—or worse, just made to go away entirely! We've actually encountered an SSH installation with this configuration:

```
# /etc/ssh/ssh_config
GlobalKnownHostsFile    /dev/null
UserKnownHostsFile      /dev/null
StrictHostKeyChecking   no
```

Scary, but understandable; SSH had cried wolf one too many times. Unfortunately, effectively skipping server authentication disables a vital part of SSH security: resistance to server host spoofing and man-in-the-middle attacks! This situation also makes it impractical to replace server keys periodically, as should be done, or to revoke a key in case it is known to be compromised (i.e., tell clients to no longer trust it).

All these remarks apply to the usual modes of SSH public-key user authentication, as well. Authorizing a user for login means modifying an authorization list on every host to which the user requires access, adding his key. Revoking that access means tracking all those files down—including files he may have modified himself, perhaps to allow access to accounts other than his own, that you know nothing about. Changing keys may be essentially impossible; after a while, the user himself may have no idea where that key has gotten to! Eventually, a compromised key is almost sure to work on some machine where it's lying forgotten in a dusty *authorized_keys* file (or *~/.ssh2/authorization* file, or registry key, or ...).

Now, none of these issues is new or unique to SSH. The problem of large-scale, centralized authentication and authorization (AA) has been studied for a long time, and standard solutions exist. Fortunately, besides simplicity, another strength of SSH is flexibility. The common devices that we're complaining about are not implied by the SSH protocol; they're just widespread implementations. The protocol says nothing about how a server key should be verified or a user key authorized for access, and SSH software is free to use more sophisticated methods. Moreover, the protocol is extensible so that new elements such as key types or authentication exchanges can be defined as needed in order to support such methods.

Of course, flexibility doesn't help much if there *are* no such "sophisticated methods" actually available. For years, there weren't—but recently, maturing SSH products have incorporated support for scalable AA. We will discuss two here: X.509 public-key infrastructure (PKI) with Tectia, and Kerberos with OpenSSH.

A word before we start: both Kerberos and X.509 PKI are substantial topics on their own, and we can't do more than scratch the surface of them here. We'll give just a brief (incomplete!) sketch of each system, present a simple working configuration, and make some comments about other features to look at. Beyond that, you'll need to read up on these systems yourself in order to delve into their use.

11.5.1 Tectia with X.509 Certificates

11.5.1.1 What's a PKI?

"X.509 PKI"—a forbidding term; it sounds like part of a warp engine that needs calibration, right after you reinitialize the field coils. Let's break it down: PKI stands for Public Key Infrastructure, and refers to a system for dealing in scalable fashion with the trust issues raised by deploying asymmetric (public-key) cryptography, including:

- Binding public keys to identities: users, hosts, routers, etc.—these are the *principals* in the system
- Indicating or controlling the use of keys (encryption, signing, email, web/SSL, etc.)
- Replacing keys
- Renewing or revoking previously made bindings
- Securely communicating all these properties

Although the term sounds generic, in practice it has come to refer specifically to hierarchical systems in which so-called Certifying Authorities (CAs) vouch for the identity of principals and certify ownership of cryptographic keys. CAs can themselves be vouched for by higher CAs, arranged in a *tree of trust*. This reduces the trust problem to distributing the keys of a small number of well-known authorities, avoiding the combinatorial explosion of dealing individually with every pair of principals who might need to communicate securely.

X.509 is the name of a standards document of the International Telecommunications Union (ITU, formerly the CCITT). Its original intent was to describe an authentication system for another ITU standard: X.500 directories (the title is "Recommendation X.509: The Directory Authentication Framework"). However, in the process it specified a format for *digital certificates*: data structures which embody the key/principal binding we mentioned, and that portion of X.509 has become widely used in PKI systems.

X.509-style PKIs also use a great many other standards. To get an idea of the scope of the subject, just take a look at the home page of the IETF PKIX working group, at:

http://www.ietf.org/html.charters/pkix-charter.html

It's a daunting list...but we'll just sum up the essentials here. The most important components of a certificate are:

- Issuer name
- Subject name
- Public key
- Validity dates
- Signature

The *signature* is a cryptographic function of the entire certificate data structure, and is made by the issuer using *its* private key (which does not appear here). The meaning of the certificate is: "the issuer vouches that the subject owns the private counterpart to this public key (but this affidavit is only good between the given validity dates)."

Now in reality, certificates can be much more complex, containing many more attributes. Also, the interpretation may be different: "owns" might mean "is authorized to use," or "has access to sign with but does not actually know," etc. And there are many unanswered questions here, such as how carefully did the issuer check the subject's identity? But we'll leave all that alone and concentrate on the basics.

The *issuer* and *subject name* are expressed as *Distinguished Names* (DNs), as defined by X.509. These are attribute/value sets, represented in text like this:

```
/C=US/ST=New York/O=Mad Writer Enterprises/CN=Richard E. Silverman/
emailAddress=res@oreilly.com
```

The attribute abbreviations here are Country, STate, Organization, and Common Name (and there are more).

Now, let's see how all this helps with SSH host key verification.

11.5.1.2 Using certificates with Tectia host keys

When an SSH client connects to a server, it needs to verify that the server's host key actually belongs to the host it intended to contact. The usual way is to compare it to a local list of already known keys, but that has many drawbacks, as we pointed out earlier. Instead of managing an unwieldy, changing set of host keys, with PKI each client needs only one public key: that of a CA shared by all hosts in the system. Each time you deploy a new Tectia host, you generate a new hostkey as usual—but you also obtain a certificate, binding the host's name to its public key. That certificate is signed by the CA, and every client has the CA's public key. During the key-exchange phase of the SSH protocol, the client receives the certificate along with the server's hostkey; there are key types *x509v3-sign-rsa* and *x509v3-sign-dss* for this purpose instead of the usual *ssh-rsa* and *ssh-dss*. Instead of looking up the hostkey in a list, the Tectia client:

1. Compares the subject name in the certificate to the server hostname and verifies that they match

2. Verifies the server's signature on the key-exchange transaction, proving it actually holds the corresponding private key

3. Verifies the issuer signature on the certificate using the CA's public key, to be sure it's genuine (i.e., that the certificate was actually issued by the trusted CA)

If the key passes all these tests, then the client considers the key valid, and server authentication succeeds. You'll notice this doesn't completely remove the need for key distribution: the clients do still need to get the CA key in a trusted manner. But it's much easier to distribute or update a single key that changes very infrequently, than to manage a constantly changing known-hosts list!

Now we'll get down to specifics with a simple example.

11.5.1.3 A simple configuration

For our example, we'll start with a new instance of Tectia Server installed on a Linux host; first, we need to generate a hostkey with a certificate. This is not something we can describe very comprehensively, because it relies on outside factors: what actual PKI system is in use. You might be using anything from a home-brew CA using the free OpenSSL software that comes with most Unix variants these days, to a managed PKI service outsourced to a major security vendor, involving multiple layers of hierarchy, cross-certification among organizations, separate Registration Authorities, private-key escrow, etc.

If the PKI in question uses the Certificate Management Protocols (CMP, RFC-2510), then you can use *ssh-cmpclient* to communicate with the PKI system: generate keys; request, receive, revoke, or update certificates; etc. You should consult your PKI vendor or managing staff as to how to proceed in this case. To keep our example simple, we'll follow an older but still widely used process: generating a keypair and certificate request using OpenSSL, which we then supply to the CA by some simple method (email and the Web are the usual ways).

11.5.1.4 Getting a certificate

Suppose our company is Vogon Construction, Inc., and the server hostname is jeltz. vcon.com. To generate a key pair and certificate request:

```
% openssl req -nodes -config -new rsa:1024 -out request.pem \
    -outform pem -keyout private.pem -days 1095 \
    -subj '/C=US/ST=New York/L=Manhattan/O=Vogon Construction, Inc./CN=jeltz.vcon.com'
```

This generates a new 1024-bit RSA key pair and produces two files:

private.pem
> The unencrypted private key

request.pem
> An X.509 certificate request

The *request.pem* file contains the public key and asks to bind the hostname *jeltz. vcon.com* to that key for a period of three years (1095 days). The DN contains other information besides the hostname, and typically the CA will require set values for some of that, e.g., that the Organization field match that of the CA.

Next, send the request to the CA, and engage in whatever authentication procedures it requires: call Bob in IT, verify receipt of an email at your given address, swear an oath and sign in blood—whatever it takes. When the CA is satisfied, it will return to you a certificate, which you save in a file, *certificate.blob*. If it is an ASCII file looking like this:

```
-----BEGIN CERTIFICATE-----
MIIDbzCCAtigAwIBAgIDA9GvMAoGCSqGSIb3DQEBBQUAME4xCzAJBgNVBAYTAlVT
MRAwDgYDVQQKEwdFcXVpZmF4MSOwKwYDVQQLEyRFcXVpZmF4IFNlY3VyZSBDZXJ0
...
VdrJ1Z4HLT7PL+nEuvRJcpyw+A==
-----END CERTIFICATE-----
```

then it is in a format called PEM; if it's not, then it's in another format called DER.

The two files, *private.pem* and *certificate.blob*, contain the host private key and our desired certificate; you can delete *request.pem*. Now, we need to convert these to Tectia's format for host keys, in a two-step process. First:

```
% openssl pkcs12 -export -out jeltz.p12 -in certificate.blob -inform {pem|der} -inkey
private.pem
```

Choose "pem" or "der" depending on the format of the certificate. This stores the combined public key, private key, and certificate in a single file using yet another format, PKCS-12. You will be prompted for a passphrase to protect the file. This is a good format in which to store the keypair and certificate in case you need to rebuild the host and restore the key, so keep that file. Next:

```
$ ssh-keygen -k jeltz.p12 -p ''
```

This will, of course, prompt you for the passphrase (twice, in fact), and finally produce the two files we want:

jeltz.p12-1_ssh2.crt
    Certificate in DER format

jeltz.p12_ssh2
    Unencrypted private key in SECSH format used by Tectia [6.1.2]

Now, to get Tectia *sshd* to use them.

11.5.1.5 Hostkey verification: configuring the server

Install the new key and certificate in the Tectia configuration directory:

```
# install -o root -m 444 jeltz.p12-1_ssh2.crt /etc/ssh2/jeltz.crt
# install -o root -m 444 jeltz.p12_ssh2 /etc/ssh2/jeltz
```

and add this to *sshd2_config*:

```
HostCertificateFile jeltz.crt
HostKeyFile jeltz
```

If you want to continue offering the existing plain ssh-dss host key as well as the new certificate, you may need to add or uncomment the following:

```
PublicHostKeyFile hostkey.pub
HostKeyFile hostkey
```

These are the defaults if no hostkey is specified, but once you add the HostCertificateFile, the defaults will not apply. For our example, though, we suggest you turn or leave off all other hostkeys so that successful server authentication by the client depends on this one key working.

Lastly, restart Tectia Server:

```
# service sshd2 restart
```

and try to connect with *ssh*:

```
% ssh jeltz.vcon.com
warning: Received host certificate is not valid, error:
search-state = { certificate-was-not-found database-method-search-failed } warning:
Authentication failed.  Disconnected (local); key exchange or algorithm negotiation
failed
(Key exchange failed.).
```

This error message shows that we succeeded: the client received a certificate along with the host key. A debug trace will show more specifically that the host-key type has changed:

```
% ssh -d4 jeltz.vcon.com
...
debug: Ssh2Client/sshclient.c:244/ssh_client_key_check: Got key of type x509v3-sign-
rsa
debug: Ssh2Client/sshclient.c:286/ssh_client_key_check: Checking certificate validity
...
```

Now, we just need to arrange for the client to be able to verify the certificate.

11.5.1.6 Hostkey verification: configuring the Client

For this, we need the CA's public key, itself in the form of a certificate. This should be readily available from your CA; after all, the CA isn't much use unless everyone has it. Get it in DER format; if they provide it in PEM, convert it thus:

```
$ openssl x509 -inform pem -outform der -in <certificate file> -out cacert.der
```

Now install the CA certificate:

```
# install -o root -m 444 cacert.der /etc/ssh2
```

configure *ssh* to use it:

```
# /etc/ssh2/ssh2_config
# Note that this path must be absolute, unlike in the server config, since otherwise
it is relative
# to the user's ~/.ssh2 directory.
HostCANoCRLs /etc/ssh2/cacert.der
```

...and try!

```
# Tectia
$ ssh -v jeltz.vcon.com
...
```

```
debug: Ssh2Client/sshclient.c:984/keycheck_cert_cb: Host certificate valid and signed
by a trusted CA, accepting
...
```

If all has gone according to plan, this works, using whatever user authentication method you have available; the debug message shown indicates that the certificate validation succeeded.

11.5.1.7 User authentication: configuring the client

We have just set up server authentication using a server-supplied certificate. In fact, the converse is possible as well: Tectia Server can authenticate users by certificate as well. As before, we need a new keypair and certificate, this time for a DN matching a user. We follow the same procedure we used earlier [11.5.1.4], but with the following subject name:

```
/C=US/ST=New York/L=Manhattan/O=Vogon Construction, Inc./CN=Prostetnic V. Jeltz/
subjectAltName=email:pvj@vcon.com
```

It is critical to include a `subjectAltName` of type `email` as shown—even if the user has no email address at all, in fact, and you have to make one up. It is a very confusing and thoroughly undocumented fact that Tectia Server requires the presence of this attribute for user certificates, even if it's not used. Otherwise, Tectia mysteriously rejects the certificate with no reason. It cost us several hours of bewilderment, culminating in an intense threesome with *gdb* and the Tectia source, to uncover this fact.

In a related bit of confusion, there's a bug in OpenSSL whereby this attribute will *not* be automatically copied into the certificate request, like everything else next to it. You must edit the OpenSSL configuration file (often in */usr/share/ssl/openssl.cnf*), and add or uncomment the following:

```
[ usr_cert ]
```

Once you have your private key and user certificate, place them in *~/.ssh2,* say:

~/.ssh2/pvj.crt
> Certificate

~/.ssh2/pvj
> Private key

and configure *ssh* to use this key:

```
# ~/.ssh2/identification
CertKey pvj
```

We know it won't work, since we haven't configured the server yet—but as a test:

```
% ssh -l pvj jeltz -o AllowedAuthentications=publickey
warning: Authentication failed.
Disconnected (local); no more authentication methods available (No further
authentication methods available.).
```

We set *ssh* to try only public-key authentication since that's what we want to test; this way it doesn't end up asking for a password. The interesting message will be in the server log, typically */var/log/secure*:

```
sshd2: Authorization check for user pvj's certificate rejected, reason: No
certificate authorization configured.
```

And now finally, we tell the server how to authorize users based on their certificates.

11.5.1.8 User authentication: configuring the server

With the old method, there was an implicit correspondence between an account and a public key authorized to log into it: the key sat in a special file in the account's home directory. With PKI, there is only the certificate, so we need a rule whereby Tectia can determine whether a particular certificate grants access to the requested account. In fact, Tectia allows great flexibility in expressing such rules. First, add this to the server configuration:

```
# /etc/ssh2/sshd2_config
PKI cacert.der
PKIDisableCrls yes
MapFile cert.users
```

This tells Tectia Server to trust user certificates signed by our CA, and to use the rules in */etc/ssh2/cert.users* to authorize access to accounts. The rule language is described in the manpage for *ssh_certd_config*, section "MAPPING FILES." We'll give a few examples here:

```
# allow a certificate issued to Prostetnic V. Jeltz in our company, access to account
pvj
#
pvj subject C=US,ST=New York,L=Manhattan,O=Vogon Construction, Inc.,CN=Prostetnic V.
Jeltz

# allow any certificate issued to Prostetnic V. Jeltz, whether by our organization or
not
#
pvj subject CN=Prostetnic V. Jeltz

# allow certificate serial number 17 issued by our CA
#
pvj SerialAndIssuer 17 C=US,ST=New York,L=Manhattan,O=Vogon Construction, Inc.

# allow any certificate issued by us to access account "shared"
#
shared Issuer C=US,ST=New York,L=Manhattan,O=Vogon Construction, Inc.

# allow certificate with email address pvj@vcon.com
#
pvj email pvj@vcon.com

# pattern rule: allow certificate with email address <foo>@vcon.com to access account
<foo>
#
%subst% EmailRegex ([a-z]+)@vcon\.com
```

You would think we'd now restart *sshd* to have these changes take effect, but in fact Tectia has a separate daemon responsible for certificate validation: *ssh-certd*. So:

```
# service ssh-certd restart
```

Now, try logging in again:

```
% ssh -l pvj jeltz -o AllowedAuthentications=publickey
```

If all has gone well, it will work, with the following telltale message in syslog:

```
sshd2: Certificate authentication for user pvj accepted.
```

You can have multiple PKI blocks in the server configuration, directing trust of various CAs and each with its own account mapping.

We have presented the simplest possible view of PKI; it may be much more complicated. You might interact with something called a Registration Authority for obtaining your certificate, for example, rather than directly with the CA. Verifying a certificate might involve following a chain of certificates and signatures back to a trusted "root" certificate, rather than just one—or there might be multiple trust paths, if cross-certification is available, etc.

11.5.2   OpenSSH and Tectia with Kerberos

Kerberos is an authentication system that addresses the same set of problems as PKI: providing a scalable system for mutual authentication and secure communication. Kerberos simply uses a different basic model and set of technologies. It was originally developed as part of Project Athena, a wide-ranging research and development effort carried out at MIT between 1983 and 1991, funded primarily by IBM and Digital Equipment Corporation. Project Athena contributed many other pieces of technology to the computing world, including the well-known X Window System. There is now an IETF Kerberos working group:

http://www.ietf.org/html.charters/krb-wg-charter.html

which coordinates work on and standardization of the current version of the Kerberos protocol, Kerberos-5.

There are two main distinctions between Kerberos and PKI:

- Kerberos is based on symmetric encryption rather than public-key techniques.
- Kerberos is an *active* third-party system.

Both the Kerberos and PKI models have trusted third parties: in PKI it is the CA, and in Kerberos it is a service called the Key Distribution Center (KDC). Both are trusted in the sense that principals depend on them to correctly identify other users, and not to reveal certain cryptographic secrets. However, Kerberos requires the real-time, online participation of the KDC when two principals wish to communicate. This is in contrast to PKI: once two principals have obtained certificates from the CA, they may communicate at any time by speaking only to each other; the CA is not involved. It may be necessary to contact the CA for related services, such as checking for certificate revocation or obtaining issuance policies—but it is not required for the basic mutual authentication procedure.

This added availability requirement would seem to be a liability over PKI—but as usual, it's all about trade-offs. In exchange, Kerberos offers a much simpler administration and user experience, as well as some different security properties. For instance, with Kerberos, users' long-term secrets are never stored outside the KDC, whereas in PKI each user has the secret component of his keypair, which must be stored and protected.

11.5.2.1 How Kerberos works

Since it is based on symmetric cryptography, Kerberos is perforce a *shared-secret* system. The basic unit of Kerberos administration is called a *realm*, which consists of a set of principals and single KDC database they trust. When a principal joins a Kerberos realm, it shares a secret key with the KDC; the KDC database essentially consists of a list of principals and their keys. For user principals, the key is derived from a password. Principals may also correspond to software services, such as an SSH server, IMAP server, etc.; their keys are randomly generated and stored in protected files where the services can access them. A principal name looks like 1/2/3/.../ n@REALM. There can be any (positive) number of initial parts as shown, but in practice there are usually either one or two. A plain-user principal name would be res@REALM. A user principal name for particular uses, such as a privileged administrative instance, might be res/admin@REALM. And a principal representing a service—say, an IMAP server on host *mail.foo.org*—would have the name imap/mail.foo.org@REALM.

When principal A wants to communicate with another—say, B—principal A first tells the KDC that it wants to talk to B. Principal A needs to do two things: prove its identity to B, and establish a shared secret with B for secure communication, called a *session key*. The KDC provides these things in a message called a *ticket*, which it sends back to A. The ticket is sealed with A's secret key, known only to the KDC and A—hence A trusts that it is genuine, and it is protected from network snooping. Unsealing the ticket, A finds the needed session key—and yet another ticket! This one, however, is sealed with B's secret key (known only to the KDC and B). A can't read this at all, but that doesn't matter; all A needs to do is send this ticket as-is to B. When B unseals its ticket, it finds A's name and another copy of the session key. Just as before, since B's ticket is sealed with B's key, B trusts that the ticket is genuine. The meaning of each ticket is that the KDC has shared the session key with A and B. The two principals then execute a protocol which proves to each that the other does in fact hold that key—at which point, mutual authentication is accomplished. Further, the session key can be used for subsequent security functions, such as encrypting a conversation between them.

Now, this explanation is very basic.* It doesn't exactly describe the Kerberos protocol, but rather, a simpler one. However, it gives the essential flavor of how the third-party shared-secret model works. The real Kerberos-5 protocol can be viewed as an elaboration on this basic idea, to address various possible attacks and provide more features. We won't get any more detailed than we already have, except to list a few of the real-life differences:

- Our model requires the user to type his password for every Kerberos transaction. Real Kerberos instead involves first issuing to a user a special ticket, called a *ticket-granting ticket* (TGT). Subsequent tickets for other principals involve presenting the TGT back to the KDC, proving that the requestor has been recently authenticated. TGTs (and indeed all tickets) expire after a period of time, typically 10 hours. So, the user need only type his password infrequently, and it need not be locally stored. The TGT must be stored, but it is of limited value (and can't be used to change the user's password).

- The ticket expiration feature involves timestamps, which in turn require that all principals have synchronized clocks. Some skew is allowed (typically up to five minutes), but Kerberos will not function properly if hosts' clocks drift too far from one another.

11.5.2.2 Kerberos support in SSH

Kerberos support for SSH is not defined directly; rather, there is a draft that extends SSH to use GSSAPI, as documented in "Generic Security Services/Application Programming Interface (RFC-2743)."

GSS is a sort of security meta-protocol, with a role and implementation structure similar to that of PAM or SASL. GSS allows two communicating peers to negotiate security parameters abstractly, in terms of types of protection and relative strength rather than particular protocols, ciphers, or algorithms. The GSS layers on either side will pick the strongest compatible mechanisms available to each which meet their clients' needs, without the higher-level software needing to bother with the details. Typical GSS implementations allow adding new mechanisms in the form of system dynamic libraries, which then automatically become available to GSS clients without recompilation.

In particular, there is a GSS mechanism supporting Kerberos-5, documented in "The Kerberos Version 5 GSS-API Mechanism (RFC 1964)."

Of course, this is a bit convoluted; why not simply support Kerberos directly as its own SSH protocol extension? This was in fact done in SSH-1. The answer is that GSS is becoming a widely used standard. By defining a method for using GSS in SSH, implementers can take advantage of existing GSSAPI software libraries. And in doing

---

* And in fact, in some ways an outright lie.

so, SSH can automatically use new GSS security mechanisms as they become available, without further standards work. For example, Tectia Windows Server provides both Kerberos and NTLM user authentication via GSSAPI. The relevant SSH protocol draft is "GSSAPI Authentication and Key Exchange for the Secure Shell Protocol" (draft-ietf-secsh-gsskeyex).

Just a few years ago, this whole area was a work in progress, with only patches and experimental implementations. Now, however, it has solidified and is present in several mainstream SSH products and platforms, including OpenSSH, OS X, and Tectia on both Windows and Unix. This matches the widening adoption of Kerberos in general. And amazingly...for the most part, they all interoperate! It is now possible to have strong authentication and single-signon among various OS/SSH combinations, using Kerberos.

Note that while it has been possible for a while to get something similar using SSH public-key authentication with *ssh-agent*, Kerberos is a win for two different reasons. The issue of central management and scalability for larger organizations, we've already discussed. The other important point is that public-key authentication is SSH-specific. You go to all the trouble to teach people about generating keys, using agents, enabling agent forwarding, etc.; and after all that work, you get a solution that works *only* for SSH. Suppose you log into a domain account on a Windows machine, then SSH to another one. Public-key authentication may let you log in, but you'll have to type your password again at some point to gain access to resources such as network shares—your Windows domain credentials did not follow you over SSH. With Kerberos, however, the same credentials which allowed login can also be forwarded to the remote host and used there for other purposes. And since Kerberos is a standard, the same can be true connecting from a Windows to a Unix host. This provides a much more pervasive and useful single-signon system.

11.5.2.3 Kerberos interoperability with OpenSSH and Tectia

As an example, we will take a lone Debian GNU/Linux box, attached to a network of Windows machines in an Active Directory domain named AD.ORG. The Linux box, lonely.ad.org, is running Debian-unstable and has the following packages installed; krb5-user, krb5-doc, and ssh-krb5 (which as of this writing is based on OpenSSH 3.8.1). The Windows machines are running the Tectia Windows Server, Version 4.2 or later. Suppose you have an account, "joe," in the Windows domain, you're logged into the Debian machine, and you want to connect to the Windows server, "winnie," You simply type:

```
lonely% kinit -f joe@AD.ORG
```

Amazingly, this prompts for your Windows password, and (assuming you type it in correctly)—it works! No errors, no complaints, no "DANGER! WARNING! WINDOWS INCOMPATIBILITY DETECTED!" Disbelievingly, you type:

```
lonely% klist
Ticket cache: FILE:/tmp/krb5cc_11500
```

```
Default principal: joe@AD.ORG

Valid starting       Expires            Service principal
01/30/05 02:28:35  01/30/05 10:28:41  krbtgt/AD.ORG@AD.ORG
        renew until 01/30/05 03:28:35
```

You have just received Kerberos credentials from a Windows Domain Controller—
say, "dc1." No local configuration was necessary, because *kinit* found the domain
controller via the DNS, using records like this:

```
$ORIGIN ad.org
_kerberos                 TXT     "AD.ORG"
_kerberos._udp            SRV     0 0 88  dc1
_kerberos-master._udp     SRV     0 0 88  dc1
_kpasswd._udp             SRV     0 0 464 dc1
_kerberos-adm._tcp        SRV     0 0 749 dc1
_kerberos-iv._udp         SRV     0 0 750 dc1
```

These tell a DNS client that machines with names under *ad.org* belong to the AD.ORG
Kerberos realm, and that a Kerberos KDC is available on *dc1.ad.org* via UDP to port 88
(among other Kerberos services: some of these records might be absent or unnecessary
in your DNS). The Windows DNS servers for the domain will publish such records
automatically. If you have an alternate or more complicated configuration—say, using
non-Windows nameservers—then you may have to add these records yourself (or you
could resort to local configuration; see the manpage for *krb5.conf*).

Trembling with technological anticipation, you forge onward:

```
lonely% ssh winnie
The authenticity of host 'winnie (10.2.17.4)' can't be established.
DSA key fingerprint is b6:b2:09:81:f4:c7:96:43:4a:0c:cc:12:9d:61:54:1f.
Are you sure you want to continue connecting (yes/no)?
```

Remember that SSH server authentication happens first, before user authentication;
this shows that we're still using the usual SSH key-based server authentication
(assuming you don't already have winnie's key in your known-hosts list). That's dis-
appointing, but we'll talk about that later. Assuming you say yes and continue,
though...

```
Warning: Permanently added 'winnie,10.2.17.4' (DSA) to the list of known hosts.
Microsoft Windows XP [Version 5.1.2600]
(C) Copyright 1985-2001 Microsoft Corp.

C:\Documents and Settings\joe>
```

You have been logged into the Windows machine! Furthermore, you'll find that you
have Windows domain credentials there; you could, for example, map a network
share (via the *net use* command) that requires the joe identity to access—without
retyping your password. Repeating the *ssh* command with *–v* will show the details:

```
lonely% ssh -v winnie
OpenSSH_3.8.1p1 Debian-krb5 3.8.1p1-7, OpenSSL 0.9.7e 25 Oct 2004
debug1: Reading configuration data /etc/ssh/ssh_config
```

```
debug1: Connecting to winnie [10.2.17.4] port 22.
debug1: Connection established.
...
debug1: Remote protocol version 2.0, remote software version 4.2.0.21 SSH Secure
Shell Windows NT Server
debug1: no match: 4.2.0.21 SSH Secure Shell Windows NT Server
debug1: Enabling compatibility mode for protocol 2.0
debug1: Local version string SSH-2.0-OpenSSH_3.8.1p1  Debian-krb5 3.8.1p1-7
...
debug1: Authentications that can continue: gssapi-with-mic,gssapi,publickey,password
debug1: Next authentication method: gssapi-with-mic
debug1: Authentication succeeded (gssapi-with-mic).
```

The user authentication method chosen is gssapi-with-mic, an improvement which
fixes a security flaw in the earlier method named simply gssapi. A subsequent *klist*
on the client side shows the new Kerberos ticket acquired for the connection:

```
lonely% klist
Ticket cache: FILE:/tmp/krb5cc_11500
Default principal: joe@AD.ORG

Valid starting     Expires             Service principal
01/30/05 02:28:35  01/30/05 10:28:41  krbtgt/AD.ORG@AD.ORG
        renew until 01/30/05 03:28:35
01/30/05 02:45:00  01/30/05 03:45:00  host/winnie.ad.org@AD.ORG
        renew until 01/30/05 03:28:35
```

Now, of course, there are many possible combinations of client, server, and Kerberos systems, and some of them will require more work. For example, going the
other way in this scenario (Windows to Linux) would mean joining the Debian box
to the Windows Kerberos realm. You could do this using Resource Kit utilities to
add its host principal, host/lonely.ad.org@AD.ORG, to the domain controller; extract a
Unix-compatible *keytab* file from it; and copy it to */etc/krb5.keytab* on the Linux
machine. Or, you might solve the problem a different way by placing the non-
Windows hosts in a separate realm, perhaps with Linux-based KDCs, and establishing inter-realm trust between them. These issues are more specific to Kerberos
administration than to SSH proper, and are beyond our scope here.

Before leaving this case study, let's discuss some final details of SSH configuration,
server authentication, and network address translation (NAT).

SSH configuration. The Debian *ssh-krb5* package is built with Kerberos authentication
turned on by default; that's not normally true. In other situations you would have to
set some configuration options:

```
# ~/.ssh/config
GSSAPIAuthentication        yes
GSSAPIDelegateCredentials   yes
```

You might not want to delegate credentials automatically for all connections,
though, just as you might not set X forwarding on by default: it could give access to
an attacker if the remote host has been compromised.

Server authentication. The secsh-keyex draft defines Kerberos server authentication as well, in the form of new SSH-TRANS key exchange methods using GSSAPI. This part of the draft is not as widely implemented as user authentication, however; for example, the Debian and OS X versions of OpenSSH support it, whereas the main OpenSSH and Tectia do not. Its use is controlled with the GSSAPIKeyExchange server keyword. To see that the client supports it, look in the -v trace for lines like this:

```
debug1: Mechanism encoded as toWM5Slw5Ew8Mqkay+al2g==
debug1: Mechanism encoded as A/vxljAEU54gt9a48EiANQ==
```

The "mechanisms" here are GSSAPI mechanisms, and these messages occur during the key-exchange phase.

Kerberos server authentication, when available, has several advantages:

It relieves you of managing known-hosts lists
> The client doesn't consult these files at all; instead, it relies on Kerberos to validate the server's identity. In fact, depending on the server implementation, you may be able to dispense with even generating host keys at all; the draft defines a "null" host key type for just this situation, where none is required. Of course, this would keep non-Kerberized clients from connecting at all, so you might want to keep host keys anyway for compatibility's sake.

It automatically deals with host aliases
> With known-host lists, every possible name a host might be called must be listed with that host's key in the file. Kerberos, though, uses the server's canonical name from the DNS, obtained by mapping the given name to an address and then mapping that address back to a name. As long as you maintain your hosts' canonical names properly and use them for corresponding Kerberos service principals, aliases will be handled automatically.

> Note that this does entail some security trade-off: an attacker who can subvert the DNS can cause an SSH client to authenticate the server against the wrong name. Of course, the server it contacts must still actually validate against Kerberos with this name, so it can't be just any machine—but it might have credentials from a host the attacker previously compromised. This level of risk may be acceptable, but should be considered. This isn't really a Kerberos-specific problem; the same feature could be used with hostkey authentication, with the same usability/security trade-off.

It's much faster
> Since Kerberos uses symmetric cryptography, it is noticeably faster than public-key methods. If both server and user authentication happen via Kerberos, new SSH connections can be very fast. In fact, the Kerberos exchange that affects server authentication does client authentication as well, and some implementations support a userauth method named external-keyx that takes advantage of this fact. external-keyx says to the server, "Look back at the key exchange— you'll find it already authenticated me, so please let me in!"

There are some limitations, though. One is name uniqueness: hosts must have unique names known beforehand in order to be joined to the Kerberos realm. This shows up most immediately with the "localhost" problem: *ssh localhost* doesn't usually work with Kerberos server authentication, even when it works for connecting to the same machine using its hostname. This is because the name "localhost" means a different host on every machine—so there can't be an entry in the Kerberos database for "localhost," because it can only have one key. You can make it work by arranging */etc/hosts* files so that on each host, 127.0.0.1 maps back to that host's canonical name—but the way that hosts files work, this means the name must also forward-map to the loopback address, not the host's "real" address. This has some advantages, actually, but is likely to break some things also; it may not be worth it.

The problem can also show up with more complicated network situations such as proxies, tunnels, or clusters of machines with dynamically assigned and shared addresses—anything in which the simple server/hostname/address correspondence Kerberos needs is violated. Furthermore, it won't work for batch jobs if those don't also use Kerberos for authentication, which is often not the best choice. The bottom line is that while Kerberos server authentication can be useful, hostkey-based authentication usually needs to be available as well for exceptional situations.

Network address translation (NAT). Kerberos originally bound credentials to the address of the machine to which they were issued, to make attacks harder: if someone managed to steal a ticket, it would be harder to (mis)use it. However, in today's sad world of ubiquitous NAT, this can cause more trouble than it's worth. Most recent Kerberos deployments have this address-matching feature turned off, but you may need to do it yourself if not, e.g., with a statement like:

```
# /etc/krb5.conf
[libdefaults]
noaddresses = true
```

This actually controls whether clients include addresses in ticket requests, so when you change it you will need to run *kinit* again. Situations involving multiple credential-forwarding connections may have addresses creep back in anyway, due to forwarding code which requests them anyway even if the original ticket had none; again, most recent Kerberos code has eliminated this problem, but you may still see it.

11.6   Tectia Extensions to Server Configuration Files

In Chapter 5, we described the server configuration files in detail, including OpenSSH's *sshd_config* and Tectia's *sshd2_config*. Tectia provides several levels of configuration not found in OpenSSH, called *metaconfiguration* and *subconfiguration*, and also some unusual rules for quoted values. We now cover them in detail.

11.6.1 Metaconfiguration

Tectia recognizes specially structured comments at the beginning of configuration files. These lines determine the syntax rules for the rest of the file, and are therefore called *metaconfiguration information.*

Configuration files distributed with Tectia all start with lines of the form:

```
## SSH CONFIGURATION FILE FORMAT VERSION 1.1
## REGEX-SYNTAX egrep
## end of metaconfig
## (leave above lines intact!)
```

The first line specifies the syntax version number, and defines the start of the meta-configuration information. Increasing syntax version numbers allow the syntax rules to be extended, possibly in incompatible ways. As long as older configuration files explicitly specify their syntax versions, they can still be correctly understood by newer versions of the Tectia server.

The default syntax version (used if there is no metaconfiguration information) is 1.0. This refers to the "traditional" syntax rules understood by Tectia versions before Version 3.0.0 (when the metaconfiguration information syntax was introduced). The latest syntax version at press time is 1.1.

Syntax rules are further refined by lines that immediately follow the syntax version. These lines contain pairs of metaconfiguration parameter names and values, and look similar to the keyword lines in the rest of the configuration file, with two important differences:

- The pairs occur within comment lines.
- The metaconfiguration parameter names must always be uppercase.

Syntax Version 1.1 adds support for the REGEX-SYNTAX parameter, which determines how regular expressions are interpreted. The three standards are:

> egrep (the default for syntax version 1.1)
> zsh_fileglob or traditional (the default for syntax version 1.0)
> ssh

These values are case-insensitive, unlike the parameter names. Full syntax rules are described in Appendix B.

Metaconfiguration information ends when an unrecognized comment line (or a standard, uncommented keyword line) is encountered. It's a good idea to mark the end with an ordinary comment line (like "end of metaconfig" as shown earlier) that does not look like a metaconfiguration parameter, to prevent possible misinterpretation of adjacent comment lines and to enhance readability. Use of ## instead of # is just a stylistic convention to allow the metaconfiguration information to be more easily distinguished from unrelated comments.

Pitfalls with Tectia Metaconfiguration

Since metaconfiguration information in Tectia is represented as structured comments, there is an unfortunate consequence: typos can cause the information to be ignored silently, because unrecognized lines are just ordinary comments. This can cause subtle (and dangerous) misinterpretation of the rest of the configuration file.

We therefore recommend using the boilerplate metaconfiguration information in the sample configuration files from Tectia as a template. Edit carefully and sparingly, if you need to make changes (e.g., to use a different regex syntax). Resist the temptation to omit the metaconfiguration information, however, because explicitly specifying the syntax rules will protect you in the future if the default rules change.

For troubleshooting, the *sshd -d* command-line option [5.9] with the SshConfigParse module and a relatively high debug level can be informative:

```
# Tectia
sshd -d SshConfigParse=9
```

More precise rules for recognizing metaconfiguration information are:

- Metaconfiguration information must be at the beginning of the configuration file. It can only be preceded by empty lines or whitespace, but not by ordinary comments or uncommented keyword lines.

- Metaconfiguration information lines can only be separated by empty lines or whitespace. Don't try to add ordinary comments (or standard keywords) within the metaconfiguration information.

- The syntax version line must match the (*egrep*) regular expression:
    ```
    #.*VERSION[[:space:]]+[[:digit:]]+\.[[:digit:]]+.*
    ```
  Note that VERSION must be uppercase, but can be preceded by any other characters, which are ignored. At least one space must separate VERSION from the version number, which must have two numeric components, separated by a period. Any trailing characters are ignored. Here's a valid example:
    ```
    #VERSION 1.1 -- Tectia Configuration File for server.example.com
    ```

- Metaconfiguration parameter lines must match the (*egrep*) regular expression:
    ```
    #[#[:space:]]+[[:upper:][:digit:]-]+\s+.*
    ```
  Note that at least one space or extra # character must appear between the first # comment character and the parameter name (in contrast to the VERSION line), so a line like #REGEX egrep does not work.

  Parameter names can contain only uppercase letters, digits, or hyphens. At least one space must separate the parameter name from the value. Values can contain whitespace.

- Unrecognized parameter names are ignored, but metaconfiguration information continues as long as the parameter line is well formed.

11.6.2 Subconfiguration Files

It is sometimes useful to customize the SSH server configuration depending on the type of connection or session. For example, a system administrator might want to impose stronger authentication requirements if a connection originates from a client outside of a firewall, or to record more detailed logging information about the activities of special-purpose guest accounts.

Tectia servers support these kinds of conditional configuration modifications with host- and user-specific configuration files, which are known collectively as *subconfiguration files*. The subconfiguration files use the same syntax as the main configuration file, except as noted later. Each file starts with its own, independent metaconfiguration information.

The `HostSpecificConfig` keyword is used to update the configuration based on the client host:

```
# Tectia with zsh_fileglob or traditional regex syntax
HostSpecificConfig *.example.com    /etc/ssh2/subconfig/ourhosts

# Tectia with egrep regex syntax
HostSpecificConfig .*\.example\.com /etc/ssh2/subconfig/ourhosts
```

The first value is a pattern that matches hostnames or addresses, as described for the `AllowHosts` keyword. [5.5.3] For example, if all of the machines inside a firewall are assigned to a range of addresses, it might be convenient to use a netmask for the pattern:

```
# Tectia
HostSpecificConfig \m10.1.1.0/24 /etc/ssh2/subconfig/insiders
```

The second value is the filename containing the host-specific configuration.

Similarly, the `UserSpecificConfig` keyword specifies a pattern describing user accounts, and the filename with user-specific configuration settings that apply to those accounts. In the simplest case, the pattern matches usernames or numerical user IDs, as for the `AllowUsers` keyword: [5.5.1]

```
# Tectia with zsh_fileglob or traditional regex syntax
UserSpecificConfig guest[[:digit:]]## /etc/ssh2/subconfig/guests

# Tectia with egrep regex syntax
UserSpecificConfig guest[[:digit:]]+ /etc/ssh2/subconfig/guests

# Tectia
UserSpecificConfig 12[3-6][[:digit:]] /etc/ssh2/subconfig/guests
```

More generally, patterns have the form *user*[%*group*][@*host*]. The optional *group* matches either group names or numerical group IDs, as for the `AllowGroup` keyword: [5.5.2]

```
# Tectia with zsh_fileglob or traditional regex syntax
UserSpecificConfig *%[x-z]guests /etc/ssh2/subconfig/xyz-guests
```

```
UserSpecificConfig *%800[[:digit:]] /etc/ssh2/subconfig/guests-8k

# Tectia with egrep regex syntax
UserSpecificConfig .*%[x-z]guests /etc/ssh2/subconfig/xyz-guests
UserSpecificConfig .*%800[[:digit:]] /etc/ssh2/subconfig/guests-8k
```

Users can (and often do) belong to multiple groups: they are all checked.

The optional *host* matches the client hostname or address, as for the AllowHosts keyword [5.5.3] or HostSpecificConfig:

```
# Tectia with zsh_fileglob or traditional regex syntax
UserSpecificConfig guest@*.friendly.org /etc/ssh2/subconfig/friends
UserSpecificConfig *%trusted@\m10.1.1.0/24 /etc/ssh2/subconfig/trusted-insiders

# Tectia with egrep regex syntax
UserSpecificConfig guest@.*\.friendly\.org /etc/ssh2/subconfig/friends
UserSpecificConfig .*%trusted@\m10.1.1.0/24 /etc/ssh2/subconfig/trusted-insiders
```

The *user* cannot be omitted from the pattern. If the pattern has two or more components (*user*, *group*, or *host*), then *all* of them must match for the user-specific configuration to be read.

The Tectia server starts by reading the main configuration file, and sets up the default configuration, which can include references to the subconfiguration files, and an associated pattern for each. When a connection is accepted from a client host, the server forks, and the child process that handles the session inherits its own private copy of the configuration. This private configuration is discarded when the child process exits at the end of the session, so the private configuration can be modified without affecting the default configuration that is used as the starting point for other sessions.*

The metaconfiguration parameters are not considered part of the configuration and are not inherited by subconfiguration files. Metaconfiguration information is independently associated with each file, because it describes the syntax of that file's contents. Although it's possible to use different metaconfiguration parameters for subconfiguration files, this is confusing, and we strongly recommend starting each subconfiguration file with the same, explicit metaconfiguration information as the main configuration file.

Immediately after the server accepts a new connection, but before any conversation ensues with the client, the server uses the client hostname or address to check the patterns for all HostSpecificConfig keywords, in the order that they were specified in the main configuration file. The server reads each host-specific configuration file for patterns that match, and modifies its private configuration as it does so.

---

* If debugging options [5.9] prevent forking, then the single server process exits after handling a single session, so only a single copy of the configuration is needed.

Later, when the username has been specified by the client (and group memberships have been determined by the server for the user), the server checks the patterns for all UserSpecificConfig keywords, again in the order indicated by the main configuration file, and reads user-specific configuration files for matching patterns to further customize the configuration.

The order for reading the configuration files is important because it determines how keywords apply to the final configuration that is used for each session. Keywords that are read later either override or append to the values for earlier keywords—this principle applies whether the keywords appear multiple times in a single file, or in separate files.

For example, suppose our main configuration file contains:[*]

```
# Tectia: /etc/ssh2/sshd2_config
PasswordGuesses 1

UserSpecificConfig guest[[:digit:]]+    /etc/ssh2/subconfig/guests
UserSpecificConfig          .*%[x-z]guests /etc/ssh2/subconfig/xyz-guests

HostSpecificConfig       .*\.example\.com /etc/ssh2/subconfig/ourhosts
HostSpecificConfig .*\.foo\.example\.com /etc/ssh2/subconfig/foohosts

PasswordGuesses 2
```

When the server starts, it reads this main configuration file, and sets the value for the PasswordGuesses keyword first to 1, and then to 2. The server also records the filenames and patterns for the subconfiguration files.

Later, the server checks the patterns for the host-specific configuration files, in order. If a connection is accepted from *laptop.foo.example.com*, then both host patterns match. So, if the files contain:

```
# Tectia: /etc/ssh2/subconfig/ourhosts
PasswordGuesses 3

# Tectia: /etc/ssh2/subconfig/foohosts
PasswordGuesses 4
```

then the value for the PasswordGuesses keyword is overridden to 3, and subsequently to 4.

Finally, the server checks the patterns for the user-specific configuration files, again in order. If the client specifies the username as guest33, and the server determines that this user belongs to the group yguests, then both user patterns match. So, if the files contain:

```
# Tectia: /etc/ssh2/subconfig/guests
```

---

[*] We'll use *egrep* regex syntax exclusively in this running example for simplicity, but of course other regex syntaxes could be used as well.

```
PasswordGuesses 5

# Tectia: /etc/ssh2/subconfig/xyz-guests
PasswordGuesses 6
```

then the value for the PasswordGuesses keyword is overridden to 5, and eventually to 6, which is the value that is actually used for authentication.

The order for reading keywords is determined primarily by the order for reading files, and secondarily by the order of occurrence of the individual keywords within each file. In our example, even though the last PasswordGuesses keyword in the main configuration file appears after the subconfiguration keywords, the settings in the subconfiguration files still override the default configuration. Similarly, even though UserSpecificConfig keywords appear before HostSpecificConfig keywords in the main configuration file, the server always reads host-specific configuration files before user-specific configuration files.

It's therefore a good idea to order the keywords in the main configuration file to reflect the order imposed by reading subconfiguration files, with default settings first, followed by HostSpecificConfig and UserSpecificConfig keywords at the end. Our example would be more clearly written as:[*]

```
# Tectia: /etc/ssh2/sshd2_config
PasswordGuesses 2

HostSpecificConfig       .*\.example\.com /etc/ssh2/subconfig/ourhosts
HostSpecificConfig .*\.foo\.example\.com /etc/ssh2/subconfig/foohosts

UserSpecificConfig guest[[:digit:]]+    /etc/ssh2/subconfig/guests
UserSpecificConfig        .*%[x-z]guests /etc/ssh2/subconfig/xyz-guests
```

Because host- and user-specific configuration files are read in the order specified in the main configuration file, the patterns should be listed starting with general patterns first, followed by increasingly specific patterns.[†] Patterns can be carefully constructed and ordered to encode arbitrarily complicated logic for customizing almost any aspect of the configuration based on the client host, users, or groups: a very powerful feature.

Subconfiguration files can be further divided into sections, which are marked by even more specific patterns, each followed by a colon, on separate lines.[‡] The keywords in each section are used only if the pattern for the section matches. Sections end when a

---

[*] We have removed the first PasswordGuesses keyword, since it is always overridden by the second occurrence anyway.

[†] The order for reading files can also be viewed as a consistent progression from general settings in the main configuration file to increasingly specific settings for hosts and users in the subconfiguration files.

[‡] The Tectia documentation also refers to sections as *configuration blocks*, or *stanzas*. Subconfiguration sections have the same structure as those used in client configuration files [7.1.2], except for the interpretation of the patterns.

---

new pattern line is encountered, or at the end of the subconfiguration file. The section patterns in host- and user-specific configuration files are interpreted in the same way as the patterns for the HostSpecificConfig and UserSpecificConfig keywords, in the main configuration file, respectively.

Any line that ends in a colon character (":") is considered to be a section pattern line.

Sections are a useful alternative to separate subconfiguration files. We might choose to combine the host-specific configuration files from our original example as:

```
# Tectia: /etc/ssh2/subconfig/ourhosts
PasswordGuesses 3
# ... other general keywords for all hosts in example.com

.*\.foo\.example\.com:
  PasswordGuesses 4
  # ... other more specific keywords for foo.example.com

.*\.bar\.example\.com:
  PasswordGuesses 8
  # ... other more specific keywords for bar.example.com

.*\.baz\.example\.com:
  PasswordGuesses 9
  # ... other more specific keywords for baz.example.com
```

This is especially convenient if there are many general keywords for the primary domain, but only a few, more specific keywords for each subdomain. It's also handy if there are lots of subdomains, because we can add or remove subdomains without modifying the main configuration file.

Sections cannot be used in the main configuration file. This makes sense: it isn't at all clear what would be used to match such patterns. The server warns if any section pattern lines are detected in configuration files where sections are inappropriate, like the main configuration file.

Sections for user-specific configuration files work similarly. We can override settings for specific users:

```
# Tectia: /etc/ssh2/subconfig/guests
PasswordGuesses 5
# ... other general keywords for all guest usernames

guest[0-4][[:digit:]]*:
  PasswordGuesses 10
  # ... other more specific keywords for guest usernames with [0-4] digits

guest[5-9][[:digit:]]*:
```

```
    PasswordGuesses 12
    # ... other more specific keywords for guest usernames with [5-9] digits
```

or for specific groups:

```
    # Tectia: /etc/ssh2/subconfig/xyz-guests
    PasswordGuesses 6
    # ... other general keywords for all [x-z]guests groups

    .*%xguests:
      PasswordGuesses 15
      # ... other more specific keywords for the xguests group

    .*%yguests:
      PasswordGuesses 16
      # ... other more specific keywords for the yguests group

    .*%zguests:
      PasswordGuesses 17
      # ... other more specific keywords for the zguests group
```

Several other important aspects of server behavior follow directly as consequences of the order and timing for reading the configuration files. The server normally reads its main configuration file only when it starts, and must be signaled to reread the configuration later, if changes are made. [5.2.4] In contrast, subconfiguration files are reread for each connection, so no signaling is necessary if the files are modified. In fact, a "match anything" pattern can be used to store frequently changed keywords in a subconfiguration file, to avoid the need for frequent signaling:

```
    # Tectia with zsh_fileglob or traditional regex syntax
    HostSpecificConfig  * /etc/ssh2/subconfig/volatile

    # Tectia with egrep regex syntax
    HostSpecificConfig .* /etc/ssh2/subconfig/volatile
```

If an error is detected while reading the main configuration file, then the server exits. Errors within host-specific configuration files cause the connection to be terminated. For user-specific configuration files, errors result in denial of access.

Some keywords cannot be specified in subconfiguration files. In some cases, the keywords control server behavior that happens before the subconfiguration files are read. For example, it doesn't make sense to specify the Port keyword [5.3.3.1] in subconfiguration files, because the port (or ports) must be chosen to listen for incoming connections before any connections can be accepted. Certain other keywords are forbidden in subconfiguration files because they would be too confusing. For example, the HostSpecificConfig and UserSpecificConfig keywords are restricted to main configuration files: imagine trying to understand the pretzel logic resulting from nested subconfiguration files! Tables 11-1, 11-2, and 11-3 list the keywords permitted in each kind of configuration file.

Table 11-1. Tectia keywords permitted only in the main configuration file

AllowHosts	CertdListenerPath	DenyHosts
ExternalMapper	ExternalMapperTimeout	FIPSMode
HostCa	HostCAMoCRLs	HostCertificateFile
HostKeyFile	HostSpecificConfig	HostKeyEkInitString
HostKeyEkTimeOut	HostKeyEkProvider	KeepAlive
LDAPServers	ListenAddress	MapFile
MaxBroadcastsPerSecond	MaxConnections	NoDelay
OCSPResponderURL	PKI	PKIDisableCrls
PasswordAuthentication	Port	ProtocolVersionString
PubkeyAuthentication	PublicHostKeyFile	RSAAuthentication
RandomSeedFile	RequireReverseMapping	ResolveClientHostName
SocksServer	SshPAMClientPath	UseSOCKS5
UserSpecificConfig	XauthPath	

Table 11-2. Tectia keywords permitted in the main and host-specific configuration files, but not user-specific ones

AllowGroups	AllowTcpForwardingForGroups	AllowTcpForwardingForUsers
AllowUsers	AuthPassword.ChangePlugin	BannerMessageFile
ChRootGroups	ChRootUsers	Ciphers
DenyGroups	DenyTcpForwardingForGroups	DenyTcpForwardingForUsers
DenyUsers	DisableVersionFallback	ExternalAuthorizationProgram
ForwardACL	LoginGraceTime	MACs
PermitRootLogin	Ssh1Compatibility	Sshd1ConfigFile
Sshd1Path		

Table 11-3. Tectia keywords permitted in all configuration files

AllowAgentForwarding	AllowSHosts
AllowTcpForwarding	AllowX11Forwarding
AllowedAuthentications	AuthInteractiveFailureTimeout
AuthKbdInt.NumOptional	AuthKbdInt.Optional
AuthKbdInt.Plugin	AuthKbdInt.Required
AuthKbdInt.Retries	AuthPublicKey.Cert.MaxSize
AuthPublicKey.Cert.MinSize	AuthPublicKey.MaxSize
AuthPublicKey.MinSize	AuthorizationFile
Cert.RSA.Compat.HashScheme	CheckMail
DenySHosts	FascistLogging
ForwardAgent	ForwardX11
HostbasedAuthForceClientHostnameDNSMatch	IdleTimeout

Table 11-3. Tectia keywords permitted in all configuration files (continued)

IgnoreRhosts	IgnoreRootRhosts
NoOp	PGPPublicKeyFile
PGPSecretKeyFile	PasswdPath
PasswordGuesses	PermitEmptyPasswords
PrintMOTD	QuietMode
RekeyIntervalBytes	RekeyIntervalSeconds
RequiredAuthentications	SecurIdGuesses
SettableEnvironmentVars	SftpSysLogFacility
StrictModes	StrictModes.UserDirMaskBits
Subsystem-...	SysLogFacility
UserConfigDirectory	UserKnownHosts
Verbose	VerboseMode[a]
X11Forwarding	

[a] The VerboseMode keyword (or the Verbose synonym) [5.8] prevents forking only if used in the main configuration file. In subconfiguration files, it merely enables debug output.

11.6.3 Quoted Values

Tectia removes double quotes from values. The following lines are all valid:*

```
# Tectia
PermitEmptyPasswords "no"
PermitEmptyPasswords "y"es
```

In most cases, there is no reason to use quotes, but they are handy in a few, rare situations. If a value ends with a colon (:) character, it will be misinterpreted as a section pattern: [5.2.1]

```
# Tectia: misinterpreted as a section pattern!
AuthKbdInt.Plugin /usr/local/sbin/kiplugin --prompt color:
```

This is a particularly insidious error if it occurs in a configuration file that supports sections (e.g., subconfiguration files), because the section pattern will probably never match, so the rest of the configuration file is silently ignored![†]

To prevent this, enclose the value in quotes:

```
# Tectia
AuthKbdInt.Plugin "/usr/local/sbin/kiplugin --prompt  color:"
```

This works because the recognition of section pattern lines occurs before quotes are removed. Since the quoted line doesn't end in a colon, it isn't considered a section

---

* Single quotes have no special significance.

† The server does warn about section patterns in configuration files that should not have them, like the main configuration file, which makes the error easier to detect.

pattern line. Equivalently, you can also enclose only part of the value in quotes, as long as the quoted part includes the final colon:

```
, # Tectia
  AuthKbdInt.Plugin  /usr/local/sbin/kiplugin --prompt "color:"
  AuthKbdInt.Plugin  /usr/local/sbin/kiplugin --prompt  color":"
```

To include a literal quote character in a value, precede it with a backslash. For example, to construct a shell command that uses (shell) quotes to protect a command-line argument with embedded whitespace from being split:

```
# Tectia
AuthKbdInt.Plugin /usr/local/sbin/kiplugin --prompt \"Enter your favorite color:\"
```

When configuration files are read, the whitespace between the keyword and value is discarded, and any trailing whitespace at the end of each line is removed from the value.* Quotes can be used to retain this whitespace as part of the value. As a devious example, you can hide user configurations in a temporary directory named as a single space character:

```
# Tectia
UserConfigDirectory /tmp/" "
```

11.7   Tectia Plugins

The Tectia server can use external programs, known as *plugins*, for flexible handling of tasks like changing passwords [5.4.2.3], driving the process for keyboard-interactive authentication [5.4.5.2], or performing arbitrary checks for access control. [5.5.6] We'll demonstrate how to use plugins with several examples:

- Handling expired passwords
- Extending keyboard-interactive authentication
- Authorization

11.7.1   A Plugin for Changing Expired Passwords

Remember our discussion of expired passwords in Chapter 5? [5.4.2.3] We showed how Tectia's SSH server can detect an expired password at authentication time, and prompt the user to change it:

```
$ ssh server.example.com
rebecca's password: < ... old, expired password ... >
Authentication successful.
< ... the following output is from running the passwd forced command ... >
Changing password for user rebecca.
```

---

* Keywords that use multiple values separated by whitespace also discard the whitespace between those values. Otherwise, whitespace that is embedded within a single value is left unchanged.

```
Changing password for rebecca
(current) UNIX password: < ... old, expired password, again ... >
New password: < ... new password ... >
Retype new password: < ... new password, again ... >
passwd: all authentication tokens updated successfully.
Connection to server.example.com closed.
```

The SSH server accomplishes this by calling either the system password-change program (e.g., *passwd*) or an alternative program specified by the PasswdPath configuration keyword. This technique, which is the default, uses a forced command to change the password. This method is conceptually simple but has several drawbacks:

- No explicit indication is given that the password is expired, or that a forced command is being used. Of course, the prompts from the password-change program are a clue, but a user might be (understandably!) suspicious about prompts that demand passwords for no apparent reason. Furthermore, if the user intends to run some other command with similar prompts for unrelated passwords, she might be confused by unexpected interactions with the password-change program.

- While it makes sense to ask the user to type his *new* password twice, to avoid mistakes, it's annoying and unnecessary to require entering the *old* password twice. This happens because the first old password is sent to the SSH server while the second is demanded by the password-change program, and the server doesn't forward the password.

- The connection is closed after the forced command finishes, whether the password change was successful or not, and the user must then repeat the authentication with a separate *ssh* command, which in turn requires entering the new password yet again.

- The username isn't passed from the SSH server to the password-change program, since most programs only allow non-root users to change their own passwords, and some allow only root to specify a username on the command line. If several usernames use the same numerical user ID (a bad practice, but it does occur), then only the first user's password is changed.

Fortunately, the SSH-2 protocol provides a better mechanism for changing passwords during authentication, and Tectia allows a separate program, known as a *password-change plugin*, to manage the process. This mode of operation is enabled by the AuthPassword.ChangePlugin keyword:

```
# Tectia
AuthPassword.ChangePlugin /usr/local/libexec/ssh-passwd-plugin
```

Here's an example of a password change using the plugin:

```
$ ssh server.example.com
rebecca's password: < ... old, expired password ... >
Your password has expired.
New password: < ... new password ... >
```

```
Enter password again: < ... new password, again ... >
Authentication successful.
< ... login session starts ... >
```

As before, the client collects the user's password and sends it to the server, which verifies it. When the server discovers that the password is expired, it sends an expiration message back to the client, which informs the user about what's happening. The client then prompts for the new password and sends it to the server, which passes all of the necessary information (the username, plus the old and new passwords) to the plugin program to change the password. If the plugin tells the server that the change was successful, then the server considers authentication complete, and continues. Otherwise (if the change failed), the server tells the client, which can prompt the user to try again, without starting a new session or using a separate *ssh* command. Much better!

The plugin program runs with the privileges of the user, not those of the server. If the plugin program isn't found or can't be run for some other reason, then password changes always fail.

11.7.1.1 The ssh-passwd-plugin program

Tectia includes a generic plugin program, *ssh-passwd-plugin*, in most binary distributions.* *ssh-passwd-plugin* runs the system's password-change program within a pseudo-terminal, effectively acting as an intermediary between the SSH server and the program that actually performs the password change, as shown in Figure 11-14.

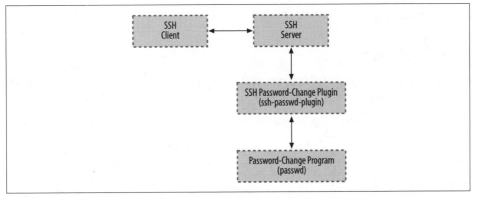

Figure 11-14. Tectia password-change plugin

The actions of *ssh-passwd-plugin* are controlled by the configuration file */etc/ssh2/ plugin/passwd_config*, which uses the same syntax as other server configuration files.† [5.2.1] The configuration file is read every time the plugin runs.

---

* Alternatively, the *ssh-passwd-plugin* program can be built from the source distribution.

† Including metaconfiguration information.

The *ssh-passwd-plugin* configuration consists of a series of `Request` and `Response` (or `FinalResponse`) keywords, which should occur in pairs:

```
# Tectia: /etc/ssh2/plugin/passwd_config with egrep regex syntax
Request "\(current\) UNIX password:"
Response $old_password$\n

Request "New password:"
Response $new_password$\n

Request "Retype new password:"
FinalResponse $new_password$\n
```

This example describes the behavior of the password-change program used for the preceding forced-command example.

Request values are regular expressions that match output from the password-change program.

 Quotes are required if the `Request` pattern ends with a colon (`:`) character, to prevent misinterpretation as a section pattern line [5.2.1], or if the pattern ends in whitespace, which is normally discarded. It's a good idea always to quote `Request` values.

Response values are strings that are sent to the password-change program when the preceding Request value matches. These strings can contain the following special tokens:

* `$user_name$`
* `$old_password$`
* `$new_password$`

which are replaced by the values supplied by the client and forwarded via the server. Use $$ in the string to send a single $ character, or \n to send a newline.*

The last expected response is indicated by the `FinalResponse` keyword; its value uses the same format as `Response`.

Response strings can also be one of the following special result values:

$ERROR_DISPLAY
    Send the match for the preceding `Request` value back to the client via the server and terminate, indicating that the password change failed.

$ERROR_LOG
    The same, but only send the match to the server for logging, not to the client.

---

* Newlines are not supplied automatically, so most response strings will need at least one explicit \n, usually at the end.

$SUCCESS

Indicate that the password change was completed successfully whenever the preceding Request value matches.

The special result values for the response strings have a $ character at the beginning only, not at the end, unlike the tokens for the username and passwords.

The result values are case-insensitive, but it's best to use uppercase to distinguish them from the tokens, which *must* be lowercase.

Unrecognized output from the password-change program is ignored, so expected error messages should be matched and sent to the user:

```
# Tectia: /etc/ssh2/plugin/passwd_config
Request "BAD PASSWORD: it's WAY too short"
Response $ERROR_DISPLAY
```

If error messages contain sensitive information, or aren't interesting for users, then they can be logged instead:

```
# Tectia: /etc/ssh2/plugin/passwd_config
Request "internal error: database corruption"
Response $ERROR_LOG
```

Similarly, if the password-change program prints a success message, *ssh-passwd-plugin* can use it to determine that the operation went well:

```
# Tectia: /etc/ssh2/plugin/passwd_config
Request "all authentication tokens updated successfully"
Response $SUCCESS
```

Some password-change programs succeed silently, however. In this case, *ssh-passwd-plugin* can examine the exit status returned by the password-change program to detect success, using the GetSuccessFromExit keyword:

```
# Tectia: /etc/ssh2/plugin/passwd_config
GetSuccessFromExit yes
```

A zero exit status indicates success. The default value for GetSuccessFromExit is no, meaning that the exit status is ignored. Unless you are using a broken program that returns random exit status values, we recommend configuring *ssh-passwd-plugin* to enable GetSuccessFromExit.

By default, *ssh-passwd-plugin* waits up to four seconds for output from the password-change program. This can be changed using the DataTimeout keyword:

```
# Tectia: /etc/ssh2/plugin/passwd_config
DataTimeout 10
```

The value is a number of seconds; time units are not recognized.

An alternate password-change program can be specified using the `PasswdPath` keyword:

```
# Tectia: /etc/ssh2/plugin/passwd_config
PasswdPath /usr/local/bin/goodpasswd $user_name$
```

This differs from the `PasswdPath` keyword in the server configuration file in that *ssh-passwd-plugin* expands tokens, as shown for the username.

> The server is supposed to supply the value for its `PasswdPath` keyword to the plugin as a default; the `PasswdPath` keyword in *ssh-passwd-plugin*'s own configuration file would then override the server's value. However, this isn't actually done (as of Tectia Version 4.1), so it's necessary for *ssh-passwd-plugin* to always specify the `PasswdPath` if the value needs to be changed.

Debugging the interactions between *ssh-passwd-plugin* and the password-change program can be challenging. Because unrecognized output is simply discarded, the usual symptom of mismatches in the configuration file is the error:

```
Timeout when waiting for exit status.
```

ssh-passwd-plugin recognizes the *–d* or *--debug* command-line options, but these are not passed automatically from the *sshd* command line to the *ssh-passwd-plugin* command line, so it's necessary to specify the option in the value for the `AuthPassword.` `ChangePlugin` keyword. Use the `GenPasswdPlugin` module and a high debug level to see all of the data exchanged between the programs:

```
# Tectia
AuthPassword.ChangePlugin /usr/local/libexec/ssh-passwd-plugin -d GenPasswdPlugin=9
2>> /tmp/plugin.dbg
```

Alternately, *ssh-passwd-plugin* uses the value of the environment variable `SSH_DEBUG_LEVEL`, which can be set before starting the server. If both the environment variable and the command-line option are used, the option wins.

Debug output is written to the standard error stream, but the server runs the plugin using the (Bourne) shell, so we append the output to a file with the `2>>` redirection. This is needed when the SSH server runs in the background as a daemon, because stderr is discarded. If the server is also running in debug mode, so stderr is already being sent to some convenient location, then the `2>>` redirection can be omitted, and *ssh-passwd-plugin* will send its debug output to the same place as the server.

11.7.1.2   A Perl package implementing the Tectia plugin protocol

All Tectia plugins use a simple, line-oriented protocol designed to facilitate scripting. Here we discuss some of the common elements of the protocol, and illustrate them by writing a Perl package, `Net::SSH::Tectia::Plugin`, containing handy functions that we'll use in our example plugin scripts. We chose the `Net::SSH` prefix to correspond with other Perl packages for SSH available on CPAN.

General Rules for Plugins

When working with plugins, be aware of the following important points:

Use absolute pathnames to specify plugins
> This is true even though some Tectia sample configuration files suggest using only command names as values for plugin keywords. The server intends to search the *libexec* and *bin* subdirectories of the Tectia install directory for plugin programs. However, bugs prevent this feature from working (as of Tectia Version 4.1), so only the PATH inherited by the SSH server is actually used.

Command-line arguments are supported
> Use quotes carefully in the values for plugin keywords if the command-line arguments include whitespace or colons. [11.6.3]

Know your stdin, stdout, and stderr
> The server runs a plugin program with pipes connected to the plugin's standard input and output streams for communication with the server. The standard error stream is discarded by both the server and the plugin, and should therefore be avoided.

As we discuss each type of plugin, we'll provide examples written in Perl, but any language can be used; in fact, the Tectia source distribution includes some sample plugins written as Bourne shell scripts.

The package starts with the usual preliminaries, identifying the names of the exported functions, and a version number for the package:

```
package Net::SSH::Tectia::Plugin;
use strict;
BEGIN {
    use Exporter;
    use vars qw(@ISA @EXPORT $VERSION);
    @ISA = qw(Exporter);
    @EXPORT = qw(
        &ssh_plugin_recv
        &ssh_plugin_params
        &ssh_plugin_send
        &ssh_plugin_success
        &ssh_plugin_failure
    );
    $VERSION = 1.01;
}

1;  # return true for import
```

The server sends lists of (key,value) pairs to the plugin, which reads them on its standard input. Each pair is formatted as "key:value" on a separate line, and the end of the list is marked by a line of the form "end_of_words" where "words" describes the kind of information in the list.

Keys and the end marker are case-insensitive. The plugin is supposed to ignore keys that it does not understand, to allow for future extensions to the protocol. If the end marker is not seen, the plugin must fail, as described shortly.

The ssh_plugin_recv function conveniently reads information lists from the server:

```
# Read a list of "key:value\n" pairs from the server.
# Usage: &ssh_plugin_recv($words), where "end_of_$words\n" (case-insensitive)
# marks the end of the list.
# Returns ("end_of_$words", key1, value1, key2, value2, ...) on success,
# or an empty list on failure.
sub ssh_plugin_recv
{
    my $words = shift;
    my @pairs;  # accumulated list of (key, value) pairs

    # read each line from the server
    while (<>) {
        chomp;  # discard newlines
        # return the end marker and list of pairs if the end marker is seen
        return ($_, @pairs) if /^end_of_$words$/i;  # case-insensitive

        my ($key, $value) = split(':', $_, 2);
        $key = lc($key);    # keys are case-insensitive: translate to lowercase

        push(@pairs, $key, $value);
    }

    return undef;   # return an empty list if no end marker was seen
}
```

All plugins start by reading a list of parameters from the server, so we provide a shorthand function for that:

```
# Read a list of parameters from the server.
sub ssh_plugin_params   { &ssh_plugin_recv("params"); }
```

The plugin sends messages back to the server by writing single-word tokens or "key: value" pairs, each on a separate line, to the plugin's standard output stream:

```
# Send a message to the server.
# Usage: &ssh_plugin_send($token) to send "$token\n"
#     or &ssh_plugin_send($key, $value) to send "$key:$value\n".
sub ssh_plugin_send
{
    local $| = 1;   # flush data to pipe after every write, to avoid buffering
    print join(':', @_), "\n";
}
```

Special messages are used to indicate success or failure of the operation performed by the plugin:

```
# Send success or failure messages to the server.
sub ssh_plugin_success  { &ssh_plugin_send("success"); }
sub ssh_plugin_failure  { &ssh_plugin_send("failure"); }
```

The server doesn't examine the exit status values returned by the plugin; it only notices success or failure messages. Nevertheless, it's good form to return a zero or nonzero exit status value for success or failure, respectively.

11.7.1.3 Creating a customized password-change plugin

Now that we've created the Net::SSH::Tectia::Plugin package, let's write our own password-change plugin script with it. This might be useful if passwords are stored in some kind of nonstandard external database, and are changed by a mechanism other than a traditional *passwd* program, so that *ssh-passwd-plugin* can't be used.

The plugin starts by reading parameters from the server, which include the user-name as well as old and new passwords supplied by the client:

```
#!/usr/bin/perl -w
use strict;
use Net::SSH::Tectia::Plugin;
my ($end, %params) = &ssh_plugin_params();
```

The keys and values for the parameters are stored in the %params hash for easy retrieval.

The plugin sends error messages back to the server using error_msg and error_log keys, which correspond to the $ERROR_DISPLAY and $ERROR_LOG special response values used by *ssh-passwd-plugin*:

```
sub ssh_plugin_error_msg    { &ssh_plugin_send("error_msg", @_); }
sub ssh_plugin_error_log    { &ssh_plugin_send("error_log", @_); }
```

It's a good idea for the plugin to check for and log protocol violations:

```
sub ssh_plugin_die
{
    &ssh_plugin_error_log(@_);
    &ssh_plugin_failure();
    exit(2);
}
&ssh_plugin_die("missing end marker for params")    unless defined($end);
&ssh_plugin_die("missing user_name")    unless exists($params{"user_name"});
&ssh_plugin_die("missing old_password") unless exists($params{"old_password"});
&ssh_plugin_die("missing new_password") unless exists($params{"new_password"});
```

Finally, the plugin changes the password, in our example using a change_password function that updates the database, and indicates the result of the operation to the server, which forwards it back to the client:

```
my $result = &change_password($params{"user_name"},
                              $params{"old_password"},
                              $params{"new_password"});

if ($result eq "success") {
    &ssh_plugin_success();
    exit(0);
} else {
```

```
        &ssh_plugin_error_msg($result);      # tell the client why it failed
        &ssh_plugin_failure();
        exit(1);
    }
```

The complete code for our plugin is shown in Example 11-1.

Example 11-1. Our password-change plugin

```
#!/usr/bin/perl -w

use strict;
use Net::SSH::Tectia::Plugin;

my ($end, %params) = &ssh_plugin_params();

sub ssh_plugin_error_msg   { &ssh_plugin_send("error_msg", @_); }
sub ssh_plugin_error_log   { &ssh_plugin_send("error_log", @_); }

sub ssh_plugin_die
{
&ssh_plugin_die("missing end marker for params")    unless defined($end);
&ssh_plugin_die("missing user_name")    unless exists($params{"user_name"});
&ssh_plugin_die("missing old_password") unless exists($params{"old_password"});
&ssh_plugin_die("missing new_password") unless exists($params{"new_password"});

my $result = &change_password($params{"user_name"},
                              $params{"old_password"},
                              $params{"new_password"});

if ($result eq "success") {
    &ssh_plugin_success();
    exit(0);
} else {
    &ssh_plugin_error_msg($result);      # tell the client why it failed
    &ssh_plugin_failure();
    exit(1);
}
```

The server is supposed to pass the value for its PasswdPath keyword to the plugin using the SSH2_PASSWD_PATH environment variable, which could be accessed as:

```
    my $passwd = $ENV{"SSH2_PASSWD_PATH"};
```

However, the server doesn't currently do this (as of Tectia Version 4.1).

11.7.2 A Plugin for Keyboard-Interactive Authentication

Keyboard-interactive authentication, including one-time passwords and challenge-response authentication, was covered in Chapter 5. [5.4.5] Here we'll show how to construct a plugin with our Net::SSH::Tectia::Plugin package to hook into keyboard-interactive authentication. It will prompt the user for some personal information, which is recorded (perhaps at account creation time) in a database.[*]

The plugin starts by reading parameters from the server:

```
#!/usr/bin/perl -w
use strict;
use Net::SSH::Tectia::Plugin;

sub ssh_plugin_die
{
    &ssh_plugin_failure();
    exit(2);
}

my ($end_params, %params) = &ssh_plugin_params();
&ssh_plugin_die() unless defined($end_params);
```

The plugin checks for protocol violations, such as a missing end marker for the parameters, and indicates failure using the ssh_plugin_die function.

The parameters are stored in the %params hash for easy retrieval. Keys supplied by the server include:

user_name
> The username requested by the client (to be used on the server).

host_ip
> The local (server) host address.

host_name
> The local (server) hostname.

remote_user_name
> The remote (client) username. This is sent only if it is known by the server from an earlier hostbased authentication.

remote_host_ip
> The remote (client) host address.

remote_host_name
> The remote (client) hostname.

> The *RFC.kbdint_plugin_protocol* file in the source distribution only defines the parameter's user_name, remote_host_ip, and remote_host_name. The Tectia plugin protocol requires plugins to ignore unrecognized parameters.

---

[*] See the file *RFC.kbdint_plugin_protocol* in the Tectia distribution for details, and *kbdint_plugin_example.sh* for another example implemented as a shell script.

The keyboard-interactive plugin next sends a list of prompts to be displayed by the client:

```
&ssh_plugin_send("instruction", "Please provide some personal information.");
&ssh_plugin_send("req",         "Favorite color: ");
&ssh_plugin_send("req",         "Pet's name: ");
&ssh_plugin_send("req_echo",    "Do you like chocolate? ");
&ssh_plugin_send("end_of_requests");
```

The optional "instruction" message is used to display introductory information.

 Although the SSH-2 protocol (as described in the IETF SECSH draft) supports newlines in the instruction string, there is no way to send them using the Tectia plugin protocol, which uses newlines as delimiters. If multiple instruction strings are sent, only the last one is used by the server.

Responses collected by the client are not echoed for prompts specified by req messages. If the response should be echoed, then the req_echo message can be used instead.

The list of prompts ends with the end_of_requests marker. When the server reads the marker, it sends the list of requests to the client.

After the client collects the replies and sends them back to the server, the server forwards them to the plugin using the same kind of list:

```
my ($end_replies, @replies) = &ssh_plugin_recv("replies");
&ssh_plugin_die() unless defined($end_replies);
```

The replies are stored in the @replies list as a series of (key,value) pairs; each reply pair corresponds to a request prompt. We use a list rather than a hash because the server uses a reply message for each response value, but the plugin can step through the list to set up a %replies hash for easy retrieval, checking for and rejecting protocol violations as it does so:

```
my %replies;
foreach my $reply qw(color petname chocolate) {
    my ($key, $value) = splice(@replies, 0, 2);
    &ssh_plugin_die() unless defined($key) && $key eq "reply" &&
                            defined($value);
    $replies{$reply} = $value;
}
&ssh_plugin_die() if @replies;  # too many replies
```

Finally, the plugin uses any subset of the parameters and the replies collected from the user for authentication, in our example using a verify_personal_info function, and indicates the result of the operation to the server, which forwards it back to the client:

```
my $result = &verify_personal_info($params{"user_name"},
                            # ... and other params, if relevant ...
```

```
                            $replies{"color"},
                            $replies{"petname"},
                            $replies{"chocolate"});

    if ($result eq "success") {
        &ssh_plugin_success();
        exit(0);
    } else {
        &ssh_plugin_failure();
        exit(1);
    }
```

Here's an example of keyboard-interactive authentication in action, shown from the client's perspective:

```
$ ssh server.example.com
Keyboard-interactive:
Plugin authentication
Please provide some personal information.
Favorite color: green < ... not echoed ... >
Pet's name: Elvis < ... not echoed ... >
Do you like chocolate? yes < ... echoed ... >
Authentication successful.
< ... login session begins ... >
```

Of course, a GUI-based SSH client could display the information in a different format.

The plugin can perform additional rounds of request/reply interactions if needed.

For example, if some of the responses were malformed, the plugin can ask again; in this case, an instruction message is often used to provide guidance about allowable values:

```
unless ($replies{"chocolate"} eq "yes" ||
        $replies{"chocolate"} eq "no") {
    &ssh_plugin_send("instruction", "Please answer \"yes\" or \"no\".");
    &ssh_plugin_send("req_echo",    "Do you like chocolate? ");
    &ssh_plugin_send("end_of_requests");
}
```

Subsequent interactions are sometimes needed to collect follow-up information whose relevance is based on previous responses:

```
if ($replies{"chocolate"} eq "yes") {
    &ssh_plugin_send("instruction", "Tell us more about how you like chocolate!");
    &ssh_plugin_send("req",         "Light or dark? ");
    &ssh_plugin_send("req",         "With nuts? ");
    &ssh_plugin_send("end_of_requests");
}
```

More realistic examples of additional queries would be prompting to update expired passwords, multistage challenge-response protocols, etc.

Only a single plugin can be specified by the `AuthKbdInt.Plugin` keyword. If multiple keyboard-interactive authentication techniques must be supported by the plugin, then it should ask the user to pick a technique during an initial round of interactions, and pose follow-up queries for specific techniques during subsequent rounds.

 To use Tectia's SecurID plugins along with other techniques that are supported by a custom plugin, the custom plugin can be written to forward information between the server and the SecurID plugins, according to the Tectia plugin protocol. An alternative is to recompile the server with built-in support for SecurID, eliminating the need for separate SecurID plugins.

The plugin should *not* implement its own retry logic for failed authentications. Instead, it should simply indicate failure and let the server manage retry attempts, according to the value for the `AuthKbdInt.Retries` keyword.

The plugin program must be written carefully, since it runs with all of the privileges of the SSH server (typically root). For example, it's important to treat all data supplied by the user as potentially hostile: consider buffer overruns, special characters used to construct filenames, etc. Perl's "taint mode" is useful for detecting possible security problems.

A more subtle danger is information leakage. For example, it might seem reasonable for a plugin to fail immediately after the initial parameters have been received from the server, if (say) the username is found to be invalid. After all, why ask for more information if the authentication will fail anyway? The problem with this approach is that it allows remote attackers to determine which usernames are valid, without authenticating. A system administrator might notice large numbers of failed authentications in the system logs [5.9], but by then, the damage has already been done.

A better approach is to always collect *all* information from the user, and make authentication decisions only after this has been done. The design of the prompts can be tricky when later interactions depend on the validity of previous responses. In some cases, it's necessary to use "fake" information so that all of the interactions will seem plausible when early replies are incorrect.

Even timing can be a concern. If authentication is computationally expensive, or requires a measurable amount of time to complete for other reasons, it may be necessary for the plugin to sleep for an equivalent interval when those costly authentication steps are skipped, so an attacker can't tell what's happening.

11.7.3   A Plugin for External Authorization

Next we'll write a plugin, once again using our `Net::SSH::Tectia::Plugin` package, to perform external access control. Our plugin will allow guest accounts to log in from untrusted systems, but only at certain times.* We covered external access control in Chapter 5. [5.5.6]

The plugin starts by reading parameters from the server:

```
#!/usr/bin/perl -w
use strict;
use Net::SSH::Tectia::Plugin;

my ($end, %params) = &ssh_plugin_params();

unless (defined($end)) {
    &ssh_plugin_failure();
    exit(2);
}
```

The plugin checks for protocol violations, such as a missing end marker for the parameters, and indicates failure (causing access to be denied) if any are detected.

The parameters are stored in the %params hash for easy retrieval. The server supplies the same keys as for keyboard-interactive plugins. [11.7.2]

The program then uses any of the parameters and other information at its disposal to determine if access should be allowed or denied:

```
my $restrict =
    &account_type($params{"user_name"}) eq "guest" &&
    &host_trust_level($params{"remote_host_ip"},
                      $params{"remote_host_name"}) eq "outside" &&
    &schedule(time) eq "prime";
```

Our example uses an &account_type function to categorize usernames, perhaps based on the username itself (like AllowUsers or DenyUsers [5.5.1]) or by looking up group memberships (like AllowGroups or DenyGroups [5.5.2]). Similarly, an &host_trust_level function classifies remote hosts, based on the address or hostname (like AllowHosts or DenyHosts [5.5.3]).

External authorization programs are especially useful when access control decisions must be based on complicated logic or information that is not understood directly by the Tectia server. For example, netgroups or other databases could be used by the &account_type or &host_trust_level functions to evaluate users or hosts, respectively, and other factors such as the time can be incorporated, in our example by a &schedule function.

Finally, the program indicates success or failure to the server to allow or deny access:

```
if (! $restrict) {
    &ssh_plugin_success();
    exit(0);
} else {
```

---

* See the file *RFC.authorization_program_protocol*.

```
    &ssh_plugin_failure();
    &ssh_plugin_send("error_code", "generic_error");
    &ssh_plugin_send("error_msg",  "Remote guest logins are not allowed during prime
time.");
    exit(1);
}
```

The program can send an error code and message to the server to describe failures. The protocol defines only two error codes:

password_too_old
> The user's password has expired.

generic_error
> Some other error occurred.

If the program informs the server about password expiration, then the server runs the system password-change program (either the default, or the value for the PasswdPath keyword) as a forced command. [8.2.3] It does not, however, run a password-change plugin, because the plugin applies only to the authentication phase, which has already been completed when the external authorization program runs.

In practice, password expiration isn't very useful for external authorization programs, since the programs don't interact (even indirectly) with clients, and passwords are really associated with separate authentication techniques that are performed earlier. Instead of using the password_too_old error code with an external authorization program, use a keyboard-interactive plugin [11.7.2] to flexibly handle password expiration.

Because that leaves only the generic_error code, the error_code message is itself not very useful. Perhaps someday the protocol will be extended to define other, more meaningful error codes, if they are needed to modify server operation.

The error message is an arbitrary string that explains why access has been denied.

Unfortunately, the server doesn't currently (as of Tectia V476 Version 4.1) use the error message string for any purpose whatsoever. It isn't forwarded to the client, so it can be displayed by the user, and it isn't even recorded in the system log or mentioned in debug output. [5.9]

It's still a good idea for external authorization programs to send an error message back to the server, however, so that future versions of the server might be able to use it.

The external authorization program should be written carefully, since it runs with all of the privileges of the SSH server (typically root). Perl's "taint mode" is useful for detecting possible security problems.

Troubleshooting and FAQ

OpenSSH and Tectia are complex products. When a problem occurs, your plan of action should be, in order:

1. Run the client and server in debug mode.

2. Consult archives of questions and answers to see if anyone else has encountered and solved this problem.

3. Seek help.

Many people jump immediately to Step 3, posting questions in public forums and waiting hours or days for a reply, when a simple *ssh –v* or FAQ can clarify the problem in moments. Be a smart and efficient technologist, and use your available resources before seeking help from the community. (Although the SSH community is eager to help if you've done your homework.)

12.1   Debug Messages: Your First Line of Defense

SSH clients and servers have debugging built in. When invoked with appropriate options, these programs emit messages about their progress and failures. You can use these messages to isolate problems.

12.1.1   Client Debugging

Most clients print debug messages when invoked with the *–v* (verbose mode) option: [7.4.17]

```
$ ssh -v server.example.com
$ scp -v myfile server.example.com:otherfile
```

So many problems can be identified in verbose mode. This should be your first instinct whenever you encounter a problem.

Please take a deep breath and repeat after us:

"*ssh –v* is my friend...."

"*ssh –v* is my friend...."

"*ssh –v* is my friend...."

12.1.2   Server Debugging

The OpenSSH and Tectia servers also print debug messages when asked: [5.9]

```
# OpenSSH
$ sshd -d -e

# Tectia
$ sshd -v
$ sshd -d debug_spec
```

In either case, the server enters a special debugging mode. It accepts a single connection, operates normally until the connection terminates, and then exits. It doesn't go into the background or create a child process to handle the connection, and it prints information on its progress to the screen (that is, to the standard error stream).

Tectia has a more complicated system for debugging: numeric debugging levels, specified with the *–d* option, where a higher number means more information. [5.9] In fact, *–v* for verbose mode is actually just a shorthand for *–d2*. At higher debug levels, the output is so huge that only SSH developers will likely find it of use in tracking down obscure problems. But you may need to crank up the level beyond 2 to see the information you need. For example, to have it report which algorithms are negotiated for a connection, use *–d3*. If you get the error message "TCP/IP Failure," turning up to *–d5* shows the more specific OS-level error message returned from the connection attempt.

When debugging a server, remember to avoid port conflicts with any other running SSH server. Either terminate the other server, or use an alternative port number for debugging via the Port keyword or *–p* option. For example, using OpenSSH syntax, run the server:

```
# OpenSSH
$ sshd -d -e -p 54321
```

Then use the *–p* option in the client when testing this debugging instance of the server:

```
$ ssh -p 54321 localhost
```

This way, you don't interrupt or affect another *sshd* in use.

12.2 Problems and Solutions

In this section, we cover a wide range of difficulties, organized by category. The sidebar "The Top 10 SSH Questions" lists what, in our experience, are the most frequently asked of the frequently asked questions. We focus on problems that may occur in many versions of the SSH software on diverse operating systems. We don't address the sorts of questions shown next that rapidly become obsolete.

- Compilation problems specific to one operating system, such as "HyperLinux beta 0.98 requires the --with-woozle flag"

- Problems and bugs that are specific to one version of SSH, particularly older versions

In all questions, we will assume you have already used debug or verbose mode (e.g., *ssh –v*) to isolate the problem. (If you haven't, you should!)

12.2.1   General Problems

Q: *The commands ssh, scp, ssh-agent, ssh-keygen, etc., aren't doing what I expect. Even the help messages look weird.*

A: Maybe they are Tectia programs when you are expecting OpenSSH, or vice versa. Try running these commands to find out:

```
$ ssh -V
$ ssh --help
```

Q: *When I try to connect to an SSH server, I get the error "Connection refused."*

A: No SSH server is running where you tried to connect. Double-check the hostname and TCP port number: perhaps the server is running on a port different from the default?

Q: *When I log in, the message of the day (/etc/motd) prints twice.*

A: Both *sshd* and the *login* program are printing it. Disable *sshd*'s printing by setting the serverwide configuration keyword PrintMotd to no.

Q: *When I log in, I see two messages about email, such as "No mail" or "You have mail."*

A: Both *sshd* and the *login* program are checking for mail. Prevent *sshd* from checking by setting the serverwide configuration keyword CheckMail to no.

12.2.2   Authentication Problems

12.2.2.1 General authentication problems

Q: *The SSH server says "Permission denied" and exits.*

A: This occurs if all authentication techniques have failed. Run your client in debug mode and read the diagnostic messages, looking for clues. Also read our solutions to specific authentication problems in the rest of this section.

Q: *How do I authenticate without typing a password or passphrase?*

A: The four available authentication methods for this are:

- Public-key with *ssh-agent*
- Public-key with an unencrypted key on disk (empty passphrase)

- Trusted-host
- Kerberos

Automatic authentication has a number of important issues you should carefully consider before selecting from the preceding list. Read our case study on this topic. [11.1]

Q: *I get prompted for my password or passphrase, but before I have time to respond, the SSH server closes the connection.*

A: Your server's idle timeout value may be too short. If you are a system administrator of a Tectia server machine, set IdleTimeout to a larger value in the server-wide configuration file. [5.3.3.5] If you are an end user of OpenSSH, set an idle-timeout value in *authorized_keys*. [8.2.7]

12.2.2.2 Password authentication

Q: *Password authentication isn't working.*

A: Use *ssh –v*. If the connection is being refused altogether, the SSH server is probably not running, or you are connecting to the wrong port. Port 22 is the default, but the remote system administrator might have changed it. If you see "permission denied," password authentication might be disabled in the server.

Make sure the server permits password authentication in the serverwide configuration file (PasswordAuthentication yes for OpenSSH, Allowed-Authentications password for Tectia). Also check your client configuration file to make sure you don't have PasswordAuthentication no.

If you are prompted for your password, but it is rejected, you might accidentally be connecting to the wrong account. Does your local username differ from the remote username? Then you must specify the remote username when connecting:

```
$ ssh -l my_remote_username server.example.com
$ scp myfile my_remote_username@server.example.com:
```

If this still doesn't work, check your local client configuration file (*~/.ssh/config* or *~/.ssh2/ssh2_config*) to make sure you haven't accidentally set the wrong value for the User keyword. In particular, if your configuration file contains Host values with wildcards, check that your current command line (the one that isn't working) isn't matching the wrong section in the file. [7.1.2.4]

One common problem on the server side involves OpenSSH and Pluggable Authentication Modules configuration. PAM is a general system for performing authentication, authorization, and accounting in an application-independent fashion. If your operating system supports PAM (as Linux and HPUX do, for example), OpenSSH will probably have been automatically compiled to use it. Unless you take the extra step of configuring PAM to support SSH, all password authentication will mysteriously fail. This is usually just a matter of copying the appropriate *sshd.pam* file from the *contrib* directory in the OpenSSH distribution, naming the copy "sshd," and placing it in the PAM configuration directory (usually */etc/pam.d*). The *contrib* directory contains several example files for different flavors of Unix. For example, on a Red Hat Linux system:

```
# cp contrib/redhat/sshd.pam /etc/pam.d/sshd
# chown root.root /etc/pam.d/sshd
# chmod 644 /etc/pam.d/sshd
```

If OpenSSH isn't using PAM, and password authentication still isn't working, the compilation options --with-md5-passwords or --without-shadow might be relevant. These make no difference if PAM support is enabled in OpenSSH, because they deal with how OpenSSH reads the Unix *passwd* map. When using PAM, the OpenSSH code doesn't read the *passwd* map directly; the PAM libraries do it instead. Without PAM, though, if your system is using MD5-hashed passwords instead of the more traditional *crypt* (DES) hash, you must use --with-md5-passwords. You can tell which hash your system is using by inspecting the */etc/passwd* and */etc/shadow* files. The hashed password is the second field in each entry; if the password field in */etc/passwd* is just "x", then the real entry is in */etc/shadow* instead. MD5 hashes are much longer and contain a wider range of characters:

```
# /etc/shadow, MD5 hash
test:$1$tEMXcnZB$rDEZbQXJzUz4g2J4qYkRh.:...

# /etc/shadow, crypt hash
test:JGQfZ8DeroV22:...
```

Finally, you can try the compilation option --without-shadow if you suspect OpenSSH is trying to use the shadow password file, but your system doesn't use it.

Q: *The server won't let me use an empty password.*

A: Empty passwords are insecure and should be avoided. Nevertheless, you can set PermitEmptyPasswords yes in the serverwide configuration file. [5.4.2.2]

12.2.2.3 Hostbased authentication

Q: *Hostbased authentication isn't working.*

A: Use *ssh –v*. If everything looks right, check the following. Suppose the client user is orpheus@earth, and the target account is orpheus@hades—that is, on host *earth*, user orpheus invokes *ssh hades*.

For OpenSSH:

- `PubkeyAuthentication yes` belongs in the server and client configurations.
- `EnableSSHKeysign yes` must be in the server configuration.
- A copy of earth's public host key must be in *hades:/etc/ssh/ssh_known_hosts* (or *hades:~orpheus:/.ssh/known_hosts2*).
- The entry may be in the target account's known hosts file instead, i.e., in *hades:~orpheus/.ssh/known_hosts*. Take care that "earth" is the canonical name of the client host from the server's point of view. That is, if the SSH connection is coming from the address 192.168.10.1, then `gethostbyname(192.168.10.1)` on hades must return "earth," and not a nickname or alias for the host (e.g., if the hostname is *river.earth.net*, the lookup must not return just "river"). Note that this can involve multiple naming services, since `gethostbyname` can be configured to consult multiple sources to determine a translation (e.g., DNS, NIS, */etc/hosts*). See */etc/nsswitch.conf*. If your systems don't agree on canonical hostnames, you'll have no end of trouble with hostbased authentication. You can work around such problems to an extent by manually adding extra host nicknames to the known hosts file, like this:

      earth,gaia,terra 1024 37 716416478851403631403090131934...

For Tectia:

- `AllowedAuthentications` must include the value `hostbased` in the server and client configurations.
- *ssh-signer* must be setuid root. More precisely, it needs to be able to read the private host key, which in the normal installation means it must be setuid root.
- A copy of earth's public host key in *hades:/etc/ssh2/knownhosts/earth.ssh-dss.pub* (or *hades:~orpheus:/.ssh2/knownhosts/earth.ssh-dss.pub*, if you specified `UserKnownHosts yes` on the server).
- Regarding canonical hostnames, the same comments as for OpenSSH apply.

12.2.2.4 Public-key authentication

Q: *How do I install my public key file on the remote host the first time?*

A: Here's the general method:

a. Generate a key pair.

b. Copy the text of the public key into your computer's clipboard or other cut/paste buffer.

c. Log into the remote host via SSH with password authentication, which doesn't require any special files in your remote account.

d. Edit the appropriate authorization and key files on the remote host:

- For OpenSSH, append the public key to *~/.ssh/authorized_keys*. Alternatively, run the program *ssh-copy-id*. [2.4.3]

- For Tectia, paste the public key into a new *.pub* file in *~/.ssh2* (say, *newkey.pub*), and append the line `Key newkey.pub` to *~/.ssh2/authorization*.

e. Log out from the remote host.

f. Log back into the remote host using public-key authentication.

When editing the remote authorization file, make sure your text editor doesn't insert line breaks into the middle of a public key. OpenSSH public keys are very long and must be kept on a single line.

Q: *I put my SSH public-key file, mykey.pub, into my remote SSH directory, but public-key authentication doesn't work.*

A: Placing a valid public-key file (e.g., *mykey.pub*) in your SSH directory isn't sufficient. For OpenSSH you must append the key (i.e., the contents of *mykey.pub*) to *~/.ssh/authorized_keys*. For Tectia, you must add a line of text to *~/.ssh2/authorization*, `Key mykey.pub`.

Q: *Public-key authentication isn't working.*

A: Invoke the client in debug mode (*ssh –v*). Make sure:

- Your local client is using the expected identity file

- The correct public key is on the remote host in the right location

- Your remote home directory, SSH directory, and other SSH-related files have the correct permissions [5.3.2.1]

Q: *I'm being prompted for my login password instead of my public-key passphrase. Or, my connection is rejected with the error message "No further authentication methods available." (Tectia)*

A: There are several possible causes for both of these problems:

- Public-key authentication must be enabled in both the client and server (OpenSSH `PubkeyAuthentication yes`, Tectia `AllowedAuthentications publickey`).

- Specify your remote username with *–l* (lowercase L) if it differs from your local username, or else the SSH server will examine the wrong remote account:

  ```
  $ ssh -l jones server.example.com
  ```

- Check the file permissions in your server account. If certain files or directories have the wrong owner or careless access permissions, the SSH server refuses to perform public-key authentication. This is a security feature. Run *ssh* in verbose mode to reveal the problem:

```
$ ssh -v server.example.com
...
server.example.com: Remote: Bad file modes for /u/smith/.ssh
```

In your server account, make sure that the following files and directories are owned by you and are *not* world-writable: ~ (your home directory), *~/.ssh*, *~/.ssh/authorized_keys*, *~/.ssh2*, *~/.rhosts*, and *~/.shosts*.

- For Tectia, if you use the *–i* option to specify an identification file:

```
$ ssh -i my-identity server.example.com
```

check that *my-identity* is an identification file, not a private-key file. (In contrast, *ssh –i* for OpenSSH expects a private-key file.) Remember that Tectia identification files are text files containing the names of private keys.

Q: *I'm being prompted for the passphrase of the wrong key.*

A: Make sure your desired public key is in your authorization file on the SSH server machine. Also check for typographical errors in any options specified for the key. [8.2] A mistyped option causes the associated key line to be skipped silently. Remember that options are separated by commas, not whitespace.

Q: *I ran ssh-agent, but when I run ssh-add to add keys, it cannot find the agent.*

A: *ssh-add* can communicate with *ssh-agent* only if certain environment variables are set. These variables—SSH_AUTH_SOCK for OpenSSH and SSH2_AUTH_SOCK for Tectia—direct *ssh-add* to the socket used by *ssh-agent*. The environment variables are set automatically if you run the agent correctly. [6.3.2] This implies that any shells run before *ssh-agent* won't know how to contact it.

In the shell where you're running the failed *ssh-add*, check for the presence of the appropriate environment variable:

```
$ env | grep SSH
SSH_AGENT_PID=7206
SSH_AUTH_SOCK=/tmp/ssh-gckksA7161/agent.7161
```

If you don't see it, then either you didn't run the agent correctly, you ran this shell before you ran *ssh-agent*, or you're not properly exporting the SSH_AUTH_SOCK variable. If you do see the socket variable, then perhaps it has an old value (from a previously run and now-dead agent). Try opening a new shell and running *ssh-add*.

12.2.2.5 PGP key authentication

Q: *After the PGP passphrase prompt, I am being prompted for my login password.*

A: If you get prompted for your PGP key, and then your password:

```
Passphrase for pgp key "mykey": ********
smith's password:
```

first make sure you're typing your PGP passphrase correctly. (For instance, PGP-encrypt a file with that public key and decrypt it.) If so, then there might be an incompatibility between the PGP implementations on your client and server machines. We've seen this behavior when the PGP key (generated on the client machine) doesn't have sufficient bits for the PGP implementation on the server machine. Generate a new key on the server machine.

Q: *I get "Invalid pgp key id number '0276C297'".*

A: You probably forgot the leading "0x" on the key ID, and SSH is trying to interpret a hexadecimal number as a decimal. Use `PgpKeyId 0x0276C297` instead.

12.2.3   Key and Agent Problems

12.2.3.1 ssh-keygen

Q: *I generated an OpenSSH key and tried using it with Tectia, but it didn't work. (Or vice versa.)*

A: This is normal. OpenSSH and Tectia (SECSH) keys aren't compatible. However, you can convert one to the other with *ssh-keygen*. [6.2.1]

Q: *Each time I run ssh-keygen, it overwrites my default identity file.*

A: Tell *ssh-keygen* to write its output to a different file. For *ssh-keygen* in OpenSSH, use the *–f* option. For Tectia, specify the filename as the last argument on the command line; no option is needed.

Q: *Can I change the passphrase for a key without regenerating the key?*

A: Yes. For *ssh-keygen* in OpenSSH, use the *–N* option, and for Tectia use the *–p* option.

Q: *How do I generate a host key?*

A: Generate a key with an empty passphrase and install it in the correct location. The OpenSSH source distribution has a *Makefile* target to do this:

```
# cd directory_containing_source_code
# make host-key           Will not overwrite existing keys
# make host-key-force     Will overwrite existing keys
```

or you can do it manually:

```
# ssh-keygen -t rsa1 -f /usr/local/etc/ssh_host_key -N ""
# ssh-keygen -t dsa -f /usr/local/etc/ssh_host_dsa_key -N ""
# ssh-keygen -t rsa -f /usr/local/etc/ssh_host_rsa_key -N ""
```

Likewise, the Tectia source distribution has a *Makefile* target:

```
# cd directory_containing_source_code
# make generate-host-key   Will not overwrite existing key
```

or you can do it manually:

```
# ssh-keygen -P -t dsa -c "DSA hostkey" /etc/ssh2/hostkey
```

Q: *Generating a key takes a long time.*

A: Yes it may, depending on the speed of your CPU and the number of bits you have requested. DSA keys tend to take longer than RSA keys.

Q: *How many bits should I make my keys?*

A: We recommend at least 1024 bits for strong security.

Q: *What does oOo.oOo.oOo.oOo mean, as printed by Tectia's ssh-keygen?*

A: The manpage calls it a "progress indicator." We think it's an ASCII representation of a sine wave. Or the sound of a chattering gorilla. You can hide it with the *–q* flag.

12.2.3.2 ssh-agent and ssh-add

Q: *My ssh-agent isn't terminating after I log out.*

A: If you use the single-shell method to start an agent, this is normal. You must terminate the agent yourself, either manually (bleah) or by including appropriate lines in your shell configuration files. [6.3.2.1] If you use the subshell method, the agent automatically terminates when you log out (actually, when you exit the subshell). [6.3.2.2]

Q: *When I invoke ssh-add and type my passphrase, I get the error message "Could not open a connection to your authentication agent."*

A: Follow this debugging process:

   a. Make sure you are running an *ssh-agent* process:
```
$ /usr/bin/ps -ef | grep ssh-agent
smith 22719    1  0 23:34:44 ?       0:00 ssh-agent
```
   If not, you need to run an agent before *ssh-add* will work.

   b. Check that the agent's environment variables are set:
```
$ env | grep SSH
SSH_AUTH_SOCK=/tmp/ssh-barrett/ssh-22719-agent
SSH_AGENT_PID=22720
```
   If not, then you probably ran *ssh-agent* incorrectly, like this:
```
# Wrong!
$ ssh-agent
```
   For the single-shell method, you must use *eval* with backquotes:
```
$ eval `ssh-agent`
```
   Or for the subshell method, you must instruct *ssh-agent* to invoke a shell:
```
$ ssh-agent $SHELL
```
   c. Make sure the agent points to a valid socket:
```
$ ls -lF $SSH_AUTH_SOCK
prwx------   1 smith   0 May 14 23:37 /tmp/ssh-smith/ssh-22719-agent|
```

If not, your SSH_AUTH_SOCK variable might be pointing to an old socket from a previous invocation of *ssh-agent*, due to user error. Terminate and restart the agent properly.

12.2.3.3 Per-account authorization files

Q: *My per-account server configuration isn't taking effect.*

A: Check the following:

- You might be confused about which versions of SSH use which files:

  OpenSSH
  > *~/.ssh/authorized_keys*

  Tectia
  > *~/.ssh2/authorization*

- Remember that the *authorized_keys* file contains keys, whereas the Tectia *authorization* file contains directives referring to other key files.

- You might have a typographical error in one of these files. Check the spelling of options, and remember to separate OpenSSH *authorized_keys* options with commas, not whitespace. For example:

  ```
  # correct
  no-x11-forwarding,no-pty 1024 35 86975112479875257784866526224505...

  # INCORRECT (will silently fail)
  no-x11-forwarding no-pty 1024 35 86975112479875257784866526224505...
  # ALSO INCORRECT (note the extra space after "no-x11-forwarding,")
  no-x11-forwarding, no-pty 1024 35 86975112479875257784866526224505...
  ```

12.2.4 Server Problems

12.2.4.1 sshd_config, sshd2_config

Q: *How do I get sshd to recognize a new configuration file?*

A: You can terminate and restart *sshd*, but there's quicker way: send the "hangup" signal (SIGHUP) to *sshd* with *kill –HUP*.

Q: *I changed the sshd config file and sent SIGHUP to the server. But it didn't seem to make any difference.*

A: *sshd* may have been invoked with a command-line option that overrides that keyword. Command-line options remain in force and take precedence over configuration-file keywords. Try terminating and restarting *sshd*.

12.2.5 Client Problems

12.2.5.1 General client problems

Q: *A feature of ssh or scp isn't working, but I'm sure I'm using it correctly.*

A: The feature might have been disabled by a system administrator, either when the SSH software was compiled (Chapter 4) or during serverwide configuration (Chapter 5). Compile-time flags cannot be checked easily, but serverwide configurations are found in the files */etc/ssh/sshd_config* (OpenSSH) or */etc/ssh2/sshd2_config* (Tectia). Ask your system administrator for assistance.

12.2.5.2 Client configuration file

Q: *ssh or scp is behaving unexpectedly, using features I didn't request.*

A: The program might be responding to keywords specified in your client configuration file. [7.1.2] Remember that multiple sections of the *config* file apply if multiple Host lines match the remote machine name you specified on the command line.

Q: *My OpenSSH ~/.ssh/config file doesn't seem to work right.*

A: Remember that after the first use of a Host directive in the *config* file, all statements are inside some Host block (because one Host block is terminated only by the start of another). The *ssh* manpage suggests that you put defaults at the end of the *config* file, which is correct; when looking up a directive in the *config* file, *ssh* uses the first match it finds, so defaults should go after any Host blocks. But don't let your own indentation or whitespace fool you. The end of your file might look like this:

```
# last Host block
Host server.example.com
 User linda

# defaults
User smith
```

You intend that the username for logging into *server.example.com* is "linda", and the default username for hosts not explicitly listed earlier is "smith". However, the line User smith is still inside the Host server.example.com block. And since there's an earlier User statement for *server.example.com*, User smith never matches anything, and *ssh* appears to ignore it. The right thing to do is this:

```
# last Host block
Host server.example.com
 User linda

# defaults
Host *
 User smith
```

Q: *My Tectia ~/.ssh2/ssh2_config file doesn't seem to work right.*

A: See our answer to the previous question for OpenSSH. However, Tectia has the opposite precedence rule: if multiple configurations match your target, then the *last*, not the first, prevails. Therefore, your defaults go at the beginning of the file.

12.2.5.3 ssh

Q: *I want to suspend ssh with the escape sequence but I am running more than two levels of ssh (machine to machine to machine). How do I suspend an intermediate ssh?*

A: One method is to start each *ssh* with a different escape character; otherwise, the earliest *ssh* client in the chain interprets the escape character and suspends.

Or you can be clever. Remember that if you type the escape character twice, that's the meta-escape: it allows you to send the escape character itself, circumventing its usual special function. So, if you have several chained *ssh* sessions all using the default escape character ~, you can suspend the *n*th one by pressing the Return key, then *n* tildes, then Control-Z.

Q: *I ran an ssh command in the background on the command line, and it suspended itself, not running unless I "fg" it.*

A: Use the *–n* command-line option, which instructs *ssh* not to read from stdin (actually, it reopens stdin on */dev/null* instead of your terminal). Otherwise, the shell's job-control facility suspends the program if it reads from stdin while in the background. Or better: use *ssh -f* (possibly with *–N*). [9.2.6]

Q: *ssh prints "Compression level must be from 1 (fast) to 9 (slow, best)" and exits.*

A: Your CompressionLevel is set to an illegal value for this host, probably in your ~/.ssh/config file. It must be an integer between 1 and 9, inclusive. [7.4.14]

Q: *ssh prints "Cannot fork into background without a command to execute" and exits.*

A: You used the *–f* flag of *ssh*, didn't you? This tells the client to put itself into the background as soon as authentication completes, and then execute whatever remote command you requested. But, you didn't provide a remote command. You typed something like:

```
# This is wrong
$ ssh -f server.example.com
```

The *–f* flag makes sense only when you give *ssh* a command to run after it goes into the background:

```
$ ssh -f server.example.com /bin/who
```

Q: *ssh prints "No host key is known for <server name> and you have requested strict checking (or 'cannot confirm operation when running in batch mode')," and exits.*

A: The client can't find the server's host key in its known-hosts list, and it is configured not to add it automatically (or is running in batch mode, so it can't prompt you about adding it). You must add it manually to your per-account or system-wide known-hosts files.

Q: *ssh prints "Selected cipher type...not supported by server" and exits.*

A: You requested that *ssh* use a particular encryption cipher, but the SSH server doesn't support it. Normally, the SSH client and server negotiate to determine which cipher to use, so you probably forced a particular cipher by providing the *–c* flag on the *ssh* command line or by using the `Cipher` keyword in the configuration file. Either don't specify a cipher and let the client and server work it out, or select a different cipher.

Q: *ssh prints "channel_request_remote_forwarding: too many forwards" and exits.*

A: *ssh* has a static limit of 100 forwardings per session, and you've requested more.

12.2.5.4 scp

Q: *scp printed an error message: "Write failed flushing stdout buffer. write stdout: Broken pipe." or "packet too long".*

A: Your shell startup file (e.g., *~/.cshrc*, *~/.bashrc*), which is run when *scp* connects, might be writing a message on standard output. These interfere with the communication between the two *scp* programs. If you don't see any obvious output commands, look for *stty* or *tset* commands that might be printing something.

Either remove the offending statement from the startup file, or suppress it for noninteractive sessions:

```
if ($?prompt) then
    echo 'Here is the message that screws up scp.'
endif
```

Q: *scp printed an error message, "Not a regular file."*

A: Are you trying to copy a directory? Use the *–r* option for a recursive copy. Otherwise, you may be trying to copy a special file that it doesn't make sense to copy, such as a device node, socket, or named pipe. If you do an *ls –l* of the file in question and the first character in the file description is something other than "–" (for a regular file) or "d" (for a directory), this is probably what's happening. You didn't really want to copy that file, did you?

Q: *Why don't wildcards or shell variables work on the scp command line?*

A: Remember that wildcards and variables are expanded by the *local* shell first, not on the remote machine. This happens even before *scp* runs. So if you type:

```
$ scp server.example.com:a* .
```

the local shell attempts to find local files matching the pattern server.example.com:a*. This is probably not what you intended. You probably wanted files matching a* on *server.example.com* to be copied to the local machine.

Some shells, notably the C shell and its derivatives, simply report "No match" and exit. The Bourne shell and its derivatives (*sh*, *ksh*, *bash*), finding no match, will actually pass the string server.example.com:a* to the server as you'd hoped.

Similarly, if you want to copy your remote mail file to the local machine, the command:

```
$ scp server.example.com:$MAIL .
```

might not do what you intend. $MAIL is expanded locally before *scp* executes. Unless (by coincidence) $MAIL is the same on the local and remote machines, the command won't behave as expected.

Don't rely on shell quirks and coincidences to get your work done. Instead, escape your wildcards and variables so that the local shell won't attempt to expand them:

```
$ scp server.example.com:a\* .
$ scp 'server.example.com:$MAIL' .
```

Q: *I used scp to copy a file from the local machine to a remote machine. It ran without errors. But when I logged into the remote machine, the file wasn't there!*

A: By any chance, did you omit a colon? Suppose you want to copy the file *myfile* from the local machine to *server.example.com*. A correct command is:

```
$ scp myfile server.example.com:
```

but if you forget the final colon:

```
# This is wrong!
$ scp myfile server.example.com
```

myfile gets copied locally to a file called "server.example.com". Check for such a file on the local machine.

Q: *How can I give somebody access to my account by scp to copy files, but not give full login permissions?*

A: Bad idea. Even if you can limit the access to *scp*, this doesn't protect your account. Your friend could run:

```
$ scp evil_authorized_keys you@your.host:.ssh/authorized_keys
```

Oops, your friend has just replaced your *authorized_keys* file, giving himself full login permissions. Maybe you can accomplish what you want with a clever forced command, limiting the set of programs your friend may run in your account. [8.2.3.3]

Q: *scp -p preserves file timestamps and modes. Can it preserve file ownership?*

A: No. Ownership of remote files is determined by SSH authentication. Suppose user smith has accounts on local computer L and remote computer R. If the local smith copies a file by *scp* to the remote smith account, authenticating by SSH, then the remote file is owned by the *remote* smith. If you want the file to be owned by a different remote user, *scp* must authenticate as that different user. *scp* has no other knowledge of users and uids, and besides, only root can change file ownership (on most modern Unix variants, anyway).

Q: *OK, scp -p doesn't preserve file ownership information. But I am the superuser, and I'm trying to copy a directory hierarchy between machines (scp -r) and the files have a variety of owners. How can I preserve the ownership information in the copies?*

A: Don't use *scp* for this purpose. There are better ways, with *tar*:

```
# tar cpf - local_dir | (ssh remote_machine "cd remote_dir; tar xpf -")
```

or *rsync*:

```
# rsync -ra -e ssh local_dir remote_machine:/remote_dir
```

The *rsync* method has the advantage of being interruptible and resumable without retransferring files.

12.2.5.5 sftp

Q: *sftp reports "Cipher <name> is not supported. Connection lost."*

A: Internally, *sftp* invokes an *ssh* command to contact *sftp-server*. [3.7.3] It searches the user's PATH to locate the *ssh* executable rather than a hardcoded location. If you have more than one SSH product installed on your system, *sftp* might invoke the wrong *ssh* program. This can produce the error message shown.

Q: *sftp reports "ssh_packet_wrapper_input: invalid packet received."*

A: Although this error appears mysterious, its cause is mundane. A command in the remote account's shell startup file is printing something to standard output, even though stdout isn't a terminal in this case, and *sftp* is trying to interpret this unexpected output as part of the SFTP packet protocol. It fails and dies.

You see, *sshd* uses the shell to start the *sftp-server* subsystem. The user's shell startup file prints something, which the SFTP client tries to interpret as an SFTP protocol packet. This fails, and the client exits with the error message; the first field in a packet is the length field, which is why it's always that message.

To fix this problem, be sure your shell startup file doesn't print anything unless it's running interactively. *tcsh*, for example, sets the variable $interactive if stdin is a terminal.

12.2.5.6 Port forwarding

Q: *I'm trying to do port forwarding, but ssh complains: "bind: Address already in use."*

A: The port you're trying to forward is already being used by another program on the listening side (the local host if it's a *–L* forwarding or the remote host if it's a *–R*). Try using the *netstat –a* command, available on most Unix implementations and some Windows platforms. If you see an entry for your port in the LISTEN state, you know that something else is using that port. Check to see whether you've inadvertently left another *ssh* command running that's forwarding the same port. Otherwise, just choose another, unused port to forward.

This problem can occur when there doesn't appear to be any other program using your port, especially if you've been experimenting with the forwarding feature and have repeatedly used the same *ssh* to forward the same port. If the last one of these died unexpectedly (you interrupted it, or it crashed, or the connection was forcibly closed from the other side, etc.), the local TCP socket may have been left in the TIME_WAIT state (you may see this if you used the *netstat* program as described earlier). When this happens, you have to wait a few minutes for the socket to time out of this state and become free for use again. Of course, you can just choose another port number if you're impatient.

Q: *How do I secure FTP with port forwarding?*

A: This is a complex topic. [11.2] FTP has two types of TCP connections: control and data. The control connection carries your login name, password, and FTP commands; it is on TCP port 21 and can be forwarded by the standard method. In two windows, run:

```
$ ssh -L2001:name.of.server.com:21 name.of.server.com
$ ftp localhost 2001
```

Your FTP client probably needs to run in passive mode (execute the passive command). FTP data connections carry the files being transferred. These connections occur on randomly selected TCP ports and can't be forwarded in general, unless you enjoy pain. If firewalls or NAT (network address translation) are involved, you may need additional steps (or it may not be possible).

Q: *X forwarding isn't working.*

A: Use *ssh –v*, and see if the output points out an obvious problem. If not, check the following:

- Make sure you have X working before using SSH. Try running a simple X client such as *xlogo* or *xterm* first. Your local DISPLAY variable must be set, or SSH doesn't attempt X forwarding.

- X forwarding must be turned on in the client and server, and not disallowed by the target account (that is, with no-X11-forwarding in the *authorized_keys* file).

- *sshd* must be able to find the *xauth* program to run it on the remote side. If it can't, this should show up when running *ssh -v*. You can fix this on the server side with the XAuthLocation directive (OpenSSH), or by setting a PATH (that contains *xauth*) in your remote shell startup file.

- Don't set the DISPLAY variable yourself on the remote side. *sshd* automatically sets this value correctly for the forwarding session. If you have commands in your login or shell startup files that unconditionally set DISPLAY, change the code to set it only if X forwarding isn't in use.

- OpenSSH sets the remote XAUTHORITY variable as well, placing the *xauth* credentials file under */tmp*. Make sure you haven't overridden this setting, which should look like:

```
$ echo $XAUTHORITY
/tmp/ssh-maPK4047/cookies
```

  Some flavors of Unix actually have code in the standard shell startup files (e.g., */etc/bashrc, /etc/csh.login*) that unconditionally sets XAUTHORITY to *~/.Xauthority*. If that's the problem, you must ask the sysadmin to fix it; the startup file should set XAUTHORITY only if the variable is unset.

- If you are using an SSH startup file (*/etc/ssh/sshrc* or *~/.ssh/rc*), *sshd* doesn't run *xauth* for you on the remote side to add the proxy key; one of these startup files must do it, receiving the proxy key type and data on standard input from *sshd*.

- Try *ssh -Y* (OpenSSH) or *ssh2 +X* (Tectia) to make forwarded X clients "trusted" by the display server. [9.4.5.3]

12.3 Other SSH Resources

If we haven't answered your questions in this chapter, try the following good sources of help available on the Internet.

12.3.1   Web Sites

The SSH home page, maintained by SSH Communications Security, is also a good resource of general information and links to related content:

http://www.ssh.com/

Information on OpenSSH can be found at:

http://www.openssh.com/

And of course, check out this book's web sites:

http://www.oreilly.com/catalog/sshtdg/
http://www.snailbook.com/

12.3.2   Usenet Newsgroups

On Usenet, the newsgroup *comp.security.ssh* discusses technical issues about SSH. If you don't have Usenet access, you can read and search for its articles on the Web at Google Groups:

http://groups.google.com/

or any other site that archives Usenet posts.

Before posting a troubleshooting question, run the SSH client and server in debug or verbose mode and include the full text of the debug messages in your note.

Overview of Other Implementations

SSH products are available not only for Unix, but also for Windows, Macintosh, Amiga, OS/2, VMS, BeOS, PalmOS, Windows CE, and Java. Some programs are original, finished products, and others are ports of OpenSSH or of Tectia ancestors, undertaken by volunteers and in various stages of completion.

In the remaining chapters of this book, we cover several robust implementations of SSH for Windows and the Macintosh. But first, in this chapter, we quickly survey SSH products for many platforms.

We have set up a web page pointing to SSH-related products that we know. From this book's catalog page:

http://www.oreilly.com/catalog/sshtdg/

follow the link labeled Author's Online Resources, or visit us directly at:

http://www.snailbook.com/

Also check out this third-party page listing many free SSH implementations:

http://www.freessh.org/

13.1 Common Features

Every SSH implementation has a different set of features, but virtually all have one thing in common: a client program for logging into remote systems securely. Some clients are command line–based, and others operate like graphical terminal emulators, opening windows with dozens of configurable settings.

The remaining features vary widely across implementations. Secure file copy (*scp* and *sftp*), remote batch command execution, SSH servers, SSH agents, and particular authentication and encryption algorithms are found in only some of the products. Most include a generator of public and private keys.

13.2 Covered Products

For Microsoft Windows, we cover in full chapters:

- OpenSSH, ported to Windows using the Cygwin library (Chapter 14)
- Tectia's commercial products for Windows (Chapter 16)
- SecureCRT, a commercial SSH client by VanDyke Software (Chapter 17)
- PuTTY, a small, free suite of SSH clients (Chapter 18)

For Macintosh OS X, we cover in a full chapter:

- OpenSSH, as included with Macintosh OS X (Chapter 15)

13.3 Other SSH Products

Unfortunately we can't cover every SSH implementation, but here are summaries to aid your explorations. Because SSH products need to remain secure, we list only products that are in active development (or at least have been updated in the past year or two) and that support the SSH-2 protocol. This means we've intentionally left out dozens of older SSH products with respected histories, like NiftyTelnet SSH for the Mac, Top Gun SSH for Palm, FISH for VMS, and Sergey Okhapkin's classic Windows port of the original SSH1. Old-timers like these have their place in history, but have been supplanted by more modern implementations.

We've organized the products by platform. Some products are free and others are shareware or commercial, usually quite inexpensive. Additionally, many of the commercial products have free evaluation versions available, so you can try before you buy.

13.3.1 BeOS

At press time, we have found no modern SSH clients for BeOS. There are a bunch of ancient ones (2000–2002) supporting the old SSH-1 protocol: search *http://www.bebits.com/* to find them.

13.3.2 Commodore Amiga

At press time, we have found no modern SSH clients for the Amiga. The closest is an Amiga port of OpenSSH (*http://www.chernoff.org/amiga/*, free). However, it's a port of Version 3.0.2, which is several years out of date.

13.3.3 GNU Emacs

ssh.el (*http://www.splode.com/~friedman/software/emacs-lisp/src/ssh.el*, free) is an Emacs interface for SSH client connections. It does not implement SSH itself, but invokes an external client (e.g., *ssh* from OpenSSH or Tectia) within Emacs.

13.3.4 Java

JavaSSH (*http://javassh.org/*, free), a.k.a. Java Telnet/SSH Applet, is just what it sounds like: an SSH client applet.

JSch (*http://www.jcraft.com/jsch/*, free), a.k.a. Java Secure Channel, is an implementation of the SSH-2 protocol.

MindTerm (*http://www.mindbright.se/*, commercial, but free for personal or limited commercial use) is an SSH client and terminal emulator. The same company sells Appgate Security Server, an enterprise-level security product with SSH capabilities.

SSHTerm Professional (*http://www.sshtools.com/*, commercial, but free for personal or limited commercial use). The same vendor also produces Maverick SSHD, an SSH server written in Java; J2SSH Maverick, a Java SSH library for programmers; and Maverick.NET, an SSH API for Microsoft's .NET platform.

13.3.5 Macintosh OS 9

MacSSH (*http://www.macssh.com/*, shareware) is the premier SSH client for OS 9. It supplanted NiftyTelnet SSH, which we covered in the first edition of this book.

MacSFTP (*http://www.macssh.com/*, shareware) is an SFTP client by the maker of MacSSH, for copying files securely between computers.

13.3.6 Macintosh OS X

Macintosh OS X comes with OpenSSH installed. However, MacSFTP is also available. [13.3.5]

13.3.7 Microsoft Windows

Windows SSH products have exploded in number in the past few years. Frankly, there are so many commercial SSH terminal clients it's almost ridiculous. On the other hand, it's nice to have choices.

Axessh 2.6 (*http://www.labf.com/axessh/*, commercial) is a terminal emulator and file-transfer program supporting SSH.

Ericom PowerTerm (*http://www.ericom.com/*, commercial) is a whole suite of SSH products for the enterprise.

F-Secure SSH (*http://www.f-secure.com/*, commercial) is an SSH-based terminal emulator.

Kermit 95 (*http://www.columbia.edu/kermit/k95.html*, commercial) is the classic program and protocol from the 1980s, updated to support SSH by borrowing code from OpenSSH.

OpenSSH on Cygwin (*http://www.cygwin.com/*, free) is a port of the whole OpenSSH suite to Windows and is the subject of Chapter 14.

PenguiNet (*http://www.siliconcircus.com/penguinet/*, commercial) is an SSH terminal emulator and secure file-copy program.

Pragma Fortress (*http://www.pragmasys.com/*, commercial) is an enterprise-level SSH server.

PuTTY (*http://www.chiark.greenend.org.uk/~sgtatham/putty/*, free), is a small but mighty suite of SSH clients covered fully in Chapter 18.

RemotelyAnywhere (*http://www.remotelyanywhere.com/*, commercial) is a remote system administration package that includes an SSH server.

Secure iXplorer (*http://www.i-tree.org/*, commercial) is a Windows Explorer-like program for accessing remote files. It is based internally on PuTTY.

Secure KoalaTerm (*http://www.foxitsoftware.com/*, commercial) is an SSH terminal emulator with particular focus on terminal emulation features.

SecureCRT (*http://www.vandyke.com/*, commercial) is a terminal emulator with SSH support, covered in Chapter 17. SecureFX is VanDyke's secure file-transfer program with a graphical user interface. It is not an SSH terminal program.

ShellGuard (*http://www.shellguard.com/*, commercial) is an SSH-capable terminal emulator with secure copy capability.

Tectia (*http://www.ssh.com/*, commercial) is the Windows implementation of the major product we've been covering throughout this whole book, from SSH Communications Security.

VShell (*http://www.vandyke.com/*, commercial) is an SSH server from the maker of SecureCRT.

WinSSHD (*http://www.bitvise.com/winsshd.html*, commercial) is an SSH server.

WiSSH (*http://www.wissh.com/*, commercial) is a "remote desktop" program that operates over the SSH protocol, encrypting traffic between your local machine and the remote PC.

ZOC (*http://www.emtec.com/zoc/*, commercial) is an SSH terminal emulator.

13.3.8 Microsoft Windows CE (PocketPC)

PocketPuTTY (*http://pocketputty.duxy.net/*, free) is a port of PuTTY.

PocketTTY (*http://dejavusoftware.com/pocketty/*) is another SSH terminal client.

13.3.9 OS/2

ZOC, the Windows client, is also available for OS/2. [13.3.7]

13.3.10 Palm OS

The only Palm implementation used to be Top Gun SSH, but it supports only the SSH-1 protocol and is quite old. Fortunately there are some new kids on the block.

pSSH (*http://www.sealiesoftware.com/pssh*, free) is an SSH client for PalmOS 5 and up.

TuSSH (*http://www.tussh.com/*) is an SSH client for PalmOS 4 and up.

13.3.11 Perl

Several free Perl modules (*http://www.cpan.org/*) are available that provide an SSH API for software developers:

Net::SSH::Perl
> An implementation of the SSH protocol, written in Perl

Net::SSH
> An SSH API that provides wrappers around the *ssh* command

Net::SCP
> An SSH API that provides wrappers around the *scp* command

Net::SCP::Expect
> Another wrapper around *scp*, this one supporting Expect (*http://expect.nist.gov/*) so that passwords can be passed to it programmatically

13.3.12 Unix Variants (Linux, OpenBSD, etc.)

We've covered OpenSSH and Tectia extensively in this book, but there are others....

Dropbear (*http://matt.ucc.asn.au/dropbear/dropbear.html*, free) is an SSH client and server intended to run in as little memory as possible.

Kermit (*http://www.columbia.edu/kermit/ssh.html*, free), the venerable communications program of long ago, has been updated with SSH protocol support.

lsh (*http://www.lysator.liu.se/~nisse/lsh/*, free) is an SSH-2 client (*lsh*) and server (*lshd*).

PuTTY runs on Linux as well as Windows. [13.3.7] In addition, there is an unrelated program gPutty (*http://www.defora.org/index.php?page=gputty*), that is a PuTTY clone for the GNOME environment.

SecPanel (*http://www.pingx.net/secpanel/*, free) is a graphical, point-and-click manager for SSH client connections. It's written in the programming language *tcl* and invokes SSH clients from your installed OpenSSH or Tectia distribution.

13.3.13 VMS

BAMSE (*http://www.free.lp.se/bamse/*) is an SSH client. It has not been updated since 2002 but is supposedly the best VMS client available.

OpenSSH for Windows

OpenSSH, though originally written for Unix-like operating systems, runs well under Windows too. If you prefer command-line programs rather than a GUI, OpenSSH is probably your best bet for a free SSH implementation.

In order to run OpenSSH on Windows, you must install the Cygwin library (*http://www.cygwin.com/*) and associated programs. The installation is pretty simple but large: some users complain about the added "bloat" of Cygwin's many programs. If this concerns you, check out OpenSSH For Windows (*http://sshwindows.sourceforge.net/*), a minimal installation of OpenSSH and Cygwin. Our perspective, however, is that Cygwin comes with so many mind-bogglingly useful tools (ported from Unix) that you might as well do a full install.

In most cases, OpenSSH operates the same way under Windows as it does under Unix. In this chapter we'll cover only the differences; in Chapter 15 we will cover OpenSSH on the Macintosh similarly.

 Like Unix, Cygwin uses the term "directory" to refer to a folder. We will use the Cygwin terminology.

14.1 Installation

Cygwin is available from *http://www.cygwin.com/*. Download the installation program and run it. Make sure to install the following packages:

openssh
> The full suite of programs and support files

cygrunsrv
> A program needed to run *sshd* as a Windows service

Once Cygwin is installed, complete the setup:

1. Make sure that *c:\cygwin\bin* is in your search path.

2. Create an environment variable called CYGWIN, and give it the value ntsec tty.

14.2   Using the SSH Clients

The client programs *ssh*, *scp*, and *sftp* work just as they do on Unix:

```
# Log into server.example.com as user smith
$ ssh -l smith server.example.com

# Copy myfile from your local machine to server.example.com
$ scp myfile server.example.com:

# Run an interactive file-copy session with sftp
$ sftp server.example.com
```

The only bit of trickiness is locating your *~/.ssh* directory via Windows. On Unix platforms, your home directory is located in an obvious place, usually */home/ yourname*. And in fact, if you run a Cygwin shell, you can literally refer to */home/ yourname* as well. But what if you're using a standard Windows command shell (e.g., *cmd*) or browsing files with Windows Explorer: how can you find your *~/.ssh* directory? Simply type this command from a Windows command shell:

```
C:\> cygpath -w ~
C:\cygwin\home\smith
```

The *cygpath* command converts Cygwin paths into Windows paths, and the lone tilde (~) represents your Cygwin home directory. In this example, *cygpath* reveals your home directory to be *C:\cygwin\home\smith*. Thus, your SSH-related client files will be stored in the directory *C:\cygwin\home\smith\.ssh*.

14.3   Setting Up the SSH Server

The SSH server, *sshd*, runs under Cygwin as a standard Windows service, called (not surprisingly) Cygwin SSH Service. Cygwin provides a script, called *ssh-host-config*, to set this up. Here's what to do:

 The Cygwin SSH Service (a.k.a. *sshd*) runs only on flavors of Windows that support services: NT, 2000, XP, 2003, etc.

1. Make sure you've set up the path and environment variables for OpenSSH and Cygwin. [14.1]

2. From an account with administrative privileges, run:

```
C:\> ssh-host-config
```

3. Answer yes to all questions.

4. When *ssh-host-config* completes, your service should be ready to run. Open your Services control panel, look for Cygwin SSHD Service, and start the service. Alternatively, use the command line:

```
C:\> net start sshd
```

You might also want to set the service startup to Automatic, so it runs whenever you boot the computer. To stop the service, again use the Services control panel or type:

```
C:\> net stop sshd
```

If the service refuses to run, here are some things to try:

- Make sure the file */var/log/sshd.log* is writable by the SYSTEM account.
- Read */var/log/sshd.log* for error messages.

To test the server, connect to yourself:

```
C:\> ssh localhost
```

You should be prompted for your password and be able to log in.

 Serverwide configuration files are found in */etc*, such as */etc/sshd_config*. This is in contrast to Unix-like systems that usually keep these files in */etc/ssh*.

14.3.1 Opening Remote Windows on the Desktop

If you want to run graphical applications via *ssh* that open windows, such as *notepad* or *regedit*:

```
C:\> ssh my-pc-name notepad
```

this will not work unless you grant *sshd* permission to do so. Here's how to do it on Windows XP and 2000:

1. Open the Services control panel.

2. Stop the *Cygwin sshd* service.

3. Double-click the *Cygwin sshd* service to view its properties.

4. Select the Log On tab.

5. Under "Log on as," select the Local System account and check the box "Allow service to interact with desktop."

6. Click OK and restart the *Cygwin sshd* service.

Before doing this, however, carefully consider the security implications. You're permitting *any* user with SSH privileges—not just the logged-in user, not just administrators—to open windows on the desktop remotely.

14.4 Public-Key Authentication

The OpenSSH clients—*ssh*, *scp*, and *sftp*—and the key-related programs—*ssh-key-gen*, *ssh-agent*, and **ssh-add** (covered in Chapter 6)—use public-key authentication just as they do under Unix. You might need to know where your *~/.ssh* folder is to refer to keys. [14.2]

When connecting to the Cygwin SSHD Service (*sshd*) from the outside world, there are a few things to think about:

- Make sure your *~/.ssh/authorized_keys* file contains the appropriate public keys. [6.1.1]

- Check the `Cygwin SSHD Service` in the Services control panel, and note the NT user account under which it is running. Then make sure that this account:

  — Has read access to your *~/.ssh* directory and your *~/.ssh/authorized_keys* file.

  — Has read access to the host keys in the Cygwin */etc* directory.

  — Has write access to the log file */var/log/sshd.log*.

  — Is in the local Administrators group, if you plan to invoke operations by SSH that require administrative privileges. Then authenticate using this account. (For more flexible credentials, consider a PKI solution. [11.5] Cygwin includes a Kerberos package.*)

  — Is listed in the Cygwin */etc/passwd* file. Use the Cygwin *mkpasswd* program to generate this file if you need; for example, in the Cygwin shell:

    ```
    $ mkpasswd -l > /etc/passwd
    ```

    but make sure you understand what you're doing so that you don't wipe out vital accounts! Run *man mkpasswd* to learn more.

14.4.1 Running an Agent

An agent is a program that keeps private keys in memory and provides authentication services to SSH clients. If you preload an agent with private keys at the beginning of a login session, your SSH clients won't prompt for passphrases. Instead, they communicate with the agent as needed. [2.5] The OpenSSH agent program is *ssh-agent*.

In order for *ssh-agent* to work, it communicates via environment variables. [6.3.2] If you're using the Cygwin shell (*bash*), you can start the agent via the same methods as

---

* For Kerberos or GSSAPI support., you might need to recompile OpenSSH. At press time, `KerberosAuthentication` and `GSSAPIAuthentication` are disabled in the Cygwin binaries for OpenSSH. You'll need to download the OpenSSH source code and recompile it with the GNU C compiler, *gcc*, also included with Cygwin. Once things are set up, they do work as in our case study. [11.5.2]

on Unix. Unfortunately, these methods don't work immediately on Windows if you're using the command shell (*cmd.exe* or *command.exe*), so here is a quick recipe:

1. Run the agent:

```
C:\> ssh-agent
SSH_AUTH_SOCK=/tmp/ssh-agent.1468; export SSH_AUTH_SOCK;
SSH_AGENT_PID=3212; export SSH_AGENT_PID;
echo Agent pid 3212;
```

2. Notice the output includes some environment variables:

```
SSH_AUTH_SOCK=/tmp/ssh-agent.1468; export SSH_AUTH_SOCK;
SSH_AGENT_PID=3212; export SSH_AGENT_PID;
```

3. Set the environment variables by hand:

```
C:\> set SSH_AUTH_SOCK=/tmp/ssh-agent.1468
C:\> set SSH_AGENT_PID=3212
```

4. Your agent is ready to load with keys: [2.5]

```
C:\> ssh-add
Enter passphrase for /home/you/.ssh/id_dsa: ********
Identity added: /home/you/.ssh/id_dsa (/home/you/.ssh/id_dsa)
```

14.5 Troubleshooting

The following lists some ideas for troubleshooting:

* If */var/log/sshd.log* says "Privilege separation user sshd does not exist," then either turn off privilege separation in */etc/sshd_config*, or create the "sshd" account (e.g., with Cygwin's *useradd* command).

* Run *filemon* from the command line, and look for accesses to the *~/.ssh* directory.

* In the Local Security Policy administrative tool, turn on auditing for object access: this is found under Local Policies/Audit Policy. Set it to audit both success and failure. Then select the *~/.ssh* folder and enable this auditing for all accesses to the folder and its contents (Properties/Security/Advanced/Auditing).

14.6 Summary

The full-featured OpenSSH suite runs on Windows for free. What could be better?

OpenSSH for Macintosh

OpenSSH is supplied with Macintosh OS X and runs much like it does for other Unix-like operating systems. The primary differences and distinguishing features are:

- Some extra setup before the OpenSSH server, *sshd*, can be accessed by the outside world
- The software, which is a modified version of OpenSSH maintained by Apple
- Some important differences in the way *sshd* is configured by default, such as invocation and Kerberos support

15.1   Using the SSH Clients

The usual OpenSSH clients, *ssh*, *scp*, and *sftp*, work normally without any extra effort on your part:

```
# Log into server.example.com as user smith
$ ssh -l smith server.example.com

# Copy myfile from your local machine to server.example.com
$ scp myfile server.example.com:

# Run an interactive file-copy session with sftp
$ sftp server.example.com
```

15.2   Using the OpenSSH Server

Before you can use *sshd* on Mac OS X, you'll need to enable the server and possibly open up the Mac's firewall. In addition, you'll want to know about some configuration differences as compared to most other OpenSSH installations.

15.2.1   Enabling the Server

SSH server startup is controlled from the Sharing pane in System Preferences, under Services, as in Figure 15-1. To enable *sshd*, select Remote Login and click the Start button.

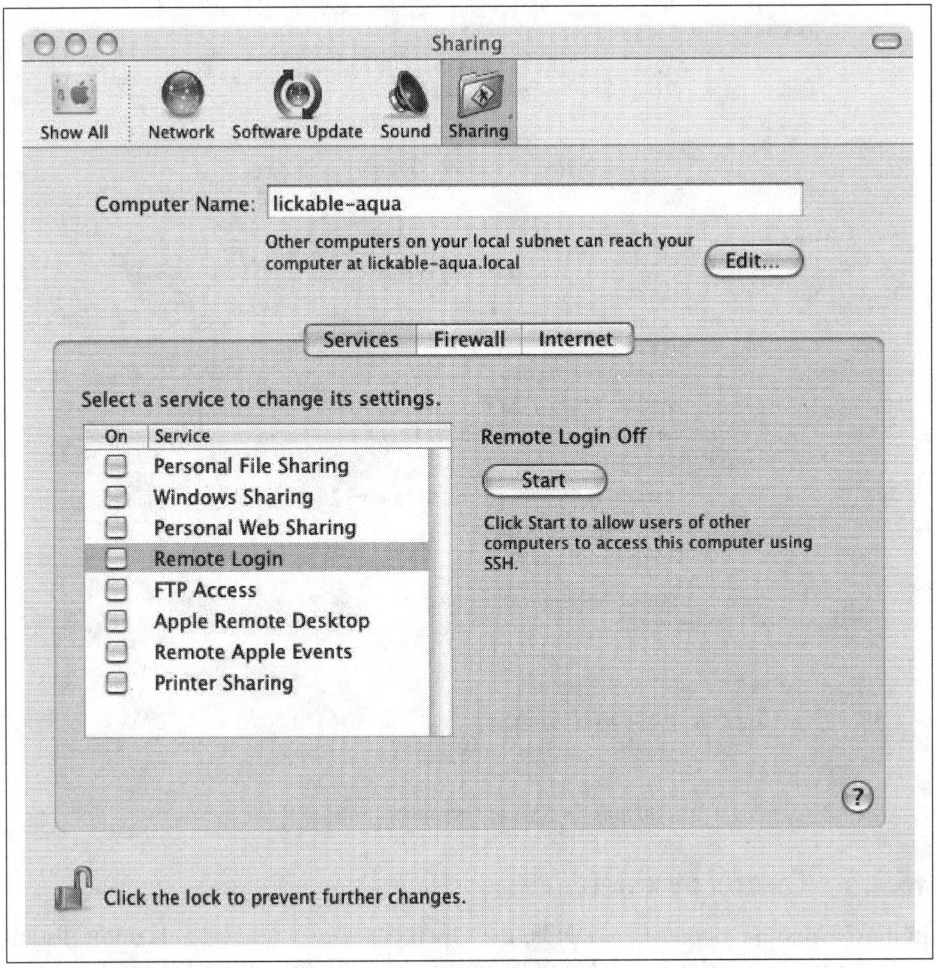

Figure 15-1. Enabling the SSH server in System Preferences

15.2.2   Opening the Firewall

By default, the Mac OS X personal firewall will block SSH connections from the outside world. If you have this firewall enabled, you must manually permit SSH traffic through it. This is done from the Sharing pane in System Preferences, under Firewall, as in Figure 15-2.

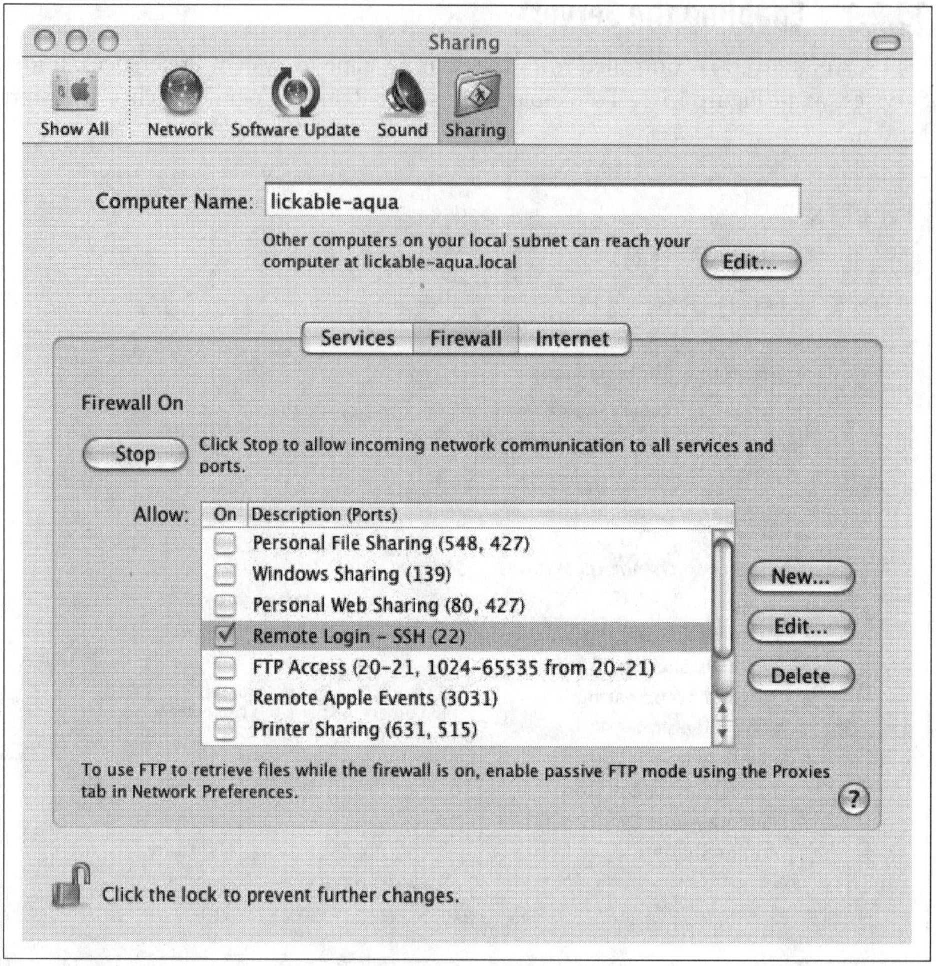

Figure 15-2. Opening a firewall hole for SSH in System Preferences

15.2.3   Control by xinetd

In most Unix-like operating systems, the OpenSSH server runs as a daemon, listening for SSH connections. On Mac OS X, however, *sshd* is controlled by the super-server daemon, *xinetd*. [5.3.3.2] Whenever an SSH client attempts to contact *sshd* on TCP port 22, *xinetd* notices the attempt and invokes a single instance of *sshd* (specifically, *sshd -i*) to serve that connection.

The *xinetd* configuration file for *sshd* is */etc/xinetd.d/ssh*:

```
# /etc/xinetd.d/ssh:
service ssh
{
        disable = no
```

```
        socket_type    = stream
        wait           = no
        user           = root
        server         = /usr/libexec/sshd-keygen-wrapper
        server_args    = -i
        groups         = yes
        flags          = REUSE IPv6
        session_create = yes
    }
```

Note the use of the wrapper script *sshd-keygen-wrapper*: it will generate new host keys if they are missing, as after a fresh OS install.

15.2.4 Server Configuration Details

On Mac OS X, the serverwide configuration files are found in the */etc* directory instead of the more common */etc/ssh*: for example, the serverwide configuration file is */etc/sshd_config* rather than */etc/ssh/sshd_config*.

The SSH software is a modified version of OpenSSH maintained by Apple; they backport security fixes to it whenever required.

 At press time, version "OpenSSH_3.6.1p1+CAN-2004-0175" has a bug whereby dynamic port forwarding (*–D*) doesn't work: it listens on the specified port, but actual connection forwarding fails.

15.2.5 Kerberos Support

The OS X OpenSSH build has protocol 2 Kerberos support for both user and server authentication, following the major Internet-Drafts on these (*draft-ietf-secsh-gsskex* and draft-*ietf-galb-secsh-gssapi*). It implements user authentication via the gssapi and external-keyx methods; it does not yet have the improved gssapi-with-mic method. In case a Kerberos-secured key exchange has been used for server authentication, the external-keyx method allows the userauth protocol to refer back to the previous Kerberos exchange for user authentication, skipping an unnecessary extra authentication phase.

This Kerberos support is also fully DNS-enabled, meaning it will find Kerberos authentication servers from information in the DNS if it is available. In a network of compatible and correctly configured Kerberos and OpenSSH servers, *no* extra configuration is needed for a plain OS X host newly attached to the network to use Kerberos for secure, single-signon client SSH connections. All that is required is to run:

```
$ kinit user@REALM
Please enter the password for user@REALM: ********
$ ssh user@host
```

Place the following lines into *etc/krb5.conf* to relieve the user from having to specify the realm—and if the Kerberos principal and OS X account usernames are the same, then a simple *kinit* will suffice:

```
[libdefaults]
default_realm       = REALM
```

Instead of the command-line utility *kinit*, you can use the OS X GUI Kerberos utility: */System/Library/CoreServices/Kerberos.app*.

Tectia for Windows

Our treatment of Tectia in previous chapters has focused on Unix implementations, but Tectia is fully supported on Microsoft Windows platforms. It's packaged as a suite of products, including:

Tectia Client
> A GUI application that initiates outgoing SSH connections, with a terminal emulator, supporting key-management functionality, port forwarding, and file transfers using SFTP, plus command-line programs for scripting

Accession Lite
> An authentication agent

Tectia Connector
> Transparent, dynamic port forwarding for selected applications

Tectia Server
> A service to accept incoming SSH connections

At press time, the Tectia products can be installed on the versions of Windows listed in Table 16-1. Consult the latest documentation for a complete list of supported platforms.

Table 16-1. Supported Microsoft Windows platforms for SSH Tectia

Program	95	98	Me	NT	2000	XP	Server 2003
Tectia Client	-	any	any	4.0SP6	SP2	any	any
Accession Lite	-	any	any	4.0SP6	SP2	any	any
Tectia Connector	-	-	-	4.0SP6	SP2	SP1	-
Tectia Server	-	-	-	4.0SP6	SP2	any	any

16.1   Obtaining and Installing

Tectia products are shipped as Windows Installer Packages.* The easiest way to install is to use Windows Explorer to double-click on the included *.msi* files:

- TectiaClient-*version.msi*
- TectiaConnector-*version.msi*
- TectiaServer-*version.msi*

These files can be found in the *install/windows* folder on your distribution media, or downloaded from the *ssh.com* web site, depending on how you purchased the products. The installers must be run by a user with administrative privileges. Installing the Connector package requires a reboot.

During interactive installation, you'll see a series of dialogs; use these to specify the install directory if the default location is not appropriate. By default, Tectia products are installed within the Program Files folder in a Tectia subfolder named *SSH Communications Security*.† Files for each product are collected in separate subfolders under the *Tectia* subfolder:

- SSH Secure Shell
- SSH Accession Lite
- SSH Tectia Connector
- SSH Secure Shell Server

We'll refer to these as the "installation folders." The installers also create entries in the Start/Programs menu, under the program groups:

- SSH Tectia Client
- SSH Tectia Connector
- SSH Tectia Server

The installer for the Client package optionally creates desktop icons for the GUI client application:

- SSH Tectia Client
- SSH Tectia Client – File Transfer

The PATH environment variable is updated to include the installation folder for the Client package, so scripts can easily access command-line programs.

---

* Accession Lite is included with the Client and Connector packages and is not available as a separate package.

† The Program Files folder can be determined by examining the value of the PROGRAMFILES environment variable. It is typically *C:\Program Files*.

The Server installer generates host key files by running *ssh-keygen2* in a command window: this can take several minutes to complete.* The server is added as a service that starts automatically whenever the system boots.

Tectia products can also be installed silently, using the *msiexec* command-line tool:

```
C:\> msiexec /q /i Tectia<Product>-<version>.msi INSTALLDIR="<path>"
```

If the INSTALLDIR argument is omitted, the default locations are used. Silent installation is handy for rolling out products to a large number of systems.

To remove Tectia products, use the Add/Remove Programs section of the Control Panel, or the command:

```
C:\> msiexec /q /x Tectia<Product>-<version>.msi
```

The Tectia Server must be stopped before it is uninstalled.

16.2   Basic Client Use

When you run the GUI client application (typically via the desktop icon or the Start menu), it displays a terminal window. To initiate an outgoing connection, do one of the following:

- Click on the Connect toolbar icon.
- Use the File/Connect menu item.
- Press the Enter key or space bar within an unconnected terminal window.

This brings up the Connect To Remote Host dialog shown in Figure 16-1. Fill out the values for the server's hostname, the remote username (on the server), and the port number (if different from the default 22); select an authentication method from the drop-down menu; and finally click Connect. If the host key for the server has not been seen before, the client prompts for confirmation before saving it, as in Figure 16-2. Respond to the prompts demanded by subsequent dialogs, which depend on the authentication method chosen.

If authentication succeeds and the server grants access, you can work within the terminal window in Figure 16-3.

You can create additional sessions on the same server by using the New Terminal Window toolbar icon or the Window/New Terminal menu item. These sessions run in separate terminal windows, and are tunneled through different channels within the existing SSH connection, so no additional authentication is required.

---

* If you run Server installer in silent mode, the host key is not generated automatically. Use *ssh-keygen2* to generate the host key manually.

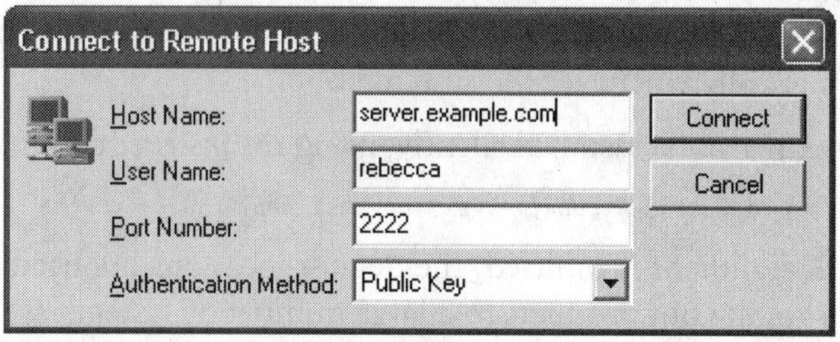

Figure 16-1. The Connect to Remote Host dialog

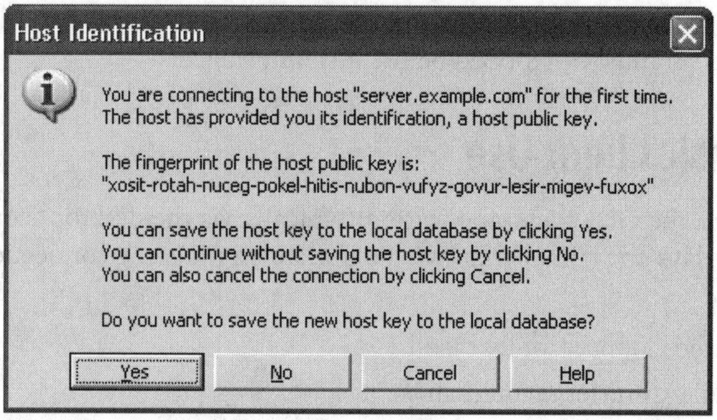

Figure 16-2. Encountering a previously unknown host key

The client disconnects automatically when the last session terminates. If you need to disconnect manually for some reason, use the Disconnect toolbar icon or the File/ Disconnect menu item.

16.3 Key Management

To manage the key pairs that are used for public-key authentication, use the Keys page (Figure 16-4) of the Settings dialog, which is accessed by either the Settings toolbar icon or the Edit/Settings menu item. The Settings dialog is a GUI-based interface to the functionality provided by the *ssh-keygen2* command-line program.

Click Generate New Keypair to start the Key Generation Wizard, which presents a dialog that prompts for the key type (DSA or RSA) and key length, generates the key (this can run for several minutes, which provides plenty of time to appreciate an animated display of random bits), and finally prompts for a filename to store the key, an optional comment, and the passphrase.

To copy a key pair from files in some other location to the user profile folder, click Import. If an existing key is selected, click Export to copy the key pair from the user

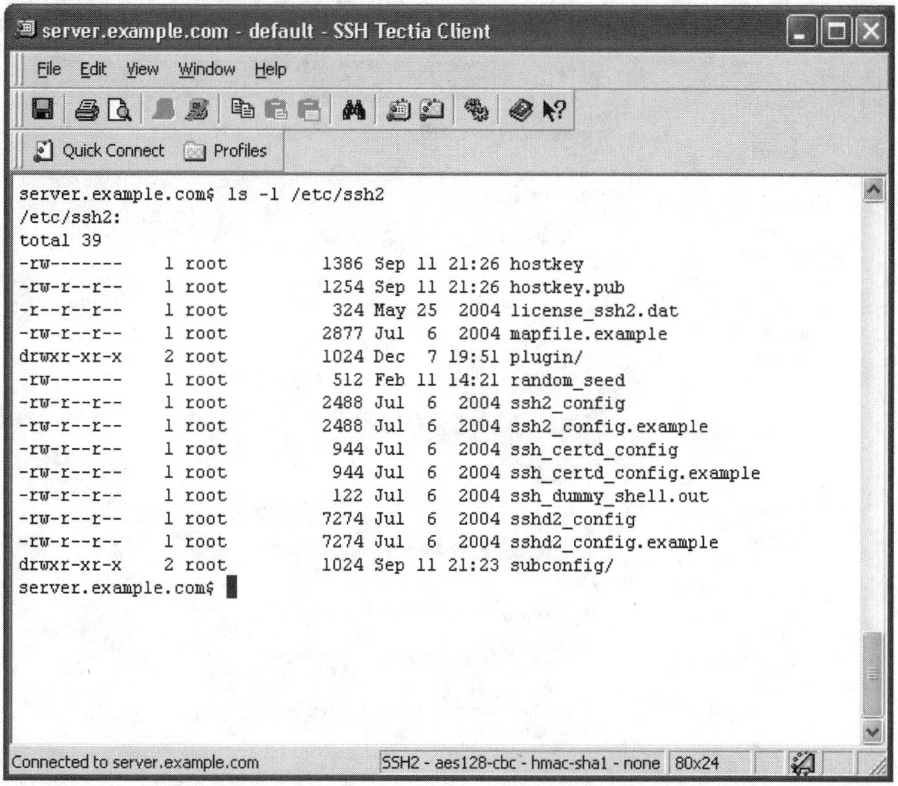

Figure 16-3. Terminal window

profile folder to some other folder, or Delete to remove the key pair, or Change Passphrase to present a dialog that prompts for the old and new passphrases.

Click Upload to conveniently transfer a selected public key to a server using *sftp*, and automatically add an entry in the authorization file so that the key will be used.* This assumes you have already authenticated using some other mechanism. A dialog allows the destination folder and authorization filename to be changed if the default locations on the server are not appropriate.

To view the contents of the public-key file (using the Notepad editor), double-click on a key in the list, or select a key and click View.

Finally, click Configure to update the identification file that is used by the *ssh2* command-line program. All keys in the list are included; the identification file must be edited manually if some keys should be excluded.

---

* Uploading is also offered as an option by the Key Generation Wizard whenever new key pairs are produced.

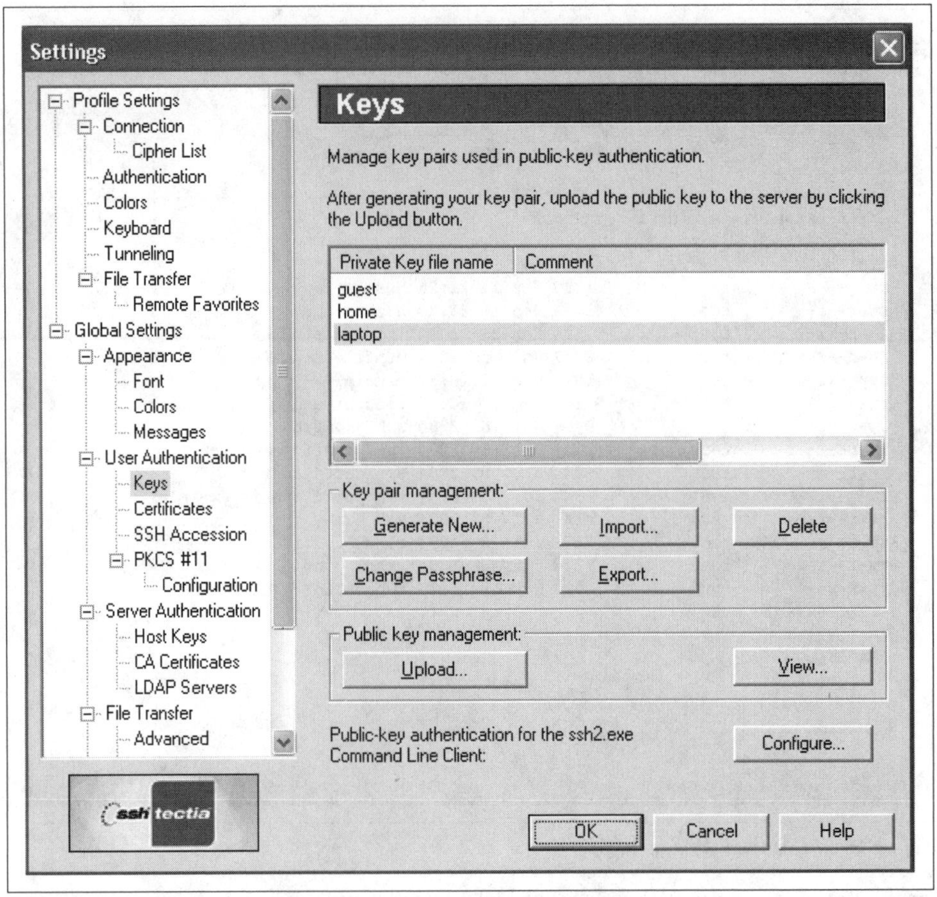

Figure 16-4. Keys page of the Settings dialog

16.4 Accession Lite

Accession Lite is started automatically when each user logs in; it acts as an authentication agent.[*] The GUI application provides the same functionality as the *ssh-agent* and *ssh-add* programs that are used on Unix systems.[†]

The easiest way to access the Accession Lite GUI, shown in Figure 16-5, is to double-click the icon in the tool tray on the taskbar. The Tectia Client and Connector applications also have icons and menus for Accession Lite. Normally, Accession Lite stops

---

[*] By default, a splash screen is briefly displayed when the program starts. This can be disabled if you find it annoying.

[†] These command-line programs are not provided with the Tectia Client product on Windows. Only Accession Lite can be used as an authentication agent.

automatically when the user logs out (or the system is shut down), but if it needs to be stopped manually for some reason, use the File /Quit menu item.

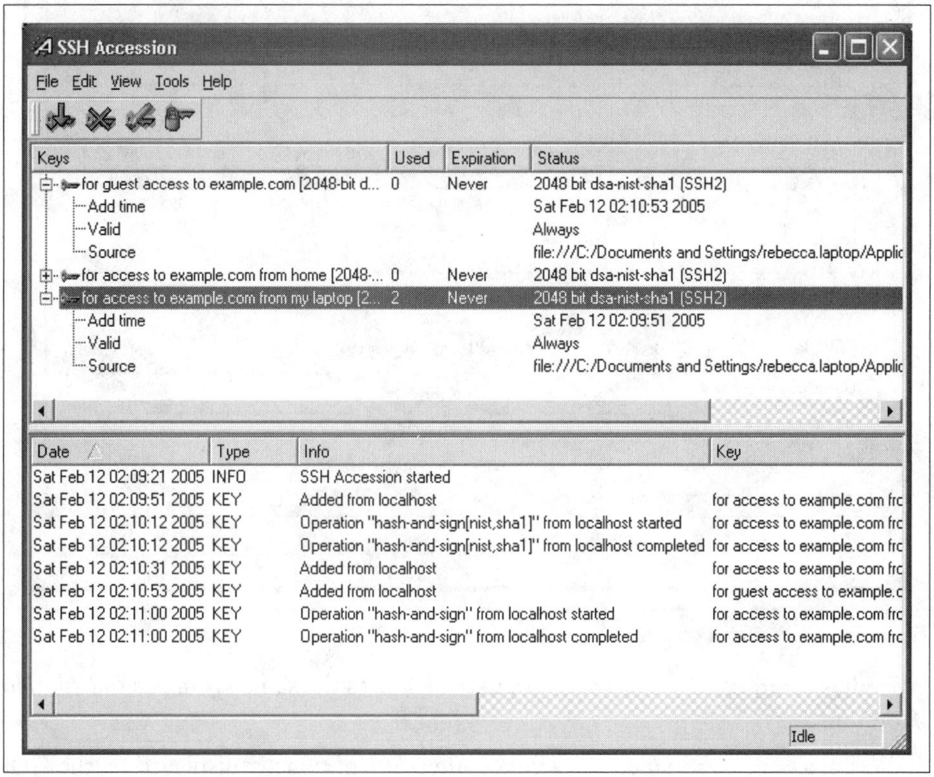

Figure 16-5. Accession Lite

The main Accession Lite window displays information about the loaded keys and a log of its operations in separate panes.

The toolbar icons or equivalent items in the Tools menu can be used to perform actions:

- Add a key to the agent: a series of dialogs prompt for the filename and a passphrase.
- Delete a selected key from the agent.
- Lock or unlock a selected key: dialogs prompt for a passphrase.
- Edit attributes for a selected key: this presents the Key Attributes page (Figure 16-6) of the Settings dialog, which can also be obtained via the Settings toolbar icon or the Edit/Settings menu item.

The default attributes apply to all of the keys, unless overridden for specific keys. Keys can be set to expire after a specified time, and can be limited to a maximum number of uses. Forwarding can be restricted to a limited number of hops, or more

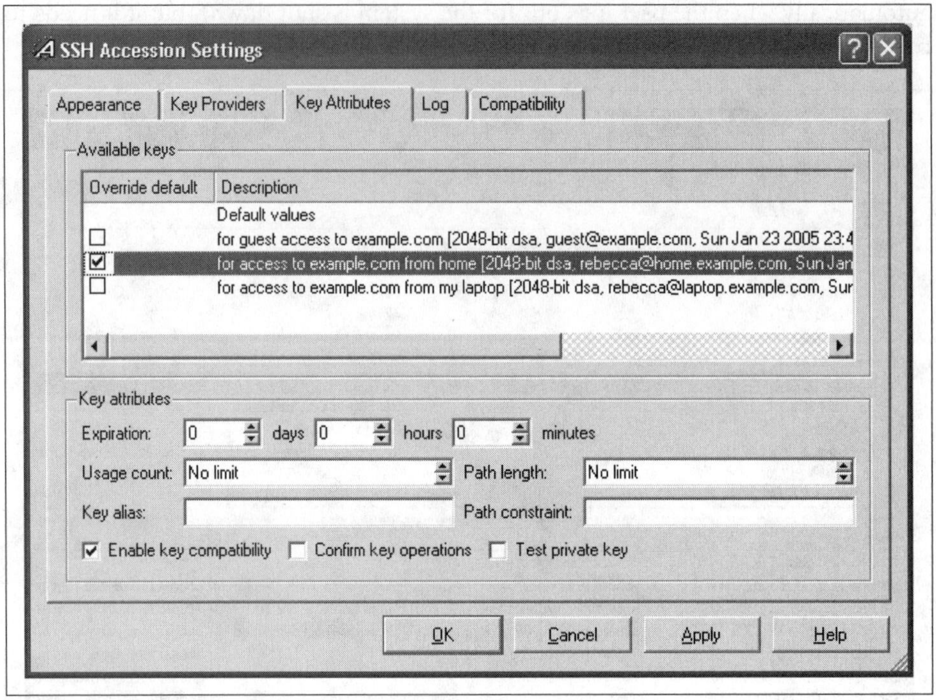

Figure 16-6. Key Attributes page of Accession Lite

generally according to a constraint string, which uses the same syntax as the *ssh-add -F* option. [6.3.3]

A short alias can be assigned to each key; these are optionally displayed by the GUI instead of the more verbose descriptions according to settings on the Appearance page.

"Enable key compatibility" means that SSH-1 keys can be used by SSH-2 clients, and vice versa. Support for SSH-1 and SSH-2 client connections is controlled independently by checkboxes on the Compatibility page.

If "Confirm key operations" is checked, then the agent prompts for each use of the key. "Test private key" requires the agent to verify that the certificate corresponds to the key whenever it is used.

The Compatibility page allows a single key to be loaded automatically when Accession Lite starts. To load an entire collection of keys automatically, use the Key Providers page and add the Software provider. This emulates a smart card by monitoring a specified folder, and automatically adding or deleting keys in the agent as they are created or removed from the folder.

The Log page allows the transaction log that is displayed in the log pane of the main window to be saved to a file.

By default, all configuration settings are saved automatically; this can be disabled by a setting on the Appearance page. The File/Save Configuration menu item is used to manually record configuration changes.

16.5 Advanced Client Use

Most of the time, the Tectia GUI applications effectively act as configuration editors, allowing users and administrators to change and save the configuration without worrying about the location or format of configuration files. In some other circumstances, however, an understanding of these details is useful, so we'll provide a brief guided tour through the internal structure of Tectia's configuration on Windows.

The system client configuration file *ssh2_config* is stored in the Tectia client installation folder. This file has the same format and function as the */etc/ssh2/ssh2_config* file on Unix systems.[7.1.2.2]

Most other parts of the configuration are separately maintained for each user, and are stored in the user profile folder* in the application data subfolder.† Tectia configuration files are collected in a subfolder named *SSH*. This folder is analogous to the user configuration folder on Unix systems (typically *~/.ssh2*, but ultimately determined by the `UserConfigDirectory` keyword), although the specific files and folder layout are different for Windows, as we'll see. [5.3.1.5]

 If roaming profiles are used, then the user profile folder is replicated on a server, and files are transmitted to client machines via the network, where they can be seen by anyone who is able to sniff traffic en route. To prevent this, either disable roaming profiles for Tectia users, or store the Tectia configuration files in a different, local folder. If the `SSHCLIENT_USERPROFILE` environment variable is set, its value specifies an alternate location to be used for the Tectia configuration files, instead of the user profile folder.

The Tectia user configuration folder contains:

RandomSeed
> A pool of random data. [7.4.18]

HostKeys
> A subfolder to store public keys for known hosts. [7.4.3]

---

* The user profile folder can be determined by examining the value of the `USERPROFILE` environment variable. It is typically *C:\Documents and Settings\username.hostname* or (on older systems) *C:\WINNT\Profiles\username*.

† The full pathname for the application data folder, including the user profile folder components, can be found in the value of the `APPDATA` environment variable. The subfolder is typically named *Application Data*.

UserKeys
> A subfolder for storing user identities.

identification
> A list of keys used by the command-line client, *ssh2.exe*. This file can be produced automatically by the GUI client. [16.3] If the *identification* file is missing, then all keys in the *UserKeys* folder are used.

*.ssh2
> Profile settings for the GUI client, which are used to store configuration information based on the connection target (discussed shortly).

global.dat
> Global settings for the GUI client, which apply to all connections (discussed shortly).

SSH Accession\config.cfg
> The configuration settings for Accession Lite, stored in XML format.

The *All Users* profile folder is conceptually merged with each user profile folder.* Host keys and profile settings can be copied from a user profile folder to the *All Users* profile folder to provide systemwide access.

 The *All Users* profile folder isn't available on older platforms such as Windows 98 or Me.

To provide a systemwide default configuration for Accession Lite, copy a suitably crafted *config.cfg* file from a user profile folder to the Accession Lite installation folder.

 Accession Lite doesn't use the *All Users* profile folder.

The **.ssh2* files for profile settings and the *global.dat* configuration file are usually updated by the GUI client (discussed shortly). However, they are ordinary text files that use the venerable DOS **.ini* format and are easy to edit directly.

Settings are grouped in sections that are identified by names with square brackets, on separate lines. Each setting is a keyword and value, separated by an equals sign, with one pair per line. Values have prefixes to indicate the type of data:

---

* The *All Users* profile folder can be determined by examining the value of the ALLUSERSPROFILE environment variable. It is typically *C:\Documents and Settings\All Users* or (on older systems) *C:\WINNT\Profiles\All Users*.

N:
> Decimal number

H:
> Hexadecimal number

S:
> String

Boolean values are represented as decimal numbers, with zero and one indicating false and true, respectively. For example:

```
[Security]
...
FIPS mode=N:0
```

Direct editing of these files is required to update a few settings that are not displayed by the GUI client: e.g., the FIPS mode setting. It is also occasionally convenient to use a script to generate a large number of profile setting files that differ only by a few settings.

The files *default.ssh2* and *defaultsftp.ssh2* contain default settings for the GUI client's terminal and SFTP modes, respectively. If these files are missing, then hardwired default settings are used.

Profile settings files can be used in several ways:

- Double-click on **.ssh2* files in Windows Explorer. This works because the installer arranges to associate the *.ssh2* file suffix with the GUI client.

- Create desktop shortcuts to the profile settings files, and then double-click on the desktop icons. The Tectia client installer automatically creates desktop shortcuts for the default profiles using the terminal and SFTP modes.

- Click on the Profiles toolbar icon, and then select one of the defined profile settings from the drop-down menu.

- Use the File/Profiles menu item to present the same drop-down menu.

The drop-down profiles menu also contains items that allow new profiles to be added, and existing profiles to be edited. When new connections are initiated using unsaved profile settings, a dialog is briefly displayed that allows the new profile settings to be added. The Settings toolbar icon or the Edit/Settings menu item provides access to the Profile Settings page of the Settings dialog for editing the current profile.

Use the File/Save Settings menu item to save the current profile settings, as well as the global settings. The File/Save Layout menu item performs the same function, but also records the current position of all the GUI client's windows.

Profile settings include connection parameters (e.g., the remote hostname, username, and port number), encryption and MAC algorithms, authentication methods, optional port forwarding (which is discussed in the next section), and *sftp* file transfer modes.

Global settings include key pairs (which we've discussed previously: see Figure 16-4), host keys, other *sftp* options, and SOCKS firewall specifications.

Except for settings that are related to the appearance or behavior of the GUI client itself, all of the profile and global settings correspond to keywords discussed in Chapter 7.

16.6 Port Forwarding

Port forwarding allows Tectia to tunnel TCP connections through multiplexed channels within an existing SSH connection. [9.2] To set up forwarding, use the Tunneling page (Figure 16-7) of the Settings dialog which is accessed by either the Settings toolbar icon or the Edit/Settings menu item. Local and remote forwarding (specified by the *–L* and *–R* options for the *ssh2* command-line client) correspond to outgoing and incoming tunnels, respectively, for the GUI client.

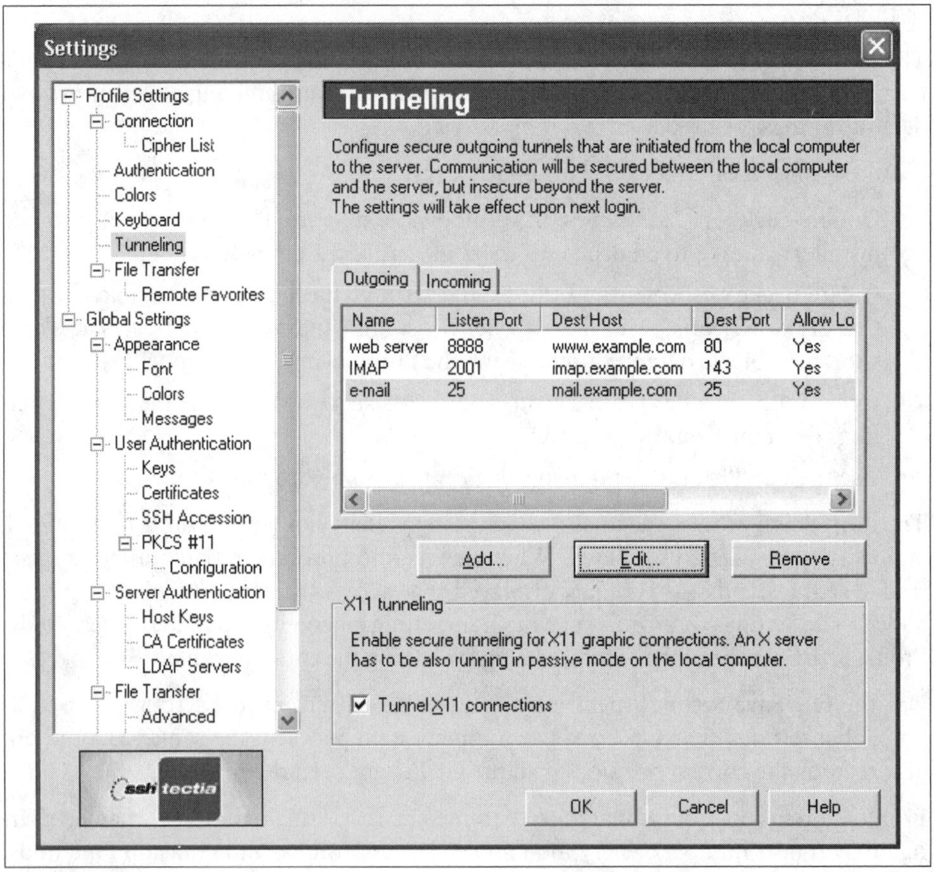

Figure 16-7. Tunneling page

Configure forwarding by first selecting the Outgoing or Incoming tab. Click Add to define settings for a new port forwarding, using a separate dialog (Figure 16-8), or click Edit to redefine settings for a selected existing forwarding, using a similar dialog. Click Remove to destroy a selected forwarding.

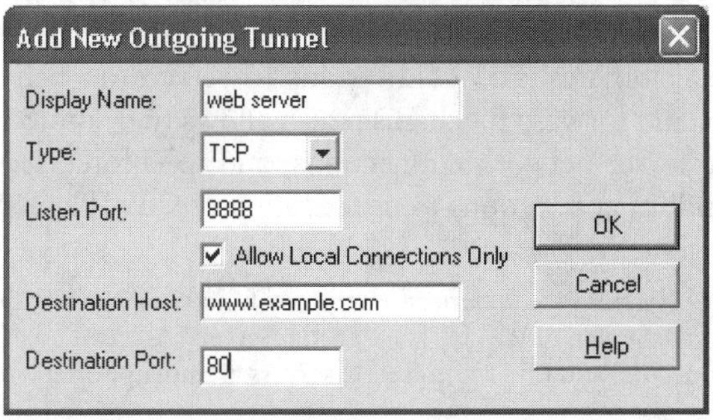

Figure 16-8. Defining settings for a new port forwarding

Settings for each forwarding include:

- A descriptive name, for the displayed list
- The port on which to listen, either on the client side (for local forwarding or outgoing connections) or on the server side (for remote forwarding or incoming connections)
- The destination host and port, to which connections should be forwarded on the opposite side
- A checkbox to allow only local connections (only for local forwarding or outgoing connections), which is usually left enabled
- The type of forwarding: usually TCP to indicate no special processing, or FTP to create temporary forwarding in the reverse direction for FTP data channels in active mode

Forwarding changes are effective only for the next session, except for removals, which happen immediately.

X forwarding is controlled by a checkbox. This is used with a separate X server running on the same system as the Tectia client.

16.7 Connector

We have previously seen how static port forwarding can be extended for SOCKS-aware applications to provide dynamic port forwarding. [9.3] SOCKS is fully supported by the Tectia client, but you have to reconfigure each application to use the SOCKS proxy, which can be annoying.

Tectia Connector extends this concept further to achieve complete transparency: applications can use dynamic port forwarding without any reconfiguration whatsoever, because the applications are entirely unaware that the forwarding is happening.

To accomplish this feat, Connector worms its way into the Windows TCP/IP protocol stack (which includes hostname lookup functionality). This allows it to intercept networking operations by applications and reroute them to its own Connector engine, which then initiates SSH connections to servers on behalf of the applications. The capture and forward mechanism also allows the Connector engine to exercise precise control over network connections, and to enforce security policies that require certain kinds of connections to use secure protocols, like SSH.

 As of Version 4.2, Connector requires functionality provided only by "Tectia Server (T)." [16.11] "Tectia Server (A)" can't be used with Connector, and other non-Tectia servers are unsupported.

Connector only affects outgoing TCP connections. Applications can still accept incoming connections directly, and other protocols (like UDP, ICMP, etc.) are completely ignored by Connector. Note, however, that all applications can be affected by Connector's interception of hostname lookups.

Connector uses only the SSH-2 protocol, never SSH-1. It is fully self-contained, and does not rely on the Tectia client. Instead, Connector implements the SSH-2 protocol and initiates its own connections.

The Connector engine starts automatically when each user logs in. If it has been stopped for some reason, it can be restarted manually using the SSH Tectia Connector item from the Start/Programs/SSH Tectia Connector menu, or by running the *SSHConnector* program in the Connector installation folder.

In normal operation, Connector is unobtrusive, presenting only a small icon in the tool tray on the taskbar to announce its presence. Right-click the icon to produce a menu that displays a list of applications currently using Connector, a checkbox that allows the Connector engine to be enabled or disabled, and an Exit item that shuts down the Connector engine.

The Connector Status dialog can be displayed by double-clicking the tool tray icon or selecting the Status item from the tool tray icon menu. The Tunnels view shows each forwarded port, with the program using the connection, the destination server, and usage statistics (data sent and received). The Logs view displays messages (with timestamps) about authentication, creation of forwarded ports, connections by applications, etc. The Connector engine maintains its own log; it doesn't send messages to the Windows event log.

Privileged users can use the Administration dialog or edit the configuration file directly to configure the Connector engine. The administrative GUI interface is accessed by selecting the SSH Tectia Connector Admin item from the Start/ Programs/SSH Tectia Connector menu, or a similar item in the Connector tool tray icon menu, or by running the *SSHConnectorAdmin* program in the Connector installation folder.

16.7.1 General Settings

The Connector engine itself is configured by the General Settings view of the Administration dialog (Figure 16-9), which applies to all outgoing connections.

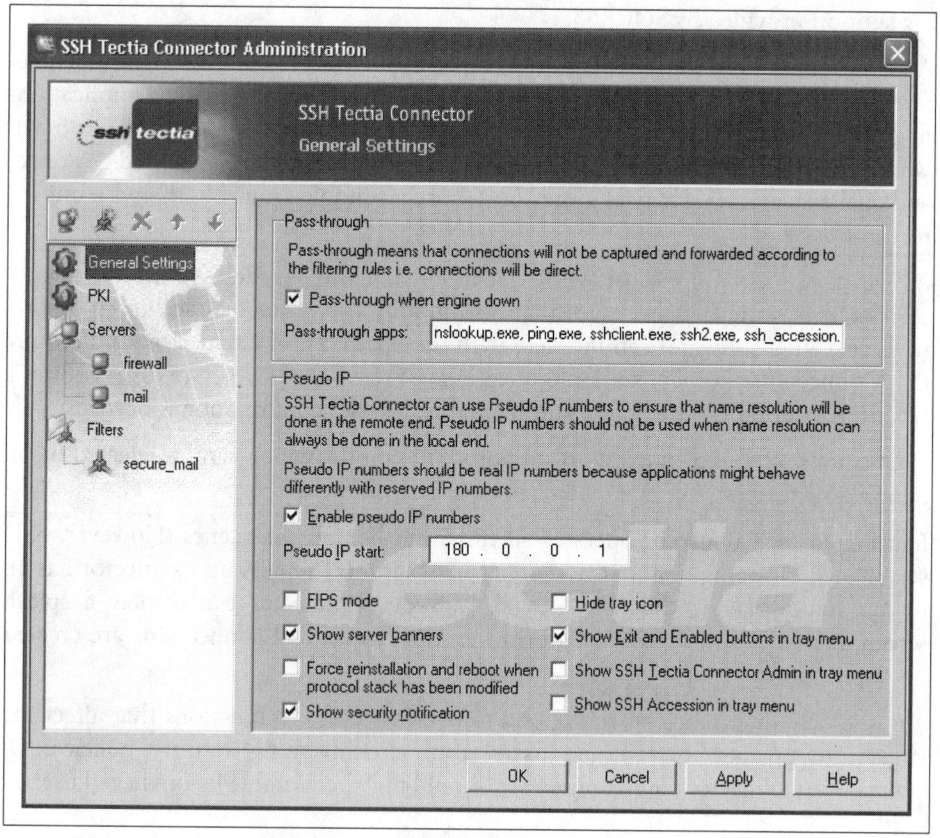

Figure 16-9. Configuring the Connector engine

Sometimes it is necessary or convenient to bypass Connector and allow applications to initiate their own connections directly: this is known as pass-through mode. An option is provided to allow pass-through if the engine is disabled or shut down. If this pass-through option is disabled, then connections will be blocked, which might be appropriate if security policies mandate that only secure connections are allowed. A comma-separated list of applications can also be exempted from interference by

Connector. Typically these applications are for network diagnostics (e.g., *nslookup* or *ping*) or related to direct use of SSH (e.g., the Tectia client, Accession Lite, etc.).

Applications frequently need to connect to secure servers within internal networks from outside of firewalls. External hostname lookups are commonly prevented, to avoid leaking information about the internal network, and because direct access to the secure servers is blocked by the firewall anyway. In such cases, Connector can be configured to return dynamically assigned pseudo (or fake) IP addresses to applications in response to hostname lookups. When the connection is forwarded across the firewall via SSH, the hostname lookup is done internally. This is similar to the naming support provided by SOCKS5.

A base address must be identified for the pseudo IP addresses. This should be chosen carefully to avoid conflicts with real addresses of machines that applications might need to contact. It is natural to use reserved addresses (e.g., the 10.0.0.0/8 network) for this purpose, but if applications detect the use of such reserved addresses and misbehave, then it may be necessary to use a suitable range of otherwise unused real addresses.

As we have seen, Connector works by modifying the Windows TCP/IP protocol stack. Other, unrelated packages that also modify the protocol stack (such as firewalls and VPN software) can interfere with the operation of Connector, and require that Connector's protocol stack modifications be reinstalled, which in turn requires a reboot. An option is provided to automate this; no user confirmation is needed.

Connector's SSH implementation supports FIPS mode, which can be selected by an option. [5.3.5]

In most cases, Connector operates silently, and behind the scenes. However, SSH servers can be configured to send banner messages to clients, and Connector has an option for displaying them. [5.6.1] In addition, Connector can display a splash screen as a brief security notification when new forwarded connections are created for applications.

The tray icon menu can be configured to control access to functions that affect the engine, to prevent unprivileged users from circumventing security policies. Of course, the Connector configuration file should only be writable by privileged users.

16.7.2   Servers for Outgoing SSH Connections

Settings for each server used for an outgoing SSH connection must be defined by the Servers view of the Administration dialog in Figure 16-10.

A display name is assigned to the collection of settings for the server. Connections to a server can be routed via a previously defined server, to set up chains of port forwardings, if required for nested firewalls.

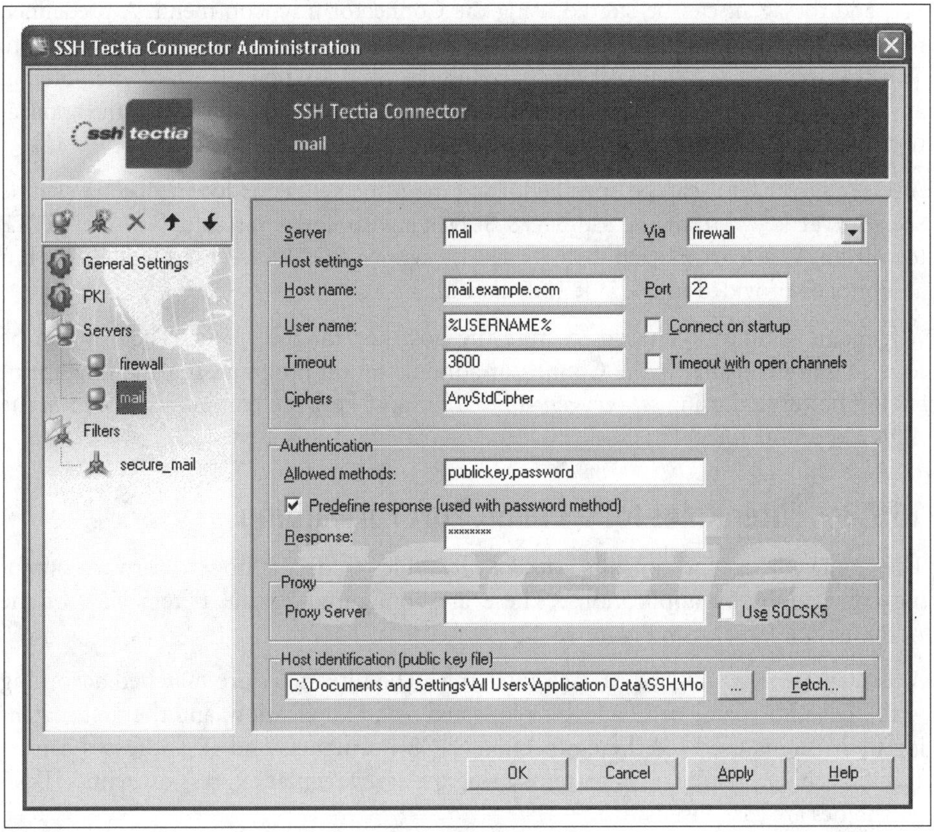

Figure 16-10. Defining settings for outgoing SSH connections

The most important characteristics of the SSH connection can be specified for the server. The special token %USERNAME% means that the local Windows username is used for the remote username as well.

By default, Connector initiates SSH connections only when required to forward connections from applications, but an option is provided to initiate the connection when the Connector engine starts. Idle SSH connections are terminated by Connector after a specified timeout interval elapses.[*] Normally, SSH connections are retained (even when idle) if any forwarding channels are still active, but Connector can be configured to ignore active channels when it closes idle connections.

The allowed authentication methods are specified as a comma-separated list, chosen from the set: gssapi-with-mic, publickey, keyboard-interactive, and password. Public-key authentication is especially convenient with Accession Lite acting as an authentication agent. [16.4] Accession Lite is included with the Tectia Connector pack-

---

[*] The timeout interval is expressed as a number of seconds.

age, and the agent can be started using the Connector tray icon menu. A predefined response can be stored in the Connector configuration for password authentication. This is insecure, since the password saved in the configuration file is not encrypted in any way, and the predefined response is intended only for situations when the application handles its own authentication using some other secure mechanism.

A proxy server URL can be specified using the same syntax as for the Tectia client's SocksServer keyword or the SSH_SOCKS_SERVER environment variable. [7.4.7.2] HTTP forwarding is also supported, using a similar syntax. SOCKS4 is used by default, but an option is provided to use SOCKS5 instead.

A filename should be chosen to store the host key for the server. The key can be fetched automatically by the Connector administration program, but the fingerprint should be verified using *ssh-keygen -F*. [6.2.2] Host keys are commonly stored in the *All Users* profile folder.

16.7.3   Filter Rules for Dynamic Port Forwarding

The Connector engine consults a list of filter rules to decide how to forward outgoing connections by applications. These are configured by the Filters view of the Administration dialog in Figure 16-11.

A display name is assigned to each filter rule. The filter rules are matched according to the DNS hostname or IP address requested by an application, and the first matching filter rule is used for the connection. DNS hostnames and IP addresses can be specified either literally or as patterns using the *egrep* regular expression syntax. DNS hostnames are case-insensitive.

In the usual case when an application connects using a DNS hostname, Connector scans the filter rule list. If a hostname match is found, then the first matching filter rule is used. The IP address returned to the application is taken from the filter rule if one is specified, or is otherwise dynamically assigned from the pool of pseudo IP addresses.* If no matching filter rule is found, then the connection is initiated directly, with no port forwarding.

When an application connects using an IP address, Connector similarly scans the filter rule list, looking for a filter rule with a matching address, and uses the first filter rule that is found. Otherwise, if there is no matching filter rule, then Connector does a reverse hostname lookup using the IP address. If this lookup succeeds, then Connector performs a DNS hostname match, as described previously. Otherwise, if the reverse hostname lookup failed, then Connector blocks the connection. Any hostname specified for the filter rule is passed to the other side of the forwarded connection so that the server can perform the hostname lookup for the real IP address on an internal network.

---

* If pseudo IP addresses are disabled in the General Settings, then the actual IP address of the server is used.

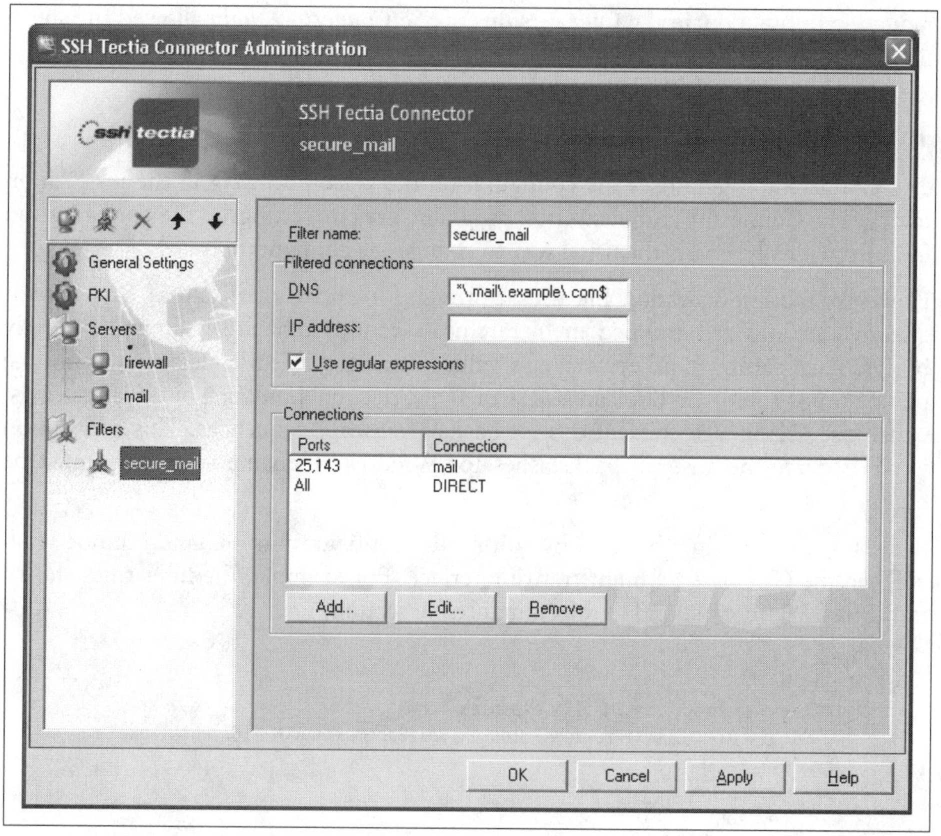

Figure 16-11. Filter rules for forwarding outgoing connections

Connections are forwarded based on the target port requested by the application, according to a list of connection rules for each filter rule. Each connection rule consists of a comma-separated list of ports, or the special value All, plus one of the following actions:

DIRECT
> Initiate a connection directly, without port forwarding.

BLOCK
> Block the connection, so the application will see the error "connection refused."

server
> Initiate an SSH connection, according to the settings for the named server.

The first matching connection rule for the requested port is used. If no connection rule matches, then a direct connection is initiated.

Connections are also forwarded according to the full pathname for the application. The Connector administrative interface allows the specification of only a single application. This restriction was imposed as of Version 4.2, and is actually a reduction in functionality. Earlier versions of *SSHConnectorAdmin* allowed the specification of an application for each filter rule.[*]

16.7.4 Configuration File

The Connector engine uses the configuration file *sshcorpoeng.cfg* in the installation folder. The Connector administration program saves its settings in the configuration file automatically, and is the usual way to change the configuration.

However, the configuration file uses a straightforward format and is easy to edit directly. Settings are grouped in hierarchical sections that are delimited by curly braces. Each setting is a keyword and value, separated by an equals sign, with one pair per line. Values are Boolean (FALSE or TRUE), decimal numbers, or quoted strings, which use C-language conventions for backslash escape sequences. This convention is unfortunate, because all backslashes for Windows filename separators must be doubled.

Some features can only be used by editing the configuration file, and are not available via the GUI-based administrative interface. For example, the filter rules shown in Figure 16-11 correspond to the configure file section:

```
Filters = {
  secure_mail = {
    DNSNameRegexp = ".*\\.mail\\.example\\.com$"
    Application = "C:\\\\Program Files\\\\WhizBangMail\\\\MailClient\\.exe"
    RealIP = FALSE
    Connections = {
      connection1 = {
        Via = "mail"
        Port = "25,143"
      }
      connection2 = {
        Via = "DIRECT"
        Port = "0-65536"
      }
    }
  }
}
```

Regular expressions or literal values can be selected independently for DNS hostnames and IP addresses by using any combination of the following keywords:

- DNSNameRegexp
- DNSName
- IPAddressRegexp
- IPAddress

---

[*] You can specify multiple applications if you use Tectia Manager to configure Connector. The restriction also does not apply if you edit the configuration file directly.

The `RealIP` keyword controls assignment of pseudo IP addresses for each rule.

A separate application can be specified for each filter rule. The application pathname is actually a pattern, using the *egrep* regular expression syntax. The combination of C-language conventions for strings and regular expressions leads to an abundance of backslashes. For the setting:

```
Application = "C:\\\\Program Files\\\\WhizBangMail\\\\MailClient\\.exe"
```

the C-language string corresponds (collapsing the doubled backslashes) to the regular expression:

```
C:\\Program Files\\WhizBangMail\\MailClient\.exe
```

which matches the pathname:

```
C:\Program Files\WhizBangMail\MailClient.exe
```

16.8   File Transfers

The Tectia client supports file transfers using *sftp*. The File Transfer window (Figure 16-12) for the GUI client is obtained by using the New File Transfer Window toolbar icon or the Window/New File Transfer menu item, and operates similarly to Windows Explorer.

To transfer files, use any of the following methods:

- Simply drag and drop files or folders between the Local and Remote views.
- Select the files or folders to be transferred in the Local or Remote views, and then click the download or upload icons in the toolbar.
- Right-click on a file or folder in the Local or Remote view to produce a menu, and then use the Upload or Download menu items. If the Upload Dialog or Download Dialog menu items are used instead, then a separate dialog allows selection of files to be transferred.
- Select the files or folders to be transferred in the Local or Remote views, and then use the same menu items in the Operation menu.

Most other file operations can be performed within the Local or Remote views using the Operation menu, or familiar Windows Explorer gestures. These include opening files, running programs, deleting or renaming files and folders, creating new folders, etc. Some restrictions on the operations may be imposed by the remote system.

The *sftp* file transfer mode can be set to ASCII, Binary, or Auto Select using icons on the toolbar, or the Operation/File Transfer Mode menu items.

The transfer view at the bottom of the window shows progress information and statistics for each transfer.

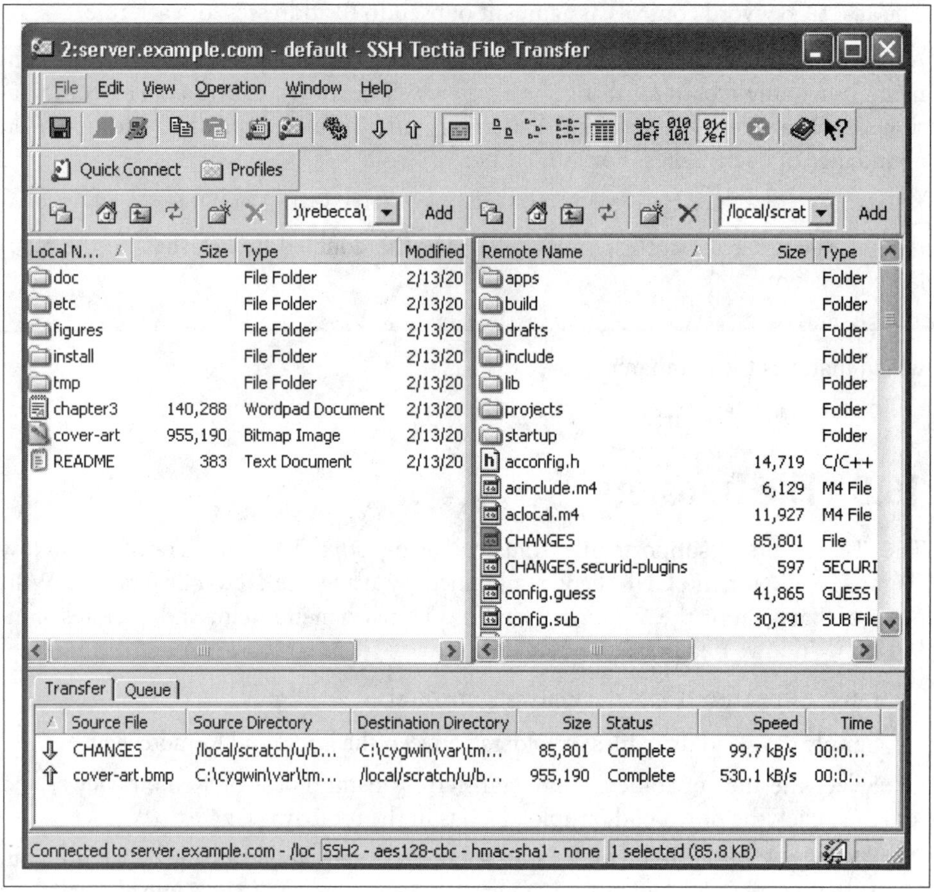

Figure 16-12. File transfer window

16.9 Command-Line Programs

The GUI client can be launched from the command line. This is useful for creating customized shortcuts, or other wrapper scripts (e.g., *.bat files).

The program is named *SSHClient*, and supports the following options:[*]

-r

Reset all customizations made to the user interface (toolbars and menus). The client asks for confirmation before doing this.

-u [username]

Specify the remote username.

---

[*] Options can also be specified with a forward slash instead of a hyphen: e.g., /f or -f.

-h [hostname]

Specify the remote hostname (where the SSH server runs).

-p [port]

Specify the port number.

-f

Start using the file-transfer window instead of the terminal window.

A profile settings file (**.ssh2*) can also be specified as the last argument on the command line.

The GUI client immediately initiates an outgoing connection if any of the *–u*, *–h*, or *–p* options, or a profile settings file, are specified. If no remote hostname is given (either by the *–h* option or a profile settings file), then the client prompts for connection parameters, with any other supplied values as defaults. Otherwise, the client starts in an unconnected state and waits for outgoing connections to be initiated manually.

The precedence for settings is (from strongest to weakest):

1. Command-line options
2. A profile settings file specified on the command line
3. Default profile settings files: either *default.ssh2* or *defaultsftp.ssh2* (if the *-f* option is used)
4. Hardwired default settings, if the default profile settings files do not exist

The Tectia Client package also supplies a set of command-line programs, including *ssh2*, *scp2*, *sftp2*, and *ssh-keygen2*.* These programs are intended for scripting, and function almost exactly as they do for Unix implementations, except that they are aware of the Windows conventions for configuration file locations. In fact, *ssh2 -h* is an easy way to list the location of the configuration files for the client (in the user profile folder). The programs understand both Windows and Unix filename conventions using backslashes and (forward) slashes, respectively. Wildcards are case-insensitive, in accordance with Windows filesystem conventions.

 Command-line variants for *ssh-agent2* or *ssh-add2* are notably absent. This functionality is provided only by Accession Lite. The command-line client program (*ssh2*) uses Accession Lite to contact an agent for authentication.

---

* Note that all of the program names end with the "2" suffix. Corresponding program names without "2" are not provided, as they are (via symbolic links) on Unix systems.

16.10 Troubleshooting

The Help menu offers two items that are useful for identifying problems.

The Troubleshooting dialog (Figure 16-13) displays a collection of useful information, including:

- Local client version
- License details
- Operating system
- Remote server version
- Algorithms used
- Connection settings
- Error messages

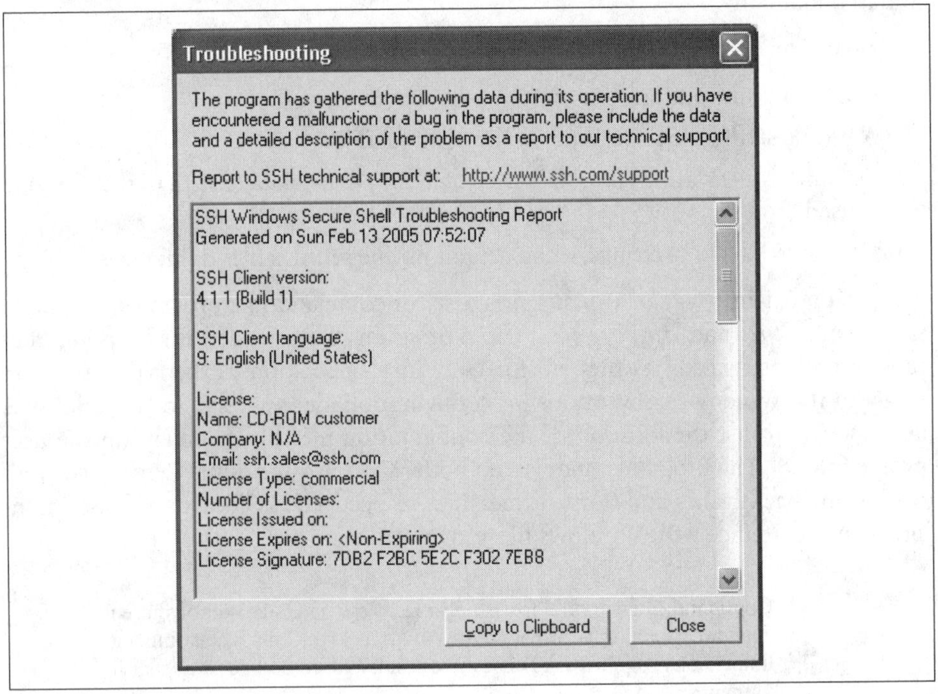

Figure 16-13. The Troubleshooting dialog

The Debugging dialog (Figure 16-14) collects diagnostic output messages from the client. A checkbox enables or disables debugging. The debug level is specified according to the syntax described for the *ssh2 -d* command-line option [7.3]; it can restrict output to specific modules.* A log file must be specified to store the debug messages, which are also displayed in a scrollable view. A checkbox allows the log file to be automatically cleared when the client starts; it can also be cleared manually at any time using the Clear File button.

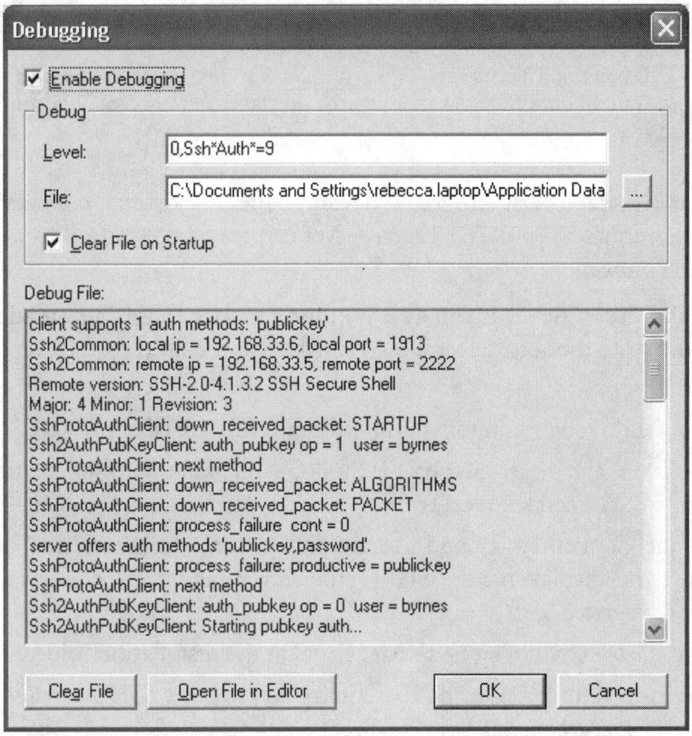

Figure 16-14. The Debugging dialog

16.11 Server

Two distinct flavors of the Tectia server are available (as of Version 4.2). The full-featured Tectia Server (T) is intended for application tunneling, and supports extra functionality needed by Tectia Connector, while the slightly encumbered Tectia Server (A) is intended only for remote system administration. All the programs that make up these products are identical; the only difference is the license file that enables or disables the additional features.

---

* Verbose log levels cause the client to run more slowly.

16.11.1 Server Operation

The Tectia server is implemented by a program, *ssh2master*, that runs as a daemon and listens for incoming connections. A separate program, *ssh2server*, is run to handle each connection when it is accepted. The *sftp* server is implemented by the program *sftp_server2*.

 If you run a Tectia server on a Windows system configured with a firewall, be sure to allow access to the port(s) used to accept SSH connections, typically port 22.

Stopping the *ssh2master* program doesn't affect existing connections, since *ssh2server* continues to run. The Tectia server can even be restarted by a session that uses an SSH connection!

Normally, the Tectia server is run as a Windows service that is automatically started whenever the system boots. Several mechanisms can be used to start or stop the service manually:

- Use the Tectia server administration program (discussed shortly).
- Select either the Start Server or Stop Server item within the menu Start/ Programs/SSH Tectia Server/Tools.
- Access the Control Panel, and use the dialogs for Administrative Tools/Services to select the display name SSH Tectia Server, and then click Start, Stop, or Restart the service.
- Run the *start-ssh.bat* or *stop-ssh.bat* scripts in the installation folder.
- Start or stop the service using the command *net start SSHSecureShell2Server* or *net stop SSHSecureShell2Server*, respectively.
- Run *ssh2master -start* or *ssh2master -stop*.

ssh2master also understands the options *–install* and *–remove* to add or delete the Tectia server from the list of Windows services.

In addition, *ssh2master* accepts a few options that we have discussed previously for *sshd2* on Unix platforms:

-p port
    Listen to the specified port. [5.3.3.1]

-f config-file
    Use an alternate server configuration file. [5.2.1]

-d level
    Run in debug mode, and specify the debug level. [5.9.2]

16.11.2 Server Configuration

The server's configuration files are stored in the installation folder (nothing is stored in the Windows registry):

hostkey
> Private host key (must be protected!)

hostkey.pub
> Public host key

server_random_seed
> Pool of random data

sshd2_config
> Server configuration

sshd2_config has the same format as for Unix systems, and almost all of the keywords have exactly the same meaning for Windows, so we'll just discuss the differences.

The server administration program, *ssh2admin*, also known as the Server Configuration tool (Figure 16-15), can display and change some keywords, but many features can be customized only by editing the file.

ssh2admin can be either run directly, or accessed by selecting the SSH Tectia Server Administration item within the menu Start/Programs/SSH Tectia Server. The Tools/ View Configuration item displays the *sshd2_config* file in the Notepad editor.

Configuration changes take effect for each new session, as they are read by *ssh2server*. Only a few configuration keywords are used by *ssh2master*. If any of these are changed, the service should be restarted:

- Port
- ListenAddress
- MaxConnections

FIPS mode is controlled by the FIPSmode keyword, with a value of yes or no (the default): [5.3.5]

```
FIPSMode    yes
```

16.11.3 Commands and Interactive Sessions

When a command has been specified by an SSH client, it is run directly by the Tectia server. For commands that are built into the Windows command interpreter *cmd.exe*, specify *cmd* explicitly for the *ssh* command:

```
$ ssh winserver.example.com cmd /c type readme.txt
```

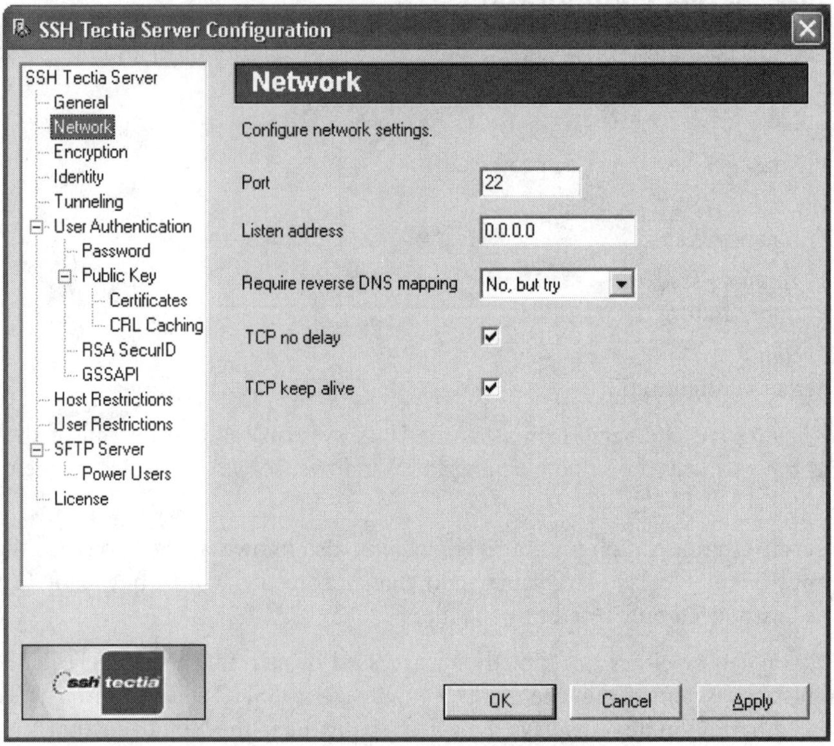

Figure 16-15. Server configuration with ssh2admin

Otherwise, if no command is given, then the server runs *cmd.exe* by default for the interactive session. An alternate program can be specified by the `TerminalProvider` keyword:

```
# Tectia
TerminalProvider    "some-other-cmd.exe"
```

This provides the same functionality as the login shell for Unix systems, except that it applies to all users. User-specific subconfiguration files can specify different programs for individual users. [11.6.2]

Users can run graphical applications from SSH sessions, but the applications have no access to the display, so this has limited usefulness. Full-screen text applications don't work correctly, because they expect to run in a real console window, and the SSH connection doesn't provide information about the window dimensions, etc.

By default, the Tectia server creates terminals for interactive sessions in a fully private window station. This is controlled by the `PrivateWindowStation` keyword:

```
# Tectia
PrivateWindowStation    yes
```

The `DoubleBackSpace` keyword copes with Japanese Windows systems, which require double backspaces to be sent by the server in response to single backspaces from the client, for each two-byte Japanese character. The value is either yes (to enable this behavior) or no (the default):

```
# Tectia
DoubleBackSpace    yes
```

Child processes that are launched from SSH sessions are not automatically terminated when the session ends. This could be construed as a bug or a feature, depending on the circumstances: beware.

The user profile folder is used as the home folder for commands and interactive sessions.

16.11.4 Authentication

Windows passwords are used for password authentication. The password authentication method is always required for domain user accounts. Public-key authentication works only for local user accounts, not domain user accounts.

The `%D` pattern for the `UserConfigDirectory` keyword refers to the user profile folder. [5.3.1.5] The user configuration folder contains the authorization file and public keys.

 The default value for `UserConfigDirectory` is `%D/.ssh2`, which works and is consistent with the Unix location. However, it is strange from a Windows perspective, and different from all of the other Tectia programs, which use the *Application Data\SSH* subfolder within the user profile folder.

16.11.5 Access Control

Accounts that use the SSH server for logins must possess the right to "log on locally." This is disabled by default on some servers, such as domain controllers. Keywords like `PermitRootLogin` that refer to the Unix superuser affect any Windows accounts with administrative privileges.

In the server configuration, domain user accounts should be specified as domain/ user (with a forward slash). The usual Windows backslash separator cannot be used.

Windows groups are not supported by the server, so keywords and values that refer to groups must not appear in the configuration files.

16.11.6 Forwarding

The Tectia server supports only TCP port forwarding on Windows, and enforces the restriction that only privileged users can use privileged port numbers (less than 1024).* X forwarding and agent forwarding are not supported.

16.11.7 SFTP Server

To support SFTP, the Tectia server configuration must include the *sftp* subsystem definition:

```
Subsystem-sftp       "sftp_server2.exe"
```

No internal implementation is built into the SSH server, as it is for the Tectia servers on Unix systems.

The SFTP server restricts access to a set of folders. This is controlled by the Sftp-DirList keyword:

```
# Tectia
Sftp-DirList    "HOME=%D, SCRATCH=S:\scratch\%U"
```

The value is a comma-separated list (with optional whitespace), where each element has the format *virtual=real*. Virtual folder names are arbitrary, and are presented to the SFTP clients. These are mapped to the specified real folders on the server. The folder names can contain the patterns %D and %U, representing the user profile folder and the username, respectively. The default value is HOME=%D.

A set of administrative (or power) users can be defined to use an alternate list of folders:

```
# Tectia
Sftp-AdminUsers     "administrator, backup.*, rebecca"
Sftp-AdminDirList   "HOME=%D, BACKUP=Z:\backup, C:=C:, D:=D:"
```

The value for Sftp-AdminUsers is a comma-separated list (with optional whitespace) of username patterns. By default, only the administrator account is included.

The Sftp-AdminDirList value has the same format as for Sftp-DirList. The default is HOME=%D, C:=C:, D:=D:.

SFTP sessions start in a home folder, which is specified by the Sftp-Home keyword:

```
# Tectia
Sftp-Home          "S:\sftp\%U"
```

The SFTP home folder must be accessible, according to Sftp-DirList or Sftp-AdminDirList. The folder can use the same patterns, %D and %U. The default is %D (the user profile folder).

---

* Windows does not normally distinguish privileged ports from higher-numbered ports.

16.11.8 Logging and Debugging

The server records log messages in the Windows event log, instead of using the standards syslog service found on Unix systems. The event log can be viewed using the Tectia server administration program, or using the Control Panel, by selecting Administrative Tools/Event Viewer.

The verbosity of the messages is controlled by the EventLogFilter keyword:

```
# Tectia
EventLogFilter      error, warning
```

Values are a comma-separated list (with optional whitespace) consisting of one or more of the following levels:

error
Serious problems that prevent operations from completing

warning
Problems that allow operations to continue

information
Normal, successful events

Note that the higher levels do not include the lower levels, as they do for syslog on Unix systems. Each Windows event log level must be specified explicitly.

The SFTP server's log messages are controlled by a separate keyword, SftpLogCategory, that specifies the kinds of messages that are sent to the event log:

```
# Tectia
SftpLogCategory     31
```

The numeric value is the sum of any of the following:

- 16 = user login/logout (the default)
- 8 = folder listings
- 4 = modifications
- 2 = uploads
- 1 = downloads

The *ssh2admin* program provides more convenient checkboxes to specify the value for SftpLogCategory.

The *ssh2master -d* option works the same way as it does for *sshd2* on Unix systems to enable debug mode and specify the debug log level: [5.9.2]

```
# Tectia
ssh2master -d4
```

Debug output is written to the console window by default, but this can be redirected to a file:

```
# Tectia
ssh2master -d4 2> debug.txt
```

The scripts *debug-ssh.bat* and *debug-ssh-file.bat* run *ssh2master* with debug level 4, as shown earlier. In addition, the *debug-ssh-file.bat* script redirects output to the file *sshd2_debug_output.txt* in the installation folder, and then displays the file in the Notepad editor after the server exits. These scripts can also be run by selecting the items Troubleshoot Server or Troubleshoot Server and Save Debug Output from the menu Start/Programs/SSH Tectia Server/Tools.

SecureCRT and SecureFX for Windows

SecureCRT, created by VanDyke Software, is a commercial SSH client for Microsoft Windows 95 through Windows 2003. It is structured as a terminal program; in fact, it started life as the terminal program CRT, another VanDyke product. As a result, SecureCRT's terminal capabilities are quite configurable. It includes emulation of several terminal types, logins via Telnet as well as SSH, a scripting language, a key-map editor, SOCKS firewall support, chat features, and much more. We will focus only on its SSH capabilities, however.

SecureCRT supports both SSH-1 and SSH-2 in a single program. Other important features include port forwarding, X11 packet forwarding, support for multiple SSH identities, and an agent. Secure file copy is accomplished not only by an *scp*-type program, *vcp*, but also by ZModem, an old protocol for uploading and downloading files. (The remote machine must have ZModem installed.) If ZModem is used while you're logged in via SSH, these file transfers are secure.

We've organized this chapter to mirror the first part of the book covering Unix SSH implementations. When appropriate, we refer you to the earlier material for more detailed information.

Our discussion of SecureCRT is based on a prerelease of Version 5.0, dated December 2004.

17.1 Obtaining and Installing

SecureCRT may be purchased and downloaded from VanDyke Software:

http://www.vandyke.com/

A free evaluation version is available, expiring 30 days after installation, so you can try before you buy. If you do purchase the program, VanDyke will provide a serial number and license key.

Installation is straightforward and glitch-free. The software is distributed as a single *.exe* file; simply run it to install the program. Follow the onscreen instructions, installing the software in any folder you like. We accepted the default choices.

17.2   Basic Client Use

Once you've installed the program, it's time to set up a new session, which is Secure-CRT's word for a collection of settings. Choose "Quick Connect..." from the File menu, and in the window that appears (see Figure 17-1), enter the following information:

Protocol
> Select *ssh2* for the SSH-2 protocol.

Hostname
> Enter the hostname of the remote SSH server, such as *server.example.com*.

Port
> Leave it at the default port number, 22, unless your server uses a nonstandard port.

Username
> Enter your username on the remote machine.

Authentication
> Select Password, unless you have another method set up already.

Also put a checkmark in the "Save session" checkbox if you plan to return to this SSH server regularly.

Now click the Connect button. You should be prompted for your login password on the remote machine, and then you'll be logged in via SSH. SecureCRT operates just like a normal terminal program. SSH's end-to-end encryption is transparent to the user, as it should be.

17.3   Key Management

SecureCRT supports public-key authentication using DSA or RSA keys. It can generate keys with a built-in wizard (in SECSH format, compatible with Tectia [6.1.2]), or you can import existing keys. It also distinguishes between two different types of SSH identities: global and session-specific. Finally, SecureCRT includes an SSH agent and supports OpenSSH-style agent forwarding.

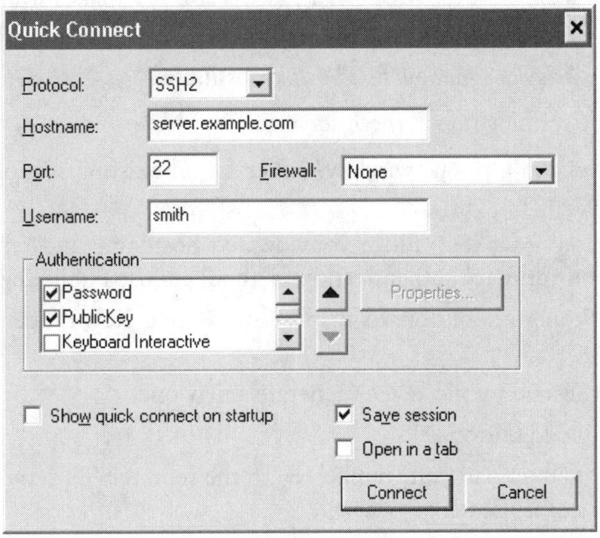

Figure 17-1. SecureCRT Quick Connect window

17.3.1   Key Generation Wizard

SecureCRT's Key Generation Wizard creates key pairs for public-key authentication. The utility is run in the Tools menu by selecting Create Public Key. Equivalently, from the Global Options window, under SSH2 or SSH1,* click Create Identity File.

Operation is straightforward. All you need to supply are the passphrase, the number of bits in the key, and some random data by moving your mouse around the screen. The RSA Key Generation Wizard then creates a key pair and stores it in two files. As with the Unix SSH implementations, the private key filename is anything you choose (say, *mykey*), and its corresponding public-key filename is the same with *.pub* added (e.g., *mykey.pub*).

Once your key pair is generated, you need to copy the public key to the SSH server machine, storing it in your account's authorization file. [6.1] SecureCRT can do this automatically, or you can do it manually.

17.3.1.1 Automatic installation of keys

SecureCRT can upload your public keys to an SSH server with the click of a button, but there's a catch: your remote SSH server must support the publickey subsystem, described in technical detail at:

http://www.vandyke.com/technology/draft-ietf-secsh-publickey-subsystem.txt

---

* VanDyke uses the terms "SSH1" and "SSH2" to mean the protocols SSH-1 and SSH-2, respectively.

VanDyke's own VShell server supports it, and VanDyke makes available a patched OpenSSH server with similar support at:

http://www.vandyke.com/download/os/pks_ossh.html

Assuming you're running one of these servers:

1. Open the Session Options window, either for an existing session or to create a new session.

2. Under Connection/SSH2, fill in your desired hostname and remote username. Then, for your primary authentication method, choose PublicKey.

3. Click the Properties button to display the Public Key Properties dialog (see Figure 17-2).

4. Select your desired public key, or generate a new one.

5. Click the Upload button.

6. SecureCRT will upload your public key to the remote SSH server machine. You will have to authenticate.

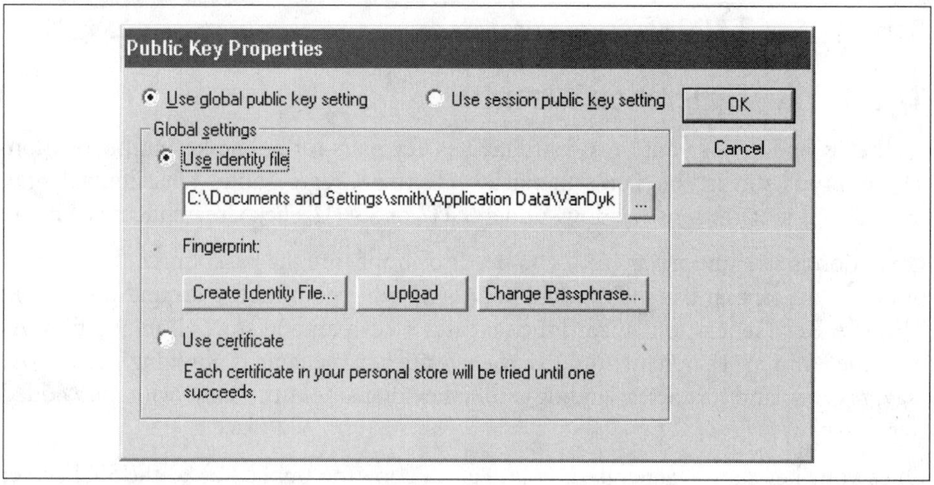

Figure 17-2. SecureCRT Public Key Properties dialog

If the server does not support the publickey subsystem, you'll see an error message like "Unable to open the subsystem for publickey assistant." Try installing the key manually.

17.3.1.2 Manual installation of keys

To install your SecureCRT public key on a remote SSH server:

1. Log into the SSH server machine using SecureCRT and password authentication.

2. View the public-key file and copy the full text of the key to the Windows clipboard.

3. Install the public key (by pasting from the clipboard as necessary) on the SSH server machine in your remote account. [2.4.3]

4. Log out.

5. In the Session Options window, select Connection/SSH2, and change Authentication from Password to PublicKey.

6. Log in again. SecureCRT prompts you for your private-key passphrase, and you'll be logged in.

17.3.2   Using Multiple Identities

SecureCRT supports two types of SSH identities. Your *global identity* is the default for all SecureCRT sessions, and is found on the Global Options window, under SSH2 or SSH1 ("Use identity file").

You may override the default by using a *session-specific identity* that may differ (as the name implies) for each session you define:

1. Open the Session Options window.

2. Select Connection/SSH2.

3. For your primary authentication type, select PublicKey, then click the Properties button to its right, to view the Public Key Properties dialog (see Figure 17-2).

4. Select "Use session public key setting," then select or generate your key of choice.

17.3.3   The SSH Agent

SecureCRT comes with an SSH agent for holding your SSH keys in memory, so you don't have to type your passphrase. (We cover agents in Chapter 6.)

SecureCRT's agent is the simplest to use of any SSH implementation we've seen. Simply open the Global Options window, select SSH2, and place a checkmark next to "Add keys to agent." From that point onward, each time you enter a passphrase for a key, the decrypted key will be stored in the agent, so you won't have to reenter the passphrase.

To enable SecureCRT's agent forwarding, which works with OpenSSH and VanDyke's own VShell servers only, open the Global Options window and select SSH2. Then place a checkmark next to "Enable OpenSSH agent forwarding." [6.3.5]

You might also notice that SecureCRT offers to remember login passwords when you use password authentication. This is not the same as using an agent: your login password on the remote machine has nothing to do with keys and passphrases on the local machine.

17.4   Advanced Client Use

SecureCRT lets you change settings for its SSH features and its terminal features. We will cover only the SSH-related ones. The others (and more details on the SSH features) are found in SecureCRT's online help.

SecureCRT calls a set of configuration parameters a *session*. It also distinguishes between session options that affect only the current session and global options that affect all sessions.

You can change session options before starting an SSH connection or while you are connected. Some options can't be changed while connected, naturally, such as the name of the remote SSH server machine. View the Session Options window (Figure 17-3) by selecting Session Options from the Options menu or clicking the Properties button on the button bar.

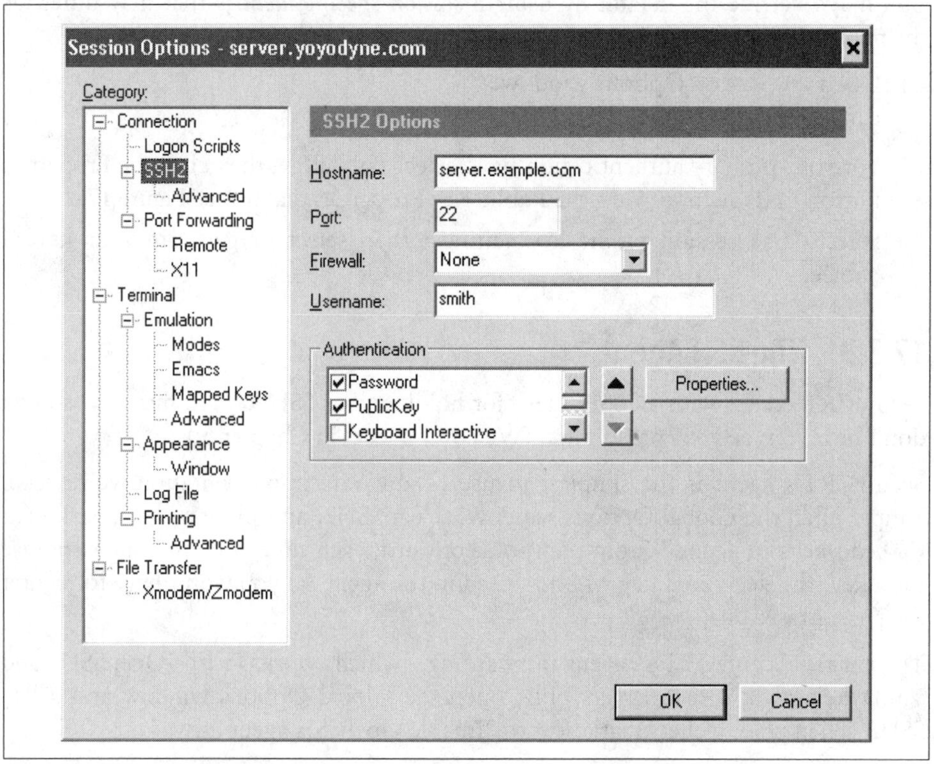

Figure 17-3. SecureCRT session options

17.4.1   Mandatory Fields

To establish any SSH connection, fill in the Connection fields in the Session Options window. These include:

Name
> A memorable name for your collection of settings. This can be anything, but it defaults to the name of the SSH server.

Protocol
> Either SSH-1 or SSH-2.

Then fill in the following fields under Connection/SSH2:

Hostname
> The name of the remote SSH server machine to which you want to connect.

Port
> The TCP port for SSH connections. Virtually all SSH clients and servers operate on port 22. Unless you plan to connect to a nonstandard SSH server, you won't need to change this. [7.4.5.1]

Username
> Your username on the remote SSH server machine. If you're using public-key authentication, this username must belong to an account that contains your public key.

Authentication
> How you identify yourself to the SSH server. This can be password (i.e., your remote login password), public key, keyboard-interactive authentication (a.k.a. challenge-response or one-time password), or GSSAPI authentication. [5.4]

17.4.2   Data Compression

SecureCRT can transparently compress and uncompress the data traveling over an SSH connection. This can speed up your connection. [7.4.14]

In the Session Options window, choose Connection/SSH2/Advanced. The "Compression" dropdown lets you select the type of compression (zlib is the most standard). You may also set a value for the compression Level. The higher the value, the better the compression, but the greater load on the CPU, potentially slowing your computer.

17.4.3   Firewall Use

SecureCRT supports connections through several types of firewalls, such as the SOCKS4 and SOCKS5 firewalls supported by various SSH servers. You can configure one or more named firewalls and select one to be the default for all new sessions.

Every individual session can use any of the named firewalls. You need to know the hostname or IP address of the firewall, and the TCP port on which to connect.

17.5 Forwarding

SecureCRT supports the SSH feature called forwarding (Chapter 9), in which another network connection can be passed through SSH to encrypt it. It is also called tunneling because the SSH connection provides a secure "tunnel" through which another connection may pass. Both TCP port forwarding and X forwarding are supported. (As well as agent forwarding, as we mentioned earlier.)

17.5.1 Port Forwarding

Port forwarding permits an arbitrary TCP connection to be routed through an SSH connection, transparently encrypting its data. [9.2] This turns an insecure TCP connection, such as Telnet, IMAP, or NNTP (Usenet news), into a secure one. SecureCRT supports local port forwarding, meaning that your local SSH client (SecureCRT) forwards the connection to a remote SSH server.

Each SecureCRT session you create may have different port forwardings set up. To set up forwarding to a particular remote host, open the Session Options window and select Connection/Port Forwarding.

To create a new forwarding, first click the Add button to display the Local Port Forwarding Properties window, as in Figure 17-4. Then enter:

Name
> Any descriptive name for your forwarding, to help you remember what it does.

Local
> The port number on your *local* machine to connect to the secure tunnel. This can be just about any number, but for tradition's sake, make it 1024 or higher. Choose a local port number that's not being used by any other SSH client on your PC. If you want to restrict the local IP address that allows connections (i.e., if your PC has multiple network addresses), check the associated checkbox ("Manually select local IP addresses...") and fill in the address.

Remote
> The port number of the remote service, such as 119 for NNTP or 143 for IMAP. The remote machine, by default, is the same one used for your SecureCRT session, but you can change this by checking "Destination host is different from the SSH server" and entering the hostname where the remote service is found. But beware: you can produce a non-secured tunnel with this kind of third-party forwarding if you're not careful.

Application

SecureCRT can run an external program for you to take part in the forwarding. For example, if you're forwarding to an IMAP mail server, SecureCRT could launch your mail client. If you want this behavior, enter the path to your desired application program.

When you're done, click OK to save the forwarding, and your desired TCP port will be forwarded for the duration of your connection.

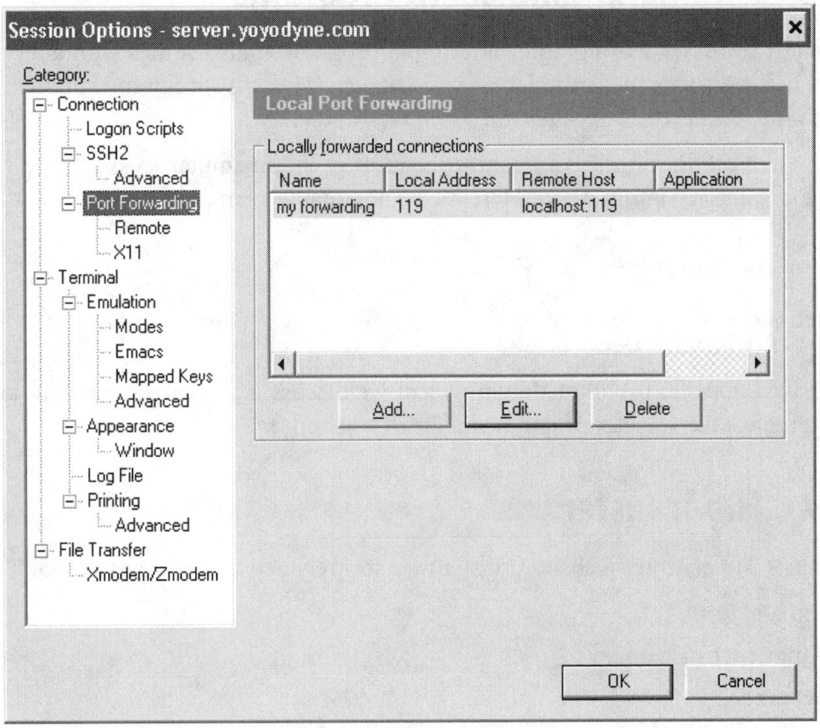

Figure 17-4. Local Port Forwarding properties window

17.5.2   X Forwarding

The X Window System is the most popular windowing software for Unix machines. If you want to run remote X clients that open windows on your PC, you need:

- A remote host, running an SSH server, that has X client programs available
- An X server running on your PC under Windows, such as Cygwin/X or X-SecurePro

SSH makes your X connection secure by a process called X forwarding. [9.4] Turning on X forwarding is trivial in SecureCRT. Simply put a checkmark in the checkbox

"Forward X11 Packets." It is found in the Session Options window under Connection/Port Forwarding/X11.

To secure an X connection by forwarding it through SSH, first run SecureCRT and establish a secure terminal connection to the SSH server machine, with X forwarding enabled. Then run your PC's X server, disabling its login features such as XDM. Now simply invoke X clients on the server machine.

17.6   Command-Line Client Programs

Although SecureCRT is a graphical terminal program, it also comes with a few command-line programs very similar to the *ssh*, *scp*, and *sftp* programs supplied with OpenSSH and Tectia. They are called *vsh*, *vcp*, and *vsftp*.

vsh is a remote login and command-execution program similar to *ssh*. Type *vsh* by itself for full usage information. Here are some notable examples:

```
# Log into server.example.com as smith
C:\> vsh -l smith server.example.com

# Invoke the remote command "who"
C:\> vsh -l smith server.example.com who
```

vcp is a file-transfer program similar to *scp*: we discuss it in the next section. *vsftp* is an interactive file-transfer program similar to *sftp* and *ftp*.

17.7   File Transfer

SecureCRT offers three ways to transfer files securely between systems via SSH:

- *vcp* and *vsftp*
- Xmodem or Zmodem
- SecureFX

17.7.1   The vcp and vsftp Commands

SecureCRT comes with a command-line program, *vcp*, for transferring files securely. It has syntax almost identical to *scp*. For example, to copy the local file *myfile* to the remote SSH server *server.example.com*, authenticating as smith, and naming the copy *newfile*:

```
C:\> vcp myfile smith@server.example.com:newfile
```

Many of *vcp*'s options are the same as *scp*'s:

-r	Recursive copy
-i	Specify a public-key identity for authentication
-v	Verbose flag for debugging

However, other options are different. Type *vcp* by itself for full usage information.

vsftp is an FTP-like client provided with SecureCRT; it should feel familiar to anyone who has used an FTP client. Run *vsftp -h* for full usage information.

17.7.2   Zmodem File Transfer

SecureCRT supports file transfer using the old Xmodem and Zmodem protocols, secured via SSH. To use these protocols, your SSH server machine will need Xmodem or Zmodem programs installed, such as *sz* and *rz* (send and receive Zmodem, respectively) or *sx* and *rx* (send and receive Xmodem, respectively), often found on Linux machines. For example, to send a file from the remote server machine to your local client machine via Zmodem:

1. On the remote system, run:

   ```
   $ sz myfile
   ```

2. SecureCRT will automatically detect the Zmodem connection and perform the download, displaying the file-transfer status in a window.

Similarly, to upload a file:

1. On the remote system, run:

   ```
   $ rz
   ```

2. In SecureCRT, choose Transfer/Zmodem Upload List, and select the files you want to transfer. Then select Transfer/Start Zmodem Upload.

17.7.3   SecureFX

If you want a graphical file transfer with a Windows Explorer-like interface, plus integration with SecureCRT, consider VanDyke's commercial product, SecureFX. Once you've authenticated and connected to a remote SSH server, you can drag and drop files between the machines with your mouse.

SecureFX also has an interesting feature called Quick Synchronize, which is roughly similar to hotsynching on a Palm Pilot. Suppose you have a set of files on your local computer and a backup copy on a remote system. The Quick Synchronize feature compares the two sets, displays the differences, and lets you make them identical by copying files securely between the two systems. Even if you've edited the files on both systems, Quick Synchronize can bring both sets up to date with the most recent changes.

17.8 Troubleshooting

SecureCRT, like any other SSH client, can run into unexpected difficulties interacting with an SSH server. In this section we cover problems specific to SecureCRT. For more general problems, see also Chapter 12.

17.8.1 Authentication

Q: *When I try to upload my public key, I get the message, "Unable to open publickey subsystem" and the upload fails.*

A: SecureCRT can upload public keys only to SSH servers supporting the publickey subsystem, an open standard created by VanDyke. If you get this message, your remote server doesn't have this support.

17.8.2 Forwarding

Q: *I can't do port forwarding. I get a message that the port is already in use.*

A: Do you have another SecureCRT window open and connected with the same port-forwarding setup? You can't have two connections forwarding the same local port. As a workaround, create a second session that duplicates the first, but with a different local port number. Now you can use both sessions simultaneously.

17.9 VShell

VanDyke Software also sells an SSH server product, VShell, that runs on Windows and various Unix platforms, including Red Hat Linux, Solaris, FreeBSD, OS X, and HP-UX. VShell has interesting features to recommend it:

File and notification triggers
VShell can execute arbitrary commands in response to events such as SFTP file transfers or failed authentication attempts.

Flexible SFTP configuration
VShell's SFTP server has an access control list (ACL) language that can assign access to individual server directories by any combination of account name or group membership. It can conveniently use the Unix chroot mechanism to restrict users to given directories, as well as define virtual directories that hide details of server file organization from clients.

Fine-grained access control
Again using ACLs, the VShell server can restrict access to services by individual accounts. One account might be allowed full access while another may use only SFTP. One group may do local port forwarding and get interactive sessions with

their defined shells, but not remote forwarding or arbitrary remote command execution, except for one user in that group, who still gets full access.

Of course, the efficacy of such measures depends on further work: it does little good to restrict remote commands, for example, if any program can be started by the user's shell. But VShell provides these restrictions at the right place: in terms of the basic SSH channel types used to invoke the services. Other SSH products often do not have this level of control, and require awkward and fragile combinations of special shells or specific authentication methods to achieve the same goal.

GSSAPI

Support for emerging GSSAPI/Kerberos SSH standards for both client and server authentication.

Very understandable debug messages

Don't underestimate the value of readable verbose messages! There will always be problems, and logging is your main tool for solving them. Reading the verbose output of some SSH products can be an art in itself. VShell's messages are particularly well done.

17.10 Summary

VanDyke's SSH products are mature, stable, and well rounded, and have good vendor support. The GUI clients SecureCRT and SecureFX both work well. The command-line clients are not as flexible as OpenSSH and Tectia's, but they cover the basics and get the job done. The VShell server supports some interesting features and is well worth checking out.

PuTTY for Windows

The world is full of rich, hyper-powerful SSH implementations, but sometimes simplicity is best. Enter PuTTY, a tiny, uncomplicated, free SSH client for Microsoft Windows.* There's no installation procedure, no steep learning curve, and in many cases, no configuration needed.

At press time, PuTTY was still labeled as "beta" software, but don't be discouraged: it's a robust and just plain useful SSH client. Thanks to Simon Tatham for creating the PuTTY suite of programs, releasing them as free software, and writing a detailed manual on his web site. Because PuTTY's manual is very good, we'll focus on the most common uses. This chapter covers PuTTY Version 0.56.

18.1 Obtaining and Installing

Installation of PuTTY is as easy as it gets. Just download the *putty.exe* executable from:

> *http://www.chiark.greenend.org.uk/~sgtatham/putty/*

and run it. This simplicity is especially handy if you're traveling and need an SSH client; PuTTY is just a quick download away.

18.2 Basic Client Use

To get started, just run (or double-click) *putty.exe*. The PuTTY Configuration dialog shown in Figure 18-1 will appear:

For a quick start, locate the box labeled "Host Name (or IP address)," enter the hostname of your remote server machine, and click the Open button. A terminal window then appears and prompts you for your login name and password. Assuming

---

* It's also available for Unix, but OpenSSH and Tectia are so widespread that we don't see much point in using PuTTY on Unix platforms.

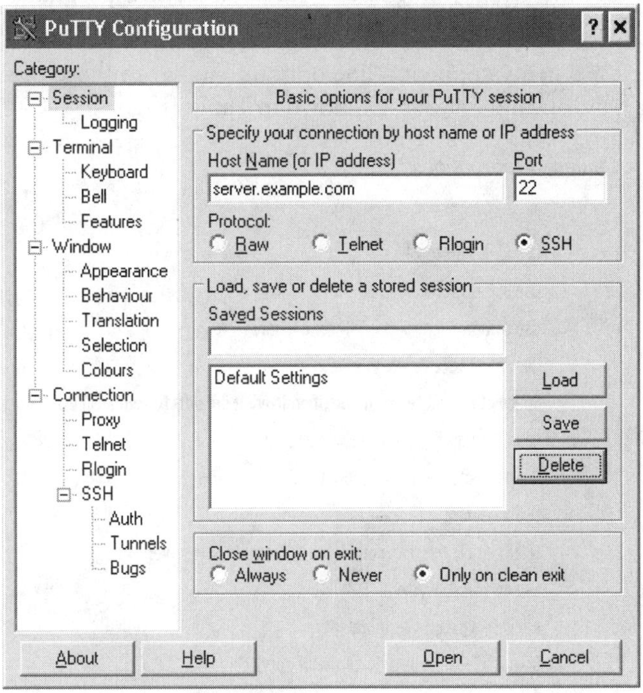

Figure 18-1. PuTTY Configuration dialog

there's nothing unusual about your SSH server, you're done: PuTTY establishes a secure login session with the server.

> PuTTY supports not only SSH, but also insecure protocols like Telnet and Rlogin. Make sure your connections are using the SSH protocol by selecting SSH on the initial PuTTY Configuration dialog. SSH is the default protocol for the other programs in the suite, such as Plink, PSFTP, and PSCP.

18.2.1 Plink, a Console Client

PuTTY comes with a second SSH terminal client, Plink, which is reminiscent of the *ssh* client of OpenSSH and Tectia. For a quick start, open a command window and type:

```
C:\> plink smith@server.example.com
```

This command connects you via SSH to *server.example.com*, logging in as remote user smith.

Plink is most appropriate for noninteractive use: for example, setting up tunnels for port forwarding, or running inside batch jobs. It can also handle interactive logins, but PuTTY is a better choice, particularly for screen-based programs like text editors. The Windows command line is not a particularly good terminal emulator.

The *plink* client has many command-line options, similar to those of *ssh*. Run *plink* by itself to see a list of valid options, as shown in Table 18-1.

Table 18-1. plink command-line options

Option	Meaning
1	Use SSH-1 protocol.
2	Use SSH-2 protocol.
C	Use compression for the SSH connection. [7.4.14]
-i *keyname*	Use the private key *keyname*.
-l *username*	Specify the remote username (if omitted, it defaults to your local username).
-load *session*	Load settings from a saved *session*.
-m *filename*	Read remote commands from the file *filename*.
-pw *P*	Use password *P*.
-P *port*	Use TCP port *port* to connect to the remote SSH server.
-s	Use an SSH subsystem. [5.8]
-t	Allocate a pseudo-terminal (pty).
-T	Do not allocate a pseudo-terminal. (pty).
-v	Print verbose diagnostics.
V	Display the program version.

18.2.2 Running Remote Commands

Instead of an interactive terminal session, PuTTY and Plink can run a single command of your choice, then exit immediately. It's simplest with Plink: just append the remote command to the Plink command line. For example, to run the *ls* (list files) command on a remote Linux machine running an SSH server, type:

```
C:\> plink smith@server.example.com ls
```

With PuTTY, visit the PuTTY Configuration dialog and look under Connection/SSH. Fill in the blank labeled "Remote command," then connect. The command will run and PuTTY will terminate afterward.

18.3 File Transfer

The PuTTY suite includes two programs for copying your files securely between machines. PSCP is a noninteractive program much like *scp*, and PSFTP is an interactive program inspired by *ftp*.

18.3.1 File Transfer with PSCP

PuTTY's *pscp* client is for copying files securely between machines, just like *scp* from OpenSSH and Tectia. Also like *scp*, *pscp* is noninteractive. (For an interactive client, see *psftp*. [18.3.2])

The syntax for PSCP is almost identical to that of *scp*. [7.5] Remote files are referenced by:

> [user@]host:path

where *user* is the remote username, *host* is the remote hostname, and *path* is the folder path to the file in question.

18.3.2 File Transfer with PSFTP

PSCP can copy files securely between computers, but the user interface is noninteractive. If you prefer a familiar FTP-like interface, try PSFTP, PuTTY's interactive file-transfer program. To start a file copying session with remote computer *server.example.com*, run:

```
C:\> psftp server.example.com
login as: smith
Using username "smith".
smith@server.example.com's password:
Remote working directory is /home/smith
psftp>
```

The prompt psftp> indicates that PSFTP is ready to accept commands. If you're familiar with FTP, the PSFTP commands will make you feel right at home. To transfer a file from your local machine to the remote server, use:

```
psftp> put myfile
```

or to copy a local file, *myfile*, as remote file *remotefile*:

```
psftp> put myfile remotefile
```

This is equivalent to the PSCP command:

```
C:\> scp myfile server.example.com:remotefile
```

In the other direction, to transfer files from the remote server to your local machine, use *get*:

```
psftp> get remotefile
psftp> get remotefile myfile
```

To traverse the directory (folder) hierarchy of the remote machine, use the *cd* command as in DOS or Unix:

```
psftp> cd my_remote_subfolder
psftp> cd ..
```

To change your working directory on the local machine, use *lcd*:

```
psftp> lcd my_local_subfolder
psftp> lcd ..
```

For a full list of commands, type *help*, or for assistance with a particular command, specify the command name as well (e.g., *help put*). Table 18-2 lists the available commands. Unfortunately, PSFTP does not include the useful *mput* and *mget* commands for transferring many files at once.

Table 18-2. PSFTP commands

Basic commands:	
open	Open an SFTP connection to a remote server.
bye, exit, quit	Exit PSFTP.
help	Get a help message.
!	Shell escape: run a command-line program on your local computer.
Directory (folder) commands:	
dir, ls	List a directory.
cd	Change directory (remote machine).
lcd	Change directory (local machine).
pwd	Print the name of the directory you're in (remote machine).
lpwd	Print the name of the directory you're in (local machine).
mkdir	Create a directory.
rmdir	Delete a directory.
File commands:	
get	Download a file.
put	Upload a file.
reget	Restart a download that you tried previously, but failed; will pick up where the previous download left off.
reput	Restart an upload that you tried previously, but failed; will pick up where the previous upload left off.
mv, ren	Rename a file.
rm, del	Delete a file.
chmod	Change permissions of a file, like the Unix *chmod* command.

18.4   Key Management

If you'd like to use public-key authentication to connect to remote hosts [2.4], PuTTY includes a key generator program, called PuTTYgen. It has a simple graphical user interface for creating and editing RSA and DSA keys, as shown in Figure 18-2.

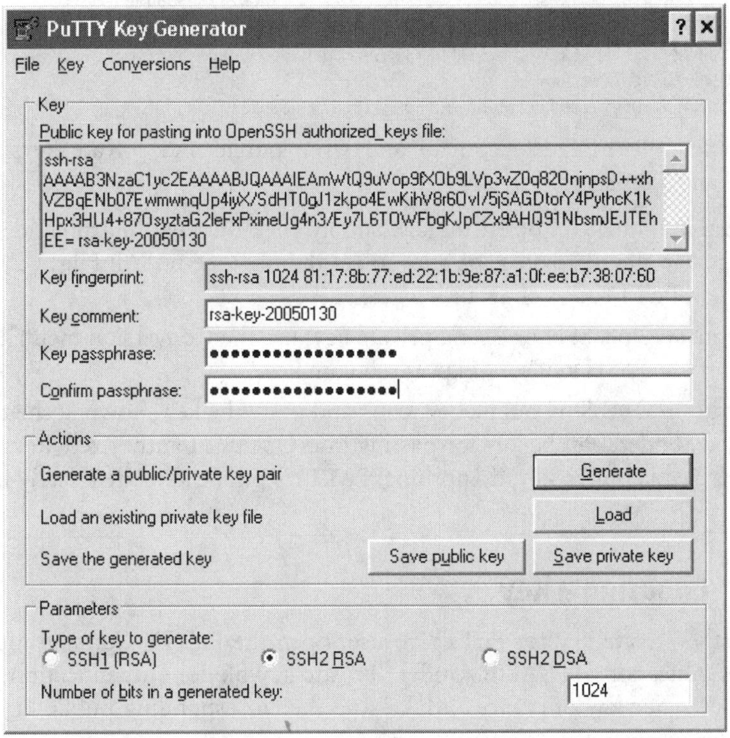

Figure 18-2. PuTTYgen, the key generator

To create a new key, simply click the Generate button. You'll be asked to waggle your mouse around to supply random numbers to the generator, then to supply a passphrase. To edit an existing key, just click the Load button.

You might remember that OpenSSH and Tectia use different file formats for their keys. PuTTYgen uses the SECSH format for public keys [6.1.2], but its own unique format for private keys. The private key is stored in a file with the suffix *.ppk* and looks like this:

```
PuTTY-User-Key-File-2: ssh-rsa
Encryption: aes256-cbc
Comment: Your comment here
Public-Lines: 4
AAAAB3NzaC1yc2EAAAABJQAAAIBltDpO1wC9qJ98peVr5y9C7N9vdOh+OrCNwbIh
lba1oSf94rrDl1TQXKXxgIHSd1ICgh7wkdxFWbyDRXSuWdur6kreTGRaw9XgCzQt
LyANMtKAPpDYVE1g8jb6jA1bOMtK8b+pGPmetbvdyBDmFcQ/oPwYyrZIjfbd8IdK
FxxJvw==
Private-Lines: 8
3ryAyuTLEnYuLGsetfNvazRYOhxQmzBWSyMLyT2i+zt7QqArlPglY1Um3NBJlYgS
caHDiLyH95tV2onEeBThJzYFAvgrr7UlXVjQTDLr29fe2FTS/bNm4OahTaKzTNV4
OEojvG1yafCucaZMVwsndB4djpm4otJja+xDVLN7Wj3ibzUT+SfodSJyazMAjBOy
Q3ndbcqcIPPg4OM3sL8cO9KTVdcuLkkyKMSV5yEgTAPORGOM+T8/ChHLFLHswwV+
```

```
/tlbOGLZRa1w3KsnzHHFKxMsM2zOdHXnSG8TXOkecdpT2p8PT3UGw2+SMESD8umc
GLai7g/oo3lMJVSOezrooDCO6p8J8OXk8h84gYeJbBIyXdELh10E3fnDSkTy5jS4
w2SCNzXX67ggWjIFtsefsx6VJ4WwJUYtNbKY35M59xMug/GRBLO7QPLu+xSh8/RB
yM/rWtUvGwXG3ygW/TVm7A==
Private-MAC: a0f9fa2204172fc6df9e0f6d5b918c8790d88611
```

But never fear: PuTTYgen can read and write public and private keys for both OpenSSH and Tectia:

- To read an OpenSSH or Tectia key, simply click the Load button and select the key file. (In the file dialog, be sure to set the file type to "All Files (*.*)" so that your non-PuTTY keys show up.)

- To write an OpenSSH or Tectia private key, use the Conversion menu and select "Export OpenSSH key" or "Export ssh.com key."

- To write an OpenSSH public key, copy and paste the key shown at the top of the window, under "Public key for pasting into OpenSSH authorized_keys file." To write a Tectia public key, do nothing: PuTTY's public keys are already in SECSH format.

18.4.1   Choosing a Key

To select the private key for PuTTY to use, open the PuTTY Configuration dialog and visit Connection/SSH/Auth. Under "Private key file for authentication," browse to and select your key of choice. (Make sure the corresponding public key is properly installed on the server. [6.2])

If you're using Plink, you can choose the key on the command line with the *–i* option:

```
C:\> plink -i c:\keys\me.ppk smith@server.example.com
```

18.4.2   Pageant, an SSH Agent

An SSH agent goes hand in hand with public-key authentication. [6.3] PuTTY has an agent, called Pageant, that caches private keys (stores them in memory) and responds to authentication-related queries from PuTTY, PSCP, and other clients in the suite. In short, Pageant is a timesaver, so you don't have to keep retyping your passphrase.

To run Pageant, just double-click it or invoke it from the command line. (Even better, add *pageant.exe* to your system startup so that it's always available when you boot or log in.) An icon will appear in the Windows System Tray on the taskbar. Right-click the icon and you can load keys into the agent, view your keys, or perform other operations, as shown in Figure 18-3. (To add a key, you'll need to know its passphrase.) Once a key is loaded into Pageant, the various PuTTY clients will use the key transparently, and you won't have to retype its passphrase.

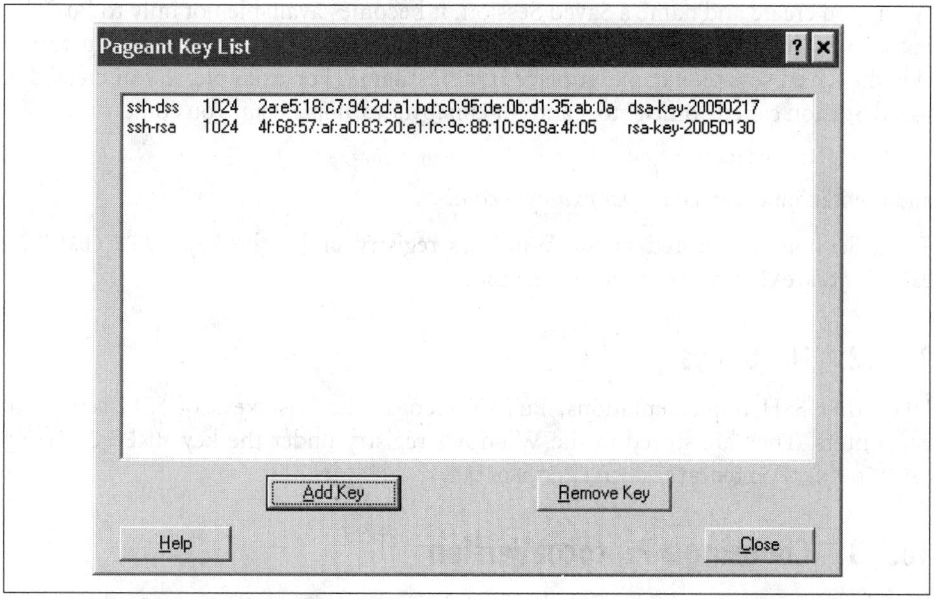

Figure 18-3. Pageant, the PuTTY agent

You can also run Pageant on the command line. Just follow it with one or more keys you'd like to load, e.g.:

```
C:\> pageant key1 key2 key3
```

and it will dutifully load them.

Speaking of agents, PuTTY also supports agent forwarding [6.3.5], but only for OpenSSH servers, not Tectia servers. Just make sure the option "Allow agent forwarding" is checked in PuTTY's configuration window; or if you're using Plink, add the *–A* option to enable agent forwarding or *–a* to disable it.

18.5   Advanced Client Use

PuTTY is simple to use in its most basic form. Nevertheless, its clients have many options that are worth trying out. We will cover the ones relating to SSH. Other terminal-related features, like settings for the window, keyboard, and mouse, we encourage you to explore on your own.

18.5.1   Saved Sessions

If you have a habit of connecting to the same remote machines often, set up a Saved Session, which remembers the settings for that connection so that you can reuse them. This is similar to the OpenSSH and Tectia feature of configuration files, but with a GUI. [7.1.2] Simply configure PuTTY the way you like it, then save that configuration under a name, such as "My Favorite Settings" or "office."

When you create and name a Saved Session, it becomes available not only to PuTTY, but also to the other programs in PuTTY's suite, such as PSCP and Plink. Just provide the saved session's name in place of a hostname. For example, if you created a Saved Session called "office" to stand for *employer.example.com*, you could run:

```
C:\> plink office
```

and it will connect to *employer.example.com*.

Saved Sessions are stored in the Windows registry under the key \HKEY_CURRENT_USER\Software\SimonTatham\PuTTY\Sessions.

18.5.2   Host Keys

Like other SSH implementations, PuTTY records the host keys of SSH servers it encounters. They are stored in the Windows registry under the key \HKEY_CURRENT_USER\Software\SimonTatham\PuTTY\SshHostKeys.

18.5.3   Choosing a Protocol Version

We always recommend you use the SSH-2 protocol, since it is more secure and robust than the original SSH-1. Nevertheless, PuTTY does support both protocols, and you can choose your preferred protocol on the PuTTY Configuration dialog, under Connection/SSH. The choices are:

1 only
> Require SSH-1, or else fail.

1
> Try SSH-1 first, then SSH-2.

2
> Try SSH-2 first, then SSH-1.

2 only
> Require SSH-2, or else fail (recommended).

With Plink, you can force the protocol version with the *-1* (SSH-1 only) and *-2* (SSH-2) options:

```
C:\> plink -2 smith@server.example.com
```

18.5.4   TCP/IP Settings

SSH uses TCP/IP as its transport mechanism, and PuTTY gives you control over some TCP-related settings.

18.5.4.1 Selecting a remote port

SSH servers almost always run on TCP port 22, but if you encounter a nonstandard server, you can choose a port in the PuTTY Configuration dialog, under Connection. Locate the Port value and fill it in.

With Plink, just specify the –P option to set the port number:

```
C:\> plink -P 12345 smith@server.example.com
```

18.5.4.2 Keepalive messages

SSH clients can optionally send TCP keepalive messages to an SSH server to recognize when a connection has failed. [7.4.5.4] If the client detects a lack of responses to these messages, it shuts down the connection. You can enable or disable this feature in the PuTTY Configuration dialog, under Connection.

18.5.4.3 The Nagle Algorithm

TCP/IP has a feature called the Nagle Algorithm, which is designed to reduce the number of TCP segments sent with very small amounts of data (e.g., 1 byte), usually as part of an interactive terminal session. This can affect performance over wide-area networks. [7.4.5.5] PuTTY lets you enable or disable the Nagle Algorithm in the PuTTY Configuration dialog, under Connection.

18.5.5   Pseudo-Terminal Allocation

SSH clients allocate a pseudo-terminal on the server machine: a software abstraction representing a computer terminal. [7.4.6.5] PuTTY does this by default, but you can prevent this in the PuTTY Configuration dialog, under Connection/SSH.

Because PuTTY is designed as a terminal client, which is interactive, you generally can leave this setting alone. But if you're using PuTTY noninteractively, say, only to set up port forwarding—you don't strictly need a pseudo-terminal. If you're using Plink, you can disable pseudo-terminal allocation with the –T option or leave it enabled with –t.

18.5.6   Proxies and SOCKS

PuTTY supports SOCKS, an application-layer network proxying system supported by various SSH implementations. [7.4.7] You can enable it in the PuTTY Configuration dialog, under Connection/Proxy.

18.5.7   Encryption Algorithms

On the Connection/SSH section of the PuTTY Configuration dialog, you can choose the encryption algorithms (ciphers) acceptable to the client. [7.4.9] Any algorithms appearing below the line "—warn below here—" will cause PuTTY to display a warning before they are used.

For most people, the defaults are fine. But if, say, a security hole were found in one of the algorithms (say, Blowfish), you could move it below the line, and PuTTY will warn before using it.

18.5.8 Authentication

PuTTY supports the following authentication types: password, public-key, challenge-response (a.k.a. keyboard-interactive), and TIS. [7.4.13] Password authentication works by default. Public-key authentication requires you to set up a key, as we've seen. [2.4] Challenge-response authentication is enabled in the PuTTY Configuration dialog, under Connection/SSH/Auth. [5.4.5]

TIS authentication is uncommon: it authenticates users via the Gauntlet firewall toolkit from Trusted Information Systems. It works only for the SSH-1 protocol so we recommend against using it. That being said, it is enabled in the PuTTY Configuration dialog, under Connection/SSH/Auth.

18.5.9 Compression

The data flowing between the SSH client and server may optionally be compressed to save bandwidth. [7.4.14] To enable compression, open the PuTTY Configuration dialog and look under Connection/SSH. If you're using Plink, add the –C option to enable compression:

```
C:\> plink -C smith@server.example.com
```

18.5.10 Logging and Debugging

If you're having a connection problem with PuTTY, you can capture the session data in a file. Open the PuTTY Configuration dialog and look under Session/Logging. Here you select the file to receive the data, and four different settings:

Logging completely turned off
   As it says, do no logging.

Log printable output only
   This simply captures the text of your terminal session, and is not very useful for debugging.

Log all session output
   This captures not only the text of your session, but also any nonprinting control characters. This is useful for debugging terminal emulation problems, e.g., if your favorite text editor isn't behaving when viewed through PuTTY.

Log SSH packet data

> This is the big one: the actual SSH data, unencrypted, that passes over the connection. It appears in hexadecimal and ASCII, annotated with high-level information such as "Doing Diffie-Hellman group exchange" and "Access denied." If you're debugging an SSH problem, this is the logging you need. However, it's not very user-friendly: you'll need substantial knowledge of the SSH protocol to figure out what's going on.

 If you select "Log SSH packet data," *always* select "Omit known password fields" as well. Otherwise, sensitive data like passwords will be captured in the log file, which is a security risk if the log file is read or stolen by a hostile third party.

If you're using Plink, you can display diagnostic information with the *-v* option:

```
C:\> plink -v smith@server.example.com
Server version: SSH-1.99-OpenSSH_3.8.1p1
We claim version: SSH-2.0-PuTTY-Release-0.56
Using SSH protocol version 2
Doing Diffie-Hellman group exchange
Doing Diffie-Hellman key exchange
Host key fingerprint is:
ssh-dss 1024 80:de:c6:fa:f7:82:4f:c7:c4:8c:1f:6f:d4:40:4b:0e
Initialised AES-256 client->server encryption
Initialised AES-256 server->client encryption
...
```

18.5.11 Batch Jobs

SSH can be used within batch jobs to secure their communications. [11.1] With PuTTY, batch jobs are most easily done with Plink and its *-batch* option:

```
C:\> plink -batch smith@server.example.com my-job
```

The *-batch* option suppresses all user prompts. But wait: just because you've disabled prompts doesn't automatically authenticate you. You'll also need to set up passwordless authentication. Otherwise, you'll simply fail to authenticate, prompts or no.

18.6 Forwarding

Forwarding or tunneling is the use of SSH to secure another network application, covered fully in Chapter 9. Both PuTTY and Plink can set up secure tunnels for this purpose.

18.6.1 Forwarding with PuTTY

Forwarding is set up with the PuTTY Configuration dialog. For local port forwarding, which is the most common type, select Tunnels. Then fill in these fields:

Source port
> Any unused TCP/IP port on your local machine.

Destination
> The remote SSH server name, followed by a colon, followed by the remote port number.

Local/Remote/Dynamic
> Choose Local.

For example, to connect to a remote VNC server (port 5900) on *server.example.com*, you'd provide a destination of server.example.com:5900, and any unused source port (say, 12345). This example demonstrates local forwarding [9.2.1], but PuTTY can also do remote [9.2.1.2] and dynamic [9.3] port forwarding.

To turn on X forwarding [9.4] for secure connections with an X Window server, simply choose Tunnels again and select the checkbox Enable X11 Forwarding.

To turn on agent forwarding [6.3.5] to allow your SSH agent to communicate with clients on other machines, navigate to Connection/SSH/Auth and select the checkbox Allow Agent Forwarding.

18.6.2 Forwarding with Plink

To enable the various kinds of forwarding with the command-line program Plink:

Local port forwarding [9.2.1]
> Use the –L option, supplying the source port, remote server name, and remote port. For example, to forward local port 12345 to remote port 5900 on *server.example.com*, run:
> ```
> C:\> plink server.example.com -L 12345:server.example.com:5900
> ```

Remote port forwarding [9.2.1.2]
> Use the –R option, supplying the remote source port, local server name, and local port. For example, to forward remote port 12345 on *outerspace.example.com* to your local port 5900, run:
> ```
> C:\> plink outerspace.example.com -R 12345:localhost:5900
> ```

Dynamic port forwarding [9.3]
> Use the –D option. For example, to perform dynamic port forwarding via proxy on port 12345, run:
> ```
> C:\> plink -D 12345 server.example.com
> ```

X forwarding [9.4]

    Use the *–X* option to enable it, or *–x* to disable it

Agent forwarding [6.3.5]

    Use the *–A* option to enable it, or *–a* to disable it.

18.7 Summary

PuTTY is a small, useful SSH client for Windows (and available for Linux if you don't already have another SSH client installed). Its major benefit is its simplicity—just download and start using it—but under the hood it has additional powerful features for the inquisitive user. For more information, see the PuTTY manual at:

    http://www.chiark.greenend.org.uk/~sgtatham/putty/

OpenSSH 4.0 New Features

Stop the presses! Just before this book was printed, OpenSSH 4.0 was released by those fine folks at *openssh.com*. While compatible with Version 3.9, it has several important new features that we discuss briefly. (We cover just features, not bug fixes.)

Server Features: sshd

The OpenSSH server has new features pertaining to logging, listening addresses, and password and account expiration warnings.

Logging of Access Control Violations

When authentication attempts are rejected by user-level access control (AllowUsers, DenyUsers) or group-level access control (AllowGroups, DenyGroups), *sshd* will log an informative message about it.

AddressFamily Keyword

The AddressFamily configuration keyword, previously available to clients only, can now be configured for the SSH server as well. If your server supports both IPv4 and IPv6, this lets you control on which sort of addresses *sshd* will listen.

Password and Account Expiration Warnings

If your password or account is going to expire (on operating systems that support expiration), *sshd* will now warn you in advance when you authenticate—for example.:

```
Your password will expire in 6 days
Your account will expire in 11 days
```

Client Features: ssh, scp, and sftp

OpenSSH clients have new features pertaining to keyboard-interactive authentication, connection sharing, known-hosts handling, port forwarding, and command-line editing and history.

KbdInteractiveDevices Keyword

The KbdInteractiveDevices keyword was undocumented in OpenSSH 3.9, but now it's officially supported. It determines the devices that the client will try for keyboard-interactive authentication.

```
KbdInteractiveDevices = pam,skey,bsdauth
```

More Control for Connection Sharing

If you're using the connection-sharing feature of *ssh*, you can now control the master process of that connection with the *–O* option. To check whether you're using connection sharing, run the following:

```
$ ssh -O check server.example.com
```

To request the master process to exit, run the following:

```
$ ssh -O exit server.example.com
```

Hashing of Hostnames

In previous versions of OpenSSH, *known_host* files contain the hostnames and IP addresses of the computer's you've visited via SSH. If you'd like to keep this information more private, use the new HashKnownHosts configuration keyword in your client configuration file:

```
HashKnownHosts yes
```

SSH clients will now hash the hostnames so they look like random strings—for example:

```
|1|Un5Q61BdVPCq65Yj3ec/HH6r+zI=|2pPQE/qjP7rrPLblvS1epjYbUOs=
```

This feature is experimental at the moment, so use it at your own risk.

Port Forwarding

When you construct a port forwarding, you can now specify a bind address: the address on which the accepting side of the forwarding will listen. This is useful either for controlling whether a forwarding is available off-host (not listening on only on the loopback), or distinguishing among multiple addresses if the listening host is multi-homed. You give the bind address on the command line, preceding the usual *–L* or *–R* value. For example, to set up a local forwarding from local port 2001 to remote server port 143 (IMAP), listening on 192.168.100.66:

```
$ ssh -L 192.168.100.66:2001:localhost:143 server.example.com
```

or for a remote forwarding:

```
$ ssh -R 192.168.100.66:2001:localhost:143 server.example.com
```

You can also do this with the LocalForward and RemoteForward configuration keywords, prepending the bind address to the second argument:

```
LocalForward 2001 192.168.100.66:localhost:143
RemoteForward 2001 192.168.100.66:localhost:143
```

Note that this forwarding will *not* be listening on the loopback address. You need to connect to 192.168.100.66:2001, even on the server itself; trying to connect to localhost:2001 will result in "connection refused." Also note that the bind address refers to the client for local forwarding and to the server for remote forwarding.

For local forwarding, the default binding is determined by the GatewayPorts keyword. For remote forwarding, the server may choose to honor or ignore a client's binding request using a new GatewayPorts value, clientspecified:

```
GatewayPorts clientspecified
```

This means the SSH client can select the binding address for the forwarding. This permits clients to bind addresses for remote forwardings

An empty binding address, or the special value *, indicates that the client or server should listen on all interfaces (including real ones and the loopback interface for localhost).

sftp Command-Line Features

The *sftp* client now supports command-line history and editing using Emacs-like keystrokes. You'll need the *libedit* library installed on your computer, available from *http://sourceforge.net/projects/libedit*. This feature is controlled at compile time with the flag --with-libedit.

ssh-keygen

If you're using the experimental hostname hashing feature described earlier, *ssh-keygen* has some new command-line options to support it.

Hashing Your Known Hosts File

ssh-keygen can convert your *known_hosts* file to use hashes with the –H option:

```
$ ssh-keygen -H
```

The *ssh-keygen* manpage claims that the results of *ssh-keygen -H* are written to standard output, but this is not true. The command modifies your *~/.ssh/known_hosts* file directly. It also stashes a copy of the old file in *~/.ssh/known_hosts.old* for safety, but don't depend on this: running *ssh-keygen -H* twice obliterates the safe copy.

Managing Hosts

Once you've hashed your hostnames, it's hard to edit the *known_hosts* file because you can't read which line corresponds to which host. *ssh-keygen* provides new commands for locating and removing hosts from the file. To locate a particular host in the file, use the *–F* option:

```
$ ssh-keygen -F server.example.com
# Host server.example.com found: line 3 type RSA1
server.example.com 1024 35 1301302858553510086.....
```

To remove a known host, use the *–R* option and provide the original hostname:

```
$ ssh-keygen -R server.example.com
/home/smith/.ssh/known_hosts updated.
Original contents retained as /home/smith/.ssh/known_hosts.old
```

Tectia Manpage for sshregex

This document describes the regular expressions (or globbing patterns) used in file-name globbing with *scp2* and *sftp2* and in the configuration files *ssh2_config* and *sshd2_config*.

Regex syntax used with *scp2* and *sftp2* is ZSH_FILEGLOB.

Regex Syntax: Egrep Patterns

The escape character is a backslash (\). You can use it to escape metacharacters to use them in their plain character form.

In the following examples, literal E and F denote any expression, whether a pattern or a character:

(Start a capturing subexpression.

)   End a capturing subexpression.

E|F

    Disjunction, match either E or F (inclusive). E is preferred if both match.

E*

    Act as Kleene star, match E zero or more times.

E+

    Closure, match E one or more times.

E?

    Option, match E optionally once.

.   Match any character except for newline characters (\n, \f, \r) and the NULL byte.

E{*n*}

    Match E exactly *n* times.

E{*n*,} *or* E{*n*,0}

    Match E *n* or more times.

E{,*n*} *or* E{0,*n*}
> Match E at most *n* times.

E{*n*,*m*}
> Match E no less than *n* times and no more than *m* times.

[Start a character set. See "Character Sets for Egrep and ZSH_FILEGLOB."

$ Match the empty string at the end of the input or at the end of a line.

^   Match the empty string at the start of the input or at the beginning of a line.

Escaped Tokens for Regex Syntax Egrep

The following list describes the tokens:

\0*n..n*
> The literal byte with octal value *n..n*.

\0
> The NULL byte.

\[1-9]..*x*
> The literal byte with decimal value [1-9]..*x*.

\x*n..n or* \0x*n..n*
> The literal byte with hexadecimal value *n..n*.

\<
> Match the empty string at the beginning of a word.

\>
> Match the empty string at the end of a word.

\b
> Match the empty string at a word boundary.

\B
> Match the empty string provided it is not at a word boundary.

\w
> Match a word-constituent character, equivalent to [a:zA:Z0:9-].

\W
> Match a non-word-constituent character.

\a
> Literal alarm character.

\e
> Literal escape character.

\f
> Literal line feed.

\n

Literal newline, equivalent to C's \n so that it can be more than one character long.

\r

Literal carriage return.

\t

Literal tab.

All other escaped characters denote the literal character itself.

Regex Syntax: ZSH_FILEGLOB (or Traditional) Patterns

The escape character is a backslash (\). With this you can escape metacharacters to use them in their plain character form.

In the following examples, literal E and F denote any expression, whether a pattern or a character:

*

Match any string consisting of zero or more characters. The characters can be any characters apart from slashes (/). However, the asterisk does not match a string if the string contains a dot (.) as its first character, or if the string contains a dot immediately after a slash. This means that the asterisk cannot be used to match filenames that have a dot as their first character.

If the previous character is a slash (/), or if an asterisk (*) is used to denote a match at the beginning of a string, it does match a dot (.).

That is, the asterisk (*) functions as normal in Unix shell fileglobs.

?

Match any single character except for a slash (/). However, do not match a dot (.) if located at the beginning of the string, or if the previous character is a slash (/).

That is, the question mark (?) functions as normal in Unix shell fileglobs (at least in ZSH, although discarding the dot may not be a standard procedure).

**/

Match any sequence of characters that is either empty, or ends in a slash. However, the substring /. is not allowed. This mimics the ****/** construct in ZSH. (Please note that ** is equivalent to *.)

E#

Act as Kleene star, match E zero or more times.

E##

Closure, match E one or more times.

(
Start a capturing subexpression.

)
End a capturing subexpression.

E|F
Disjunction, match either E or F (inclusive). E is preferred if both match.

[
Start a character set (covered next).

Character Sets for Egrep and ZSH_FILEGLOB

A character set starts with [and ends at non-escaped] that is not part of a POSIX character set specifier and that does not follow immediately after [.

The following characters have a special meaning and need to be escaped if meant literally:

- *(minus sign)*
A range operator, except immediately after [where it loses its special meaning.

^ *or* ! *(latter applies to ZSH_FILEGLOB)*
If immediately after the starting [, denotes a complement: the whole character set will be complemented. Otherwise, literal.

[:alnum:]
Characters for which isalnum returns true (see *ctype.h*).

[:alpha:]
Characters for which isalpha returns true (see *ctype.h*).

[:cntrl:]
Characters for which iscntrl returns true (see *ctype.h*).

[:digit:]
Characters for which isdigit returns true (see *ctype.h*).

[:graph:]
Characters for which isgraph returns true (see *ctype.h*).

[:lower:]
Characters for which islower returns true (see *ctype.h*).

[:print:]
Characters for which isprint returns true (see *ctype.h*).

[:punct:]
Characters for which ispunct returns true (see *ctype.h*).

[:space:]
Characters for which isspace returns true (see *ctype.h*).

[:upper:]

Characters for which `isupper` returns true (see *ctype.h*).

[:xdigit:]

Characters for which `isxdigit` returns true (see *ctype.h*).

Example

```
[[:xdigit:]XY]
```

is typically equivalent to:

```
[0123456789ABCDEFabcdefXY] .
```

It is also possible to include the predefined escaped character sets into a newly defined one, so:

```
[\d\s]
```

matches digits and whitespace characters.

Regex Syntax: SSH Patterns

The escape character is a tilde ~. With this you can escape metacharacters to use them in their plain character form.

> In configuration the backslash (\) is used to escape the list separator (',').

In the following examples literal E and F denote any expression, whether a pattern or a character.

(

Start a capturing subexpression.

)

End a capturing subexpression.

{

Start an anonymous, noncapturing subexpression.

}

End an anonymous, noncapturing subexpression.

E|F

Disjunction, match either E or F (inclusive). E is preferred if both match.

E*

Act as Kleene star, match E zero or more times.

E*?

Act as Kleene star, but match nongreedily (lazy match).

E+

Closure, match E one or more times.

E+?

Closure, but match non-greedily (lazy match).

E?

Option, match E optionally once.

E??

Option, but match non-greedily (lazy match).

.

Match ANY character, including possibly the NULL byte and the newline characters.

E/*n*/

Match E exactly *n* times.

E/*n*,/ *or* E/*n*,0/

Match E *n* or more times.

E/,*n*/ *or* E/0,*n*/

Match E at most *n* times.

E/*n*,*m*/

Match E no less than *n* times and no more than *m* times.

E/*n*,/? , E/*n*,0/? , E/,*n*/? , E/0,*n*/? , E/*n*,*m*/?

The lazy versions of above.

[

Start a character set. See the section "Escaped Tokens for Regex Syntax SSH."

>C

One-character lookahead. 'C' must be either a literal character or parse as a character set. Match the empty string anywhere provided that the next character is 'C' or belongs to it.

<C

One-character lookback. As above, but examine the previous character instead of the next character.

$

Match the empty string at the end of the input.

^

Match the empty string at the start of the input.

Escaped Tokens for Regex Syntax SSH

The following list describes the tokens:

~0n..n

    The literal byte with octal value *n..n*.

~0

    The NULL byte.

~[1-9]..x

    The literal byte with decimal value *~[1-9]..x*.

~xn..n or ~0xn..n

    The literal byte with hexadecimal value *n..n*.

~<

    Match the empty string at the beginning of a word.

~>

    Match the empty string at the end of a word.

~b

    Match the empty string at a word boundary.

~B

    Match the empty string provided it is not at a word boundary.

~d

    Match any digit, equivalent to [0:9].

~D

    Match any character except a digit.

~s

    Match a whitespace character (matches space, newline, line feed, carriage return, tab, and vertical tab).

~S

    Match a nonwhitespace character.

~w

    Match a word-constituent character, equivalent to [a:zA:Z0:9-].

~W

    Match a non-word-constituent character.

~a

    Literal alarm character.

~e

    Literal escape character.

~f

    Literal line feed.

~n

    Literal newline, equivalent to C's \n so that it can be more than one character long.

~r

    Literal carriage return.

~t

    Literal tab.

All other escaped characters denote the literal character itself.

Character Sets for Regex Syntax SSH

A character set starts with '[' and ends at non-escaped]' that is not part of a POSIX character set specifier and that does not follow immediately after '['.

The following characters have a special meaning and need to be escaped if meant literally:

:

    A range operator, except immediately after [, where it loses its special meaning.

- *(minus sign)*

    Until next +, the characters, ranges, and sets will be subtracted from the current set instead of being added. If appears as the first character after [, start subtracting from a set containing all characters instead of the empty set.

    Until next -, the characters, ranges, and sets will be added to the current set. This is the default.

[:alnum:]

    Characters for which isalnum returns true (see *ctype.h*).

[:alpha:]

    Characters for which isalpha returns true (see *ctype.h*).

[:cntrl:]

    Characters for which iscntrl returns true (see *ctype.h*).

[:digit:]

    Characters for which isdigit returns true (see *ctype.h*).

[:graph:]

    Characters for which isgraph returns true (see *ctype.h*).

[:lower:]

    Characters for which islower returns true (see *ctype.h*).

[:print:]

    Characters for which isprint returns true (see *ctype.h*).

[:punct:]

    Characters for which ispunct returns true (see *ctype.h*).

[:space:]
>   Characters for which isspace returns true (see *ctype.h*).

[:upper:]
>   Characters for which isupper returns true (see *ctype.h*).

[:xdigit:]
>   Characters for which isxdigit returns true (see *ctype.h*).

It is also possible to include the predefined escaped character sets into a newly defined one, so:

>   [~d~s]

matches digits and whitespace characters.

Also, escape sequences resulting in literals work inside character sets.

Example

>   [[:xdigit:]-a:e]

is typically equivalent to :

>   [0123456789ABCDEFf]

Authors

SSH Communications Security Corp.

For more information, see *http://www.ssh.com/*.

See Also

ssh2_config(5), sshd2_config(5), scp2(1), sftp2(1)

Tectia Module Names for Debugging

AnsiX962Rand
ArcFour
CmiStress
CryptoRandomPoll
DUMMY_ACC
GenHash
GenMac
GenPasswdPlugin
GenRand
GenTestCipher
GenTestMac
GenTestMain
GenTestMisc
GenTestPkcs
GenTestRand
GetOptCompat
Hash_Test
ModuleName
Pkcs1
PkcsImportExport
Scp2
Sftp2
SftpCwd
SftpPager
ssh-certview
Ssh-F-ConfigD
Ssh-F-ConfigD-Log
Ssh-F-ConfigD-Ssh-Configure
Ssh-F-ConfigD-SshD-Conf
Ssh1KeyDecode

Ssh1Protocol
Ssh2
Ssh2AuthCommonServer
Ssh2AuthGSSAPI
Ssh2AuthGSSAPICommon
Ssh2AuthHostBasedClient
Ssh2AuthHostBasedRhosts
Ssh2AuthHostBasedServer
Ssh2AuthKbdInteractiveClient
Ssh2AuthKbdInteractiveServer
Ssh2AuthKbdIntPAM
Ssh2AuthKbdIntPasswd
Ssh2AuthKbdIntPlugin
Ssh2AuthKbdIntRadius
Ssh2AuthKbdIntSecurID
Ssh2AuthKbdIntSubmethods
Ssh2AuthKerberosClient
Ssh2AuthKerberosServer
Ssh2AuthKerberosTgtClient
Ssh2AuthKerberosTgtServer
Ssh2AuthPAMClient
Ssh2AuthPAMCommon
Ssh2AuthPAMServer
Ssh2AuthPasswdClient
Ssh2AuthPasswdServer
Ssh2AuthPubKeyClient
Ssh2AuthPubKeyServer
Ssh2AuthSecurIDClient
Ssh2AuthSecurIDServer
Ssh2ChannelAgent

Ssh2ChannelSession
Ssh2ChannelSsh1Agent
Ssh2ChannelTcpFwd
Ssh2ChannelX11
Ssh2Client
Ssh2Common
Ssh2KeyBlob
Ssh2PgpPublic
Ssh2PgpSecret
Ssh2PgpUtil
Ssh2SftpServer
SshAdd
SshADT
SshADTArray
SshADTAssoc
SshADTAvlTree
SshADTConv
SshADTList
SshADTMap
SshADTPriorityHeap
SshADTRanges
SshAgent
SshAgentClient
SshAgentPath
SshAppCommon
SshAskPass
SshAsn1
SshAsn1Ber
SshAsn1Create
SshAsn1OidDB
SshAsn1VM
SshAuthMethodClient
SshAuthMethodServer
SshAuthServerPasswdChange
SshBuffer
SshBufferAux
SshBufZIP
SshCAEK
SshCert
SshCertCheck
SshCertClient
SshCertCMi
SshCertCMiKey

SshCertCMiTrust
SshCertCMiUtil
SshCertCrmf
SshCertd
SshCertDB
SshCertDNDer
SshCertDNEncode
SshCertDNLdap
SshCertEdb
SshCertEdbHttp
SshCertEdbLdap
SshCertEdbOcsp
SshCertEncode
SshCertEval
SshCertIDCheck
SshCertMap
SshCertOid
SshCertReqEncode
SshCertServer
SshCertX509
SshCipherAlias
SshCipherRabbit
SshCipherRijndael
SshClientExternalKey
SshCmiPolicyTree
SshCmpClient
SshConfig
SshConfigParse
SshCopyStream
SshCryptHmac
SshCryptoAuxInit
SshCryptoAuxKeyExpand
SshCryptoAuxOldImport
SshCryptoGenpkcs
SshCryptoInit
SshCryptoPKGroup
SshCryptoPKPrivate
SshCryptoRGF
SshCryptoRSA
SshCryptoSSL3MAC
SshCryptoTests
SshCryptTwofish
Sshd2

SshdCheckConf
SshDebug
SshDecay
SshDirectory
SshDLib
SshDumpCert
SshDumpCRL
SshEcCmp
SshEKAcc
SshEKDummy
SshEkGenAccDevice
SshEkGenaccProv
SshEKPKCS11
SshEKProv
SshEKSystem
SshEkView
SshEncode
SshEventLoop
SshFastalloc
SshFCGlob
SshFCRecurse
SshFCTransfer
SshFCTransferCore
SshFdStream
SshFileBuffer
SshFileCopy
SshFileXferClient
SshFileXferInternal
SshFilterStream
SshFSM
SshFtpFilter
SshGafpClientInterface
SshGafpFragmentStore
SshGafpKeyEncode
SshGenCiph
SshGenMPAux
SshGenMPInteger
SshGenMPPrime
SshGenPlugin
SshGenPluginCmd
SshGetCwd
SshGetOpt
SshGlob

SshGlobals
SshHostKey
SshHostKeyIO
SshHS
SshHSBackEndSymlink
SshHttp
SshHttpClient
SshHttpFilterProxy
SshHttpProxy
SshHttpServer
SshHttpTests
SshHttpUtils
SshInet
SshInetEncode
SshKeyFile
SshKeyGen
SshKneel
SshLdapBind
SshLdapConnect
SshLdapConvenience
SshLdapExt
SshLdapFilterFromString
SshLdapFilterToString
SshLdapInit
SshLdapInput
SshLdapModify
SshLdapObject
SshLdapOutput
SshLdapSearch
SshLdapTest
SshMiscString
SshMP2Adic
SshMPArithmetic
SshMPArithmeticExtra
SshMPInit
SshMPIntegerCore
SshMPIntegerMisc
SshMPIntMod
SshMPKernel
SshMPMont
SshMPPowM
SshMPSieve
SshMtTimeouts

SshNameList
SshNameServer
SshObstack
SshOcsp
SshOcspClient
SshOcspHttp
SshOcspTest
SshOcspTestUtil
SshPacketImplementation
SshPacketWrapper
SshPAMClient
SshPdbDummy
SshPgpCipher
SshPgpFile
SshPgpGen
SshPgpKey
SshPgpKeyDB
SshPgpPacket
SshPgpStringToKey
SshPipeStream
SshPKB
SshPKCS12
SshPKCS12Conv
SshPkcs6
SshPkcs7Common
SshPkcs7Decode
SshPkcs7Encode
SshPkExport
SshPKIDiscovery
SshPkiEnroll
SshPkiEnrollPkix
SshPkiEnrollScep
SshPrivateKeyRead
SshProbe
SshProcess
SshProtoAuthClient
SshProtoAuthServer
SshProtoCompat
SshProtoConnection
SshProtoCross
SshProtoKex
SshProtoTransport
SshProtoTransportAppl

SshProxyKey
SshPrvFile
SshPswbMac
SshRadius
SshRadiusConfig
SshRadiusUrl
SshRandomAnsiX917
SshRandomDev
SshRandomPool
SshReadLine
SshReadPass
SshRegex
SshSecSHAlgName
SshSerialStream
SshServer
SshServerProbe
SshSftpServer
SshSftpStandaloneServer
SshSha
SshSigChld
SshSigner2
SshSKB
SshSNList
SshSocks
SshSocksFilter
SshSPrintf
SshStdIOFilter
SshStr
SshStream
SshStreamConnect
SshStreamPair
SshStreamstub
SshTcp
SshThreadedMbox
SshThreadPool
SshThreadStubs
SshTime
SshTimeMeasure
SshTimeout
SshTtyFlags
SshUdp
SshUdpGeneric
SshUnixLocalStream

SshUnixPtyStream
SshUnixPtyStreamPTMX
SshUnixTcp
SshUnixUser
SshUserFile
SshUserFileBuffer
SshUserFiles
SshUtilFile
SshWinSyslog
SshX509CertReqDecode
SshX509Cmp
SshX509CmpDecode
SshX509CmpEncode

SshX509CmpUtil
SshX509CrlEncode
SshXmlCompress
t-ldapconv
TestCertdStresser
TestParser
TestRandom
TestSshFileCopy
TestSshGlob
TestTtyFlags
TPassExploit
X509Private

SSH-1 Features of OpenSSH and Tectia

This appendix describes the SSH-1 protocol features of OpenSSH and Tectia. Since we recommend against using SSH-1, you might never encounter these features, but we mention them for completeness.

OpenSSH Features

Serverwide Configuration

KeyRegenerationInterval *(or sshd -k)*
> Set the number of seconds between generations of the SSH-1 server key. This temporary key is used only for SSH-1 connections. The default is 3600 seconds (1 hour), and a value of zero disables regeneration.

RhostsRSAAuthentication
> Permit or deny authentication by the RSA key together with authentication by *rhosts* files.

RSAAuthentication
> Permit or deny authentication by the RSA key.

ServerKeyBits *(or sshd -b)*
> Set the number of bits in the SSH-1 server key: see KeyRegenerationInterval above. The default is 768 bits, and the fewest allowable is 512 bits.

Client Configuration

Cipher
> Replaced by Ciphers for SSH-2 protocol connections

RhostsRSAAuthentication
> Same as for serverwide configuration

RSAAuthentication
> Same as for serverwide configuration

Files

~/.ssh/identity, ~/.ssh/identity.pub
> These files contain your default private and public keys, respectively, for public-key authentication.

/etc/ssh/ssh_host_key
> This system file contains the SSH-1 protocol (RSA) host key.

Tectia Features

Tectia provides limited support for SSH-1, mostly by running programs from some older implementation whenever the SSH-1 protocol is required. Some of the Tectia programs do have built-in support for SSH-1, however.

Serverwide Configuration

The Tectia server has no built-in support for SSH-1, but it can be configured to run a separate SSH-1 server for SSH-1 clients. See "Compatibility Between SSH-1 and SSH-2 Servers" in Chapter 5.

The following keywords in the */etc/ssh2/sshd2_config* file control SSH-1 compatibility mode:

Ssh1Compatibility
> Run the SSH-1 server when SSH-1 clients connect (if yes).

Sshd1Path
> The pathname for the SSH-1 server.

Sshd1ConfigFile
> An alternate configuration file for the SSH-1 server, replacing the one specified for the Tectia server by the *–f* command-line option.

Client Configuration

The *ssh -1t* option runs an SSH-1 client program, and *ssh -1i* uses built-in SSH-1 emulation. See "Choosing a protocol version" in Chapter 7.

The following keywords in the */etc/ssh2/ssh2_config* file control SSH-1 compatibility mode:

Ssh1Compatibility
> Use SSH-1 if the server supports only supports the older protocol (if yes), or otherwise fail (if no).

Ssh1InternalEmulation
> Use the Tectia client's built-in SSH-1 functionality (if yes), or otherwise run an external SSH-1 program (if no).

Ssh1Path

The pathname for the external SSH-1 program.

Ssh1MaskPasswordLength

Send SSH_MSG_IGNORE packets with SSH-1 sessions to obscure the length of the password (if yes, the default). Otherwise, the unencrypted length fields used by SSH-1 can be easily intercepted.

Ssh1AgentCompatibility

Specifies whether and how to do agent forwarding. The value is one of:

Don't forward SSH-1 agent connections (the default).

traditional

Forward SSH-1 agent connections with no information about the forwarding path.

ssh2

Forward SSH-1 agent connections, and add information about the forwarding path as for SSH-2. This requires using the Tectia agent in SSH-1 compatibility mode.

File Transfers

scp can run a program *scp1* for file transfers using SSH-1. No mechanism is provided to specify an alternate name for the compatibility mode program (or a complete pathname: the *scp1* program is always found by searching the PATH).

If the *scp -1* option [7.5.9] is specified as the first option on the command line, then *scp1* is run for SSH-1 compatibility, with the rest of the arguments passed verbatim.

scp1 is also run if the *–t* or *–f* command-line options are used. These options were used for old implementations of the remote *scp* server.

Key Management

The *ssh-keygen -1* option converts a key (in a file specified as an argument for the option) from an older format used by some SSH-1 implementations to the new format used by Tectia.

Authentication Agent

The *ssh-agent -1* option causes the agent to handle requests from SSH-1 clients.

Keys added with the *ssh-add -1* option are an exception: they are not allowed to be used for SSH-1 operations.

The *ssh* client uses the keyword Ssh1AgentCompatibility to control agent forwarding, as described previously.

SSH Quick Reference

Legend

Mark	Meaning
✓	Yes: feature is supported/included
1	SSH-1 protocol only, not SSH-2
2	SSH-2 protocol only, not SSH-1

sshd Options

OpenSSH	Tectia	Option	Meaning
✓		−4	Use IPv4 addresses only
✓		−6	Use IPv6 addresses only
✓		−b bits	# of bits in server key
✓		−d	Verbose mode
	✓	−d debug_spec	Enable debug messages
	✓	−D debug_spec	Enable debug messages, keep listening
✓		−D	Don't detach into background
✓		−e	Send error messages to stderr
✓	✓	−f filename	Use other configuration file
✓	✓	−g time	Set login grace time
✓	✓	−h filename	Use other host key file
✓	✓	−i	Use *inetd* for invocation
1		−k time	Regeneration interval for SSH-1 server key
✓	✓	−o "keyword value"	Set configuration keyword
✓	✓	−p port	Select TCP port number
✓	✓	−q	Quiet mode

OpenSSH	Tectia	Option	Meaning
✓		−Q	Quiet if RSA support is missing
✓		−t	Test mode
✓		−u length	Set length of *utmp* structure
	✓	−v	Verbose mode
	✓	−V	Print version number

sshd Keywords

OpenSSH	Tectia	Keyword	Value	Meaning
✓	✓	#	Any text	Comment line
✓		AcceptEnv	Variables	Copy client environment variables to server
	✓	AllowAgentForwarding	Yes/no	Same as ForwardAgent
	✓	AllowedAuthentications	Auth types	Permitted authentication techniques
✓	✓	AllowGroups	Group list	Access control by Unix group
	✓	AllowHosts	Host list	Access control by hostname
	✓	AllowSHosts	Host list	Access control via *.shosts*
✓	✓	AllowTcpForwarding	Yes/no	Enable TCP port forwarding
	✓	AllowTcpForwardingForUsers	User list	Per user forwarding
	✓	AllowTcpForwardingForGroups	Group list	Per group forwarding
✓	✓	AllowUsers	User list	Access control by username
	✓	AllowX11Forwarding	Yes/no	Same as ForwardX11
	✓	AuthInteractiveFailureTimeout	Seconds	
	✓	AuthKbdInt.NumOptional	# submethods	Set number of optional submethods required for authentication
	✓	AuthKbdInt.Optional	Auth methods	Set optional authentication submethods for keyboard-interactive auth
	✓	AuthKbdInt.Plugin	Filename	Path to plugin for keyboard-interactive auth
	✓	AuthKbdInt.RADIUS.NASIdentifier		Client identifier for RADIUS keyboard-interactive authentication
	✓	AuthKbdInt.RADIUS.Server	Server spec	RADIUS server for keyboard-interactive auth
	✓	AuthKbdInt.Required	Auth methods	Set required authentication submethods for keyboard-interactive auth

OpenSSH	Tectia	Keyword	Value	Meaning
	✓	AuthKbdInt.Retries	# retries	Permitted retries for keyboard-interactive auth
	✓	AuthorizationFile	Filename	Location of authorization file
✓		AuthorizedKeysFile	Filename	Location of authorization file
	✓	AuthPassword.ChangePlugin	Filename	Location of password-change plugin program
	✓	AuthPublicKey.MaxSize	# bytes	Max size of public key
	✓	AuthPublicKey.MinSize	# bytes	Min size of public key
2		Banner	Filename	Location of banner file
	✓	BannerMessageFile	Filename	Location of banner file
	✓	Cert.RSA.Compat.HashScheme	md5/sha1	Set hash compatibility
	✓	CertdListenerPath	Filename	Location of certificate validation daemon
✓		ChallengeResponseAuthentication	Yes/no	Permit Challenge-Response authentication
✓	✓	CheckMail	Yes/no	Check new mail on login
	✓	ChRootGroups	Group list	Run chroot( ) on login
	✓	ChRootUsers	User list	Run chroot( ) on login
2	✓	Ciphers	Cipher list	Select encryption ciphers
✓		ClientAliveCountMax	# messages	Upper limit on client-alive messages
✓		ClientAliveInterval	Time	Frequency of sending client-alive messages
✓		Compression	Yes/no	Enable compression
✓	✓	DenyGroups	Group list	Access control by Unix group
	✓	DenyHosts	Host list	Access control by hostname
	✓	DenySHosts	Host list	Access control via .shosts
	✓	DenyTcpForwardingForUsers	User list	Per user forwarding
	✓	DenyTcpForwardingForGroups	Group list	Per group forwarding
✓	✓	DenyUsers	User list	Access control by username
	✓	DisableVersionFallback	Yes/no	Compatibility with old versions of software
	✓	ExternalAuthorizationProgram	Filename	Location of authorization program
	✓	ForwardACL	Forwarding spec	Access control over port forwarding
	✓	ForwardAgent	Yes/no	Enable agent forwarding
✓	✓	ForwardX11	Yes/no	Enable X forwarding
✓		GatewayPorts	Yes/no	Gateway all locally forwarded ports

OpenSSH	Tectia	Keyword	Value	Meaning
	✓	GSSAPI.AllowedMethods	kerberos	Permitted GSSAPI methods
	✓	GSSAPI.AllowOldMethodWhichIsInsecure	Yes/no	Use fallback code for old GSSAPI methods
	✓	GSSAPI.Dlls	Directory	Path to GSSAPI libraries
2		GSSAPIAuthentication	Yes/no	Enable GSSAPI authentication
2		GSSAPICleanupCredentials	Yes/no	Destroy credentials on logout
2		HostbasedAuthentication	Yes/no	Enable hostbase authentication
	✓	HostbasedAuthForceClientHost-nameDNSMatch	Yes/no	Fail authentication on DNS mismatch
	✓	HostCertificateFile	Filename	Location of X.509 certificate key file
✓		HostKey	Filename	Location of host key file
	✓	HostKeyEkInitString	Init string	Initialization string for external host key provider
	✓	HostKeyEkProvider	Provider spec	External host key provider
	✓	HostKeyEkTimeOut	Time	External host key provider timeout
	✓	HostKeyFile	Filename	Location of host key file
	✓	HostSpecificConfig	Filename	Location of subconfiguration file for hosts
	✓	IdleTimeout	Time	Set idle timeout
	✓	IgnoreLoginRestrictions.PasswordExpiration	Yes/no	Ignore password-expiration policy of operating system
	✓	IgnoreLoginRestrictions.Rlogin.AIX	Yes/no	Ignore remote login restriction on IBM AIX
✓	✓	IgnoreRhosts	Yes/no	Ignore .rhosts files
	✓	IgnoreRootRhosts	Yes/no	Ignore .rhosts for root
✓		IgnoreUserKnownHosts	Yes/no	Ignore user's known-hosts keys
	✓	KeepAlive	Yes/no	Send keepalive packets
✓		KerberosAuthentication	Yes/no	Permit Kerberos authentication
✓		KerberosGetAFSToken	Yes/no	Attempt to get AFS tokens (Kerberos)
✓		KerberosOrLocalPasswd	Yes/no	Kerberos fallback authentication
✓		KerberosTicketCleanup	Yes/no	Destroy ticket cache on logout
✓		KeyRegenerationInterval	Time	Key regeneration interval
✓	✓	ListenAddress	IP address	Listen on given interface
✓	✓	LoginGraceTime	Time	Time limit for authentication
✓		LogLevel	Syslog level	Set syslog level
✓	✓	Macs	Algorithm	Select MAC algorithm

OpenSSH	Tectia	Keyword	Value	Meaning
✓		MaxAuthTries	# attempts	Maximum number of authentication attempts per connection
	✓	MaxBroadcastsPerSecond	# broadcasts	Listen for UDP broadcasts
	✓	MaxConnections	# connections	Maximum # of simultaneous connections
✓		MaxStartups	# connections	Maximum # of simultaneous connections
	✓	NoDelay	Yes/no	Enable Nagle Algorithm
✓		PasswordAuthentication	Yes/no	Permit password authentication
	✓	PasswordGuesses	# guesses	Limit # of password tries
		PasswordExpireWarningDays	# days	Warn user before expiration
✓	✓	PermitEmptyPasswords	Yes/no	Permit empty passwords
✓	✓	PermitRootLogin	Yes/no/nopwd	Permit superuser logins
✓		PermitUserEnvironment	Yes/no	Permit users to set environment variables
	✓	PGPPublicKeyFile	Filename	Default location of PGP public-key file for authentication
✓		PidFile	Filename	Location of pid file
✓	✓	Port	Port number	Select server port number
✓		PrintLastLog	Yes/no	Print date/time of last login
✓	✓	PrintMotd	Yes/no	Print message of the day
✓		Protocol	1/2/1,2	Permit SSH-1,SSH-2 connections
	✓	ProxyServer	Server spec	Set SOCKS server
2		PubKeyAuthentication	Yes/no	Permit public-key authentication
	✓	PublicHostKeyFile	Filename	Location of public host key
	✓	QuietMode	Yes/no	Quiet mode
		RandomSeed	Filename	Location of random seed file
	✓	RandomSeedFile	Filename	Location of random seed file
	✓	RekeyIntervalSeconds	Seconds	Frequency of rekeying
	✓	RequiredAuthentications	Auth types	Required authentication techniques
	✓	RequireReverseMapping	Yes/no	Do reverse DNS lookup
	✓	ResolveClientHostName	Yes/no	Should server resolve client IP addresses
1		RhostsRSAAuthentication	Yes/no	Permit combined authentication
1		RSAAuthentication	Yes/no	Permit public-key authentication
✓		ServerKeyBits	# bits	# of bits in server key
	✓	SettableEnvironmentVariables	Patterns	Environment variables that may be set in server

OpenSSH	Tectia	Keyword	Value	Meaning
	✓	SftpSysLogFacility	Syslog level	Set syslog level for *sftp*
✓		SkeyAuthentication	Yes/no	Permit S/Key authentication
	✓	Ssh1Compatibility	Yes/no	Enable SSH1 compatibility
	✓	Sshd1ConfigFile	Filename	Configuration file for SSH-1 sessions
	✓	Sshd1Path	Filename	Path to *sshd1*
	✓	SocksServer		Same as ProxyServer
✓	✓	StrictModes	Yes/no	Strict file/directory permissions
	✓	Subsystem-*name*	Name | URL	Define a subsystem
✓		Subsystem	Name	Define a subsystem
✓	✓	SyslogFacility	Syslog level	Set syslog level
	✓	Terminal.AllowGroups	Group list	AllowGroups for terminal access
	✓	Terminal.AllowUsers	User list	AllowUsers for terminal access
	✓	Terminal.DenyGroups	Group list	DenyGroups for terminal access
	✓	Terminal.DenyUsers	User list	DenyUsers for terminal access
✓		TCPKeepAlive	Yes/no	Send keepalive packets
✓		UseDNS	Yes/no	Do reverse DNS lookups
✓		UseLogin	Yes/no	Select login program
✓		UsePAM	Yes/no	Use Pluggable Authentication Modules (PAM)
✓		UsePrivilegeSeparation	Yes/no	Enable privilege separation
	✓	UserConfigDirectory	Directory name	Location of user SSH2 directories
	✓	UserKnownHosts	Yes/no	Respect ~/.ssh2/knownhosts
	✓	UserSpecificConfig	Filename	Location of subconfiguration file for users
	✓	UseSOCKS5	Yes/no	Use SOCKS5 instead of SOCKS4
	✓	VerboseMode	Yes/no	Verbose mode
✓	✓	X11Forwarding	Yes/no	Same as ForwardX11
✓		X11DisplayOffset	# offset	Limit X displays for SSH
✓		X11UseLocalhost	Yes/no	Bind X server to loopback or wildcard address
✓		XAuthLocation	Filename	Location of *xauth*
	✓	XAuthPath	Filename	Location of *xauth*

ssh Options

OpenSSH	Tectia	Option	Meaning
✓		−1	Use SSH-1 protocol only
	✓	−1(t |i)	Use SSH-1 protocol via *ssh1* executable (t) or internal emulation (i)
✓		−2	Use SSH-2 protocol only
✓	✓	−4	Use IPv4 addresses only
✓	✓	−6	Use IPv6 addresses only
✓	✓	−a	Disable agent forwarding
	✓	+a	Enable agent forwarding
✓		−b bind_address	Select a network interface
✓		−A	Enable agent forwarding
✓	✓	−c cipher	Select encryption cipher
✓		−C	Enable compression
	✓	−C	Disable compression
	✓	+C	Enable compression
	✓	−d debug_spec	Enable debug messages
✓		−D port	Do dynamic port forwarding
✓	✓	−e character	Set escape character
	✓	−E name	Use external key-provider *name*
✓	✓	−f	Fork into background
	✓	−fo	Fork into background once
✓	✓	−F filename	Use other configuration file
✓	✓	−g	Gateway locally forwarded ports
	✓	+g	Don't gateway locally forwarded ports
	✓	−h	Print help message
✓	✓	−i filename	Select identity file
	✓	−I string	Initialization string for external-key provider
✓		−I device	Choose smartcard device
✓		−k	Disable Kerberos ticket forwarding
✓	✓	−l username	Remote username
✓	✓	−L port1:host2: port2	Local port forwarding
✓	✓	−m algorithm	Select MAC algorithm
✓		−M	Do not execute remote command
✓	✓	−n	Redirect stdin from */dev/null*
2		−N	Execute no remote command
✓	✓	−o "keyword value"	Set configuration keyword

OpenSSH	Tectia	Option	Meaning
✓	✓	–p port	Select TCP port number
✓	✓	–P	Use nonprivileged port
✓	✓	–q	Quiet mode
✓	✓	–R port1:host2: port2	Remote port forwarding
✓	✓	–s subsystem	Invoke remote subsystem
	✓	–S	No session channel
✓		–S socket	Choose control socket for connection sharing
✓	✓	–t	Allocate tty
✓		–T	Don't allocate tty
✓	✓	–v	Verbose mode
	✓	–V	Print version number
✓	✓	–x	Disable X forwarding
	✓	+x	Enable X forwarding
	✓	+X	Enable trusted X forwarding
✓		–X	Enable X forwarding
✓		–Y	Enable trusted X forwarding

scp Options

OpenSSH	Tectia	Option	Meaning
✓	✓	–1	Use SSH-1 protocol
✓		–2	Use SSH-2 protocol
✓		–4	Use IPv4 addresses only
✓		–6	Use IPv6 addresses only
	✓	–a [src:|dest:[unix |mac |dos]]	Transfer files in ASCII mode
✓		–a	No file-by-file statistics
✓		–A	Print file-by-file statistics
✓	✓	–B	Batch mode: disable prompting
✓	✓	–c cipher	Select encryption cipher
✓		–C	Enable compression
✓		––checksum (yes |no)	Compare files by checksum (optimization)
✓	✓	–d	Require target to be a directory when copying a single file
	✓	–D debug_spec	Enable debug messages
✓	✓	–f	Specify copy FROM (internal use)
✓		–F filename	Specify alternative configuration file
	✓	––force-lower-case	Rename destination files in all lowercase
	✓	–h	Print help message

OpenSSH	Tectia	Option	Meaning
✓	✓	−i filename	Select identity file
	✓	−I	Interactive mode: prompt before overwriting
✓		−l kilobits_per_second	Limit bandwidth
	✓	−M num	Set maximum number of requests to num
	✓	−n	Print actions, but don't copy
✓	✓	−o "keyword value"	Set configuration keyword
	✓	−−overwrite (yes|no)	Do/don't overwrite existing files
✓	✓	−p	Preserve file attributes
✓	✓	−P port	Select TCP port number
✓	✓	−q	Quiet mode
	✓	−Q	Don't print statistics
✓	✓	−r	Recursive copy
✓	✓	−S filename	Path to ssh executable
	✓	−−statistics (yes|no |simple)	Verbosity level for statistics
✓	✓	−t	Specify copy TO (internal use)
	✓	−u	Remove original file after copying
✓	✓	−v	Verbose mode
	✓	− V	Print version number
	✓	−W	Always transfer whole files; don't optimize

ssh and scp Keywords

OpenSSH	Tectia	Keyword	Value	Meaning
✓	✓	#	Any text	Comment line
✓		AddressFamily	any | inet | inet6	Set IP address type
	✓	AllowAgentForwarding	Yes/no	Same as ForwardAgent
	✓	AllowedAuthentications	Auth types	Permitted authentication techniques
	✓	AuthenticationNotify	Yes/no	Print message on stdout on successful authentication
	✓	AuthenticationSuccessMsg	Yes/no	Print message on stderr on successful authentication
✓	✓	BatchMode	Yes/no	Disable prompting
✓		BindAddress	Interface	Select a network interface
	✓	Cert.DODPKI	Yes/no	Certificates must be DoD PKI-compliant
	✓	Cert.EndpointIdentityCheck	Yes/no	Verify server hostname versus certificate

OpenSSH	Tectia	Keyword	Value	Meaning
	✓	Cert.RSA.Compat.HashScheme	md5/sha1	Set hash compatibility
✓		ChallengeResponseAuthen-tication	Yes/no	Enable challenge-response authentication
✓		CheckHostIP	Yes/no	Detect DNS spoofing
1		Cipher	Cipher	Request encryption cipher
2	✓	Ciphers	Cipher_list	Supported encryption ciphers
✓	✓	ClearAllForwardings	Yes/no	Ignore any specified forwarding
✓	✓	Compression	Yes/no	Enable data compression
✓		CompressionLevel	0–9	Select compression algorithm
✓		ConnectionAttempts	# attempts	# of retries by client
✓		ConnectTimeout	Time	Timeout for connecting to SSH server
✓		ControlMaster	Yes/no/ask	Enable connection sharing
✓		ControlPath	Socket	Location of socket for connection sharing
	✓	DebugLogFile	Filename	File for debug messages
	✓	DefaultDomain	Domain	Specify domain name
	✓	DisableVersionFallback	Yes/no	Compatibility with old versions of software
	✓	DontReadStdin	Yes/no	Redirect stdin from */dev/ null*
✓		DynamicForward	Port, socket	Set up a dynamic forwarding
	✓	EkInitString	Init string	Initialization string for external host key provider
	✓	EkProvider	Provider	External host key provider
✓		EnableSSHKeysign	Yes/no	Enable *ssh-keysign*
✓	✓	EscapeChar	Character	Set escape character (^ = Ctrl key)
	✓	ForcePTTYAllocation	Yes/no	Allocate a pseudo-tty
✓	✓	ForwardAgent	Yes/no	Enable agent forwarding
✓	✓	ForwardX11	Yes/no	Enable X forwarding
✓		ForwardX11Trusted	Port, socket	Set up a trusted X forwarding
✓	✓	GatewayPorts	Yes/no	Gateway locally forwarded ports
✓		GlobalKnownHostsFile	Filename	Location of global known hosts file
	✓	GoBackground	Yes/no	Fork into background
	✓	GSSAPI.AllowedMethods	kerberos	Permitted GSSAPI methods
	✓	GSSAPI.AllowOldMethodWhichIsInsecure	Yes/no	Use fallback code for old GSSAPI methods

OpenSSH	Tectia	Keyword	Value	Meaning
	✓	GSSAPI.DelegateToken	Yes/no	Delegate GSSAPI tokens
	✓	GSSAPI.Dlls	Directory	Location of GSSAPI libraries
✓		GSSAPIAuthentication	Yes/no	Enable GSSAPI authentication
✓		GSSAPIDelegateCredentials	Yes/no	Delegate GSSAPI tokens
	✓	Host	Hostname	Real name of a host
✓		Host	Pattern	Begin section for this host
	✓	HostCa	CA spec	CA certificate for authentication
	✓	HostCAMoCRLs		Same as HostCa but disables CRL checking
✓		HostKeyAlgorithms	Algorithm list	Set precedence of host key algorithms
✓		HostKeyAlias	Alias	Set alias for a host key
✓		HostName	Hostname	Real name of host
✓		IdentitiesOnly	Yes/no	Ignore *ssh-agent*
✓	✓	IdentityFile	Filename	Name of private-key file (RSA)
	✓	KeepAlive	Yes/no	Send keepalive packets
	✓	LDAPServers	LDAP URL	Locate LDAP servers
✓	✓	LocalForward	Port, socket	Local port forwarding
✓	✓	Macs	Algorithm	Select MAC algorithm
	✓	NoDelay	Yes/no	Enable Nagle Algorithm
✓		NoHostAuthenticationForLocal-host	Yes/no	Ignore localhost when checking host keys
✓	✓	NumberOfPasswordPrompts	# prompts	# of prompts before failure
✓		PasswordAuthentication	Yes/no	Permit password authentication
	✓	PasswordPrompt	String	Password prompt
✓	✓	Port	Port number	Select server port number
✓		PreferredAuthentications	Auth list	Permitted authentication techniques
✓		Protocol	1/2	SSH protocol version
✓		ProxyCommand	Command	Connect to proxy server
	✓	ProxyServer	Server spec	SOCKS server
✓		PubkeyAuthentication	Yes/no	Public-key authentication
	✓	QuietMode	Yes/no	Quiet mode
	✓	RandomSeedFile	Filename	Location of random seed file
	✓	RekeyIntervalSeconds	Time	Frequency of key exchange
✓	✓	RemoteForward	Port, socket	Remote port forwarding

OpenSSH	Tectia	Keyword	Value	Meaning
1		RhostsRSAAuthentication	Yes/no	Permit combined authentication
1		RSAAuthentication	Yes/no	Permit public-key authentication
✓		SendEnv	Variable list	Which environment variables are sent to SSH server
✓		ServerAliveCountMax	# retries	Upper limit on retries to contact SSH server
✓		ServerAliveInterval	Time	Timeout to contact SSH server
	✓	SetRemoteEnv	var=value	Set environment variable
✓		SmartcardDevice	device	Smartcard device
	✓	SocksServer	Server	Same as ProxyServer
	✓	Ssh1AgentCompatibility	Yes/no	Enable SSH1 agent compatibility
	✓	Ssh1Compatibility	Yes/no	Enable SSH1 compatibility
	✓	Ssh1InternalEmulation	Yes/no	Do SSH-1 internally
	✓	Ssh1MaskPasswordLength	Yes/no	Mask password length
	✓	Ssh1Path	Filename	Path to *ssh1*
	✓	SshSignerPath	Filename	Path to *ssh-signer2*
✓	✓	StrictHostKeyChecking	Yes/no/ask	Behavior on host key mismatch
✓		TCPKeepAlive	Yes/no	Send keepalive packets
	✓	TrustX11Applications	Yes/no	Enable trusted X11 forwarding
✓		UsePrivilegedPort	Yes/no	Permit privileged port use
✓	✓	User	Username	Remote username
✓		UserKnownHostsFile	Filename	Location of user known hosts file
	✓	UseSOCKS5	Yes/no	Use SOCKS5 instead of SOCKS4
	✓	VerboseMode	Yes/no	Verbose mode
✓		VerifyHostKeyDNS	Yes/no/ask	Verify a remote host key via DNS
✓		XAuthLocation	Filename	Location of *xauth*
	✓	XAuthPath	Filename	Location of *xauth*

ssh-keygen Options

OpenSSH	Tectia	Option	Meaning
	✓	−1 *filename*	Convert SSH1 key file to Tectia
	✓	−7 *filename*	Convert PKCS #7 key file to Tectia

OpenSSH	Tectia	Option	Meaning
	✓	−a trials	DH-GEX: number of primality
✓	✓	−b bits	# of bits in generated key
	✓	−B positive_integer	Specify numeric base for displaying key
✓		−B	Print fingerprint of key in BubbleBabble format
✓		−c	Change comment (with −C)
	✓	−c comment	Change comment
✓		−C comment	Specify new comment (with −c)
✓		−d	Generate DSA key
	✓	−D filename	Derive public key from private-key file
✓		−D reader	Download public key from smartcard reader
	✓	−e filename	Edit key file interactively
✓		−e	Export OpenSSH public key to Tectia format
✓		−f filename [a]	Output filename
	✓	−F filename	Print fingerprint of public key
✓		−G filename	DH-GEX: output file to generate candidate primes
	✓	−h	Print help and exit
	✓	−i	Display key information
✓		−i	Convert Tectia public key to OpenSSH
	✓	−k	Convert PKCS #12 key file to Tectia
✓		−l	Print fingerprint of public key
✓		−M memory	DH-GEX: set amount of memory to use
✓		−N passphrase	Specify new passphrase
	✓	−o filename	Output filename
	✓	−−overwrite (yes|no)	Overwrite output file or not
✓		−p	Change passphrase (with −P and −N)
✓		−P passphrase	Specify old passphrase (with −p)
	✓	−P	Use empty passphrase
✓	✓	−q	Quiet: suppress progress indicator
	✓	−r	Stir in data from random pool
✓		−S hexnumber	DH-GEX: starting point
✓		−r hostname	Print DNS record
✓		−R	Detect RSA (exit code 0/1)
✓	✓	−t algorithm	Select key-generation algorithm
✓		−T filename	DH-GEX: output file for test primes
✓		−U	Upload public key to smartcard reader
	✓	−V	Print version string and exit
✓		−W generator	DH-GEX: choose generator

OpenSSH	Tectia	Option	Meaning
	✓	−x filename	Convert key from X.509 to Tectia
✓		−y	Derive public key from private-key file
	✓	−?[b]	Print help and exit

[a] The output filename is given as the final argument to *ssh-keygen*.
[b] You may need to escape the question mark in your shell, e.g., −\?.

ssh-agent Options

OpenSSH	Tectia	Option	Meaning
	✓	−1	SSH1 compatibility mode
✓		−a socket	Bind to given socket
✓		−d	Debug mode
	✓	−d debug_spec	Debug mode
✓	✓	−c	Print C-shell-style commands
✓		−k	Kill existing agent
✓	✓	−s	Print *sh*-style commands
✓		−t time	Set maximum lifetime of identities

ssh-add Options

OpenSSH	Tectia	Option	Meaning
	✓	−1	Limit SSH-1 compatibility
✓		−c	Confirm identities before loading them
✓	✓	−d	Unload key
✓	✓	−D	Unload all keys
✓		−e reader	Remove key in smartcard reader
	✓	−f step	Limit agent-forwarding hops
	✓	−F host_list	Limit agent-forwarding hosts
	✓	−I	PGP keys are identified by ID
	✓	−l	List loaded keys
✓		−l	List fingerprints of loaded keys
	✓	−L	Lock agent
✓		−L	List loaded keys
	✓	−N	PGP keys are identified by name
	✓	−p	Read passphrase from stdin
	✓	−P	PGP keys are identified by fingerprint
	✓	−R filename	Specify PGP keyring file

OpenSSH	Tectia	Option	Meaning
✓		−s reader	Add key in smartcard reader
✓	✓	−t timeout	Expire key after timeout
	✓	−u	Read key from URL
	✓	−U	Unlock agent
✓		−x	Lock agent
✓		−X	Unlock agent

Identity and Authorization Files, OpenSSH

~/.ssh/authorized_keys key options: use one public key per line, preceded by options.

Option	Meaning
command="Unix shell command"	Specify a forced command
environment="variable=value"	Set environment variable
from=host_or_ip_address_specification	Limit incoming hosts
no-agent-forwarding	Disable agent forwarding
no-port-forwarding	Disable port forwarding
no-pty	Don't allocate TTY
no-x11-forwarding	Disable X Window forwarding
permitopen ="H:P"	Permit forwarding to local port P from remote host H

Identity and Authorization Files, Tectia

~/.ssh2/authorization keywords: use one keyword/value pair per line.

Keyword	Meaning
Command Unix_command	Old way to specify a forced command; now obsolete, use Options
Key filename.pub	Location of public-key file
Options comma-separated-list-of-options	Options for the key immediately preceding it; see Options table below
PgpPublicKeyFile filename	Location of PGP public-key file
PgpKeyFingerprint fingerprint	Select PGP key by fingerprint
PgpKeyId id	Select PGP key by ID
PgpKeyName name	Select PGP key by name

~/.ssh2/authorization key options: one or more options separated by commas.

Option	Meaning
`allow-from=`*host_or_ip_address_ specification*	Accept connections from incoming hosts
`command="`*Unix shell command*`"`	Specify a forced command
`deny-from=`*host_or_ip_address_ specification*	Reject connections from incoming hosts
`environment="`*variable=value*`"`	Set environment variable
`idle-timeout=`*time*	Set idle timeout
`no-agent-forwarding`	Disable agent forwarding
`no-port-forwarding`	Disable port forwarding
`no-pty`	Don't allocate TTY
`no-x11-forwarding`	Disable X Window forwarding

~/.ssh2/identification keywords: one keyword/value pair per line.

Keyword	Meaning
`IdKey` *filename*	Location of private-key file
`IdPgpKeyFingerprint` *fingerprint*	Select PGP key by fingerprint
`IdPgpKeyId` *id*	Select PGP key by ID
`IdPgpKeyName` *name*	Select PGP key by name
`PgpSecretKeyFile` *filename*	Location of PGP private-key file

Environment Variables

Variable	Set by	In	Meaning
SSH_ASKPASS	*ssh user*	OpenSSH	Path to *askpass* program
SSH_AUTH_SOCK	*ssh-agent*	OpenSSH	Path to socket
SSH2_AUTH_SOCK	*ssh-agent*	Tectia	Path to socket
SSH_CLIENT	*sshd*	OpenSSH	Client socket info
SSH2_CLIENT	*sshd*	Tectia	Client socket info
SSH_CONNECTION	*sshd*	OpenSSH	Client and server socket info
SSH_ORIGINAL_COMMAND	*sshd*	OpenSSH	Client's remote command string
SSH_ORIGINAL_COMMAND2	*sshd*	Tectia	Client's remote command string
SSH_SOCKS_SERVER	*ssh user*	Tectia	SOCKS firewall information
SSH_TTY	*sshd*	OpenSSH	Name of allocated TTY
SSH2_TTY	*sshd*	Tectia	Name of allocated TTY

Index

Numbers

3DES, 88

Symbols

$HOME environment variable, 6
-- (double dash), 103
~ (tilde), 21

A

AAA (authentication, authorization, and accounting), 109
AcceptEnv keyword, 199
Accession Lite, 536–539
   Enable Key Compatibility, 538
account access control, 185–191
account permissions and security, 25
active-mode (FTP), 419
Address Space Layout Randomization (ASLR), 151
AddressFamily keyword, 294, 591, 620
addressing, single name, multiple address issue, 71
Advanced Encryption Standard (see AES)
AES (Advanced Encryption Standard), 87
AFS (Andrew File System), 406
agents, 28–32, 45, 242–260
   access control, 253
   agent forwarding, 30–32, 256–259, 350
      connections in series, 32
      enabling, 259
      firewall example, 256

      operation, 257
      server configuration, 206
   authentication agents, 8
   automatic loading
      single-shell method, 251
      subshell method, 252
      X Windows, 253
   automation and, 29
   client identification, 255
   cpu usage, 259
   debugging (OpenSSH), 259
   double-remote copying with scp, 30–32
   environment variable command format, 247
   identities, listing and deleting, 248
   invocation, login accounts, 243
   keys, 29
      listing, 29
      loading, 28, 247–253
   locking and unlocking, 29, 249
   protected memory, 255
   security aspects, 253–256
      agent cracking, 255
   single-shell invocation, 243–245
   subshell invocation, 246
   switching identities, 261
   troubleshooting, 504
AllowAgentForwarding keyword (Tectia), 206
AllowedAuthentications keyword (Tectia), 172
   gssapi, 182
   hostbased, 175
   keyboard interactive, 178

We'd like to hear your suggestions for improving our indexes. Send email to *index@oreilly.com*.

allow-from keyword, 197, 340
AllowGroups keyword, 191, 192, 195, 201,
    371, 400, 402, 477, 493, 591, 613
AllowHosts keyword, 115, 158, 192, 193,
    198, 225, 250, 340, 347, 402, 471,
    472, 477, 493, 613
AllowSHosts keyword, 193, 198, 412, 477,
    613
AllowTcpForwarding keyword, 201, 205,
    370, 371, 400, 403, 477, 613
AllowTcpForwardingForGroups
    keyword, 201, 371, 477, 613
AllowTcpForwardingForUsers
    keyword, 201, 205, 371, 477, 613
AllowUsers keyword, 185
    pattern matching, 186
AllowX11Forwarding keyword, 205, 381,
    477, 613
ARCFOUR (see RC4)
ASLR (Address Space Layout
    Randomization), 151
asymmetric cryptography, 41
attacks, 91–96
    agent cracking, 255
    brute-force attacks, 40
    connection hijacking, 91
    covert channels, 96
    dictionary attack, 27
    eavesdropping, 91
    IP attacks, 94
    IP spoofing, 91
    keystroke timing data and potential
        attacks, 96
    man-in-the-middle attacks, 19, 92
    name service spoofing, 91
    password cracking, 93
    replay attacks, 37
    TCP attacks, 94
    traffic analysis, 95
    user or administrator carelessness and, 97
authentication, 3, 38
    agents, using (see agents)
    authorization in hostbased authentication
        (SSH), 71
    failure messages, 20
    passwordless, 32
    per-account configuration and, 328
    public-key authentication (see public-key
        authentication)
    scalability case study, 452–468

SecurID hardware-based
    authentication, 180
server configuration for (see serverwide
    configuration, authentication)
ssh (client) configuration, 307–310
troubleshooting, 498–504
(see also SSH (Secure Shell), SSH-AUTH)
AuthenticationNotify keyword, 308, 309,
    620
AuthenticationSuccessMsg keyword, 308,
    309, 620
AuthInteractiveFailureTimeout keyword
    (Tectia), 173, 179
AuthKbdInt.NumOptional keyword
    (Tectia), 179
AuthKbdInt.Optional keyword, 179, 180,
    477, 613
AuthKbdInt.Plugin keyword, 180, 477, 478,
    479, 492, 613
AuthKbdInt.RADIUS.NASIdentifier
    keyword, 613
AuthKbdInt.RADIUS.Server keyword, 613
AuthKbdInt.Required keyword, 179, 180,
    477, 613
AuthKbdInt.Retries keyword (Tectia), 179
authorization, 39
authorization files, server accounts, 329–331
AuthorizationFile keyword, 145, 330, 477,
    614
authorized_keys, 24, 346
AuthorizedKeysFile keyword, 145, 614
AuthPassword.ChangePlugin keyword, 477,
    480, 484, 614
AuthPublicKey.MinSize and MaxSize
    keywords (Tectia), 175
autoconf, 102
Axessh, 517

B

BAMSE, 520
Banner keyword (OpenSSH), 198
BannerMessageFile keyword (Tectia), 198
bastion host, 256
batch jobs, 408–415
    hostbased authentication, 412
    Kerberos authentication, 413
    password authentication, 408
    public-key authentication, 409–412
        agents, 410–412
        filesystem passphrase storage, 409
        plaintext keys, 410

security precautions, 413
   least-privilege accounts, 414
   locked-down automation
     accounts, 414
   restricted-use keys, 414
   ssh options, 414
BatchMode keyword, 295, 415, 441, 620
BeOS SSH implementations, 516
binary distributions, 99
binary packet protocol, 50
BindAddress keyword, 291, 620
Blowfish, 88
bogus ICMP attacks, 94
boot versus manual invocation, 129
brute-force attacks, 40
bulk keys or bulk ciphers, 41
bzip2 and bunzip2, 101

C

cancel-tcpip-forward request, 65
case studies
   authentication, 452–468
   batch and cron jobs (see batch jobs)
   FTP, 415–436
   gateway hosts, connecting
     through, 444–452
   Pine email client, 436–444
CAST, 89
CertdListenerPath keyword, 477, 614
Cert.DODPKI keyword, 620
Cert.EndpointIdentityCheck keyword, 620
certificate authorities, 14
Cert.RSA.Compat.HashScheme
   keyword, 477, 614, 621
challenge/response authentication, 22
ChallengeResponseAuthentication
   keyword, 171, 178
channels, 47, 64
   channel numbers, 64
   channel requests, 66
CheckHostIP keyword, 285, 621
CheckMail keyword (Tectia), 199
ChRootGroups keyword, 195, 477, 614
ChRootUsers keyword, 195, 477, 614
Cipher keyword, 163, 509, 609, 621
ciphers, 40
Ciphers keyword, 53, 162, 167, 169, 306,
   477, 614, 621
ClearAllForwardings keyword, 357, 358, 621
client configuration, 266
   debugging messages, 495

setup recommendations, 404
troubleshooting, 507
ClientAliveCountMax keyword, 154, 614
ClientAliveInterval keyword, 154, 155, 614
Command keyword, 626
Commodore Amiga SSH
   implementations, 516
compression algorithms, 91
Compression keyword, 171, 268, 272, 273,
   276, 280, 311, 614, 621
CompressionLevel keyword, 508, 621
configuration, 101
   compile-time configuration, 101–105
   configuration files, 45
   configure script, 102
     command-line flags, 103–104
     options, 105
     pathname embedding versus PATH
      variable, 104
   make command, 105
   "none" encryption, 53
   OpenSSH (see OpenSSH)
   per-account configuration (see
     per-account configuration)
   serverwide configuration (see serverwide
     configuration)
   Tectia (see Tectia)
   (see also client configuration)
connection hijacking, 91
ConnectionAttempts keyword, 621
Connector, 543–551
ConnectTimeout keyword, 293, 621
control connections (FTP), 418
   forwarding, 420–424
     choosing the target, 421
ControlMaster keyword, 64, 288, 621
ControlPath keyword, 64, 288, 621
covert channels, 96
CRC (Cyclic Redundancy Check) hash, 43
CRC-32 (Cyclic Redundancy Check), 89
cron jobs (see batch jobs)
cryptanalysis, 40
cryptography, 39–43
   hash functions, 42
   public-key cryptography, 41
   secret-key cryptography, 41
   security, 40
CVS (Concurrent Versions System), 125
Cyclic Redundancy Check (CRC-32), 89
Cygwin, 518

D

data connections (FTP), 418
Data Encryption Standard (DES), 87
debugging
    messages, 495
    serverwide configuration
        syslog files, 131
DebugLogFile keyword, 621
default identity, 229
DefaultDomain keyword, 621
deny-from keyword, 197, 340
DenyGroups, 402
DenyGroups keyword, 191, 192, 201, 400,
        402, 477, 493, 591, 614, 617
DenyHosts keyword, 115, 158, 193, 198,
        250, 340, 347, 477, 493, 614
DenySHosts keyword, 193, 198, 412, 477,
        614
DenyTcpForwardingForGroups
        keyword, 201, 205, 477, 614
DenyTcpForwardingForUsers keyword, 201,
        205, 477, 614
DenyUsers keyword, 185
    pattern matching, 186
DES (Data Encryption Standard), 87
dictionary attack, 27
Diffie-Hellman key agreement algorithm, 86
digital certificates, 14
Digital Signature Algorithm (DSA), 85
digital signatures, 41
DisableVersionFallback keyword, 477, 614,
        621
display, 382
DNS (Domain Name Service), 11
DontReadStdin keyword, 298, 621
DropBear, 519
DSA (Digital Signature Algorithm), 85
dynamic port forwarding, 373–377
DynamicForward keyword, 304, 621

E

eavesdropping, 91
Egrep, sshregex (Tectia), 595
    character sets, 598
    escaped tokens, 596
EkInitString keyword, 264, 621
EkProvider keyword, 264, 621
email clients (see Pine email client)
EnableSSHKeysign keyword, 347, 501, 621

encryption, 4, 40
    algorithms, 40
        ssh (client), 306
    programs, 1
env channel request, 66
environment variables, 627
    agents and, 247
    per-account settings, 340–343
    ssh (client), 275
Ericom PowerTerm, 517
escape characters and sequences, 21
EscapeChar keyword, 272, 301, 302, 621
exec channel request, 66
Expect, 519
ExternalAuthorizationProgram
        keyword, 194, 477, 614

F

file transfers
    sftp, 323
filesystems, recommended settings, 404–407
firewalls, 1, 15
    FTP passive mode and, 424
    port forwarding, bypassing with, 364
forced commands, 326, 332
    command menu, displaying, 335
    logging, 338
    rejecting connections, 334
    scp and, 338
    security concerns, 333
    SSH_ORIGINAL_COMMAND
        environment variable, 336
ForcePTTYAllocation keyword, 296, 621
ForwardACL keyword, 201, 203, 204, 205,
        477, 614
ForwardAgent keyword, 259
forwarding, 39, 350
    limiting or disabling per-account, 344
    (see also port forwarding; agents, agent
        forwarding)
ForwardX11 keyword, 116, 380, 381, 477,
        614, 621
ForwardX11Trusted keyword, 383, 621
Friedl, Markus, 10
F-Secure SSH, 518
FTP (file transfer protocol), 417, 429–434
    case study, 415–436
        control connection
            forwarding, 420–424
        static port forwarding, 417

Tectia client, 416
VanDyke's SecureFX tool, 416
data connections, forwarding through
SSH, 434–436
default data port mode, 432
TCP protocol and, 433
NAT and, 426–429
passive mode, 422–426, 431
firewalls and, 424
PASV port theft problem, 423
SSL-enhanced, 14
troubleshooting, 511
typical data transfer mode, 429

G

gateway hosts, 256
case study, 444–452
port forwarding (SSH-in-SSH), 449
scp, 448
SSH connection, making, 445–448
tunnelled SSH
withProxyCommand, 450
GatewayPorts keyword, 355, 356, 357, 364,
389, 390, 397, 404, 422, 593, 614,
621
GlobalKnownHostsFile keyword, 621
GNU Emacs and SSH, 517
GnuPG (GNU Privacy Guard), 11
GoBackground keyword, 367, 621
gPutty, 520
group access control, 191
GSSAPI, 463
GSSAPI.AllowedMethods keyword
(Tectia), 182
GSSAPI.AllowOldMethodWhichIsInsecure
keyword, 182, 615, 621
GSSAPIAuthentication keyword
(OpenSSH), 181
GSSAPICleanupCredentials keyword, 182,
615
GSSAPIDelegateCredentials keyword, 622
GSSAPI.DelegateToken keyword, 622
GSSAPI.Dlls keyword (Tectia), 183
gzip and gunzip, 101

H

hash functions, 42, 89
collision-resistance and
pre-image-resistance, 43
HOME environment variable, 6

host keys, 20, 284–287
implementation dependency, SSH, 69
Host keyword, 270, 271, 272, 273, 274, 281,
447, 499, 507, 622
hostbased authentication
batch jobs and, 412
per-account configuration and, 347
security of, 412
server configuration for, 175–177
troubleshooting, 500
HostbasedAuthentication keyword
(OpenSSH), 175
HostbasedAuthForceClientHostnameDNSM
atch keyword, 177, 477, 615
HostCa keyword, 477, 622
HostCAMoCRLs keyword, 477, 622
HostCertificateFile keyword, 458, 477, 615
host-key generation, 130
HostKey keyword, 142, 615
HostKeyAlgorithms keyword, 307, 622
HostKeyAlias keyword, 286, 449, 451, 622
HostKeyEkInitString keyword, 477, 615
HostKeyEkProvider keyword, 615
HostKeyEkTimeOut keyword, 477, 615
HostKeyFile keyword, 142, 477, 615
HostName keyword, 273, 280, 622
hosts, 19–21
HostSpecificConfig keyword (Tectia), 471
hostspecs, 73

I

IDEA (International Data Encryption
Algorithm), 86
identification files (Tectia), 232
identities, 227–242, 281–283
creating, 233–242
Diffie-Hellman key exchange, group
generation, 241
default identity, 229
listing and deleting, 248
manual switching, 261
multiple identities, 260–262
OpenSSH, 229
switching with agents, 261
tailored sessions, 262
Tectia, 230
IdentitiesOnly keyword, 283, 622
IdentityFile keyword, 157, 232, 261, 262,
273, 281, 282, 283, 410, 622
IdKey keyword, 232, 627
IdleTimeout keyword, 155

idle-timeout keyword, 155, 343, 403, 499
IdPgpKeyFingerprint keyword, 263, 627
IdPgpKeyId keyword, 263, 627
IdPgpKeyName keyword, 263, 627
IgnoreLoginRestrictions.PasswordExpiration
        keyword, 615
IgnoreLoginRestrictions.Rlogin.AIX
        keyword, 615
IgnoreRhosts keyword, 76, 175, 176, 197,
        198, 405, 412, 478
IgnoreRootRhosts keyword (Tectia), 176
IgnoreUserKnownHosts keyword
        (OpenSSH), 176
IMAP (Internet Message Access
        Protocol), 437
    authentication, 437
inetd
    server configuration and debugging, 223
    server invocation using, 150
initialization scripts, SSH servers, 200
installation
    prerequisites, 100
    signature verification, 100
    software inventory, table, 124
    source code, 100
    source files
        extraction, 101
    symbolic links created during, 123
    Tectia (see Tectia, installation)
    Unix implementations, 99–101
        binary distributions, 99
    on Unix systems, 99
integrity, 37
integrity checking, 4, 167–169
interactive sessions, authentication without
        passwords, 32
International Data Encryption Algorithm (see
        IDEA)
IP attacks, 94
IP spoofing, 91
IPSEC (Internet Protocol Security), 12

J

J2SSH Maverick, 517
Java SSH implementations, 517
JavaSSH, 517
JSch, 517

K

kadmin command, 413
KDC (Key Distribution Center), 461
KeepAlive keyword, 153
keepalive messages, 152–154
Kerberos, 12, 461–468
    batch job authentication using, 413
    integration in SSH, 12
    OpenSSH and Tectia
        interoperability, 464–468
    OpenSSH implementation, 111
    server configuration for, 181–183
    support in SSH, 463
    tickets, 12
KerberosAuthentication keyword
        (OpenSSH), 181
KerberosOrLocalPasswd keyword
        (OpenSSH), 182
KerberosTgtPassing keyword
        (OpenSSH), 182
KerberosTicketCleanup keyword, 182
Kermit, 518, 519
KEXINIT messages, 51
Key keyword (Tectia), 232, 330
keyboard-interactive
        authentication, 177–180
    one-time passwords, 177
    Tectia plugin for, 488–492
KeyRegenerationInterval keyword, 609, 615
keys, 8, 22, 40, 44
    changing, 27
    host keys, 20, 284–287
        implementation dependency, SSH, 69
    key exchange, 51
    key generators, 45
    key management, 227–265
        programs for key creation, 227
        setup recommendations, 404
    key pairs, 228
    key-distribution problem, 41
    secrecy, 24
    session keys, 462
    Tectia external keys, 264
    troubleshooting, 504
keywords, 134
known hosts, 19–21
    known hosts mechanism, 20
    known-hosts databases, 45, 284–287

L

launch-sshd shell script, 139
LDAPServers keyword, 477, 622
limiting simultaneous connections, 157
Linux SSH implementations, 519
ListenAddress, 148
local computers, securing, 29
LocalForward keyword, 355, 356, 357, 593, 622
LoginGraceTime keyword, 155, 156, 477, 615
LogLevel keyword, 312, 313, 615
lsh, 520

M

MAC (message authentication code), 53, 167–169
Macintosh
  OpenSSH, 526–530
    SSH clients, 526
    SSH server, 526–530
  SSH implementations, 517
Macs keyword, 168, 615, 622
MacSFTP, 517
MacSSH, 517
man-in-the-middle attacks, 19, 92
masquerading, 426
Maverick SSHD, 517
Maverick.NET, 517
MaxAuthTries keyword, 156
MaxBroadcastsPerSecond keyword, 159
MaxConnections keyword, 157
MaxStartups keyword, 157
MD5, 90
message authentication code (see MAC)
metaconfiguration, 469
Microsoft Windows (see Windows)
MindTerm, 517
motd (message of the day), 198

N

Nagle Algorithm, 159
name service spoofing, 91
NAT (Network Address
    Translation), 426–429
  masquerading, 426
  server-side issues, 427
netgroups, 74
network applications, security issues, 1
Network Information Service (NIS), 11
network interface server settings, 148

networking terminology, 6
NEWKEYS, 57
NFS, recommended settings, 404–407
NiftyTelnet SSH, 517
NIS (Network Information Service), 11
nmap, 161
no-agent-forwarding keyword, 334, 344, 403, 414
NoDelay keyword, 115, 159, 293, 477, 616, 622
NoHostAuthenticationForLocalhost
    keyword, 287, 622
"none" encryption, 53
no-port-forwarding keyword, 330, 331, 334, 344, 371, 403, 414
no-pty keyword, 296, 334, 345, 346, 403, 414, 506
no-X11-forwarding keyword, 381, 414, 513
NumberOfPasswordPrompts keyword, 295, 622

O

one-time pad, 40
one-time passwords, 111, 177
OpenBSD, 5, 10
  SSH implementations, 519
OpenSSH, 5, 10, 99
  account authorization files, 329
  authorization files, 626
  configuration, 107–111
    access control with
      TCP-wrappers, 111
    command-line flags, 107–111
    dependencies, 106
    file locations, 107
    Kerberos support, 111
    networking, 109
    PAM authentication, 109
    pid file, 108
    turning on support for Internet
      Protocol Version 4 (IPv4), 109
  conversion, SSH-1 to SSH-2 keys, 231
  environment variables, 627
  help command, 278
  host access control, 338
  host keys implementation, 70
  identities, 229, 626
  installation, 106–111
    build and install, 107
    extraction of zipped files, 106
    verification with PGP, 107
  Macintosh operation, 526–530

OpenSSH (*continued*)
    SSH clients, 526
    SSH server, 526–530
  popularity of, xi
  prerequisites, 106
  privilege separation, 80, 184
  public-key installation, 24
  quick reference, 612–627
  random number generation, 108
  random number storage, 79
  scp keywords, 620–623
  scp options, 619
  server configuration, 157
    logging and debugging, 211–215
  server host-key generation, 130
  server protocol version string, 170
  serverwide configuration
    authentication keywords, 171
    configuration files, checking, 135
    debugging messages, 496
    hostbased authentication, 175
    Kerberos authentication, 181
    password authentication, 173
    public-key authentication, 174
    recommended settings, 398–401
    reverse IP mapping, 158
    SSH protocol settings, 169
    user welcome, 198
  smartcard support, 241
  software inventory, 124
  SSH configuration directory, key storage
    file, 24
  ssh keywords, 620–623
  ssh options, 618
  SSH-1, 609
  ssh-add options, 625
  ssh-agent options, 625
  sshd keywords, 613–617
  sshd options, 612
  ssh-keygen options, 623
  SSH_ORIGINAL_COMMAND
    environment variable, 336
  subsystem command syntax, 208
  Version 4.0 new features, 591–594
    AddressFamily configuration
      keyword, 591
    clients, 592
    connection sharing, 592
    hostname hashing, 592
    KbdInteractiveDevices keyword, 592
    logging of access violations, 591

    password and account expiration
      warnings, 591
    port forwarding, 592
    server, 591
    sftp command line, 593
    ssh-keygen command-line
      options, 593
  Windows and Cygwin operation, 518,
    521–525
    agents, 524
    Cygwin installation, 521
    opening remote windows, 523
    public-key authentication, 524
    ssh clients, 522
    SSH server setup, 522
    troubleshooting, 525
OpenSSL, 14, 106
  directory path, flagging, 108
Options keyword, 330, 331, 371
OS/2 SSH implementations, 519

P

packet filters, stateful, 424
PalmOS SSH implementations, 519
PAM (Pluggable Authentication
    Modules), 109, 183
  OpenSSH authentication, 109
  serverwide configuration, 183
passive mode (FTP), 419, 422–426
  firewalls and, 424
  PASV port theft problem, 423
passphrases, 24
  changing, 27
  limitations, 28
PasswdPath keyword (Tectia), 174
password authentication, 173–174
  batch jobs, issues with, 408
  empty passwords, 173
  expired passwords, 173
  failed password attempts, 173
  troubleshooting, 499
password cracking attacks, 93
PasswordAuthentication keyword, 171, 173,
    272, 307, 400, 402, 499, 616, 622
PasswordExpireWarningDays keyword, 616
PasswordGuesses keyword (Tectia), 156,
    473
PasswordPrompt keyword, 295, 622
passwords
  one-time passwords, 111
  security risks, 21

PenguiNet, 518
per-account configuration, 102, 326–348
  advantages, 326
  authentication, 328
    access restriction by host or
      domain, 338
    forced commands, 331
    OpenSSH authorization files, 329
    public-key based
      configuration, 328–346
    Tectia authorization files, 330
  environment variables, setting, 340–343
  forwarding, disabling, or limiting, 344
  hostbased access control, 346
  idle-timeout option, setting (Tectia), 343
  limitations, 326
  setup recommendations, 403
  troubleshooting, 506
  TTY allocation, disabling, 345
  user's rc file, 348
Perl modules for SSH implementation, 519
PermitEmptyPasswords keyword, 173
permitopen keyword, 344
PermitUserEnvironment keyword, 199
PGP (Pretty Good Privacy), 11
  authentication in Tectia, 262–264
PgpKeyFingerprint keyword, 263, 331, 626
PgpKeyId keyword, 263, 331, 626
PgpKeyName keyword, 263, 331, 626
PGPPublicKeyFile keyword, 478, 616
PgpPublicKeyFile keyword, 263, 331, 626
PgpSecretKeyFile keyword, 264, 627
PidFile keyword, 143, 212, 616
Pine email client, 126, 436–444
  connection scripts, 444
  mail relaying, 442
  remote usernames and, 442
PKI (Public Key Infrastructure), 55, 454
plaintext, 40
PocketPuTTY, 519
PocketTTY, 519
port forwarding, 8, 349, 351–372
  dynamic port forwarding, 373–377
  firewalls, bypassing, 364
  forwarding off-host, 361–364
  ftp protocol forwarding, 371
  listening port number, 367
  local forwarding, 352–356
    gateway ports, 355
    remote forwarding, compared
      to, 358–361

  multiple connection issues, 357
  remote forwarding, 356
  remote logins, without, 366–367
  server configuration, 201–205, 370
  target forwarding address, choosing, 368
  TCP-wrappers (see TCP-wrappers)
  termination, 369
    TIME_WAIT problem, 370
  troubleshooting, 512
  X forwarding (see X forwarding)
Port keyword, 148
port number
  server settings, 148
Pragma Fortress, 518
PreferredAuthentications keyword, 308, 622
PrintLastLog keyword (OpenSSH), 199
PrintMotd keyword, 198, 398, 498, 616
privacy, 37
private keys, 228
privilege separation, issues with, 80
privileged ports, 10
PRNGs (pseudo-random number
    generators, 79
Protocol keyword (OpenSSH), 223
protocols, 3
ProxyCommand keyword, 445, 450, 451,
    452, 622
ProxyServer keyword, 616, 622
pseudo-random number generators
    (PRNGs), 79
pSSH, 519
pty-req channel request, 66
PubKeyAuthentication keyword
    (OpenSSH), 174
public key files, 229
Public Key Infrastructure (PKI), 55
PublicHostKeyFile keyword, 142, 477, 616
public-key authentication, 21–32
  agents, using (see agents)
  algorithms, 84–86
  authenticator, 22
  batch jobs, 409–412
    agents, 410–412
      filesystem passphrases storage, 409
      plaintext keys, 410
  client/server interaction, 22
  key pair generation, 23
  keys, changing, 27
    OpenSSH, 27
    Tectia systems, 27

public-key authentication (*continued*)
    password authentication, compared
        to, 26
    private keys, 22
    public keys, 22, 228
        installing in remote accounts, 24
        OpenSSH installation, 24
        Tectia systems, installation, 25
    server configuration for, 174
    Tectia systems, key generation on, 23
    troubleshooting, 501
public-key cryptography, 41
PuTTY, 518, 520, 576–589
    batch jobs, 587
    configuration and settings
        authentication, 586
        compression, 586
        encryption algorithms, 585
        logging and debugging, 586
        Proxies and SOCKS, 585
        pseudo-terminal allocation, 585
    configuration and use, 576
        host keys, 584
        saved sessions, 583
        SSH protocol selection, 584
        TCP/IP settings, 584
    file transfers, 578
        PSCP, 579
        PSFTP, 579
    forwarding, 587
    installation, 576
    key management, 580–583
        agents, 582
        key selection, 582
    Plink console client, 577
    remote commands, 578
    TCP/IP settings
        keepalive messages, 585
        Nagle algorithm, 585
        remote port selection, 585

Q

QuietMode keyword, 211, 313, 478, 616,
    622

R

random number generation, 78
    OpenSSH, 108
random seed, 45
RandomSeed keyword, 616

RandomSeedFile keyword, 143, 477, 616,
    622
RC4 (ARCFOUR), 88
r-commands, 10
    disabling, 398
    insecurity, 11
    SSH, replacing with, 125–127
        in CVS, 125
        in GNU Emacs, 126
        in Pine, 126
        in rsync and rdist, 127
rcp, 81
rdist, 127
realms, 462
regex syntax, SSH patterns (Tectia), 599–603
    character sets, 602
    escaped tokens, 601
regular expressions manpage
    (Tectia), 595–603
    egrep patterns, 595
    ZSH_FILEGLOB, 597
RekeyIntervalSeconds keyword, 155, 162,
    307, 478, 616, 622
remote account name, 279–281
remote program invocation and security, 333
RemoteForward keyword, 356, 357, 593,
    622
RemotelyAnywhere, 518
replay attacks, 37
requests, 65
RequiredAuthentications keyword
    (Tectia), 172
    gssapi, 182
    hostbased, 175
    keyboard interactive, 178
RequireReverseMapping keyword, 158, 189,
    193, 477, 616
ResolveClientHostName keyword, 189, 477,
    616
restricted shell, 414
reverse IP mappings in server
    configuration, 158
RhostsRSAAuthentication keyword, 172,
    175, 347, 609, 616, 623
RIPEMD-160, 90
Rivest-Shamir-Adleman public-key algorithm
    (see RSA)
RPM packages, 99
RSA (Rivest-Shamir-Adleman) public-key
    algorithm, 84
RSAAuthentication keyword, 172, 174, 477,
    609, 616, 623

rsh (restricted shell), 414
rsh suite, 10
rsync, 127

S

ScanSSH program, 161
scp (Secure Copy Program), 7, 17, 81, 82,
    313–323
    authentication through local agents, 31
    bandwidth settings, 320
    batch mode, 319
    Cygwin under Windows, 522
    data compression, 320
    directories, recursive copying, 316
    double-remote copying using
        agents, 30–32
    encryption algorithms, setting, 319
    file conversions, 320
    file transfers, 17
    forced commands and, 338
    gateway hosts, using through, 448
    help, 322
    internal options, 322
    keywords, 620–623
    Macintosh, 526
    optimization, 321
    options, 619
    original file, automatic removal
        (Tectia), 317
    permissions, 317
    safety features, 318
    ssh executable, locating, 322
    SSH protocol settings, 319
    statistics, display of, 321
    syntax, 18, 313–316
    TCP/IP settings, 319
    troubleshooting, 509
    user identity, 319
    wildcards, 316
scp2, 82, 84
sealed servers, 438
SecPanel, 520
secret-key algorithms, 86–89
secret-key cryptography, 41
SECSH (Secure Shell) working group, 10
secure file transfers, 7
Secure Hash Algorithm (see SHA-1)
Secure iXplorer, 518
Secure KoalaTerm, 518
secure remote logins, 5
Secure Shell protocol (see SSH)

Secure Socket Layers (SSL), 14
SecureCRT, 518, 563–573
    client configuration and use, 568–570
    command-line programs, 572
    file transfers, 572–573
        vcp and vsftp commands, 572
        Zmodem over SSH, 573
    forwarding, 570–572
        port forwarding, 570
        X forwarding, 571
    key management, 564–567
        agents, 567
        key generation, 565
        key installation, automatic, 565
        key installation, manual, 566
        multiple identities, 567
    session configuration, 564
    troubleshooting, 574
SecureFX, 573
SecurID, 180
SecurIdGuesses keyword (Tectia), 180
security
    agent forwarding and untrusted
        machines, 206
    batch job precautions, 413
    carelessness and, 97
    compile-time configuration setup
        recommendations, 397
    forced commands and, 333
    forwarding and, 205
    multiple identities, advantages, 260
    network applications and, 1
    shell escapes and, 333
    Tectia SSH-1 compatibility mode
        issues, 225
SendEnv keyword, 199, 289, 623
    server settings and, 199
server authentication, 38
ServerAliveCountMax keyword, 154, 293,
    623
ServerAliveInterval keyword, 154, 293, 623
ServerKeyBits keyword, 609, 616
serverwide configuration, xv, 102, 128–226
    access control, 184–198
        account access control, 185–191
        chroot, restricting directory access
            with, 195
        external access control, 194
        group access control, 191
        hostname access control, 192
        root access control, 194
        shosts access control, 193

serverwide configuration (*continued*)
  authentication, 171–184
    authentication syntax, 171–173
    hostbased authentication, 175–177
    Kerberos, 181–183
    keyboard-interactive
      authentication, 177–180
    login programs, selecting, 184
    PAM, 183
    password authentication, 173–174
    PGP, 181
    public-key authentication, 174
  configuration files, 133–138
    checking, 135
    time values in, 155
  file locations, 142–146
    host-key files, 142
    per-account authorization files, 145
    process ID file, 143
    random seed file, 143
    server configuration files, 144
    utmp file structure, 145
  file permissions, 146
  forwarding, 201–206
    agent forwarding, 206
    port forwarding, 201–205
    X forwarding, 205
  host-key generation, 130
  initial setup, 141–171
    data compression, 170
    encryption algorithms, 162–167
    integrity-checking (MAC)
      algorithms, 167–169
    key regeneration, 161
    numeric values, configuration
      files, 149
    protocol version string, 170
    restart for each connection, 151
    SSH protocol settings, 169
    TCP/IP settings (see TCP/IP settings,
      server)
  logging and debugging, 209–223
    syslog, 210
  making changes, 139
  metaconfiguration information, 134,
    468–479
  per-account configuration (see
    per-account configuration)
  port forwarding, 370
  port selection, 131
  reconfiguration example, 141

  server compatibility, SSH-1 and
    SSH-2, 223–226
  setup recommendations, 397–403
  startup file script, 129
  subconfiguration files, 134
  subsystems, 206–209
    definition syntax, 206
  troubleshooting, 506
  user logins and accounts, 198–201
    client environment variables, setting
      permissions, 199
    initialization scripts, 200
    user welcome messages, 198
session keys, 462
sessions, 44
  identity-based tailoring, 262
SetRemoteEnv keyword (Tectia)
  server settings and, 199
SettableEnvironmentVars keyword
  (Tectia), 200
setup recommendations, 396–407
  client configuration, 404
  compile-time configuration, 397
  key management, 404
  per-account configuration, 403
  remote home directories, 404–407
  serverwide configuration, 397–403
sftp, 33, 81, 84, 323–325
  ASCII vs. binary transfer, 34
  command-line options, 34, 325
  Cygwin under Windows, 522
  interactive commands, 323–325
  Macintosh, 526
  vs. ftp, 34
SftpSysLogFacility keyword, 211, 617
SHA-1 (Secure Hash Algorithm), 90
shadow files, 110
Shannon, Claude, 40
shell channel request, 66
SHELL environment variable, 28
shell escapes, 333
ShellGuard, 518
SIGHUP signal, 140
signers, 45
single-shell agent invocation, 243–245
S/Key in OpenSSH, 111
SkeyAuthentication keyword, 617
slogin (SSH1), 34
SmartcardDevice keyword, 623
SMTP (Simple Mail Transfer Protocol), 437
sniffing, 37

SocksServer keyword, 120, 304, 477, 548, 617, 623
source distributions, 100
SRP (Secure Remote Password), 13
ssh (client), 5
    configuration, 266–313
        authentication, 307–310
        command-line options, 267
        configuration files, 268–275
        connections, 294–302
        data compression, 310
        encryption algorithms, 306
        environment variables, 275
        forwarding, 305
        host key types, 307
        host keys and known-hosts
            databases, 284–287
        integrity-checking (MAC)
            algorithms, 306
        logging and debugging, 312
        precedence, 276
        protocol settings, 287–289
        proxies, 302, 302–305
        random seeds (Tectia), 313
        remote account name, 279–281
        session rekeying, 307
        SOCKS, 302–305
        subsystems, 311
        TCP/IP settings, 290–294
        user identities, 281–283
    Cygwin under Windows, 522
    debugging messages, 495
    escape character, 21
    keywords, 620–623
    known and unknown hosts, 19–21
    Macintosh, 526
    remote terminal sessions, 16
        client/server channel, establishing, 17
        login, 17
    ssh options, 618
    ssh-add options, 625
    ssh-agent options, 625
    ssh-keygen options, 623
    troubleshooting, 508
    unexpected behaviors, handling, 19
    verbose mode, 19, 277
SSH Communications Security, 5, 9
SSH (protocol)
    quick reference, 612–627
SSH (Secure Shell), xii, 1–15, 36–98
    address name with multiple numeric
        address, problems, 71

algorithms, 84–91
    hash functions, 89
    public-key algorithms, 84–86
    secret-key algorithms, 86–89
authentication, 38
    supported methodologies, 38
authorization, 39
authorization in hostbased
        authentication, 71
    control file details, 72
    hostbased access files, 72
    netgroups, 74
    netgroups as wildcards, 76
backward compatibility, 78
clients, 16–35, 44
    scp (see scp)
    sftp (see sftp)
    slogin, 34
    ssh (see ssh)
client/server architecture, 2
compression algorithms, 91
configuration directory
    key storage files, 24
configuration (see configuration)
cryptography (see cryptography)
denotation of protocols, products and
        clients, 4
features, 5–9, 36–39
    keys and agents, 7
    port forwarding, 8
    remote commands execution, 7
    remote logins, 5
    scp (see scp)
    secure file transfers, 7
file transfers, 81–84
flexibility in prosecution of services, 47
forwarding, 39
    supported types, 39
function and purpose, 1
history, 9
implementation-dependent features, 48,
        69–81
    host keys, 69
included component protocols, 46–49
installation (see installation)
integrity, 37
keys, 44
known-hosts mechanism, 20
PKI, supported types and supporting
        implementations, 55
privacy, 37
privilege separation (OpenSSH), 80

SSH (Secure Shell) (*continued*)
 pronunciation, 1
 protections provided by, 91–93
 random number generation, 78
 r-commands, replacing, 125–127
  in CVS, 125
  in GNU Emacs, 126
  in Pine, 126
  in rsync and rdist, 127
 related technologies, 10–15
  firewalls, 15
  IPSEC and VPNs, 12
  Kerberos, 12
  PGP and GnuPG, 11
  SRP, 13
  SSL, 14
  SSL-enhanced telnet and FTP, 14
  stunnel, 15
 security vulnerabilities, 93–98
 server, 43
 sessions, 44
 software inventory, 124
 SSH agent (see agents)
 SSH-1, 36, 68
  Tectia compatibility support, 122–123
 SSH-1 protocol, 9
 SSH-2, 36, 45–67
  SSH-1 compared to, 68
 SSH-2 protocol, 9
 SSH-AUTH, 47, 57–63
  authentication request, 57
  authentication response, 58
  host-based authentication, 62
  "none" request, 59
  password authentication, 61
  public-key authentication, 60
 SSH-CONN, 47, 64–67
  channel requests, 66
  channels, 64
  completing the connection process, 67
  global requests, 65
  requests, 65
 SSH-SFTP, 48
 SSH-TRANS, 47, 49–57
  connection, 49
  initialization of encryption, 56
  key exchange algorithm, 51
  key exchange and server
   authentication, 54
  message authentication code and
   algorithms, 53
  parameter negotiation, 51
 protocol version selection, 50
 server authentication and
  anti-spoofing, 56
 supported encryption algorithms, 37
 system architecture, 43–45
 Unix implementations (see OpenSSH;
  Tectia)
 Unix versions, xvi
SSH Secure Shell product (see Tectia)
SSH1 product, 9
Ssh1AgentCompatibility keyword, 611, 623
Ssh1Compatibility keyword, 224, 477, 610,
  617, 623
Ssh1InternalEmulation keyword, 610, 623
Ssh1MaskPasswordLength keyword, 611,
  623
Ssh1Path keyword, 611, 623
ssh-add command, 28, 247–253
 command-line options, 250
 listing keys, 29
 reading input, 28
 troubleshooting, 505
ssh-agent command, 28
 locking agents form unauthorized use, 29
 troubleshooting, 505
ssh-askpass program, 28
 password piping, 409
ssh-copy-id command (for key
  installation), 26
sshd (server), 129
 authentication syntax, 171–173
 client environment variables and, 199
 command-line options, 138
 configuration (see server configuration)
 debugging messages, 496
 hushlogin and, 199
 inetd, 223
 initialization scripts, 200
 key regeneration, 161
 keywords, 613–617
 launch-sshd shell script, 139
 public keys file, 176
 running as ordinary user, 129
  disadvantages, 131
 running as superuser, 129
 setup recommendations, 397–403
 SIGHUP signal, 140
 sshd command options, 612
 user SSH directory, 144
 user welcome messages, 198
 xinetd, 223

Sshd1ConfigFile keyword, 225, 477, 610, 617
Sshd1Path keyword, 224, 477, 610, 617
sshd-check-conf program, 136–138, 219
ssh-keyconverter (OpenSSH), 231
ssh-keygen command, 23, 233
    command line options to change passphrases, 27
ssh.pid file, path specification, 108
ssh-probe program (Tectia), 160
sshrc files, 200
sshregex (Tectia) manpage, 595–603
    egrep patterns, 595
    syntax, 595
    ZSH_FILEGLOB, 597
SshSignerPath keyword, 311, 623
SSHTerm Professional, 517
SSL (Secure Socket Layers), 14
    TCP-based applications, enhanced with, 14
StrictHostKeyChecking keyword, 284, 285, 286, 623
StrictModes keyword, 25, 146, 147, 149, 478, 617
stunnel, 15
subconfiguration files, 471
    forbidden keywords, 476
    keyword order, 473
    sections, 474
subshell agent invocation, 246
subsystem channel request, 66
Subsystem keyword, 207
symbolic links, created by SSH installations, 123
symmetric ciphers, 41
SYN flood attack, 94
SyslogFacility keyword, 210
system administration, xv

T
tar format, 101
TCP attacks, 94
TCP/IP settings, server
    ASLR (Address Space Layout Randomization), 151
    failed logins, 156
    idle connections, 155
    invocation by inetd or xinetd, 150
    keepalive messages, 152–154
    Nagle Algorithm, 159
    port number and network interface, 148
    reverse IP mappings, 158
    server discovery, 159
    simultaneous connections, limiting, 157
tcpip-forward request, 65
TCPKeepAlive keyword, 153
TCP_NODELAY bit, 159
TCP-wrappers, 389–395
Tectia, 5, 99
    account authorization files, 330
    authentication
        authorization file, 232
        external keys, 264
        identification files, 232
        identities, 230
        PGP, using, 262–264
        X.509 certificates, 454–461
    authorization files, 626
    client for FTP, 416
    configuration, 113–122
        authentication, 117–120
        debugging, 120
        encryption, 117
        file locations and permissions, 113
        networking, 115
        random number generation, 115
        SOCKS proxies, 120
        TCP port forwarding, 117
        X Window system, 116
    configuration extensions, 468–479
    configuration files
        keywords, 477
        quoted values, 478
    debugging
        module names, 604–608
    environment variables, 627
    file-naming conventions, 130
    help command, 278
    host access control, 340
    host keys implementation, 70
    host-key generation, 131
    identity files, 626
    idle-timeout option, setting, 343
    installation, 111–113
        build and install, 113
        file extraction, 112
        md5 verification, 112
        prerequisites, 112
    metaconfiguration, 134, 468–479
    plugins, 479–494

Tectia (*continued*)
    customized password-change
        plugin, 487
    expired passwords,
        changing, 479–484
    external authorization, 492
    general rules, 485
    keyboard-interactive
        authentication, 488–492
    Perl package for plugin
        implementation, 484
    public keys, changing, 27
    public-key generation, 23
    public-key installation, 25
    quick reference, 612–627
    random number storage, 79
    scp keywords, 620–623
    scp options, 619
    scp2, 84
        scp, contrasted with, 82
    server debugging messages, 496
    serverwide configuration
        access control files, 196
        authentication syntax, 172
        authentication techniques, 172
        configuration files, checking, 136
        hostbased authentication, 175
        host-key generation, 130
        Kerberos authentication, 182
        keyboard-interactive
            authentication, 178
        limiting simultaneous
            connections, 157
        logging and debugging, 215–223
        password authentication, 173
        public-key authentication, 174
        recommended settings, 401–403
        rules for quoted strings, 135
        server discovery, 159
        SSH protocol settings, 170
        SSH-1 and SSH-2 compatibility
            issues, 223–226
        ssh-probe, 160
        user welcome, 198
    software inventory, 124
    SSH configuration directory, key storage
        file, 24
    ssh keywords, 620–623
    ssh options, 618
    SSH Secure Shell product, name
        change, xi
    SSH-1, 610–611

    client configuration, 610
    key management, 611
    scp file transfers, 611
    serverwide configuration, 610
    SSH-1 protocol compatibility and
        support, 121–123
    SSH2_ORIGINAL_COMMAND, 336
    ssh-add options, 625
    ssh-agent options, 625
    sshd keywords, 613–617
    sshd options, 612
    ssh-keygen options, 623
    sshregex manpage, 595–603
        egrep patterns, 595
        syntax, 595
        ZSH_FILEGLOB, 597
    subconfiguration files, 471
        forbidden keywords, 476
        keyword order, 473
        sections, 474
    subsystem command syntax, 208
    Windows operation (see Tectia for
        Windows)
Tectia for Windows, 531–562
    Accession Lite, 536–539
    client application, 533–534
        configuration and profiles, 539–542
    command-line programs, 552
    Connector, 543–551
    file transfers, 551
    installation, 532
    key management, 534
    port forwarding, 542–543
    supported Windows platforms, 531
    Tectia Servers A and T, 555–562
        access control, 559
        authentication, 559
        commands, 557
        configuration, 557
        forwarding, 560
        logging and debugging, 561
        operation, 556
        SFTP server, 560
    troubleshooting, 554
telnet
    SSL-enhanced, 14
terminal locking, 29
Terminal.AllowGroups keyword, 617
Terminal.AllowUsers keyword, 617
Terminal.DenyGroups keyword, 617
Terminal.DenyUsers keyword, 617
tickets, 462

time values, server configuration files, 155
TIME_WAIT state, 433
TLS (Transport Layer Security), 14
Top Gun SSH, 519
traffic analysis, 95
transparency, 349
transparent proxies, 424
Triple-DES, 88
Trojnara, Micha, 15
troubleshooting, 497–513
TrustX11Applications keyword, 383, 623
TTY allocation, disabling per-account, 345
tunneling, 39, 351
    advantages, 451
tunnels, 8
TuSSH, 519
Twofish, 89

U

Unix
    hushlogin convention and SSH, 199
    "message of the day" (motd), 198
    syslog, 210
UseDNS keyword, 158
UseLogin keyword, 184, 205, 617
UsePAM keyword, 110, 171, 178, 183, 617
UsePrivilegedPort keyword, 292, 623
UsePrivilegeSeparation keyword, 184, 617
user authentication, 38
User keyword, 279, 499, 623
UserConfigDirectory keyword, 137, 144,
    145, 269, 539, 559, 617
UserKnownHosts keyword, 176, 617
UserKnownHostsFile keyword, 287, 623
UserSpecificConfig keyword (Tectia), 471
UseSOCKS5 keyword, 477, 617, 623

V

VanDyke Software, 563
VerboseMode keyword, 216, 219, 312, 478,
    617, 623
VerifyHostDNS keyword, 286
VerifyHostKeyDNS keyword, 623
version-control systems, 125
VMS SSH implementations, 520
VPNs (Virtual Private Networks), 12
VShell, 518, 574

W

Windows
    OpenSSH on Cygwin, 521–525
        agents, 524
        enabling remote windows, 523
        installation, 521
        public-key authentication, 524
        ssh clients, 522
        SSH server setup, 522
        troubleshooting, 525
    PuTTY client (see PuTTY)
    SecureCRT (see SecureCRT)
    SSH implementations, 517
    Tectia (see Tectia for Windows)
Windows Pocket PC SSH
    implementations, 519
WinSSHD, 518
WiSSH, 518
wu-ftpd, 423

X

X forwarding, 349, 377–389
    limiting or disablig per-account, 344
    server configuration, 205
X11DisplayOffset keyword, 381, 617
X11Forwarding keyword, 205, 617
x11-req channel request, 66
X11UseLocalhost keyword, 617
xauth, 108
XAuthLocation keyword, 381, 389, 513,
    617, 623
XAuthPath keyword, 617, 623
xinetd
    server configuration and debugging, 223
    server invocation using, 150

Y

Ylönen, Tatu, 4, 5, 9

Z

zlib, 91, 106
ZOC, 518, 519
ZSH_FILEGLOB, sshregex (Tectia), 597
    character sets, 598

About the Authors

Daniel J. Barrett, Ph.D., has been immersed in Internet technology since 1985. Currently working as a software engineer, Dan has also been a heavy metal singer, Unix system administrator, university lecturer, web designer, and humorist. He is the author of O'Reilly's *Linux Pocket Guide*, and is the coauthor of *Linux Security Cookbook* and the first edition of *SSH, The Secure Shell: The Definitive Guide*. He also writes monthly columns for *Compute!* and *Keyboard Magazine*, as well as articles for the O'Reilly Network.

Richard E. Silverman has a B.A. in computer science and an M.A. in pure mathematics. Richard has worked in the fields of networking, formal methods in software development, public-key infrastructure, routing security, and Unix systems administration. He coauthored the first edition of *SSH, The Secure Shell: The Definitive Guide*, and he loves to read, study languages and mathematics, sing, dance, and exercise.

Robert G. Byrnes, Ph.D., has been hacking on Unix systems for 20 years, and has been involved with security issues since the original Internet worm was launched from Cornell University, while he was a graduate student and system administrator. Currently, he's a software engineer at Curl Corporation. He has worked in the fields of networking, telecommunications, distributed computing, financial technology, and condensed matter physics.

Colophon

Our look is the result of reader comments, our own experimentation, and feedback from distribution channels. Distinctive covers complement our distinctive approach to technical topics, breathing personality and life into potentially dry subjects.

The animal on the cover of *SSH, the Secure Shell: The Definitive Guide* is a land snail (*Mollusca gastropoda*).

A member of the mollusk family, a snail has a soft, moist body that is protected by a hard shell, into which it can retreat when in danger or when in arid or bright conditions. Snails prefer wet weather and, though not nocturnal, will stay out of bright sun. At the front of a snail's long body are two sets of tentacles: its eyes are at the end of one set, and the other set is used for smelling and navigation.

Land snails are hermaphrodites, each having both female and male sex organs, though a snail must mate with another snail in order for fertilization to occur. A snail lays eggs approximately six times a year, with almost 100 eggs each time. Young snails hatch in a month and become adults in two years. A snail's life span is approximately 5–10 years.

Known as a slow mover, a snail moves by muscles on its underside that contract and expand, propelling the snail along at a slow pace. It leaves a wet trail of mucus, which protects the snail from anything sharp it may need to crawl over as it searches for food. The snail's diet of plants, bark, and fruits causes it to be a pest in many parts of the world where it is notorious for destroying crops.

Mary Brady was the production editor for *SSH, the Secure Shell: The Definitive Guide*. Audrey Doyle proofread the book. Marlowe Shaeffer and Mary Anne Weeks Mayo provided quality control. Lydia Onofrei provided production assistance. John Bickelhaupt wrote the index.

Ellie Volckhausen designed the cover of this book, based on a series design by Edie Freedman. The cover image is an original engraving from the book *Natural History of Animals* by Sanborn Tenney and Abby A. Tenney, published by Scribner, Armstrong & Co. in 1873. Karen Montgomery produced the cover layout with Adobe InDesign CS using Adobe's ITC Garamond font.

David Futato designed the interior layout. This book was converted by Keith Fahlgren to FrameMaker 5.5.6 with a format conversion tool created by Erik Ray, Jason McIntosh, Neil Walls, and Mike Sierra that uses Perl and XML technologies. The text font is Linotype Birka; the heading font is Adobe Myriad Condensed; and the code font is LucasFont's TheSans Mono Condensed. The illustrations that appear in the book were produced by Robert Romano, Jessamyn Read, and Lesley Borash using Macromedia FreeHand MX and Adobe Photoshop CS. The tip and warning icons were drawn by Christopher Bing. This colophon was written by Nicole Arigo.